CHOREOGRAPHY & NARRATIVE

CHOREOGRAPHY & NARRATIVE

BALLET'S STAGING OF STORY AND DESIRE

SUSAN LEIGH FOSTER

INDIANA UNIVERSITY PRESS BLOOMINGTON & INDIANAPOLIS

Illustrations are courtesy of the Bibliothèque Nationale de France, Paris, unless otherwise indicated.

The paper used in this publication meets the minimum requirements of American National Standard for Information Sciences—Permanence of Paper for Printed Library Materials, ANSI Z39.48-1984.

Manufactured in the United States of America

Library of Congress Cataloging-in-Publication Data

Foster, Susan Leigh.
Choreography and narrative : ballet's staging of story and desire / by Susan Leigh Foster.
p. cm.
Includes bibliographical references and index.
ISBN 0-253-33081-5 (cl : alk. paper)
1. Ballet—France—History—18th century. 2. Ballet—France—History—19th century. 3. Choreography—France—History—18th century. 4. Choreography—France—History—19th century.
I. Title.
GV1649.F67 1996 96-2237
792.8'0944—dc20

1 2 3 4 5 01 00 99 98 97 96

for

Hayden White

who taught me to read history

CONTENTS

ILLUSTRATIONS

PREFACE

Pointed leg, stiff skirt, diminutive wings, garlanded head, tousled hair, curving arms, adoring look—all hovering in a tree's branch five feet above the ground. How did she get there? Perhaps small buoyant leaps have carried her from center stage into the downstage exit where she maneuvers past other dancers and technicians to the third bay, grabs her flower, and runs up the stairs and out to the end of the seesaw, leaning against the support struts as she tips forward into arabesque. Extended enticingly, she meets the gaze of an infatuated prince who gestures his longing, one hand on his heart, the other sweeping from it toward her. Either her ethereal beauty or her unpredictable appearance has impelled him to his knees, a further sign of his devotion. Through her partially eclipsed, floating figure and the sweet diagonal of their mutual affection, these two can now enact the haunting mood and alluring spectacle that the audience beyond the footlights is eager to behold. Backstage, her assistants, ever attentive and knowing that one false jerk might cause her to tumble, hold steady, ready to float her up and away. Their canny assessment of size, weight, and fulcrum physics underpins her apparitional charm.

How did she get there? Since the curtain opened, he, the prince, has been chasing after her because haunted by her. She has repeatedly evaded him, all the while re-exciting him with her seeming availability. She appears unpredictably from behind the bushes; she stirs up all his yearnings. The ambiguous curve of her arms conveys reciprocal attraction, but also her familiarity with the bounds of propriety. Positioned precariously between the virginal and the wanton, she is the girl "who loved to dance too much."[1] Powerless to pursue her because of her lightness and enigmatic illusivity, the prince is nonetheless authorized to demonstrate his tender sensibility, his allegiance to the ideal, and his lonely destiny as she vanishes before his eyes. Her next appearance sets this machinery of desire in motion again. She is the thing he is wanting; her movements chart the syntax of passion. Even more crucial, they propel the narrative forward. And this is her function. Harnessed to convey a lightness not her own, pinned among the gazes of technicians, suitor, and audience members, she embodies the fleeting gesture of desire itself, without which the story could never be told.

How did she get there? Born into one of the many performing arts families that populated the stages of European theatres or else a waif of working-class origin, she began studying dance at an early age. Over the years she veers away from the feminine domain of domestic responsibilities and intrudes instead upon the masculine space of public spectacle. She acquires technical facility at the vocabulary of classical steps and pantomimic gestures, and at their transfer from dancing studio to proscenium theatre. She learns to navigate among choreographers' demands, dancers' rivalries, administrators' dictates, and critics' tastes in order to make her dancing seen. She conspires with the backstage hands, costumers, machinists, conductor, and even members of the claque on

1. "The Floating Wili in *Giselle* Act 2," From Albert Hopkins, *Magic: Stage Illusions and Scientific Diversions.*

whose support her favorable reception depends. And she negotiates with admirers for monetary backing and advocacy that would gloss her hard work with the luster of stardom.

How did she get there? Each of these explanations—stories about performance, choreography, and production—privileges distinct facets of ballet that this study incorporates as partial, linked responses to the questions it poses. Taken together these explanations contour the topos of this study's inquiry: How, in the course of ballet's mid-eighteenth-century practice, did dancing bodies begin to tell stories in performance? How, over the subsequent century of ballet's development, did the storying of dancing bodies affect their performances as dancers, as manifestations of choreography, and as members of the production? How might the narrativization of theatrical dance link with the increasing assimilation of narrative into other cultural practices accomplished toward the end of the eighteenth century, and, in turn, with the larger social and political movements of that period? And finally, what insights does the example of dance's history offer into the interplay of body, gender, desire, and narrative?[2]

Most histories of dance and of ballet have chosen to explain the dancing body's significance in the same way that an enthusiastic viewer admires the production, exercising the most discerning version of the audience member's expectations about the value and meaning of spectacle. Written as if positioned in the auditorium, these histories endow dancers with heroic attributes. They account for choreography largely through references to the collaborative involvement of dancing with music, costumes, and scenery. The ballet—a pristine, aesthetic accomplishment—remains separate from and barely influenced by other forms of spectacle, much less a social and cultural context. These histories record the crucial, and often neglected, facts of the performance (dates, names, and places); they never attempt to evoke the phenomenal experience that danced spectacle offers, or the embedded choreographic intelligence that gives the spectacle meaning.

This history reverses the traditional trajectory of ballet history's inquiry. Written from a position upstage, it peers through the back curtain at both the stage action and the audience, all the while feeling dancers and stagehands brush past as they cross from one side to the other. Rather than contemplating the performance as a sublime coordination of strokes of genius, it examines each moment's action as the embodiment of representational strategies implemented by choreographer and dancers. It treats dancing as a form of labor and dancers as skilled workers. It dwells on choreographic choices, attempting to discern their stance toward the construction of bodily, individual, gendered, and social identities. It thinks its way into the choreographic decisions, made throughout the rehearsal process and in performance, that theorize corporeality. Here the theoretical, rather than a contemplative attitude achieved afterwards and at a distance, is taken to be embedded (embodied) within the practical decisions that build up, through the active engagement of bodies, during the making of the dance.

Dance is uniquely adept at configuring relations between body, self, and society through its choreographic decisions. Many of these are documented in the partial records of dance practice that remain. Sifting through ballet programs, choreographers' journals, newspaper reviews, dancing manuals, published and unpublished letters by amateurs, musical scores with marginal notes, historical and philosophical treatises on dance, administrative records documenting contracts, salaries, and programming policies, costume and scenery sketches—the lineaments of a corporeal practice called ballet begin to coalesce. Performances by contemporary artist-scholars, working to reconstruct accurate versions of past dancing from these same documents, flesh out the images of a historical dance tradition with the palpable presence of dancing.[3]

Yet the persuasive power of dancing's articulate physicality and choreographic ingenuity only comes into focus when its dancing bodies perform alongside the bodies fashioned by other cultural pursuits. In order to decipher the ballet's choreographic theorizations, to resurrect and place in motion the ballerina's engraved image, this history positions in frictive encounter bodies engaged in distinct corporeal pursuits. It derives the significance of dance in any one historical moment from several distinct discursive and institutional frameworks that touch dance, operating upon and through it in different ways. When thrown together with bodies engaged in various other endeavors, the dancing body's meaning becomes more perceptible. Thus this study uses the concept of a culturally constructed, historically specific body to cut across disciplinary boundaries such as those of medical history, physical education, the practices of fashion, etiquette and comportment, and the science and art of representing the passions in order to elucidate pervasive values toward the body and the changes in these values over time. In an effort to track the broad development of dance alongside other corporeal pursuits, this study has narrowed its focus to a single locale: Paris. Judged repeatedly as home to the most lavish danced spectacle and the most talented and highly trained dancers, this capital catalyzed enormous enthusiasm for theatrical and social dance, and it also nurtured a lively debate concerning the body's aesthetic, moral, and political significance. By comparing dance with the corporealities instantiated in other practices, the ballet's choreographic conventions can be seen as particular stagings of the body's participation in the larger performance of the body politic.[4]

To approach choreography as theory is to open up a space where dancing and all body-centered endeavors have an integrity equivalent to that of written documentation of them.[5] They establish their own lexicons of meaning, their own syntagmatic and paradigmatic axes of signification, their own capacity to reflect critically on themselves and on related practices. This parity between the danced and the written invites new approaches to the act of translating dancing into a verbal description. Translation comes to entail a recognition of the distinctiveness of each medium, and then a series of tactical decisions that draw the moved and the written into an interdisciplinary parlance.

The tactics of this history work at one level to fashion a descriptive text that adheres to the moved example. In many passages, the description of dancing attempts to trace out the patterns, shapes, and energies enacted by historical dancing bodies. At another level, the historical narrative is choreographed so as to present a text quite unlike the performances it describes. Where the story ballets attempted to achieve a coherence based on the logical sequence of seamlessly related events, this text designates distinct parts for the textual bodies found in the chapters, the evaluations of selected ballets, the analyses of narrative conventions, and the notes. The chapters synthesize evidence concerning the overall appearance and impact of dance performances with choreographic process, training procedures, and more general attitudes toward the dancing body. These chapters are followed by descriptions and analyses of specific ballets, chosen not for their popularity but for what they reveal about the workings of danced narrative and its development over time. Accompanying the analyses of ballets are short, whimsical meditations that probe the effectiveness of conventions within ballet productions that were used repeatedly to move the story forward. Notes supplement information provided in the text concerning attitudes toward dance, and they also connect dance-making to analogous practices in other fields. All these parts of the history have been staged as semiautonomous acts whose performance generates a multibodied co-motion. From its upstage position this history acknowledges the divides between stage, wings, and auditorium, and between performed illusion and illusion-producing machinery, and it reproduces those fissures in the nonseamless construction of its text. At still another level, it meditates on its own relation to its subject matter by interrogating and historicizing the presumed relations between words and movements and between the acts of writing and of dancing.

The historian's body that produced this text, trained in ballet but dedicated to experimental, postmodern choreography, embarked on this research as a means to contextualize the stories it has danced and also those it has witnessed in performances by contemporary artists who collage text, mediatized imagery, site-specific interrogations of the body, and movement in their efforts both to tell stories and to reflect on the telling of those stories. The dancing bodies placed in motion by these efforts exude an intense physicality and a reflexive generativity. Deeply marked by Cunningham's aesthetic legacy, they perform gender as a set of vocabularies and attributes, and they repeatedly declare their fierce independence from music.[6] But they are also haunted by a dichotomy between the figural and the discursive (sometimes known as the abstract and the representational), a dichotomy that Cunningham's storyless dances eschewed.[7]

Cunningham's aesthetic predispositions—to affirm the body's idiosyncratic physicality and to inscribe autonomous functions for dance and music—have embedded and embodied themselves in this text. Post-Cunningham choreographers' struggles—to contest traditional roles for male and female dancers, to reconfigure discursive and figural elements within performance, and to elaborate strategies for commenting reflexively on the work of art—are equally palpable and present on these pages. This postmodern body of choreographic work, never directly addressed here, operates as transparent partner to the ballerina on her seesaw, observing the tremor of her foot as she strives to satisfy both prince and viewer, testing the weight and substantiality of her position, offering her some new moves. In their duet, the ballerina and her postmodern partner explore the historical conditions, both political and aesthetic, necessary to the emergence of danced narratives, and they examine the effects of danced stories upon the bodies who performed them. The trajectory of their duet moves them from the historical stage of vanished dancing to the theoretical stage of choreographic strategies for representation.

On this new stage of representation, the ballerina, seesaw and all, holds her position as the embarrassed gestures of the exposed technicians and the obsessive repetitions of the prince—of intrinsic interest as varieties of signing—surround her. Her magical presence, all the more uncanny because of its newly acquired critical reflexivity, fascinates viewers, but enthralls them equally with the story of the production of their fascination. Perhaps as she leads them through the story's story, seeing what they saw, she develops a desire to choreograph the very balancing act she knows so well. Perhaps she contrives a descent from the seesaw and, inspired by the new mechanics of representation that such a descent entails, runs to the studio to begin work on her own dance. But wait: not unaware of her own charisma, she pauses before exiting to throw her flower to the audience, signaling her gratitude for their attention and also her complicity in the cycle of desire that her dancing has always performed.

Before exiting into this text, I extend my deepest thanks to all those who danced with me during the seesaw of research and writing that composed it, commemorated in the incorporation of their names into this moment's textual body: tp Cynthia Novack, Richard Bull, Susan Manning, Mark Franko, and Marion Kant for their collective efforts in helping to envision "dance as culture"; to Victor Gourevitch, Henry Abelov, George Haggerty, Ellen D'Oench, Christina Schlundt, and Linda Tomko for generously sharing with me their knowledge of the eighteenth century; to Ronald Kuivila, Nancy Roberts, Cheryl Cutler, Richard Stamelman, Alvin Lucier, Wendy Stokes, Linda and Jean-Claude Mézières, Allegra Fuller Snyder, Margaret Brose, Sharon Salinger, Susan Rose, Philip Brett, and especially Sue-Ellen Case for their sustained support of the project; and to Sarah Cordova, John Jordan, Barbara Ras, LuAnne Holladay, Joan Catapano, Nicole Wilde, and staff members at the New York City Library for the Performing Arts at Lincoln Center, the Bibliothèque de l'Arsenal, and the Bibliothèque de l'Opéra. I also wish to acknowledge the support of the National Endowment for the Humanities, whose fellowship enabled the crucial first stages of archival research, Wesleyan University, and the University of California at Riverside.

CHOREOGRAPHY & NARRATIVE

INTRODUCTION
Pygmalion's No-Body and the Body of Dance

In 1734 a letter published in the *Mercure de France* described for the edification of her adoring Parisian audience the latest accomplishments of renowned dancer and choreographer Marie Sallé.[1] Performing in the pantomime-rich London theatre world, Sallé had introduced a radical new interpretation of Ovid's story about the sculptor Pygmalion. As detailed in the letter, Sallé had chosen to appear uncorseted, without wig or mask, and to adapt movement from the vocabulary of pantomime in order to depict a faithful likeness of Greek sculpture. Her scandalously realistic choreographic choices achieved instant acclaim, prompting republications of the letter in newspapers across Europe and inspiring numerous plagiarized productions of her *Pygmalion*.[2]

The whole ballet, lasting perhaps twenty minutes,[3] commences with Pygmalion in his atelier surrounded by six assistants, mallets and chisels in hand; their spirited frolic plays one tour de force against another. At Pygmalion's request, they open the back of the workshop, where they find a statue of uncommon perfection. Pygmalion regards it tenderly, touching its feet and waist, kissing its hands, adding bracelets to its arms, and a necklace. His passionate transports give way to anxious frustration and then a dreamlike stupor. Finally, rousing himself, he prays to the goddess Venus to bring his beloved statue to life. A sudden change in the music, accompanied by three sudden shafts of light, signals Venus's acquiescence to his plea. Galathea, much to the astonishment of Pygmalion and his assistants, slowly stirs to life. As the sculptor offers her his hand so that she might descend from her platform and touch the ground, she begins to dance, forming simple steps with an elegant ease. Pygmalion then demonstrates more complicated sequences of steps, each of which she repeats and even embellishes with graceful aplomb. This dancing lesson culminates in mutual expressions of love, celebrated in a final dance performed by assistants, sculptor, and living work of art.

Two aspects of Sallé's *Pygmalion* must have struck Parisian audiences as especially arresting. The first derived from her status as *première danseuse* at the Paris Opéra, the most elite institutionalization of the arts of music and dance in all Europe. Sallé was an employee at the Opéra and hence an emissary of the King, and it seemed remarkable that she would abandon the decorous trappings that signaled both her identity as an artist and the accomplishments of her art form—all in order to implement a new choreographic concept. Second, her ballet used pantomime to portray faithfully the sincere feelings of danced characters. Pantomime had become a familiar staple at fair and street performances all across urban Europe, where it played the subversive role of satirizing or circumventing narrative, but it had seldom been invoked as the principal medium for sustaining a coherent exchange of thoughts and feelings on a stage featuring the most elevated aesthetic values.[4] Thus Sallé's production simultaneously transgressed boundaries in the hierarchical systems of professional status, class, and genre.

But this audacious initiative reverberated with an import that extended far beyond the innovative and fashionable trends of the moment. Her dance did not simply evidence a new generation's tastes and sensibilities coming to embodiment. Rather, it gestured toward an aesthetic and political rupture of enormous proportions. Sallé's *Pygmalion* demonstrated an unprecedented individual initiative in its control and direction of artistic creation. It likewise intimated a new conception of individual identity in prefiguring the Enlightenment value of *sensibilité*, whose focus on emotion, motivation, and empathy would command the body's authentic participation in hosting and communicating feelings. This new notion of the individual, contained within and supported by the physical body, provided the foundation for the political ideal of citizenship and the supporting definitions of public and private space and masculine and feminine behavior upon which the Revolution would be based.[5]

Fifty-five years later, at the very close of the Revolution, the aspiring choreographer Louis Milon selected the Pygmalion myth as subject for his first full-length ballet.[6] Its premiere at the Théâtre Ambigu-Comique enjoyed such success that it was produced at the Paris Opéra the following year.[7] Divided into two substantial acts, each probably the length of Sallé's entire ballet, Milon constructed his version within the larger frame of an anacreontic pastorale. The first act expands on the differences between Constant and Inconstant Love, personified by two cherublike figures, one with arrows of gold, the other with arrows of paper, who vie to determine the fate of shepherd Pygmalion's love for the shepherdess Delphide. Inconstant Love triumphs with a series of maneuvers that embroil Delphide in other amorous liaisons. Pygmalion's repeated attempts to attract her end in dejected despair. As act 1 draws to a close, a cloud covering the stage lifts to reveal a sculptor's studio with several apprentices busily at work on a group of statues. Inconstant Love hands Pygmalion a chisel and mallet and then exits.

The second act seems to have been heavily influenced by Jean-Jacques Rousseau's *Lyric Scene* of the Pygmalion story, published in 1762 and first performed at the Paris Opéra in 1772.[8] Like Rousseau's mimed monologue, Milon's choreography consisted almost entirely of a long solo for the sculptor in his atelier. As the curtain parts, Pygmalion can be seen holding open a corner of the drape surrounding a large pedestal. After gazing with charmed approbation at the statue beneath the drape, he commences work on one of the several partially formed stones in the room. The results disappoint him, and he moves on to the next stone. Again he becomes disillusioned with his own gestures, so much so that he throws his tools on the table and slumps to the floor. Soon, however, he is back on his feet, dismissing each stone in turn as inadequate to his task. He approaches the draped pedestal and slowly opens the curtain to reveal the perfectly executed Galathea, an exact replica of his unloving Delphide. Captivated by her grace and proportions, Pygmalion moves closer, then farther away, examining the statue from all angles. He perceives a possible flaw and retrieves his chisel to amend it, but then reconsiders, fearing that he could do irreparable damage. He casts his tools across the room and starts to close the drape, but cannot. Again his passionate devotion to the statue inspires him to alter it slightly, this time by adding a garland of flowers around her neck. He steps back to admire his work, but immediately determines that she is more beautiful without ornament and rushes to remove the necklace. He stands still, absorbed in tender regard. Eventually aware of his reverie, he becomes embarrassed, and then full of resolve. He tours the studio, gathering up his tools, which he hangs on the wall before leaving for the night. Still, he cannot resist one last glance at the statue, and the sight impels him to her. He falls on his knees and expresses his love. Suddenly the studio and sculptures vanish, and Galathea and Pygmalion find themselves transported into the gardens of Cythera, where Venus brings the statue to life. Graces, Amours, and Pleasures join in the festive ballet that ends the act.

Milon's version of the Pygmalion story presented a striking contrast between the pastoral idyls of shepherds, shepherdesses, and Amours in act 1 and Pygmalion's long, introspective soliloquy in act 2. The revolving flirtations of young men and women in the first act conformed to many of the eighteenth-century conventions for ballets representing rural life. The hunting and chasing, hiding and seeking, and chance amorous encounters created the kind of pleasing, perpetual change that had delighted audiences for a century. Act 2, however, required viewers to focus exclusively on a single individual's conflict-ridden actions. Here they saw the inner life of the character portrayed more fully than ever before. Pygmalion's extended deliberations, full of doubts and new resolve, focused on an immobile image incapable of returning his gaze. Repeatedly, he gestured toward her, demonstrating his attachment to her, but in its unresponsiveness the statue pointed him back toward his new role as artist. The statue thus functioned as a manifestation of ideal form, a source of inspiration but also of distraction from his ongoing work as sculptor. Charged with these two contradictory roles, and utterly impassive, the statue created the narrative conditions under which Pygmalion's mental and emotional life could unfold.[9]

Sallé's immobile statue had sustained the erotic encounter between sculptor and work of art during moments when he touched her feet and waist or decorated her with jewelry. But she had not served as the stationary measure of his feelings, the mute and stony partner in his internal dialogue. In Sallé's ballet, the artwork, once created, was attributed a life of its own. Not only did the major portion of the action center on the interplay between Pygmalion and Galathea, but both artist and artwork coordinated their actions so as to enable a series of discoveries, shot through with eros, about their own identities. Galathea systematically assimilated society through her instruction in that most consummate of all civilized pursuits—dancing. Pygmalion likewise discovered how to translate his artistic sensibilities into mobile form, responding to each of her exquisitely interpreted phrases with an elegant proposal for the next dance. The cadre of assistants, a social frame around their evolving relationship, underscored the inseparability of self from society.

Milon, in contrast, used the statue's immobility to focus the action on the artist's appraisal of himself and his work. His Pygmalion, entirely alone, danced out an interiorized subjectivity and also a new conception of art as the sublimation of desire. In the same way that he divided Amour into constant and inconstant types, Milon fashioned Galathea as a real person in act 1 and as Pygmalion's projected desire in act 2. For the first time viewers were given an explanatory origin for the identities of both artwork and artist: Delphide's fickle abuse of Pygmalion's devotion caused his conversion to sculptor. The fidelity and intensity of his love for her, sublimated into art, produced a masterpiece. The magnificence of his artistic creation, like the depth of his character, could be traced to her inconstancy.

Thus Pygmalion's ability to transform life into art and his striking revelations of doubt and desire ultimately depended upon a series of non-negotiable distinctions. Life and art, constancy and inconstancy, creator and created became essentialized opposites embodied in the characters of the two Amours, Delphide, and Galathea. Sallé had staged her ballet at the intersection of categories such as life and art, elaborating a spontaneous exchange between artist and sculpture that heightened the eros of their communication. Milon's Pygmalion, in his encounters with the real and then the ideal, could gesture his sentimental longing for an ideal love, but never dance out the consequences of a love come to life.

This technique of configuring dichotomous oppositions, so evident in Rousseau's theorization of the social contract, resonated throughout the political and artistic production of the late eighteenth century. It enabled a new conception of human agency by stipulating an actor and an acted-upon that rationalized the political reforms undertaken throughout the Revolution. In place of the mutually defining identities of monarch and subject, participants in the Revolution argued that autonomous, individually active agents might collectively determine their own destiny.[10] Yet this liberatory agenda, as Foucault has clearly shown, included new strategies of control and new subjects of domination that served only to redistribute rather than abolish oppressive structures of power. Galathea, for example, icon for the feminine and the bodily, had in Sallé's ballet been able to descend from her pedestal and dance, whereas Milon's statue remained fixed in place.

In 1847 Arthur Saint-Léon choreographed yet another version of Pygmalion and Galathea, *La Fille de Marbre,* which he organized into two acts preceded by a lengthy series of virtuoso dances that showed off the dancers in their Spanish dress.[11] A lavish production that moved from the palace of the Genii of Fire to the crowded streets of fifteenth century Seville, the ballet nonetheless received substantial criticism from journalists who found the plot unnecessarily complicated, the extravagant scene changes dutifully presented, and the dancing labored.[12] Saint-Léon had varied the plot by imbuing the woman-statue with the power, unknown to her, to determine her ultimate destiny. Where both Sallé and Milon structured their ballets along a trajectory that culminated in the union of sculptor and statue, Saint-Léon fashioned the statue's character such that her choice of love could only end tragically.

When the curtain opens, the sculptor has just concluded negotiations with Satan to exchange his own soul for the enlivenment of his beloved statue, provided that the Genii of Fire agrees to inspire her with the breath of life. The Genii places his own further stipulation on the deal: this woman-statue can never fall in love, or she will suffer the return to inanimate stone. The sculptor, relegated to the role of fatherly chaperone, then watches in wonder as the unattainable object of his desire slowly comes to life as the gypsy girl Fatma. (See fig. 2.) Satan follows his new property who, in turn, follows his beloved creation up from the bowels of the earth and into the center of Seville. Bewitching the passers-by, guards, religious penitents, and even the city's mayor, the beautiful gypsy cannot herself resist the impassioned overtures of a young Moorish prince imprisoned in the palace where she is to dance for the King of Spain. Yet a revolt has already been planned, and at a preordained signal the prince leads his subjects into fierce battle, eventually reclaiming the city and his crown. He returns triumphant to his gypsy-queen, but as he draws her up the stairs to the throne she suddenly turns to stone. The sculptor, ever vigilant but increasingly powerless, swoons with grief and dies. The ballet's final image presents Satan resting his foot on the body whose soul he has just received. (See fig. 3.)

Satan, and not Venus, presided over the fates of characters in Saint-Léon's ballet, his dark will triumphing over love in the end. Rather than a classical Greek sculpture whose purity of form could easily assimilate to societal norms, the female character Fatma displayed all the elements of the classic orientalist fantasy: she descended from an exotic community whose mysterious way of life elicited fascination and terror; her unabashed interest in fleshly desires enhanced the appetites as well as the status of all those who could contain her exuberant body. Sensuous, joyous, and certainly not immobile as in Milon's ballet, Fatma was nonetheless pinned among the controlling gazes of five male characters: the adoring creator who determined her appearance; Satan and the Genii who constructed her fate; the lecherous mayor who authorized her public life; and the amorous prince who defined her love. Like Milon's Galathea, who fulfilled contradictory functions of inspiration and distraction, Fatma's identity revolved around the prohibition and the desire to love. Unlike Milon's heroine, whose power resided solely in her ability to attract her creator's attention, Fatma was given one "act of free will"—the suicidal acknowledgment of love on which narrative closure depended.

In Milon's *Pygmalion* the statue constituted the masculine projection of the feminine through which the male sculptor could manifest interiority. Here the statue functioned as a feminized commodity whose exchange among men ensured their potency. Milon's sculptor, full of emotion yet utterly ineffectual, was divided in Saint-Léon's ballet into a range of male character types whose interactions mutually enhanced their power and influence. In a period

TOP: 2. Costume by Paul Lormier for Fanny Cerito as Fatma in *La Fille de Marbre* (1847).

BOTTOM: 3. Lormier's costume for M. Elie as Almir (Satan) in *La Fille de Marbre*.

4. Fanny Cerito as Fatma, surrounded by the sculptor, the governor of Seville, and other officials in act 2 of *La Fille de Marbre.*

of intense political disillusionment and on the eve of another revolution, Saint-Léon's ballet referenced the masculine domain of public governance struggling to assert itself in the face of a powerful, burgeoning capitalist market and a massive, obfuscatory bureaucracy. Implicit within the ballet's homosocial world of rulers and reformists was a new conception of human agency, one in which actor and acted-upon no longer maintained a clear, causal connection. The economic momentum of capitalism, with its abstraction of product from labor, on the one hand, and the civil bureaucracy's tortuous routinization of governance, on the other, intervened to render seemingly ineffectual any attempts at shaping a social destiny.

Serving as a cipher for the disrupted connection between actor and action, the gypsy girl Fatma shimmered like attractive merchandise on display in the new capitalist martketplace. (See fig. 4.) Alienated from the labor that produced them, the commodities arranged in the stores invited consumers to acquire them as accoutrements to their social identity, as prophylactics patching over the discrepancy between concrete labor and symbolic capital.[13] Similarly, the gypsy girl supplemented male political and sexual agency, giving it an illusory sense of efficacy. As in Milon's ballet, the sculptor's creation never attained any personhood. The sculpture's identity in both ballets resulted exclusively from behavior prescribed by male characters that fulfilled their amorous and sexual desires. In Milon's *Pygmalion* these desires were cast as autoerotic, whereas in Saint-Léon's they appeared as homoerotic.[14] In both ballets Galathea's behavior was essential to the story's getting told: her *inaction* created narrative suspense, and her actions—coming to life or falling in love—permitted narrative closure.

5. A 1758 production of *Pygmalion* at the Schouwburg Theatre in Amsterdam featuring child dancers.

Only in Sallé's ballet did the primitive and protean structure of the narrative enable the woman-statue to participate in the construction of her own identity. She and her creator, through their seemingly spontaneous danced dialogues, mutually defined their relationship as well as their individual contributions to it. (See fig. 5.) Their ongoing reciprocity similarly signaled the self-generating, polysemic properties of art itself. Once created, the art object generated meanings that expanded and changed as one continued to interact with it. Unlike Milon's ballet, where art endured as the fixed product of sublimated desire, or Saint-Léon's production, where art, entirely commodified, carried a different purchase price for each potential buyer, Sallé's depiction of art celebrated its renewability as erotic, passionate, and intelligent, in turn.

The period punctuated by Sallé's, Milon's, and Saint-Léon's versions of the Pygmalion myth witnessed the emergence of theatrical dance as an autonomous art form, separate and distinct from opera and capable of conveying a story entirely through danced movement. For the first time in the development of Western theatrical dance, performance presented characters whose relationships with one another spawned logical motivations, credible responses, and resolute actions; and over the course of the performance, those interactions orchestrated the sense of a beginning, middle, and end. Drawing on well-known myths and romances for their scenarios, and reducing these to the simplest of plot structures, the ballet productions of the late eighteenth and early nineteenth centuries achieved a coherence and autonomy for dance as a form of spectacle that it never before enjoyed. Sallé's ballet was one of the first experiments leading to the development of the danced story. Milon's production testified to the vitality and durability of the new art form in the wake of the turbulent decade of the 1790s. Saint-Léon's work occurred at the end of an era of development that had balanced in productive tension all the elements of this new genre of spectacle—novel character types and plot structures, the movement vocabularies of dance and mime traditions, changing structural and stylistic values in musical composition, and innovations in architectural design and technological support for the theatre. In the course of its development from Sallé's time to Saint-Léon's, this new art form achieved a kind of monumental influence on theatrical dance equivalent to the novel's impact on literature.

As the dance tradition molded itself to the contours of narrative structure, new divisions of labor coalesced. The principal female character, like the immobile Galathea in Milon's ballet, came to serve as a fixed function around which characters' interior subjectivities and even the story itself unfolded. Variations on her immobility proliferated: the woman-statue reincarnated as victim, as captive, and eventually as a rendition of the abstract concept of ephemerality. In all these roles, she exhibited the most intense, the greatest range of feeling, and the least ability to effect change. The male character, like the solicitous sculptor, searched for her, saved her, agonized over her, ever protective but also desirous to display her beauty for all to see. As the new genre developed, impediments to the felicitous union of male and female characters loomed increasingly large. Eventually narratives of loss predominated in which the female characters, as in Saint-Léon's gypsy or the illusive sylph, embodied an essential difference that invited but then prohibited an enduring alliance.

The repertoire of dance movements evolved alongside these new roles for characters. Dramatic interactions on stage came to be based less on the hierarchies of status, class, and profession, and more on the exchanges of heartfelt emotion. In response, choreographers no longer crisscrossed the stage space with orderly symmetries, and began instead to assemble dynamic hedrons of bodies. They animated high and low, and front and back stage spaces with tensile diagonals that configured characters within organic volumes. Male and female characters began to manifest unique repertoires of steps that included long balances and intricate footwork, sometimes *en pointe*, for the female dancer and higher jumps and multiple beats and turns for the male dancer. Male and female characters also began to engage in functionally distinct partnering roles. Rather than execute complex patterns in unison alongside one another, couples now intricately entwined so as to create unified sculptural wholes.

In order to accommodate the story ballet's need to substitute gestures for words, choreographers drew from the rich vocabulary of pantomimed expressions of the hands and face that could be used to depict all the flirtations, arguments, schemes, and discoveries that propelled the action forward. Always markedly different in tempo and phrasing from classical steps and poses, these semaphoric signals interrupted the virtuoso performance of dancing prowess at the same time that they clarified the story. Considerable choreographic ingenuity was needed to soften the transitions between the didactic indication of thoughts and feelings and the elegant execution of ideal forms. When successful, choreographers mingled the two vocabularies by overlaying complicated sequences of steps with gestures of the hands and face and by invoking magnificent turns, leaps, or balances as part of characters' emotional responses to a situation. Stories for ballets also facilitated the reconciliation between mime and dance by always including characters who loved to dance as well as scenes recreating festivals, dances, or sports events that capably contained more concentrated sequences of virtuoso display.

The persistent tension between dramatic action and danced elegance resulted, in part, from the immense gratification experienced by dancers and viewers alike as they witnessed the accomplished dancing body toss off one tour de force after another. As the demands of the danced narrative grew so did the desire for physical excellence. At the time of Sallé's *Pygmalion,* the dancing lesson between sculptor and sculpture referenced the necessary mastery over social protocols required of all members of the aristocracy for which dancing provided the essential preparation. Not only did vocabularies for theatrical and social forms overlap, but many of the movements alluded to those required for polite social interaction. By the time of Saint-Léon's ballet, the expertise embodied in the theatrical dance vocabulary far exceeded the abilities of the most avid social dance practitioners, and it shared with social protocol only an abstract notion of feminine grace. In the intervening years, dance teachers had adapted insights from the new science of anatomy to help fashion a self-regulating and disciplining body capable of exceptional feats, and choreographers had mined the basic set of positions and steps for variations and ornamentations of extraordinary complexity for that body to perform.

Although the impetus to display these physical accomplishments contravened the objectives of the danced narrative, the body trained in these skills ultimately met the story's needs. The anatomically informed regimen designed to enhance dancing prowess isolated and contained the body over the course of the eighteenth century. Segregated from the behavioral specifications of social protocol, the storytelling body, like Milon's statue of Galathea, became a fixed and neutral entity capable of serving as a site for the production of danced narrative. Just as Milon's Galathea presented a mute and stable surface onto which Pygmalion's desire was projected, so the dancing body itself acquired the kind of autonomous solidity that enabled it to become a vehicle for narration. But its role as vehicle consisted in two mutually enhancing functions. First, the body's autonomy and interiority, the product of its dance training, endowed it with the ability to host its own feelings, to change them as the result of a seeming dialogue with the self, and to reproduce them for the viewer. Second, the body's virtuosity, its mastery of an abstract set of physical feats, verified its trainability, its capacity to display whatever was required.

In Sallé's *Pygmalion* the dancing body, like her characterization of Galathea, existed at the interstices of several different discourses: it partook of the social codes of comportment, it displayed a virtuoso level of competence, it presented with painterly accuracy the individual's passionate responses to others. It moved among these discourses, gliding across their representational fields without centering in any one domain. Like her Galathea, the work of art that was nonetheless alive, the body dialogued with other bodies in all these discourses. By the time of Milon's *Pygmalion,* the representational division between discursive and figural repertoires had solidified. The dancing body, detached from its social moorings and objectified through scientific investigation, could either imitate feelings and actions or perform a series of sensuous, virtuoso physical accomplishments. Like Milon's version of the sculpture, the body had become a malleable yet opaque volume for the display of the representational language of pantomime or the abstract ideals of physical discipline and desire. Contained within these two discursive realms, the body could no longer engage in simultaneous or improvised dialogues with other bodies such as those choreographed by Sallé for her artist and work of art. Instead, the body became embroiled in the causal logic of call and response dictated by the constraints of classical narrative form. Like Saint-Léon's gypsy, it functioned only as an expressive instrument, an object of beauty, responsive to each new demand the story might make.

The dancing body, leached of any power to signify outside narrative's boundaries, congealed into a physical thing, and ballet provided the framework in which to showcase this body. At the time that Sallé had choreographed her *Pygmalion,* dance enjoyed a reputation as the presentation of ideal classical forms and also as the process through which both a healthy body and a graceful social identity could be achieved. Galathea's dancing lesson celebrated, by building upon, dance's role in the socializing pursuits that fashioned the proper lady or gentleman. By the time of Saint-Léon's production, dance's specialized program for training the body had removed it from social discourse so that the ballet offered only diversionary escape. Within its fantasy realm inhabited by beautiful bodies, ballet no longer referenced the acquisition of social skills, and instead connoted the playful and voluptuous actions surrounding sexual intercourse. The separateness of virtuoso and mimetic vocabularies helped to objectify further the newly autonomous body by asking it to move effortlessly back and forth between abstract physical accomplishment and impassioned nonverbal speech. At the same time, its participation in each distinct repertoire endowed the body-object with the perfect blend of anonymity and personality to host the projected desires of its viewers.

Thus the division of labor that cast female characters as objects of desire and male characters as their pursuers extended to include the relationship between dance and its viewers and dance and the other arts. The male *corps de ballet* vanished, leaving only the token principal male figure to partner a seemingly endless supply of female dancers. In this casting of characters and in the display of the beautiful body, ballets privileged the heterosexual male as the ideal spectator, eager to construct and then consume the eroticized feminine form that repeatedly vanished before him. Where Sallé's woman-statue was empowered to return the adoring gaze of her creator, Saint-Léon's gypsy could only entertain through dancing for the powerful men that surrounded her. Her one assertion of desire erased her from the narrative.

Similarly, dance assumed an increasingly feminine role with respect to music, painting, and poetry even as it achieved a certain autonomy in reward for its ability to narrate. The other arts' capacities to edify and educate their audiences and to leave behind definitive documentation of their composition carried a masculine weight and authority that the pleasure-filled and ephemeral dance could not match.[15] Where Sallé's Galathea had stood on a par with exemplars from all the arts, Saint-Léon's gypsy, a captivating waif, an exotic coquette, could charm but not persuade her audience. Her existence, commemorated, ironically, in the form of a statue in the king's palace, traced intangibilities for which no adequate record existed.

This changing status for dance finds eloquent expression in the distinctive stages of textual recording through which the existence of dance performance was documented. Sallé's use of pantomime initiated a line of experimentation in dance that rendered useless the Feuillet notation system that had been responsible for widespread dissemination of dance vocabulary and syntax since the end of the seventeenth century. The Feuillet system, with its abstract characters indicating the movements of the legs and feet and the trajectory of the body through space, could never trace out the gestures of despondency, astonishment, or flirtation that Pygmalion performed. Feuillet's indexical documentation of the body was eventually replaced with blow-by-blow verbal descriptions of the action that functioned as program notes for the production and also as the choreographer's working draft of the composition. Milon, one of a generation of choreographers who assumed a more transparent translatability between scenario and choreographed performance, wrote the published account of his ballet *Pygmalion*. By the 1830s, however, choreographers had relinquished the role of drafting the storyline to a scenarist whose narrative sketch guided the construction of choreography, music, and scenery. Although it presented the story, dance no longer operated as a translation of the words, but rather expressed all that words never could. The performance by Saint-Léon's gypsy Fatma, in its invitation to the most ephemeral pleasure, symbolized a joy and a loss that words could never evoke.

The dancing that took place in the Pygmalion ballets has, like Saint-Léon's gypsy, long ago frozen into disparate residual traces. The dance historian's project, consonant with the sculptor's desire, concerns the resurrection of that dancing body and, like Galathea's danced response, the translation of its significance from one medium to another. In this process the dance historian necessarily assumes the roles of both choreographer and historian, first reconstructing in the imagination a version of that dancing body, then producing it on the stage of the written text. Many moments in the dance historian's performances as choreographer and historian are congruent. Both choreographer and historian, like Sallé's sculptor, work collectively: their labor is never accomplished single-handedly, and both, as part of their working process, construct an imagined dancing body that, like the sculptor's creation, incorporates many techniques, many desires. The imaginary body they construct reflects their own experience as well as the desire to find embodiment for aesthetic, moral, and political values shaped within the choreographer's or historian's own lifetime. The imaginary body also reflects the assimilation of the formal constraints imposed by the disciplines of dance-making and history. Both choreographer and historian work within representational guidelines that determine the selection of material and the procedures for its presentation within their respective mediums.

As much as they coincide, the roles of choreographer and historian also diverge in ways that foreground what is unique to their disciplinary callings. Those long moments where the sculptor gazes upon the statue pining for it to come to life resemble the historian at work in the archives but not the choreographer, who looks into the empty space of the rehearsal studio and asks, "What did I accomplish here? What did the dance I made look like?" The dancing body in the relentlessness of its motion and the inevitability of its evanescence leaves in its wake so little from which to reconstruct its presence, either in the imagination or in history. Whereas choreographers have accustomed themselves to this disappearance act, historians have typically focused on projects informed by more permanent kinds of records. They have privileged information that moves within the textual field from historical document to historian's text and tended to ignore events and actions outside the textual that are unavailable or resistant to the process of translation. Yet, as the choreographer must ask of the historian, "Do not all records of human accomplishment document the motions of bodies?"

The dance historian, witness to this dialogue between choreographer and historian, can stage its conclusions in different ways. As in the different versions of Pygmalion's story, the body of historical facts can, like the gypsy Fatma, take on an exotic allure; or, resembling Milon's Galathea, assume objective permanence; or, in keeping with Sallé's lively artwork, become an active partner in the production of history. If, following Sallé's scenario, the historian and the historical dancing body dance together, then they may reenact a kind of improvised choreographic process that occurs throughout the research and writing of dance history. In this process the practices of dancing and writing partner each other, following the historian's own movement among historical documents, celebrating the historian's creative role in choreographing the historical performance, and imbuing the body of history with choreographic knowledge so that the writing of history may dance.

This dance history, following the lineaments of the Pygmalion trilogy, tells the story of ballet's acquisition of the ability to perform a story and the concomitant silencing of other registers of expression through which dance had formerly communicated. It tracks the development of a new genre of spectacle, the action ballet, as part of the massive changes in social structure and cultural values occurring in France during the same period. The development of the action ballet coincided with the collapse of monarchical rule and the rise of the middle class, with the consolidation of a separate-sphere ideology for masculine and feminine pursuits, and with a new scientific and technical interest in the body. The changing conceptions of the body and of gender that occurred as part of these massive social changes partnered the ballet's ability to narrate. As indicated in the successive versions of the Pygmalion myth, both the dancing body and the female dancer suffered a fate equivalent to that of Galathea refigured as gypsy girl. Both became mute, malleable instruments used by the ballet in order to produce a story. The ballet achieved its narrative voice and coherence by turning the female dancer into a commodity and the dancing body into a no-body.

In tracing these turns, this history allies itself with and takes inspiration from Sallé's version of the Pygmalion story. Experimental, proto-feminist, poised on the brink of dance's narrativization, her choreography depicted fluid and continually renewing identities for bodies and subjects dancing alongside one another. And it intimated at least one kind of explanatory framework—improvised choreography—that could support this protean vision of human and bodily identity. The credit for the choreographic breakthroughs that Sallé initiated and that led to the development of danced narrative has always gone, not to Sallé, but to Jean Georges Noverre, who may have been a member of the audience at her performances.[16] Noverre not only choreographed, but also wrote about the choreographic reforms necessary to enable dance to narrate.[17] His books and scenarios for his productions made history where her dances did not. In its attempt to choreograph a dance history and to historicize the opposition between the written and the danced that Sallé anticipated and Noverre put into place, this history privileges Sallé's spirited dancing lesson over Noverre's dogmatic dramas. Her savvy staging of art's creation performed a story that lies at the origin of this one.

ORIGINARY GESTURES

A gesture is only beautiful when it has painted sadness, tenderness, fierceness—in a word, the soul.[1]

Painting the situations of the soul

Choreographers, historians, aestheticians—all those writing about dance in the eighteenth century—moved quickly in their accounts of dance's origins to a consideration of the Greek and Roman mimes.[2] For almost every author, the most significant moment in the development of dance, the dancing against which all subsequent dances would necessarily be compared, occurred in the ancient Greek and Roman amphitheaters. The persuasive synthesis of music, dance, and gesture rendered by Greek theatre together with the expressivity attained in Roman pantomime constituted landmarks, if not the pinnacle, of choreographic achievement. For many the expressive power of gesture as it was developed by Greek and Roman pantomimes provided both a justification and an ultimate model for contemporary theatrical dance.[3] Captivated by the notion that dancers could depict a story through gesture and movement alone, each author recounted the famous rivalry between Pylades and Bathyllus, two immensely popular Roman mimes whose repertoires included hundreds of myths and fables, all told in movement without the aid of spoken or written texts. These ancient choreographers had developed formulae for perfecting human movement as the most eloquent form of representation, but unfortunately their techniques had been lost during the decadent decline of the art that followed the reign of Augustus. What remained for eighteenth-century choreographers was the concept and intent of ancient pantomime—to paint, using only the body's gestures, a realistic account of human feeling and action.

The verb "to paint" was utilized in virtually every eighteenth-century text on dance to describe the choreographic processes of selection and refinement that transformed

Nature into art. Painting in movement required the choreographer to choose a vivid and telling moment from Nature as the subject matter for the dance and then to perfect the rendition of that moment by presenting a judicious arrangement of the body's movements. The stage, referred to as a canvas, provided the surface upon which to assemble parts, like interlocking puzzle pieces, into a pleasing whole. The body, also conceived as a kind of surface, could, through the careful arrangement of its vibrant, segmented parts, portray human action and interaction. Writers occasionally acknowledged the discrepancy between the three-dimensional body and the two-dimensional painted image by noting similarities between dance and the bas-relief. Yet in selecting the bas-relief rather than a free-standing sculpture, they only emphasized the importance of a two-dimensional image in dance, one that appealed to the eye more than it evoked a muscular or kinesthetic response.

Painting frequently served as the principal metaphor in discussions about all the arts because it best illustrated the ostensible rationale for art—the project of imitating Nature.[4] Using an extended version of this metaphor, aesthetician Charles Batteux described the creative process common to all the arts in this way:

> But one must observe that just as the Arts select the designs of nature and perfect them, they also must choose and perfect the expressions they borrow from Nature. They must refrain from using all sorts of colors or all different sounds: it is necessary to create a judicious selection and a delicate mixture: one must unite all the images and place them in proportion and nuance and harmonize them. Colors and sounds have among them sympathies and repulsions. Nature has the right to unite them according to its desires, but Art must do so according to the rules.[5]

In attempting to evaluate how well each art "painted" life, judgments could be made concerning the appropriate combinations and proportions of elements, the nuances of execution, and the harmony of the assembled parts. The value of art conceived as an imitation of life lay in its ability to provide a perfect image, one that both celebrated and exemplified social ideals. Surrounded by such images, viewers would be educated about the true value of life, gratified at the achievements attained by civilization thus far, and inspired to continue improving the world around them.

Like most other dance viewers of his time, Batteux believed that the rules discovered by the ancients that enabled choreographers to "paint" in dance were in the process of being rediscovered. After a millennium of negligible choreographic experimentation, ballets were now palpably close to realizing the beauty of the ancient productions. Perhaps they could even improve upon the excellence of their forerunners, but only if certain changes could be affected. Batteux, like others writing about dance, used the theatrical practices of ancient Greece and Rome as justifications for theatrical dance but also for recommended aesthetic alterations to its practice.

Throughout the eighteenth century, those who wrote about dance consistently raised the same objections to performances they saw. The dance did not "paint" as well as it might. It certainly failed to achieve the painterly eloquence and accuracy of the ancient mimes. Performances often fell short in their representation of a range of emotional expression. The movements, although brilliantly executed, appeared mechanical, and the overall production needed greater narrative coherence. While commentators agreed on the nature of the disparity between ancient and contemporary dances, they disagreed on the extent of reforms necessary to bring dance up to ancient standards. Early in the century, they admitted only a modest discontent with dance practice, but in the 1750s, writers began to urge a comprehensive overhaul of theatrical dance practices.[6]

In order to secure their claims, dance writers of that period identified a new origin for dance, one existing prior to the ancient performances, one promising a more essential role for dance in society.[7] The first movements, they argued, occurred as the physical expression of the soul's feelings. In the first humans' prehistoric wanderings, as in the infant's cradle, dance movement signed the stirrings of the soul.[8] Along with song, originally comprised of disjointed cries and inflections, crude but diverse bodily movements offered the first means of communication and the basis on which verbal language subsequently developed. No longer merely one of the many civilizing endeavors that enhanced personal and social appearances, dance became a vital form of human expression and communication, an innate human response prior to any social conventions that came to govern it.

This assertion of a prior and more fundamental role for dance shifted the performance of dancing to new conceptual ground.[9] Rather than a communal endeavor that accomplished religious or social goals, dancing became an act unique in its ability to represent individual human feelings. Because it originated in the soul's first movements, dancing constituted an intrinsic response, part of human behavior. Furthermore, it had a power to convey—to paint—with uncanny accuracy the individual's true feelings. Yet unlike painting, which could only seize the telling and climactic moment to render in pictorial form, dancing could document each successive moment in the dramatic sequence of human interaction. It could provide an ongoing, affecting account of the soul's movements.

The new conception of a prehistorical dance did not elaborate a sequential causality between the soul's feelings and the body's movement. No pressing expressive needs pent up inside people caused them to move. Instead, accounts of the first moment of dancing suggested a synchronicity of bodily and spiritual states. The individual felt and moved, rather than felt and then moved. Even accounts that identify an excessive amount of feeling as the state during which the first expressive movements occurred did not analyze the growth of feeling or define the moment at which there was sufficient feeling to provoke movement. The danger or joy necessary to wrest the first cry, the first movement, occurred suddenly and even coincidentally with the movement itself. The original dancer, overcome with joy, was simply seized with joyful movement.

Louis de Cahusac, historian, librettist, and author of several articles for Diderot's *Encyclopedia*, exemplified this view of dance's spontaneous generation, describing it in these dramatic terms:

> Man experienced sensations from the first moment that he breathed; and the sounds of the voice, the play of features across his face, the movements of his body, were simply expressions of what he felt.
>
> There are naturally in the voice sounds of pleasure and of sorrow, of anger and of tenderness, of distress and of joy. There are similarly in the movements of the face and of the body gestures of all these traits; the ones were the primitive sources of song, and the others of dance.

This was the universal language understood by all nations and even by animals, because it is anterior to all conventions and natural to all the creatures that breathe on the earth.

These inarticulate sounds, which were a kind of song and (if I may express myself in this way) natural music, as it developed little by little, painted in an unequivocal manner, even though coarse, all the different situations of the soul; and they were preceded and followed externally by gestures relative to all these diverse situations.

The body was peaceful or agitated; the eyes flamed or dulled; the face colored or paled; the arms opened or closed, rose toward heaven or fell back to the earth; the feet formed slow or rapid steps; all the body, in short, responded by postures, attitudes, leaps, shudders to the sounds with which the soul painted its movements. Thus song, which is primitive expression of feeling, developed from itself a second which is in man, and it is this expression that we have named dance.[10]

Emphasizing the affinities between music and dance, Cahusac, along with many other writers of his time, proposed that the first expressive sounds and gestures, as rudimentary as they might have been, constituted a language shared by all humans and even animals.[11] These simple but powerful articulations vividly depicted the situations of the soul. And whether dance developed alongside or out of music, both, virtual templates of one another, maintained a proximity to the soul which no other arts shared.

As the direct product of fundamental human feelings, the universal language of movement manifested potential as a medium through which to communicate directly, globally, and in an orderly fashion. Far from a congeries of incoherent, erratic impulses, this language consisted of a standard repertoire of gestures which could be studied and classified. The study of the visual representation of the passions had already established that such a classification was possible. Under the guidance of court-appointed painter Charles Le Brun, a comprehensive categorization of facial expressions revealed a basic human repertoire.[12] An analogous knowledge of human movement, one of the areas of the classical mime's expertise, now required rediscovery.

Aesthetic knowledge, such as that demonstrated by the ancient mimes, enhanced and developed the expressive gift received from Nature by inculcating it with grace and measure. Thus the original universal language of movements became the raw material out of which historical dance was formed. The rules and regulations discovered by culture for lending clarity and proportion to movements only enhanced their expressivity.[13] The original language, while unique, was not longed for or sought after. Its existence rationalized the enduring importance of dance as a civilized pursuit. As Cahusac put it, "Nature furnished the circumstances, and experience provides the rules. Thus one learns to dance even though one has within oneself all the steps from which the dance is formed, as one learns to sing even though one has in the voice all the sounds of which song is formed, because one develops, through the help of Art, the talents received from nature."[14]

The postulated existence of a primeval dance only lent greater prestige to the ancient artists who had developed the necessary techniques for representing the essential relationship between movement and feeling. The classical mimes had learned both to regulate bodily movement and to refine its expressions. But for midcentury writers, such performances realized not only the painterly accuracy that the body could attain, but also the unique capacity of dance to produce a succession of images that detailed the unfolding of events over time. Pantomimes demonstrated dance's capacity to translate a story directly into movement, word by word. Their choreography painted a story from beginning to end, achieving the narrative's setting, argument, overall coherence, and unified point of view. In imagined reconstructions of these classical performances, writers found a perfect merger, via dance, of the rich yet arrested visuality of painting with the causal and logical unfolding of events through time.

Those arguing for urgent reforms in choreographic practice focused especially on the lack of narrative coherence in contemporary productions and on the meaningless display of virtuoso dance movement. Jean-Jacques Rousseau summed up over a decade of arguments in his annoyance at the absurd alternation between singing and dancing as expressed through the hero in his novel *Julie, ou La Nouvelle Heloïse*:

> It remains for me to speak of the Ballets which are the most brilliant attraction of this Opéra. . . . In every act the action is generally interrupted at the most interesting moment by a dance performed before the actors who are seated, while those in the parterre watch standing. It thus results that the protagonists of the drama are completely forgotten, or else the spectators watch the actors watching something else again. The way in which these festivities are brought on is simple.
>
> Is the prince joyous? His courtiers participate in his joy and they dance.
>
> Is he sad? He must be cheered up and they dance again. I do not know whether it is the fashion at Court to give balls to kings when they are out of humor, but I know that I cannot admire too much the stoicism of the buskinned monarch who watches gavottes and listens to songs while his crown is in danger, his life in peril and his fate being decided off stage. And there are even other subjects for dancing: the most serious events of life unfold in dance. Priests dance; soldiers dance; gods dance; devils dance; one dances at funerals and everyone dances in response to everything.
>
> The dance is then the fourth of the fine arts employed in the construction of the lyric scene; but the other three adhere to imitation; and this one, what does it imitate? Nothing.[15]

Along with other advocates of the new dance, Rousseau was troubled by the lack of narrative continuity presented in the opera-ballets and also by the inexplicable popularity of the dancing. His critique emphasized the disparity between sung drama and dance as vehicles for representing dramatic action. His sensible, bourgeois character from the country was at a loss to explain why the derivative and ornamental entrées which intervened abruptly in the middle of the action commanded such an enthusiastic response.[16]

Similarly, Denis Diderot, more critical and outspoken than most writers on dance from the period, railed against the many dance forms of which ballets were composed—the minuet, rigaudon, and sarabande—because they seemed to have no significance beyond the graceful manner in which they were performed. The noble lines traced by the dancer's body in space offered no message. The entire production, while beautifully executed, evidenced no narrative content. The dance meant nothing because it did not paint, it did not imitate life:

> The dance? The dance still awaits a man of genius; because one seldom finds it used as a genre of imitation, the dance one sees is terrible everywhere. The dance should be to pantomime as poetry is to prose, or more precisely as natural speech is to song. It is a measured pantomime.

I would like someone to tell me what all these dances performed today represent—the minuet, the passe-pied, the rigaudon, the allemande, the sarabande—where one follows a traced path. This dancer performs with an infinite grace; I see in each movement his facility, his grace, and his nobility, but what does he imitate? This is not the art of song, but the art of jumping.

A dance is a poem. This poem must have its own way of representing itself. It is an imitation presented in movements, that depends upon the cooperation of the poet, the painter, the composer, and the art of pantomime. The dance has its own subject which can be divided into acts and scenes. Each scene has a recitative improvised or obligatory, and its ariette.[17]

What dance needed, according to Diderot, was a genius, someone of synthetic vision, who could develop dance as an imitative art. The dance required a new vocabulary of movements so that it could depict human action, so that it could tell a story in its own unique way. Instead of jumping about, the dance should celebrate the great exploits, adventures, and experiences of humankind. Like song, the dance should originate inside the body; like poetry it should evidence a careful choice of, and rhythmic structure for, its movements. Its new vocabulary should borrow from pantomime all the postures, gestures, and expressions necessary for the accurate depiction of human sentiment. Once this new system of movements had been constructed, dance would be able to tell a story in its own unique way. It would organize its subject, much like opera, into acts and scenes. It would develop as an independent art form, collaboratively employing the contributions of related arts, but nonetheless manifesting an integrity all its own.

The overhaul of choreographic conventions that would enable dance to tell a story through movement thus required facility at translation—from the languages of painting and poetry to that of movement, and from the telling scenes of life to those of danced art. Choreographers were not asked to render the development of feeling into form, but instead to depict one formal image of feeling after another. They were not asked to chart the process of expression, but rather to display a range of feelings with accuracy and candor. The transitional moments between one feeling and the next were less important than the vividness with which the full-blown passion was portrayed. These successive states needed only to be encompassed by a simple plot that would justify the feelings displayed.

In the same way that choreographers were asked to move the danced action directly from one passionate scene to the next, so writers categorized the history of dance into types, making little attempt to trace their evolution or determine how one type might have grown out of another. Maximilien Gardel, for example, first-ranking dancer and Ballet Master at the Opéra, succinctly described the transition from the original dance to sacred dance this way:

Dance in the earliest times was nothing more than a naive expression of joy and recognition. Keener eyes, a vaster genius, a love of pleasure, everything revealed the more striking effects to which dancing was susceptible. Soon after, the arrival of Apis provided more elevated subjects; one celebrated the birth of Osiris, his exploits, his loves, and his coronation.[18]

The subject matter and occasion of performance implied a format for the dance that concerned most writers far more than the transformation of dances over time. Scholarly and aesthetic interest focused on the enumeration of types of dances and the sorting out of various instances of dancing based on an analysis of key features. Just as the assertion that sensation manifested itself in movement was self-evident and seemed to require no investigation into the dynamics of that process, so, too, the fact of different types and functions of dance took precedence over the relationships among them.

For example, Cahusac, having located the original dance in the psychological and universal space of primitive being, was able to organize all his observations about different dances into a typology of forms based on function and occasion. The same human need to communicate feelings informed each instance of dancing. Sacred dances, resulting from the apprehension of God as an enduring focus for human feeling, were practiced throughout the ancient world. Examples included Egyptian rites that celebrated the birth and exploits of Osiris, and specific Hebraic occasions of dancing—Moses and Miriam at the parting of the Red Sea, the daughters of Silo in the fields, David and his people before the Ark of the Covenant. Dances that occurred at civic celebrations and public festivals belonged to another broad category often referred to as secular or profane dance. Throughout the ancient and modern world, these dances improved one's health, posture, and general social skills. Theatrical dance became a third variety, perfected in ancient Greece and Rome as a medium for representing life's situations through gestural enactment.

A simple yet compelling narrative structure encapsulated these different types of dances past and present. Following the powerful birth of the primitive dance and its perfection by the ancients, dance suffered a tragic fall. Then, in a single dramatic progression, but with epicycles of refinement and vulgarity, it began its subsequent rise toward an even greater glory, one which Cahusac and other midcentury authors imagined as palpably near. If dance's practitioners, who had already achieved an extraordinary level of proficiency, could swiftly implement specified reforms, and if dance historians, categorizing the successive steps in choreographic innovation, could explicate the failures and triumphs of dancing's dramatic progress toward its final goal, then dance could easily attain perfection. Its elevated status in theatre and society would be assured, and it would reclaim the esteem of its most ardent and educated admirers.

Such a linear and unified trajectory for dance history relied upon placing dance's new origin within the enduring structure of the human psyche in order to explain the connection between past and present dance. The notion of a single drive to express the soul through movement—not the mere fact of disparate dance performances at various moments in history—spawned a narrative of dance's evolution. Dance's newly primitivized beginnings also allowed writers and choreographers of the period to refresh their arguments concerning dance's intrinsic worth and meaning. The unfathomability of the soul's first stirrings and the body's first response effectively rationalized their arguments for dance's new mission just as this pristine origin empowered dance, and their representation of it, with a universal significance.

Vanishing physicalities

For Diderot, Cahusac, and many other theatre-goers in the 1750s, the evocative impact of the Baroque opera-ballet had played itself out. The Watteau-like melancholy of its

6. An early-eighteenth-century masked dancer from the Opéra.

masked figure appeared vacant rather than suggestive. (See fig. 6.) The symmetrical use of the dancers in their placement on stage, the floor patterns wherein two dancers mirrored each other throughout a duet, the just and regulated exchange of bodies in space—were now found boring rather than ennobling.[19] The meaning of gestures and stances, clear references to noble conduct in former times, was no longer intelligible. An increasingly secularized and bourgeois viewer searched for relevance in the dancers' movement-made allusions and found none. The physicality through which dance imparted its meanings, desiccated and faint, could not muster the charisma necessary to make an impression on an audience's eyes, much less their souls.

Cassanova anticipated this disenchantment when he remarked on his own bafflement in response to seeing the superb but ephemeral, and above all, irrelevant dancing of Louis Dupré in *Les Fêtes Vénitiennes* in 1745:

> Suddenly I hear the whole of the pit burst into applause at the appearance of a tall, well-made dancer, wearing a mask and a black wig, with long curls reaching half-way down his back, and dressed in a robe open in front and reaching to his heels. . . . I see this fine figure coming forward with measured steps, and, having arrived at the front of the stage, raise slowly his rounded arms, move them gracefully, stretch them completely, then contract them, move his feet with precision and lightness, take a few small steps, make some battements at mid-calf, then a pirouette, and after disappear by walking backwards to the wings. The whole had not lasted half a minute. The applause burst from every part of the house; I ask my friend the meaning of all these

7. The dancing lesson foregrounded with riding and fencing instruction in the background, from the *Gymnasium of the Academic Arts*, 1690.

bravos, and he answers that we applaud the grace of Dupré and the divine harmony of his movements. He is now sixty years of age, and as he was forty years ago.

"What! Has he never danced in a different style?"

"He could not have danced better, the development you saw is perfect, and what is there above perfection?"[20]

Accustomed to the frequently changing styles of the Italian dancers and their extensive reliance on pantomime, Cassanova was perplexed by Dupré's popularity. He could not fathom the significance of the dancer's delicate display, the encoding of perfection into movements of the arms, legs, and stance.

Like many other French dancers of his background and training, Dupré had perfected a kind of dancing whose origins resided in the drive to regulate the body's comportment and to refine the body's every action in each endeavor it performed throughout the day.[21] His carriage, the easy articulation of his arms and legs, the carefully measured gestures, his alacrity—all demonstrated an ideal way of moving through social as well as artistic worlds. Quick, darting motions of the legs, the coordinated rise and fall of arms, and a responsive torso conducted hands, feet, and head along desired pathways that resembled those prescribed by proper social intercourse.

Dupré's performance gestured back to late-seventeenth- and early eighteenth-century conceptions of dancing as a metadiscipline that prepared the body for its movement in any endeavor. Rather than being another of many bodily pursuits and pastimes, dancing was *the* medium through which the body was cultivated for action in the practices of rhetoric, comportment, etiquette, defense, health, and art. (See fig. 7.) The opening lines from Louis XIV's 1662 charter authorizing the establishment of an Academy of Dance indicated the centrality of dance's role in providing a base for all other physical activities, including bearing arms:

> [T]he Art of Dance has always been recognized as the most honest and most necessary at forming the body, at providing the most basic and natural foundation for all sorts of exercises, among others the bearing of arms, and consequently, one of the most advantageous and useful to our nobility, and to others who have the honor of approaching us, not only in times of war in our armies, but also in times of peace in the entertainment of our ballets. . . .[22]

The charter did not distinguish between dance as a theatre art, as a social art, and as a kind of physical training. Instead, it observed that with the properly formed body, nobility could signal to each other and to foreigners their high social rank, their intrepidness in making war, and their charm in times of peace. The charter went on to designate twelve original members and those who replaced them or were initiated into the institution by them as responsible for maintaining standards of excellence in dancing and in teaching dance. In addition, they were asked to be ready to contribute choreographed divertissements, when appropriate, for the King's pleasure.[23] Their professional duties thus included choreography, but also required them to pursue dance as a system of knowledge that would provide its practitioners with an underlying foundation of bodily training useful in all situations.

Louis XIV's decision to establish the Academy of Dance, political, aesthetic, and practical, concretized dance's central role in the cultivation of the body. It likewise reinforced decisions he had made consistently since the early years of his reign regarding the rules governing the courtier's bearing and comportment. Although formulae for behavior had long been part of French aristocratic life,[24] Louis XIV organized etiquette into an immense hierarchical web that governed virtually all actions performed throughout the day at court.[25] These decisions were made as a way to control, literally, the bodies of those around him. The adherence of each body to its specifically assigned tasks and of all bodies to a generalized manner of interaction was mandated by the king as a primary means of consolidating and protecting monarchic authority.

Whether walking or standing, greeting or acknowledging one another, courtiers followed rules that stipulated how each action should be accomplished. Courtiers practiced the performance of every task, whether mounting a horse, playing a game of tennis, bowing as the sovereign entered, or moving a chair from one part of the room to another. Along with their king they also devoted themselves to dancing in ballets, at

8. A social dance performance at court.

general *bals* held after the ballets, and during divertissements. (See fig. 8.) These evenings of mixed entertainment and social dancing, no less formal than the court ballets presented for a large audience, often required couples to perform for one another. Under the scrutinizing gazes of their associates, they were asked to demonstrate their command of the key vocabulary of dance movement—and by association, their command of all other courtly skills. Facility and composure in dance signaled competence at and stature within general courtly life. Courtiers' status could thus be enhanced or jeopardized at such gatherings as a result of their level of expertise.

The artist William Hogarth, in his *Analysis of Beauty*, provided an important insight into how this expertise might have been evaluated. He identified as a central aspect of bodily comportment the gracefulness of the body's traces through space, a feature that he applied by extension to dancing. In presenting one's hand, for example, the curve traced from

9. William Hogarth's drawing of the proper S shape to be traced when passing a fan, indictated here as fig. 49, from *The Analysis of Beauty.*

one's own body toward that of another person must neither exaggerate nor underinflect the ideal S shape. (See fig. 9.) In walking, the waving trace created by the head must alternate smoothly between low and high. The minuet, the most perfect of all dances, amplified this trace by exploring a range of heights for the erect body.

> The ordinary undulating motion of the body in common walking (as may be plainly seen by the waving line, which the shadow a man's head makes against a wall as he is walking between it and the afternoon sun) is augmented in dancing into a larger quantity of *waving* by means of the minuet-step, which is so contrived as to raise the body by gentle degrees somewhat higher than ordinary, and sink it again in the same manner lower in the going on of the dance. The figure of the minuet-path on the floor is also composed of serpentine lines. . . . when the parties by means of this step rise and fall most smoothly in time, and free from sudden starting and dropping, they come nearest to Shakespear's idea of the beauty of dancing. . . .[26]

The body, as it moved through space, thus signaled its graceful presence through the traces it made. Courtiers performing their duties left in their wake a perpetual tracery. The moderated schemata that guided their movements conveyed a calm easefulness—neither too erect nor too floppy, neither mercurial nor phlegmatic.[27] By mastering these judicious spatial and temporal guidelines, they physicalized an identity that was always agile, always cool.[28]

Even the system for notating dances such as the minuet, developed at the request of Louis XIV, focused on this capacity of bodily motion to trace lines in space. Feuillet notation, so called after one of its originators, Raoul Auger Feuillet, simulated the rectangular floor of the dancing area with the rectangular layout of the printed page.[29] The

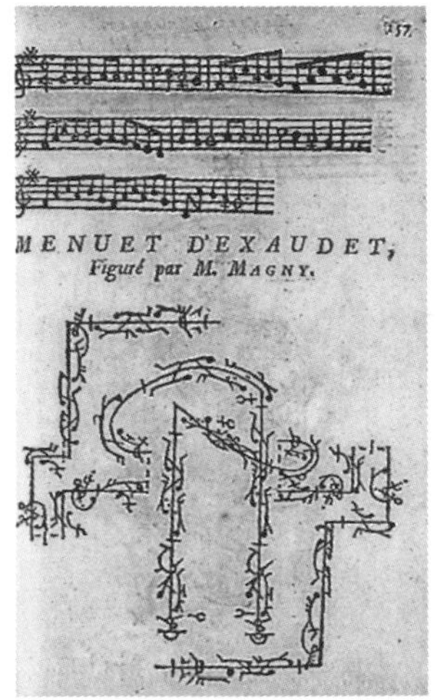

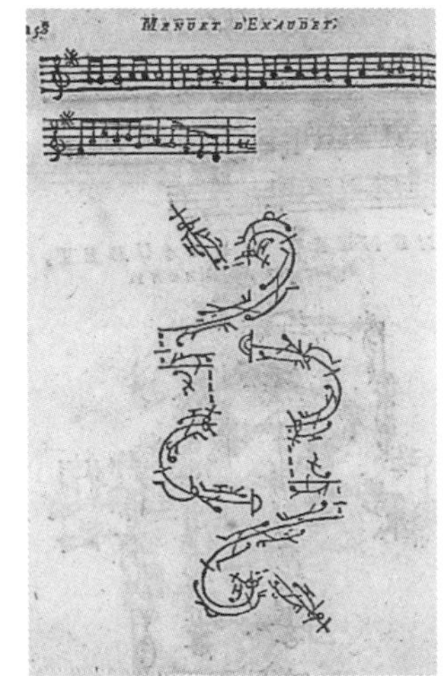

10. Feuillet-derived notation from the 1760 dance manual by Magny for his choreography entitled *Menuet d'Exaudet.*

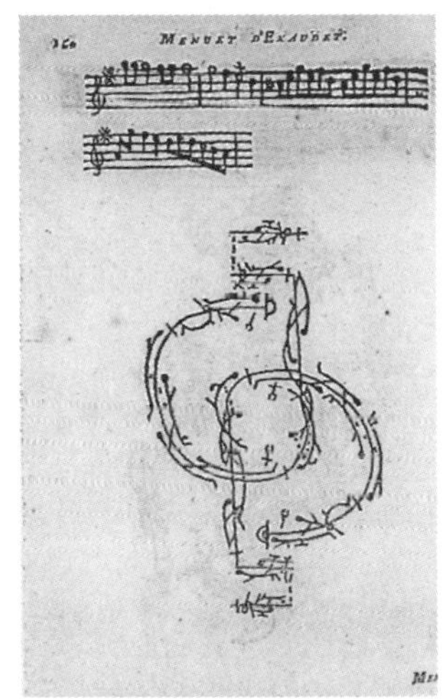

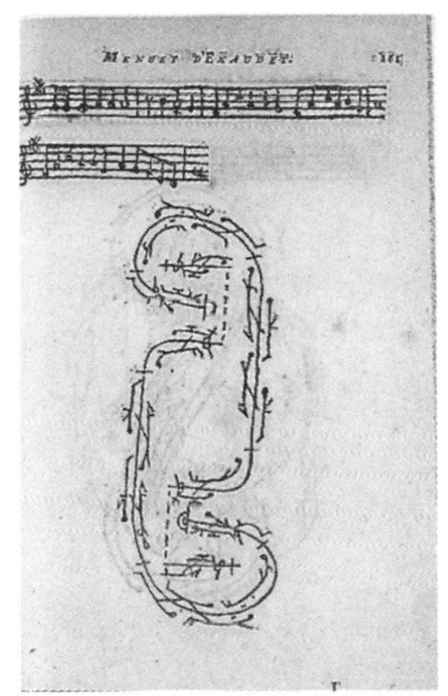

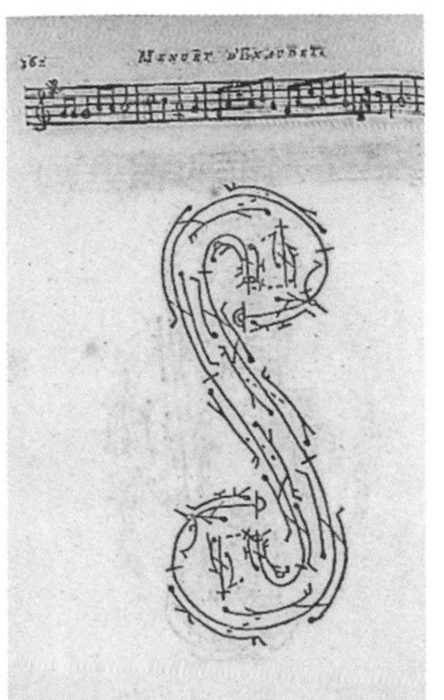

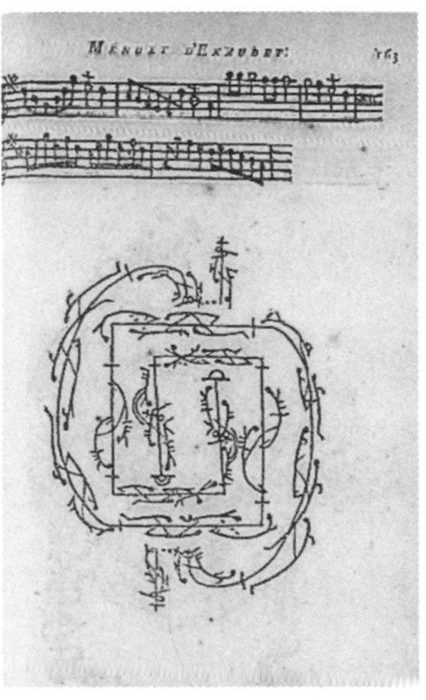

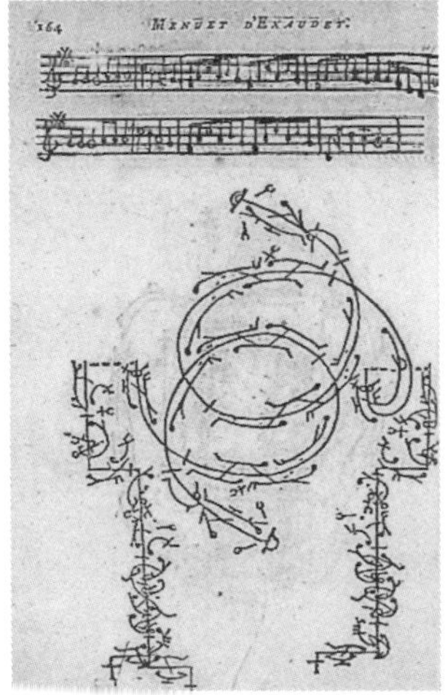

system marked the path of the dancer's whole body through that space with a track line, on either side of which were indicated the traces made by the legs and feet in their individual paths through horizontal space. (See fig. 10.) Each foot's gestures merited a mark on the page: a simple line from beginning position to ending position noted the exact trajectory accomplished by the moving foot, and even the back and forth action of the foot during a beat was recreated with back-and-forth concentric curved lines around the notation for the standing leg. Through its graphic annotations, the symbols indicated steps to be performed by the legs and feet and the precise path to be taken by the dancer through space.

Feuillet notation also represented movements in the vertical dimension, important in the dance form, but with a different sort of visual marking. Pliés, relevés, jumps, and leaps were indicated through the addition of more arbitrary symbols that attached to the trace of the body and limbs' paths through horizontal space. Similar in their horizontal trace, a leap and a step were differentiated by the addition of a small mark for bending and then rising into the air. The notation system thereby identified the horizontal trace form as the primary organizing feature of dance. Both horizontal and vertical measuring systems, however, commemorated the spatial awareness between body and surround and among all the bodies that dancing required. This carefully measured spacing out of each courtly task and interaction, celebrated in dancing, served as the mechanism for controlling and evaluating all bodies as they moved throughout the court.

As the inheritor of Louis XIV's courtly protocols and its artistic endeavors, Dupré not only offered a consummate rendition of proper comportment, but had also realized a defectless body—agreeably apportioned, with each part exercising an easeful, moderated aplomb. Noble identity depended not only on one's knowledge and proper execution of the correct actions, but also on the body's image in a given position. Undesirable attributes with which anyone might be born, such as knock-kneed legs, a thrusting chin, or sunken chest, impeded the realization of a successful aristocratic identity. As Dancing Master Pierre Rameau observed, no better remedy than dancing existed for enhancing one's bodily position and consequently one's social position:

> If dancing were confined to the theatre, it would provide occupation for a few people only; but it may be said that it merits the attention of almost every one, even if they be destined to make use of it from their earliest years. Dancing adds grace to the gifts which nature has bestowed upon us, by regulating the movements of the body and setting it in its proper positions. And if it does not completely eradicate the defects with which we are born, it mitigates or conceals them.[30]

The study of dancing, even if it did not manage to render the body perfectly erect and well-apportioned, nonetheless imparted the graceful ease that would allow the body to simulate perfection. The movements of its limbs could coordinate with one another and with those of other bodies to achieve a harmonious geometry. (See fig. 11.)

By shaping the body into the proper position, dancing fashioned an appealing physique. By cultivating the qualities of suppleness and resiliency, dancing established one's facility at moving through the social world. As perfect shapes propelled along harmonious trajectories, all persons would be able to enter into and even improve upon a gracious social intercourse:

11. Illustrations from Pierre Rameau's *The Dancing Master.*

> France has long recognized Dance as the necessary foundation for all graceful accomplishments; it is Dance that corrects the natural defects of the body, and changes its bad habits; by bringing such agreeable harmony into all its actions; it is Dance that teaches those who cultivate it, the art of entering gracefully into social gatherings, and gaining the immediate approbation that determines their destiny, and always the enjoyment of those who view them; it is Dance that teaches them to disentangle themselves gently from the most embarrassing situations; it is Dance that gives facility at horseback riding, and at bearing arms; it is Dance that prepares them to serve their Prince in battles and to please him in entertainments.[31]

Mastery of the art of dancing promised all this. And, when necessary, fluency at dancing would even help to disentangle courtiers from any awkward or unseemly occasions by distributing charm throughout their actions.

If dancing formed the exterior of the person, it also cleansed the interior. Dance created a moving body whose manners and bearing signaled its stature, but it also enhanced the body's appearance by improving its health. Composed as it was of endless tubing through which vital fluids seeped, sluiced, and churned, the body required mild agitation to keep all its substances flowing smoothly. Jean Pierre Burette justified the beneficial effects of exercise with this vivid description of the body:

> To be completely convinced of the importance of exercise in general . . . it is only necessary to envision carefully the structure of the human body. The body is a marvelous assemblage of tubes of different diameters, interlaced and folded upon themselves in a thousand ways, through which different liquids must travel ceaselessly and without disturbance so that the liquids will complete their tour. It is certain that exercise brings the muscles of the body into motion, and gives assistance to all

> parts of the body, both interior and exterior. Through exercise, the body's fibers acquire flexibility that facilitates its vibrations; and the blood refined and thinned by the frequent percussion of these fibers, travels with greater speed through all the routes troubled by poor circulation that must convey it to the furthest reaches of the labyrinth of vessels. As a result of these several advantageous effects, the machine is maintained in the best of its possible states. . . .[32]

As a result of proper maintenance of the body-machine, Burette argued, one could enjoy good digestion, good respiration, effective work from the glands in separating the blood from superfluous fluids, and a correct tension among the animal spirits. He continued:

> But what distinguishes Dance, and places it far above the other exercises, is that it maintains a naturalness and avoids the kind of violent action that characterizes most varieties of gymnastics; Dance knows how to distribute a moderate agitation to all parts of the body, which it rouses with cadence and meter; such that there is no muscle that does not enliven, and enter to contribute its part to the actions necessary to form the steps, the gestures, and the attitudes of the Dancer.[33]

Dancing contributed to the effective management of bodily fluids by keeping them from becoming stagnant. The same qualities of moderation and economy that made dancing a basis for other activities also identified it as the most effective form of exercise. The advantage of proper stimulation and circulation of bodily fluids lay not only in the feelings of well-being one would experience, but also in the attractive appearance one would acquire and then preserve.

Dupré's physicality referenced all these healthful, social, and aesthetic values of dancing. His apportioned physique and the nobility of his bearing conveyed the ideal body. His every step, his successive positionings in space traced out the most harmonious paths a body could follow. The choreography likewise drew upon, even as it aggrandized and theatricalized, social dance forms of the period. Vocabularies of both social and theatrical dance overlapped to a large extent, and they related to musical structure and phrasing in the same way.[34] Dupré's repertoire included many steps of greater intricacy, with each step fashioned for presentation by a dancer on stage to an audience seated below and in front. Audience members, however, most of whom had received instruction in dance, could discern subtle aspects of Dupré's style based on their experience of dancing as well as their frequent opportunities to view dance. His prowess, while clearly beyond their grasp, nonetheless depicted an extension of their skills.

If the vocabulary and style of Dupré's performance resonated with the dancing experience of many viewers, the theatrical image offered by his costume, mask, cloak, and the stage setting presented a finely wrought alterity. Cloaked and plumed with exaggerated elaborateness against a backdrop of comparable visual complexity, Dupré's every gesture established incidental resonances between costume and scenery. Curves and shapes of the costume's embroidery, cut, and accessories reiterated architectural detail and ornamentation built into the set, causing an over-abundance of visual messages.[35] The dancing itself, a further compounding of these privileged trace forms, moved one form nearer its likeness, another into symmetrical opposition, while occluding previous perceptions of design continuity, only to allow them to reappear moments later. Each moment's meditation on these geometries imbued the dancer with a precious otherness. How could any one figure operate as the repository of so many careful calibrations?

When masked, the dancer's face stared back at the audience, rebuffing their search for familiar forms, similarly transforming the known into the exotic. The face, normally the vehicle for a mute form of discursive exchange among dancers and between dancers and audience, was stilled by the mask. The absence of such highly specific information as the face would convey imparted a greater articulateness to the gestures of the limbs, the swaying of the torso, and the tiniest inclinations of the head.[36] At the same time, the face's impassive stillness made the dancing look effortless. The failure of the face to change attitudes when the body did created a haunting dissonance. This wrenching of bodily and facial dispositions accomplished by the mask constructed the reservoir for feeling which the specific dance form then directed toward the joyous, the saddened, the regal, or the melancholic.

Each of the dances in Dupré's repertoire, the minuet, rigaudon, and sarabande—the very dances that Diderot had dismissed as meaningless—articulated a structuring of feeling through its vocabulary and syntax. For example, dancing could occur at a moment of nostalgic reverie for the character, and thereby expand, through the execution of a slow sarabande, the inexpressible loss the character was confronting.[37] In the sarabande, the poignant suspensions, the stately slow pacing of steps imparted a sense of restraint from full-blown physical exertion. Dancers seemed to hold back from any invigorating athleticism, and they also indulged in the weighty and languorous phrasing of steps. The following description of a solo sarabande performance, although performed at court rather than onstage, gives a sense of the hesitations and shifts in mood through which melancholy would be constructed:

> Sometimes he would cast languid and passionate glances throughout a slow and languid rhythmic unit [cadence]; and then, as though weary of being obliging, he would avert his eyes, as if he wished to hide his passion; and, with a more precipitous motion, would snatch away the gift he had tendered.
>
> Now and then he would express anger and spite with an impetuous and turbulent rhythmic unit; and then, evoking a sweeter passion by more moderated motions, he would sigh, swoon, let his eyes wander languidly; and certain sinuous movements of the arms and body, nonchalant, disjointed, and passionate, made him appear so admirable and so charming that throughout this enchanting dance he won as many hearts as he attracted spectators.[38]

Rather than look like a melancholy person, the dancer manifested qualities—sudden changes in tempo, weighty suspensions, quick retractions of the eyes and body from fulsome physicality—shared with the state of melancholy.

This approach to representation infused the entire performance with a perpetual sense of a lack of sufficient discursive information. In its references to other realms of physical endeavor, dancing gestured a manner of physical being but no specific physical behavior. In its cultivation of a "nonchalant, disjointed, and passionate" physicality, the dance vectored significance away from specific messages and toward a manner of messaging. Each ballet interlude danced out states of feeling but also referenced the body's expressiveness, and this provided a source of power and identity for dance within the opera-ballets.

This exquisite refinement of the body's articulateness was what viewers had admired about dancing like Dupré's for so many years. It celebrated the body as a principal

12. A ballet from *La Princesse de Navarre,* given at Versailles in honor of Louis XV's marriage in 1745.

13. Couples dancing in a ballet from *La Princesse de Navarre.*

medium through which the aristocracy established individual identity and accomplished social interaction. The body did not merely enhance communication or provide subliminal clues to the person's state of mind. Rather, its physicality both set the stage for and performed values of central social importance. Social dancing elaborated on the deft moderation in all actions that helped determine one's stature. Theatrical dancing summoned up the full range of the body's interstitial relations—to health, comportment, politesse, as well as the arts of warfare, courtship, sportsmanship, and theatrical display. It vivified the metadisciplinary bodily techniques that infused every action with an illustrious nobility.

And Dupré's kind of dancing showed even more. It demonstrated the profound sense in which any achievement of noble stature, by Dupré or any other dancing body, never occurred in isolation. Status of any kind, like the guidelines for how bodies should move—in relation to one another and to horizontal and vertical grids—was defined in relation with all other bodies participating in the courtly system. (See fig. 12.) The symmetrical to and fro, the calculated clusters of individuals, the graceful resolve from one configuration to the next—showed bodies suspended within and reticulated by the linear patterns of requisite social behavior. Even as a soloist Dupré demonstrated in his every gesture full cognizance of his relation to space, to metered time, and to a momentarily absent sociality.

The ballets in which Dupré appeared charged the pristine, rational perspective defined by the proscenium and stage with various kinds of spatial inscription—traceries of feet on the floor, arms and hands in the air, the collocations of bodies distributed across the stage. (See fig. 13.) Just as monarch, courtiers of differing ranks, and all subjects assumed their mutually defining roles within the same rigidly fixed social and political hierarchies, so dancers displayed the perfect coordination of all bodies within an analogous set of fixed forms. A single, favorable viewing location and a hierarchy of less optimal perspectives surrounding it mirrored the structuring of space on the stage. For those privileged to occupy the central seats, a feeling of omniscience and all-knowingness resulted from gazing into the carefully modulated infinity in which each character assumed a decorous and appropriate place. For those not so privileged, there remained the grandeur of the spectacle itself, mitigated perhaps by the tacit sense of one's placement slightly askew.

Corporeality, as cultivated and epitomized by dancers like Dupré, enabled the graceful negotiation and perpetual reaffirmation of these hierarchized social roles. Yet the power and eloquence of those bodies had eroded entirely for Diderot and others championing a new dance.[39] The originary chain of meaning descending from god to king to social classes that had empowered the body but also required it to become so articulate had rusted through. They found in Dupré's agile maneuvers only an ornamental silliness. They found in his masked moderation not a breathtaking display of tact and nuance, but an annoyingly ambiguous avoidance of the dancer's precise thoughts and feelings. For them Dupré and his fellow dancers increasingly gestured like haunting melancholic apparitions toward a vacant expressivity.

Transgressive gestures

Those arguing for a new approach to danced theatricality, Diderot included, hoped to replace Dupré's virtuoso performance with a realistic, moving image of human nature. Unmasked and clothed in accurate historical costume, dancers would abandon decorative geometry and instead depict actual human beings embroiled in the issues and conflicts of social life. These danced characters would evoke the dramas inherent in all human relationships and dance out a succession of interactions that developed from a beginning point through an essential conflict to a synthetic resolution. The vividness of these actions would allow viewers both to see and to feel the characters' experiences.

This agenda for reform for dance fit within a larger aesthetic project that conceptualized a new role for all the arts as capable of cultivating an innate sensibility on the part of one human being for another.[40] Exposure to the arts would not only enhance the capacity for empathy, but also expose one to the variety of predicaments, injustices, tensions, and pleasures that formed the fabric of social life. If theatrical productions were to succeed in realizing this new vision of art, they would necessarily develop new forms and contents for performances.[41] Specifically, the theatre should explore new genres, neither tragic nor comic, and new subject matters based on quotidian life rather than exceptional and heroic situations. And it should pursue a new narrative coherence, one that traced the inevitable logic of human actions and thereby avoided reliance on sudden interventions by supernatural forces.[42]

For Diderot, the successful reformation of theatrical dance depended upon a careful choreographic elaboration of gesture.[43] Gesture most readily conveyed the experience of great passions because it spoke the superior language of the heart. From the needs, desires, and feelings which it expressed could be derived a sense of wisdom as opposed to mere intelligence. Unextractable from the site of the body performing it, gesture always pronounced its message in a specific social situation that anchored its meaning in a given place and moment. But if its bodily location gave it concreteness, gesture's mobility imparted a unique ability to represent the flux of life.[44] Gesture had the uncanny capacity to represent the dynamic ebb and flow, the assertive presence and fleeting disappearance of events in the mind and the world.

A unique biological alliance between bodily motion and consciousness allowed movement to show thought and feeling directly. As aptly described by Le Brun, complex but straightforward anatomical mechanisms were responsible for bodily expression of the passions:

> First, Passion is an emotion of the Soul, residing in the sensitive part, either upon her pursuing what she judges to be for her good, or shunning what she thinks hurtful to her; and, commonly, whatever causes Passion in the soul, creates also some Action in the Body.
>
> As therefore it is granted that most of the Passions of the soul produce some Corporeal Actions, it is necessary to know which are the Actions of the Body that express those Passions, and what Action is.
>
> Action is nothing else but a motion of some part, and motion is made only by the elasticity of the muscles, which receive their motion from the nervous juice, which passes through them; the nerves act only by the spirits contained in the cavities of the brain; and the brain receives the spirits immediately from the blood, that passes continually through the heart, which heats and rarifies it so, that, being straight conveyed to, and filling the cortex of the brain, a certain fluid juice is there produced called Animal spirits.
>
> The brain thus filled, sends back a supply of these spirits to other parts by the nerves, which are like so many little Threads or Pipes, that convey them into the muscles, in proportion to their need, for the Action to which they are called.
>
> Thus the muscle that acts the most, receives the greatest quantity of spirits, and consequently becomes more swelled and puffed up, than those that are not immediately employed in Action, which appear more lank and relaxed than those that are.[45]

As a result of this complex hydraulic machinery, the body registered the soul's movements instantaneously with its own exact replica. The body thus stood as the sign for the soul, the principal means through which the soul could make itself known.

By the 1740s when Diderot had begun to formulate his views on gesture, research and debate on the exact nature of bodily responsiveness had supplanted the hydraulic imagery utilized by Le Brun with metaphors deriving from the resonating string, yet the instantaneous and inevitable response of body to soul remained unquestioned. Passions now resulted from patterns of resonating nerve fibers, the same fibers that produced bodily motions.[46] The excitation of the nerves, whether by the outer world or the inner imagination, afforded the perception of the passion and at the same time created a physical enactment of the passion known as gesture. Trains of images resonating in the mind produced identical trains of muscular contractions. The body, seized by the soul's passions, stamped them out, imprinting them in space, and vibrating with them in time. The passions, as vibrating strings, caused an analogous oscillation in the body's nerves.

Art, through its careful depiction of the passions, could cultivate the sensibility of any human to perceive these patterns of excitation in another. Gesture's role in promoting sensibility had long been recognized in painting, but had never been sufficiently explored in movement, pantomime, and theatre, so that viewers could observe not single, selected moments but the development through time of human experience. Compared with spoken language, gesture afforded a more powerfully synthetic and also a more precise form of communication. It did not, however, promise to convey aspects of human experience inexpressible in any other form of discourse, nor did gesture claim a special authenticity or uniqueness as a language. It possessed the didactic and declarative capacity of words, and it could dissimulate as words could by being enacted without sincere feelings. As languages, both verbal and gestured vocabularies consisted of sets of conventions to be deciphered. Gesture simply transmitted its messages more vividly. Diderot's exultation following his famous experiment of watching a play with his ears covered[47] resulted both from the inimitable power of gesture and from his own ability to respond appropriately, laughing or crying when the scene called for it, because the gestural language could be deciphered so easily.

The prevalent acting style of the period left little room for expressive gesture.[48] Actors privileged the verse they spoke by assuming a posture of imperturbable reserve, reinforcing their delivery with an occasional and well-timed wave of the arm. Stationed in a symmetrical semicircle at the front of the stage, they rarely directed their speech toward one another. Their infrequent shifts of weight or location, walking, kneeling, or extending the hand, while flawless, derived from studies in correct comportment rather than the representation of the passions. The characters whose roles they played were meant to crystallize out of the speech, the writing within the play itself, rather than from a physical approximation of their appearance and actions. The actors' minimalist gestures graced the occasion and referenced, from the same distance as Dupré's dancing, the feelings summoned up within the text.

The English actor David Garrick's revelatory visits to Paris in 1751 and again in 1763 had a profound impact on artists and aestheticians searching for alternatives to this static, if dignified, display.[49] Notorious for his animated gestures, vivid facial expressions, and full-bodied commitment to the character's circumstances, Garrick traveled perpetually around the stage, sank to the ground, rose up precipitously and even showed, with the help of a specially designed wig, his hair standing on end.[50] Partly because he lacked a powerful stage voice and also suffered from frequent respiratory congestion, he pioneered in the development of bodily movements that could say what his voice could not.[51] He carefully observed, practiced, and then enacted each aspect of a given feeling. He introduced lengthy moments of introspection into his performance of a character in order to highlight the character's private emotional states.

Garrick's approach to acting strengthened reformists' convictions that the theatre could and should provide an occasion for the experience of profound emotion, and perhaps more importantly, it gave them an image of how that theatre might look. The actor's innovations, however, may have resulted less from a choreographic facility for inventing movement or from the desire to overhaul acting technique than from his ability to apply the language of one medium to the situation of another. Like Sallé twenty years earlier, Garrick witnessed pantomime as part of the daily performances that took place in small London theatres. These productions, along with those at the fair theatres that periodically opened in urban centers across Europe, presented an exuberant melange of singing, acrobatics, tightrope walking, slapstick, pantomime, exotic animal acts, and

14. Jean Baptiste Nicolet's refurbished theatre at the Foire St. Germain.

fireworks against opulent, frequently changing scenic backdrops.[52] (See fig. 14.) These heteroglot evenings of entertainment, with their fast-paced sequences of satiric and erotic commentary, greatly amused their audiences, although according to one indignant witness of the period, they would have been "much embarrassed to recount what so diverted them."[53] Although the bawdy, acrobatic, interventionist style descendant from the Commedia dell'Arte tradition prevailed in these productions, they incorporated an impressive repertoire of choreographic strategies for substituting gesture for dialogue. (See fig. 15.) It remained for Garrick to apprehend the applicability of this gestural vocabulary to the more refined and idealistic setting of classical drama.

A significant augmentation to the repertoire of pantomimic gestures had occurred in the early decades of the eighteenth century.[54] In both London and Paris, an intense and prolonged rivalry sprang up at the beginning of the eighteenth century between the fair theatres and the main theatrical establishments. As the popularity of the scandalous, irreverent fair productions began to affect audience size and consequently profits at the large theatres, administrative staff at the main houses marshaled government support to harass their legal and cultural inferiors. In Paris the Opéra, Comédie Française, and Comédie Italienne used the charters received from Louis XIV that defined their exclusive rights to perform opera, drama, and musical comedy, respectively, to extract royalty fees from the fair theatres and also prohibit them from presenting works in any of their genres. Censors, suddenly pressured to uphold the charters' delegation of responsibilities, exercised unpredictable, despotic control over texts submitted by fair theatre entrepreneurs for their approval. New regulations not only enjoined the fair theatres from

15. A late-seventeenth-century harlequin surrounded by sellers of various goods at the Foire St. Germain.

presenting comedies, tragedies, or entire operas, but also restricted their use of dialogue and even sung lyrics. Between 1745 and 1751, for example, spoken or sung dialogue was banned entirely.[55]

Capitalizing on an inconsistent and slow-moving bureaucracy, the fair theatres responded with a riotous profusion of strategies for altering presentational formats.[56] Dialogues would be presented with one actor at a time on stage; players would appear speaking nonsense syllables in perfect alexandrines while pantomiming the action; an offstage actor would deliver lines for an onstage actor who would mouth them; child actors were used in place of adults; actors would carry their lines on signs around their necks; or verse would be displayed on huge placards which the audience would then sing to popular tunes while the actors mimed the action. Because prohibitions usually denied producers the right to present extended sequences of spoken or sung dialogue, gesture was frequently substituted to convey part or all of the drama.

The demand placed on bodily movement to carry the narrative along must have inspired substantial changes in the vocabulary inherited from the Commedia repertoire. Players added to the starkly stereotypic attitudes of the Commedia routines facial and bodily positions that indexed a fuller range of emotional experiences. They began to fashion sequences of such positions that delineated the narrative structure. They adapted the intricate spatial relations developed in acrobatic routines to illustrate relationships among different types of characters. And they began to extend the length and scope of coherent narrative that could be rendered by movement and music alone.

While the pressure on the fair theatres to avoid classical theatrical genres forced an exploration of pantomime as a medium capable of telling a story, the thrust of the performances remained resolutely antinarrative. They thrived on the parodic, iconoclastic, and spectacular display rather than the coherent, sentimental tale. They used pantomime to mimic in such a way as to deflate power. Many of the productions relied upon the audience's familiarity with a classic plot. As they mercilessly satirized, for example, Lully's famous Opéras and Corneille's dramas, the unorthodox sequences or juxtapositions of events in different mediums eroded any sense of continuity. The parodic tactics unraveled or even exploded all narrative logic. A 1745 production parodying the Pygmalion story cast a sentimental puppetmaker named Brioché (a word whose English equivalents include "bun," "cake," or "blunder") opposite a practical-minded puppet named Gigogne (whose English equivalent is "the old woman who lived in a shoe").[57] Folly, instead of Venus, brought not only Gigogne to life but all the puppets in the shop. Gigogne's instruction by Folly's Graces in the arts of singing and dancing satirized aristocratic fashion and protocol.[58]

The combination of humor, shock, and eros served up in these productions appealed not only to the working-class community for whom they were a familiar staple, but also to the aristocracy whose conduct they openly satirized.[59] While the working classes relished the opportunity to appropriate and then violate the ennobling myths of the period, the aristocracy delighted in the sexy affront to elevated values. Secure in their birthright, the nobility enthusiastically patronized the fair theatres, intrigued perhaps more by their erotic than their political appeal. By providing a kind of entertainment to which the aristocracy and working classes could enthusiastically respond, the fair theatres complicated and compromised a policy designed to maintain distinct kinds of art for distinct classes of people. Police and other city authorities expressed ambivalent opinions about the fair theatres. They felt the pressure to uphold the standards of the high art tradition exemplified by productions at the Opéra and Comédie Française, but they also subscribed to the prevalent belief that a populace, diverted by entertainment, would be more controllable and less given over to discussions of flagrant social injustice.

The subversive impact of the productions, however, may have extended further than authorities could anticipate by involving viewers from disparate social classes in a commentary on social class itself. Because of the audience's physical proximity to the stage, the productions simultaneously assaulted and involved all viewers with their unpredictable sequencing of events in different mediums. (See fig. 16.) The small size of the theatres, when compared with the main houses at the Opéra or Comédie Française, situated viewers close to the explosive barrage of sensations on stage, but it also required them to rub shoulders with one another. Although boxes were available for aristocratic spectators, the small size of the house permitted members of all classes to examine and interact with one another at close range. Tidy boundaries between populations dissolved in such an intimate space, where theatrical lighting and makeshift architecture destabilized clear indications of rank—one's dress, comportment, and companions. The fact that these theatrical productions, like any others, required actors to represent identities not their own further problematized the grounds on which social identity was determined. Could one assume the rank of an aristocrat simply by acting like one?

16. A tightrope act at one of the fair theatres.

One anonymous description, apparently by a lady of high birth, elaborated on the disquieting confusion generated by these productions in a wonderfully vivid account of preperformance "performances" by actors and audience members. Having entered the well-known fair theatre, the Opéra Comique, early because of the cold, she was confronted by a number of players gearing up for the performance:

> A young Musketeer, one knee on the floor, declaimed tragicomically at the feet of a fairly pretty actress and kissed the hand that she indifferently allowed him to hold; another actress feebly fought without any difficulty against the advances of a dull councillor who desired to return to its place the garter she had removed so as to show him its fine workmanship; a third dallied with an impudent fop whose hand carressed her bosom.[60]

A Duke with whom she was acquainted arrived and escorted her to her seat, but the performers continued to regard her with such effrontery "that I changed appearance twenty times from embarrassment which in turn served as the subject of a vast number of nasty jokes which they delivered loudly enough to be heard."[61] Seated, she was assaulted by a new series of impertinences, as twenty sets of eyeglasses turned toward her, and she overheard loud inquiries as to her identity and comments on her appearance. Soon she was rescued from this scrutiny by the arrival in an adjacent box of another young woman who seemed to relish the opportunity to perform for the audience:

> [She] made faces, took some snuff, whispered to some kind of servant who had accompanied her, took from her embroidered purse a small gold box which she handled so as to assure its visibility to the spectators below, and returned it to the purse, ostentatiously tying its knot; then, to dispell the fatigue that this pitiful exercise had caused, but also to be able to display a portrait ringed with diamonds that she wore as a bracelet, she leaned her head on her elbow and tried out for a fairly long time an interesting pose. Unfortunately for her, the actors then appeared, stealing from her the better part of the viewers' attention.[62]

This description cast audience members and actors in a series of scenes performed in the lobby, and it likewise described audience members performing for one another—all prior to the commencement of the production. It even intimated the continuation of audience performances throughout the onstage performance. The snide irreverence of the actors and the hyperbolic gestures of the young woman who could afford a box seat derived their meaning from a class-conscious critique of aristocratic privilege. If this anonymous account is at all accurate, then the performances encouraged audience members and actors to demonstrate their knowledge of the codes of class-based comportment both on and off the stage.

Immersed in the performance of these codes from an early age, Marie Sallé, daughter of fair theatre performers and niece of a famous harlequin, began her career in the fair theatres and enjoyed sustained exposure to the innovative use of pantomime, gesture, and physical theatre in productions at both Paris and London theatres.[63] Her ascendancy to the role of *première danseuse* at the Opéra marked another, although far more rare, example of blurred class boundaries. Although her *Pygmalion* was never presented at the Opéra, where its brevity and narrative integrity contravened the grand aesthetic objectives of the five-act opera-ballets, her extraordinary artistry won her the opportunity to choreograph several ballets as acts within larger operas that appeared at the Opéra throughout the 1730s and '40s.[64] Framed by the larger spectacle and plot structures of *Les Indes Galantes* (1735), *L'Europe Galante* (1736), and *Les Fêtes d'Hébé* (1739), she began to work out the intercalation of mimed gesture and danced step.[65] These dances, viewed by a number of younger choreographers including DeHesse, Hilverding, and possibly Noverre, were noted by aestheticians and critics as pioneering works in the new genre. Sallé also made several trips to London where her choreographic experimentation may well have been witnessed by Garrick.[66]

Among those who followed Sallé's lead in extracting from the fair theatre repertoire representational strategies that could be utilized in more elevated contexts, Jean Baptiste DeHesse, a Dutch choreographer living in Paris, was hired in 1747 by Madame de Pompadour to choreograph for her private theatre. Like Sallé, DeHesse came from a family with a long history of involvement in music, acting, and pantomime in the fair theatres, and he received his training there and began presenting pantomime ballets at the

17. Jean Baptiste François DeHesse's *La Guinguette, divertissement pantomime* (1750), produced at the Théâtre Italien, as depicted by Gabriel-Jacques de St. Aubin.

Théâtre Italien in 1734.[67] (See fig. 17.) More often comical diversions than serious dramas, DeHesse's pantomimes for Pompadour's audiences were infused with the characters and vocabulary of the Commedia tradition. *Le Pédant* (1748), a typical pantomime, sketched out the misadventures of a tutor continually outmaneuvered by his half-witted assistant and his students. Scenes such as the assistant's attempt to clean the tutor's robe with a mop or to place a hat on the tutor's head using a ladder combined with rowdier chase scenes and revelations of mistakened identity to produce a hilarious if frivolous entertainment. Unlike Sallé's *Pygmalion,* which progressed toward the union of sculptor and artwork, DeHesse's *Le Pédant* arranged discrete, independent scenes one after another. The scenario offered no development toward a climax or sense of resolution at the end beyond the happy, but momentary, accord between all the characters. Neither *Pygmalion* nor *Le Pédant* offered a complex narrative structure, yet their ability to sustain narrative involvement without words struck viewers as innovative and intriguing.

Similarly, Jean Georges Noverre's production at the Opéra Comique, *Les Fêtes Chinoises* (1754), organized groups of exotic characters in a dazzling parade, using as pretext the occasion of a Chinese festival. *La Fontaine de Jouvence* (1754) demonstrated the joyful effects of the rejuvenating waters of the Fountain of Love on peoples from Europe, Africa, Asia, and America.[68] Full of pomp and glitz provided by exotic costumes, these performances also incorporated short, pantomimed interactions among characters such as the mandarin and slaves, shepherds and shepherdesses, and citizens from the corners of the world.

18. Mme. de Pompadour playing the role of Galathée in *Acis et Galathée* with Louis XV and the court as audience.

Experiments such as Sallé's and DeHesse's gave momentum to theatrical reform initiatives in the 1750s by providing vivid pictures of actual situations. They made use of fair theatre characters and their situations to create new danced images. Rather than the majestic pomp evoked by an orderly procession, they suggested tensile, asymmetrical, bodily configurations whose push and pull depicted passion-filled responses. (See fig. 18.) Instead of a stage highly charged with various kinds of spatial inscription, these presentations built upon the tableau vivant—frozen moments of angst, joy, intrigue, or anger in which each character registered a unique and vivid participation. No tangential and oblique references, no decorous restraint, these performances suggested that it was possible literally to capture what was occurring in life and catapult it onto the stage. There audiences might study a re-presentation of life in order to understand what humankind is and does.

Originating the action ballet

Although evidence that gesture could substitute for speech surrounded them—in all the marginal theatres of Paris, and increasingly in the elite venues—writers campaigning for changes in theatrical dance never referred to those theatrical experiments as examples of what the new dance might look like.[69] Instead, they preferred to ground their aesthetic arguments in a timeless past, one that registered only innate expressive predispositions rather than specific historical practices. Even their references to the performances of ancient Greece and Rome emphasized general aesthetic intentions of the dances rather than enumerating specific dances as part of historical customs and traditions. By locating dance's origins in an absolute, ahistorical time and place, advocates of the new dance helped to rationalize its new role as accessible yet educative, as the medium that would inculcate greater sensitivity in all viewers. The existence of gesture as anterior to speech explained its immediate legibility. The fact that dancing had originated prior to any specific historical record of dance explained its popular and universal appeal.

The first cause of dancing—the result of individual feeling rather than social occasion—removed dance from the realm of actions with immediate political consequences. Yet this new origin for dance contained its own tacit ideological argument. Because dancing developed from human and not godly predispositions, it operated with absolute validity outside the purview of the church. Because its prehistorical originators dwelled in a classless community, dancing constituted one of the endeavors of a diverse urban society rather than the project of a hierarchically organized court. These Enlightenment goals of decentering church and monarchy were complemented by a third line of argument, imperialist in its objectives, that used the presumption of movement as universal language to rationalize expansionist foreign policies. Because productions claimed universal accessibility to and significance for the portraits of life they performed onstage, they helped to justify the exportation of French culture just as they provided reassurance that Paris, sited at the center of the world, spoke to and represented all other cultures.

The fair theatres, in their transgressive experimentation with bodily movement and gesture, had already constructed critiques of both church and state. By satirizing the very conventions through which religious and aristocratic identities were maintained, the performances intimated the existence of a more egalitarian site from which to exercise the state's power. Their ironic egalitarianism, however, differed from the humanistic characterization of people and circumstances that the dance reformists envisioned. In the reformists' idealized ancient past and staged future, no bodies behaved outrageously. All bodies faithfully portrayed the characters assigned to them, manifesting qualities of good samaritanism, domestic loyalty, and the work ethic, qualities that resonated with the concepts of *sensibilité* and true gesture elaborated by Diderot and others. The ironic pantomime, in contrast, cultivated a protean body capable of conformity and then excess, docility and grotesquerie. It satirized sensibility as well as the pompous decorum of the aristocracy. Any consistency in its satiric stance resided in its relentless critique of absolutist values and not in the body through which such a critique was manifested.

Reformist arguments complemented bourgeois expectations about the function of art by focusing on the educative value of presenting true-to-life images of current social conditions. Viewers, they argued, would enjoy the opportunity to witness the most appropriate human conduct and the most desirable resolution of social dilemmas. At the same time, viewers would cultivate their own ability to respond empathetically to the problems of others. Art in general, and gesture in particular, had the capacity to communicate the most noble and elevated of human conscious experiences—the feelings deriving from a moral response to the human condition. As a universal language, gesture allowed for the immediate apprehension of such feelings, and therefore could function as an effective vehicle for this didactic, moralizing, and above all, serious mission for art.

The reformists gave a variety of names to the new dance they envisioned. They called it "ballet-pantomime," "ballet en action," "ballet héroïque," or "ballet d'action."[70] With these descriptive labels, they hoped to sum up the aesthetic goal of enacting life in danced form. The new genealogy of dance, with its primal origin, tabulated varieties, and linear development, complemented the strategic plan for the necessary choreographic innovations: select the most vivid storyline, map out the passions, and realize the connections between motivation and action. The careful omission of populist versions of these innovations, like the establishment of a primal origin for dance, disengaged choreography from any overt participation in politics and helped to construct a new level from which ideological and political content was conveyed. Rather than the clear flexing of monarchic musculature conveyed by the opera-ballets, whose movements of gods and goddesses reaffirmed the requisite hierarchies of behavior, the action ballet should depict realistic images of people. Rather than a vicious parody of the absolutist anatomy by naughty misadventurers, the action ballet promised sincere depictions of social justices and injustices. It did not originate at the king's court or from his behest, nor did it derive from the critique forged in response to the oppressive tactics of the institutions that represented him. Instead, the new dance was designed to embrace monarch and subjects, both loyal and rebellious, enlivening and affecting them all through the universal language of gesture.

Interlude

The Bank of Grass [Le banc de gazon]

Beginning with the earliest action ballets, scenarios indicate that the productions made use of that rich symbolic property known as "the bank of grass." In a remarkable number of ballets, characters, overwhelmed by their feelings, sink onto it. Occasionally they throw themselves, but more often they incline slowly away from the vertical, prolonging their descent with a series of momentary arrests, succumbing, eventually, to the horizontal. The taut, bell-like frame that allows female dancers to appear as ships under full sail gliding across the stage suddenly creases, shifts off center, folds still further, causing the elegant lines of the dress to crinkle, and finally topples. The male body, so perfectly erect, its arms and legs inflated with propriety and confident in their calibrated distance from one another, suddenly folds in on itself, limbs askew.

Rather than welling up inside the characters, feelings overtake and engulf them. No contortions of the torso signal the birth and development of feeling. The character remains erect, looks anxiously from side to side as the feelings arrive, and then slowly capsizes under their weight. Perhaps these feelings are a kind of liquid or gaseous mass, the chemical results of frictional interactions with others. They seem to hover above and around the dancer. When their density is sufficient, they press down with an irresistible force.

The manicured green expanse nurtures and supports the characters upon their arrival from culture into nature. Here, on the carefully cultivated and apportioned terrain, they can give themselves over fully to their emotions. Here, they lose all awareness of others. Here, they lie fainted, sleeping, or dreaming.

After so many hours of resolute verticality, this violation of erectness is extreme. It creates an illicit, antisocial, utterly captivating image. The character is both down and out, unable to fulfill any semaphoric function as a conveyance of public meaning. Prone and incapacitated, oblivious to the surrounding world and the viewer's gaze, the character transforms viewers into voyeurs. Awakened to the delights and privileges of their own sensibility, viewers savor this horrifying and delicious moment, signaled from the very beginning by the presence, stage left or stage right, of the bank of grass.

Télémaque dans l'île de Calipso (1759)

Télémaque's choreographer, Antoine Buonaventure Pitrot, was one of several itinerant professionals who traveled throughout Europe securing appointments at various courts and in the main theatres of principle cities. Trained in Italy, Pitrot's competence at the classical vocabulary and his exposure to Italian uses of gesture and pantomime prepared him well for experimentation with the new action ballet, and he was referred to in dance writing of the period as one of the chief proponents of the new genre.[1] In addition to *Télémaque*, he was commissioned by the Comédie Italienne to produce two other ballets there in the early 1760s. Although not entirely successful, these works played an important role in alerting Parisian audiences to the new directions in ballet.[2]

The published scenario for *Télémaque* divides the single-act ballet into twenty-three scenes, the first twenty of which take place in a clearing on the island with the sea in the distance and Calipso's cave-palace to one side. The last three scenes set the action at the water's edge and feature a large burning boat, a second rescue boat, and a population of tritons and nereides dancing on the water. No record of the music remains, but we know from the witty, detailed review of the ballet by Ange Goudar that it lasted about forty minutes.[3] The opening scene consists of several dances by the sorceress Calipso, her nymphs, and eventually a troupe of fauns, who perform before Télémaque and his guide Mentor in an attempt to persuade them to remain on the island. The clever spacing of the dances pairs nymphs with fauns in various ways as Calipso repeatedly entices Télémaque away from the action in order to propose marriage to him. Mentor, disapproving and ever-watchful, prohibits Télémaque from any further involvement. Calipso's attempts to seduce Mentor also fail, and she retreats sullenly to one side. Venus appears, possibly in a gloire lowered from above, and orders Amour to help Calipso. The mischievous, androgynous cherub, by dancing with each in turn, has soon enflamed the hearts of all gathered. Télémaque, in particular, as he takes Amour in his arms, feels the awakening of a new kind of desire, and Eucharis, the most beautiful of all the nymphs, feels a similar expansive affection. Mentor's sudden reappearance and his rejection of Amour's advances causes all the dancers to disperse.

Eucharis, left alone, discovers that she has fallen in love with Télémaque. Her danced soliloquy, reflecting a range of feelings associated with love—anxiety, fear, hope, joy—builds to such a state of agitation that she falls delirious on the bank of grass. Télémaque, in search of Eucharis, discovers her there, and they dance out their love for one another. Mentor interrupts them and reprimands Télémaque, who listens respectfully. Amour then arrives with nymphs and fauns to accompany Télémaque on a hunt, and they leave together. Mentor, who remains behind, and Calipso, who has emerged from her cave, discover their common interest in transporting Télémaque off the island. Calipso, enraged at Télémaque's preference for Eucharis, indicates to Mentor where and how to build a boat that will take them away. Calipso then joins and disrupts the hunting party, railing at all the nymphs, Eucharis and Amour, each in turn. Télémaque, hearing sounds of the construction of the boat in the distance, learns from Calipso of Mentor's plans. The scenario represents their exchange in dialogue form:

> "What do I hear, he cries out? That Mentor is abandoning me, I'm done for. Oh, Eucharis, if Mentor leaves, I will have no one but you." "What are you saying,

> Télémaque, you cruel ingrate," responds Calipso. "I swear by the Stix that you will leave my island, and you, Amour, tyrant of hearts, will flee my presence."[4]

Amour dismisses Calipso with laughter and she falls to the ground in despair. When Eucharis comes to Calipso's aid she rallies, enraged at Eucharis's generosity and Télémaque's indifference, and then exits into her cave. Mentor arrives to take Télémaque away; they argue as Eucharis looks on. Then as Mentor draws Télémaque reluctantly toward the boat, Amour comforts Calipso with the proposal to burn down the boat. The scene then changes to seaside. Nymphs and fauns armed with torches follow Amour toward the boat. Télémaque's delight at the burning boat turns to despair as Mentor dives into the water. Télémaque dutifully follows, much to the dismay of nymphs and fauns. A Tyrien boat picks up the two swimmers, and in celebration of their rescue the sea churns up innumerable dancing tritons and nereides. Amour exits laughing as the fauns attempt, in vain, to console Calipso.

No mention of Eucharis was made at the end of this classic coming-of-age story in which wisdom triumphed over desire. Although the ballet reiterated a theme prominent in all opera ballets of the period—resistance and final accession to love—duty ultimately won out, causing men to go their way, women to wait for love's reconfiguration elsewhere. In its interpretation of the myth the ballet emphasized the importance of becoming familiar with the charms and pleasures of love. However, no enduring coupling necessarily followed from the acquisition of this knowledge.

On Calipso's island, women, as supernatural characters, served as objects of desire but also sought love actively. Both Calipso and Eucharis (once she had been sensitized by Amour to the feeling of love) asserted their romantic interests. Télémaque, the only mortal, acquiesced to Mentor's age and authority. Although known to an audience familiar with the myth as Minerva/Athena in disguise, Mentor played a resolutely masculine and patriarchal role. Amour, in contrast, presented a mischievous, nonaligned, ironic, and seemingly androgynous figure that resembled the swerving nature of desire itself. Described in both scenario and review as a figure small enough to be cradled in Télémaque's arms, Amour may well have been played by a child of either sex. The size and sexual indistinctness of the child would have underscored Amour's polysexual character.

The scenario offered striking opportunities to view individual characters engaged in soliloquies and dialogues that revealed a range of feelings. Of the twenty-three scenes four featured single characters undergoing several distinct feelings and nine presented pantomimed dialogue between two characters. Eucharis's solo, typical of this new genre, showed her exploring various aspects of her newfound love for Télémaque: ". . . worry, fear, hope, and joy are some of the different movements that she feels and that agitate her to such a point that she falls onto a bank of grass to rest."[5] According to the scenario, Télémaque then arrived looking for Eucharis and fell at her feet. Eucharis awakened "frightened, but soon joy overtook her fear: and the two lovers tenderly expressed their feelings in character dances."[6] After their tableau-like encounter, the two lovers executed a duet composed of classical steps. They gazed at one another; their facial expressions and gestures, clearly visible throughout the dance, smoothed the transition from pantomime into dancing, and also gave the familiar duet form a new cast. Less the danced expression of abstract love, the duet depicted the personal awakening to love by two characters.

The preponderance of solos and duets shifted the emphasis away from large group pomp and pageantry, although the scenario seems to have offered a good balance between small and large group scenes. Reviews of *Télémaque,* however, found substantial fault with the ballet. Both Goudar and the *Mercure de France* critic complained that the plot, with its extensive dialogues, did not hold together. The characters expressed themselves using far too many cabrioles. Many of their conversations contained indecipherable references to other people and events, complex arrangements, and negotiations. Calipso's change of heart, for example—first advising Mentor to build the boat and then accepting Amour's proposal to burn it down—might well have seemed incomprehensible. With all the commotion surrounding them, characters never developed their feelings in a sustained way.

Thirty years later, Pierre Gardel presented his version of *Télémaque* at the Opéra—a production whose conclusion contained telling differences. In 1790, a Télémaque more devoted to Eucharis chooses her repeatedly over Mentor. Calipso, with Medea-like deception, suggests to Télémaque that Eucharis hide on board the ship. At the moment where flames engulf her, Amour flies in and carries Eucharis off in a cloud. Télémaque, who has watched from shore, is pushed into the water by Mentor, and the curtain falls as the nymphs run toward the water's edge. In Gardel's version the relationship between Télémaque and Eucharis took on greater solidity—they conspired together, he saved her from Calipso's rage, and was eventually forced to leave her. Eucharis's entrapment on the burning boat became the main focus of the climax. Amour, far less ironic, dutifully saved her as Venus, a benign ruler, looked on.

Pitrot's version of the ballet did not congeal plot or characters as effectively. Both scenario and reviews left the impression that vivid displays of feeling arrested only momentarily a generalized hubbub. The unmotivated entrances and exits of characters and the seeming inability of a gestural language to communicate complex ideas prohibited characters from attaining consistency or depth. The need to display both technical prowess and scenic diversity forced a choreographic compromise in which crystalline moments of emotional fervor never added up.

On One Side, On the Other; Above and Below

Scenery in the action ballets is used effectively to establish the structural tensions between private and public and between one kin-group and another. Often the scene represents two families' dwellings placed on either side of the stage and divided by a central common space, or it shows a single house with public space surrounding. Habitations further divide into upper and lower stories connected by balconies, interior and exterior staircases, or even a tree. This architecture of the above and below, the one side and the other offers many possibilities for intricate avoidances, secretive encounters, and elaborate circumnavigations.

He knocks at the door; she appears on the balcony above to sign that she will descend and open the door. (This is how the minutes pass at the theatre.) Not long after he has entered, the husband returns, and, finding that he has forgotten his key, knocks as well. He knocks again, again, and again. Only after several more minutes does his wife appear at the balcony. Just as she lets him in the door, the lover appears on the balcony, grabs a rope attached to a pulley, and slides safely on the diagonal to the other side of the stage. Or two young lovers have rigged up a signaling system between their balconies. They send love letters; they flirt and blow kisses above, while the adults go about their business below. Or those above, the knowing, poke contrapuntal fun at those below, the ignorant.

All this animates the space framed by the proscenium in a lively way. The viewer's eyes must move rapidly from down to up to across, never quite taking in all that is presented. The choreography cleverly promotes key moments in each couples' exchange by allowing for periods of calm and repetition in other ongoing encounters. Still the visual distance among events allows one to see only the blur of some actions while focusing on others.

The shift in the viewer's gaze across the various demarcations of social space underscores the inherent conflicts upon which the plot thrives, whether they involve the distinctiveness of kin-groups, the disparity between domestic and village affairs, the divergence of erotic attraction and domestic obligation, or the incommensurability between parental inclinations to fulfill the social contract and the ardent, impossible love of their offspring. At the same time, the rapidity and intricacy of the action as staged in the various locales reinforce the plot's frantic constructions of eros and deceit.

19. An early-eighteenth-century Harlequin and Columbine.

20. A midcentury Harlequin and Columbine.

Arlequin Soldat Magicien, ou le Canonier, Pantomime (1764)

Jean-François Mussot Arnould wrote and directed this comic episode in the ongoing adventures of Arlequin, the immensely likeable Comedia character whose arrival on the scene always meant trouble.[1] (See figs. 19 and 20.) Nicolet performed the role of the cuckolded husband in his own recently opened Théâtre du Sr. Nicolet, and his wife played the deceitful and quixotic match to both husband and Arlequin. The success of Nicolet's entrepreneurial efforts, centering a newly stabilized kind of theatre in an unproven area of Paris, depended upon matching opulent visual display with a more conservative storyline. *Arlequin Soldat Magicien*, less risqué than fair theatre productions but with the same fast pacing and complex stage business, satisfied the bill. Not so sentimental as the musical comedies of his competitor Favart,[2] but lacking the aggressive irreverence of fair theatre pantomimes, this production was pitched to a growing population of shopworkers, artisans, and servants willing to spend their spare change at the theatre. With sentimental scenes and the triumph of an embattled love, it registered the influence upon the fair theatre tradition of reforms focused on sensibility. At the same time, its resolute satire situated it as a kind of hybrid spectacle, neither action ballet nor pure pantomime, whose gestural inventiveness would provide an ongoing source of choreographic solutions for the action ballet.

The first scenes take place at the wigmaker's shop. Preparing to go out into the city, the wigmaker is shaved by his servant Pierrot while his daughters dress his hair. Just after he and Pierrot depart, Arlequin, dressed as a soldier, appears with a billet demanding lodging. The wife, unwilling to accommodate him on the pretext that her husband's approval is required, finally accedes to his remonstrations by sequestering him in the attic. Her own lover, a solicitor's clerk, then arrives much to the surprise of her two sons, who threaten to expose the couple. The sons are silenced by a bag of money the clerk produces, and they exit promising to drink to his health. The clerk requests a meal, and the daughter is sent out for comestibles. Arlequin, vastly amused by all he sees from the attic window, provides a running gestural and facial commentary on all the players. The daughter returns with a soup, and they sit down to eat, but the husband's sudden knock at the door sends the soup under the table and the clerk into the armoire. In response to her husband's scolding, the wife explains the soldier Arlequin's presence. Pierrot escorts him downstairs, and as they sit to eat, Arlequin in an aside to the wife signs that he has seen all. He then entertains the group with stories of war and imitations of battles. Warming to his role center stage, Arlequin announces that he is also a magician and, much to the wife's distress, brags that he can produce a soup from under the table. Husband, wife, and Pierrot all tremble with fright as Arlequin performs a magical incantation. Pierrot, ordered to look for the soup, resists, and is enchanted by a swat from Arlequin's wand. The husband pleads with Arlequin to restore his servant, who upon regaining mobility finds the soup. Only a few moments into their meal, Arlequin now claims that he can produce a clerk from the closet. The wigmaker is aghast, the wife pretends to faint, Pierrot faints for real, and Arlequin calls for help. The sons rush in and make the cuckold sign behind their father, who attempts to reinstate order by asking Arlequin to leave. On his way out Arlequin passes the wife a letter demanding a meeting.

Now in the street, Arlequin, awaiting the wife, is approached by the clerk, who gratefully bestows a bag of money on the soldier for his protection. The wife arrives and determines to run away with Arlequin. When the clerk protests, Arlequin hits him with the wand and they flee. Husband and sons learn from the clerk about the desertion and exit in hot pursuit. Arlequin and the wife are drinking in a café when Pierrot finds them. Arlequin immobilizes him, then restores him and offers the bag of money in exchange for silence. Although Pierrot agrees, he soon slips out to tell the husband, and the new couple beseech the owner to hide them, the wife in another room and Arlequin in a large sack. When Pierrot and the husband arrive on the scene, Pierrot claims to have seen Arlequin diving into the sack and they demand to look inside. After a long debate with the owner, Pierrot is allowed to open it. A large monkey jumps out and chases him around the room. Back in the street, the husband heads for home, and the couple finally escape the indefatigable Pierrot with a strike of the wand that changes the scene to a military camp. Arlequin hides in a tent, but the husband, back on the chase, enlists the help of a cannoneer, who captures Arlequin when he pokes his head out and then stuffs him in the cannon. As Arlequin soars through the air, the husband grabs the wife and runs off. Devastated, Arlequin lands near a cave. A compassionate magician emerges and restores Arlequin, promising assistance.

Making their way back to town, husband and wife are spotted by Arlequin, who rushes in and reunites with the wife while the husband's back is turned. Again Pierrot tattles, and the couple flees. The husband, accosted by the magician, proffers his explanation; the magician responds by inviting him and Pierrot to sit at the edge of the stage while he rescues the wife. But then the magician attaches large rocks to their legs and marries Arlequin and the wife. When the husband agrees to accept this turn of events gracefully, he is released. But when he attacks Arlequin, the magician strikes him down, and the curtain closes on Arlequin embracing the magician.

The familiar kinds of stage business on which this production relied—relentless yet always sudden poppings on and off stage, unpredictable reversals of characters' motivations, voyeuristic metacommentary, surprising spectacle (the changes of scene, the monkey, or the cannon shot)—formed the staple routines that garnered for these performances their widespread appeal. Each of the hundreds of pantomimes produced annually on boulevard stages combined and modified these basic theatrical premises in exhilarating new ways. In *Arlequin Soldat Magicien* the wand worked to alter radically both the movement vocabulary of an individual character and the full scenic location of the action. Arlequin's attic location bifurcated the stage space so as to provide the simultaneous pantomimed commentary and metacommentary of which viewers never tired. The circulation of the money bags from clerk to sons and from clerk to Arlequin to Pierrot recontextualized this prop at the same time that it gestured irreverently toward the power that money seemed to hold. Supporting this fast-paced satire was the seemingly endless repertoire of hiding, chasing, and fighting, acrobatics and stunts, pantomimed phrases, and specific gestures (such as that of the cuckold) from which the action ballet would continue to develop in subsequent decades.

Not noble and not empowered, these characters from the boulevard stage nonetheless created a compelling presence onstage. Full of contradictions and failings—the husband's vanity, the wife's fickleness—their interactions with one another signaled a reflexive self-awareness of the preposterous situations in which they found themselves. This reflexivity was made possible by the richness of the gestural repertoire. Phrases of movement could be performed as statements, simulations, or critiques depending upon the precise choreographic inflection they were given. From his attic vantage, Arlequin could affect surprise, doubt, or bemusement at events below. And he could also pretend to direct and control the lovers' actions and to register varying degrees of involvement with their developing romance. Along similar lines, Arlequin's claim to magical powers produced a fear infused with skepticism in the husband, a fear based on knowledge (of the soup's origins) in the wife, and a fear driven by gullibility in the servant. A few moments later both wife and Pierrot faint, but one performs an obvious simulation of the swoon while the other appears to succumb for real.

Like Arlequin's metacommentary, these simultaneous performances of the same action, each with a different kind and degree of motivation constructed an ironic depth within the performance. They fleshed out the sociality of the interacting bodies with a sophisticated mutual awareness of society's functioning.[3] Any individual character, a thin stereotype when considered separately, could never achieve this kind of ironic distance on the social regulation of individual aspirations. Only collectively could the ensemble stage its own awareness of social roles. This awareness, sometimes bitter, sometimes despairing, showed the group pressing against the futility of their social immobility. It was this subtle irony that had most threatened police and government officials about the fair theatre productions, and that marked the boulevard as a possible site of protest and collusion against the state. To show the role as a role—as Arlequin, the classic impersonator who interlopes through all walks of life—with such eloquence, intimated the possibility of changing other roles as well.

The Comedia's nineteenth-century descendant, not Harlequin but a white-satined Pierrot, would achieve analogous popularity as a symbol for populist disenchantment. Focused at the site of his body, so as to render him an everyman, were the unrealized hopes and dreams of an entire society. Yet his mute gesturing of the unjustness of his plight retained little of the mobilizing critique of the previous century. Unlike eighteenth-century Comedia pantomimes, the nineteenth-century Pierrot was a lone figure, realized by the famous mime Jean Dubureau and those who copied him, all of whom performed as soloists.[4] Because he stood alone, deserted by all co-conspirators, he could never muster the necessary ironic distance on a social situation. Instead, he invited only individuated empathic responses of discontentment from each viewer who saw him. Because his gestures, as poignant as they were, took place in a world apart from speech, they performed frustration but never critical appraisal of social problems. *Arlequin Soldat Magicien* blended different kinds and levels of bodily movement, treating gesture as both substitute for and commentary on speech. Its choreography thus carried an activist weight that nineteenth-century pantomime and gesture could not.

2 STAGING THE CANVAS AND THE MACHINE

A ballet is a type of more or less complicated machinery . . .[1]

Spectacular dancing bodies

If the meaning of dancing such as Dupré's had eroded for many dance viewers by midcentury, dancing in a variety of venues nonetheless enjoyed enormous popularity.[2] If the life of dance as a metadisciplinary practice yielding a graceful bodily engagement in all actions had expired, dancing in pursuit of health, sociability, and spectacle retained an avid and plentiful following. Dancing like Dupré's, poignant in its restraint, its understated elegance, may no longer have captivated viewers, yet dancers' virtuoso command of an expanding, demanding vocabulary of steps met with enthusiastic adulation. The exquisite geometry of bodily shapes and group configurations, the enchanting élan with which one image resolved into another, intimated a perfectability of body and spirit that confirmed expectations of progress toward human enlightenment.

The locus of activities that mattered to those who tracked the improvements in bodily cultivation developed in the city and not at court. Dancing Masters, drawn to the city in large numbers, taught the latest social dances to an aristocratic and bourgeois clientele. They also published notated versions of social dance compositions that circulated out to the provinces as the latest fashion in dancing, further reinforcing the centrism of Paris. Viewers enjoyed theatrical dancing in a wide variety of locations and genres throughout the city. In 1760 some of the more successful fair theatre producers established year-round houses on the newly built Parisian boulevards.[3] Dance contributed generously to the heterodox entertainments produced at these theatres, and it formed part of the diverse entertainments enacted by both professionals and aristocrats at their own private theatres.[4] It not only figured prominently in productions at the Académie Royale de la

21. The African from a 1779 production of *Aline, Reine de Golconde*.

22. Neptune as costumed for productions of *Acis et Galathée* (1749) and *La Journée galante* (1750).

Musique et de la Danse (the Opéra), but was also featured in interludes between acts of classical dramas presented at the Comédie Française.[5] It blended with the lyrical action of the *opéras comiques* offered at the Comédie Italienne, and sometimes merited a special slot in the programming.[6] Some of these entertainments toured to Versailles or Saint-Cloud, and others originated there before showing in the capital. The city, however, hosted the largest group of discerning viewers. Paris attracted foreigners and tourists from around the country and the world. It housed the publishing and newspaper industries that gave critical attention to dance. And it radiated a charisma and energy that the court could no longer muster.

The movement to reform theatrical dance centered in the city and specifically on the productions at the Opéra, whose royal charter identified it as the unique institution dedicated to the presentation of theatrical dance. The Opéra offered two formats in which dancing was featured—the opera-ballet and the ballet—both of which relied on sung lyrics rather than pantomimed action to narrate the story. The opera-ballet, so condescendingly described by Rousseau, was a lengthy production in three to five acts that incorporated sporadic intervals of dance throughout the performance and often concluded with a longer danced divertissement. Dancers in these productions most frequently formed the entourage of a principal singing character, or they populated the landscape where the action occurred—fauns, satyrs, and nymphs in the mythological forest; shepherds and shepherdesses in the rural countryside; Turks, Indians, or Africans from "the nations of the globe;"[7] demons and furies from hell. Regardless of characters' land of origin, cultural difference was signaled only through tiny modifications to standardly cut garments and through modest augmentation in the form of adding stereotypic gestures or stances to the standard vocabulary of steps. (See figs. 21 and 22.) Dancing intervened at moments of festivity or crisis, courtship or pageantry, and it celebrated the resolution of dramatic conflict portrayed through the sung lyrics.

The ballet, a shorter form that usually followed the longer opera-ballet to complete the evening's entertainment, consisted of several short acts connected by a metaphorical theme. *Les Fêtes Vénitiennes,* in which Dupré danced, used the Venetian carnaval as a pretext for the presentation of diverse dancing ensembles. *L'Europe Galante,* choreographed in part by Sallé, catalogued different nationalities throughout Europe and even Asia. Singing characters navigated the festivities, introducing and describing each group. Their presence lent the only continuity to the production as a whole.

Although aestheticians, critics, and choreographers conducted an extensive campaign for reforms in both the opera-ballet and the ballet, the Opéra resisted implementation of the proposed improvements with the full force of its bureaucratic and royally sanctioned weight. Despite its reputation for innovation, the grandeur of its productions, and the incomparable talents of the dancers, its legacy as designated instrument of court policy did not encourage experimentation.[8] The Opéra's administrative organization, as hierarchized, complex, and magisterial as the ballets it produced, rendered it unresponsive to new aesthetic agendas.[9] The popularity of pantomime on the boulevard stage may also have tainted its reputation, especially among Opéra administrators eager to maintain the appearance of class-based genres of spectacle. Furthermore, administrators at the Opéra, sensitive to the strong lobby of players, instrument-makers, singers, and composers in its employ, saw in the proposed choreographic reforms a disturbing devaluation of music and a heightened visibility for dance.[10] In their estimation the danced portions of their programming were already too popular; they drew in audiences in large numbers and received the most enthusiastic applause. Reviews repeatedly acknowledged that the only reason to attend the Opéra was to view the dancing. Any further cultivation of dance's presence at the Opéra threatened to compromise the very nature of the Opéra's aesthetic responsibilities.[11]

Still, the Opéra's stodginess seems remarkable, especially since experimentation with the action ballet was taking place in other European cities. In Stuttgart, Noverre, sponsored by the Duke of Wurtemberg, systematically worked out his ideas on the action ballet in more than a dozen full-length productions. These ballets, based on historical and mythological subjects from Greek antiquity, introduced a complete range of passions to the stage. Where productions in Paris tended to focus on the lighter themes entailed in romance, Noverre's ballets, six of which were tragedies that concluded in destruction and despair, depicted the intricate actions and interactions of classical drama.[12] In Vienna, Franz Hilverding, followed by his student Gaspare Angiolini, introduced the new genre sponsored by the monarchy and also by its forward-thinking director of the Theater am Kärntnertor, Francesco Algarotti. The most notable of the Viennese productions, Angiolini's *Don Juan, ou le Festin de Pierre* (1761), achieved instant acclaim for its choreography and also for the new dramatic support from the music evident in Gluck's score. In St. Petersburg, Hilverding, at the request of Catherine the Great, created several action ballets on themes drawn from Greek antiquity.[13] Throughout Italy, experimentation with pantomime was far advanced, as evidenced in the capabilities of Italian-trained itinerant choreographers such as Pitrot.

Even as word filtered in from abroad concerning the success of the new forms, the Opéra persistently cultivated other values, continuing to produce the lavish and spectacular opera-ballets for which it had achieved international renown. In a time when the populace experienced spectacle at the circus, fireworks displays, freak shows, and in experiments with electricity and magnetism, the Opéra stood out as the most optically opulent of all. (See fig. 23.) Like most other theatres built in the eighteenth century, the Opéra featured several sets of flats on each side, corresponding draperies hanging overhead, and a backdrop, all painted to create a single scene that receded in perfect perspective toward a central vanishing point. The scenery could depict a wide variety of contrasting locales, including ornate gardens, marble-columned rooms, or city squares replete with distant harbors and sailing ships. Trap doors permitted statuary, fountains, or altars to complement a given decor. Platforms known as gloires, capable of carrying several characters at a time, could also descend from the ceiling masked as a god's chariot or cupid's clouds. Due to the clocklike workings above, behind, and underneath the stage, new flats could slide into place with new overheads and backdrops unfurled in three to five seconds. The new scene would jiggle its way into clarity before the viewers' eyes, and the resolve from colorful chaos into well-composed picture charmed audiences repeatedly throughout the evening's entertainment.[14]

Backstage machines simulated thunder and the roar of the wind, and phosphorus ignited in the rafters replicated lightning. Rotating reflectors positioned next to the vertical columns of candles in each wing cast intense light on designated areas of the stage and left others in shadow. Bowls full of colored liquids held in front of candles bathed the stage in blue, red, or green light. As arresting as these effects were, they competed with the fashionable display created by the onlookers themselves in the dimmed but never

23. A production of *Iphigénie en Tauride* showing the grandeur of the late-eighteenth-century Opéra. Seating is inaccurately depicted by the nineteenth-century anonymous engraver.

darkened auditorium.[15] The viewer's attention, diverted by the suggestive positioning of bodies, the sumptuous arrangement of fabrics and jewels in one of the many boxes, would be recaptured by a stunning new scene onstage, only to wander out across the audience in search of additional visual and social stimulation.

The Opéra's well-deserved renown for lavish visual display was surpassed only by the reputation of its ballets, whose luxurious harmony of decor, costume, and choreography achieved great notoriety throughout Europe. After periods of minimal action in which singing characters formally declared their feelings and intentions, bodies encrusted with feathers, ribbons, satin, and lace would suddenly sweep onto the stage. Each dancer, individually adorned and coiffed, contributed to the extraordinary assemblage of colors, lines, and textures that decorated the stage. The ballets involved large numbers of dancers in patterns that embroidered the space with a never-ending series of configurations. Dancers transited from pinwheel formations to columns, they processed downstage, turned away to either side, reformed in small circles, exchanged single dancers among the circles, and then suddenly reappeared in neatly spaced rows. Single dancers led others along complex paths that braided groups together in intricate assemblages, each smoothly resolving into the next.[16]

Dancers executed this parade of patterns invoking a moderated but dynamic energy. Phrases exemplified a range, but not the extremes, of quickness and slowness. Steps from the basic vocabulary propelled dancers along their designated paths, allowing them to make decorous contact with one another. Female dancers' bell-shaped skirts tilted from side to side, occasionally revealing the inclination and trajectory of the ankle. (See figs. 24 and 25.) Men's stiff tunics (*tonnelets*), while they emphasized the entire leg's movements, still segmented the body like the female's dress into articulate periphery and composed central body. (See figs. 26 and 27.) The partially disclosed steps of the female dancer and the fully evident execution by the male created a pleasant exercise in comparison during their frequent unisons. Large circles of the leg (*ronds de jambes*); shifts of weight to the side, front, or back; jumps; turns—all signaled the dancers' synchronicity. Unison could also be deduced by tracking the precise location of the body within a vertical grid. The vocabulary of steps elaborated several heights for the body—degrees of plié and relevé—and equally subtle but precise facings for the dancer. Even when dancers directed their movements toward each other around a central point, the shifts of facing and of height confirmed their unified endeavors.

The raked stage lent added complexity and dynamism to the action. Upstage dancers attained sufficient elevation to be distinguished over the heads of downstage dancers, and this enhanced the visual variety within the proscenium's frame while at the same time directing the viewer's attention to the floor patterns delineated by the dancers as they navigated across the space. The slope of the stage also differentiated paths directed upstage from those coming forward toward the audience. As dancers toiled up the moderate but perceptible hill, their movements, although no less decorous, filled with effort, and their bodies appeared suspended in the receding perspective. By contrast, the phrases performed while moving downstage exhibited a carefree abandon, moderated only by the restraint necessary not to exceed the bounds of appropriate comportment. The moment when a dancer pivoted upstage to begin a descent transmitted an ecstatic effervescence, whereas the turn to begin an ascent confirmed the need to mask any extremes of feeling with a sophisticated, accomplished ease. The push and pull created by the dancers' changing efforts enlivened the symmetrical hierarchies of their groupings and also enriched the geometrical patterning of the floor.

Each of the bodies within the complex geometry continued, as in Dupré's performances, to reference the social regulations for correct comportment. Just as the singing elaborated verbal and sonoral worlds appropriate to the characters, so the dancing developed the discourse of the body as it should appear at all social occasions. Dancers displayed with daring and whimsical accuracy the proper comportment in greeting, touching, and gazing, while also maintaining the proper proximities to one another. Singers assumed along with dancers an elegant and polished comportment. Their minimal gestures originated in the same bodily stance and reflected the same values of ease and grace demonstrated in the dancers' performance. When they were swept into the choreographed patterns, they promenaded from pinwheel to column and executed simple footwork with an assured competence. When regarding the dance from the periphery of the stage, they presented a stationary version of the body that dancers put in motion.

If the overall visual spectacle of decorous bodies promenading through an opulent space seemed to have attained an extraordinary level of refinement, the individual skills

24. Costume design for a solo *Chaconne* danced by Marie Allard in a production from the 1750s of *Les Fêtes de l'Hymen* (1747).

25. Costume design for a female dancer in the role of a happy shadow from 1764.

26. Costume design for M. Laval in a noble role from *Les Fêtes de l'Hymen.*

27. Costume design for a male dancer in the role of a happy shadow from 1764.

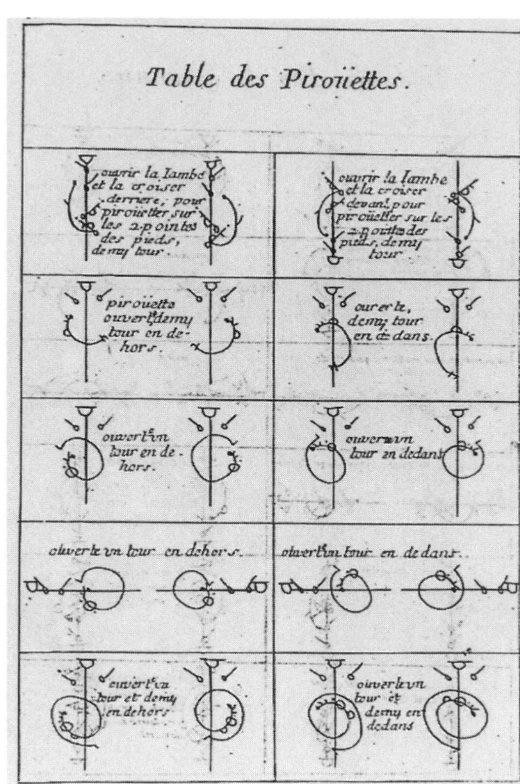

28. Table of pirouettes from Raoul Auger Feuillet's *Chorégraphie.*

of the dancers in executing a demanding vocabulary reflected an equivalent level of accomplishment. With the academization of dance in the late seventeenth century, dancers had devoted increasing amounts of time to mastery of the form. Identified early in the eighteenth century as professionals, dancers quickly raised the standards of beauty and accomplishment for theatrical dancing. Although an Opéra school for the study of dance was not established until 1780, principal dancers regularly tutored promising students. The ability to focus for several hours daily on the practice of dancing yielded new levels of physical confidence and dexterity.

The drive to achieve new standards of physical accomplishment was fueled, in part, by the ballet vocabulary's innate capacity to generate hierarchies of movements requiring various degrees of skill. The five true positions (and their five inverse counterparts, known as the false positions) along with the seven basic steps—*plier, élever, sauter, cabrioler, tomber, glisser,* and *tourner*[17]—offered countless possibilities for recombination and ornamentation. Steps could be sequenced in innovative patterns that demanded expert coordination, balance, or timing. They could also be enlarged or multiplied so as to feature a greater range of movement in several parts of the body. And the steps could be decorated with tiny gestures—additional circles of the wrist or foot, a toss of the head—that called for quick, precise control.

A turn, for example, could execute one-quarter, one-half, three-quarters or a full revolution. (See fig. 28.) A cabriole could involve single or multiple beats of the leg. A jump could be performed with ranging heights and degrees of lightness. A relevé could be held for greater or lesser amounts of time. Corresponding to each step, positions and movements of the arms reiterated or complemented the legs' patterns, and these, too, could be elaborated so as to increase the complexity of the movement phrase. Subtle articulations of the shoulder, elbow, wrist, and fingers, in concert with the legs, coordinated to produce phrases of substantial rhythmic complexity. In the very best choreography, the rhythmic dialogue set up between dance and music phrasing constructed counterpoints of suspension and accentuation that consistently arrested viewers with the degrees of dissonance and similitude that they produced.[18] What enthralled them equally was the dancers' fluid mastery over the entire sequence of patterns.

Choreographers and dancers were caught up in the project of exploring and mastering this seemingly limitless but well-organized repertoire. The hierarchies of expertise that helped to organize the vocabulary provided dancers and viewers with clear standards of proficiency. As in Dupré's time, viewers familiar with the basic vocabulary savored both the innovations and the technical expertise necessary to accomplish them. Learning to dance and to watch dancing, one assimilated the same well-defined set of criteria for evaluating action.

The ballets within an opera celebrated the hierarchical valuing of vocabulary and expertise by ranking both dancers and genres. Dancers employed at the Opéra assumed the titles *Premier Danseur, Figurant,* or *Corps* based on their proficiency and their charm as performers. A small and usually equal number of male and female dancers held the titles Premier Danseur and Première Danseuse. They performed exclusively in solos and duets featured within each ballet. The most esteemed among these dancers, like Dupré, appeared only in the final ballet of the evening. Dancers of the second rank performed in small group *entrées* and sometimes as exotic solo figures. The corps served as decorous background to these encounters and then swept soloists into the large processional patterns that most often concluded each section.

The three genres of dancing—*noble, semi-noble,* and *caractère*—cut across the rankings of dancerly expertise, infusing the criteria of proficiency with additional, more complex values.[19] The genres categorized ways of moving that affected the vocabulary dancers learned and the characters they represented. Noble or serious dancing, for example, emphasized the eloquence of the body in moving from one harmonious pose to the next. It required both regal composure and an elegant physique. Dancers expert in this genre typically assumed the stately roles of gods, nobility, heroes, and heroines. In contrast, the semi-noble (or semi-caractère) style encouraged a more sprightly approach associated with pastoral figures. (See fig. 29.) Dancers' well-proportioned but more compact bodies evidenced the strength and resiliency necessary to perform with alacrity a wide range of steps. The caractère or grotesque dancer undertook mastery of the athletic, acrobatic, and aerial vocabulary, and frequently invoked false as well as true positions and steps. The most spectacular and animated of all the characters, these dancers performed the roles of clowns, demons, and soldiers.

The privileging of the noble over the caractère, of the majestic over the extraordinary, mitigated the technocratic tendency to cultivate the biggest, highest, and most in developing the ballet vocabulary. The values of finesse and fire, of force, lightness, nobility, decency, and vivacity which constituted superior performance in dancing evidenced the productive tension that existed between technical and stylistic achieve-

Paysan Galant
Habit en usage dans plusieurs Ballets

29. Country gentleman costume by Jean-Baptiste Martin used in several ballets.

ment. Dancers and viewers alike examined and compared the nuances that such a system could generate. As exponents of a given genre, dancers were evaluated in terms of their abilities to realize its highest aesthetic goals. They distinguished themselves by possessing certain notable features of the genre, or by contributing modest innovations in vocabulary or style that further refined it. Thus Vestris exemplified the very best aspects of the noble genre by performing, despite its extreme difficulty, with absolute ease.[20] Mlle Heinel, making her debut at fifteen in the semi-caractère genre, combined a seductive face with the graces of a nymph, and an aplomb most remarkable for her age. And the young Madeleine Guimard, despite the impediment created during one season by her broken arm carried in a sling, dazzled viewers with her lightness and grace.[21]

If the performance confirmed a hierarchical and perfectly ordered structuring of bodily accomplishment, it also elaborated a highly refined but nonetheless compelling orchestration of desire. The most common subjects for dances within opera-ballets or ballets centered around resistance to and ultimate capitulation in the act of love. The female corps de ballet, frequently cast in the role of Diana's nymphs, would devote themselves to hunting until suddenly interrupted by a surprise attack from the male corps cast as fauns. Scenes of evasion, flirtation, and protestation would eventually culminate in the triumph of fauns over nymphs, of love over virtue. Principal characters often replicated the peregrinations of the corps, surrendering to love with Cupid's and Hymen's blessing. A more pastoral version of this scenario depicted shepherds in pursuit of shepherdesses across meadows and through forests. Still other versions sketched the same plot utilizing the exotic trappings of foreign lands. *Peruviennes* succumbed to *Peruviens*; *Persiennes* refused, but then finally acceded to the wishes of *Persiens*; *Phryigiens* eventually prevailed over *Phrygiennes*.

In their daily lives, dancers frequently played out similar scenarios of resistance and capitulation, of pursuit and conquest, achieving a notoriety that increased their onstage appeal.[22] Whether they came from one of the large families of professionals whose members staffed theatres as singers, musicians, actors, and dancers throughout Europe, or from middle- or working-class backgrounds, once they were hired by the Opéra, they became employees of the King. As such they occupied a special category within society, one that resisted strictures governing behavior based on family identity.[23] Working-class women, unhappily obligated to family or marriage, often took advantage of the status given to Opéra staff to escape their father's or husband's jurisdiction. As independent women secure within the institution of the Opéra, they manifested a unique erotic charge. Not only were they available for liaisons, but they displayed considerable skills in matters of fashion and comportment as well as mastery over the codes of flirtation.[24] Male dancers also functioned as objects of sexual fascination and speculation.[25] Like their female counterparts, they enjoyed a social mobility due to their great proficiency at the skills of self-presentation necessary to mingle with the highest echelons of society.

Dancers of both sexes were invited regularly to social gatherings of the elite; they performed alongside nobility in entertainments produced by aristocrats in their own private theatres;[26] and they hosted gatherings attended by nobility that included performances. This blurring of social with theatrical contexts complicated the onstage identities of the dancers. The ambiances of sexual intrigue constructed both onstage and off reinforced each other. Watching dancers court one another onstage, viewers not only witnessed a reiteration of offstage behavior they had enacted or heard about, but could also imagine the dancers flirting, by a quick gesture of the head or forearm, with the audience.

The masks sometimes worn by dancers heightened the intrigue by obscuring their identity and de-clarifying any messages directed out toward the audience. The viewers' gaze traveled across the dancer's body in search of clues to the real-life self. The immobile faces invited viewers to project a variety of feelings onto the performer, and allowed them to find confirmation in the abstract articulations of the body's joints. At the same time, the choreography kept dancers interlocked in a social organization created by the patterns of all bodies moving in space. Gestural inflections, interpreted by viewers as momentary expressions of individual desire, were immediately woven into the overall choreographic design. The spectacle thus assured the dancer's unavailability onstage by placing a number of barriers in the path of desire—the mask, the choreography, and the distance between stage and audience. These same conventions, however, also heightened the viewer's erotic fascination by preserving the ambiguity of the dancer's sentiments. The dancer's fleeting gestures, their grace, and their level of abstraction all provided multiple attachments for the viewers' ongoing fantasies.

The choreography for the ballets fused the sensuous and erotic connotations of dancers' movements to the structural organization of the music. Dance offered a physical visualization of instrumental music in the same way that vocal music transformed poetry into sound.[27] Where sung lyrics were thought to amplify written poetry with multiple complementary rhythms, dancing, it was argued, added inflection and coloration to music. And where the music's harmony and instrumentation augmented the depth and intensity of the feelings expressed in the poetry, the dance's energy and vitality enhanced music in a similar way. Dance functioned like a poetics scripted alongside the music that both clarified and enhanced the music's meaning. As one Dancing Master put it:

> One must please the eyes, without doubt, when one dances; that is the primary consideration: but since the Dance must, as an auxiliary language, lend color, and a new intelligibility to music, it is necessary for the dance to speak to the soul, to excite and bring to mind ideas, and demonstrate the movements of the soul which the poet and composer would have desired.[28]

Technical facility at articulation, deftness at the skills that pleased the eyes, could not alone satisfy the astute viewer. Choreographers and dancers needed to identify qualities of spirit in the music—the products of a careful collaboration between poet and composer—and exemplify these qualities in the articulations of the dance. The dance would then coexist with music and text as the last in a series of faithful transcriptions.

The physical analogies that dance provided to musical phrasing, rhythm, inflection, and mood gave the performance its meaning. This description of Maximilien Gardel praised choreography and execution for the breathtaking physicality exhibited in partnering the music:

> One remarked especially in the Couplet du *Crescendo* on the manner in which the accelerating and interlinked steps of the young dancer exactly wrote for the eyes the notes of the couplet. He joins to the faithful and lively expression in this section, a lightness and surprising aplomb with an energy that leads one to believe, by the end of the *entrée,* that one has seen one of the strongest and lengthiest dances yet to appear in the Theatre.[29]

Gardel's steps *wrote* the notes for the viewers' eyes to read. His physical forcefulness or languor, voluptuousness or buoyancy supplemented both music and lyrics to create a polyphonic, or rather, polyarticulate spectacle.

Gardel's dexterity, precision, and agility held intrinsic value for viewers who saw in bodily articulation another of many discourses for expressing human existence. Engaging this physicality the viewer could not help but be drawn into the framed space of the stage and then backward in admiration of the dancers' skill and beauty and the choreographer's inventiveness. The boxlike universe of the stage with its perfect perspective seemed to order and regulate all human motion. Reviews from the period repeatedly described the ballets as "brilliant," "agreeable," "fast-paced," and "ingenious."[30] By presenting such elegantly costumed personages engaged in a seemingly endless sequence of smoothly flowing, innovative patterns, ballets seemed to affirm the general belief that human perfection was imminent.[31] The careful calibration of bodies in relation to one another and to space, the inventiveness of their repositionings, the masterful display of their geometric articulation provided a sumptuous spectacle that left nothing to be desired.

The exceptional popularity of the ballets derived, in part, from a generalized social preoccupation with and enthusiasm for dancing.[32] Performances by nobility at court were no longer mandated, nor was dancing envisioned as a foundation for all other pursuits. The repertoires of steps for salon and stage had begun to diverge so that audience members attending the opera-ballets saw performed phrases only distantly related to those they were able to execute. Still, for upper- and middle-class inhabitants of the city, the multiple benefits to be derived from the practice of dancing were undeniable: dancing provided moderate yet comprehensive exercise; it improved the visual appearance of the body; it imparted ease to one's comportment in all social settings; and it promised the most diverting and elevated form of entertainment.

Treatises on social dance reeled off the valuable functions performed by dance in the same way that they distinguished between sacred, profane, and theatrical forms.[33] They continued not only to connect to the protocols for correct comportment but also to incorporate extensive analyses of proper social behavior as part of the study of dancing. Chavanne's *Principes du Menuet,* for example, included lengthy descriptions of the greetings required for such distinct occasions as entering a private house, arriving at a large assemblage of people, leaving the church or one's house, passing by someone in the street, encountering someone by chance, or being introduced purposefully to someone.[34] Through the study of dancing, one learned the codes of behavior, the movements they entailed, and the style—graceful and unaffected—with which they should be performed. In this way dancing improved one's comportment, just as it contributed to one's understanding and appreciation for nature. Its effects on health, society, and art, as earlier in the century, continued to be conceptualized as an ensemble of mutually complementary benefits.

What distinguished midcentury approaches to the practice and evalution of dancing was the emphasis on the body's appearance at each moment in time. In learning to dance, the establishment of a trace—the evidence of the relationship between moving gesture and spatial surround—mattered far less than the configuration of the body at each moment. The body should assume an agreeable stance while still, and it should exhibit equally graceful shapings and harmoniously crafted rhythms while in motion. All bodies, as they moved alongside one another, should demonstrate not so much their mutual awareness of their own participation in motion's flux, but rather their adeptness at placing themselves congenially and clearly in the general socialscape.

In its fulfillment of spatial and temporal specifications, the body increasingly resembled nothing so much as a machine.[35] The endless strings, tubes, and sacks described by Burette had been analyzed in greater detail by midcentury and acquired new functional attributes. The joints operated like levers;[36] the muscles resembled springs;[37] and the whole body constituted so many mechanical parts that could be brought into good working order. Dancing Masters frequently referred to the body as the human machine and believed that their pedagogical strategies effectively calibrated and aligned its workings. Like Pygmalion's statue, the body could be made to come to life and move beautifully if the proper care were taken.[38]

Dancing built the body-machine by strengthening its parts and aligning and lubricating their interfaces. Then it maintained the machine through gentle, prudent use. The desired physical shape produced by dancing might even be thought to approximate the lifelike mechanical puppets frequently displayed in fairs and at court throughout the eighteenth century.[39] The body's easeful and moderated movement in all social situations shared with the machine a detached, well-timed precision. Humans aspired to perfectly guided actions, so much so that the formal protocols regulating all social intercourse could easily seem like instruction manuals for a vast social mechanism.

Even those Dancing Masters who advocated a less "mechanical" execution of steps treated the body like a complex machine. A mechanical or lifeless performance resulted when complicated steps were featured in a meaningless array. The principles of mechanical efficiency, however, should necessarily inform the performance of all steps. From the first lessons, Dancing Masters made an effort to impart an internal fortitude necessary to support correct positioning for what they conceived as a self-regulating rather than mutely malleable machine. Their increasing awareness of anatomical structure only confirmed and lent greater precision to the notion that what was mechanical was natural:

> I would like the instructor to explain to the student the cause of everything, that the student understand that what he or she is being asked to do is natural and conforms to reason, and that disagreeable attitudes or movements are not natural. For example, in walking, the center of weight in the body alternates between the two legs: this conforms to the laws of mechanics, it is natural; if the head and the shoulders fall forward, or if the hips rest behind the legs, these movements are not natural.[40]

The natural as the mechanical was that which conformed to universal principles of mechanical efficiency which, in turn, derived from an analysis of abstract spatial forms.

Dancing enhanced one's physical appearance by forming, first of all, the perfect image of the person standing. The simple, open shape assumed by the body in second position created the most natural and hence most desirable impression:

> If one wants to pay attention to the manner in which the human being is constructed, one will see that the body is never so well composed nor cuts so fine a figure as during the times when one stands equally on both feet, slightly apart, letting the arms and hands fall naturally with their own weight; this is what one calls, in terms of dance, being in second position, with the hands on one's pockets. This stance is the most natural and the simplest, even though it is always very difficult to teach to someone who is learning to dance. It seems that nature is perpetually in opposition to itself.[41]

At the first lesson, Dancing Masters began to construct the body-machine by demonstrating and then molding the student into the first basic and then the other four true positions. This exercise enabled them to begin to correct any physical defects their students might display, such as a sunken chest, a sour countenance, or the most prevalent problem of all: the unsightly curvature of the leg that rendered the person bowlegged or knock-kneed. It also allowed them to monitor poor social habits such as the awkward protruding of the elbows or the tendency to titter.[42]

In achieving the best overall bodily design, the position of the head was considered by some Dancing Masters to be of key importance,[43] where others emphasized the role of the foot,[44] with its toes actively spread, and still others focused on the alignment of the legs. All agreed, however, that the proper assemblage of bodily parts was necessary to demonstrate ease and assuredness in standing and walking. The famous dancing master Marcel was praised by his son for his ability to teach the assured step as follows:

> He would have said that in order to take an assured step, it is first necessary to flex at the knee of the leg one wants to start with; lift ever so slightly the foot of the same leg; carry it forward by stretching the thigh, in such a way that the leg, very straight, moves in the same direction as the hip. Then having placed the foot totally on the ground, and advancing the body over the leg on which one began, he would have said, "Sir, there's one step accomplished."[45]

Marcel's description focused on the importance of achieving the same facing for both hip and thigh by stretching or extending the leg correctly. The ability to soften and then extend the leg in designated directions gave to all the steps a spongy resiliency, one of the requisite attributes of great dancing.

At each lesson Dancing Masters gestured, touched, and described the correct placement of all parts. Using the same pedagogical techniques, they also inculcated skills at social intercourse by practicing with the student much of the vocabulary of proper etiquette. The lesson began when the Dancing Master arrived at the door. Protocol demanded that he be greeted properly and ushered into the dancing room politely.[46] Dancing Masters scrutinized the position and demeanor of the student in between dances and corrected comportment as well as dancing. The *Révérence*, one of the first movements learned by any dance student, acknowledged and honored one's partner before and after a dance. Variations on this bow were used in the formal greetings required at all social occasions.[47] The same facility at the bow learned in dance class applied equally to manipulations of the hat or fan and to walking, sitting, and passing by one another.

Thus the dancing lesson alternated, without distinguishing between them, instruction in polite comportment and practice at dancing. Over months and years, students mastered etiquette as they embarked on a systematic inventory of dance steps conveyed through a gradated series of short dances. They learned to dance by practicing dances. A few simple, preliminary exercises—pliés to improve the pliancy of the knee, kicks to increase the flexibility of the leg—served to prepare students to perform dances they had mastered and to learn and practice new dances. Beginners spent their time on the simplest minuet. More advanced students might perform a range of dances selected by the Dancing Master to emphasize different qualities and timings. The apprentice body-machine imitated and repeated these dances so as to routinize the proper spatial pathways and temporal markings that defined its course.

Spatially, this practice at dancing developed a graceful harmony of legs, arms, and head as one traveled across the floor. It treated the body's parts as semi-independent fleshy masses whose orientation in space should be coordinated during each step. No abstract principle located in the body's interior regulated the alignment of the parts. Rather, a silhouette-like ideal image of the body and the pathways of motion intrinsic to the steps themselves, when correctly learned, guided the body's parts into proper positioning. Thus students were admonished not to place the head too far in front or in back because this would give the appearance of a foreshortened neck, with the head sunken in between the shoulders.[48] Dancing Masters also warned their students not to lift the leg to a height too great, or circle it in a circumference too large for its length. Otherwise, the rest of the body, in order to compensate for the compromised alignment of hip and thigh, would be thrown into an unsightly, strained position.[49]

Temporally, dancing emphasized the measuring or parsing out of the body's movements in accordance with the musical structures of rhythm, meter, and harmony. Dancing Masters frequently composed the pieces they taught their students, and sometimes accompanied them on a violin or pianoforte, at the same time closely observing the correctness and elegance of their execution. The role of Dancing Master as teacher of dancing and accompanist epitomized the close association between music and dance. At each lesson students could hear and then discuss with their teachers how dance and music fit together. They learned the rudiments of music theory—aspects of meter, rhythm, and harmony—and their import for dancing. They expanded their knowledge of types of musical forms and the choreographic structures appropriate to them. And they developed their musicality—the ability to phrase and time movement to correspond to the music.

Through the discipline of matching movement to music, students inculcated the techniques of regulating and modulating the body's energy and momentum. Like the spatial forms and traces to which the body conformed while standing and moving, the temporal demands placed on the body's motion originated outside it. Phrasing of the movement never conformed to the dancer's breathing patterns, nor were there extensive opportunities for improvising with musicians as there had been one hundred years earlier. Instead, dancing taught the body how to fit itself to spatial and temporal structures whose significance permeated social as well as aesthetic domains.

Learning the dances increased one's flexibility, and lent grace and economy to all one's movements. It also infused movements with a moderated sense of timing and a sustained energy. These skills of suppleness, efficiency, and moderation, more than any others, could be applied to any situation.[50] The flexibility acquired in dancing expanded the range of one's movement and gave the body more agility. It eliminated stiffness, an undesirable social as well as physical trait, and consequently, affectation.[51] Students of dance always evidenced the necessary aplomb, both because they manifested familiarity with the appropriate decorum, and also because their limbs were at ease.

Dancing functioned as a regimen for bodily improvement with equal effectiveness on all types of bodies and all varieties of defects:

> But even as to those of either sex, the practice of dancing is attended with obviously good effects. Such as are blessed by nature with a graceful shape and are clean-limbed, receive still greater ease and grace from it; while at the same time, it prevents the gathering of those gross and foggy humors which in time form a disagreeable and inconvenient corpulence. On the other hand, those whose make and constitution occasion a kind of heavy proportion, whose muscular texture is not distinct, whose necks are short, shoulders round, chest narrow, and who, in short are, what may be called, rather clumsy figures; these will greatly find their account in a competent exercise of the art of dancing. . . .[52]

For those who labored with a thick and undifferentiated physique, dancing carved from it a proper and articulate shape. For those who suffered from constitutional weaknesses—

thin limbs, slumped shoulders, paleness—dancing built up and animated the body. Furthermore, dancing incited joy and gaiety, which gave the body an uplifted, light-hearted appeal. Other forms of exercise, tennis for example, produced frustration and anger.[53] In social as well as theatrical contexts, the joyful countenance of the dancer pleased spectators in the same way that the carefully constructed body set them at ease.

For those gifted students who might distinguish themselves with a career in dance, a further set of abstract criteria existed which they were required to fulfill. Students not only assimilated the complex vocabulary of theatrical dance and the modifications in bearing and in the size and quality of movements necessary for the stage, but also began to gear their aptitudes toward one of the three genres. Dancing Masters directed students with the slim, elegant physique and sustained simplicity required by the noble genre toward that repertoire of dances, whereas those with a more compact, athletic musculature learned the caractère steps. Those with a talent for quick or light movement were given semi-caractère dances that developed and extended their abilities to fuse graceful forms with a certain degree of tour de fource dancing.

The three genres, like the spatial and temporal forms of the dancing, existed as predefined roles into which the dancer's body was cast. They collated movement qualities and physical attributes so as to fashion character types that represented three categories of being. Although differences in execution were permitted, they were perceived as variations on a standard type rather than as unique contributions by an exceptional artist. Artistic achievement was measured in terms of how well one exemplified the genre rather than how well one interpreted one's role.[54] The fact that most lessons were private allowed Dancing Masters to focus intimately on the student's innate capabilities and channel them in the appropriate direction.

The spatial and temporal demands for mechanical efficiency placed on the body served as well to define what was desirable choreographically. The ballet as a whole was conceived as a more or less complicated machinery, an intricate organization of interlocking parts, which if treated economically would create visual liveliness and appropriateness, and if insufficiently organized would produce a disjointed muddle:

> Cannot those ballets which, on the contrary, bring only disorder and confusion in their train, whose development is disjointed, whose figures are muddled, which betray the expectations of the artist and the anticipation of the public, because they err alike in a sense of proportion and accuracy, be compared to ill-arranged pieces of machinery, over-burdened with cogs and springs?[55]

In likening the ballet to a machine, choreographers considered the smooth interaction between its contributing parts—scenery, costumes, lighting, music, and movement. Overburdened with the ornate cogs and springs of virtuoso accomplishment and the decorum of soloists' privileges, or derailed by a plot with no pretext for dancing, the ballet could not achieve a harmonious whole. But where the body evinced the surety of correct placement and an economy of motion, and where the ballet, as each scene gave way to the next, demonstrated an analogous well-crafted efficiency, then both body and ballet could undertake, with ease and deftness, their proper mission—to present living images of a perfected physicality.

Challenging hierarchy

Both the beauteous spectacle that the ballets provided and the perfectly tuned body-machine that performed them were threatened by the new imitative dance. The action ballet challenged existing notions of theatricality with its careful weighting of music, lyrics, and dance, and the very vocabularies out of which choreography and pedagogy had developed. Rather than the transcriptive process through which dance rendered music into visual and corporeal form, the action ballet translated a story into danced dramatic action. It would not implement steps to "write" musical and poetic structures on the body, but instead, translate a narrative into progressional scenes whose characters danced and gestured the plot. This radical redefinition of choreographic process implied new skills for dancers to master, new standards of virtuoso accomplishment, and a new kind of collaborative relationship among all the artists producing the ballet.

Of all the texts to discuss the actual aesthetic implications of the new dance, Jean Georges Noverre's *Letters on Dancing and Ballets* (1760) set forth the most comprehensive and influential arguments concerning the changes it entailed. Cited repeatedly by other choreographers and writers on dance,[56] this text delineated both the aesthetic ambitions of the action ballet and the practical alterations in dancers' and choreographers' professions necessary to accomplish them. A mediocre dancer by the standards of 1743, when he made his debut, Noverre established his reputation as a choreographer through the series of ballets he created for the Opéra Comique and his tours to London at the invitation of Garrick. By the end of the 1750s, Noverre had synthesized his observations on the innovative uses of pantomime seen at the fair theatres and in London with his own choreographic discoveries and with the reformist arguments of writers like Diderot and Cahusac into a comprehensive, hyperbolic, beautifully written manifesto. Written from the point of view of the choreographer or even the teacher of choreography[57] rather than that of Dancing Master, aesthetician, historian, or amateur viewer, his book offered an energetic critique as well as a detailed formulation of the new approach to theatrical dance practices.

In his critique of dance at the Opéra, Noverre identified as the cause of its many failings the lack of collaboration among poet, composer, and choreographer. Because choreographers were excluded from the process of determining the theme of the opera, ballets did not form an integral part of the dramatic action. Choreographers thus assumed a subsidiary artisanal role similar to that of machinist or designer, caustically but accurately described by Noverre as follows:

> Let us see what the *maître de ballet* usually does at this spectacle, and let us examine the work he is given to do. He is presented with a prompt copy: he opens it and reads: PROLOGUE: *passepied* for the dancers representing Games and Pleasures; *gavotte* for the Laughs, and *rigaudon* for the Pleasant Dreams. FIRST ACT: march for the Warriors, second air for the same, *musette* for the Priestesses. SECOND ACT: *loure* for the People, *tambourin* and *rigaudon* for the Sailors. THIRD ACT: march for the Demons, lively air for the same. FOURTH ACT: entry of Greeks and *chaconne*, without counting Winds, Tritons, Naiads, Hours, Signs of the Zodiac, Bacchantes, Zephyrs, Shades and Fatal Dreams—because there is no end to them . . .
>
> Sir, says the *premier danseur* to the *maître de ballet*, I take the place of such a dancer and must dance to such an air; by the same token a certain *danseuse* insists on

> dancing the *passepieds,* another the *musettes,* this one the *tambourins,* that one the *loures,* and a third the *chaconnes;* and this imaginary privilege, this dispute about rights and style, supplies each opera with twenty solo *entrées* which are danced in costumes totally opposed in style and manner, but which differ neither in character, atmosphere, combinations of steps nor in the poses. . . .[58]

As characterized by Noverre, choreographers worked with a list of types of dances and characters to be composed for each act. The choreographer arbitrated in the matching of dancers to parts and constructed new ensemble sections that suited the temperaments of the populations to be portrayed—demons, shepherds, etc. Principal dancers, however, exercised considerable control over their own appearance by selecting dances and costumes, and choreographers' success often depended upon their ability to introduce pleasing new configurations that fit individual dancers' stylistic preferences with the overall requirements for each act of the opera.

Noverre hoped to ennoble the choreographer's role by making it the central coordinating position in the production.[59] Choreographers would determine the subject of the ballet and oversee the efforts of scene and costume designers, machinists, poet, and composer. They would structure the various scenes of the ballet and direct the dancers in the kind of action necessary to realize the plot. They would also teach dancing, both its expressive and mechanical aspects, and thereby assure a reliable cadre of dancers trained in the appropriate techniques.

So that choreographers could acquire the necessary expertise for their new role, Noverre advised them to read widely, learn a variety of disciplines, and to observe life around them.[60] For inspiration in choosing subjects for ballets, Noverre recommended a thorough knowledge of literary and dramatic classics as well as history.[61] Close study of painting would enable choreographers to envision the great subjects of history translated into action and also improve their understanding of the principles of ordering color and shape.[62] From geometry choreographers could learn the variety of shapes usable in composing large group patterns,[63] and from anatomy and drawing the proper representation of the passions for each individual body and face.[64] The study of music, essential to choreographers' success, permitted them to craft phrases with precision and accuracy, to sequence steps in accordance with musical phrasing, and to communicate with the composer.[65]

Choreographers well versed in all these areas could use their skills to direct and shape rather than dictate the staged action. They should not demonstrate specific steps or expressions to be copied, but rather surround dancers with the action and allow them to respond. If dancers only imitated and then reproduced what choreographers demonstrated, then the ballet would lack any fire or liveliness.[66] Noverre encouraged choreographers preparing for a rehearsal to write out a scenario of the scene they were about to choreograph. Through this exercise they would gain a deeper understanding of the characters' motivations necessary to evaluate and guide dancers' responses. Noverre likened the relationship between choreographer and dancer to that of the poet and the reciter of poetry.[67] The choreographer produced and orchestrated a script for dancers to interpret.

But this role for the choreographer, as coordinator and final judge over all aspects of the production, violated the existing distribution of responsibilities at institutions like the

Opéra. It reversed the established flow of the collaborations in which poet and composer determined the shape of productions long before choreographic labor began. Even more significant, the action ballet challenged the preeminence of composer and music. Dancing in the opera-ballets had illustrated the music, whereas in the action ballet, the dramatic needs of a plot devised by the choreographer would dictate both movement and music. The choreographer was not only authorized to confer with the composer about the ballet's musical needs, but dancing became the central and defining activity.

The powerful new position for choreographers predicted by the action ballet disturbed dancers as well. Principal dancers who enjoyed celebrity status typically exercised strong influence over the nature of the performance in any production. The classical operatic tradition permitted lead dancers to arrange their own solos, and accommodated their preferences for the kind of character or dance they would perform. In Noverre's vision of the new dance, lead dancers would contribute poses and even phrases of movement to the overall choreography, but these initiatives from dancers would be evaluated by the choreographer in terms of their suitability to the character and to the narrative as a whole. Furthermore, the often murky distinction between main and supporting characters in the new ballets did not map neatly onto the existing, clearly defined boundaries between principal dancers and *figurants*. Principals could no longer count on the structuring of the scenes to confirm their superiority. And their requisite participation in the entire ballet entailed lengthier rehearsals. Principals and figurants would necessarily work together in order to apprehend their own parts within the complex choreographic whole.

As described by Noverre, the action ballet promoted a more egalitarian working relationship among dancers with varied skills and dispositions. Still, the criteria for evaluating excellence, because of their resistance to quantification, did not identify for dancers a clear system of accomplishments and rewards. And the new dance demanded a substantial investment from dancers in learning the arts of pantomime and facial expression. The new choreography emphasized the dancer's ability to play a character convincingly as much or more than the deft execution of a complicated jumping pattern or the sensitive inflection of a phrase.[68] To express fury perfectly, or to appear as the most ardent lover[69]—these standards of imitative excellence would join criteria based on the elegance and alacrity of the step or movement phrase. Dancers were still asked to display a perfected body and to evidence mastery over the traditional lexicon. Unmasked, they would also need to acquire skills at two kinds of facial control. They would be asked to add to the body's postures and gestures the facial expressions necessary to convey the character's every sentiment. They would also need to hide any evidence of the effort entailed by a given movement or phrase. Noverre found especially repugnant any registering in the face of the effort required to perform a movement, and he encouraged choreographers to eliminate such effort-filled movements from their dances. With no established method of instruction for gestural or facial pantomime, however, dancers' reticence to convert to the new dance seems understandable.[70]

For Noverre, the performers necessarily became the characters they played, but these characters were not autonomous beings with spontaneous needs and desires. The full range of the character's feelings and action could be known by the performer in advance. Dancers could practice each passion in all the shades of its intensity and thereby cultivate their innate capacity to respond to imagined emotions as well as their knowledge of how each passion should look. As part of the dancer's preparation, Noverre advocated a training program analogous to that undergone by the student of painting:

> They begin by making them draw an oval, they next pass to the different parts of the face and then combine them to make a head; so with the other parts of the body. When the pupil has arrived at that stage when he can put together a whole figure, the master teaches him to recognise natural movements, shows him how to arrange with art those pencil strokes which bestow life and imprint on the features the passions and affections with which the soul is affected.
>
> The dancing-master, like the painter, after having taught the pupil certain steps, the manner of combining one with the other, the opposition of the arms, the *effacements* of the body and the positions of the head, must still show him how to give value and expression to them by the help of the features. In order that he may succeed, it will only be necessary to arrange *entrées* for him in which he would have many passions to represent. It would not be sufficient to make him depict these same passions in all their force, it would still be necessary for him to be taught the succession of their movements, their degrees of light and shade, and the different effects which they produce on the features. From such lessons, dancing would learn to speak, and the dancer to reason. . . .[71]

The body should be treated as a kind of painting surface on which the passions could be rendered in so many strokes. A character's every action could be constructed, part by bodily part, passion by passion, and practiced repeatedly.

But this kind of bodily training had no danced precedent. The interdisciplinary skills it demanded subverted not only the hierarchies of rank and expertise but also the system of genres. The standard repertoire of noble or caractère behaviors seemed insufficient to represent the uniqueness of the characters and of the situations in which they found themselves. A given character could, over the course of the story, undergo a complex range of emotional responses. The consolidation of physical and psychological traits offered by each of the three genres lacked the flexibility necessary to evoke this palette of expressions.

At the same time, Noverre and other choreographers interested in the new form were careful not to advocate the abandonment of the basic vocabulary of steps or the stylistic achievements of each genre's best practitioners. Even as he denounced the erotic, allusional inscriptions of the masked dancer as artifice, Noverre extolled the gradations of intensity that infused the execution of complex physical skills and approved of the dancers' musicality, which would enable them to inflect the phrasing of such skills so as to complement and reinforce musical structure. He never acknowledged the allusions made by such inflections to the play of feelings across the soul or to the syntax of desire itself, but the range of stylistic qualities that had been developed in the classical dance, along with the intensity of conviction it demanded, were vital to the project of the action ballet. Thus, even as he railed against cabrioles and entrechats,[72] steps that impressed too strongly upon viewers the physical skills necessary to accomplish them, he emphasized the importance of speed, brilliancy, and precision.[73] If he disdained the vacuousness of arm movements, he nonetheless desired a graceful proportioning of parts that would lead to a harmony of the whole body. He believed in the firmness of foundation, the equilibrium necessary to create pliancy in movement.[74] And he hoped to display the same easeful aplomb, the playful springiness and assured nobility, so admired in dancers like Dupré.[75]

The action ballet required new kinds of expertise not only from dancers and choreographers but also from viewers. The criteria of grace, alacrity, and precision used to evaluate dancing were retained by the new choreographic project, yet new categories of accomplishment were also instituted. Like the criteria for judging a dancer's excellence, however, the viewer's ability to perceive and evaluate dancing relied on intangible qualities. According to Noverre, the ballet would be successful if it transferred the dancers' sentiments and passions to the souls of the viewers.[76] To accomplish this task, choreographers, dancers, and viewers all had to resist the attraction of pyrotechnic displays of virtuosity and acquire the discrimination necessary to identify the just depiction of passions. By observing the world around them, viewers would cultivate the taste necessary to discriminate between false gestures, the products of artifice and deception, and true gestures, resulting from the unanimous commitment of body, mind, and soul to a given feeling. Once viewers had achieved a certain level of discrimination and susceptibility to just imitation, then dancers could

> captivate the public by the force of the illusion and make it experience all the emotions by which they are swayed. That realism, that enthusiasm which distinguishes the great actor and which is the life-blood of the fine arts is, if I may so express myself, like an electric spark. It is a fire which spreads rapidly, and in a moment captivates the imagination of the spectator, stirring his soul and rendering his heart susceptible to every emotion.[77]

Those who failed to study the passions, to learn what a realistic representation of them might be, remained impervious to the electric moment when the characters' feelings leapt from stage to auditorium.

The passionate portrayals that such systematic study could produce "spoke to the soul through the eyes."[78] More visual than visceral, their power to awaken in the viewer analogous passions resulted from their imitative accuracy. They would teach the viewer about the world through their detailed, realistic enactment of it. This didactic form of dance left little room for indulgence in erotic fantasy or sumptuous visual ornamentation. It championed the sensible and the sentimental over the sensate, and replaced the ambiguous nuances of the masked tracer of forms with the enthusiastic clarity of the feeling-filled personage.

The more sensible machine

As radically as the action ballet diverged from the opera-ballets, it shared an aesthetic interest in surfaces and in the machinelike workings of theatrical spectacle that made surfaces lustrous. Noverre and others hoped to reposition the choreographer at the origin and center of ballet production, but this centralization of authority was construed as improving the efficiency with which plot, virtuosity, and scenic liveliness might interface. They intended that dancers extend their repertoire to include the pantomimic, but this challenge to dancers' skillfulness constituted an augmentation more in amount than in kind of expertise. The pantomimic vocabulary itself emphasized the appearance of passions, not the process of their development. The crystalline display of each feeling mattered in a way that either the evolution from one feeling to the next or the difficulty in expressing a feeling did not. The contiguity of perfectly painted images was what counted, making the transformation into and out of those images register only in the efficiency and cleverness with which they facilitated change.

In the social world as in the world of art, the body—wigged, painted, beauty-marked, and jeweled—reveled in contiguous surfaces. Fashionable dress celebrated the intersection of one richly textured surface with another—of sleeve with glove with ring, or of hem with stocking with shoe. It did not explore the play between an undisclosed interiority and an approved exteriority. The woman's bosom, for example, largely exposed, was treated as another surface where the cut of each neckline spoke more significantly than the disclosure of an expanse of powdered flesh. The man's waistcoat and vest framed the groin area, but as a series of openings of one surface onto the next. Bodies, whether on stage or in the salon, intercoursed with one another like parts in a complicated machine. The perfection of mechanical dolls, so much an interest at midcentury, set standards for bodily appearance and aplomb which live bodies aspired to meet.

Proponents of the action ballet hoped to deepen the appearance of bodies, to render them more vivid and more sensible, and to orchestrate a causal logic for their interactions. They did not intend to alter the clocklike timing or spatial precision that the opera-ballets had attained or to sacrifice a single moment of spectacle. The careful sequencing of a range of feelings would draw the viewer further into the action, making all the more miraculous the transitions from one compelling scene to the next. The project of representing the passions, like the construction of the stage machinery responsible for changing scenes, required choreographers to coordinate looks and gestures for each dancer and to fit all bodily postures and motions together using the plot as blueprint. The plot gave their motions coherence and integrity just as mechanical drawings elucidated the machine's purpose. Exhibiting their purpose, dancing bodies would thereby continue to signal their horizontal and vertical perfectability even as they began to stand at the center of the grid that measured them.

Interlude

Make the Scheme Known

As Noverre succinctly observed, the action ballet must organize itself into a beginning, a knotted middle (*noeud*), and an end. But how to make that knot visible? Perhaps one of the characters has put into motion an insidious scheme. Some hideously evil or mildly mischievous plot will soon engulf the oblivious others. But in the meantime, the schemer must act with obsequious civility toward them. No one must know what has been contrived, except, of course, the audience. In order to remind the audience of the impending disaster, to whet their appetite, the character, scarcely capable of maintaining the mask of cordial normalcy, must frequently revert to the scheming mastermind who has contrived the oncoming misery. In private, off to one side of the stage but in full view of the audience, this character's politesse suddenly falls away. True motivations and aspirations flicker into visibility. Will anyone notice? Will the seizure provoke suspicion? Will the character resume a deceptive role in time? When might this delirious self-revelation occur next?

The suspense of the impending doom is aided and abetted by the character's inner struggle. Each seizure by, each return to, the "true" self that concocted the scheme augments anticipation. At the same time, the very fact of the deception is a perfect vehicle for the display of interiority. A thousand different sequences connect the public social drill which the character must play out to the private inner life of tumultuous emotions. "You are about to die, but I am kissing your hand with great affection." "The kidnappers are going to spirit you away, but first I will throw a party for you." "I will pretend we have never met before even though I have already arranged your demise." The body forces the mask of friendliness over itself, a transformation either arduous or eerily sudden. If the body's struggle is intense, the scheme must be very dire, or the character not so malevolent; but if the return to civility lacks any hesitation, then the character must be very evil, indeed.

These are the delicious intricacies that both choreographer and performer launch into with relish. The raising eyebrow, curling lip, shrugging shoulder, whisking cape, frozen torso, trembling hand—so many different codes, timings, sequences. Choreographer and performer discuss the possibilities, try out various sequences, map a course of action. Each performance, the dancer digs into the role with a slightly different attack. Efforts and timings of individual expression readjust so as to achieve maximum dramatic impact. It is a triumph. The dancer has gone to the limits of self-revelation. Now the audience knows what a human is and can be.

Jason et Médée (1771)

Gaetano Vestris's *Jason et Médée,* one of the first complete action ballets to be performed at the Opéra, occurred as a danced play within the second act of the opera *Ismène et Isménias,* warning the opera's main characters of their possible fate. Along with Maximilien Gardel, another of the principal dancers at the Opéra, Vestris had traveled to Vienna at Noverre's encouragement and danced in several of his ballets, including the role of Jason in the premiere of Noverre's *Jason et Médée.* He had likewise performed the role in Vienna.[1] In his review of the ballet, Grimm accused Vestris of plagiarism, and Noverre blamed him for the indifferent response his own five-act version received when it premiered at the Opéra in 1780.[2] Vestris, however, was supported by the critic for the *Mercure de France,* who claimed a long and illustrious performance history for Vestris's production:

> It has been said that the production was already seen in foreign courts, but long before this, the charming author of *Daphnis et Cloé, d'Eglé,* and *Silvie* had the idea to use this theme and produce it on stage, because the music was composed in 1755 and in 1763 a production took place before their Majesties at Choisi, and it was this same ballet that Vestris reproduced, in its appearance and its spirit.[3]

Whether or not Vestris copied Noverre, (no record remains of a 1763 production at court), Vestris enjoyed a reputation as one of the most distinguished performers of the time and could easily ride out the controversy.[4]

The plot of *Jason et Médée,* like the third act of *Les Horaces,* provided a perfect vehicle for the expression of strong and vivid emotions. (See fig. 30.) It also offered one of the few tragic ballets performed in Paris. Noverre choreographed several tragedies while in Stuttgart, as did Angiolini in Vienna,[5] but these brooding and vengeful plots whose climaxes filled the stage with death and destruction—so horrifying that they caused one audience in Stuttgart to run out of the theatre in fright[6]—seldom appeared on the French stage. Audiences may have tolerated the level of terror achieved in Vestris's production because the ballet cohered with and was subsumed by the overall plot of the opera. Although no scenario for Vestris's version of *Médée et Jason* has survived, a review in the *Mercure de France* of a 1776 production indicates both the scope of the production and the division of the ballet into scenes:

> The inconstancy of Jason who abandons Medea to marry Creuse, their new love, Medea's resentment, the efforts she makes to revive her unfaithful husband's love, reminding him of his children; the fury of this jealous woman, her schemes, the marriage festival of Creuse, the insidious reconciliation that Medea effects toward her rival, the poisoned present she offers; the tormented death of Creuse, Jason's despair, the Furies' agitation, the insulted rage of Medea drawn up into the sky in a chariot of dragons; the murder of her children which she stabs in full view of their father, a rain of fire and the destruction of the palace; all this action produced a spectacle of the grandest effect.[7]

Rather than a panoramic or processional beginning that would briefly introduce all characters, the review suggests that the ballet immersed spectators immediately in the

30. An English illustration satirizing the strong display of emotions in a scene from *Jason et Médée*.

noeud, the knot of the action. The ballet apparently opened with the depiction of Jason's inconstancy. He abandons Medea for Creuse in paired scenes that first show him dancing amorously with Creuse and then depict Medea's consequent feelings of rejection. Medea reminds Jason of their children, but he remains engrossed in his new love. Her sense of degradation then transforms into a furious anger, represented through a danced interlude with the figures of Jealousy, Vengeance, and Despair: "The principal dancers, that is, Jason (Vestris), Médée (Allard), Creuze (Guimard), are each in their character and express themselves vividly. Jealousy, Vengeance, and Despair, the three infernal divinities, dance a scene in which the tableau is most striking."[8] These infernal figures may even have haunted the stage during Medea's interactions with Jason and Creuse, helping to illustrate Medea's painful predicament.

Following the intimate encounters among the three main characters and the three infernal divinities, which occupy the first third of the ballet, the scene opens up onto the marriage festival of Jason and Creuse. The large group dances would have provided a hiatus in the inevitable progression of events and returned the audience briefly to the world of classical dancing. Once the festivities are well under way, Medea takes Creuse aside, seemingly reconciled to Jason's change of heart, and offers the poisoned mantle. Creuse dances out her life's final moments as Jason and his companions look on, horrified. After Creuse's tormented death and Jason's demonstration of despair, the action accelerates. The Furies arrive to torture Jason; Medea, in full rage, mounts her dragon-led chariot and slays her children in front of Jason, as the palace finally crumbles under a fiery rain.

The ballet revolved around Medea and the development of her feelings toward Creuse and Jason. Far more wicked and powerful than the sorceress Calipso, Medea projected a frightening image of woman's capacity for revenge. Jason, an older Télémaque, had assumed that love relations could be reordered as desire dictated. Cast simultaneously as betrayer and betrayed, he pursued Creuse actively, yet stood a helpless victim before Medea's rage. Creuse, like Eucharis, served as the object of love, but also invited love. Interactions among these main characters and also between Medea and the Furies were rendered even more vivid by the resolves into dramatic tableaux, where the tensions inherent in the relationships could crystallize into spatial design.[9]

During the course of the ballet, the relationships among these three characters traversed three distinct landscapes. The opening scenes, probably set in a chamber designed to suggest intimacy, emphasized the power of characters' individual actions. Here, the ratio of dancer to surroundings strongly privileged the body's signs. In contrast, the decorous motion of the ballroom scenes foregrounded those actions against a social backdrop as if to remind characters and viewers of the social context for their behavior. The contrast between this large-scale setting and the earlier scenes must have created the visual stimulation and variety to which viewers were accustomed, and, at the same time, cultivated a sense of suspense as they awaited a return to the dramatic action. The concluding natural disasters—far more horrific than any form of social condemnation—would have engulfed all individual gestures.

In its movement from bedroom to ballroom to fiery rain, the scale and magnitude of the theatrical settings buttressed the plot's powerful message. The settings also established nature over society as a final regulatory and condemnatory force. Earlier ballets typically resolved after a concluding gesture from the gods supported, often, by a change in natural conditions. The story of Jason and Medea linked their tragic fate directly to their own feelings and actions; no intervention from social or supernatural worlds modified the progression of events. Nature, rather than operating in response to the gods, manifested a will of its own. When compared with the potency of individual gestures and the spectacle of nature, society as a controlling force receded in importance.

Grimm, no friend of Vestris, nonetheless admitted the popularity of the production. His account of the performance, however, pointed to several inadequacies in both the choreography and the performance:

> The ballet that Noverre gave in Vienna was replicated by Vestris, who had danced in Noverre's production in Vienna. It would have been better at least to retain that production's superb music; but M. de la Borde preferred to substitute his own without power and without taste. Vestris failed to observe another essential feature of the music: that in Noverre's ballets, dancing and cadenced walking are very distinct; one only danced during the great moments of passion, in the decisive moments; during the scenes one walks in time to the music, but without dancing. The transitions from measured walking to dancing and from dancing to measured walking are necessary to the spectacle in the same way that opera moves from recitatif to aria and back again; but dancing for the sheer sake of dancing shouldn't occur until the end of the piece. . . . Noverre's imitator, Vestris, having no understanding of these elements, made a ballet with no dramatic effect. In spite of this, the novelty of the spectacle made it a

> success and attracted large audiences to the Opéra. Some said that it was good, while others found the contorsions of Vestris-Jason to be ridiculous and those of Medea-Allard to be disgusting. Creuse-Guimard, after having been poisoned by her rival, danced in the third act as a simple shepherdess, costumed in a dress so elegant that all the ladies have abandoned the carnival domino in order to dance in dresses "à la Guimard." This costume was none other than a dress elegantly styled worn over a skirt of another color. The invention of this style should be accorded to the actresses of the Comédie Italienne who played roles at the Opéra Comique. It remained only for Mlle. Guimard or her costumer to add pompoms, garlands, and other ornaments.[10]

Grimm intimated that Vestris was unaware of the necessary distinction between the dramatic scenes of cadenced gesture and step and scenes where dramatic dialogue resolved into dancing, and he judged Vestris unable to craft the transitions from such dramatic movement to classical dancing and back again. He also implied that the acting was overblown, preposterously exaggerated.

Equally damning, in terms of the action ballet's aesthetic goals, was Grimm's account of Guimard's impact both on and off stage. Possibly shorthanded, Vestris brought Guimard back in the final act of the opera to dance as one of the shepherdesses. For that ballet she chose to dress in the audacious style of the Comédie Italienne actresses, apparently a first for the Opéra stage. Such an appearance, however, would probably not have generated the fashion response that it did without Guimard's flamboyant presentation. Making no attempt to fit in, Guimard starred her own performance persona over those of Creuse or shepherdess, thereby compromising the theatricality of both dances. Viewers, tuned to several levels of spectacle at the Opéra, not only accommodated her behavior but were inspired by it.

The Invigilant Dancer

Stealthily, the invigilant dancer tiptoes onto the stage. Somewhere to the front and side of the action, this dancer assumes a position entirely visible to the audience, yet undisclosed to the other characters onstage. From this privileged vantage, the dancer spies on the action, learning the motivations and desires of fellow characters. The presence of the invigilant dancer opens up spatial and temporal dimensions distinct from those of the main action. Through the presence of the invigilant dancer, the narrative can advance.

The invigilant dancer's presence cordons off a space from which a new genre of gaze is possible. This mode of viewing is different from the evaluative observation directed by the audience, and also different from the reciprocal regards that characters engrossed in the action give one another. Spectators stare at the stage, but they also scan the audience, occasionally exchanging glances with other viewers. Characters engrossed in the action onstage look at and engage one another. Or they may turn away, look up or down or off into the distance, indicating through these occipital gestures that they are fantasizing, remembering, ruminating—that is, projecting themselves into some other time or place. Still, these reside within and result from the social system of motivations shared by all characters. The invigilant dancer's gaze, in contrast, is notable for its fixedness. Postural and gestural shifts mark changes in this character's feelings, but seldom are they so violent as to pull his or her eyes away from the object of their regard. This fixedness disciplines the audience by guiding and sustaining their focus on the spied-upon dancers' actions.

Invigilant dancers stand outside the social worlds of both characters and audience. The act of spying endows these characters with an unusual kind of individual initiative. Often pathetic characters, they are willing to violate social proprieties for some individual need. Yet because of their unorthodox espionage, they learn something that would not have been revealed until much later. Their knowledge positions them to intervene in the dull course of things, to expose, to provoke, to make or break another's fate. This knowledge endows the character with both hindsight and resolve, opening the narrative into the past and future. In its stealthy stillness, the invigilant dancer's gaze thus layers the narrative.

Apelles et Campaspe (1776)

Noverre chose *Apelles et Campaspe,* which premiered in Vienna in 1772, as the first of his ballets to be presented at the Opéra after assuming his duties there as Maître des Ballets. His appointment, the result of having served as Marie Antoinette's Dancing Master in Vienna, was resisted by many of the Opéra's leading dancers.[1] They would have objected to the fact that Noverre, an outsider whose reputation was made in the provinces, could be awarded the appointment over the assistant Ballet Masters who ordinarily succeeded to the position. They may also have resisted the mandate, implied by Noverre's presence, to develop skills necessary for performing the action ballet.

Noverre arrived at the Opéra during a period of considerable administrative upheaval. Dancers, singers, musicians, and designers employed by the institution had all begun to voice objections to disadvantageous or inept administrative practices. Dancers in particular, recognizing the popularity of their art and their own star value, began to demand higher salaries, more benefits, and a greater voice in the kind and number of roles they performed. As part of their bargaining tactics, they often failed, at the last minute, to appear for performances. Attempts by the administration to sanction them for their breaches of contract only augmented their renown.[2] In 1776, the general unrest within the institution resulted in the formation of a committee of artists responsible for decisions concerning programming and salaries for all Opéra employees. This model of governance, utilized for many years at the Comédie Française, brought together representatives from the various arts involved in opera productions—musicians, singers, dancers, and scenic designers. It proved a relatively successful approach to administration at the Opéra, given that it functioned consistently throughout the Revolution and up until Napoleon's reorganization of all the theatres in 1807. From its inception through the early 1780s, however, it maintained especially hostile relations with the Opéra's directors and their staff, causing the downfall of De Vîsmes, appointed director in 1777, after only three years.

Noverre was doubly compromised upon his arrival at the Opéra by this antagonism between employees and administration. As Maître des Ballets and consequently a member of the committee, he necessarily represented the interests of the artists. Support for his appointment, however, could only come from the directors, who were responsible for executing the monarchy's wishes. And even the Opéra directors could not be counted as reliable allies, since their allegiances to opera as a musical form in which dance played a supporting role were well established. Noverre's arrival signaled the possible ascendancy of dance over music, because the action ballet gave to dance both a greater visibility and an autonomy from music, a revised weighting of artistic mediums that could ultimately undermine the administrative structure of the Opéra.

If any ballet could help ease the various tensions generated by Noverre's appointment, it was *Apelles et Campaspe.*[3] Based on a lighter theme than many of his ballets, it elided any possible allegorical references to the struggles between dancers and administration by focusing on the classic preoccupation of the artist with the art object. The production contained opportunities for both pantomimic and classical dancing as well as highly ornamented and novel scenic designs. It also offered to Madeleine Guimard, one of the most powerful figures in Opéra politics, a perfect vehicle for the display of her talents.

The ballet begins in the painter Apelles' studio as he anticipates the arrival of his patron Alexandre. An array of his work provides a decorative backdrop; assistants, dressed as nymphs, zephyrs, graces, and Amours busily engage in final preparations. Alexandre's martial entrance, Ephistion on his left, Campaspe followed by her ladies-in-waiting on his right, causes a final flurry of activity before the assistants coalesce around his veiled portrait. Having greeted Alexandre, Apelles presents his depiction as Jupiter and is gratified at Alexandre's approval. Alexandre then asks to see any portraits of women, and Apelles shows him one representation of Venus. Alexandre, again admiring Apelles' work, commands him to produce a likeness of his consort Campaspe. The simple gestures of his pantomimed dialogue give way to more fluid movement on stage as Campaspe, at Alexandre's request, assumes a series of poses gracefully framed by Apelles' costumed assistants. Apelles looks on, overwhelmed by her beauty, while Roxanne, Alexandre's principal mistress, enters and becomes increasingly agitated. At the end of the display, Alexandre greets and calms Roxanne, and leaving Campaspe behind, they exit together followed by the rest of the retinue.

Subsequent scenes chart Apelles' growing frustration as he repeatedly attempts to portray Campaspe in a role worthy of her beauty. Each new character he asks Campaspe to assume requires new costuming and setting. Apelles' assistants rush to provide the lance, helmet, and pedestal for Athena, the flowers surrounding Flore, and the tiger skin for Diana. The clever interlocking of bodies and tasks as the assistants make over each scene entirely provides a lively counterpoint to the steadily increasing fascination which painter and subject show in their gazes toward each other. As each new configuration is achieved, Apelles attempts to draw Campaspe, but overwhelmed by his feelings for her, finds his sketches woefully inadequate. Finally, he determines that the role of Venus is the only appropriate setting, and his assistants begin to construct the charming landscape in which she might recline surrounded by Graces and Amours. Apelles, more enchanted than ever, burns incense and prostrates himself before her. At this moment, Roxanne surreptitiously enters and witnesses the amorous display. Her voyeuristic framing of the scene increases its erotic charge by recalling the quotidian social strictures from which the couple have strayed and also emphasizing the seductiveness of the gaze with which Apelles has held Campaspe in place. Roxanne exits, jubilant with the knowledge that will compromise her rival.

Having entered the mood necessary for painting, Apelles finally begins to draw uninterruptedly. At Roxanne's behest, Alexandre quietly enters, but finds nothing amiss and leaves. Apelles works earnestly at first but soon succumbs again to frustration at his own inadequacies, which now builds into a tormented rage. He destroys all his drawing materials and eventually slumps in despair against one of the columns in his studio. Campaspe, who can endure her mute role no longer, rushes to him. They reveal their mutual affection just as Alexandre reenters. Furious at this double betrayal, Alexandre lashes out, recomposes himself, shuns the couple, and then threatens menacingly again. Campaspe faints at his feet, and Apelles runs to her. Ephestion, attempting to mollify Alexandre, eventually persuades him that a compassionate acknowledgment of the couple's love would best manifest his kingly virtues. Alexandre's decision to condone the couple's involvement results in a final tableau for the act: Roxanne, having run to Alexandre to express her gratitude at his tacit commitment to her, then kneels to help Campaspe, who revives and kisses Alexandre's knees as Apelles throws himself at his patron's feet. This triangular composition emphasizes Alexandre's beneficent greatness; his gesture beckoning them to rise and follow reinforces his leadership.

The second act of the ballet takes place in the throne room of Alexandre's palace, where both couples and other members of the court celebrate their love. The general dancing in which Alexandre, significantly, deigns to participate shows the full technical skills of the Opéra dancers and the sumptuous spectacle for which the stage was notorious. The celebration reaffirms Alexandre's commitment to Roxanne, his beneficence, and the triumph of true love over social prohibitions.

Apelles et Campaspe staged yet another version of the male artist's fascination with the female as work of art. Unlike Sallé's *Pygmalion*, which cast both artist and work of art in active roles, *Apelles et Campaspe* focused on the inability of the artist and the passivity of his subject. Unlike Rousseau's and Milon's productions, which explored exclusively Pygmalion's interior dilemmas after having fashioned the perfectly lovable artwork, Apelles was shown in the act of painting a subject whose desirability increased with every brush stroke. Both Apelles and Campaspe struggled openly and inwardly with the difficulties of art-making. Both were held in place by the social and artistic contracts they had made. Still, their predicament was not without its erotic allure for both male and female characters. Where Campaspe, as gazed upon by Apelles, remained helpless within the representational field of artistic project, Apelles, as viewed by Campaspe, remained equally helpless in his futile efforts to represent the beautiful. The unavailability and vulnerability of each character fueled their mutual erotic interest. Their steadily increasing desire climaxed in Apelles' final gesture of despair as he slumped against the column. Campaspe's single explosive gesture, running to Apelles, read less as a conscious decision than an uncontrolled act of compassion. The genuineness of both these actions released the characters from their social and artistic obligations. Movement, conceptualized as a universal and original language, assumed here the ability to convey a message deeper and more compelling than any indicated social protocols. Painter and subject thus expressed their mutual affection in a world momentarily removed from imposed social strictures.

The *Mercure de France* reviewer, while impressed with the vividness and accuracy of both acts, found the second too strong a contrast with the first:

> If one wanted to find something lacking in this magnificent composition; it is that the painter of this pantomime has enclosed a double subject in the same frame; that is the crowning of Roxanne suggests a second action that, while noble and charming, contrasts too little with the gracious love of Apelles and Campaspe; which is to say that he has framed together a dignified image by Albane or Corregio with a painting by Raphael or Michelangelo. Dare we also ask of this grand master whether Alexander, Ephestion, and Roxanne should actually join in the dancing, or whether it would not be more appropriate for them to appear as dramatic characters, full of passion and interest in the action, but distinct from the others in the rank and in their countenance. Certainly we see very little of their *entrées* or of their dances with Apelles, Campaspe, Apelles' students, and the soldiers. As for the rest, we can hardly express our admiration for this genre of dance that replicates the beauty of poetry and the rules of painting.[4]

Relying heavily on the analogy to painting, the reviewer suggested that Noverre as a painter of pantomime had framed as a diptych two pieces of vastly contrasting style. According to the critic, not only did the first and second acts clash in their tone and quality, but the dancing in Act II by the principal dramatic characters for Act I—Alexandre,

Roxanne, and Ephestion—failed to make an impact. Two forms of conservatism may have been evident in this critique: as the official spokespiece of the crown, the *Mercure de France* may have found it advantageous to comment indirectly on the implications of Alexandre's dancing for the role of the King, whose status required a more dignified and removed conduct. The review could also have signaled a sophisticated critique of Noverre's theatrical reforms. Using Noverre's own criteria, the review praised each act individually, yet faulted the ballet's overall coherence.

Noverre met with subtle yet substantial resistance from Opéra employees and administration during his tenure there.[5] He was allotted insufficient numbers of productions and funds with which to costume and decorate them.[6] Although recognized for his choreographic achievements in the action ballet, he primarily worked to contrive the standard divertissements required for most opera-ballets.[7] Critical reviews maintained a respectful tone while always finding fault with some aspect of the choreography.[8] Rather than persevere under hostile conditions, Noverre petitioned for and received a pension from the Opéra in 1781.

3 NARRATING PASSION AND PROWESS

The first human beings, strongly moved by their surroundings, expressed their feelings through metaphors, through lively and accentuated articulations, through energetic gestures. Poetry, Music, and Dance were born with this primitive language, or rather, they comprised its essence.[1]

Dancing the action

Throughout the 1760s and early '70s, Paris audiences witnessed the incremental introduction of various elements associated with the new action ballet—an increased reliance on pantomime, a new use of the face in expressing emotion, an emphasis on asymmetry and diversity in large group forms, historical accuracy in costuming.[2] No single production can be identified as ushering in the new genre.[3] Writers from the period reflecting back on the development of the form cited Pitrot's productions at the Comédie Italienne and Lany's ballets for the Comédie Française as well as shorter entrées performed by Dauberval and Allard within the rubric of the Opéra's ballets.[4] (See fig. 31.) These experiments along with Laval's *Aeglé* in 1770, Gaetano Vestris's single-act version of the story of Jason and Medea in 1771, Maximilien Gardel's *L'Avènement de Titus à l'Empire* in 1775, and Noverre's *Apelles et Campaspe* in 1776 began to establish a new autonomy for dance. This autonomy was reflected in the addition of a new category, that of "Danse," which was added to the *Mercure de France* headings for various kinds of spectacles in 1777. Under this category summaries and reviews of productions in the new genre at the Opéra, Comédie Française, and Comédie Italienne were printed, a sign that via the action ballet dance had achieved programmatic distinctiveness as a category of production.[5]

Other Parisian theatres had long since begun to cultivate different visions of the body—more spectacular, domestic, or erotic—and to explore new fusions of movement and text. The prolonged and substantial popularity of the fair theatres and ineffectual monitoring by government authorities eventually resulted in acceptance of their performances as part of Parisian theatrical life. In 1760 the Opéra Comique joined forces with the Comédie

31. Jean Dauberval and Marie Allard in a pas de deux.

Italienne in order to resuscitate its moribund reputation. The instant success of Jean-Baptiste Nicolet's Les Grands Danseurs de Corde, a transplant from the fair theatres to the Boulevard du Temple, encouraged other entrepreneurs to develop permanent houses there. While harassment from the chartered institutions continued, more stable financial agreements contracted with them enabled boulevard theatres to plan seasons of entertainment and employ performers long-term. Although the theatres' reputation for the risqué persisted, owners worked hard to surround viewers with sumptuous decor to promote an impression of stability if not respectability and to diffuse their antagonistic political heritage.

Boulevard theatres proffered a strange amalgam of extraordinary acrobatic feats, grotesque displays of the freak body and its accomplishments, and death-defying stunts. These elastic or misshapen bodies violated all rules of decorum. Acrobats assumed any and every position with slippery ease, oblivious to the social requisites for an open and vertical carriage and for a moderate, measured effort in all actions. (See figs. 32–35.) The distended and deformed appearances of midgets, hunchbacks, and other "freaks" likewise perverted established norms of desirable posture and comportment. Earlier in the century such physical oddities had been marginalized by the six-week run of the fair and by the foreign identities of most performers. In the 1760s and '70s, however, they came to be viewed as an established and continuing form of entertainment, a consistent alternative physicality.

During an evening's program at the boulevard theatres, acrobatic and deformed bodies often framed a more lyrical and familiar image of the body, that articulated in the musical comedy. In these works actors moved agreeably from one medium to another. They burst into song and dance at celebratory moments; they adopted mime over dialogue during the humorous plotting of escapades, and they utilized the tableau-vivant at moments of

32. Acrobatic juggling and balancing maneuvers of midcentury.

33. The Theatre of Exercises presenting spectators with an array of astonishing stunts.

34. Mlle. Mioly's entertaining contortions.

35. The Famous Prussian [*La Fameuse Prussienne*] showing her accomplishments on the tightrope in the 1780s.

overwhelming passion.[6] (See fig. 36.) None of the performers' varied abilities as actor, mime, singer, and dancer was developed to an extreme level of accomplishment. Opera-ballets apportioned singing and dancing to experts in those disciplines and often dwelt on a single impassioned interaction, reiterating it through a series of musical elaborations for minutes at a time; the comedies, however, integrated all discourses within each performer and told their stories with a timing that more closely resembled that of an analogous real-life scene. Transitions between each activity appeared smooth and facile. Similarly, the quick-smooth pace of the entire evening modulated the contrast between spectacular, contorted, misshapen and lyricized bodies, even as the range of physical types rendered the body presented in musical comedy all the more normal in appearance and conduct.

The wholesome bodies of the comedies played out relatively complicated adventures that briefly evoked a range of passions. The subversive use of pantomime often gave way

36. The last scene tableau from *Les Adieux,* produced at the Théâtre de l'Ambigu-Comique in 1784.

to the sentimental as productions focused on simple love themes told in song, drama, and dance. Embroiled in the exigencies of middle-class life, characters displayed a responsiveness to feelings, both endearing and lively. The action did not allow them to dwell in any one emotion, but instead required rapid, vivid responses in each new situation. As a result, the comedies allowed viewers to indulge in empathic identification with a character's feelings, while maintaining a dynamic, fast-paced progression of events. In the process, however, gesture became increasingly adapted to paralinguistic use, enhancing spoken or sung action rather than serving as a primary means of communication. Characters still danced, as in the opera-ballets, at moments of celebration, during festivities, or during courtship, but the dancing served more to mark the joy or exoticism of a given occasion. Thus the performances projected a greater narrative coherence, although movement told less of the story. Even the narrative, however, often served as a pretext for a series of eye-catching displays.[7]

Although pantomime, song, and dance all played more subdued roles as they became integrated into the lyric drama, the comedies continued to poke fun at the serious and grand works produced at the Opéra. (See fig. 37.) Some continued to parody operas by adapting and then altering well-known plots and characters.[8] Or they spoofed the very conventions of sensibility that were coming into vogue in grand theatre and opera.[9] Others, by privileging dramatic flow over musical form, exposed as artificial and arcane the operatic conventions. Still others used novel mixtures of pantomime performed to well-known songs, played without their lyrics as a way of ensuring accessibility to the pantomime but also spoofing conventional relations between music and dance.[10] The productions as a whole, however, de-emphasized the pornographic and scatological and built instead on dramatic suspense through complicated chase scenes that entailed quick changes of scenery and multiple special effects. They rounded out the evening's entertainment with wild animal acts, acrobats, puppet shows, tightrope walkers,[11] contortionists, and fireworks displays, the specific combination of which gave to each theatre its distinctive reputation. (See fig. 38.)

If the boulevard theatre programs played off and against the classical standards of both art and physicality, so too the more clandestine performances held in the private theatres of aristocrats and performing artists challenged established protocols.[12] A tradition of hiring players for private entertainments extended back to the beginning of the century, when aristocrats found the fair theatre acts irresistibly titillating. Throughout the 1760s, '70s and '80s, luminaries of French society, and even the dancers Madeleine Guimard and Jean Dauberval, built or acquired large domiciles in Paris with theatres attached. Here they entertained substantial numbers of the elite with suppers, general dancing and amusements, and performances. (See fig. 39.)

Like many of the boulevard theatre productions, the private theatre diversions satirized standard dramatic texts. The private productions, however, typically distorted accepted protocol by presenting a more openly sexual body concerned with explorations of its own desires. Where the boulevard theatres increasingly sanitized and sentimentalized their offerings, some of the private performances pushed hard at the boundaries of social and sexual deco-

TOP 37. An actress playing the role of a tragicomic low-life character in the 1783 production of *Le Directeur Forain* at the Variétés Amusantes in the Foire St. Germain.

BOTTOM 38. Tightrope dancing and other acrobatic feats.

rum. The risqué and pornographic encounters depicted on stage produced just the opposite of the impassioned, storytelling body constructed in the musical comedies. They unraveled the unintegrated body even further, allowing viewers to contemplate a substantial erosion of regulations concerning physical and social comportment.

Not only did the private productions transgress the regulations concerning proper

9. A late-eighteenth-century full-dress ball.

sexual conduct, they also blurred boundaries between the social and the theatrical. Certain parts were played by daring amateurs, who, along with the professional performers, mingled with the audience before and after the presentations. Costumes blended with high fashion; candlelight and sumptuous furnishings lent an aura of theatricality to all nonstage spaces. Where the boulevard theatres with their varied versions of accomplished physicality increasingly differentiated between audience and performers, the private theatres perpetuated the opportunity, established in the earlier fair theatre productions, to play with the trappings of social identity. In the context of the fairs, however, where audiences were composed of all social classes, the effect of such play had tended to subvert the hierarchical rankings of class. The privacy afforded by the elite theatres encouraged a far more decadent inquiry into social identity. Here professional performers who had transcended their lower- or middle-class origins facilitated a testing of social roles among members of a privileged class.

When viewed alongside these other theatrical bodies, more spectacular and erotic, the Opéra's first experiments with the action ballet must have appeared somewhat staid or even pedantic. When compared with the natural, lyrical bodies of the musical comedies, the Opéra's mute gesturing must have seemed arcane, if novel. Still, the novelty of gestured storytelling attracted the viewer's eye in two ways. Viewers repeatedly remarked on the new range of expression portrayed by facial and bodily gestures and the subtle gradations in each feeling depicted, and they were captivated by the opportunity presented in the ballets to interrogate the relationship between motivation and action. The newly mobile face and semaphoric arms and hands lent visual intrigue to an already complex yet familiar setting. Extended solos, duets, and trios developed themes of romance or intrigue with all the attendant emotions of doubt, jealousy, modesty, joy, coquetry, etc. These innovative sequences, in which the face played the central role of clearly enunciating the emotion expressed, allowed viewers to track the progression of distinct emotions and to note whether and how the situation produced a logical response from all the characters.

Not only were the interactions between principal characters portrayed with greater realism, but large group scenes took on a less regimented, more naturalistic appearance. The crowd in tumultuous hubbub had been featured in fairground theatre productions and at the Opéra Comique throughout the 1750s, but even at the Opéra choreographers began to experiment with new group forms.[13] Rather than the symmetrical exchanges by even rows of similar characters, ballets began to be replaced by irregular dispositions of dancers in space. In reviewing the 1765 production of *Castor and Pollux*, for example, the *Mercure de France* critic praised the choreographer Laval for having

> broken the symmetrical ordering of group configurations used in all ordinary *entrées*. The characters are distributed in groups of unequal number that change and reconfigure endlessly, but as though by chance. There is an infinite multiplicity of different dances that produce a totality always striking and true, and formed through apparently fortuitous positions that however are the result of a profound synthesis of art and order, hidden with a genius and skill that one cannot too strongly applaud. The dancers, whose sizes are gradated so as to achieve perspective and placed upstage, sustained their motion, which left no void in any part of the dance and which supported the illusion without distracting from the principal objects of the spectacle.[14]

Choreographers also began to experiment with diagonal crossings and a greater range of speeds of locomotion in order to affect a more casual and lively array of bodies. Some ballets incorporated diverse character types—children, adults, and elderly actors—into the action in order to suggest the chaotic effervescence of a crowd. Others followed through on Noverre's recommendation that shorter dancers be positioned upstage so as to create a more accurate semblance of perspective.[15]

During the 1770s and '80s a series of action ballets were staged alongside the opera-ballets, revived and new, that embodied many of the reforms Noverre had envisioned while still conforming to the standards for spectacle and virtuosity that the Opéra required. Choreographers began by selecting a well-known story drawn from mythology or from a highly popular story or play. They necessarily chose narratives with a great range of feelings and actions, a small but diverse number of characters, a clear set of relationships between motivations and consequences. They also needed to assure a lively progression from one kind of scene and scenery to the next.

Sometimes they added characters or changed locations in order to achieve a balance between coherence and visual variety.[16] Frequently, they resorted to some kind of natural disaster as a way simultaneously to move the plot forward and create scenic spectacle. Sometimes they could only convey necessary information verbally in which case signs or banners explaining the dramatic premise suddenly unfurled onstage.

In addition to a clearly realized plot and a lively progression of visual images, choreographers could not neglect the display of virtuoso dancing. Neither dancers nor viewers could have accepted the new form without a thorough infusion of the complex, ornamented vocabulary of classical steps and also the creation of special sections of dancing devoted solely to its display. In order to ensure this blend, choreographers evaluated all possible scenarios for their ability to support the display of dancing, and they also mined each storyline for all possible instances where the full-blown display of dancing might reasonably occur. The successful action ballet production needed characters who could dance their interactions, but it also contained two, three, four, or more major occasions for the presentation of virtuoso dancing performed both by soloists and large groups. Scenarios that rationalized these displays, through the staging of festivals, competitions, or social dances, allowed the felicitous conjunction of sentimental drama with elegant physical discipline. The longest and most spectacular of these virtuoso displays usually concluded the ballet. Lasting fifteen to twenty minutes, as much as a quarter of the length of the entire ballet, these sequences reviewed all characters and showed off their dancing skills while consolidating and celebrating alliances among the contrasting social groups within the ballet—the bride's and groom's families, the shepherds and shepherdesses, the Creoles and the French. In contrast to the pantomimic scenes arranged with asymmetrical spacings among small numbers of characters, the large group scenes often used the stately patterning of the earlier opera-ballets—crisscrossing lines and circles and peripheral groupings of dancers that framed the soloists. They sustained the sensuous and grand presentation of corporeal form that had been a celebrated staple of all eighteenth-century productions while adding to this the more intimate portrayal of human feelings.

An appropriate idea for a ballet, then, necessarily afforded the opportunity to synthesize visual contrast and appeal with a unifying plot. It introduced distinctive characters whose relations were varied and whose actions were highly motivated. A theme like the seasons or the nations of the globe that held together the multiple, distinct scenes of the early eighteenth-century opera-ballets did not qualify as the kind of unifying force sought by the action ballet choreographers. The orderly presentation of distinct populations based on their rank within a social hierarchy or their attributes—whether lively, subdued, fierce, or exotic—no longer sufficed. Choreographers searched instead for a human dilemma, a conflict among characters and their circumstances that would dictate individuals' behavior. The overarching allegorical taxonomies of the opera-ballets had to be replaced by an underlying premise that impelled all characters organically into action.

Choreographers not only staged the story, but also wrote their version of it for publication as the program for the performance. Published librettos for the opera-ballets had consisted of an opening description of the setting for each act and the lyrics and names of the characters who sang them. At the end of each act and at other appropriate moments, the italicized indication, "On danse," would appear. With rare exceptions this phrase was the only description of any movement onstage in the entire libretto. In contrast, programs for the action ballets often included a preface by the choreographer that presented general views on dance and background information on aesthetic decisions made while choreographing the piece, followed by a complete description of the danced action. The account read like a story. It told who the characters were, what they felt, how they acted, and any other relevant events taking place around them. Sometimes it even included dialogue "spoken" by characters.

The genre's commitment to portraying feelings and interactions with greater accuracy impelled viewers to assess its success as a form of mimetic representation. Viewers discerned and condemned discrepancies between the well-known story, the printed program, and the danced version. Sometimes, they took issue with the story selected, or they objected when the action degenerated into vague gesticulations, or when the choreography failed to express with sufficient emphasis a character's situation, or when the action became embellished with sequences of "meaningless" virtuosity.[17] They took great interest in the staging of the story—whether it should be divided into scenes or acts and, if so, how many. And they examined the characters' motivations, deliberating over whether their actions were justified, the inevitable product of the situations in which they found themselves.

The danced story's stipulation of motivation and consequent action began to construct a new kind of personality for danced characters, evident in both their onstage and offstage behavior. Each new production offered a new constellation of passions brilliantly enacted.[18] And as more and more characters came to life in the various stories presented, they created opportunities for a more individualized style of dancing causing a proliferation of styles and character types among principal dancers. Dancers were increasingly identified with and by the types of roles they performed. This new variety of characters subtly altered the strict, tripartite genre system used to classify dance styles since the beginning of the century. Because of the range of expression required, individual dancers' performances were no longer necessarily compared to a single, ideal form. Instead, dancers were perceived as initiating their own styles, so much so that young dancers making their debut were often described as performing in the genre of a well-known principal.[19] Early in the century dancers like Prévost, Camargo, or Sallé had pioneered in the development of a classical tradition with their highly distinctive contributions to dancing style and vocabulary. Such contributions, however, were seen to embody, as they improved upon, an absolute form. By the late eighteenth century, general notions of noble, semi-noble, and caractère continued to organize pedagogy, the administrative structure of the Opéra, and the large number of opera-ballets presented. The stylistic requirements of each genre, however, began to expand and blur as the new vocabulary of gestures was fashioned to each character's needs.[20] (See figs. 40 and 41.)

The same association between character type and style imbued performers with new identities offstage as well. In their dealings with Opéra administrators, they exerted a new kind of individual initiative.[21] In the streets of Paris, leading dancers were less the emissaries of the court, emblems of a royal style, a courtly life, and a

40. A ballet danced by countryfolk with aristocratic characters looking on, from the first act of *Le Carnaval du Parnasse* as rendered by Gabriel-Jacques de St. Aubin.

classical comportment, and now evidenced "personality," flamboyant and often disobedient, in their public and private dealings.[22] Society followed with great interest their amorous liaisons, their affairs in the worlds of art and real estate, their wranglings over contracts and rights, and the nights spent in Fort L'Évêque for refusing to perform or some other violation of their obligations. Not that the performers' offstage identities fused with those of the parts they typically played.[23] Rather, the dancers' ability to represent characters lent depth to their own personhood, which became increasingly an object of the public's interest.

Both female and male characters showed a greater range of responses to situations, a more complex blending of diverse feelings than in earlier ballets. Female characters, more frequently than in earlier ballets, began to find themselves the victims of some natural disaster or social predicament. Dislocated from their usual resources, they struggled and resisted, suffered and lamented, and finally rejoiced in the resolution of their plight. Unlike the Dianas and nymphs of the opera-ballets, they did not offer categorical resistance to male characters' advances, but instead wavered between protestation and acceptance. Male characters, no less emotional, displayed a variety of emotional responses, often evoked by the heroine's plight. Their angst could now derive not only from the tragic events affecting country or family, but also from the failure of more personal ambitions or desires.

Access to the new characters' personalities was enhanced by changes in costuming accomplished slowly over the 1770s and 1780s. Rather than the visual opulence of single, lavishly varied forms, costumes began to achieve visual diversity through contrasting and unique types. These changes gave characters a softer, less formalized appearance. The open-laced sandal came to replace the ornate high-heeled slipper worn by both men and women. Dresses for women lost their exaggerated waistline definition and skirts their bell-shaped rigidity, featuring instead midcalf, flowing layers and loose bodices. Men's breeches even replaced the stiff tonnelets worn by men dancing in the noble genre. Cuts and textures of fabric were more diverse, conforming to the faithful depiction of wardrobes of the various professions represented. The female character's

41. Countryfolk celebrating alongside a performance by noble opera characters from André Ernest Modeste Grétry's *La Double Epreuve ou Colinette à la Cour* (1782).

flowing dress underscored her vulnerability, whereas the breeches enabled the male character's complementary accessibility.

These developments of character were achieved more through the repertoire of pantomimic postures and gestures together with the costuming rather than through the vocabulary of classical steps. The classical vocabulary offered little support for characters' emotional accessibility or for gender-based difference in character types. It continued to stipulate nearly identical repertoires of movements for male and female dancers in which both men and women mastered turns, beats, balances, and complicated sequences of steps. They continued to perform these combinations alongside one another or in symmetrically patterned oppositional paths as they had since the beginning of the century. Male principals performed a greater number of beats or turns and presented a palette of stronger and more forceful dynamic qualities, whereas female leads developed a softer and more nuanced execution. Occasionally, the male dancer partnered the female dancer by supporting her at the waist for a balance or guiding her turning body as she swept beneath his extended arm. In general, however, the classical repertoire upheld an isomorphism of masculine and feminine identities. Male and female dancers were identical in all but size.

Salaries for both sexes reflected this equivalence.[24] Even though the distinctive performances of individual dancers had begun to erode the system of genres, pay scales reflected a perception of equality between male and female dancers at each rank. The Maître de Ballet, compensated at the same rate as other leading dancers for his work as a performer, received an additional handsome salary for choreographic and administrative labor. Dancers in each rank, of which there was always an equal number of men and women, received equal pay and equal pensions.

From their equal yet distinctive positions, newly complex male and female characters acted out their attraction to one another using new conventions of courtship. The opera-ballets' characterizations had encoded romance in the proximities of dancers to one another, the angle of the head's tilt, or the softness or abruptness of a gesture. Now, dancers assumed the role of characters depicting the story of love. The earlier ballets parsed desire into a series of feeling states, each the subject of a given dance or scene. Because of the extended length of each dance and the need to sequence dances that diverged in tempo and mood, the relationship of one sentiment to the next was deemphasized. In contrast, the new choreography crafted a range of emotions into long phrases executed by a single dancer. The quickness and vividness with which each emotion was portrayed focused attention on the accuracy of its rendition and also on the logical order in which feelings were presented. Dancers no longer functioned as the agents through which choreographed form combined with musical structure to create allusions to specific sentiments as they had in the operas. Nor did they enact highly predictable character types deriving from the Commedia dell'Arte tradition as they had in the fair theatre productions. Instead, they emerged as characters whose personal feelings and desires followed a certain developmental form.

This new kind of character seduced viewers in a novel way.[25] No barriers, such as the opera-ballet's masks, costumes, and interlocked choreographic patterns, stimulated the viewer's desiring imagination. No scandalous scenes of sexual intercourse like those of the private theatres aroused viewers' appetites. Instead, coquetry in all its chaste variations was faithfully depicted, plainly evident. What evoked attachment to the characters was their winsomeness or courage, their woeful plight, or their audacious valiance. The erotic power of a shoulder, a glance, a tilting sweep of the body, the power of physicality itself, dissipated. The desirable became wrapped instead within a personality, a character one could get to know over the course of the story and whose nature could easily be summoned up in the imagination via review of the narrative for a re-eroticized encounter after the performance was long past.

Viewers found these characters enormously appealing. The candid display of all the nuances of courtship, all the distress of hardship, spoke to their souls through their eyes:

> The dance of our day has acquired a perfection that allows it to dominate our operas . . . even though within the structure of the poems, it is only an accessory to the action. But when it will take a part and play a role, then it will be all the more essential and

> even necessary for dance, seconded an elegant and picturesque music, to make apparent how many resources it offers to express all the passions and all the feelings. Dance could even become the foremost art; because it is proven that sight is of all the senses the one which strikes the soul with the most rapidity and energy.[26]

The persuasive force of these spectacles promised to imbue dance as an art form with added prestige. No longer an agreeable accessory,[27] dance was on the verge of realizing the ancients' secrets and thereby assuming a central role among all the arts.

A passion for anatomy

In order to become the feeling-filled personages required by the action ballet, dancers necessarily developed new facility at acting and learned to integrate facial, gestural, and postural representations of emotional states with their dancing. Yet for all their advocacy of the action ballet, proponents of the new form seldom mentioned the skills necessary to its execution, much less the sources or availability of knowledge addressing the representation of the passions. Where Noverre had advised choreographers to study history, anatomy, painting and geometry for inspiration in choosing and staging the most telling scenarios, dancers seem to have pioneered piecemeal their own techniques of danced acting, following the lead of Italian dancers who had been trained in pantomime, and perhaps drawing upon theories of painting and acting that were widely available.

Le Brun's *Méthode pour apprendre à dessiner les passions* had established a direction for eighteenth-century inquiries into the passions with its identification and scrutiny of forty fundamental facial expressions, each drawn to the same scale so that positions of eyes, cheeks, lips, and eyebrows (the most telling facial feature in Le Brun's opinion) could be compared. Designed to acquaint practitioners in several disciplines—drama, painting, the declamatory arts, medicine, physiognomy—with the true and just expression of basic and compound feelings, the *Méthode* presented static images that delineated the schematic features of each passion, but it also organized the images in a particular sequence with accompanying narration that indicated what addition, deletion, or negation of feeling transformed one passion into another. According to Le Brun, for example, admiration could lead to esteem and esteem heightened to veneration; it could also result in ecstasy, or, if "the object, which at first raised our Admiration, has nothing in it deserving our Esteem, Contempt."[28] Treelike systems of classification housed each passion and indicated its nearest relations, its positive or negative weight. Versions of Le Brun's drawings with their accompanying explanations appeared in paintings of diverse subjects and also in portraits of actors in performance. His accompanying descriptions of the drawings were summarized or even plagiarized by many of the treatises on painting and acting throughout the eighteenth century.[29]

Le Brun's careful tabulation of the passions, taken up in treatises on painting and acting, invited a precise mapping out of the physical characteristics of each passion in great detail. Nowhere was this project more fully realized than in Johan Jakob Engel's *Idées sur le Geste et L'Action Theatrale,* a guide to the execution and interpretation of bodily movement in dramatic performance.[30] Building on nearly a century of investigation into Le Brun's basic premises, this two-volume work considered every kind of visible bodily change as a communicative sign.[31] Claiming a close alliance with both physiological and physiognomic research,[32] Engel organized his observations around a simple principle of analogy: as the soul expanded or contracted, so would the body. Pages upon pages of Engel's book presented detailed summaries of the look and behavior of the person's individual body parts as they experienced a given passion, all ranked according to the degrees of expansion or contraction entailed. In suffering, for example,

> expressions and movements together reveal the anxiety and the interior struggle of the soul with the painful feelings of the hurt. The person who suffers is no longer the melancholic, weak and dejected; but instead oppressed, full of anguish; the angles of the eyebrows raise toward the middle of the wrinkled forehead, and more, so to speak, toward the front of the brain, troubled and agitated by a strong tension; all the muscles of the face are taut and moving; the eye is full of fire, but this fire is vague and vacillating; the chest heaves rapidly and with violence; the walk is both urgent and heavy, the whole body stretches out, spreads and contorts itself, as if it had a generalized assault to sustain; the head thrown to the back, turns to the side with a violent contraction; (an easy movement and thus rather ordinary, similar to pity or ironic complaint) all the muscles of the arms and feet stiffen; the hands, clasped in torsion, disengage and then often turn themselves over, detaching themselves from the front of the body where they hang toward the ground with the fingers completely entwined. When, finally, the tears cover the face, they are not large, swollen, and isolated as those which issue from the eyes of the person who cannot satisfy his or her anger; nor are they the soft, taciturn tears of the melancholic that flow freely from full and relaxed vessels; it is a torrent from the lacrymal glands which a visible commotion of the entire machine and of the convulsive shakes of the face's muscles express with force.[33]

The body, parsed into tiniest increments, each capable of registering distinct kinds of movement, pronounced its state of distress. The angle of the eyebrows, the weight of the walk, the tilt of the body, the tension of the arms, the wandering, gripping, and interlocking of fingers—all distinguished the subject's state of suffering from adjacent feelings of melancholy or pity.

The astounding level of detail in Engel's portraits of the passions brought to fruition the kind of descriptive project Le Brun had envisioned. Nevertheless, Engel's work contained crucial differences that registered the impact of decades of physiological research. As early as 1709, Pierre Polinère's dissection of the frog, whose leg remained responsive and whose heart continued to beat long after its brain had been severed, raised questions as to the exact nature of the body's responsivity to the soul. Muscles seemed not only to respond by degrees to the soul's movements, but also to manifest a unique life force, a fundamental vitality which caused them to reverberate with the soul's initiatives. Research on the inherent sensitivity of the musculature conducted over the course of the century had inspired by midcentury the acoustical metaphors which likened both the passions and the nerves to resonating strings.[34]

By the time of Engel's study, research intimated an additional degree of autonomy for the physical body, reflected in his division of gesture into two basic kinds: those uniquely tied to the mechanism of the body, such as quick breathing after running or heaviness of the eyelids prior to sleep, and those such as the passions that conveyed desires and motivations.[35] Both kinds of gestures depended upon, just as they revealed, the soul's inclinations. Yet the first, a physiological type of response, demonstrated an involuntary level of bodily functioning, whereas the second, more conscious type of action, established the repertoire of standardized signs on which nonverbal communication was based. It was this second type of gesture that actors needed to study carefully for use in performance.[36] The more involuntary type of bodily movement, subtle and uncontrollable, was subject to gross and inaccurate treatment on stage. Typically, in attempting to approximate the grasping motions of the fingers at death or the drooping eyelids of sleep, the actor would so exaggerate the gesture as to break the desired illusion of verisimilitude, unless, of course, the actor was seized spontaneously by the exact emotion he or she was attempting to represent.[37]

The distinction between voluntary and involuntary bodily responses implicit in physiological research and recognized in Engel's analysis paralleled the long-standing debate in the acting community over the nature of the actor's experience while performing.[38] In its most succinct formulation, the debate centered around the relative merits of "imitating" or "following" Nature.[39] To imitate Nature the actor faithfully copied and tirelessly rehearsed each of the character's expressions detail by detail. A text like Le Brun's or Engel's would benefit the actor by providing a comprehensive and reliable guide to any passion needed. In contrast, the actor who followed Nature made an effort to think and feel as the character would so as to achieve complete emotional congruity with the character's role. Both approaches called for the actor to study the play carefully and to analyze thoroughly the motivations of its characters. "Imitation," however, did not require any synchrony in performance between the feelings of the actor and those of the character, whereas "following" implied complete identification.

The project of imitation sent actors out into the world (and the world of painting) in search of analogous characters and situations from which they could fashion the appropriate behavior. If actors followed nature instead, they enhanced their innate capacity to feel, their sensibility, by subjecting themselves to situations in which they would be moved. Imitating nature, the actor practiced the part, in front of friends or even a mirror; following nature, the actor read great books and was inspired by them to feel. The value of imitation resulted from the reliability and perfectability of the performance, whereas following Nature promised a special, intangible charge, a kind of fiery or electrical impulse transmitted from actor to spectator. The disadvantage of imitation lay in its potential for a lifeless, sterile performance, whereas the weakness of following could be seen in the tendency of actors to degenerate into unstructured, self-indulgent bathos. Actors imitating characters were evaluated, in part, on the suitability of their stature and looks for the part they played.[40] Actors following characters were limited not by appearance so much as by their innate disposition to be affected by particular passions more than others.

Whether in support of imitating or following, treatises on acting seldom contained more specific instructions on how to practice acting. In one of the few references to actual training procedures, François Riccoboni advised against practice in front of a mirror, claiming that actors, whose mission fundamentally differed from that of dancers, would distort the natural timing and positions by playing to their own visual image:

> The dancer only shows spectators the movements of his or her body. The actor must focus all their attention on the experience of his or her soul. Those who dance must always exhibit themselves in a painterly attitude, all the positions of this kind are sought after. Those who act must utilize these brilliant positions only rarely when they find themselves forced to. Ordinarily the actor must present him or herself more simply. This is why I say that one must not study one's gestures in front of a mirror. The person who looks in the mirror becomes accustomed to measuring and slowing the movements too much, which removes any spontaneity; such an actor learns to dwell for too long in positions that are most pleasing to the eye and to return to them far more often than to those which appear less striking, and thus becomes mannered. The dancer, in contrast, could never find a better teacher than the mirror, because all the things which come into play become perfections when they are found in the one who dances.[41]

Riccoboni encouraged dancers to work in front of the mirror in order to achieve the most striking line and elegant proportions in their execution of the classical steps. Their task was to make evident the movements of the body in accordance with the measured meter of the music. If, like actors, they were also to undertake the non-metered representation of the soul's movements, then, presumably, the use of the mirror would undermine their spontaneity and their persuasiveness.

Very little of the debate over the status of the player's soul in performance found its way into writings on dance. Noverre, although ambiguous in his several references to the issue, disagreed with Riccoboni by suggesting that the choreographer should imitate and the dancer follow Nature. Where choreographers were advised to study Nature in an effort to fashion a perfect sequence of striking images, dancers were encouraged to listen to their own feelings, to let their bodies respond to the powerful movements of their souls:

> Gesture is the countenance of the soul, its effect must be immediate and cannot fail to achieve its aim when it is true.
>
> Instructed in the fundamental principles of our art, let us follow the movements of our soul; it cannot betray us when it is subject to a lively feeling, and if at those moments it cause the arms to make such and such a gesture, this gesture is always just and correct and sure in its effect. The passions are the springs which actuate the machine; whatever movements result from it, they cannot fail to be expressive. After this, it cannot but be concluded that the sterile rules of a school must disappear from the action ballet to give place to natural expression.[42]

Assuming the immediate and total connection between soul and bodily machine, Noverre proposed that dancers who simply displayed their muscular responses to lively feelings would deliver the truest image. Whether such responses were appropriate in rehearsal, performance, or both, he did not specify. Undoubtedly influenced by the doctrine of sensibility, highly popular during the period in which he formulated his treatise, he invoked the electric spark imagery frequently used to describe the best performances by actors who followed Nature.[43]

Noverre justified his privileging of the spontaneous over the academic by invoking movement as a universal language. The dancers' spontaneous responses would be true, and could be understood by all peoples of the globe, because they were the same as those made by the first primitive humans responding to the stirrings of their souls. The soul infused movement with both fire and intelligence. The training necessary to fashion the harmonious body-machine would not inhibit it from responding fully and accurately to the soul's impulses, so long as dancers did not devote themselves too much to the mastery of complicated *cabrioles* and *entrechats*. Unlike the body-machine, however, which could easily be disciplined, the dancer's soul could not be trained. The dancer thus became a unique individual who combined the physical skills necessary to produce graceful and harmonious movement with the innate capacity to feel the passions strongly. Yet, as much as Noverre and the other action ballet choreographers endowed the dancer with a special temperament, the performer's responsiveness remained circumscribed by the languagelike repertoire of feelings available. Especially passionate performers produced no new or unique feelings. Rather, they imbued the standard repertoire of passions with added fervor. The body-machine, not an instrument for registering the individual soul's peregrinations, remained a canvas for displaying a fixed quantity of images.

To what extent dancers followed the debates within acting technique or studied the manuals that classified the passions is hard to discern. Certainly they attended the salons where paintings that exercised a knowledge of representational strategies were exhibited and discussed. They also attended performances at the Comédies Française and Italienne and on the boulevards, where approaches to acting ranging from the most hyperbolic to the most understated could be found. And they certainly explored anatomy, a science that developed hand in hand with the painterly project of investigating the passions. It seems likely, however, that they developed their skills at acting and pantomime by borrowing extemporaneously from one another and from acting and painting rather than by undertaking a systematic study of acting. Their obligations as masters of the classical dance vocabulary took precedence over other inquiries on a daily basis.

If dancers sporadically gathered what they could of acting techniques, their pursuit of a pedagogy to enhance dancing prowess followed a clear progression, one in which anatomy became a principal analytical tool both for understanding students' physical problems and for guiding the general cultivation of the body. Through their studies of the skeleton, Dancing Masters had observed, for example, that outward rotation of the leg originated in the hip joint.[44] This insight caused them to encourage dancers to abandon the use of turn-out machines—contraptions designed to crank the legs open by securing the feet to two outward turning platforms—that had been much in vogue at the beginning of the century. Likewise, a thorough understanding of skeletal structure enabled Dancing Masters to identify principles that related deficiencies in students' movement to their physical structure. Noverre commented on one such relationship as part of his profile of knock-kneed dancers, who, he claimed,

> have very little elasticity and rarely strike with the toe. I believe I have discovered the true reason for this when I consider the long and flat shape of their feet. I compare this part to a lever of the second order, that is to say, a lever where the weight is between the fulcrum and the power, so that the fulcrum and the power are at its extremities.

> Hence the fixed point or fulcrum corresponds to the extremity of the foot, the resistance or weight of the body is carried on the instep, and the power which raises and sustains this weight is applied to the heel by means of the Achilles tendon. Now as the lever is stronger in a foot that is long and flat, the weight of the body is further distant from the fulcrum and nearer the power; hence the weight of the body must be greater and the strength of the Achilles tendon diminish in equal proportion. I have said then that this weight not being in as exact a proportion in dancers that are *arqués* as it is in those who are *jarretés,* who have usually a high and strong instep, the former have necessarily less ease in raising themselves on the extremity of the toes.[45]

By analyzing bodily functioning as the movement of a series of levers, the structural imperfection at the knee joint could be connected to deficiencies at the ankle and foot, problems that explained the visible properties of the dancer's movement.

Informed by their burgeoning awareness of anatomical structure, Dancing Masters increasingly emphasized the need to structure teaching to suit the unique physical needs of each student.[46] Classification of types of physical impediments and deformities, and a growing knowledge of the specific exercises best suited to remedy a given problem, led teachers to advocate a highly individualized course of study. They believed that dances appropriate for the cultivation of one student's body could be ineffective for another. As Dancing Master Giovanni-Andrea Gallini observed: "Who does not know that almost every individual learner requires different instructions? The laying of a stress on some particular motion or air which may be proper to be recommended to one must be strictly forbidden to another."[47]

To accommodate students' individual needs, Dancing Masters began to develop a greater number of preliminary exercises designed to remedy specific defects. Italian choreographer and teacher Gennaro Magri recommended that

> the Master should also observe whether some are weak in the knees and the insteps or in one of these two said parts. For this he should use a remedy and make them do a long daily exercise practicing walking round the room only on the balls of their feet, keeping the knee and instep stretched without any bend whatsoever and, thus exercising for a few hours daily, the weak parts will be fortified.[48]

Dancing Masters also initiated exercises that facilitated the students' acquisition of basic skills. Noverre, for example, suggested that in place of the turn-out machine, students should practice *battements* and *ronds de jambe*—movements that rotated the leg in the hip socket by directing it to the front, side, and back.[49] Where earlier in the century the performance of simple dances served to instruct the body in the correct execution of steps, Dancing Masters in the 1760s and 1770s introduced specific exercises to prepare the body to dance correctly.

These changes in dance pedagogy coincided with innovations in the science of human posture, whose techniques for correct postural alignment explored unique individual exercises that reflected an awareness of the body's structure.[50] Throughout the seventeenth and early eighteenth centuries, the corset, for example, was considered the proper corrective guide to good posture and advocated for both normal and deformed adults and children. Around the middle of the eighteenth century, doctors and physical educators began to reject this uniform, external body mold in favor of programs of simple exercises designed to teach the body to align itself. As in dance, the properly aligned body was one that had achieved a correct spatial positioning for each of its parts—head, chest, shoulders, lower back, hips, thighs, and legs. Body parts were adjusted forward or back, higher or lower, to conform to an ideal visual schema, a kind of silhouette, of perfect posture. Where early in the century, the corset, like the turn-out machine, was thought to accomplish this correct spatial positioning with the body's passive participation, educators in the middle of the century began to introduce regimens that would enable the body actively to achieve rectitude.

The emphasis on individual anatomical structure and on self-alignment had implications for the comportment of the Dancing Master while instructing the student. Teachers were discouraged from pushing or pulling the student's body into the correct shape, and advised, instead, to facilitate the student's growth through a gentle support. Gennaro Magri described the appropriate style of instruction this way:

> a bad Master can spoil that which is good. The first laziness of one of these who understands the Art poorly . . . is that in the first exercises he takes the Pupil by the hands, gripping them firmly in his own, forcing [the pupil] to bend and rise, accompanying him with the movement of the hands. The result of this is that the Scholar, if young in years, is in consequence delicate and unsteady because of the weakness of the nerves and of the bones; because of his stupidity he leans strongly on the Master who acts as a support. Behold the bad effect. In that effort which he makes to support himself, he lifts the elbows outwards, thrusts out the shoulders, and the chest goes in; by becoming accustomed to this posture it happens that, freed from the Master's hands, he continues in this ill-composed attitude. . . . Therefore, I will advise here below how to deal with giving the first rudiments. First of all place the Pupil in fourth position, the knees well stretched and turned out; then with a noble and gentle air he should prepare his body with the head high, the chest forward, shoulders down, the stomach and the abdomen held in, the waist inclined forwards, the arms falling naturally with the elbows a little behind, and take care to do everything without overemphasis because too much affectation leads to impropriety. Then the Master must gently lift his hands with palms upward without leaning, but only to steady him. . . . the Pupil must not be supported by the Master when rising, nor pressed when bending, but must have a gentle, subtle guide, and thus becoming accustomed to being without support when he is released from the slight support of the hands, he will be elegant and well composed.[51]

Magri predicted that if the Dancing Master did not allow the student to acquire slowly the strength and awareness necessary to establish the body's own uprightness, he ran the risk of imparting irremediable bad habits. If, instead, he applied a subtle series of directives, he could eventually launch the student with a full-blown, self-sustaining, upright bearing.

With the establishment of a school at the Opéra for aspiring dancers in 1780, these kinds of pedagogical insights could find their way into standardized classroom practices.[52] Students repeated simple movements to increase their strength and stability. Repetition of these isolated movements segmented dance sequences in the same way that anatomy dissected the musculature in search of the passions. But it also lent a new awareness of muscle groups as masses that could be controlled and harnessed for the purpose of enhancing expertise at dancing. Only the practice of dancing itself had served to improve performance in the past. Now the dancer could feel the incremental adjustments worked on the body by exercise and enjoy the measured advances in competence that such a regimen afforded.

By working assiduously at the routines presented in class, dancers mastered an unprecedented level of control over the burgeoning vocabulary. They learned to perform *entrechats* while turning in the air, and double and triple *pirouettes*.[53] Expansions in number and complexity to the language of dance evidenced its elasticity. Just as the study of anatomy provided new pedagogical insights, so too the study of dance vocabulary by the newly competent anatomized bodies would yield new directions in virtuosity. The vocabulary's apparently infinite expandability only proved the perfectability of the body.

The language of dance

Insofar as choreographers and aestheticians conceived of the action ballet as the visual and moving representation of a story, they relied heavily on the analogy between dance and painting in order to elucidate the visual impact of the dance. But in their efforts to explain this new aesthetic project, they also elaborated a comparison between dance and language. The linguistic elements of vocabulary and syntax and the larger features of narrative such as the beginning, dramatic knot, and resolution served repeatedly as the analogies through which the action ballet might be explained and understood. This analysis of dance as language differed from notions of choreographic writing developed earlier in the century. Instead of dance as a visual articulation of the poetic qualities of music—its meter, phrasing, and harmony and their attendant emotional states—choreography now demonstrated a moment-by-moment enunciation of the plot. The action ballet did not "write" a dialogue with the music that expanded on a state of feeling. Instead, it required both music and choreography to "write" the story of characters' progression of feelings.

A vivid critique of the conception of writing was offered in one anonymous letter to the *Mercure de France* from 1762. Signing as an "ancien maître de ballet" critical of contemporary choreographic practices, the author drew the comparison between dance movement and language in these terms:

> the result is that what we call steps in our profession take the place of words in our language; that their combinations form phrases more or less well turned; that all this methodically ordered, will be seen correctly written; but that the execution of these parts, no matter how perfectly it is accomplished, can never produce anything else, by comparison, than normal reading, with agreeable inflections and correct pronunciation: it will never have within it anything that originates in genius, anything which is related to it. To invoke the exaggerated pronouncements of their aficionados, dancers, whose steps write the notes, have probably, to a very great degree, the merit of good articulation. But what do they articulate? Here is the important question, to assess not only whether there is genius but even soul in their dancing.[54]

Like earlier aesthetic mandates upon which the performances of dancers like Dupré had been based, this Ballet Master claimed for dance the ability to "write" visually. Dancing should demonstrate articulateness, intelligence, and intelligibility. Dancing's steps, like the notes of the music, formed phrases, inflected with the same lucid and spirited motivation as that summoned up in the musical composition.

Even in the Ballet Master's eyes, however, this esteemed aesthetic was being supplanted by another approach to composition, that of writing the story. (See fig. 42.) In this approach dancing incorporated the painterly postures of the emotions, and also the kinds of behavior in which an angry person would typically engage. Take, for example, the point in *Armide* where "hate grows out of the most ardent love":

> We find for the dancers, following Hate, several actions that could take place in Armide's presence, such as fighting furiously among themselves over a headband, turning a quiver upside down, distributing the arrows among themselves, and breaking them in different ways: the execution of Amour's torch alone could produce a dance performed in a thousand different ways; the play of this torch with those of the Furies after presenting it to Armide; all this finally could produce the most fertile material for a poem rendered entirely in dance.[55]

The patient explanation of the Ballet Master in enumerating choreographic possibilities reveals the logical, even scientific, approach taken in the action ballet and also the newness of the project. Never before had such a close examination of the connection between feelings and behavior been entailed by the art of choreography. Yet the writings of both music and of story could not easily be contained in any single ballet. Danced characters, once constructed, could not reintegrate into the choreographic rendition of music's intensities, moods, and inflections. In order to remain credible, they consistently required new and compelling motivations, actions, and responses, the design of which depended upon pantomimic rather than classical repertoires.

Noverre pointed to the syntactical dimension of this new kind of choreographic writing in his comparison between dance and language:

> When all these movements are not directed by genius, and when feeling and expression do not contribute their powers sufficiently to affect and interest me, I admire the skill of the human machine, I render justice to its strength and ease of movement, but it leaves me unmoved; it does not affect me or cause me any more sensation than this arrangement of the following words:
>
> Fait . . . pas . . . le . . . la . . . honte . . . non . . . crime . . . et . . . l'échafaud.
>
> But when these words are ordered by a poet they compose this beautiful line spoken by the Comte d'Essex:
>
> Le crime fait la honte, et non pas l'échafaud.[56]

Movements, like words, could be arranged so as to depict an idea, a character's thoughts or feelings, or they could follow one another in a chaotic jumble that represented only nonsense. In order to achieve a lucid sequence of movement, the choreographer was pressed to ask what each character should logically do at each moment.

Each character necessarily manifested the appropriate behavior, but groups of characters in their expressions and in their configurations should also conform to the developing plot. Extending the analogy between language and dance even further, Maximilien Gardel proposed that the choreographer's ability to position dancers in space and

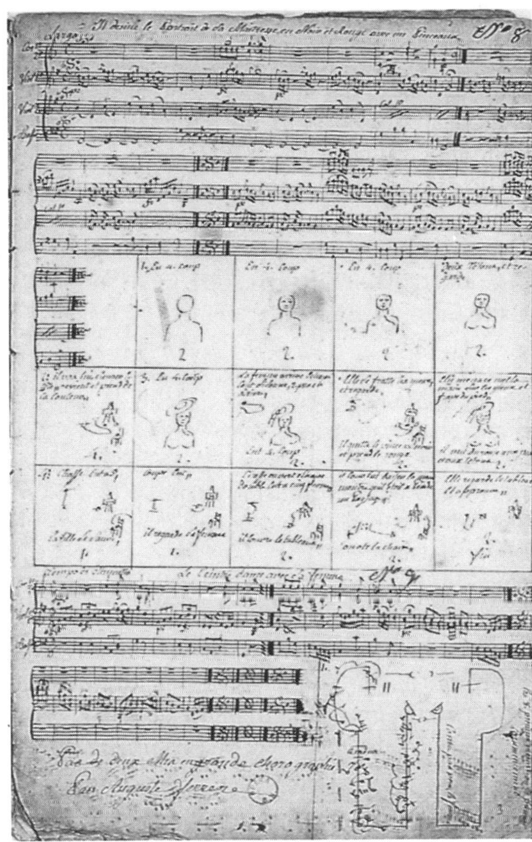

42. A page from Auguste Frederic Joseph Ferrêre's 1782 notation for the ballet *Le Peintre Amoureux de son Modelle,* in which he used verbal description, drawings, and Feuillet-derived notation to document the danced action.

coordinate their expressions and their movements as a group corresponded to the poet's style and versification.

> It is necessary for the reader, to judge the project effectively, to have a good idea of the tableaux, the groups, the attitudes, and the actions that produce each situation. The tableaux, groups, and attitudes are for the Ballet Master what style and versification are for the Poet, and they come into their proper proportion when the work is being made, so that all that remains for the execution of the dance is the fire, the taste, and the knowledge of theatrical effects and of the identity of each character.[57]

The disposition of the dancers in accordance with the plot, Gardel argued, formed the basis or foundation of each scene and of the ballet as a whole. Once this structure had been determined, then all that remained for the choreographer to attend to was the fire and taste of the execution and the appeal of the overall theatrical effect.

Analogies such as Gardel's between dance and prose or poetry permeated critical writing on the action ballet but were most commonly applied in discussions of the relationship between the ballet and its program notes. Should the program notes provide the reader with historical background on the story, its sources in antiquity, or with explanations of the relationships among characters prior to the beginning of the ballet? Or should they concentrate on a blow-by-blow account of feelings and actions in the performance?[58] Should the choreography translate verbal metaphors word for word, or should choreography and notes represent the plot each in their own way? Could the choreographer introduce an entirely new story to the stage, or was it necessary to utilize a plot and characters with which viewers were already familiar? While each choreographer and aesthetician answered these questions differently, debates were grounded in the assumption that an absolute equivalence between text and dance could be reached.

Critics in their reviews presumed that the published scenario should and could represent precisely what had occurred onstage. Frequently, they reprinted verbatim the program notes as a description of the performance. To these they appended an evaluation of dancers' execution, the qualities of style, grace, vivacity, proportion, and precision with which dancers met the challenge of dancing out the story. When they took issue with the production, their disapprobation most often stemmed from the perceived failure to adhere to the notes. Critics complained vociferously about sections or entire ballets for which they were required to consult the program notes in order to comprehend the dancing. The choreography could be vague, making it impossible to tell what the character was "saying," or it could be misleading by dictating actions for a character that did not conform to the scenario.[59] Alternatively, the production might suffer from an excessive attention to spectacle. If the choreographer broke the unity of action in order to present a lively progression of scenic changes, or if dancers engaged in a grotesque display of meaningless virtuosity, or if the festive divertissements that displayed complex group patternings dragged on, then the ballet failed. Each of these criteria, however, shared the expectation that the performance would render the story as written, with vivid clarity and transparent ease.

Exasperated at the literalness with which choreographers and critics invoked the dance-as-language metaphor, one viewer challenged Gardel to make a ballet using as the scenario his introductory treatise on the history and theory of dance.[60] Dance movement, he argued, was incapable of expressing many things, not only the abstract concepts of historical discourse, but even the sad passions: "It would therefore be quite ridiculous, in my opinion, to see Terpsichore expressing her pain by dancing and pirouetting sadly around a tomb."[61] The dance, emblematic of lighter, more joyous emotions, should be restricted in its choice of topics to the levity of love, the delight and festivity of celebration.

By restricting the choice of subject to lighter themes, some choreographers and viewers may have hoped to achieve a better integration of pantomimic gesture and classical steps. Portrayal of the stronger, more violent passions often entailed a static staging of tableau-like images. Seized by hatred, terror, jealousy, or vengefulness, the body became rooted, its limbs contorted, its focus downward, whereas the joyous emotions lifted one's body up, freeing the legs for various cabrioles and entrechats that would signal an animated state. Even during those phases of courtship when a character might experience rejection or doubt, the dispirited body could remain mobile, if somewhat droopy. And any such downcast moments would predictably resolve into felicitous reunions, unlike revenge, which would likely segue into remorse. Even if they agreed, however, that the dance vocabulary lent itself to lightness, choreographers nonetheless persevered in exploring a full range of passions. Ballets enacted terror, aggression, hatred, and remorse along with surprise, delight, and desire. The complex palette of passions as much as the vocabulary of classical steps was what made dance like language.

But was the gestural repertoire truly a language? could it say everything that words could? Of all the works to undertake an investigation of this question, Engel's *Idées sur le Geste et l'Action Théâtrale* offered by far the most exhaustive and persuasive answer. In conjunction with his comprehensive analysis of the passions, Engel undertook a thorough inquiry into the numerous claims for a direct correspondence between language and movement. According to Engel gesture depicted a full range of feelings. As a means of communication, it had the capacity not only to speak eloquently,[62] but also, like its sister art, poetry, to engage in rhetorical figurement. Engel provided examples in movement of metonymy, synecdoche, and irony, three of the many tropes, as follows:

> I could present an infinite number of examples of figurative gestures. Do you want to see a metonomy that uses the effect for the cause? The footman, speaking of the disagreeable way in which his master could repay his pranks, rubs his back with his hand as if he felt already the pain of the beating stick. Do you ask for another, one that, instead of an object, indicates an exterior relationship? In designating the real God or those of the pagans, the language of gesture uses their supposed home in the heavens. In the same way, the raised hands, the eyes directed heavenwards, call the gods to witness innocence, implore their help, and solicit their vengeance. Or would you prefer a synecdoche? One can designate through a single person an entire family or with a single enemy an entire army of the enemy. Or do you prefer an irony? The young beauty who refuses the hand of the suitor she despises makes a deep curtsy to him, but ironically. The number of allusions is no less in gesture than in language. The action of washing the hands signals innocence; two fingers planted in front of the forehead indicates the infidelity of the woman; by blowing softly over an open hand, one indicates the idea of nothing.[63]

Engel granted gesture the declamatory and rhetorical capabilities of poetry. He also attributed to movement the ability to convey abstract thought.[64] The sheer number of detailed comparisons that he undertook, however, eventually led him to doubt the linguistic abilities of movement.

Through speech, Engel argued, people could indicate both the idea of the object to which they referred and also the manner in which that object affected them.[65] Communication through movement alone, when the object of reference and the feeling it engendered were not united, entailed a bifurcation of the body, or even a dual role for some parts of the body that would be impossible to perform. Even though the languages of words and gestures seemed hypothetically equivalent, the physical complications entailed in communication using movement argued for a simultaneous deployment of both systems, each making its contribution to the expressive act. The value of gesture thus lay in its paralinguistic potential—as a supplementary sign system that could lend complexity and nuance to all verbal pronouncements.[66]

If gesture was to tell a story without the aid of words, a project which Engel as playwright and aesthetician of dramatic theatre did not ultimately recommend, it could only be used to present well-known events (a point which was emphasized by Engel's translator in the preface to the French edition of the work).[67] Successful ballets, both ancient and modern, certainly relied on the viewer's prior knowledge of the narrative's plot, characters, and setting. Ballets like Noverre's, he argued, never presented an original story whose action viewers could easily follow. Instead, they adapted well-known narratives whose details were provided in the program notes. The choreography itself, Engel observed, offered a paralinguistic interpretation of the story. Where the original advocates of the action ballet had invoked classical texts that claimed an equivalence for gesture and language, Engel straightforwardly asserted that these texts must have inflated the degree to which movement could speak a story.[68] The stories the ancient pantomimes enacted were well known, and the music, through its rhythm, mode, and phrasing, helped to elucidate the choreographic narrative. Furthermore, Engel observed, the choreography could not depict line by line the story on which it was based. As evidence of this he described a deplorable production of Noverre's *Les Horaces* in which Camille, rendering the line "Puisse la terre engloutir Rome" (May the earth swallow up Rome), had repeatedly stuffed her fist into her mouth as if her fist was Rome and her body the earth.[69]

In the action ballet a spirited faithfulness to the written text from which it derived was the standard against which both the choreography and performance were judged. Viewers looked for imaginative solutions to the representation of a well-known passage—scenes that would demonstrate, perhaps for the first time, how famous characters looked and felt as their lives unfolded. A literal, line-by-line enactment such as Engel attributed to Noverre's choreography could only result in deadly sections of vague gesticulation. Although it was not inconceivable that a languagelike system of bodily signs could be invented, Engel concluded that the movement from feeling to action to indication of which the current repertoire was capable did not offer the precision or range necessary to constitute a language. Expressive movement thus had more in common with music and declamation than language and painting.

Although he did not elaborate extensively on this paralinguistic definition for movement, Engel sketched out its basic features, energy and sensibility, and argued for the need to study the development of the passions through time. Citing the famous analogy between the passions and a plucked string, he observed that emotions never seize the soul completely and instantaneously, but rather take time to grow and pass away. Certain emotions, because of their energy, could follow in natural succession one from another, whereas others could not. Musical principles of thematic development as well as rhetorical guidelines for oral presentations demonstrated these natural laws of succession. Choreographers and dancers as well as actors could increase their effectiveness by adapting these principles to their use of expressive movement.

Through its exhaustive comparisons Engel's analysis laid the foundation for an antilinguistic conception of dance, yet his emphasis on categorization according to visual schemata proscribed any functionalist theory of expressive movement. He never claimed that a particular style of movement or movement itself was uniquely capable of representing specific feelings or motivations. Instead, his theory of the relationships among passions relied on a pictorial analysis of each and a comparison of their relative sizes and weights. Each passion was constituted by a certain degree of involvement for each part of the body. Complex passions or the passage from one passion to the next could be calculated by adding or subtracting the correct amount of bodily presence.[70] Still, his analysis exposed flaws in the analogy between dance and language that had been accepted only a decade earlier as the perfect explanation for dance's capacity to narrate events.

Whether or not choreographers agreed, action ballets were most successful when they used not only a well-known plot, but also one that had recently circulated through public space as a popular novel or boulevard production.[71] Relying on viewers' familiarity with the story, choreographers then enjoyed more latitude in the actual staging of events. Certainly, the enormous success of a ballet like Pierre Gardel's *Le Déserteur* (1788),[72] (see

43. A scene from Pierre Gardel's *Le Déserteur* (1788).

fig. 43) depended upon viewers' knowledge of the plot, as this critic for the *Mercure de France* observed:

> In general, this pantomime is very interesting and enjoyed great success. Even though it is nothing other than the play already so well known, faithfully reproduced from beginning to end, it seems to create more of an effect than the play itself; either because the events following each other more quickly seem to give a more vivid jolt; or because the pantomime, obligated, without the possibility of words, to exaggerate the expression, has greater means to electrify us than simple dialogue.[73]

Unencumbered with the need to establish backgrounds for each character, choreographers might move directly to the critical interactions, the dramatic engagements that the action ballet depicted so well. They might also bestow greater attention on the scenes of virtuoso dancing and on their integration into the action.[74]

If choreographers of the action ballet and their advocates persevered throughout the 1770s and 1780s in the use of linguistic analogies to explain the new genre, they spent equal time denigrating the "cabrioles and entrechats" from the classical ballet repertoire. These steps came to epitomize dancing that was unlike language. When the choreographer failed to make evident the character's clear motivation, or when the choreographer succumbed to the pressure to introduce tour de force dancing unsupported by the dramatic action, then the scene immediately degenerated into meaninglessness. The phrase "cabrioles and entrechats" handily referenced the sterile and mechanical display of routine skills or simply a regression to earlier versions of choreographic writing.[75] In choosing these terms, however, critics belied an underlying concern with the potential conflict between danced action and dancing prowess.[76]

Some action ballet enthusiasts hoped to do away with the virtuoso vocabulary of dancing altogether:

> One can observe from such a composition, that pantomime dance is the art that most closely approximates painting. Both speak to the eyes, and they form in the same way tableaux where the passions and sentiments of the characters are rendered with the help of gesture, attitudes, positions, and groupings. Painting fixes its compositions. Pantomime dance varies them. Painting can only catch one interesting moment of a single composition; pantomime dance must on the contrary search for an action most generative of a sequence of tableaux. Painting employs color, shading, and light to give depth and life to its figures; dancing borrows from the art of music in order to bring intelligence to its designs. These are the principal correspondences that effect one's evaluation of the pantomime dance; and it is by making dancing as close to painting as possible that M. Noverre has created a new art, or at least, brought back the dance pantomimes of the ancients, perfecting the designs that one had roughly sketched. We wonder, in keeping with the principles of dance, which must always paint and become part of a reasoned action or composition, what is the significance of these solos, these duets, these complicated steps, in which one or more dancers develops with grace, if one wants, their legs and their arms, their beats of *entrechats,* the comings and going from left to right, their thrusts forward and back, their turnings upon themselves, and their whirlings as if they were delirious. One feels that all these diverse movements are good studies to be applied at an occasion; but when they are not integrated into the principal action, they paint nothing. What could one say of a painter who created a work from the formal studies of the academy? Each figure might be marvelously colored and drawn with great precision and elegance, but wouldn't the ensemble of figures be ridiculous and untenable?[77]

If the ballet was to construct a moving version of a painting, why was it necessary to continue to include virtuoso solos and duets? Their complicated phrases, the very fact that they traveled, unmotivated, from one side of the stage to the other and back again in a delirium of cabrioles demonstrated their unsuitability to the plot.

Grimm, in his report on Noverre's productions for the Duke of Wurtemberg, published this description, which confirmed the incompatibility of dancing and dramatic movement:

> I have also seen in this genre very beautiful productions at the court of Mannheim; but these ballets follow a completely different system from the French operas. The dancers walk more than they dance. One sees fewer steps and symmetrical dances than gestures and groupings; one never sees the two rows, one of male and the other of female dancers, that line each side of the stage. This arrangement as if at a ball can at the most take place after the denouement when it is only a question of ending the ballet with a general divertissement.[78]

The action ballet's aesthetic mandate to track characters' feelings and interactions through time carried with it the strong implication that the classical vocabulary was irrelevant. Yet, as Grimm astutely observed, Noverre's productions at Mannheim had not reckoned with the French devotion to dancing and the Opéra's institutionalization of that enthusiasm. For the action ballet to succeed on the French stage, choreographers would have to negotiate between drama and virtuosity, suturing them together whenever and however possible.

The self-filled body

The action ballet embodied a new conception of individuality as contained within and supported by individual bodies. Each body could undergo, just as it could faithfully depict, self-generating sequences of passion. Each body could be compelled into reactive responses to other bodies according to the causal logic of emotional syntax. Choreography imitated feelings and interactions common to all people. Dancers represented peasants, soldiers, artists, and daughters, and not gods, goddesses, fauns, and nymphs. Their movements placed all bodies on the same footing. The choreography thereby disentangled the aristocratic subject from the requisite protocols of courtly behavior, and extended to all human beings regardless of class or profession the same capacities to feel and to empathize with another's feelings. These mimetic bodies were no longer suspended within a web of gestures oriented to provide the monarch, seated in the single most favorable viewing location, with the perfect perspective on the stage as universe. Dancers could now open up the spectacle to a wider range of viewing positions from which their discursive messagings could be apprehended. Their asymmetrical, tensile group configurations and their evolving sequences of passions could be seen best, but not most perfectly, from the center of the auditorium.

In this revolutionary overhaul of choreographic conventions, the action ballet performed alongside other Enlightenment theories of the human condition, exploring an egalitarian vision of humanity that would participate in the radical political events of the 1790s. The project of detaching each French citizen's body from religious and courtly constraints had focused the political and philosophical arguments of authors as diverse as Voltaire, Diderot, Rousseau, and Condillac. Well in advance of the actual seizure of power by the "people" of France, distinct cultural practices including dance provided images of the individuality that subjects would necessarily acquire in order to participate in the governance of the state. Boulevard theatres, in their relentlessly hilarious and scathing satires of seventeenth-century classics and of religious topics, accomplished one kind of detachment from absolutism. Their melange of grotesque, subversive, and sentimental performances leveled hierarchies at the same time that it radically expanded the kinds of bodies eligible for inclusion in the body politic.

The action ballet worked another kind of detachment by providing images of self-motivating, self-supporting, and self-sustaining bodies. Dancers in the opera-ballets, through their gracefully calibrated distances from one another and the traceries of arms, legs, and heads they fabricated, had all celebrated the reticulated social space which the king and his subjects inhabited. Identity within that space, established as much by how one moved as what one said, never existed apart from the patterns of all bodies in regulated motion together. The action ballet, in contrast, designated each body as the site of an autonomous individuality. Each body had been trained individually, learning to align itself without the aid of postural props, relying instead on the fortifying exercises that it initiated. Each body's actions on stage caused reactions registered in the behavior of surrounding characters. But their identities did not depend upon a set of mutually recognized and executed patternings of movement. Instead, characters propelled themselves autonomously around the stage. Their gestured proclamations marked the individual implementation of a seemingly universal and innate system of communication. The motivation and facility for communication originated within each body and not in a socially constructed and politically imposed codification of conduct.

If the creation of autonomous danced characters exhilarated viewers with its liberatory vision, it nonetheless generated a choreographic dilemma of enormous proportions. Why did these characters ever perform entrechats, cabrioles, and pirouettes—the hallmark of achievement in the classical repertoire of steps? What meaning beyond the breathtaking speed or height or lightness of the maneuver did these steps claim? In becoming individuated characters, dancers lost their entitlement to the domain of virtuoso physical articulateness. As generic fauns or nymphs, their dancing had corporealized the values of grace, agility, sweetness, and appropriate daring. As Jason, Médée, Mirza, or Le Déserteur, their performances of phrases from the classical repertoire manifested a physical accomplishment, one that evidenced the attributes of grace and dexterity, but that first and foremost required skill rather than passion-driven motivation.

The very project of rendering a story using danced characters thus threw into opposition and conflict the repertoires of danced steps and pantomimic gestures. Fauns, nymphs, or Roman gods such as Dupré portrayed had encompassed the passionate and the virtuoso within a single aesthetic standard. Their conception of choreographic writing imbued each danced phrase with signification as articulation, as superior physical accomplishment, and as an intensity of feeling. Now, dancers onstage necessarily turned from the enactment of character to the display of dancerly prowess, and choreographers worked to contrive justifications for that transformation.

Stories sited at celebrations, festivals, parties, or games worked effectively to reconcile the two repertoires. During these scenes lengthy and large-scale stagings of the classical repertoire could credibly represent the buoyant spirits of all participants. Yet the technical skills of dancers demanded visibility at other moments as well, and this pressure to display dancerly prowess threatened at every moment to compromise the congenial development of the narrative. Critics consistently found fault with the frequent deviations from the story that occurred as a result of the insertion of virtuoso steps. Yet the increasingly specialized and highly technical preparation of the dancer, the benefits derived from anatomical insights applied to dance, had resulted in an expertise—a physical eloquence, a penchant for the spectacular—that proved strongly resistant to the goals of a narrative dance. Dancers wanted to show their physical competence, and the audience wanted to see it.

Interlude

The Duel

The pace of events onstage has slowed; the forces of good and evil have been carefully specified, perhaps even too clearly delineated. What's next? Let's have a duel! Let's break out of dancing and into fighting! The crisp clink of metal on metal, faster than any move except the beat of the leg or flick of the wrist, comes as such a welcome intervention into the measured moderation with which the danced step fits the music's meter. Not that the swordplay isn't rhythmically phrased and perfectly metered. It, too, conforms to the music, but with explosive eruptions of engagement, one body/blade against another. A bursting lunge forward, a deft feint backward, up on the bridge, down on one's back: the diagonal thrusts of swordsmen swirl around the stage. The fierce interconnectedness of the duo—they never face forward when presenting their dueling dialogue to the audience—galvanizes a different quality of attention from that presumed by dancing. Even though the body must uphold standards of "cool," the musculature commits with notable force and purpose to the rhythmic parries. In a duel, one distracted glance away could mean death. Onlookers know this. The crowd parts to make room for the duo. Women wring their hands anxiously and men stand back, restraining themselves from intervention in a matter of honor.

How is it that dueling fits so easily into the scenario? The swordplay's virtuosity contains dramatic emplotment. These two characters are angry, hostile, and aggressive, or else brave and good. The clever crafting of the fight shows a level of bodily articulation parallel to dancing, and the swordsmen display many of the cherished physical skills necessary to dancing—agility, lightness, élan. But also, when dancing bodies shift suddenly from decorousness to aggression, they reinvigorate all those ancient protocols of the courtier that connected comportment to combat and to choreography. Precious survivor from a time long ago, the duel provokes exquisite nostalgia for the moment when honor operated as an unquestioned moral code and the path taken by the hero's sword exemplified the choreography of the good and true.

Mirza (1779)

For action ballets produced at the Opéra, *Mirza* marked a shift in focus from mythological to historical characterization. Set in the colonial Caribbean, the work capitalized on the exoticism of locale and inhabitants to create one of the most popular theatrical presentations of the decade. Like Vestris, *Mirza*'s choreographer, Maximilien Gardel, had danced for Noverre in Stuttgart. He made his debut with the Opéra in 1759 and assumed the position of Ballet Master at the Opéra in 1781. Unlike Noverre, whose appointment at the Opéra resulted from his political ties, Gardel worked his way up through its institutional ranks. He commanded the respect of dancers at all levels, and he comprehended the bureaucratic and political complexities that were inherent in each production. Familiar as well with the protocols of city and court, Gardel choreographed two versions of *Mirza*, one performed at Versailles in March of 1779, and the other for the Opéra the following November. The published scenarios for the performances indicate significant differences, both in the magnitude of the production—the Opéra version included an extra act and several additional supporting characters—and also in moral tone.[1]

The Opéra version opens at the heroine Mirza's family house. Her close ties to her Creole mother and her father, the French governor of the island, are established, as well as her attachment to the French officer Lindor and her repudiation of the villainous Corsair's advances. At the climax of the Opéra version, when the heroine has fainted, Lindor's calls for help summon Mirza's parents, with whom the hero intercedes for permission to marry. In the shorter Versailles version, in which Mirza's parents never appear, Lindor's kisses slowly revive her. The couple then exits and reappears at his estate in a final celebration of their betrothal. Although both versions focus primarily on the young couple's attachment and the Corsair's challenge to it, the presence of Mirza's parents would have made a telling difference by locating the lover's relationship within the generational lines of authority. Their absence in the Versailles version would have robbed the heroine of a social origin and consequently imbued her with an alluring availability suitable for the private entertainment of the court.

Both the second act of the Opéra version and the opening of the ballet at Versailles set the action in the countryside, the sea in the distance, a bridge crossing a small stream to one side. Mirza and Lindor's evening tryst is interrupted by a skirmish between four Negroes and the Corsair. Lindor rushes to the aid of the Corsair, saving his life. Although he leaves the couple after expressing his gratitude to Lindor, the pirate returns the following morning once Lindor has left to rejoin his troop. Mirza rejects his advances, his offer of jewels, his insinuating and overbearing manner. Still, he pursues her and finally grabs her in an effort to abduct her. In the Opéra version, she struggles free and runs off stage just as Lindor arrives. In the other version, the Corsair casts Mirza aside in order to meet Lindor's challenge, and she runs from the scene in horror as the two men battle. Although Lindor is wounded and loses his sword, he eventually prevails, throwing the Corsair into the river. Lindor then exits in search of Mirza, just as she arrives to find only his sword and the water stained with blood. In the Versailles ballet, Mirza, assuming the worst, seizes the sword with the intention of killing herself, but Lindor returns and arrests her hand. In both versions she faints, overwhelmed by grief, but is revived by Lindor's kisses in one case and by her mother's solicitous hand in the other. The couple, either by themselves or with the parents' blessing, then reaffirm their mutual love. The final act—at Lindor's home in the Versailles version, at the family home in the Opéra version—shows guests and servants celebrating the couple's marriage with dancing. The more elaborate Opéra production concludes this act with a display of troops in review, a mock battle, and a dance by the local inhabitants, followed by a contredanse for all.

The ballet's simple story concerned an already declared love interrupted by outside forces and then reestablished. At both Versailles and the Opéra, the compelling action choreographically and dramatically occurred in the scenes depicting the struggle between the Corsair, Mirza, and Lindor. The sinister pursuit and intended rape of Mirza, the timely appearance of the hero, the rejection of the desired woman in favor of the challenge of the duel—all these appeared as crystalline actions, full of excitement and easily legible. Mirza, exoticized as a Creole while at the same time elevated in status as daughter of the governor, is the figure desired by both honorable and corrupt forces. The abbreviated version produced for the court portrayed Mirza as more sexually available—operating without parental governance—and also more active—she was willing to contemplate suicide having deduced Lindor's death. In the Opéra version, she became a more passive character; her liaison with Lindor developed at her parents' house, and her mother and father returned at the end to reinstate their authority over her. In both, she fled the site of combat and succumbed to her own feelings in a faint. Her double vulnerability—first struggling in the arms of the Corsair and then fainting in the arms of her lover—evoked in Lindor the attachment necessary to commit to marriage.[2]

The ballet's strongly motivated actions, the kinesthetic thrill of elaborately choreographed duels, and the suspenseful stage business of one character rushing offstage in one direction while another bursts onstage from the other direction, all captured viewers' enthusiasm. The *Mercure de France* described the ballet as a congenial, even ideal, balance between this kind of rousing action and a simple plot:

> This pantomime enjoyed the greatest success; and one can vouch that it was deserved. One can rightly say that the intrigue was minimal; perhaps one should have added that an overly complicated plot does not suit the ballet; that only a simple action, easy to develop in a succession of scenes in which the help of a gestural vocabulary is only used to paint things and not words should be approved for works of this type: perhaps one should add also that the author demonstrated a deft ability to utilize contrasts, to present tableaux of a different genre without breaking the rules or abandoning the subject. One laughs in the first act; one is deeply moved in the second; in the third, one shares equally in the feelings of admiration and joy: it seems that nothing more could be asked of the choreographer. There might be a few nuances still to be desired, a few cuts to be made; because where is perfection to be found? The choice of musical airs that accompanied the action is done with a great deal of intelligence and discernment; one cannot say as much for the choice of music for the dances.[3]

The critic heartily approved of the adept way that Gardel moved the action from comic family intrigue to treacherous combat to festive celebration, while keeping within the confines of the plot.[4]

As exciting and well integrated as the action was, the energy of the production was powerfully augmented by the exotic setting and its local inhabitants. Unlike Circe's island, the Caribbean had a geographical reality and exoticism for Parisians developed over decades of colonial settlement there. This exoticism blended heightened senses of sexual desire and danger into an unknown that circumscribed the simple plot, saving it from banality while at the same time giving the story focus. As a Creole Mirza was worth fighting for. Raised in this exotic locale, she manifested an extra sensual allure plus the privilege that her father's position bestowed. The Negro population provided a colorful, alternative look and style of movement as well as the menacing possibility of revolt.[5] The four Negroes pursuing the Corsair would have immediately been presumed to be the evil figures, even though pirates also deserved their reputation as ruthless and lawless mavericks. In the final act, however, the Negro population participated in the celebration, thereby contributing their alterity to the general colonial good. After serving as the foreboding yet stimulating socialscape, the colonized people were then used to demonstrate France's supreme power.

If the use of foreign populations either to provide a sense of danger or to enhance the spectacle was too blatant, then the ballet might be judged a failure. Such was the case in a one-act revisitation of *Mirza* entitled *Fête de Mirza* that premiered three years later. According to the *Mercure de France*, the ballet, a hideous melange of actions, compromised the very status of the action ballet:

> . . . a so-called Ballet-pantomime, in which one lunches during the first act; where in the second, one kills the savages with rifles, a spectacle worthy of cannibals; whose third act depicts soldiers performing their maneuvers on a parade ground, the preparations for corporal punishment, and the anguish of a wife imploring the forgiveness of her husband who is about to die on a funeral pyre; whose fourth act, finally, by a miracle even more striking because it happens without any apparent force, shows deaf who can suddenly hear and dumb who can sing. . . .[6]

The unmotivated slaughter of the Negroes struck the critic as a spectacle worthy of "cannibals." It was prompted, according to him, by the increasing urgency with which audiences demanded striking images and fast action. Yet all but the parterre rejected this caricature of a ballet, leaving the critic to wonder whether ballet should return to its role as accessory to opera: "Pantomime caused the decline of Roman theatre, and it will probably accomplish the same for ours, because the Opéra cannot exist without dance; but it should remain as an accessory."[7] With its autonomy from opera barely established, choreographers looked to the popularity of ballets like the original *Mirza* for proof of the genre's viability. But the pressure to produce spectacle would continue to yield failures as well as successes.

The Earth Trembles; The Thunder Roars

Things are going well, or they are going poorly. No matter. There comes a moment when the narrative needs a boost. The earth trembles, and the thunder roars [*La terre tremble; la foudre gronde*]. A natural cataclysm has suddenly intervened in the normal course of human affairs. This predictable intervention can claim no legitimate reason for being. Nothing in the plot prefigures the arrival of such a catastrophe. Perhaps it indicates the gods' displeasure, or it stands for the arbitrary power of Nature itself. It may reprimand characters for their actions, or render their circumstances more dire. Perhaps it will serve to measure their moral and physical acumen. The plot has contrived no way for human actions to accomplish these evaluative functions. But the viewer does not notice this narrative shortfall. The persuasive grandeur of the spectacle pulls one immediately into the impending destruction.

Clouds rush in as the stage suddenly darkens. Blotchy flashes of light momentarily illuminate the scene. Large waves appear at seaside. Buildings shake and sometimes collapse. Characters rush from one side to the other and back—clutching, flailing—their swirling commotion augmenting the stage's quaking.

This technological display does not require empathy from the viewer as human actions do. The viewer knows from the outset that the machinery is simulating disaster. It is the sheer scale of the operation, the intricacies of timing and coordination, the radical alterations to the box-stage that impress themselves so strongly upon the viewer. The mechanistic and technological enormity of the interruption accomplishes a jolt that human actions never can. After witnessing such an ambitious theatrical display, they can only be convinced of the effects wrought by such a natural disaster on the lives of characters they have come to know. The catastrophe has accomplished its dual function, thrilling viewers with its stupendous, driving destruction and, incidentally, changing the course of the narrative.

44. Madeleine Guimard as Mélide in Pierre Gardel's *Le Premier Navigateur* (1785).

Le Premier Navigateur, ou le Pouvoir de l'Amour (1785)

A huge success, *Le Premier Navigateur* was one of the first action ballets presented at the Opéra to integrate dramatic action with an ambitious scenic design over three long acts. Noverre's five-act version of *Médée et Jason* (1780) failed to persuade its viewers, who found it dignified but also indecipherable,[1] of the action ballet's capacity to sustain narrative coherence over a long duration. *Le Premier Navigateur,* through its canny mixture of scenes involving dancing and sport, its scenic changes and simple dramatic action, established the kind of balance between drama and spectacle that would be used for years to come.[2] Gardel's younger brother, Pierre, who would succeed his brother two years later as the Opéra's Maître des Ballets, choreographed the ballet. He was able to make use of the enormously popular Madeleine Guimard, now in her prime, and Auguste Vestris as principles. Costumed in simple peasant garb, these dancers played the sentimental plot for all it was worth.

In the first act, the suitors of the young shepherdess, Mélide, arrive bearing gifts. (See fig. 44.) As she observes their procession, she is attracted only to Daphnis, and when the men exit to prepare for the competition that will determine her mate, she worries that he may not win. Observing her secretly, Daphnis is delighted. He rushes to her and they swear their love before he leaves for the games. Presided over by a village elder, the danced competition between men occupies the rest of the act. Daphnis wins easily, and the group exits the stage. At the beginning of act 2, the marriage is performed and then followed by general celebrations. The games that Daphnis was required to win, however, suddenly seem a small obstacle as a violent storm arises, cracking open the land and leaving Mélide stranded on what has become a small island. Backstage explosions of phosphorus, the sudden extinction and illumination of side-light candles and the use of thunder machines provide convincing proof of the storm's severity. The crack in the land, most probably a break in the flooring running horizontally across the back of the stage, lifts Mélide up and isolates her in the distance as the long, corkscrew-shaped turning rods that closely resemble waves rush into the gap. As the storm subsides and the full recognition of the catastrophe sets in, Daphnis, desolate and distraught, paces the shoreline. Mélide's mother, equally dismayed, begs him to return to the village, but he refuses. Overcome by emotion she faints, and must be transported away. Daphnis himself succumbs to a troubled reverie in which he dreams of rescuing Mélide with a boat whose sail is inscribed with the words: "Be brave enough to expose yourself to the element that separated you from all that you find dear; love will guide you." When he awakens, he finds the boat waiting. Mélide's mother rushes in and again begs him to return home, but he boards the small craft and departs as the curtain falls. The final act shows Mélide despairing, stranded without hope on one side of the island, as Daphnis lands on the other. They soon discover one another and rejoice. The dangerous journey home, however, remains before them, and both register the doubt and longing associated with the voyage. Having mustered the courage to set sail, the scene suddenly changes to the Temple of Venus, where Amour and his court preside over celebrations by fauns and bacchantes honoring the strength of the couple's love. In the last moments of the celebration, Venus descends in her chariot to acknowledge the triumph of love.

The thin plot for this ballet consolidated several themes from earlier ballets and operas: the village beauty and the practice of competing for her hand in marriage; the disruption of human affairs by catastrophic natural acts; and the intervention in human affairs by the gods, especially Venus and her followers. The staging also relied on a convention, in effect since the earliest court ballets, of indicating a dream through the appearance of a danced character. His actions, although not the fact of the dancer-as-dream, caused the *Mercure de France* to offer its only criticism of the ballet:

> One would wish that his own genius, excited only by the dream, would inspire him upon waking to fell a hollow tree, acceding to the help of his friends if necessary, in order to construct a frail canoe which one could not watch him board without trembling. Then, one says, the alarm that he inspires would be justified; can such alarm really exist with such visible protection from the gods?[3]

Had the boat not been provided by divine agency, the need for courageous action by Daphnis would have seemed more convincing.

Although the reviewer preferred the image of Daphnis constructing and then departing in the boat by himself, the dream sequence itself proved most compelling. According to the *Mercure de France* description, the success of the ballet derived not from innovations in character type, locale, or custom, but rather from several scenes, specifically the dream and the dialogue between Daphnis and Mélide's mother, that depicted and sequenced emotions in new ways:

> . . . the scene with the dream, in which the agitation of his soul, quite different from his actions while awake, makes it possible to distinguish the bewilderment of sleep; and the scene of his delirium when he pushes Mélide's mother away with fury and falls

at the same moment to his knees to beg forgiveness for his harshness. These moments seem preferable even to the expression of despair; not that M. Vestris did not render them all with great accuracy, but we believe that the violent passions need only energy, and natural sensibility to be expressed, and that these qualities are less rare than those of finesse and depth of conception.[4]

The scene showing the movement associated with a troubled dream offered a new perspective on the individual's behavior in a state other than waking. Similarly, the sequence where Daphnis became so distraught he pushed Mélide's mother away and then begged her forgiveness highlighted the conflicting impulses a single character might feel. Soliloquies and dialogues in earlier action ballets tended to illustrate a range of emotions that focused on an external object of desire or revulsion—Eucharis discovering her love for Télémaque, or Apelles attempting to paint Campaspe. In *Le Premier Navigateur,* a deeper grammar of emotions was revealed based on the character's self-awareness and this "depth of conception" demanded a new finesse on the part of the performer.

The success of *Le Premier Navigateur* seems to have provoked a long diatribe against the action ballet published in the *Mercure de France* some months after its premiere. Its author proposed several revealing arguments for discontinuing the genre:

For several years now, the public has viewed with pleasure productions of ballets-pantomimes. These ballets are separate works that demand great care, great expense, multiple studies, that can only be performed by the principal dancers. But does this genre serve the Opéra, and might it not, on the contrary, become detrimental?[5]

The expense, the range of the dancer's technical competence, the demand on principal dancers entailed by the action ballet would inevitably rob the opera-ballets of their charm. For, even if choreographers could find time to do both, wouldn't the dancers save themselves for the pantomimes and thus no longer excel at dancing in the operas? Not only would the quality of the opera erode, according to the author, but the practitioners and viewers of dance would begin to conceive of themselves as equal and separate from music:

The dance is only an accessory in Polymnie's theatre, a very useful, indispensable accessory . . . but nevertheless we regard the recently accepted notion of creating a distinct genre a dangerous innovation for this spectacle, because it is to be feared that sooner or later the dance will look to take the lead from that to which it was considered a member. And besmides, there is probably more merit in artfully bending one's ideas to those of others, to subordinating oneself in some manner in order to make shine the riches of one's own genius, rather than to create haphazardly for given or imagined subjects more for effect than for reason.[6]

Although the author advocated an immediate return to dance as a subsidiary of opera and could not imagine why his comments would shock or upset choreographers,[7] the action ballet had achieved a momentum that could not be checked. Administrators at the Opéra as well as critics worried about its increasing popularity, but their concerns only confirmed the genre's vitality. A ballet like *Le Premier Navigateur* secured its status by introducing into the Opéra the sentimental simplicity of boulevard musical comedies, integrated with the pomp and circumstance that the Opéra's scale demanded. Everyone understood the story, thrilled to the dramatic spectacle, and left the theatre gratified by the dancing.

Escape into the Heavens

No matter how rickety the ride, how obvious the ropes, there is something irresistibly delightful about flying through the air. The machinery of flight, the gloire, comes disguised as a chariot or a cloud. Typically, gods use it to move between heaven and earth in order to intervene in human affairs. They step onto a platform hidden by the cloud/painting and gesture toward their destination. The cloud begins to glide across the sky/backdrop, allowing the travelers to stand in stately ensemble as they ascend or descend.

The gods appear at preposterous times. It is all too obvious that the story has dug itself into a hole from which it cannot extricate itself without aerial aid. Enter the gods, to make things right, to tidy things up. And still, no matter how dull their heavyhanded restoration of the hierarchies of status and morality, their ride to and from the heavens is intoxicating. The gloire is large but not disproportionate with the other clouds and rays of light that occupy the heavens. It travels slowly enough to underscore the dignity of those it carries and the momentous achievement of hoisting bodies into the air, but quickly enough to seem like a miracle.[1] They are flying! Even once they attach ropes directly to the character's body and pull it up through the air, the gesture of flight remains the same: the body has defied gravity and narrative.

Only good characters get to do this, or rather, it is a sign of their goodness that they have access to the air. Descent toward earth places the character at risk. Touched by, embroiled within the affairs of humankind, they may succumb to desire and its attendant passions. Ascent toward the heavens insures liberation from all that turmoil. There, in the crystalline space of pure abstraction, characters see and do only what is right. The intimation of this heavenly existence, embodied in the act of flight, secures the dramatic tension of affairs on earth.

Hercule et Omphale, Pantomime en 1 Acte (1787)

Nicole-Médard Audinot arrived on the boulevard in 1769 where he established his Théâtre de l'Ambigu Comique just next door to Nicolet's Grands Danseurs du Roi. He soon became, along with Nicolet, one of the wealthiest and most notorious producers on the boulevard, wrangling successfully with other producers and various governmental authorities for rights to produce his entertainments. For fifteen years he operated as a maverick, demonstrating his wit and ambition in a series of tactics that thwarted government attempts to restrict his programming. Beginning in 1784, however, a new governmental initiative authorized the Opéra to grant privileges that gave theatres the sole rights to produce a given form of entertainment. Anyone could now apply for a permit to present spectacles so long as their proposal was unique. Entrepreneurs came forward in abundance and, in their eagerness to qualify, set unfeasible limits on their own operations. At the same time, administrators granting the licenses hoped to improve the financial circumstances of the Opéra, so they allowed frequent overlap. As a result, competition for talent and for audiences increased dramatically. In addition, the capitalist free-for-all eroded further the class-based distinctions between grand and popular theatrical forms. Not only had the division between patented houses and fair theatres dissolved, but now even the tripartite system that ranked boulevard theatres along a middle-class scale was destabilized.

Audinot's rendition of the story of Hercule and Omphale demonstrated the extent to which Opéra and boulevard subjects could overlap. The choice of a noble, mythological subject and its lavish treatment attained a blend of spectacle and narrative coherence normally associated with action ballets produced at the patented houses. Its elevated and tragic plot occurred as part of a season that also featured rowdy satires and acrobats, a further indication that strict control over theatres' offerings could not be maintained. The one-act performance sufficiently captivated audiences that he produced a more spectacular three-act version in 1790.

The 1787 version of *Hercule et Omphale* opens with the foreign king's courtship of Omphale. His repeated attempts to woo her are met with icy rejection, and he eventually leaves, vowing revenge. The scene changes to a deserted cove on Omphale's island, where Hercule and his soldiers land and celebrate recent victories by inspecting their bounty and recounting their adventures. When they eventually fall asleep, Amour sneaks in, startles Hercule, and as he jumps to his feet, shoots him with one of his arrows. Amour then introduces Omphale, and conqueror and queen fall in love immediately, dancing out their courtship in an extended pas de deux. The jealous king, accompanied with a battalion of soldiers, interrupts the two and a turbulent battle ensues. At one point Omphale is actually carried off by the king, but Hercule, under heavy attack, frees himself and rescues her. Once the king's troops are routed, Hercule and Omphale resume their danced dialogue, swearing eternal love to each other. Again the couple is interrupted, this time by Minerva in full battle regalia with her entourage. She portrays for Hercule the glories of battle and victory, forcing him to chose between love and war. After much deliberation, Hercule leaves Omphale to pursue his true calling. Stricken with grief, Omphale seizes a sword and is about to plunge it into her breast when Amour enters and, horrified at the unhappy conclusion to his project, appeals to his mother for help. Venus descends in a chariot and graciously draws Omphale toward her. They ascend to heaven together as the curtain falls.

The 1790 version precedes the romantic encounter between Hercule and Omphale with an act of celebrations hosted by Amour at his palace. Various tableaux depict famous romances between gods or goddesses and mortals—Diane and Endymion, Jupiter and Europe, Apollo and Daphne—decoratively framed by shepherds and shepherdesses, nymphs and hours. Envy enters and conjures up an impressive storm, an omen of the events to follow, which frightens the shepherds and creates general chaos, but Amour eventually restores order. At the beginning of the second act, Amour first seduces Omphale with a portrait of Hercule, then finds Hercule asleep after his revelry and pierces his heart with an arrow, thus causing the two to fall in love. The couple's pas de deux is interrupted this time by Hercule's own soldiers, who plead with him to return to his life as a warrior by presenting his lance, shield, and helmet. Momentarily torn between two futures, Hercule finally dismisses his soldiers and returns to a triumphant Omphale. Minerva then enters and the final scene proceeds as in the earlier one-act version.

Where the earlier scenario relied on the figure of the jealous king to produce the necessary conflict, the 1790 production focused on Hercule's internal struggle for its development. In that version, Hercule, twice tempted by a warrior's destiny, played out the conflict and its final resolution at the site of his own body. Both versions were structured effectively around Hercule's indecision, which allowed the action to build in suspense toward his final departure. Omphale's grief-stricken desperation sustained the climax. The original version of the scenario, submitted to censors for approval, called for Omphale to light a torch and set her own palace on fire, perishing in the flames. Apparently, the censors determined that this level of aggression and destruction was unsuitable for public entertainment, especially given the volatile energies that must have circulated through Paris in the last years of the decade.[1] However, the felicitous intervention by Venus that resulted in a more or less happy ending garnered their approval. Even this version allotted to Omphale a terrifying rampage around the stage before turning her anger on herself.

Omphale belonged to a minor class of female characters who prefer solitude to male companionship, autonomous power as rulers of their kingdoms to shared power as the consorts of male rulers. Extreme versions of Diana, these women required considerable cleverness on Amour's part in order to be ensnared in the apparatus of love. The typical nymph-and-faun chase scenes usually resolved when the fauns' superior endurance eventually forced the nymphs, always attracted to their male counterparts, to capitulate. The seduction of characters like Omphale, because of their pride in stature, entailed less a flirtatious scolding that jostled them into their rightful place, and more a serious reprimand for having assumed the right to govern themselves. They fell—from one social role to another—in love.

GOVERNING THE BODY

> The line the centre of gravity has to follow is indeed very simple, and in most cases . . . straight. But seen from another point of view, this line could be something mysterious. It is nothing other than *the path taken by the soul of the dancer.*[1]

The street, the stage, the nation

Throughout the eighteenth century, public life in Paris shared with theatrical presentations of the time a highly orchestrated protocol. Complex conventions governed comportment on stage and in the street. In both arenas individuals engaged one another with a sense that they were acting their parts. Protocols consolidated under the reign of Louis XIV continued to guide public conduct, and even though mandated by and most evident in the interactions of an elite aristocracy, this system of regulations modulated all social interactions. It governed forms of address, bowing and greeting, and protocols of right-of-way between and among members of each social class.[2] Criteria for evaluating one's comportment included grace and ease of movement and the relaxed erectness of bearing, qualities that would become evident in one's style through assiduous study with the Dancing Master. Additional criteria addressed the various elements that composed the visual image one presented. Considerable expertise was required to ensure that the costume and trappings of one's daily life signaled the correct identity. Social life thus entailed a regimen not unlike the performer's preparation for an appearance onstage.

During the decade of the 1790s, however, the sense of public life as theatre intensified.[3] The streets became a stage as never before, and this theatricalization of public life brought with it new grounds for engaging in and interpreting public behavior.[4] (See fig. 45.) People's actions, rather than indicating the correct response for their profession and class, began to be interpreted as signs of patriotic fervor. Criteria of grace and aplomb that had been applied to the mannerliness of self and class presentation throughout the century were replaced by evidence of authentic devotion to the new France.[5] Codes of patriotism supplanted class-based hierarchies of protocol as the foundation for public

45. The opening of the Revolution Club, a satirical portrayal of aristocratic behavior and theatrical practices.

interactions between and among members of both sexes. Instead of bowing to the degree stipulated by one's own gender and class and those of the person being greeted, all citizens waved flags together and to one another. Not only were criteria for evaluating public behavior applied to both sexes and across all classes, but the origins of those criteria no longer derived from either ancient or aristocratic sources. Instead, standards for behavior, formulated consensually, originated in the human predisposition to act sympathetically, heroically, and righteously. (See fig. 46.)

These public enactments of identity destabilized the purpose and meaning of theatrical production. For most of the century, theatre-goers had viewed performances as special, concentrated, and refined versions of life. The architectural context of the theatre and the expertise of the performers clearly delineated the separation between art and life. The mass gatherings that occurred during the 1790s—political debates and protests, parades and festivals—encouraged all citizens to view their own actions as spectators in the theatre might view those of the performers. These large-scale assemblies helped to create a shifting and shiftable framework for identifying art. The dramatic, the spectatorial could be instantiated anywhere, as if the proscenium that had cordoned off art from life could now be constructed in any number of places.

The political debates held at the National Assembly, for example, cast orators in the roles of actors. (See fig. 47.) Large audiences attended daily, encouraging dramatic approaches to debate and judging the viability of proposals partly in terms of the rhetorical persuasiveness of the député's presentation.[6] Politicians, aware of these criteria, increasingly orchestrated their debates so as to appeal to the theatrical sensibilities of onlookers. They dressed, gestured, postured, and delivered their lines in imitation of the great actors at the Comédie Française.[7] Spontaneous gatherings in the streets around a persuasive orator, always a part of Parisian life, likewise took on a new intensity. Even the

46. Dancing as the head of the Princesse de Lamballe is paraded through Paris.

47. Speeches offered to the National Assembly by Women Artists, September 1, 1789.

audience members at the theatre now claimed the same theatricality for their own actions as for the events onstage.[8]

Festivals organized by the new government to commemorate the new social order imparted a similar kind of theatricality to quotidian activities.[9] On a typical festival day, the citizenry awakened to artillery fire that summoned them to participate in the day's celebration.[10] They were asked to decorate the balconies of their dwellings with flowers or flags and then to assemble dressed in revolutionary colors, carrying the appropriate props—perhaps roses for women and olive branches for men—at designated locations around the city. Having functioned as stage hands decorating the city as a theatrical space, they then assumed their roles as actors. Citizens were organized into masses, columns, or rows according to their age, sex, profession or some combination of these. (See fig. 48.) Each group, now a representative of that constituency within society as a whole, maintained a designated distance from all others. Special orderings for groups, determined for each festival, allowed the parade to arrive at the central arena in the order suitable for the general ceremonies. Once all the parades had assembled, the general proceedings cast the marchers into the double role of audience observing the main ceremony and of participants who recited, cheered, and engaged in specific actions—mothers lifting babies into the air, men waving olive branches or flags. After speeches and ritualized commemorations and oath-taking, dancers might perform a pantomimed version of events associated with the festival. Viewers looking on from a considerable distance would discern simple scenarios of despair followed by exhilarated liberation or decadent chaos transformed into the orderly enthusiasm for a new France, all gestured carefully and didactically to the rhythmic structure of the music. At the end of the convocation, the crowd would disperse after a general cry of "Vive la République," or it might process out of the arena. Following these general gatherings by the majority of Parisians, small celebrations took place in each neighborhood. Ensembles of musicians, installed outside local taverns, accompanied men, women, and children in the Carmagnole and other popular dances. (See fig. 49.)

The choreographic formulae used in these rituals to transform daily activities into public theatre were easy to conceptualize. All those engaged in the action had only to show their synecdochic relationship to the larger social whole. A man stood for all men, a woman for all women, the young or the aged for their respective degree of maturation. Devotional acts—flag planting, banner waving, the display of olive branches—performed by any of these characters pronounced the group's allegiance to the new society. Pantomimes performed by professional dancers showed how those skills of vivid depiction and eloquent, impassioned action could contribute to the building of a liberated France. The participation by each group constructed the microcosmic version of the social macrocosm. The yoking together of the various social groups into a newly invented processional order prefigured the newly ordered society. Any quotidian activity became worthy of public consideration because of its contribution to the healthy functioning of the country.

Festival organizers championed the pedagogical value of these public assemblies.[11] The arts, they argued, complemented political and juridical forms of argumentation through their persuasive appeal to the sympathetic affections of the human spirit. Because of their capacity to awaken the most elevated sentiments, the most sublime feelings,[12] the arts would best express the "reunion of an entire people."[13] The festivals would also impart

48. The first Fête de la Liberté, April 15, 1792.

49. Fête given in memory of the General Federation, July 18, 1790.

an appreciation for the workings of society, giving each participant a better understanding of the needs and contributions of others. Thus one festival enthusiast suggested as subjects for festivals the different kinds of labor—harvesting or manufacturing—that contributed to society.[14] Another patriotic entrepreneur proposed this series of festival topics to be held at ten-day intervals:

To the Supreme Being
To Nature and to the Universe
To human genius

To conjugal love
To the love of parents and children
To love of the country

To friendship
To good feelings among all men
To those who have done good for humanity

To the support of the feeble and oppressed
To the comfort of the indigent
To the consolation of the afflicted and the unhappy

To liberty
To equality
To those martyred for the rights of man

To the sovereignty and independence of all peoples
To the union of all free nations
To peace among men

To laws
To justice
To public order

To education
To morals
To virtue

To truth
To reason
To genius

To education
To sciences
To useful discoveries

To work
To industry
To arts and crafts

To antiquity
To posterity
To immortality[15]

This carefully conceived sequence, beginning and cycling back on the subject of immortality, grouped ideas together by way of underlying themes. As a participant in this cycle of events, one would learn to equate love of family and country via the theme of love; truth and genius via the theme of reasoned thought; liberty, equality, and the martyrdom of those defending human rights via the precious opportunity to exercise those rights. With the exception of four groups of people—specifically identified as *martyrs, doers of good, the afflicted* and *the unhappy*—each subject was constructed from an abstract noun that summarized all specific instances of a given type of action. Even the terms "martyr" or "doer of good deeds" collected into one heading all types of such actions. Each of these collectivizing nouns was further reified by its thematic connection to the other two.

The reasoning that informed this series of abstractions was the same as that which allowed one patriotic action to signify all patriotic actions, and one exemplary person—young, old, male, or female—to stand for that social group. In both cases an array of human actors or actions was reduced to a single form with a single function that fit into a larger whole. Similarly, art itself contributed its ability to arouse sympathetic emotions into the full system of industries and endeavors necessary to the creation of an emancipated society. Before, the theatrical arts, as specialized versions of life, had presented characters constructed from stereotypic references to class, gender, and profession as well as a palette of human emotions that denoted the state of one's feelings. Ensembles of specific behaviors, these characters represented idealized portraits of those types of people and actions found in the real world. In contrast, the heroes and heroines of the public patriotic spectacle shared with the populations they represented a single, essential quality—manhood, womanhood, bravery, magnanimity. They did not represent idealized types found in society, nor did they exemplify conduct proper to those types. Rather, they each acted so as to trace the connection between individual and society, transforming themselves into emblems of an organic social whole.

Thus the mass spectacles along with the public behavior surrounding them leveled distinctions among social classes at the same time that they suffused life with art and art with life. Members of all classes could engage in public presentation with the same intensity of commitment and the same physical expertise. Orderings for the ceremonial processions signaled a hierarchy of importance, but the sheer number of constituencies included in each parade implied more open access to a worthy social group. Attendance at the mass gatherings imparted to all participants the means through which their own extemporized gestures and even their daily activities could attain dramatic significance.[16] All citizens could instigate a Carmagnole, plant a flag, and see in their improvements to household or neighborhood the building of a new France. Any citizen could likewise demand a patriotic justification from others for their actions. The opportunity, suddenly available to all citizens, to find in any action a charismatic symbol of the unfolding new society inspired a heady, transgressive energy that swept through the streets of Paris. (See fig. 50.)

Where the theatricalization of Parisian public space exhilarated citizens with its blurring of art and life, the famous Law Regarding Spectacles instigated an equally intoxicating dissolution of categories within the institutional framework that determined theatrical production. Issued in January of 1791, this ordinance gave living authors rights to their manuscripts and entrepreneurs a virtually unregulated opportunity to produce theatrical events. Throughout the eighteenth century the three patented houses not only

50. Fêtes and fireworks on the Champs-Elysées.

maintained control over genres and the establishments that might present them, but also over plays and scenarios submitted to them. Once a proposal was offered, its author relinquished all control over when and how it might be produced. According to the new regulations, the authority over a play's presentation resided with the writers or with their offspring for fifty years after their death. Plays became public property after that time. The three main houses also lost control over the licencing of theatrical establishments. Anyone who could obtain an appropriate space and hire guards—one to maintain order at the door, and several more inside—could now open a theatre.

Dancers and choreographers, although they participated as an integral part of almost all theatrical productions in the general opening up of venues and genres, were little affected by the new legal rights for authors specified in the Law Regarding Spectacles. Choreographers authored dances by publishing either in notated form or as printed scenarios the action in ballets. Plagiarism of the actual performance, an issue throughout the eighteenth century, was difficult to prove because choreographers often used the same story as the source for their work. Independent choreographers never submitted proposals to the patented houses unsolicited, nor did the writing of the scenario constitute the real labor of their art. For all these reasons their legal rights did not substantially alter following the decree.[17]

The general entrepreneurial response to this decree, however, underscored the popularity of all varieties of theatrical presentations as well as the enthusiasm to pursue a theatrical career, an enthusiasm that embroiled choreographers, along with artists and artisans dedicated to all aspects of theatrical productions, in new experimentation. Overnight, performance spaces sprang up throughout Paris.[18] As they folded, responding to the vicissitudes of political events and individual fortunes and expertise, they were replaced by others. Producers, composers, writers, and choreographers, all eager to exercise their new freedoms, arranged upbeat versions of classic and venerable dramas. These were presented alongside the exotic divertissements and sentimental pantomimes that had long dominated the boulevard stage. The jumbling of genres within a given evening and a specific piece resulting from these entrepreneurial initiatives must have created the same euphoric response cultivated by the festivals. The boundaries between high and low forms crumbled, leaving in their place a motley arrangement of sentiment, spectacle, and scandal.

This aesthetic free-for-all endured only briefly. Successive new governments increasingly came to view theatre as an instrument for conveying social values. While they could never maintain complete control over the protean theatrical community, they nonetheless attempted to monitor offerings for the social and moral messages they contained. As early as March of 1791, the Opéra was asked to put forward a plan for revising its repertory to reflect the values of the new society. The Opéra administration's response cited appropriate kinds of works to be retained as well as deletions and alterations. Gluck's excellent music for *Iphigénie en Tauride* and *Alceste,* for example, would be preserved by composing new patriotic lyrics to accompany it. The dance's lascivious tendencies would be replaced with a new decency through the elimination of that favorite entertainment of the aristocracy—the action ballet.[19]

Ironically, many of the criteria used to assess patriotic displays such as the realistic and passionate involvement in action had been advocated by the proponents of the action ballet since the middle of the century. The pantomimic ballets presented at the Opéra and on the boulevard stage had prepared the way for public revolutionary drama through their emphasis on the individual character rather than on monarchic social hierarchies. The rhetoric surrounding the development of the genre as well as the construction of the danced stories themselves located the origin of the characters' actions in individual feeling rather than in prescribed social comportment. By 1791, however, continued support for the action ballet threatened multiple individual and institutional agendas which seem to have conspired to propose its eradication. For both the top echelon of performers, eager to return to evaluative systems based on skills at virtuoso dancing, and the Opéra's administration, anxious to reassert music's supremacy, the government's mandate offered the opportunity to reinstate a more classical aesthetic within the repertory. Furthermore, the action ballet was closely associated with Noverre, its most vocal advocate, who had been brought to the Opéra by Marie Antoinette. The Opéra staff undoubtedly felt compelled to dissociate the Opéra from the crown as much as possible, and Noverre's allegiance to the Queen served as a handy emblem, easy to forego, of royal support. At the same time Pierre Gardel, eager to secure his position as the Maître de Ballet, may have used the dissociation from the action ballet as an opportunity to deflect close governmental scrutiny away from ballet. By indicating a willingness to eliminate the story from the ballet, he promoted an image of dance as pleasant, contentless entertainment over which he could preside without further scrutiny from the government.

If the Opéra administration hoped with its response to dissociate the institution from the action ballet, it did so in name only. Productions by Gardel and other choreographers implementing the basic conventions of the genre occurred frequently at the Opéra throughout the decade along with its other programming. Highly successful works such as *Psyché* (1790) and *Télémaque* (1791) were repeated along with new ballets like *Le*

Jugement de Paris (1793) and *Daphnis et Pandrose, ou La Vengenance de l'Amour* (1794) that continued the tradition of storylines based on well-known classical myths, although they avoided tragic or heroic subjects easily associated with the nobility in favor of plots with the lighter concerns of courtship and romance.[20] (See figs. 51 and 52.) Opéra choreographers and dancers participated in these ballets at the same time that they contributed their talents to patriotic pageants produced at the Opéra and to the great spectacles and festivals produced around the city.[21]

TOP: 51. Mme. Gardel as Psyché in Pierre Gardel's *Psyché* (1794).

BOTTOM: 52. Pierre Gardel as Télémaque in his version of *Télémaque dans l'île de Calipso* (1790).

Dancers' participation in such diverse kinds of programming reflected the influence of governmental supervision on theatrical production. The Opéra, for example, underwent a radical alteration in its institutional identity evident in the patriotic pageants and pantomimes, rallies, and restagings of outdoor festival events that occurred alongside the operas and ballets. This range of activities reflected the new welter of genres and styles of spectacle offered throughout the theatrical world, but also the mandate to forge at the theatrical site a fusion of individual expressive needs with the values of the new society. Previously, events on the Opéra stage had depicted gods or kings demonstrating ideal social comportment; now they presented patriotic newsreels—action-packed sagas of the sacrifices and brave deeds of real individuals, the ruthless evil of the enemy, the triumph of good, each situated in a specific place.[22] Where before, large assemblies of singers and dancers had portrayed the powerful entourages of principal royal characters, these gatherings now expressed the common will of the people.

The Opéra, one of the most powerful symbols of the monarchy and the principal expression of its aesthetic and political orientation, underwent these revisions to its repertoire and an analogous change in its relation to the other theatres.[23] Throughout the eighteenth century legal and illegal artistic production shared as a common reference point the express desires and dictates of the monarchy. Productions at the fairs or on the boulevard were ultimately monitored through an apparatus of censors, police, and administrators at the three patented houses authorized by the crown. To present unapproved work or work that plagiarized or perverted performances held at the patented houses was to contravene the aesthetic imperatives of the king. All individual initiatives were thus measured against the forms of expression condoned by, because they best represented, the values of the monarchy. With the instigation of the Law

Regarding Spectacles, a new conception of individual expressive rights was introduced that operated at all theatrical venues. The decree created the legal space within which individual aesthetic initiatives could exist. The new government, willing to acknowledge these rights while at the same time recognizing the state's needs, was placed in the unfamiliar position of arbitrating between the two. This kept producers and artists guessing as to what would be acceptable just as it required successive governments to undertake an analysis, for which they were clearly unprepared, of art's relation to the state.[24] During the turbulent early and middle years of the 1790s, the Opéra was plunged into this negotiation along with every other theatre, regardless of its history or its offerings.

With the assertion of individual expressive rights, witnessed daily in the streets of Paris and in its theatres, models for male and female comportment underwent considerable change. In the construction of their staged characters, in their dress, and even in their assignations as performers, women and men took on highly differentiated identities. Patriotic festivals typically marked the sexes as separate units within the social whole. Each female performer represented womankind, each male mankind. Yet underlying this distinctiveness, both sexes claimed equal status as citizens of the new France, and the conception of woman as citizen underpinned radically new roles for female characters especially during the early and middle years of the decade. A number of pantomimes and plays included women engaged in the formerly masculine and now patriotic activities of fighting, protesting, and celebrating in the name of the new republic. Heroines added to their roles as loved ones and evil forces the exemplary category of citizen helping to shape and protect the emerging society. Heroes continued to exhibit the range of emotional responses developed in the action ballet that included greater pathos, more anger and despair, usually in response to the changing fortunes of the government. All members of a village, regardless of class origins or occupation, were shown united in feeling and in action. They conferred and worked together.

In many of the new productions, whose topical content and hasty construction allowed little rehearsal time, the pantomime vocabulary combined with the simplest danced steps to form the basic movement repertory. Such a rudimentary set of skills diminished gender and class differences by giving all performers a similar set of actions and responses. Satiric versions of classic dramas presented performers with similar kinds of options for making fun of the characters they played. All characters made use of exaggeration, clumsiness, disorientation, and ineptness to poke fun at the classics.

Costuming reiterated these new gender and class identities giving performers both greater uniqueness and a greater range of movement. Beginning in the 1750s advocates of the action ballet had argued for more realistic costuming, the elimination of wigs and masks, and the introduction of clothing resembling that worn in contemporary society. These changes had been introduced incrementally throughout the latter half of the century, appearing first on the boulevard stages and much later at the Opéra. Theatrical productions during the Revolution solidified these changes through the sheer number and diversity of performers with more realistic dress. They augmented this lifelike orientation toward costuming with emblems of partisanship—hats of various sorts, belts, and weapons, many inscribed with verbal messages of patriotic dedication that also featured revolutionary colors and insignia. In some productions costumes were rendered more uniform, as if to evoke mass participation. Others made use of the toga, a popular alternative to realistic dress, in order to construct images for abstract characters such as

Nature or Truth or to render the citizenry uniform in purpose. Toga-like costumes, with their specific reference to imagined concepts of classical democracy, suggested a deep and essential desire for freedom and justice on the part of those who wore them.

The new role of citizen constructed in characters' roles and in their dress was further reinforced by a change in the customary assignation for performers as printed in the programs for a given production. Throughout the eighteenth century a strict marking of gender and character had been observed in program information, where listings of performers and their roles were divided into acts and within each act into both character type and gender. The categories of nymph (always feminine) and faun (always masculine) were simply followed by a list of the Messieurs and Mesdames or Mesdemoiselles who played them. But all other categories in which both men and women could participate (e.g. shepherds, peasants, Turks, members of the court) were separated into masculine and feminine headings. Thus Bergers and Bergères, Paysans and Paysannes, Peruviens and Peruviennes each had their list of performers. For a brief period of time from 1794–98 headings for characters remained bifurcated according to gender, but performers' titles changed. No longer Messieurs or Mesdemoiselles, they became *citoyens* or *citoyennes*. This had the effect of distinguishing their membership in the state and also indicating an equality of participation regardless of gender.

By the end of the decade this convention for surnames changed again. Male performers maintained their titles as citoyens, but female performers were returned to the assignation of Madame or Mademoiselle. As represented by the program information, the opportunity to participate along with men in the polity, briefly afforded to women, was rescinded. Analogous modifications to the range of female character types and behaviors ensued. The number of active heroines diminished while those who were in need or who provided maternal nurturance increased. As quickly as women had assumed egalitarian participation in the new republic, they were excluded from it.

These changes directly reflected the failure of the Revolution to realize a new social identity for women as argued for by Condillac and other Enlightenment thinkers and as fought for by public figures such as Olympe de Gouges.[25] They also marked the beginning of a conservative restructuring of social and theatrical practices that accompanied Napoleon's rise to power. Following his coronation as emperor in 1804, Napoleon reconfigured Parisian theatres through a series of restrictions reminiscent of those legislated by Louis XIV.[26] He limited the number of theatres in the city to seven and assigned to each a distinct repertory based on a hierarchy of refinement. The new laws left intact the author's rights of ownership over the script, but constricted severely the entrepreneur's rights of production and the influence of theatre within society. More broadly, the radical claims for sexual equality made in the 1790s soon gave way to a strict division of labor along gender lines: public and private endeavors were engendered as masculine and feminine, respectively. As blatant staging of this division, fashion, resplendent in color, texture, and cut of garments for both men and women throughout the eighteenth century, lost all its flamboyance in male costuming in the earliest years of the nineteenth century. Drab grays and browns, somber and sober vertical lines, all testified to the man's judicious and serious dedication to governance, whereas the soft, flowing, voluminous and ornamented fabrics of female dress signaled a more decorative but also nurturing garb for wife and mother. The patriotic festivals had depicted just this division of social labor along gender lines in their segregation, spatially and behaviorally, of men and women. By the end of the decade, the association of each gender with specific social functions had been moved centerstage.

The immense social and political upheaval experienced by the citizens of Paris in the 1790s produced no immediate or palpable effect on the development of the action ballet. No governmental decrees deprived dancers of work, and none challenged the viability of dance as an art form or its usefulness to society. The transgressive equation of art and life and the collapse of hierarchies of taste and genre did not result in radically new choreographic forms. Yet the postrevolution restructuring of society created an entirely new backdrop against which the action ballet was danced. Public space, masculinized and lacking the florid displays of comportment that distinguished eighteenth-century sociability, tucked theatre indoors. Outwardly, all bodies began to display the stoic composure that had been prescribed for those on their way to the guillotine.[27]

Muscular geometry

While social and artistic life in the 1790s and early 1800s underwent turbulent change, scientific inquiry into the bodily origins of human identity moved incrementally forward. The joint efforts of doctors, anatomists, and aestheticians pinpointed with increasing precision the muscular configurations and degrees of muscular contraction that produced a given display of feeling. Following the work of German anatomist Johann Caspar Lavater and also that of Felix Camper, scientists linked both emotional responses and moral predispositions to precise physical mechanisms.[28] Anatomists founding the new science of phrenology similarly traced the origins of character type to a specific shape and size of the body and the head. The science of anatomy also searched for evidence of sexual distinctiveness at ever more interior bodily locales, eventually focusing on the skeleton—the core, the hardest physical structure—as the ultimate indicator of essential difference.[29] This drive to determine exact correlations between body structure and behavior also motivated the work of rhetoric and acting theorists, who established increasingly detailed codes for expressive posture and gesture.[30]

The new anatomical studies continued the eighteenth-century tabularization of knowledge at greater levels of anatomical detail. For example, Charles Bell's *Essays on the Anatomy of Expression in Painting* reported on languor, faintness, laughter, sorrow, joy, discontent, suspicion, remorse, wonder, astonishment, fear, terror, horror, despair, and madness, each with the degree of detail evident in this description of rage:

> The expression of human rage participates of both of these [muscles used in animal rage]; the corresponding muscles of the lips and nostril, producing a similar action with that of animals; an exposure and gnashing of the teeth; a degree of sparkling of the eye, and an inflation of the nostril. And of a face under the influence of such action, a spectator would infallibly say, that the aspect is perfectly brutal, savage, and cruel. But when the Corrugator Supercilii, a muscle peculiar to human expression, is brought into action, the sign is altered. The eyebrows are knit, the energy of mind is apparent, and the mingling of human thought and emotion with the savage and brutal rage of the mere animal.
>
> In man, the action of the frontal muscle, and Corrugator Supercilii, and of the orbicular muscle of the mouth, bestows a greater latitude of expression; and if in

addition to the action of these muscles, instead of the wide drawn lips, and the exposure of the teeth, as in the rage or bodily pain of animals, the mouth is half closed; the lips inflated by the action of the circular fibers, and drawn down by the action of the peculiarly human muscle, the Depressor Anguli Oris, there is then more of agony of mind than of mere bodily suffering; a combination of muscular action of which animals are incapable.[31]

The drawings accompanying Bell's text showed the skin peeled away, the musculature in action. Passions, organized into two great classes, the painful and the pleasurable, were separated by the state of indifference. Within each type, the description of a given passion included formulae for the addition and subtraction of muscles that would produce an adjacent passion.

Like Le Brun's text from nearly a century before, Bell's anatomy provided a taxonomic ordering of passions, yet the quest for greater and greater precision in identifying muscular involvement, and the objective scrutiny given to the face in particular, laid the foundation for a new distinctiveness based on function. Certain muscles were unique to humans and appeared to have no other function than the production of a given facial expression. Certain facial expressions unique to humans communicated the capacity to think and feel. Members of each racial group exhibited shared but also distinctive profiles of physical traits that rationalized the differences in temperament, just as humans bore certain similarities to and differences from animals. The functions of the male and female, infancy, youth, and age, all could be typed according to physical characteristics exhibited:

By anatomy, considered with a view to the arts of design, I understand not merely the study of the individual and dissected muscles of the face, or body, or limbs; I consider it as including a knowledge of all the peculiarities and characteristic differences which mark and distinguish the countenance, and the general appearance of the body, in situations interesting to the painter or statuary. The characters of infancy, youth, or age; the peculiarities of sickness or of robust health; the contrast of manly and muscular strength, with feminine delicacy; the appearances of diseases, or pain, or of death; the general condition of the body. . . . all these form as necessary a part of the anatomy of painting as the tracing of the muscles of expression in their unexerted state, and of the changes induced upon them as emotions arise in the mind.[32]

Like the revolutionary fêtes of the 1790s that identified by function the social types necessary to a healthy society, and like Engel's functionalist distinction between linguistic and paralinguistic behaviors, Bell's anatomy proceeded to correlate categories of social and physiological characteristics based on the function that each performed.

Research on the structure of the human skeleton paralleled the lines of inquiry established in the anatomy of the passions.[33] Since the inception of anatomy based on real-life observation, female skeletal structure had been drawn and analyzed primarily from male skeletons. The basic structural features of both sexes were thought to differ only in relative size, with women cast as diminutive versions of men. Only toward the end of the eighteenth century did anatomists begin to use actual female skeletons as the basis for their observations. Their increasingly detailed comparisons led to the recognition of bone-deep differences between the sexes, differences that could only be accounted for by a functionalist explanation: the width of the female pelvis, the relative smoothness of bones, the pyramidal structure of the skeleton as a whole—all confirmed woman's function as child-bearer and nurturer, whereas the breadth of the male shoulder girdle and the size of the cranium supported his calling as worker and decision-maker. As Bell put it: "Women, like children, have the skin smooth, but the limbs round, polished, and pyramidal. This proceeds from the muscles being less powerful, and the bones less prominent than in man, and from the fat being in great proportion and filling up all inequalities."[34] And these differences, Bell explained, accounted for the contrasting performance styles of male and female dancers:

> Violence of gesticulation is indelicate, if not unnatural, in females, and detracts from their beauty. This strikes us strongly in the necks and limbs of Opéra dancers. That which is beauty in a young man, is deformity in a female. The nymphlike lightness of a female dance, which so much charms the eye at a distance, loses much of its grace and beauty, when, the figure advancing, the movements are perceived to be accomplished with violent straining and muscular action. This soon must destroy the natural beauty and symmetry peculiar to the female form.[35]

Studies such as these established the functionality of the body's various parts, and they also gave it a palpably objective identity. The identification of common expressive characteristics in humans and animals enhanced the perception of the body as material object by focusing on the flesh and bones common to both. The scrutiny with which each joint or muscle group was examined imbued human physicality with a concreteness and tangibility it never before achieved. Eighteenth-century anatomy retained a proximity between body and soul that endowed the body with unpredictable mutability. Its fluids moved precipitously; its muscle fibers reverberated with soulful sonorousness. New studies of the body, in their assiduous detail, expanded the divide between muscle and passion, constructing of the one an objective and material realization of the other.

The rigorous scrutiny exhibited in anatomical studies was equally evident in regimens developed to improve dancing. Preparatory exercises developed in the late eighteenth century—ronds de jambes, pliés and relevés—were supplemented with dévelopés, beats for the feet, and ports-de-bras. Combinations of basic positions and movements between them formed routines, each requiring several repetitions. The use of a barre running along one wall of the room at waist height facilitated the repetition of these routines by stabilizing dancers as they exercised one side of the body and then the other. Where the leg swings, pliés, bends, and portes-des-bras elaborated distinct spatial trajectories for body parts, the numerous repetitions challenged each part to extend further in all directions.[36]

The simpler stretches and bends that opened the eighteenth-century class had been designed to lubricate the body for dancing. The new pedagogical approach fortified, corrected, and extended the body's parts before it danced. Thus the system of preparatory exercises, rather than dancing itself, took on the responsibility for eliminating bodily defects. Teachers increasingly relied on anatomical knowledge to enhance and justify their pedagogical approach. Their written observations reflected an even more detailed acquaintance with muscular and skeletal structures. Prescriptions for correct alignment and execution of movements were cast in terms of detailed enumerations of physical features. The analysis of classic defects, such as the knock-kneed and bowlegged tendencies in the legs, also used the language of anatomy to describe both the problem and the recommended remedy, as in this analysis of bowleggedness by Dancing Master Carlo Blasis:

> He who is bowlegged must work continually to separate those parts which are too close together; the best method for success is to turn the thighs outwards, and to move in this direction while profiting from the freedom of movement of the rotating femur within the cotyloid cavity of the pelvic bones. Aided by this exercise, the knees will follow in the same direction, and will return, we might say, to their proper place. The patella which seems destined to limit the falling back of the knee joint, will realign itself perpendicular over the center of the foot, and the thigh and the leg no longer straying from the line will then draw a straight alignment that will assure the firmness and stability of the torso.[37]

A thorough knowledge of muscular and joint actions, as they conformed to and were guided by a simple geometry, could produce impressive results in the repatterning of ungainly or defective body parts. Training had become a science.

Early nineteenth-century training regimens gave the musculature a new and prominent role in maintaining correct alignment.[38] Where eighteenth-century postural pedagogy had relied on the corset as a corrective device that would prop the body up, and late-eighteenth-century teachers assisted individual students with the process of aligning bodily regions, the new pedagogy identified in the system of muscle groups the capacity for the body to erect itself. The corset, an exterior container that would mold the body, could now be replaced by the body's own discipline. Each of the body's regions, no longer conceptualized as blocklike sections to be pulled or twisted to conform with the others, potentially manifested the interior strength to accomplish alignment, and the repetition of exercises imbued each muscle group with just that strength.

Muscular strength permitted the body to pull together around a central core and thereby resist the destabilizing and disintegrating effects of gravity. Social dancing master J. H. Gourdoux reflected both the increased use of anatomical language in describing the body and the new organization of body parts in this argument for the centrality of good posture to good dancing:

> The bottom of the foot is the real base upon which all the weight of the body is carried; but it is the waist that controls uprightness and facilitates the execution of dancing. One cannot be a good dancer without being firmly aligned over the pelvis: if one abandons this it is impossible to sustain a straight line; one risks each moment the danger of losing the center of gravity. . . . The dancer who is well-aligned at the pelvis must show a chest that opens according to the shoulders' movement, and a positioning of the head slightly back: the chin should be slightly pulled back under the jaw.[39]

The maintenance of a central and core organization for the body not only helped it remain agile and at ease, but also provided assurance and strength of character:

> The effects of this art on the physique of certain individuals are extremely interesting; let us paint a young person of feeble temperament whose education has been

neglected; the head will naturally protrude forward, pressed into the shoulders, the chest sunken, the knees crooked and bent, the feet turned in, the body constantly waivering, failing to preserve a center of gravity; but see this person leave after six months of lessons under the tutelage of a good master, with the feet turned out, the hamstring stretched, the hips well placed, the chest forward, the head proud and gracious, the arms released forward, and the movements easeful.[40]

53. Drawings of correct bodily alignment with limbs encapsulating ideal lines, from Carlo Blasis's *Traité Elémentaire, Théorique et Pratique de l'Art de la Danse.*

The core served as a guideline for the assessment of postural and character problems as well as determining the ideal placement for the body at rest or in motion.[41]

Exercises for distinct bodily regions—arms, legs, torso—helped to draw the body toward a primary core, and they also helped to establish a core for each bodily region—an ideal line each set of muscle groups was to encapsulate. (See fig. 53.) The principal line, extending from the head down through the feet, replicated itself in secondary lines running from the center line out along arm and leg bones to the periphery. Eighteenth-century Dancing Masters had typically alluded to proper alignment by comparing the body's silhouette to an ideal outline. They measured the body's alignment against a set of lines running alongside its parts. Now the musculature wrapped around these lines, embodying rather than gesturing toward them.[42] The lines conveyed their existence even as the body was disciplined by them. Carlo Blasis published the clearest indication of the linear core that guided the body's presentation in his *Traité Elémentaire, Théorique et Pratique de l'Art de la Danse.* Numerous drawings of dancers illustrated the desired versions of basic positions and steps. The geometric relations among limbs and torso were indicated by a dotted line located close to the bone and extending the length of the limb.

The lines were designed to encourage those dancing and those evaluating the dance to see, embedded in the flesh, circles, lines, and angles of varying degrees.[43]

Not only did the body contain a new interior organization governing the positioning of limbs and torso, but it was also given a new framework for its orientation in space. The basic vocabulary of positions now enumerated distinct types of facings for the body—composites of arm, leg, torso, and head that regulated the possible variations on arabesque and attitude positions as well as all poses that initiated or concluded sequences of traveling steps. As the leg extended to the diagonal front or back, the torso twisted slightly to face the audience creating either an open or closed sense of the body's contours. Or else the leg gestured directly to the side, presenting a vertical body of uninterrupted lines. The facings, by providing the pivotal connections between all virtuoso steps, constituted a kind of grammar for the sculptural presentation of the body. They underscored the body's significance, for dancers and viewers, as a volume defined by the skin's surface whose shape changed as it moved through space.

The new pedagogical approach permitted a larger number of students in the class at the same time that it enabled a closer monitoring of each student's progress. Classroom exercises, effective and efficient in their cultivation of the body, assured all diligent students improvement by offering a standard format for execution with clearly specified attributes for each movement. The teacher well-versed in the ideal bodily posture and range of movement could track each student's accomplishments and provide critical commentary on the rate of improvement. Blasis went so far as to propose a new system of notating basic exercises that employed stick figures to delineate the desired shape of the body for each position. Likening his notation to an alphabet book, he argued for its dual efficiency: it increased the teacher's effectiveness by providing objective criteria for improvement and also afforded students the opportunity to study on their own at home.[44]

As students advanced in their command of the general exercises done in a large group setting, they were encouraged to begin work on individual stylistic development conducted in coaching sessions where dancers worked alone or in small groups with a famous teacher. In these tutorial sessions students learned to refine their execution of basic movement and also to model those movements for use in a particular dance. By practicing actual dances, usually composed by the teacher, they cultivated an individuated version of the teacher's style. Unlike the eighteenth-century tutorial instruction which identified early in the training process an appropriate genre for each dancer, students now trained in the same basic repertoire regardless of their constitutional and behavioral propensities. The study of dancing thus differentiated between a foundation of standard movements and an ornamental stylistic adaptation of each body to the standard.

Many of the teachers, even as they participated in the new pedagogical approach, lamented the demise of the three genres.[45] André Deshayes, a venerated teacher employed by the Opéra school, struggled to revive the three-part classification system claiming that it held the key to improving the quality of dancers' performance.[46] In correspondence with the Opéra administration, he evaluated as mediocre the current level of skill attained by dancers.[47] The training system, by not accommodating differences in physique, might produce featured soloists effectively, but could not fashion a uniform corps de ballet. Because it required students of all sizes, shapes, and proclivities to master the same generic material, it reduced each student's potential achievements. Those favoring a return to the genres refined the definition of each not only in terms of character types but also precise physical measurements. The new scientific apprehension of the body permeated their arguments. Each body's physical characteristics could be appraised and matched objectively with the most suitable genre.

Yet try as they might, the genre system was moribund. The sheer number of steps, the lists of competencies, the ever-expanding criteria for excellent dancing swept up students and teachers alike in pursuit of a genreless perfection. Everyone attended to

> placing the students, turning them, and paying particular attention to their pointes; opening out, and especially extending completely their knees; watching scrupulously to see that the movements of the head, those of the arms and movements of the body are in perfect harmony with the steps performed by the legs no matter how difficult they are.[48]

The training process immersed students and teachers in series of incremental adjustments that indicated a correct or incorrect trajectory for bodily improvement. The body's parts, more segmented and scrutinized than ever, had to be coordinated into a single pleasing assemblage.

Although anatomical studies had begun to verify bone-deep differences between the two sexes, male and female dancers continued to share much of the same vocabulary, to train according to the same guidelines, and to be accorded equal status.[49] As in eighteenth-century ballets, female dancers performed softer and more diminutive versions of the same steps that male dancers executed with aggressive brilliance. The quality of attack, height of the leg, or shaping of the arms differed slightly, but the same standards of grace, dexterity, and precision applied to both men and women. Partnering began to explore more complex entwinements of male and female bodies and featured more lifts of the female dancer than before. The novel use of pointe work—balances and steps performed on the ends of the toes—occasionally displayed by female dancers introduced the possibilities of a radically distinct repertoire of steps and competencies. Its appearance, however, fleeting and inconsequential, did not alter the tandem trajectories of dancers of both sexes.

The intense focus on training the body to master steps overshadowed study of the other principal element in the performance repertoire—the pantomime vocabulary. Although recognized by all those involved in the production of ballets as an integral competency for the dancer, pantomime classes were offered sporadically and only by private teachers. The 1807 review of the Opéra regulations undertaken by Napoleon's regime identified pantomime as a necessary component of dance training to be incorporated into the Opéra school curriculum.[50] As late as 1842, however, students submitted a petition to the Opéra administration protesting the poor quality of teaching and citing the absence of pantomime classes as a major grievance.[51] A few teachers in Paris focused on postures and gestures from the tradition as part of their classes, but for students unable to study with them, the only recourse lay in observing the Italian dancers who had received extensive training in pantomime and imitating their execution. Still, a dancer's chances for a successful career with only minimal expertise in pantomime far exceeded those of a dancer with only pantomime training. Ballet choreography afforded substantial opportunities for corps dancers to play soldiers, foreigners, peasants, or courtiers, roles that required only modest acting skills.

Evaluation of proficiency at pantomime reflected the same predilection for objectified, measurable criteria as those used in appraising skill at the vocabulary of steps. Critics' reviews of performances repeatedly emphasized the thrill of seeing such realistic portrayals of human feeling and action. This review of Jean Aumer's 1808 production of *Cleopatra* was typical in its praise of the vividness of the pantomime sequences:

> but what ensures the brilliant success of this work is the combination of the rarest artists to whom the mimed portions have been entrusted.
>
> Mlle. Chevigny is a really astounding artist in this style; her features are the faithful mirror of the passions which succeed one another with incredible rapidity; no one can express tenderness, jealousy, spite, hate, and contempt with greater truth and force. . . .
>
> Vestris, already known and distinguished in the same art of depicting the passions with movements of the face and body, surpassed himself. . . . Struggling with remorse in the midst of pleasure, dying a victim of his follies and debauches, Vestris knew how to depict in turn conjugal love, paternal tenderness, the transports of passion, the intoxication of joy, and the depths of sadness and despair.[52]

Each passion produced its own unique visual imprint. The science of duplicating these tensile shapes, advocated by Noverre and so many others, had now achieved the status of a familiar and expected component of the production. Viewers noted their energetic yet nuanced execution more than their inclusion per se within the realm of performance.

The distinctiveness of danced steps and pantomimic gestures was strikingly evident in dance enthusiast Auguste Baron's opening definition of the art:

> One has defined dancing as a sequence of steps guided by the music and accompanied by diverse movements of the body. Dance, natural in humankind, has existed in all times and all places. In its beginning, it was, like gesture, the manifestation of interior feelings; a silent language which, through attitudes, jumps and movement, expressed pleasure or sadness, anger or tenderness, affliction or joy. Little by little these simple and disorganized movements became more ordered and more controlled; imitation, that principle of the arts, took hold of them, combined them, transported them on to the stage; and the sketches, at first cruder and unpolished, but with time more refined, enlarged, and perfected, presented finally the most correct design, and the most brilliant colors.[53]

No longer the mirror of the soul as every eighteenth-century text had asserted, dancing now consisted of a sequence of steps. Its identity rested less in its ability to manifest interior sentiments than in its concreteness as a physical event. Its history as a physical spectacle consisted in the increasing orderliness of its steps and the clarity of its imitation.

Like the steps of which the dance was composed, the body that performed these steps, that assumed the revealing postures and delivered the telling gestures, had a kind of solidity absent from its eighteenth-century counterpart. Where eighteenth-century dancing had cultivated the body's capacity to shape the space through which it moved, early-nineteenth-century training procedures and dance vocabulary imbued the body—the entity encompassed by the skin—with volume so that it was perceived as a sculptural whole whose shape changed as it moved. Volume was created, in part, through the relationship established during training between an abstract set of lines embedded deep within the flesh and the surface shape of the body. It was also inherent in the new grammar of positions coordinating facings and extensions for all body parts. This volume gave the body an intrinsic interest when viewed in relative isolation from other bodies and from the space surrounding it. Space, as the medium that partnered dancers' movements and dancers' bodies so as to create an articulate tracery, mattered less now than space as the substance within the body through which it organized itself.

Virtuoso docility

As Parisians settled into the revisionist policies determining public life in the early nineteenth century, a whole host of entertainments became available that replicated in range and variety their eighteenth-century ancestors. (See fig. 54.) These spectacles offered diversion from the work of social and economic restructuring demanded in the wake of social unrest at home and aggressive military campaigns abroad. The govern-

54. Acrobats entertaining passers-by in front of the Théâtre des Variétés.

ment had allotted to each theatrical venue a specific genre of entertainment so as to maintain hierarchies of taste and refinement, although individuals moved frequently across the divides from one genre of entertainment to another. The patented houses fulfilled their mandate to produce high art, classic works, and new pieces that met

55. Charles Mazurier in two poses from the Théâtre de la Porte St. Martin production of *Polichinelle Vampire* (1823), by Frédéric-Auguste Blache.

classical standards, on a grand scale. The boulevard theatres continued to merge the sentimental and satirical (see fig. 55), but specialized in the sappy yet exhilarating melodrama. Circuses and hippodromes staged animals, acrobats, and casts of hundreds in naval battles or volcanic eruptions, sensational historical epics, or tightrope ballets.[54] (See figs. 56–58.) In addition to these entertainments, vaux-halls and parks around the city proffered relatively inexpensive divertissements that attracted spectators from all social classes.[55] Masked balls, held after hours at the Opéra or at other locations throughout the city, allowed costumed spectators from all walks of life to promenade past and intrigue with one another. Gardens on the outskirts of the city hosted evenings of dance where the public could listen and dance to different orchestras, procure comestibles at surrounding concessions, and be entertained by fireworks or other special displays.[56]

The emphasis on physical accomplishment, the training of the body as implement to virtuoso physical display, pervaded this eclectic assemblage of entertainments. At the hippodrome viewers could see stunning feats of skill performed on horseback, on the tightrope, and by groups of acrobats whose balance, flexibility, speed, and dexterity defied imagination. (See fig. 59.) Over the course of two or three hours, both male and female performers would undertake a progressively more challenging series of exercises or acts, tracking the body through its paces. The sequence of tasks tutored the spectators in the hierarchies of difficulty so that they could better appreciate the performers' skills. At the Cirque Olympique staged battles between armies of horsemen, heroines precariously stranded atop small mountains, floods and lightning storms threatening the lives of all characters—all put the body through rigorous paces. These epic tales specified distinct

56. The "abduction of the beautiful stranger" on horseback.

57. Mme. Franconi as "Fate."

58. A young American resting atop his horse, and a clown in thought beneath his galloping horse.

59. The Forioso family performing a contredance on four tightropes.

roles for each sex, yet the physical jeopardy was shared by both. The costuming and scenic effects bolstered the action, allowing the intrinsic appeal of these productions—their cycles of suspense and resolution produced as the body attempted one breathtaking challenge after another—to work its thrilling effect.[57]

The appeal of these productions lay not only in their spectacular cultivation of physical danger and prowess, but also in the conception of an objectified body they purveyed. The jumble of professional, hereditary, and economic allegiances that informed social affiliations in the first decades of nineteenth century provided little solidity upon which to base rules for comportment or conversation, much less an evaluation of art or entertainment. New social classes, no longer schooled in a homogeneous canon of artistic, literary, or political sources, could not utilize the forms of discourse, either spoken or gestured, that had helped govern social interaction in the past.[58] In the search for new occasions and formats for interaction, they saw in these entertainments the display of a seemingly neutral and egalitarian set of competencies and of criteria upon which to evaluate success. The body, as a kind of individualized blank mass available for rigorous training, lay beneath each of the spectacular and virtuoso performances they witnessed.

Nowhere was this enthusiasm for complex physical patterns successfully executed more evident than in social dance practices of the period.[59] (See fig. 60.) Public dances held around the city acquired a regular yet diverse clientele. Private social gatherings among bourgeoisie, nouveaux riches, and aristocrats featured dancing as the central activity of the evening. Hosts and guests, never assured of topics in common or even of the means to perpetuate a genteel conversation, invested in dancing as a means of passing time. The hosts made sure to invite the most prestigious dance instructors, whose participation in a single

60. Early-nineteenth-century social dance enthusiasts whose devotion to dancing is referred to as "dansomania."

dance ensured the party's success. The guest artist's decision to perform at the ball would be based on an assessment of the technical competence of all those dancing—the same criteria used by everyone present to evaluate their own relative merit.

Some dance instructors noted the shift in values from graceful aplomb to virtuoso expertise and mourned the loss of dance as a system of social parlance through which individuals could make claims about their specifically aristocratic identity. J. H. Gourdoux, for example, condemned the Revolution for the terrible loss of a tradition of elegance and amiability:

> [T]he lightness within its movements, the civil manners, amiable and gracious, the charming graces that had been developed to such a high degree of perfection during the beautiful days of France, were, in this disastrous time, held back by some, unknown to others, and replaced among several with a deformed and grotesque tone, very different from French gallantry and urbanism. . . .[60]

Not only had the Revolution obliterated or severely constrained the practice of gallantry, but it had also emphasized a crude materiality. As Gourdoux pointed out: "one only saw the material aspect of the art which defaced all its graces and charms; the public looked then toward theatrical dance and one payed attention to it as a single means to distinguish oneself in society, and the methods of the older masters were ridiculed."[61] In the absence of societal recognition for the discursive power of dancing, standards for evaluating proper social dance skill came to be set by the virtuoso style of the theatrical dance repertoire.

The vogue for dancing and the quest for expertise prompted many students to take up study with professional ballet instructors to acquire control over the body and an ability to manage movement comparable to that achieved through professional training. Instructors of both theatrical and social forms, however, discouraged the practice, arguing that the two had little in common.[62] Both demanded speed, sophisticated coordination, and stamina, but their vocabularies and stylistic demands now differed radically. The repertoire of social dances contained no entrechats, dévelopés, or pirouettes—hallmarks of the theatrical dancing body's capacity to jump, balance, and extend its parts into space. The wide variety of contredances and the equally popular three- and five-step waltzes featured patterns of small, complicated steps, sequences combining *pas de gavotte, balancé*, and *pas de rigaudon*, that formed intricate rhythmic patterns in contrapuntal accord with the music.[63] In executing these patterns, dancers in no way approximated the grand style of address—the ostentatious self-presentation evident in the size of steps, the exaggerated clarity of each motion, and the dancer's outward gaze—required of those who performed on the theatrical stages.

In the early years of the nineteenth century, complex patterns of footwork for social dances developed rapidly, assuming far greater importance than the spatial paths along which dancers moved.[64] Eighteenth-century contredances had privileged elaborate sequences of geometric floor patterns that challenged dancers to remember both locomotor path and relative distances among all dancers. The early-nineteenth-century versions increasingly focused on manipulations of legs and feet, simplifying the spatial paths so that dancers could attend to what was beneath them. It was this need for deft, detailed pattern execution that drew eager young students of social dance toward the theatrical tradition, yet the arm and leg pairings of the ballet and the extension of body parts in space had little applicability to social forms.

Social dancing called for demure simplicity, an unpretentious and genteel delivery. The rules of etiquette during and between social dances reflected a new economy of proper behavior. "Proper" meant steady, upright, well-coordinated, and nonextraneous. Bodies eagerly displayed their knowledge of the "do's" and "don'ts" that framed the social event with the same prompt directness shown in the steps. This straightforward style had little in common with the sense of composure that had linked eighteenth-century theatrical and social forms. Eighteenth-century dancers signaled neither too little nor too much and, in so doing, referenced their knowledge of the full range of codes for bodily comportment through which the nuances of identity could be communicated. Their moderated and mediated movement appeared as the perfect combination of control and naturalness. Early-nineteenth-century dancing bodies, conforming to appropriate movement, signaled instead their eager self-control. They minded their manners rather than participating in the fluid kinesthetic dialogue produced by an ensemble of bodies.

The rules established for behavior on or off the dance floor created an environment conducive to proper interactions among young people of the two sexes. Dancing Masters and bourgeois parents agreed that evenings of dancing offered one of the best occasions for controlled encounters among those just entering society.[65] Young adults could converse and dance with one another under conditions that encouraged convivial yet regulated comportment. The contredances enabled participants to survey the glamorous ballroom as they exchanged places with many other dancers. The waltzes produced a giddy euphoria, a slightly disorienting dizziness, held in check by the scrutinous gazes of all those watching the dancers. The occasion thus encouraged a certain exuberant sociability at the same time that it exerted forceful controls over each body's actions.

Just as dancing facilitated social interactions through its standardized criteria of accomplishment, so it enhanced the proper growth of the body through the measurable improvements it promoted. Dancing Masters had long made a claim about dance's contribution to graceful comportment, bodily appearance, and bodily health. Early-nineteenth-century social dance manuals continued to praise dance for its ability to enhance bodily attributes, but the focus of their claims shifted away from proper ways of moving and toward correct treatment of the body. Dancing Masters more strongly than ever encouraged the study of dance as a form of physical exercise that would ensure a more responsive and pain-free body.

Dancing's contribution to health was also taken up by instructors in the new discipline of physical education. This scientifically informed approach to maintaining bodily health recognized in dance a thorough and gentle program of exercises, especially suited for the female constitution. Of all those in need of a physical regimen to enhance bodily health, women of the middle and upper classes ranked highest. Of all the forms of exercise designed to address their needs, dance presented an ideal profile. Its emphasis on grace and lightness accorded with the generally delicate proclivities of feminine physical structure.[66] As G. P. Voarino, author of *A Treatise on Calisthenic Exercises*, put it:

> it is no exaggeration to affirm, that nine-tenths of the diseases, under which the female sex are suffering, are principally brought on by insufficient and too frequently total inattention to this important part of the animal economy: as a proof of this we need only look to the female part of the laboring classes of society, to whom disease is comparatively unknown, unless produced by vicious habits or severe privations.[67]

The body, although relegated to the status of "animal," nonetheless deserved a certain cultivation. Voarino proposed a simple series of activities—marching, skipping, crossing the legs in place, bending the knees, arm circles—that could be done with a cane or with the aid of a trapeze and were designed to increase strength and flexibility and energize the constitution. Dancing shared with these exercises the same capacity to condition and invigorate the body.

The discourses that promoted health, grace, and improved social status through dancing all emphasized the discreteness of each individual's body over the rapport generated by ensembles of bodies moving together. Lightness and ease, no longer features of a style of sociability, were identified as desirable ornamentations to one's individuality. What the study of dance as well as the occasions for dancing offered was the opportunity to increase one's ability to manage the body and then to display its robust docility.[68] Although its gentility aligned dancing with more feminine pursuits, members of both sexes enthusiastically conquered the complexities of its demanding repertoire.

The docile body produced by social dancing found a compatible partner in the theatricalized body of the melodrama, perhaps the most popular of all entertainments of the period.[69] Like the spectacular physical jeopardy produced at the circuses and hippodromes, the body in melodrama endured endless challenges. Like the well-managed display of physical expertise seen on the social dance floor, the melodramatic scenario required the body's zealous conformance to the dramatic action. The melodrama combined vivid scenic display and special effects with sudden and unanticipated interventions, reversals, discoveries, and intense struggle among characters. Storylines prolonged suspense through their elaborate variations on chase scenes, their endless confrontation between wickedness and purity. The strongly dichotomous world in which the action was situated encouraged a violent lurching between the just and unjust, between rejoicing and despair.

Most typically, melodrama located the forces of good and evil in a young virgin and a vicious villain whose relentless pursuit of the helpless heroine precipitated the spectacular scenic changes, the breathtaking escapes, the hyper-real display of passions.[70] Moments of accord between the heroine and her family or her sweetheart exploded into menacing chaos as the villain or his henchmen unleashed their latest scheme. The physical and mental torture wrought by the villain or sometimes by a natural disaster was unspeakable. The dire circumstances of innocent victims rendered them mute. They could only gesture their horrified apprehension of the injustice of events. Their bodily response thus secured a new and privileged place for gesture. Only gesture could express adequately the human experience of the sublimely awful.

By shifting into gesture at these critical junctures, melodrama helped to consolidate a new, dichotomous relationship between words and movement, the kind of relationship that Engel's analysis of gesture had anticipated but never fully established. Not only did gesture become the universal language of which Diderot and others had dreamed, but it also conveyed a special authenticity. It transcended all cultural boundaries and required no tutelage; but it also betokened a genuine state of feeling. The extremity of the actor's situation demanded unique acknowledgment. The fact that gesture was called into play at these moments defined its unique function. Where words could dissimulate, gesture could only reveal the truth.

As in Enlightenment theories of gesture, the movements and positions of the mute character were intended to awaken in the viewer an immediate, empathetic response to the crisis. Yet in its earlier use, movement, in the form of pantomime and gesture, had constituted a form of discourse itself, an alternative to verbal language that would offer a medium of communication apart from that of verbal dialogue. In many productions at the boulevard theatres, for example, movement was endowed with the ability to criticize or satirize conversation. In some cases it figured as a clandestine form of parlance through which the oppressed characters could construct a united response to tyrannical power. By the early nineteenth century, however, movement was called upon only in those moments when events extinguished speech. As such, movement no longer opposed verbal discourse in its practice, but in its essence.[71]

This essential difference between movement and speech, far from disintegrating the performance, enhanced its coherence. The action, rather than encompass two forms of communication at play simultaneously among different formations of characters on stage, was now carried by a single form of discourse whose metamorphosis from words into gesture underscored the most sublime moments. The transition from moments of speech to silence proved especially compelling. Viewers were asked to focus in on the action and attend to a new, nonverbal set of codes. Such a shift helped vary the intensity of the production, but even more important, it drew viewers into the drama by lending a sense of depth to characters' lives and struggles.

The melodrama unified its audience with a call to respond empathetically to the plights of characters. More lighthearted, satiric, or even farcical productions, such as those found on the eighteenth-century boulevard stage, had evoked a less homogeneous reaction. Productions that had poked fun at normative behavior cultivated a stance of resistance. Because they did not summon up any coherent alternative forms of social interaction, but rather elaborated varieties of deviancy, they united the audience only in noncompliance. The melodrama, in contrast, worked to fuse audience members' responses around the drama of dire situations, extremities of suffering that were reminiscent, perhaps, of events during the Revolutionary years.[72] Menaced by the villain, weeping with the heroine, and finally buoyed up by the happy conclusion, viewers moved along the narrative together. Their wet-eyed speechlessness, like the characters', forged linkages among all those present and created the basis for their assimilation into postrevolutionary society.

The surge of feeling constructed in the melodrama's moments of speechlessness depended upon the contrast between dialogue and movement. Speech surrounded the nonverbal tableaux and gestures, specifying precisely the circumstances that would motivate the characters' muteness. No such partition of functions existed for the action ballets. Productions sketched out the predicaments and tribulations of characters through pantomime and stage action and then focused in on moments of intense feelings using the same vocabularies of movement. They also incorporated long sections of virtuoso dancing that asked the viewer to attend to entirely different physical and theatrical values. Where the melodrama used movement to embroil viewers in the experience of the excruciating, the action ballets blended types of movement—expressive gesture and physical tour de force—with grace and proportion. The results were neither so suspenseful nor so extreme.

Nonetheless, this young art form emerged in the early years of the nineteenth century more popular than ever. The idea of the danced story itself retained a certain novelty, and the potential variations on standard plots with their charming possibilities for costumes and settings seemed endless. Now over an hour in length, the ballets were still programmed alongside operas, operettas, or other diversions to form the full evening's entertainment. The dancing that occurred within the operas and the ballets that followed continued to attract the most devoted attention. Fueled by the popularity of social dance and the new interest in scientific regulation of bodily movement, viewers attended ballets to see what the fullest disciplining of the body could yield.

The virtuoso body endowed the choreographer as the organizing force who invented and staged its display with a new recognition. Throughout the eighteenth century, the term "choreography" had referred to the process of transcribing a dance into notated form and to the notated score itself. The art of arranging the steps, implicit in the notated result, did not receive the attention that the carefully documented and transmittable score did. The art of making dances had no name. With the programmatic commitment to the action ballet and the objectified view of the dancing body, the term "choreography" slowly began to change its meaning so as to reflect the labor and artistry entailed in the crafting of dances. New appreciation of the craft necessary for the creation of the successful story and spectacle gave the term new meaning: "Here is the moment to say a word about choreography, this art not only of notating the steps and figures of the dance, simple technical expressions, but of putting into action all the riches of pantomime, of composing for this mute language a story, a plot, an intrigue, a knot, and an ending."[73] Dance-making, no longer transparently equivalent to the act of writing, implemented a unique, if mute, system of communication. Drawing from this system, the choreographer fashioned the entire progression of danced events. It now implemented its own mute communication system.[74]

The new tactics of scientific measurement used to train the body and to study the passions seemed to advance the performance of both classical steps and pantomimic gestures, yet it also created new distance between the two. Where mid-eighteenth-century solos featured a single well-placed pirouette and, perhaps, two short series of entrechats, dancers now eagerly displayed chains of five and six turn pirouettes, each with a different shaping of legs and arms.[75] They also relished the opportunity to demonstrate their competence at extended sequences of cabrioles and entrechats. But none of these movements carried the plot forward. Still, both dancing and expressive action could share an evaluative system based on vividness and precision that derived from a scientific interrogation of bodily movement, and the overall framework of each ballet provided ample opportunity for both. The entire ballet thus consisted of semidiscrete segments of each type—pantomime scenes *en action,* and virtuoso *pas* for variable numbers of dancers.

The segments en action developed the pathos of the situation to a fever pitch, with characters elaborating every nuance of angst or joy over a period of several minutes. Pas presented the skilled accomplishments of a soloist, a pair, or group of dancers often linked choreographically to a scenic device that supported the story in some way, such as the bamboo used in Jean Aumer's *Les Deux Créoles*:

> It tells of adventures so moving, offers tableaux so striking and so varied, that, if it suppressed three or four of its *pas,* it would be no less successful, for each situation is adroitly introduced, all the scenes are full of effect, and the catastrophe is skillfully contrived. . . . There is little dancing because everything is in action from the first act to the last; nevertheless, the *pas nègre* in the first act, which was perfectly executed, was much applauded. M. Sevin, who leads this troupe of negroes, was noticeable for the strength and skill with which he managed the bamboo. It is one of the best combat scenes on the boulevard.[76]

If presented in excess, either the en action or pas segments could undermine the buoyancy and momentum of the entire production. The fact that each functioned so distinctively, however, was not viewed as a potential compromise to the work's integrity.

What was deemed important for overall coherence was the construction of characters with clear and strong motivations. Choreographers no longer debated the need for the ballet's scenario to be taken from a well-known literature or drama. Often, they worked from a plot that had been adapted in recent memory for performance as a melodrama. Composers enhanced the tracking of the plot by incorporating tunes from well-known operas or musicals whose lyrics addressed analogous themes. Even the most familiar stories and situations, however, often required modification to ensure a lively choreographic translation. Louis Milon, for example, found it necessary to introduce a new character, Amour, for his production of *Héro et Léandre,* as he explained in the preface to his program :

> The effect produced by a reading or by a dramatization, of the charm of an easy-going and harmonious play, of a natural and delicate style, of ingenious ideas, all expressed

with energy and enthusiasm, this effect, I say, is uncertain when one hopes to transport to the soul only via the eyes, the impressions that it habitually receives via the attentive ear. Nevertheless, the subject of the love between Hero and Leander offers a situation so touching that it seemed to me capable of inspiring a real interest by putting it into action without borrowing the help of a well practiced pen, and the talents of an orator.

In presenting [this story] in its historical simplicity I was afraid that it might become monotonous. I tried to give it a more amiable tone and a dramatic progression by adding some allegorical episodes that connect to the various scenes without altering the truth of the story.

[The character of] Amour that I introduced, and that plays a principal role, seemed necessary to activate the affection that it generates within Hero; to bring about the incident when he remembers, with an allegorical dance, the triumph of Venus judged by Paris to be worthy of the prize that Juno and Pallas wanted, thereby giving greater credibility to the mythological means that, in the end, return the lovers to life and happiness.[77]

In his effort to rival the effect of literary versions of this myth, Milon determined that the introduction of Amour not only provided credible motivations for Hero's actions but also lent overall coherence to the production by reinforcing its mythological context.

Frequently, scenarios for the ballets reported introspectively on characters' thoughts and feelings. Passages in the text might summarize a character's state of mind with an interior monologue whose detail could help interpret but certainly not achieve a choreographic equivalent. In Pierre Gardel's *L'Enfant Prodigue*, for example, the protagonist was depicted as deliberating over his fate in these terms: "Each instant seemed to him the last of his life. What was to become of him? Alone in a desert, without help, repelled by the entire world; wandering without aim, without hope, betrayed by his friends, an ingrate, forsworn, disgraced; all these ideas overwhelm him at once!"[78] Choreographers understood that any dramatic action entailed a staging of the psychological states of characters involved. Where a single character's status was in question they sometimes made use of props or scenic elements in order to indicate that character's indecisiveness, longing, or dread. Other times the sequence of postures, the changing focus of eyes and head, the nuanced gesture alone could create the necessary portrait. By elaborating on the specific feelings in the program descriptions, choreographers could prepare viewers to comprehend a given tableau as well as its contribution to the overall narrative structure.[79]

As the story ballet attempted and assimilated different types of narratives, these variations on individual characters' situations seemed to thrill viewers most. Monologues in movement summoned up the private world of the character's inner thoughts and feelings. Like the gesture in melodrama, these soliloquies exuded an arresting authenticity. Yet it was not simply the representation of the passions that appealed to viewers, but rather the virtuosity of their enactment. The renowned dancer Emilie Bigottini (see fig. 61), for example, never distinguished for her expertise at the classical repertoire of steps, nonetheless astounded audiences repeatedly during the first two decades of the century with her poignant and subtle renderings of female heroines' angst. Highly successful ballets like *Paul et Virginie* (1806), *Nina* (1813), and *Clari* (1820) provided the female heroine especially with the opportunity to display a full range of passions produced either by internal romantic conflict or external dire predicament. Again, as in the melodrama,

61. Albert and Emilie Bigottini in Albert's *Cendrillon* (1823).

the female character served as convenient locus for the bulk of the pathos, although male principals also underwent moments of self-doubt and joined heroines in scenes of intimate confession or longing.

In order to unify pas and en action segments and also to justify the amount of pure dancing desired by viewers and dancers for each production, the plots continued to take shape around a festival, a soirée, or some ceremonial event where dancing would normally occur.[80] In historical ballets like Aumer's *Les Amours d'Antoine et de Cléopatre,* dancing occurred as part of processions, pageants, and festive dances performed for the royalty. Exotic ballets like *Les Deux Créoles* could draw on the supposed customs of foreign lands to present their versions of native ceremonies and festivals. Domestic ballets, often situated in the country, could make use of local village celebrations as well as incorporate upper- and middle-class balls and family festivities. These scenes rationalized the presentation of solo, duet, and large group dances throughout the ballet, even as they enlivened the production with large-scale, glamorous activity.

The overall look of a production was determined to a certain extent by its venue.[81] Following Napoleon's decree, the action ballet was restricted to the Opéra and the Porte Saint-Martin, although smaller theatres may have defied the law to experiment with the form. If so, they would have participated in a hierarchy of aesthetic values that reserved for the Opéra the most refined and for the Porte Saint-Martin cruder versions of ballet productions. Differences between productions at these two houses are evident in the *Journal de l'Empire* review of Aumer's *Les Deux Créoles,* which it claims is nothing but a burlesque rendition of Gardel's *Paul et Virginie* produced at the Opéra earlier the same year:

> Virginie, at the Opéra, is decent and modest, although lively and spirited. At the Porte Saint-Martin Theatre, this Virginie, under the name of Zoe, is cold and foolish, but much less scrupulous regarding propriety; she lightly accepts the attentions of an unknown colonist whom she meets by chance; it is true that her intentions are good; for it is in order to rescue an unfortunate negress that Zoe engages with him.
>
> As for Paul, so simple, so innocent, and so well brought up by Mr. Bernardin de Saint Pierre, here, in *Les Deux Créoles,* he is a little libertine, enterprising and determined, called Theodore. . . .
>
> At the Opéra it is a Negro who flees with his two children to escape his master's cruelty; at the Porte Saint-Martin, it is a Negress with a single child. The Opéra neglects the incident of Paul's portrait, which Virginie carries next to her heart; at the Porte Saint-Martin some importance is attached to this sentimental trifle; but one great difference between Paul and his associate Theodore is that Paul is a man and Theodore a woman; although that woman is Mme. Queriau she does not sustain the illusion, and the love of one woman for another is hardly touching. . . .
>
> One noticed, it is true, in the ballet at the Porte Saint-Martin more Negroes, and more beautiful Negroes; more devotions; more prayers and genuflections; more caresses and embraces; more agitations, more movements and disordered pathways; the tableau of the young lovers is far more exciting; the storm makes more of a clamour; Zoe remains in a faint longer at the edge of the sea; she has more difficulty in regaining consciousness: these are the only advantages that I noticed in Aumer's composition. But the ballet at the Opéra seemed to me immensely superior in terms of its taste, its precision, justice, and the elegance in both the design and the execution. . . . In short, Aumer's ballet is to Gardel's as the Porte Saint-Martin is to the Opéra.[82]

The review suggests that performances at the two theatres could be distinguished along class lines by their choice of character and the representation of that character's conduct. The Porte Saint-Martin production ignored the hero's noble disposition in favor of bourgeois entrepreneurial capabilities. And it likewise crafted a heroine whose behavior lacked the demure signs of good breeding. *Les Deux Créoles* also depicted class-specific customs, such as the wearing of the locket, that cultivated the sentimental over the stoic. The choice of the Negro mother over the father was likewise designed to raise the level of pathos beyond what the reviewer deemed appropriate for middle- and upper-class spectators.

Even more outlandish, Aumer's production featured a woman *en travesti* playing the role of the hero. At the boulevard theatres the travesty dancer, always identifiable as a woman playing the role of a male character, introduced a risqué and farcical element that offset the sentimentality of the plot. At the same time, the exceptional quality of her acting often eclipsed the awareness of the dancer's sex, as this review of Mme. Queriau's performance indicates:

> Few pieces have been played with such a cast, and in one only, that of *Jenny,* does Mme. Queriau display as much talent. In *Les Deux Créoles* she plays the part of Theodore, and invests it with all the warmth, abandon, and pathos of which she is capable. I do not know how she can support so many shocks. As the climax approaches, at the moment when she appears exhausted, she seems to acquire new strength.[83]

Because a woman played the role, the hero's capacity for feeling extended much further; she could invest the acting with greater passion. But if the hero displayed an unusual degree of warmth, the actor showed an exceptional physical strength. The male role demanded more action and stronger gestures than the typical female character would sustain. The travesty role thus presented simultaneous disruptions to the integrity of both actor and character that could be interpreted in several ways. Viewers could marvel at the woman masquerading as a man, or they could find in the performance a transgressive challenge to normative gendered behavior.

This kind of complex characterization and ambiguous message could not be tolerated at the Opéra, with its high and serious standards for the caliber of art. Consistently more conservative and resistant to change, the Opéra cultivated its reputation for presenting pure forms—the most virtuoso dancing, the most refined characters. The rowdier boulevard theatres, willing to experiment with the latest technologies (such as gas lighting) and with hybrid characters and plots, offered the most options for diversified entertainment. Even their programs, however, no longer maintained any strongly subversive agendas. The body, dominated by scientific inquiry, and its movement, happily assimilated into organic opposition with speech, no longer functioned as mediums for conspiring against and contesting dominant values.

Whether at the Opéra or the Porte Saint-Martin, the bourgeois domestic comedy was the most popular of all the story types. Plots ranged from the sentimental to the farcical, from the traumatic exercising of ruthless power to the inept display of misguided judgment. They usually centered around the familial conflict generated by the daughter's conduct in a romantic relationship and her choice of a potential spouse. Parental preferences for improved wealth or status through marriage initially prevailed, but the heroine, an inexperienced innocent, eventually won out, proving herself to be an excellent judge of character who could do no wrong. The intrinsic goodness of her love triumphed over social constraints, forcing protocol to accede to love. Often, the plight of a servant or friend replicated the structure of relationships among principal characters, creating a comic diversion from the sincere heroine's predicament. Plots usually included three or four such strata of characters, whose various enterprises resulted in a proliferation of simultaneous stage action—spying, conferring, escaping, discovering—throughout the course of the performance. No matter how dire their situations, characters found their problems felicitously resolved by the end. Unlike opera or drama, the ballet could not embrace tragedy. Dance's essential joyousness precluded a morbid or mournful conclusion. The number of pas segments and the unquestionable desirability of ending the ballet with general celebratory dancing could never be accomplished using a tragic plot.

Early nineteenth-century choreographers' and historians' publications registered this new function for dance, at once more specialized and lighthearted than eighteenth-century conceptions.[84] Their writings often located dance's origin in feelings of delight and joy rather than in the full range of passions of which the human being was capable. They also depicted dance using terms that emphasized the pleasurable,[85] the charming,[86] and the gay.[87] Their definitions of dance, epitomized in the following introductory observations by Dancing Master E. A. Théleur, focused on the pleasure of dancing and watching dance:

> There is little doubt that Dancing derives its source from pleasure and gaiety of heart, for instinct teaches us, as in all the animal creation, when we are delighted, to express

> our *allegresse* by laughing, singing, and by different motions of the body and its members: our features become animated, our eyes more brilliant—they express our inward feelings, and joy lifts us as it were off the ground: we demonstrate our happiness by clapping our hands and throwing our body into diverse positions, sometimes bending, then jumping, etc. In fact, gesticulation and motion are the natural consequences of joy; and this is dancing in its *primitive state.*[88]

Reworking Louis de Cahusac's 1757 sketch of dance's primitive origins, Théleur emphasized the capacity of the lighter emotions to produce buoyant, aerial movement. Like other writers of the period, Théleur intimated a unique role for dance as expressive of effervescent emotions. Dancing held rapturous appeal for performers and viewers alike.

Eighteenth-century writings had tracked dancing from Hebrew and Egyptian religious rites, through Greek and Roman theatres, to the court entertainments of the late Renaissance in order to justify contemporary concerns. Nineteenth-century texts offered only a cursory recitation of dance's past, one that betrayed their lack of interest in historical choreographic practices.[89] Dancing, that most charming and voluptuous of the arts, needed no agenda of reform. It now verged on perfection, not because it realized classical values, but because it had begun to develop scientifically the body's graceful prowess. Fortuitously, in recent times, dancers' understanding of the body had produced brilliant advances in physical accomplishment—multiple pirouettes and entrechats, elaborations of steps with various facings and in different directions, complex new pairings of shapes for the arms and legs. Although writings still contained admonishments against the mechanical and sterile display of physical skills, the ability to perform brilliantly this astonishing new repertoire held intrinsic satisfaction. These steps lifted the body upward, swirled it around, and drew it buoyantly from side to side. They made dancing look like joy felt.

Governing the body politic

With the new emphasis on physicality, as imitative art and as virtuoso display, dance lost irrevocably its connection to a generalized physical sociability. Dancing became one of several physical pursuits that developed specialized bodily skills, rather than a foundational undertaking that ensured a graceful performance in society and a healthy integrity in life. Dancing on stage no longer maintained a connection via social dance forms with the rhetoric of social comportment. And even social dance practices provided a diversion from, rather than a medium for, social action. Dancing as the celebration of shared physicalized values through which individuals discovered and defined identity no longer existed. Instead, dancing showed what one's body could do.

The body, scrutinized by scientific inquiry, was becoming an object to maintain and control. The very fact of a new discipline of physical education devoted specifically to the exercise of the body for health underscores the extent to which the body now functioned as neutral implement. Incapable of achieving any social standing on its own, it served the subject by staying healthy and displaying its skills. The action ballets depended upon two kinds of these physical skills—the virtuoso execution of positions and steps, and the equally demanding depiction of passionate, pantomimic action. In order to promote these skills, dance pedagogy developed new scientific approaches, at once more generic and specialized in their treatment of the body than earlier training procedures. Through dance training the body learned to erect itself by building a muscular infrastructure that supported, just as it created, volumetric space within the physique. Defined by the lines running along the cores of torso and limbs, the body's volumetric interiority provided a location, even a kind of origin for, passionate expression. By giving the body autonomous separateness from all other bodies and, at the same time, a sense of depth, dance training rationalized the sentimental soliloquies upon which characterization in the ballets depended.

These mute testimonials, like the melodrama's use of speechlessness, reverberated with the opposition between virtuoso dancing and passionate action, and also with the essential difference between speech and movement. Dancing, rather than a discursive practice through which a full range of thoughts and feelings might be articulated, now manifested the paralinguistic vicissitudes of, specifically, the lighter emotions. Pleasurable, spectacular, buoyant, and endearing, dancing diverted more than it instructed. Throughout the eighteenth century, categories of evaluation that identified theatrical production as entertainment and edification endured as distinct yet reconcilable features within a given work. Now, a subtle realignment of aesthetic values began to parse artistic attributes in dichotomous opposition. Dancing was coming to resonate more and more with the mute, the decorative, and the feminine.

The choreographic synecdoches of the revolutionary spectacles helped to establish the foundation for this new alignment. Just as society synthesized the unique contributions of men, women, old, and young, so dance provided that experience, unique among all the arts, of tasteful, lighthearted, and graceful bodily presentation. Just as women supervised domestic endeavors because of their essential capacities to nurture, dance, among all physical pursuits, provided the ideal form of exercise for women because of its intrinsic moderation and gentle thoroughness. The most recent findings in the science of anatomy supported these distinctions through their verification of bone-deep differences between the sexes.

The construction of newly gendered activities and newly responsive bodies met the changing needs of the body politic. As the hierarchies of heredity and patronage, religious affiliation, and profession crumbled at the end of the eighteenth century, new mechanisms of political control moved in to maintain the social order. These mechanisms required each body in particular and gendered bodies in general to hold themselves in the places allocated to them. Exoskeletal structures provided by church and court were thus replaced with individuated endoskeletons which each citizen necessarily learned to control. Nowhere was this reconfiguration of the body politic more evident than in the codes of conduct, even the definitions of public and private spaces. In the eighteenth century, a theatricalized display of sociability, replete with a range of ornately orchestrated responses by one individual to another, dominated public space, whereas nineteenth-century sociability revolved around the careful minding of one's manners. Each individual, rather than negotiate collective codes for proper social comportment, exuded a mastery over his or her own body. The better one danced, the more industriousness and control one displayed.

Just as the mid-eighteenth-century action ballets had opened the stage space to a more individualized vision of society, so the early-nineteenth-century ballets provided a singular model for how, precisely, such control might be exerted. First, the action ballets individuated both physicality and emotionality. Individuated characters were imbued with an interior and private emotional life and an exterior and skillful public body. Then their enactment of either passionate feeling or virtuoso dancing evidenced the same facility at implementing the body for public display. Each character in the danced story functioned uniquely to make plot and spectacle cohere. Dancing showed how to exert control over the body in order to narrate individual subjectivity and social activity. Viewers, in order to apprehend and be moved by these stories, necessarily constituted within themselves the same subordination of physicality to a narrativized subjectivity as that which the dancers displayed.

Interlude

The Magically Inscribed Message

Let us imagine that it is impossible to express certain things in gesture, and that the story requires some guiding pronouncement that explains or motivates the ongoing action. When this need to buttress the stage action with additional information presses hard on the narrative, a solution in the form of a magically inscribed message often appears onstage. This message clarifies the identity and intentions of characters, or it purveys the will and judgment of the gods. It can announce events or newcomers, or pronounce the horrible fate of any who would dare to transgress its command. Or it can enunciate an overarching thematic for the piece against which actions are measured.

The message appears like a beacon piercing the long minutes of bodily gestures with succinct clarity. Words can be so specific. Its luminous power also derives from the clever way in which it is revealed. Often some sliding or revolving panel emblazons the message across a previously opaque and seemingly unchangeable surface. The mechanical ingenuity of this contrivance renders the message adorable. Its power and authority as a verbal statement give it punch.

The narrative pivots once the worded message is unfurled. Characters take on new resolve, their actions a new momentum. Whether the message has posed a threat or promised a secure future, everyone now knows what to do. Are its words really of a higher order? One that everyone can so easily obey? Not really. Outside the theatre, even in the program notes, words have gained the final say over images, sounds, or movements. But here on the stage, surrounded by gesticulating bodies, they appear as quaint, as arcane, as any theatrical contrivance. Bodies may momentarily jump to, respond assuredly, but soon they will reengage their own self-propelled causalities. The words' presence, static and plain, eventually loses command.

Les Royalistes de la Vendée, ou les Époux Républicains, Pantomime en Trois Actes (1794)

Like many ambitious young artists in the 1790s, Jean Guillaume Cuvelier de Trie took encouragement from the radical opening up of dramatic production ordained by the 1791 Law of Spectacles and inspiration from the revolutionary scenes played out on the streets of Paris and reported from the countryside. His pantomime *Les Royalistes de la Vendée* adapted the all-good and all-evil characters conventions from boulevard productions, with their melodramatic actions and tableaux to people and situations of the contemporary political moment. Produced at the Théâtre de la Cité, one of the more enduring in the constantly changing panoply of theatrical establishments, *Les Royalistes* marked the beginning of a successful career in popular entertainment that spanned four decades. Most of Cuvelier de Tier's scenarios, numbering over three hundred, include long sections of scripted dialogue interspersed with rip-roaring action—battles conducted on horseback, large processions of troops, fireworks displays, battles at sea.[1] *Les Royalistes'* clearly structured action, while it may have used some dialogue to crystallize key concepts—the villain's challenge, "surrender or die," and the hero's response, "death"—probably entailed very little speaking.

Animated, highly sentimental, and didactic in tone, the scenario for *Les Royalistes* began with an address to "the People" which established its author's credibility as reporter at the scene: "I saw and I wrote for myself. . . . the most frightful scenes that my feeble hand attempted to trace out have been replicated in all hearts, the hatred of tyranny and fanaticism! may the clouds of blood that gather round our heads soon dissipate into well-meaning rays from the sun of Liberty!"[2] This kind of delirious evocation of a utopian future resulting from the pursuit of liberty was used more and more frequently by authors as they attempted to build their reputations as artists and as patriots. It set the stage for the newsreel-like action that followed.

Act 1 of *Les Royalistes* opens on the public square of a village in the Vendée. It is a celebratory moment: the Representative of the People honors Léon for his courage in battle, and Privat, father of Rose, announces the betrothal of his daughter to the young hero. The general festivities have just commenced when the sound of a cannon interrupts, signaling a surprise attack by brigands. The stage empties as the villagers rush into battle and then refills with small skirmishes, each group chasing after the other in turn. Privat corners the Capucin royalist, forcing him to surrender and plead for his life. Disdainful of the Capucin's groveling attitude, Privat leads his prisoner toward the Maison Commune. Surreptitiously, the Capucin draws a sword from the cross he carries and fells Privat from behind, leaving him to die at the foot of the Tree of Liberty. Rose rushes into the square in response to her father's cries, but is immediately grabbed by the Capucin. Léon, in attempting to rescue her, is seized by the Capucin's henchmen. Although vanquished, the brigands retreat with the two lovers as captives. Léon's friend Romain dresses in the attire of one of the fallen brigands and rushes after them.

Act 2 finds the lovers chained, Rose stage right and Léon stage left, to the walls of a darkened prison cell. The exhausted couple try desperately, repeatedly, to attain the comfort of each other's arms but find themselves cruelly placed just out of reach. They sink to their knees and pray to the Être Suprême. The sound of a trumpet marks dawn and the arrival of Rudemont, leader of the royalist brigands. He demands their acceptance of the white hat signifying both surrender and allegiance to the royalist faction. The couple proclaim their willingness to die rather than betray the republic, and Léon stomps on the hat that has been offered to him. Rudemont, enraged, orders a firing squad for Rose. She bears her breast to him, crying "Vive la République." This dramatic tableau dissolves with the entrance of the Capucin, who claims he will convert Rose. She repulses his attempts at seduction, choosing her own honor over the opportunity he offers to save Léon's life. In final desperation, she summons her last strength to shove the Capucin away and ring the bell for help. An aging woman jailer arrives, to whom the resentful Capucin entrusts Rose. Romain in disguise enters the cell and passes Rose a gun while the old woman is looking away. As soon as he leaves, Rose forces the jailer to unlock the door, kills the sentinel on guard, and escapes. The Capucin's expression of fury upon seeing the empty cell closes the act.

The final act, set in the countryside, begins as Rose, fleeing from the brigands, encounters Romain still in disguise. Terrified that she will be recaptured, Rose is reassured when Romain takes off his white hat (*cocarde blanche*) and rips it into pieces. They hide in the nearby woods as the royalist band arrive with Léon in chains. The Capucin orders a bonfire built around Léon. Having accomplished this task, the brigands, hearing patriots in the distance, enjoin the Capucin to leave, but he orders them to stay. Patriots burst in, and the brigands flee. Rose runs to Léon in the middle of the flames and releases him. Rudemont comes after her, but she turns on him, drawing her gun, and forces him to surrender. The Capucin approaches from behind and disarms her. Léon attacks the Capucin as Romain kills Rudemont. Léon, preparing to kill the Capucin, sees the Representative of the People surrounded by brigands and runs to help him. The Capucin then hides himself in the high branch of a tree. With the last brigands dead or fleeing, the patriots begin to celebrate. As they congratulate one another, reenact key moments in the battle, and dance the Carmagnole, the tree branch supporting the last villain cracks, conveying the Capucin toward the rushing stream and, presumably, his death.

In the middle of the 1790s many of the productions in Paris theatres dealt directly with issues pertaining to the political upheaval. Classical texts, as well as newly created divertissements, continued to be presented, and many required modest revisions in order to secure their political legitimacy. New works representing contemporary social events likewise needed a clear explication and reinforcement of patriotic ideals. *Les Royalistes*, with its didactic use of symbols and the extreme choices it forced upon hero and heroine, fulfilled all criteria for patriotism. The royalist cocarde blanche, for example, was not only stomped underfoot but ultimately shredded into "a thousand pieces." The Tree of Liberty, centerstage, provided majestic support for the community and solace for the individual in act 1, just as its counterpart in act 3 divulged the presence of evil and carried the villain to his doom. In terms of human actions, the decision to betray the republic or die was a standard dramatic confrontation throughout the decade and always elicited the same positive response. A similar choice found in the boulevard theatre repertory asked protagonists to sacrifice their own lives or situations for the well-being of a loved one. *Les Royalistes* cleverly conflated these two decisions by forcing the heroine to choose between saving her lover's life and preserving her patriotic honor. Her instantaneous championing of country over person sent a resoundingly patriotic message to all viewers.

Cuvelier de Trie constructed for the heroine of *Les Royalistes* a remarkably active role. By proclaiming allegiance to her country over her lover, Rose asserted an identity distinct from her definitions as daughter or mate. Rather than await or defer to a male character's actions, she readily escaped from jail, killing a guard in the process; rushed into a sea of flames to rescue her lover; and pulled her gun a second time in order to disarm the lead villain. As a woman fighting side by side with all other republicans, Rose signaled the preeminence of citizenship over gender. This kind of egalitarian participation in the plot, which was replicated in the program's listing of male (citoyen) and female (citoyenne) performers, marked the realization, however brief, of utopian conceptions of gender equality.

Both genders participated in the same vocabularies of movement for *Les Royalistes,* which emphasized actions such as running, chasing, sneaking, and fighting blended with didactic contestations. Dancing occurred briefly in the betrothal celebration at the opening and in the Carmagnole at the end. Only one dramatic scene, that between the couple enchained in the prison, offered the opportunity for an extended display of sentiment. Here, in the interior space of the cell, the truest feelings of Rose and Léon were poignantly revealed. Authenticating at the deepest level their patriotic fervor, the storyline could then return the action into the larger public spaces. This movement from large-scale to interior and back to an even grander scene served as a highly effective strategy for organizing scenarios throughout the nineteenth century and even in a ballet like *Petrouchka.* It demonstrated in the most simple way that what was in one heart could signal emblematically the contents of all hearts.

To Throw Oneself in the Arms of (Se Jeter dans les Bras)

Whether she has just fought alongside her lover and triumphed over the enemy or stood anxiously by awaiting the outcome of his efforts, at the moment of victory, at that second climax in the music, she throws herself into his arms. This action entails a light yet pulsional run, the head thrown back, the arms reaching ardently forward. Or does the head swing sideways as the arms open out? In whichever way she navigates through the resolving scene, she indicates that her established identity, as active combatant or as passive yet isolated observer, is untenable. The power of what she has witnessed can no longer be borne by her body alone. She requires a larger, more powerful figure in whom she can invest her being.

This may be the first and only moment in the ballet when two bodies are squeezed together into a single form. In earlier duets partnering involving lifts or closely entwined arms has kept the two bodies in motion sliding across or gliding around one another. In the fervent climactic moment, however, the two bodies stick together forming a single, static, vertical icon. His arms enfold her; their bodies press together and upward. Occasionally, it is not this man, the object of her desire, her destined mate, that she runs to, but rather her mother or even her father, both sustaining, all-knowing, long-suffering figures. Here the bodies appear more huddled together, sucked into the fused vertical stance by a sudden revelation of the direness of things, and not their rightness. Yet these are not climactic couplings but intermediary dyads, as the hero has not yet rectified things.

Throwing oneself horizontally onto the bank of grass, one transforms feelings into dreams, sleep, or simply unconsciousness, whereas by throwing oneself into the arms of the other, one gives those feelings over to that other. The heroine, thus emptied, remains vertical yet insensible. The hero, never lacking in passion, sustains the horizontal force of her arrival, assimilates the excess of feelings she brings with her, and stands taller than ever.

La Dansomanie (1800)

Having survived the enormous political and social strife of the 1790s with his job intact, Pierre Gardel worked hard to concoct a production that would delight and also reassure Opéra-goers at the turn of the century.[1] *La Dansomanie*'s incredible success can be traced to his canny selection of a rich and highly amusing subject, one that supported a wealth of comic action but that also resonated with deeper aesthetic concerns.[2] With images of public performances such as the guillotine and the raging crowd all too present in memory, and with the title "Citoyen" still attached to male performers in the Opéra program, many Parisians found both solace and diversion in this domestic comedy about the inept bourgeois gentlemen from the country who loved to dance. His character provided a brilliant resolution to the growing tension between virtuoso dancing and the mime required for storytelling because an obsessive passion for dancing guided his every action. Yet the comical pitch of the plot also contained a reflexive commentary on ballet itself and its quest for virtuoso perfection. The ballet thereby made fun and fun of itself, a doubling of wit that appealed to everyone.

La Dansomanie opens on balletomane M. Duléger, whose very name means "of lightness," devotedly practicing his steps as his wife, partisan to the romance taking place between their daughter and a young colonel living opposite the chateau, entreats him to discuss the possible marriage.[3] Servants and valet negotiate his dancing in an attempt to serve tea. The young couple, signing to each other from their upstairs windows, meet as parents exit and dance a *pas de schaal*, a popular kind of pas de deux that incorporated a long scarf. M. Duléger's Dancing Master arrives to teach him the latest steps, and the daughter, caught up in the lesson, dances the fashionable gavotte with him. Her colonel then enters to ask for her hand in marriage, but when the father interrogates him as to his expertise at the gavotte, he confesses his ignorance. Permission is denied. Flabbergasted at the father's response, the mother, Dancing Master, his assistant, and the young couple plot a performance that will bring the father around. In the meantime, peasants from the nearby countryside offer to perform their dances, and act 1 concludes with a series of popular *savoyards* in which Duléger perseveres with his incompetent attempts to dance. In act 2, the Dancing Master, his assistant, and the colonel—disguised as potential suitors from China, Turkey, and the Basque country, respectively—arrive in gaudy procession and announce a dancing competition to determine the daughter's future husband. The father, ecstatic with the fuss created around dancing, selects the Basque after all three have performed, only to discover he has been duped by the entire household. A good sport about the deception that allows both father and daughter to have their way, he requests celebratory dancing as the daughter runs to embrace her colonel.

The production's wit reverberated on several levels, not the least of which was premier dancer Auguste Vestris's own spoof of himself dancing the role of the colonel. Auguste, son of Gaetano Vestris, performed his appellation "Diou [sic] de la Danse" both onstage and off.[4] He had dazzled audiences for years with his accomplishments at turns and at jumps with beats and also with his arrogant and extravagant behavior in public. The "Pas de Vestris" whose steps the Dancing Master attempted to teach Duléger originated as one of the solos Vestris choreographed to display his talents. Shoes acquired by Duléger from a traveling salesman at the end of act 1 were inscribed with Vestris's name. The fact that

Vestris in the role of colonel responded negatively to the father's queries about his expertise at dancing would have added yet another layer of levity to the young couple's second-floor schemings and to the competition among the three suitors to determine the best dancer.

Dialogues between daughter and colonel, wife and Dancing Master, and servants and peasants occurred frequently at the periphery of the stage, while the father's bumbling pursuit of balletomania took centerstage but in a world apart. His consistently inept execution of steps, such as his floppy-footed entrechat, contained references to the regimen of dance training and the criteria for correct execution that remained accessible to viewers simply because he looked so silly. His obliviousness to those around him produced a second kind of humorous stage business as servants and family deftly accommodated his monomaniacal actions. Yet a third kind of humor issued from moments when he could be brought to focus on the group, as this review of the production relates: "everyone begged M. Duléger, who found even his son, hardly five years old, on his knees in front of him. Yet all that catches Duléger's attention in this group is the fact that the child's foot is insufficiently turned out, and he runs to correct this fault."[5] This kind of preoccupation with bodily appearance could be reiterated in innumerable ways, and it also conveyed a good-willed critique of ballet's narcissistic scrutiny of bodily form.

Milon's *Pygmalion*, produced at the Opéra the same year, also afforded the opportunity to reflect on the art of dance, yet its lofty focus on the arduous process of art-making contrasted sharply with *La Dansomanie*'s gentle satire of the making of a dancer. *Pygmalion* charted the lesser known depths of interior motivation, whereas *La Dansomanie* concerned itself exclusively with the pragmatics of presentation. *Pygmalion* exported the creative act to a timeless locale, the atelier, in order to claim the universal significance of artistic creation, whereas *La Dansomanie* specified the countryside for its action as a way of enhancing both the credibility and humor of its characters' actions. Only a country gentleman could manifest such simultaneous extremes of zeal for and incompetence at dancing. His Dancing Master, inevitably in arrears of Paris fashion, would likewise aspire but fail to achieve Parisian standards. Even the extravagant dances by the foreign suitors with their garish costumes and grandiose gestures worked as a believable burlesque because they were performed by provincials. These gentlemen had, after all, heard only secondhand of the exotic appearances by dancers from other countries, to which Parisians had long been accustomed.

The countryside locale for the ballet also defused any tensions that references to social or class-based identity might produce. The fact that the instructor toured the provinces softened the connotation of aristocratic entitlement that the role of a Parisian Dancing Master would carry. Inhabitants of the countryside, construed as generic bourgeoisie or beguiling peasants, could pursue dancing as a sign of gentility uncontaminated by class hierarchies. In a utopistic microcosm of domesticity where even the familial discord between father and daughter resolved itself through the charming display of dancing, the ballet displayed the simple aspirations of these provincials as a map to social and individual success.

Duléger's devotion to dancing guided and regulated all characters' actions so as to provide a consistent rationale for dancing. Via his balletomania, dancing suffused the entire story, and this coherence relieved viewers of the burden of justifying any outbursts of steps. Continuous eruptions of dancing, representing the exotic, the countrified, the polite, and the virtuoso, playfully teased one another. The humorous ability of multiple and various instances of dancing to comment on one another gave dance itself a kind of sophisticated awareness of its own vital strengths and its forgivable weaknesses. Duléger's insistence on dancing made everything come out better, sweeter in the end.

Duléger's passion for the acquisition of technical skills of dancing predicted the emphasis on virtuosity within the social dance craze of the first decades of the nineteenth century. In 1800, however, social and theatrical vocabularies had not yet diverged as radically as they would, and his attempts at improvement easily gestured toward both domains. *La Dansomanie* thereby quickened as it reaffirmed a public passion for dancing. In the onstage world of the provinces, dancing choreographed each individual's happiness. For a Parisian society whose professional and class-based affiliations were undergoing tumultuous change, dancing promised more than merriment. It imparted a means to regulate the presentation of one's own identity and a medium in which to discover those of others. *La Dansomanie* made this possibility for a revitalized sociality all the more plausible.

Begin and End with Dancing

The ballet begins with a festival; a gay and lively crowded scene, a bold display of colorful costumes and exhilarating physical prowess splashes the eyes as the curtain opens. Or perhaps it begins with the preparations for a festival, thereby intimating the minutes of high-energy dancing to come. As they decorate the site with garlands of flowers, practice patterns and steps, accumulate the communal energy, these characters introduce themselves and their milieu. As they enter spiritedly into the familiar sequence of the celebration, alternating large group figures with smaller group dances, they establish a kind of visual and kinesthetic excitement that will only be surpassed in the finale.

The ballet ends with a festival; an exuberant revelry stuffs the stage so full of virtuosity that the curtain finally must close. As the story finds its ending, characters almost always have something to celebrate, to delight in, to feel joyous about. And they must express this formally through the stately processions and more enthusiastic contredances, the enraptured pas des deux, the orchestrated separations and conjoinings of multiple male and female dancers. Occasionally, the dancers celebrate a darker victory, as in Don Juan's arrival in Hell, where all the creatures of the underworld unleash their demonic rapaciousness in a toast to his necessary demise. Or the ending may strike a more stately balance, one that upholds as it integrates the rowdy peasants and the magisterial nobility through the dignified figure of the monarch.

Yet whether demonic, stately, or exuberant, the ballet will end, as it began, with dancing. At the beginning of the ballet, dancing stands for amusement, recreation, and entertainment. At its end, dancing signifies celebration and rejoicing. This necessary evolution in the meaning of dancing gives the middle its credibility. Whatever else they comprehend, viewers understand that what has gone on during that middle period of dramatic gesturing has produced a noticeable change in the tenor of the dancing. And this matters as much or more than anything else.

Nina, ou La Folle par Amour (1813)

Another in the explosion of domestic comedies that dominated the first decades of nineteenth-century theatrical production, *Nina* paired choreographer Louis Milon's expertise at crafting dramatic action with the extraordinary talents of Emilie Biggotini. Biggotini had made her dancing debut in Milon's *Pygmalion* at the age of fifteen. Now in her prime as actress, mime, and dancer, she was able to bring her full talents to the role of the daughter driven mad by her father's refusal to marry her to the man she loves. Domestic comedies all reproduced in some variation the familial tension between patriarchal rights over the daughter's destiny and the intrinsic human need to love. The father negotiated for stature and wealth while the heroine/daughter boasted an instinctual ability to recognize the goodness of her desired mate, regardless of his apparent circumstances. If daughters in real life did not prevail in marrying their sweethearts, they did so onstage, where the father softened his hold in acknowledgment of the importance of happiness over status. Of course, in the end—and *Nina* was no exception—the young couple graciously triumphed in all respects: true identities were discovered, fortunes and approvals bestowed, and any pretentious suitors were matched with more suitable mates.

Nina begins with preparations in honor of a visit from the Governor to the castle of the Count. Nina, the Count's daughter, and Georgette, daughter of the steward, distribute ribbons and garlands to the women, while Germeuil and Victor along with steward Georges organize the men in various tasks. Eventually Nina and Germeuil find each other and go to sit on the grassy bank, where they express their mutual love. The Count unexpectedly comes out of the castle to inspect the preparations and discovers the couple. Germeuil asks for his daughter's hand in marriage, but as the Count deliberates, the Governor arrives and all rush to greet him. The Governor invests the Count with the rank of Grand Officer at a gathering attended by the Mayor, villagers, and castle tenants on the terrace overlooking the sea. A festival follows with numerous dances. When dancers exit to pursue their celebrations, the Governor and his son remain behind to propose marriage to Nina. The Count, never hoping to make such a match for his daughter, cannot refuse the Governor's offer. The son runs to tell Nina, who cannot believe what she hears. Not only does the Count insist, but he declares Germeuil banished from the premises. The steward delivers this decree to Germeuil who, in a desperate act, pleads with Nina's maid to arrange one final meeting between the lovers. The Governor's son overhears this conversation, and as it grows dark hides near the summerhouse in order to confront Germeuil. An aggressive assault by the son provokes a violent duel in which Germeuil is disarmed and bears his breast to the victor's sword just as Nina runs up. Her cries of distress arouse the household. The Count in fury orders Germeuil to leave, and in response, the distraught lover flings himself over the terrace into the sea. Nina faints. The son and other men run to rescue Germeuil. The Count carries Nina to the grassy bank where she revives slowly, dazed and disoriented. The sight of her father provokes absolute terror, and she runs away, then seems to recover, then mimes dancing with Germeuil, then searches frustratedly for him. When her father, full of remorse, approaches yet again, she turns and flees through the gate into the countryside.

Act 2, located in a forest glen, opens on Nina asleep, her father, maid, and steward anxiously looking on. As she stirs, the father is reluctantly led away, knowing that his presence will perpetuate her illness. Nina smiles at a flower left beside her, imagining it as a gift from Germeuil. Village girls enter to keep her company, and together they pray for Germeuil's return. Nina distributes all her possessions to them except a simple gold ring given her by Germeuil. Victor passes in the distance and Georgette longs to be with him. Nina orders them to embrace and promises to secure permission for their marriage. The Mayor, agitated because he aspired to marry Georgette, witnesses this scene along with the Count and steward. They are persuaded by Nina's eloquent argument in favor of the couple's happiness. Suddenly seeing her father, Nina runs away, and in pursuing her the Count meets the rescued Germeuil returning with Governor and son. The Count is overwhelmed with relief and hugs Germeuil as his own son. Disbelieving, Germeuil is directed toward Nina, who has returned to the grassy bank. As everyone looks on from a distance, Germeuil approaches his love and gently explains his identity. In a rush of feeling, Nina regains normal consciousness, and the couple kneel before the Count as the approving Governor, son, Mayor, and villagers look on. The ballet ends with festive dancing.

The amount and complexity of mimed dialogue in a ballet like *Nina* required skillful choreographic maneuvering. In order to sustain a series of dialogues such as the Governor's marriage request, Nina's protest, and Germeuil's banishment, and to convey abstract notions such as banishment, the choreographer carefully crafted the disposition of dancers in each grouping so that no two scenes would look alike. Milon also made use of props. The decree written by the Count authorizing Germeuil's banishment circulated to the steward who then showed it to Germeuil. In act 2 a simple gold ring allowed Nina to refer repeatedly to Germeuil as part of her sustained monologue of madness. If these kinds of choreographic inventions brought the story to life, the published scenario nonetheless conveyed details that the viewer might not otherwise absorb. Not that the scenario was necessary in order to grasp the overall plot, but the careful selection of details written into the prose could support and deepen the viewers' interpretation.

The scenario for *Nina*, following the standard format for published scenarios of ballets, began with a description of the stage set that expressed with marked clarity the division between nature and culture: "To the right the Comte's castle, with an entrance to a park a little further back. In the distance can be seen the sea which washes a terrace, protected by a balustrade running the width of the stage. To the left, an iron gate leads to the countryside; near the foreground is a grassy bank surrounded by a grove."[1] The scenic design cordoned off countryside and sea, both unruly spaces, from the castle and grounds. Heroine and hero each threw themselves into these wild places at moments of utmost despair. The grassy bank received the lovers in the first moment of ecstatic union and also framed Nina's tortured loss of identity and subsequent restoration. Earlier ballets had demarcated nature and culture, not as reinforcements of the emotional states of individual characters, but rather as indications of strata of sociability. Nature was a wilder aspect of culture. Ballets dating from the turn of the century, however, not only explored nature and culture as oppositional categories, but they also began to use these categories as enhancements to character development.

Thus Nina's transit from one landscape to another helped to articulate a parallel trajectory for the psyche, one from contented sweetheart to tormented and irrational lover. The enactment of madness, riveting in the dramatic possibilities it afforded for the portrayal of hallucination, make-believe, and delirium, already enjoyed great popularity within the world of melodrama. Madness, a state where one plausibly danced or remembered dancing, also proved a rich site for reconciling drama with dancing. In subsequent decades the unconstrained depths of the psyche yielded numerous variations in movement vocabulary and quality, as in the sleepwalking heroine of *La Somnambule* (1827), the victims of the tarantula sting in *La Tarentule* (1839), or the famous mad scene in *Giselle* (1841), a clear reiteration of *Nina*'s emplotment of madness. The extension and contortions of classic vocabulary afforded by such scenes riveted viewers as did the contrast between madness and normalcy once and if the character was restored. In 1813, however, such extended demonstrations of interiority were relatively new and made doubly compelling by Bigottini's acting abilities. She lurched from mere disorientation into a world of imagined bodies, precipitously shifted to deranged, flailing frustration, and just as suddenly commanded the attention and obedience of a young couple in whose love she had faith.

Fueled by but not contained within the parameters of madness, the character of Nina served as a barometer for most of the emotion in the ballet. Surrounded by male characters—Count, Governor, Mayor, steward, who represented the hierarchical and bureaucratic dimensions of public life—Nina, through the intensity of her feelings, channeled the changes in motivation of all characters. Her fervor inspired her father's remorse and change of heart. The intensity of her feelings surpassed those of her suicidal lover even as they galvanized both father and lover into action. And it was her ability to see the inherent goodness of the sweethearts Georgette and Victor and her conviction in arguing for their union that prevailed, even though this marriage would violate class boundaries.

Although a peasant such as Victor might ultimately marry the steward's daughter, the overall effect of domestic comedies was to uphold class boundaries for upper-class characters and to acknowledge the importance of class overall. In *Nina* and many other ballets and melodramas, the romance between hero and heroine was duplicated in a more playful and incidental courtship of a lesser-class couple which manifested more leeway in the bounds of propriety. The movement style of this second pair and the adventures that befell them entailed a cruder and more comic vocabulary. Equally ingenuous, but incapable of a rival degree of sentimentality or refined sensitivity, this couple provided verification of class-based differences. All humans yearned for love to triumph in the end, but each social class performed its own unique choreographic realization of romantic unison.

Tell-Tale Evidence

A sack of money, a glove or handkerchief, the plume from a hat—any item of noticeable yet manageable size can help to elucidate complex relations among characters. With such an item as referent, dancers can express more clearly their suspicion, jealousy, outrage, mischievousness, or glee. And the distinctiveness of individual reactions can more readily be noted. One character's confusion may be another's horror. One's ambitions are another's embarrassment. How else but with a tangible, visible prop could such intricacies be demonstrated? If characters were able only to respond to the fluid situation produced by their own moving bodies, the causal links between action and reaction could easily lose clarity. The stability of the prop's image gives each character a clear message and a steady target.

But the prop accomplishes even more. The fact of its portability suggests interesting new accommodations on the parts of all bodies that handle it. Behind the back, beneath the folds, across the room, up the stairs, its size makes it easy to convey from one context to the next, to hide and then retrieve. Each time it pops into view, it organizes the stage space, as central focus or as off-center accent. Much depends upon who sees it and who doesn't at any given moment. Even in its hiding places, it emits a signal.

The prop moves through the story collecting new identities. At one moment it stands as a badge of honor, the next it becomes a coveted acquisition, and the next it stands as proof of a secret pact between two characters. Yet although new meanings accrete to it, it retains a concreteness that characters' actions cannot muster. The prop proves love or guilt.

Les Pages du Duc de Vendôme (1820)

Jean Aumer had studied dancing and choreography under the renowned Jean Dauberval, whose oeuvre created largely for the Opéra in Bordeaux had a substantial and enduring effect on the development of the action ballet. In his long and distinguished career, Aumer demonstrated remarkable range as a choreographer, contributing several domestic comedies but also history ballets, fairy tales, and many productions set in exotic lands to the Opéra repertoire. *Les Pages du Duc de Vendôme* had first premiered in Vienna and was brought to Paris five years later as a ballet that might work effectively at the newly opened Salle Favart, a temporary location for Opéra productions before they moved to the Rue Lepeletier in 1821.[1] This romp in one act translated to choreographic action a well-known vaudeville comedy that had also served as inspiration for an opera with music by Gyrowitz, the composer of the ballet score as well. Reviewers complained about the length and irrelevance of danced divertissements and about the lack of variation from scene to scene. Viewers, however, expressed great enthusiasm for the production,[2] a fact which critics admitted reluctantly.[3]

The opening scene depicts characters engaged in preparation for the arrival of the Duke of Vendôme. Escorted gaily into the village, the Duke confers promotions on several officers and also presents to Madame de Saint Ange her niece's future spouse, the Comte de Muret. Niece Elise, however, is in love with one of the Duke's pages, Victor, and dances a scintillating bolero with him at the festivities which follow. (See figs. 62 and 63.) Some officers depart in response to the attack on a nearby outpost. The Duke orders the pages to retire for the evening, and Victor directs them to pitch a tent near to Elise's window in anticipation of his after dark rendezvous with her. The Duke, aroused by the sounds of Elise's harp, a signal to Victor, discovers one of his pages at the window and chases him back to the tent, where he removes the page's aglet so that he can be identified in the morning. Hoping with his stealthy tactics to preserve his ward Elise's honor, the Duke then retires just as Madame de Saint Ange comes out to make her inspection for the night. She is accosted, in turn, by the other three pages, each of whom believes she is a village girl whom they would like to seduce. Victor, now rejoined with Elise, looks on as the pages' mistake causes general commotion that summons the entire encampment. The Duke orders the pages to line up and is chagrined but also amused to note that none of them is wearing his aglet. He gives them one hour to produce the decorations. Especially suspicious of Victor, he interrogates him to no avail. As the Duke turns to confer with Madame de Saint Ange, however, Victor steals back the aglet from the Duke's pocket. Now when the pages reappear they are each wearing their sashes. Foiled for a second time, the Duke calls to Elise and asks the pages whose happiness depends on her love. Thinking the Duke has agreed to the marriage, the pages identify Victor. With proof of his suspicions, the Duke unleashes his wrath on Victor, but is interrupted by the victorious return of the soldiers. They intercede on Victor's behalf and the Duke finally consents to the union. Festivities celebrating the happy couple and the army's victory end the ballet.

Aumer complexified this simple plot with innumerable small scenes of courtship and intrigue, many of which occurred simultaneously on different parts of the stage. These could easily be read from the smaller scale auditorium of the Salle Favart. Even the tiniest glance or raised eyebrow would have been detected by viewers. At one point a second page, in love with one of the village girls, locks her parents in their house while he courts her. Their apoplectic faces appear in the windows. At another point all four pages conspire in their tent on various stratagems for distracting the Duke from their mischievous actions. At the moment when Victor filches his own sash back from the Duke, he waves it for Elise to see, miming to her assurances that he is safe from punishment. This intense concentration of multiple simultaneous actions, explored with great sophistication for over a hundred years by fair and boulevard theatre productions, charged the stage with competing vectors of interaction among characters. Entering and exiting, waving, spying, protesting, chasing—all these actions that connected distinct bodies across distances of stage space with different timings and intensities enriched the spectacle, giving it the appeal that delighted its viewers.

TOP: 62. Auguste Garnerey's costume design for Emilie Bigottini as the page Victor in Jean Aumer's *Les Pages du Duc de Vendôme* (1820).

BOTTOM: 63. Auguste Garnerey's costume design for Fanny Bias as Elise in Jean Aumer's *Les Pages du Duc de Vendôme* (1820).

But surely, viewers took even greater pleasure in the performances by four of the leading ballerinas of the period who danced the roles of the Duke's pages. Dressed in satin breeches, short-cropped military jackets, and jaunty cockades, these four women executed the dashing vocabulary of male dancers—surprised by the Duke, Bigottini as Victor jumped from Elise's window over his head to make her getaway—and they mingled as if identical with the other soldiers who were danced by male dancers. They also cozied up to the female characters, courting and seducing them with all the enthusiasm, or perhaps an even more exaggerated fervor, that their male role permitted. Each page, in turn, claimed the attentions of Madame de Saint Ange, drawing her hand to their breast as they declared their love. Victor and Elise entwined their arms when together and looked longingly and adoringly at one another when separated.

Given the acting abilities of dancers like Bigottini and the generally sentimental features of male characters from the period, viewers may well have forgotten from one moment to the next that they were witnessing a travesty performance. During those stretches, however, when feminine thighs, lightness of carriage, or the delicacy of facial expression brought home the sexual identity of the pages, the comedy must have reverberated with the burlesque undercutting of all serious emotional attachments. It also emitted a trace of the risqué, the delicious naughtiness of women dressing up like men laying claim to masculine actions and even the erotic voyeurism associated with female-female dalliance. Perhaps its transgressiveness extended even further: could its portrayal of women courting women have suggested the elicit sexuality of a lesbian attachment? Or could the heterosexual reality of female pages and male soldiers have camouflaged a reference to male homosexual relations?

None of the reviews makes any reference to the travesty performances in the ballet. As in most performances of male characters by female dancers, the issue of their cross-gendered identity is never mentioned. One reviewer of *Les Pages* may have commented obliquely and with disdain on the practice of travesty by observing that the ballet did not even merit production at the Théâtre de Porte Saint-Martin:

> [B]ut, as must always happen at the end of a comedy, an opera, a vaudeville, or even a ballet, the hero, after having displayed his anger with entrechats, calms himself, pardons them, and the insolent page and the seduced girl find that the only consequence to their behavior comes in the form of kisses from mother and father.
>
> Such a weak composition, so little suited to a great theatre, could only distinguish itself through the quality of the dancing and the different and varied tableaux; but nothing of that sort can be found in this new ballet, that would barely be suitable for the Porte Saint-Martin. The pages dance as though they were clog makers, or at least they contrive to produce effects by striking their feet so that the floor reverberates loudly.[4]

Boulevard theaters frequently offered entertainments that involved travesty by female performers. By condemning the quality of the pages' dancing, specifically, the loudness of their execution of a masculine repertoire of steps, and by rating the performance beneath that offered at the Porte Saint-Martin, the reviewer may have been condemning travesty without having to name it. Certainly, it was rare in the decade of the 1820s to find travesty performed on the Opéra stage.

Yet the rigidification of masculine and feminine domains accomplished in the early years of the century had established gender as a category capable of violation through travesty. When eighteenth-century female dancers performed the male role of Amour, their exposed legs, while titillating, fit within the fluid range of sexual proclivities endorsed tacitly if not practiced openly by many Parisians. Their cross-dressing did not violate masculine and feminine identities so much as contribute new dimensions to them. By 1820, however, boulevard theatres, continuing their tradition of social satire and commentary, had identified in gendered behavior a set of boundaries whose violation could be highly entertaining. Thus the highly acclaimed and popular performer Virginie Dézajet strode around the stage, sword-fighting and courting sweethearts in one travesty role after another.[5] (See fig. 64.) The Opéra, responsible for the maintenance and display of more elevated social values, could ill afford experimentation with categories as clearly defined as the masculine and the feminine. The disruption of this policy created by *Les Pages de Duc de Vendôme* apparently delighted viewers as much as it caused the critics chagrin.

64. Virginie Déjazet as Cardinal Richelieu
in act 2 of *Ozaï* (1847).

5 FUGITIVE DESIRES

Charming art! Enchanting art! what do you lack that would make you equal to the other arts that so often borrow your help? The power, as they have, to establish and perpetuate your seductions. But, alas! as fugitive as thought, you only exist in the moment, and a memory that time erases each day is the only trace that you leave behind.[1]

Cruel Nocturnal Dancing

By the late 1820s dance, although it remained joyously light, also became identified with loss. Its ephemerality impressed viewers as much as its buoyancy. This transient quality of dancing—the fact that it disappeared as rapidly as it presented itself—had never concerned late-eighteenth-century choreographers. Nor had the inability of dance to resolve into an easily decipherable form of notation mattered for their purposes. What had struck them was dance's likeness to painting and to writing, and building on that likeness, dance's special ability to depict change through time. For eighteenth-century choreographers dance shared discursive as well as aesthetic attributes with all the arts. Now, in the wake of melodrama's functionalist distinction between speech and gesture, with a burgeoning capitalist economy through which all the arts began to circulate, and with the intensified masculinization of public space, dance took on a new role in relation to the other arts. It alone lacked the capability to inscribe itself. It alone endured only in one's memory.

Dance's evanescence rendered it unique among the arts but also less powerful. It could seduce viewers momentarily but never change them. More and more a diversion, it offered the pleasurable experience of sensual, graceful forms coalescing, floating through space and then reconverging in new patterns. Through these pleasing designs it could construct a mood but not deliver a message. It could impress a virtuoso grace upon viewers or impart a melancholy sweetness, but these were sensibilities cultivated outside of speech. These were the fugitive occupations of desire.

Dance's ephemerality combined with its sensuality to enhance its delectability. Dance enthusiast, critic, and scenarist Théophile Gautier summarized general assumptions about dance's sexiness in this characterization of its aesthetic mission:

> After all, dancing has no other purpose but to display beautiful bodies in graceful poses and develop lines that are pleasing to the eye. It is silent rhythm, music made visible. Dancing is ill-suited for expressing metaphysical ideas; it expresses only the passions. Love, desire with all its coquetries; the aggressive male and the gently resisting woman—these are the subjects of all primitive dances.[2]

Dancing could make manifest the rhythmic structure of music and present the agreeable shapes identified in painting and architecture, but it could not convey ideas. In fact, for Gautier, the only plot types it could support sketched out variations on heterosexual romance between an aggressive man and a feeble woman.

Not only did dance represent erotic encounters, but dancing itself began to stand in for sexual intercourse. Often, the metaphors surrounding dance equated it with sensual, even sexual, gratification. In the prologue to his review of the ballet *Giselle,* critic Jules Janin fantasized this encounter between young man and supernatural seductress:

> It happens that an imprudent man who gets lost at the hour of this funereal ball, at the moment where the wili is let loose, will see a small hand extend toward him inviting him to dance . . . beware. Close your eyes! Not only is the hand burning and the smile burning like the hand, but also the look is soft and full of fire, the waist is slender and svelte, and the shoulder . . . rendered even whiter and more brilliant by the pale cloak of the moon—fragile lacework cut out by all the tree's leaves, by all the flowers' silhouettes—the means to resist the wili thus made, when she says to you, "Would you like to?" then it is done, you must enter into the dance. . . . You know the tune and the refrain of this round of our beautiful days:—*Enter into the dance,* and the rest? Oh, the wilis, seventeen years of age, where are they! Oh, those white girls of our poetic rounds, when they sang while dancing: *enter into the dance!,* and then miserable as I am, I know not the rest of the verse, except that it meant: *Embrace whom you will love!*[3]

To enter into dancing with someone was to abandon oneself to the embrace of the other's body, to abandon oneself to one's sexual desire, and to engage in a choreographic version of sexual intercourse with one's partner. "To love to dance too much" became a code for sexual promiscuity.

But the erotic pleasure associated with dance was tinged by feelings of loss. Like sexual intercourse, dancing enticed and aroused the participant or viewer, but then disappeared. Like flirtation it left no evidence of its existence once enacted. The enthusiasm generated by dance, therefore, contained a kind of patronizing, because fully knowledgeable, awareness of its fragility. The praise dance garnered entailed a nihilistic indulgence in its transience.

New character types and plots as well as innovations in the ballet vocabulary supported this change in dance's identity. The strategies for synthesizing plot with spectacular dancing that larded the story with festivals and parties had become predictable by the late 1820s, and choreographers had depleted variations on the standard domestic comedy. Inspired partially by literary Romanticism's interest in the exotic, two new kinds of female characters—the wispy supernatural and the robust foreigner—began to dominate the stage. Opposite yet complementary in the range of feminine attributes they represented, these characters offered new resolutions to the ongoing tension between virtuoso dancing and storytelling.

With the advent of sylphs, nymphs, sprites, undines, fairies, and nyads, choreographers now had at their disposal a character whose modus operandi was dancing itself. (See fig. 65.) These creatures danced their way from one place to the next and danced their feelings and their thoughts as well. They were believable executing intricate sissonne and pas de chat combinations in order to relocate to the other side of a room. Unlike their eighteenth-century ancestors, who formed part of Diana's entourage and claimed their appropriate place in the hierarchical structure of godly society, the new otherworldly creatures dwelled in a nature opposed to all forms of civilization. They inhabited a world apart from human or mythic communities, often living alone. Because these creatures issued from a wild, untamed topos and were often conceptualized as mute, their use of the pantomimic vocabulary of gestures and expressions carried a new persuasiveness and a greater poignancy.

These supernatural creatures symbolized the essence of muteness, with all its attendant melancholia, its thwarted impulse to speak, and they also functioned as blatant allegories for unrealized dreams and desires. Costumed in pale colors with voluminous tulle skirts and claiming the air, site of the most abstract mental processes, as their territory, these beings looked fantastical. They appeared to flit and bound, to dissolve and reinstantiate, to fly through the air, to dart unpredictably in the manner of images at the very periphery of consciousness.[4] Their dancing was both ephemeral and sexy. The diaphanous cloud of fabric that surrounded their bodies revealed arms, chest, neck, and head, as well as the misty outlines of thighs—all perceptibly flesh and blood, not at all illusion.[5] (See fig. 66.) Even more compelling, their demeanor blended naive boldness with a retiring yet erotic allure. Because they dwelled in a world apart from all civilization, they remained oblivious to the protocols governing correct comportment for the female sex. They could openly assert their feelings and their sexual desires. No monetary, familial, or social obligations attached to them. They were palpably available, their impulses to chasteness no more than endearing evidence of their primitive, uncontaminated moral

TOP: 65. Fanny Elssler as Adda in Jean Coralli's *La Chatte Metamorphosée en Femme* (1837).

BOTTOM: 66. Mlle. Brocard, an early sylphide, performing in Louis Milon's *La Mort du Tasse* (1821).

goodness. As fragile as they were unruly, these characters represented the evanescence of desire itself.

These female characters had no male counterparts. No fauns chased after them, convincing them finally to succumb to the pleasures of love over freedom. Instead, they were sought after by male characters portraying historical or contemporary mortals—clearly fictional, but nonetheless of the real world—with whom they seldom paired. They could not reciprocate the male characters' affections because of their capricious insubstantiality. Like the dancing they enacted, they evaporated in the very moment of seduction. Their mortal suitors could thus always be seen pursuing an ideal love and the idea of love at the same time. This doubling of the male character's experience lent greater depth to the ballet, a depth unavailable to it since the dissolution of the allegorical relationship between mythological and real worlds in the early eighteenth century. It also permitted the development of new tragic plots seldom implemented since Noverre's and other choreographer's earliest experimentations with the action ballet.

Ballet narratives continued to depend upon the evil force, incarnated in villainous persons or manifest as a series of natural or social disasters. The plot could also hinge upon hidden or mistaken identities whose eventual discovery resolved the suspense and reinstated the proper social order. The new and most popular alternative configuration for producing the "knot" of the story involved a supernatural female being and an unhappy, unusually sensitive male mortal. The impossibility of their mutual love, staged with increasing urgency across different social milieus, finally drew to an inevitable close with the death of one or both characters. For the first time, ballets sometimes concluded with the sad declaration of the impossibility of love.

Where the supernatural beings introduced the possibility of tragedy into the ballet repertoire, their antithetical alternates—the robust, earthy, vivacious foreigners—revitalized the comic tradition. These Dionysian characters delighted in festivities, exhibited great courage, and expressed their sexual desire quite openly. They substituted for ethereal elusiveness the colorful and intriguing habits of their society. Their origins in the vagabond community of gypsies or in a country of more warm-blooded temperaments lent them a capriciousness that could easily translate to danced steps. They also inherited a passionate disposition that imbued their pantomimic gestures with great urgency. At the same time that they broadcast their sexual availability and appetite, their naturalistic and uncivilized upbringing resulted in a pure heart and highly moral instincts.

Like their supernatural sisters, the exotics differed in their behavior from eighteenth-century representations of colonized and other foreign peoples. Utilized for the spectacle which their costumes and local setting provided, the late-eighteenth- and early-nineteenth-century foreigners danced the virtuoso steps of the classical caractère repertoire. Their foreignness served as pretext for exuberant energy, complicated rhythms, and an occasional gesture or stance reminiscent of local customs. Aside from these superficial reproductions of local dance practices, foreigners looked remarkably French. The new female exotics, in contrast, exhibited deep stylistic differences as indications of their otherness. (See figs. 67 and 68.) Serpentine arm patterns traced new pathways of sensuality. The heel planted defiantly in the ground signaled a vitality, quick shifts of weight and undulations of hips suggested a sexual appetite seemingly unavailable within contemporary Parisian society. (See fig. 69.) These evocations of otherness established the absolute uniqueness of the foreigner. She differed in her very essence from prevailing conceptions of European feminine decorum and responsibilities.

67. Costume design by Paul Lormier for Noblet as an Indian mistress in *Le Dieu et la Bayadère* (1830).

68. Costume design by Paul Lormier for an American maiden in the opera *Ozaï* (1847).

69. A country girl dressed for a celebration by Lormier in Jean Coralli's *La Tarentule* (1839).

In much the same way, the development of ballet style and vocabulary began to verify the absolute uniqueness of female and male roles. Almost like translations of medical and anatomical research on sexual difference into choreographic action, the vocabularies for both male and female dancers began to diverge markedly.[6] No longer differing only in size or quality of execution, male and female repertories began to incorporate distinct kinds of movement. Although they still danced many phrases in unison side by side, each gender now claimed a distinctive group of steps and equally distinctive criteria for evaluating their execution. Female dancers worked to master the repertoire of intricate footwork, turns, and extended balances associated with pointe work, even if most did not dance en pointe in any given ballet. Men's competence was evaluated in terms of their facility at high leaps, jumps with beats, and large multiple turns. Feminine style, always softer and more diminutive than masculine performance, acquired an even greater emphasis on lightness. The tensile quality that had signified composure in performance was replaced with a ubiquitous effortlessness. The ballerina should never appear constrained by her body's physics or physicality.

The divergence of masculine and feminine ballet vocabularies exemplified the differences between male and female dispositions ascertained in the new sciences of physiognomy and phrenology and in studies of the representation of the passions.[7] Research that focused on correlations between bodily structure and temperament observed the frailness and docility of feminine structure in comparison with masculine heartiness and the absolute uniqueness of behavioral patterns for men and women that derived from these structural differences:

> The particular predispositions of man and woman are such that, the former, having been endowed with strength, seems born to command and be obeyed. Because of this he must be subject to passions more violent than those of woman, who, feeble, soft, and submissive, seems created only to love and console, obey and please. As a consequence the attitude of the man must be noble, proud, and imperious; his posture full of firmness, the rectitude of his torso invariable, and the position of the head fixed; whereas the posture of the woman must be timid, full of softness and agreeableness: everything about her is supple and full of gracious curves; her head, softly to one side, has all the candor of an infant's pose.
>
> Throughout the ordinary functions of life, man is colder; he has a deeper sensibility in the middle of large influences than the woman; if he uses gesture, it is always with a superior expression and enthusiasm, especially during displays of energetic feelings. Woman, whose ideas are more numerous and nuanced and whose movements are more supple and feeble, employs varied gestures without energy.
>
> In his walk and expression, man, whose size is well set up and whose attitude is stronger, moves with greater strength and assurance than the woman; his walk takes on a character of virility and resolution; his look is firm and concentrated; his speech, energetic, positive and regular, his voice, sonorous, imperious, and without bursts. In woman, her walk is light and elegant; her look full of sweetness, sensuality, and finesse. Endowed with a sensibility of infinite modifications, she often speaks excessively, always in an agreeable manner; her elocution is gracious and brilliant; her voice, soft, almost fluty, and clear; her breathing, active and varied, takes on a particular character as a result of the movements she makes her breasts feel.[8]

Men and women differed in their designated purpose in life, in their emotional makeup, and consequently in their stance, walk, and habits. Speech and gestures likewise reflected the distinct sensibilities of each sex, the numerous but weak inclinations of the woman, the concentrated and regularized concerns of the man.

The varying capacities and limitations of the two sexes dictated distinct approaches to the training of male and female bodies in physical education. Where boys could engage in riding, fencing, and swimming, girls, more than ever, required a gentle form of exercise that would compensate for the sedentary and stooped activities appropriate to their sex. Social dancing, it was argued, offered the ideal practice for women to improve their posture and thus enhance their health: "When one holds the head high, and squares the shoulders, in such a way that the chest remains always open, one breathes with great facility; the conduits no longer obstructed by any curve, and the chest being continually held up, the lungs fill easily with air, and perform their functions without obstacles."[9] As a form of physical education, dance's ability to edify bodily structure, rather than supply a graceful way of moving, attracted the most attention. A firm and correct posture would eliminate blockages that inhibited proper circulation. The corset, although still implemented to address severe defects, no longer provided the external mold that would support and sustain uprightness. Women now used it, not to assist with correct alignment, but to designate the structural basis of their social identity by increasing the slenderness of their waists and the width of their hips.[10] With the corset redefined as prosthetic, women turned to dancing as a way to build up the posture and increase circulation gradually so that their delicate constitutions would not be jeopardized.

The delicacy of the female constitution and the nuance and lightness of feminine comportment found perfect expression in the new ballet vocabulary. Both supernatural and foreign characters, each in a different way, exuded the fluidity, softness, and vibrancy thought to define the essence of femaleness. New techniques for remaining en pointe during one- and two-leg balances and turns and while traveling across the floor enabled supernatural characters to appear as though floating just above ground surface. Phrases of movement that included balances en pointe had been used in ballets since the early years of the century, but because the shoe's support for the foot was provided only by heavy darning, dancers seldom balanced on their toes for any length of time. In the early 1830s Marie Taglioni set astonishing new standards for competence en pointe, the culmination of years of strenuous training.[11] Not only did she expand significantly the number of steps and poses accomplished en pointe, but she demonstrated exceptionally fluid mastery of the space between standing and elevated positions.[12] With seemingly no effort she suddenly appeared poised on the toe tips of one foot and then just as softly settled back on the ground.

Taglioni's fluidity was especially striking given the degree to which early-nineteenth-century vocabulary had cultivated the extension of the limbs. Legs often circled around the body at hip height or above. Arms likewise swept through the full space forward, to the side, and above the head. To coordinate arm and leg motions smoothly while at the same time ascending to and descending from full pointe required a new degree of strength and of control by the core musculature over the periphery. The early-nineteenth-century pedagogical reforms that had located a core line at the center of each bodily region demonstrated their effectiveness in the unsurpassed quality of Taglioni's dancing.

Pointe work also brought with it a new vocabulary of petite steps, special turns, and poised positions that signified a coquettish delight. Where Taglioni floated, Fanny Elssler, the immensely popular Austrian ballerina who developed roles as the exotic foreigner, directed her pointed feet toward and across the floor with astonishing speed and precision.[13] Tossing her head, she smiled enticingly as each thrust of legs and feet announced her proud independence and the strength of her desire. The quickness and tensility of her pointe work fleshed out the appeal of her extroverted abandon. Dancers hoping to approximate either Taglioni's or Elssler's style increased the number of repetitions of exercises involving leg extensions and also worked to strengthen the feet with innumerable relevés on one and two feet.[14]

Other innovations to the vocabulary, such as the arabesque, with its arrowlike shape, its impelling sense of forward motion, likewise imparted to both character types an evanescent quality.[15] Performed en pointe, the arabesque registered a moment of stillness at the highest possible elevation attainable without jumping. The pause it created, however, reverberated with the dynamic energy generated by the suspenseful balance and the motion-filled shape of the pose: one leg elongated high behind the body, torso inclined forward in support of the head oriented forward into the distance or turned to gaze behind at the distance already traveled, arms outstretched to the front or sides as if in flight. Poised in the arabesque, the dancer indicated both hesitancy and urgency. It allowed a moment of reflection, as if to gain one's bearings while at the same time demonstrating the compelling need to move forward.

The arabesque, like other fully extended shapes, figured within the new hierarchical organization of steps as a privileged moment. Choreography of the 1830s and '40s began to elaborate a new syntax for the phrase that featured certain movements far more than others. Balances, extensions, leaps, and turns dominated over the smaller locomotor steps that connected them. This new phrase structure differed radically from eighteenth-century step sequences, which valued far more equally each movement performed. Even early nineteenth-century combinations showed a more egalitarian interest in all kinds of steps if only by including very different ones in a single phrase. In the 1830s, however, motives composed of one important and two or three less significant connecting movements would often be repeated three or more times, each time with a slightly larger and more fervent execution. This sequencing resulted in phrases with a lilting, high-low inflection and a breathlike rhythm. The phrasing itself pressed forward and then receded, yearned again and returned to calm, then desired even more, and finally faded away.

Both male and female performers participated in this syntax of desire; however, the distinctiveness of their separate vocabularies and styles of execution cast them in complementary and mutually dependent roles. These roles, evident in the choreography for the entire ballet, were especially marked in the pas de deux, a discrete segment danced by principal characters as part of the main action or as one of the diversionary dances that portrayed balls, festivals, and concluding celebrations. The standard structure of the pas de deux—an opening duet, several alternating solos, and a concluding duet—had changed little since the eighteenth century. The form, however, took on substantially new content in the 1830s due to the unique labor that each sex contributed and the new conventions for partnering that predominated in the duets.[16] Where eighteenth- and early-nineteenth-century pas de deux featured long sequences of unison during the duets and considerable repetition from one solo to the next, the new pas de deux designated differences for male and female in both solos and duets.

70. Marie Taglioni and Herr Stullmüller as Zémire and Azor.

Duets, both the opening adagio and the concluding allegro, began to include greater physical contact. Protocols for partnering in these duets demanded unique skills from each sex. In the adagio sections partners intricately entwined to create unified sculptural wholes. The male character supported, guided, and manipulated the female character as she balanced delicately and precariously in fully extended shapes. (See fig. 70.) With his help she displayed her body's ability to maintain these positions with only the tips of her toes as foundational support. Throughout, he remained behind or to the side of his partner, solicitously, adoringly presenting her to the audience.[17] These slow moving phrases of evolving shapes would be interspersed with unison traveling patterns and also with solo phrases performed by the female who repeatedly broke away from her partner in order to dance for him. During these phrases his admiring gaze directed viewers' attention to her in the same way that his partnering displayed her body for their evaluation and appreciation. Even in the faster concluding duets where partners traveled in unison, the female dancer remained in front and was frequently guided through space by the male.

The pas de deux offered the female dancer considerable visibility but relatively little autonomy. During her solos, dancing on her own and by herself, she commanded the viewer's attention as an independent character with a particular temperament and set of accomplishments. Dancing with her partner, prominent as she was, her movements depended upon and were guided by his support. (See fig. 71.) In contrast, the male dancer, even as he controlled the pair's interaction, became a nonentity. Emerging only during his solos as the deft displayer of virtuosity, he receded into the background as he partnered her.

71. Marie Taglioni and Joseph Mazilier in a pas de deux from Filippo Taglioni's *La Fille du Danube.*

Still, the overall effect achieved through the pas de deux's structure was both pleasing and reassuring. It testified to the possibility of an organic union between functionally distinct beings. Each member of the pair initially contributed unique abilities to the formation of an intimate, constantly changing whole; then they parted to dance in their separate worlds, but eventually they returned, celebrating their reunion with animated and fast-paced unison. Within this basic structure of separation and reunion, the pas de deux offered great versatility. Choreographers could use both solos and duets to construct many different kinds of variation in character and interaction. At the same time, they could rely on the pas de deux to reinforce the intimacy of the couple's attachment. Embedded at or near the center of an act, the pas de deux consummated the love of hero and heroine.

If the pas de deux celebrated the perfect matching of male and female characters, the ballet as a whole offered a surfeit of unattached female figures. Where eighteenth- and early-nineteenth-century ballets scrupulously paired all male and female roles—shepherds and shepherdesses, nymphs and fauns, Persian men and Persian women—ballets of the 1830s and '40s abandoned most incidental male parts. Principal male characters and the requisite number of men for their entourages or for local inhabitants remained, but the vast majority of corps parts went to women. Female principal roles—young heroines, mothers, friends, soothsayers, and witches—lent themselves to a varied display of emotion. Male principals, with the exception of the sensitive hero, reflected a narrow range of governmental, aristocratic, or other institutional categories whose personalities and feelings were far less important than their position of authority. Female corps de ballet, cast as the various specimens of supernatural creatures, or as gypsies, harem girls, or peasants, rounded out the cast.

The alternative types of elusive supernatural and robust foreigner represented the ends of a spectrum of sensuality along which all female characters were located. The contrast between fantasmatic sylph and exotic, warmhearted girl was immortalized in Théophile Gautier's famous comparison of Taglioni and Elssler:

> The dancing of Fanny Elssler is completely independent of academic principles. It has a character all its own which sets her apart from other ballerinas. Hers is not the ethereal, virginal grace of Taglioni, it is something much more human which appeals more sharply to the senses. Mlle. Taglioni is a Christian dancer, if one can use such an expression about an art that is proscribed by Catholicism. She floats like a spirit in a transparent mist of white muslin with which she loves to surround herself, and she resembles a contented soul scarcely bending the petals of celestial flowers with the tips of her rosy feet. Fanny Elssler is a completely pagan dancer. She recalls the muse Terpsichore with her tambourine and her tunic slit to reveal her thigh and caught up with clasps of gold. When she fearlessly arches her back, throwing her voluptuous arms behind her, she evokes a vision of those beautiful figures from Herculaneum or Pompeii standing out in white relief against a black background and accompanying their steps with sonorous, echoing *crotala*. Virgil's verse, *Crispum sub crotalo docta movere latus* instinctively springs to mind. The Syrian slave girl he so loved to see dancing beneath the pale trellis of the little inn must have had much in common with Fanny Elssler.[18]

Taglioni's ineluctable softness and Elssler's vital buoyancy each propelled the viewer's imagination in a different way. Their contrasting styles were esteemed as the most superb realizations of vaporous, gossamer lightness—that which rendered movement the most elusive—and joyous, sensuous lightheartedness—that which rendered it most gay.

The comparison between Taglioni and Elssler exemplified in the most graphic terms new values pervasive in all the arts. Victor Hugo's *Preface to Cromwell*, a manifesto for the Romantic movement in the arts, claimed for his moment in history a new awareness of humankind's dual life. Caught between the transitory and the immortal, earth and heaven, animal nature and intelligence, body and soul—in fact, defined by the struggle inherent in these oppositions—human beings now required new artistic forms for the expression of their condition. These new forms of art and the artistic genius necessary to produce them should result from the incorporation of oppositions. Taglioni and Elssler encompassed such oppositions, each in a different way, Taglioni through her voluptuous chasteness and Elssler through her fragile vitality.

Scenarios for ballets also developed various settings and character types as polar opposites. Night and day, city and country, peasant and aristocrat, foreigner and local, all became dialectical categories that the plots traversed. The plots relied on the dichotomous opposition between these categories to achieve their dramatic tension. Where the eighteenth-century action ballets had encompassed all peoples and lands within their hierarchical tabularization of difference, these scenarios pitted one way of life against another. Racial and class differences, especially, provided the kinds of barriers and boundaries that gave the scenario its momentum. Even if they proved ultimately to be insurmountable, these differences seemed momentarily transcended by the action of dancing.

Dancing likewise embodied the oppositions of body and soul, material and spiritual, real and ideal in its every movement. Descriptions by critics, choreographers, and historians were shot through with sets of opposing qualities that an individual dancer or dance embraced. This profile of Taglioni, for example, proposed one impossible image after another, all of which she managed to encapsulate: "But what renders Taglioni inimitable, is the aerial lightness, the indefinable fluidity that only she has; she soothes you with poetry; she is an Ossianic shadow, a flower blown about by the breeze, an ideal, a dream, but a dream that is real. . . . In a word: the others seem like fallen angels, whereas she is the angel in all its primitive purity."[19] The weight of a flower and the power of the breeze to hold it aloft, a dream that is also a reality, an angel that is purely primitive—the perception of these contradictions realized in the fleeting moment of Taglioni's dancing filled viewers with ecstasy.

The art of dancing itself, demanding such strength and energy yet requiring such ease and grace, was also construed as a paragon of opposites. Praise for principal dancer Louise Noblet reflected the expectations for a correct yet mellifluous positioning of the body: "A delicate tact, an infinite grace distinguish Mlle. Noblet; her dance is light and correct; her pantomime knowing and lively. No effort, no fatigue betrays the work; everything, on the contrary, hides the art from the most clairvoyant eyes."[20] Noblet's dancing exemplified the synthesis of lightness with correctness, intelligence with vivacity. Even the most scrutinizing gaze did not find evidence of the work, known to be taking place, under the aura of inexhaustible effervescence.

With the quest to embrace within a single performance these kinds of oppositional values and with the recognition of the impossibility of sustaining such a performance either in the body of the dancer or even the memory of the viewer came a new conception of body as foil or hindrance to the realization of individual needs and desires. The new domain of physical education and the increasing scrutiny of scientific investigation construed body as an inert mass, one vulnerable to disease and requiring exercise for the maintenance of health. Body continued to stand in for the soul, to express its inclinations and mirror its desires, but it now also stood in its way. Rather than respond with docile correctness to all efforts to cultivate its health and manners, the body now required training from an early age in order to avoid the horror of deformities. The body's intransigence reflected so imperfectly the spiritual interior of the person that it often seemed like a prison: "Of all the beings who live on earth, there is only us who suffer such an oppression; we are born only to enter into a kind of prison; but what am I saying! There aren't any, I think, which do not leave the poor imprisoned person the ability to move freely."[21] The goal of dance and all other forms of physical education was no longer to induct the body into a proper way of behaving, but instead to fight against its own propensity to develop impediments to free expression.

At the theatre, dance presented the freed body for all to see, yet like the sylph, it was as unattainable as it was desirable. Similarly, dance celebrated the felicitous union of man and woman, yet often this partnership was shortlived. Dance mirrored the gendered division of labor in society in the distinct vocabularies and styles for male and female dancers, in the new roles developed for partnering, and in the range of character types. However, it endowed female principal characters especially with strange and ambiguous complexity. Supernaturals cloaked their sexual appetite with an ethereal beauty or screened a vengeful impulse with melancholy lassitude. Foreigners courted love and danger but also exuded moral virtue. The male characters who wooed these exotic creatures pursued an ideal of lustrous magnetism, but one that perpetually danced out of their grasp.

Viewers engrossed in the spectacle, the dancing, and the passion could not remain impervious to the ballet's cycles of seduction and alienation. Knowing that the ideal image of the dancing figure was unattainable, they nonetheless exhilarated in the body's charms. Knowing the ballet offered only inconsequential diversion, they still attended night after night. Drawn into the shimmering beauty of irreconcilable forces momentarily united in a single balance or a short duet, they left the theatre with only a vague and useless memory of dance's brilliance. As if the ballet summoned up a past full of promise, they enveloped themselves in a world which could never be, a world unweighted with and untainted by serious, manly concerns.

Crafting diversion

With the revolutionary struggles of 1830, the overthrow of Charles X, and the new constitutional monarchy under King Louis Philippe, "the Bourgeoisie King," the Opéra underwent yet another radical reorganization. Once an institution that received funding in order to make manifest the aesthetic standards of an absolutist government, the Opéra transformed during the 1830s into an institution whose responsibilities divided between an authorizing state and a consuming public. Experiments with private, profit-driven management altered irrevocably its identity as an emissary of France. It became another of the many institutions whose products one purchased for the price of a ticket. Still, the state did not relinquish all responsibility or control, and before leasing the Opéra to the private citizen and entrepreneur Louis Véron in 1831, it stipulated, among other things, the production each year of one grand Opéra and one grand ballet, each in three to five acts; two short Opéras of either one or two acts; and two short ballets of the same length.[22]

Originally a short novelty appended to the end of an evening's program, the action ballet had become a familiar and distinct form of spectacle meriting an exposure equal to that of its parent, the opera. Where the Opéra administration had originally seen the action ballet as a threat to the Opéra's vitality, they now viewed it as an attractive participant in the array of offerings to the public. The sustained development of the ballet vocabulary, coupled with its ability to support a range of subjects, had secured a place for dance among the classic aesthetic forms of the early nineteenth century. Dancers and danced scenes continued to form a part of most operas, but the action ballet existed alongside these performances as an autonomous entity with its own training practices that supported creative and collaborative procedures for generating new works. Ballet had achieved an autonomy firmly grounded in institutional practices that supported its independent development.

The ballet no longer aspired "to represent the manners and customs of the world" using the universal language of movement. Gautier might claim that "happily, the language of dance is understood everywhere, and the feet do not have an accent,"[23] but he referred to a highly limited domain of events and emotions about which dance might "speak and be understood." Nor did the ballet vocabulary pretend the same kind of imperialistic ordering of all human movement that it had in the eighteenth century. The influx of foreign artists—Spanish, Indian, Asian—who had performed their indigenous dances throughout Paris situated ballet as a unique form using one kind of movement among many.[24] Ballets nonetheless incorporated their own renditions of these exotic, foreign dances, relying on such scenes to infuse the spectacle with sexual and aesthetic energy. Because these scenes rendered local dances with a vivid detail far surpassing the eighteenth-century ballet's incorporation of a significant gesture or stance, they were seen to express the

72. Fanny Elssler in *La Cachucha,* from Jean Coralli's *Le Diable Boiteux* (1836).

essence of the population depicted. But they also helped to rationalize a theory of universal communication for which ballet functioned as the integrating medium. Ballet deployed the most primal of all "languages," that of heart and senses.

Thus a dance that broke with the classical tradition as radically as did Elssler's version of *La Cachucha* dazzled viewers with its seductive vitality and not the cultural distinctiveness of its aesthetic form. (See fig. 72.) Choreographed by Elssler herself as a solo pas for the new ballet *Le Diable Boiteux* (1836), this short piece mined Spanish dancing for several characteristic features, including the arched-back stance, the serpentine coordinations of arms and legs, and even the use of castanets. The degree of divergence from the classical vocabulary, and particularly the blatant sexual references, initially shocked viewers. Yet Elssler's incorporation of the lascivious into the canonical conceptions of grace and plastic beauty soon won viewers over:

> Those contortions, those movements of the hips, those provocative gestures, those arms which seem to seek and embrace an absent lover, that mouth crying out for a kiss, that thrilling, quivering, twisting body, that captivating music, those castanets, that strange costume, that shortened skirt, that low-cut, half-open bodice, and withal all Elssler's sensual grace, lascivious abandon, and plastic beauty were very much appreciated. . . ."[25]

Her ability to invest the Spanish repertoire of poses and steps with the geometrized precision of balletic vocabulary, to establish in the serpentine arm movements the same circles and arcs that defined the balletic body's core, rendered the *Cachucha* accessible and acceptable to Parisian sensibilities.

Ballet's geometry of forms, its only claim to the masculinized domain of formal structures, provided the underlying means to link ballet with other forms of dance. The parades of dances by the peoples of Scotland, Hungary, or Spain offered during each season of productions each evidenced the same formal conversion from indigenous expression to geometric precision. And this formal measuring of movement also helped to ensure ballet's autonomy as an art form. The rigorous regimens at the barre with which dancers began each day and through which the body's geometry came into being gave ballet its *techne*. (See figs. 73 and 74.) Analogous to the composer's scales or the painter's life drawings, the ballet training program inculcated the spatial and rhythmic calibrations of bodily movement, the abstract lines and shapes of body parts, that defined the formal properties of dancing. Out of these calibrated corporeal relations came the criteria for correct and virtuoso execution that delimited ballet dancing as an artistic endeavor. Eighteenth-century choreographers had used cultural difference as a novel or eccentric deviance from the ballet's virtuosity, a virtuosity that proclaimed itself as the most refined and cultivated version of bodily expression to be found on earth. Nineteenth-century viewers saw instead many different cultures' unique and developed forms of danced expression, all mediated by the colonizing transcriptive process that turned these dances into geometrized versions of themselves. Excellence at this dancing authenticated ballet as an artistic medium at the same time that it tacitly implied a connection to and mastery over the world's dance forms.

As dance came to have its own autonomy as an art form, and its own kinds of speechless messages, the choreographer's responsibilities became focused around the realization of the story and not its conception. Noverre had advised choreographers to read widely in classical literature so as to refine their ability to select and adapt a story that could be translated into dance. The eighteenth- and early-nineteenth-century choreographers had all devised and then written the scenarios for their ballets as well as created their choreographic rendition. Now the explosion of virtuoso dancing, the intricacy and sheer length of the productions required a choreographer's full-time attention, and a scenarist was called in to sketch the plot and write its published version. Writers responded to this occupational opportunity with adaptations from well-known drama, fiction, and poetry, written as vivid, poetic summaries of the danced action. The producer or director of the theatre intervened to connect the idea for a ballet with an author and a choreographer.[26] The absolute uniqueness of words and danced movement required separate artisans and a producer capable of integrating both works into the functional whole.[27]

Typically, the scenario, once approved, would be handed to choreographer and composer simultaneously, and the set designer would be alerted as to the schedule for the project. No longer the originator of the project, the choreographer now participated in collaborative discussions with producer and composer. Apprised of the parameters set by the theatre for numbers of dancers and rehearsals and any requisites for the leading roles, the choreographer could stipulate requirements for the quantity and sequencing of pas and offer ideas concerning overall staging. Sometimes composers attended rehearsals and sketched out a rhythmic and melodic framework for a given scene. Other times, the choreographer worked from a score already nearing completion.

The fact that the composer necessarily responded to the constraints of both scenario and choreography relegated ballet music to a status far inferior to that of other concert forms. Yet the decade of the '20s witnessed a significant shift in the composer's basic project, one that enhanced the profession's credibility. Up until that time composers,

28 PRINCIPES DE LA STÉNOCHORÉGRAPHIE.

CHAPITRE HUITIÈME.

DES ÉPAULEMENTS ET POSITIONS PENCHÉES DU CORPS.

LE CORPS placé sur une ou deux jambes peut S'ÉPAULER à droite ou à gauche.

Pour indiquer L'ÉPAULEMENT, on se servira d'un DIÈZE placé contre la ligne du corps, DU COTÉ OU SERA L'ÉPAULEMENT.

EXEMPLES :

Corps droit, épaulement à droite.

Corps droit, épaulement à gauche.

Si le corps n'est PAS de FACE et qu'il soit TOURNÉ d'un QUART ou d'un DEMI-TOUR, on REMPLACERA LE DIÈZE PAR $\frac{1}{4}$ ou $\frac{1}{2}$.

EXEMPLES :

Corps droit, tourné d'un $\frac{1}{4}$ de tour à gauche.

Idem. à droite.

Idem. $\frac{1}{2}$ de tour à gauche.

Idem. à droite.

Quand le CORPS aura UNE POSITION PENCHÉE (telle que dans les arabesques), la ligne indiquant le corps sera penchée DU COTÉ DU CORPS.

Corps de face penché du côté droit (avec les bras bas).

Corps de face penché du côté gauche (idem.)

Corps tourné d'un $\frac{1}{4}$ de tour et penché à droite (avec les bras en arabesque).

Idem de l'autre côté.

Corps tourné d'un $\frac{1}{2}$ tour et penché du côté GAUCHE (les deux bras haut.)

Idem de l'autre côté.

EXEMPLES DE L'ADAPTATION

DES SIGNES DU HAUT DU CORPS ET DES BRAS AUX SIGNES DES JAMBES.

3. 5.

NOTA. Comme on voit par l'exemple ci-dessus, les signes du corps doivent être placés en LIGNE DIRECTE AU DESSUS de ceux des jambes, tant pour la régularité de celui qui écrit, que pour faciliter le lecteur de sténochoré-

73. Principles of notation using the stick figure in Saint-Léon's *La Stenochorégraphie.*

32 PRINCIPES DE LA STÉNOCHORÉGRAPHIE.

SIGNE ACCESSOIRE INDIQUANT LA PIROUETTE.

PIROUETTE se dit en danse de l'action d'UN TOUR ENTIER qu'on fait de TOUT LE CORPS sur LA POINTE D'UN ou DE DEUX PIEDS. On peut pirouetter EN DEHORS ou EN DEDANS.

PIROUETTER EN DEHORS, c'est TOURNER DU COTÉ DE LA JAMBE qui est EN L'AIR quand il y en a une en l'air et l'autre à terre, ou DU COTÉ DE LA JAMBE DE DERRIÈRE, quand on est sur les deux pieds.

PIROUETTER EN DEDANS, c'est TOURNER DU COTÉ DE LA JAMBE qui est A TERRE quand il y en a une en l'air, ou de TOURNER DU COTÉ DE LA JAMBE DE DEVANT quand on est sur les deux pieds. Mais pour éviter toute confusion, j'ai adopté deux signes, l'un pour tourner à gauche, l'autre pour tourner à droite ; la position des jambes indiquera si c'est en dedans ou en dehors.

SIGNES INDIQUANT LA PIROUETTE.

Tourner à gauche.
Tourner à droite.

Lorsqu'il y aura PLUS D'UN TOUR à faire sur un ou deux pieds, on désignera par un numéro suivi d'UN *T*, et PLACÉ EN DESSOUS DU SIGNE DE PIROUETTE, le NOMBRE de tours que l'on voudra faire exécuter.

EXEMPLE :

2 t. 3 t. 4 t. 5 t. 3 t. 2 t.

EXEMPLE DE L'APPLICATION DU SIGNE PIROUETTE.

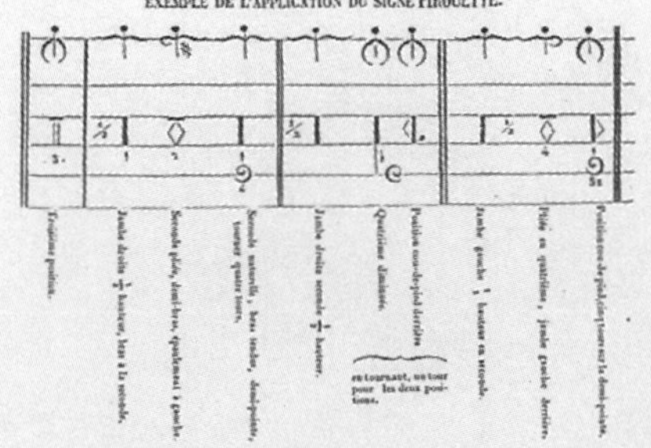

74. Varieties of pirouettes in *La Stenochorégraphie.*

following the model developed at the fair theatres and then on the boulevard stages, had incorporated into their scenes a series tunes from well-known songs whose lyrics would indicate and thereby reinforce the dramatic action. The generation that came of age in the late 1820s, however, developed new compositional techniques such as the leitmotif, the recurring phrase that lent greater coherence to the structure as a whole while still helping to identify individual characters and actions. Their compositions, while still regarded as incidental when compared to the great orchestral works, nonetheless boasted an integrity as the individual artist's work.

Working from scenario, musical score or both the choreographer would commence the process of staging the work, portrayed somewhat skeptically in this description of a rehearsal:

> It is in the rehearsal room that artists of the first rank undertake their study of pantomime; but the general rehearsals of the corps de ballet, men and women, can only take place on the stage. These lessons and these rehearsals bear no resemblance to rehearsals for the singers; here there is only noise, chattering, racket, and peals of laughter; also the ballet master who directs all these personnel wields an enormous stick whose repeated strikes on the floor barely re-establish silence. This tableau is one of the most comic and dignified from the brush of a painter both talented and ingenious. Luxury and misery! Some [of the dancers] have arrived in carriages, others in clogs; but a spirit of fraternity reigns in this little world: those who have not a penny do not act humble, and those surrounded by luxury are not insolent. . . .
>
> In all the corners, dancers nibble, they eat candies or cakes; some read a novel by Paul de Kock or Eugene Sue; the youngest parody the scene of pantomime that is being rehearsed. . . .
>
> The first rehearsals of the ballet are given with only a pitiful orchestra: one first and one second violin; whether morning or night, by the light of two or three lamps to illuminate the entire theatre. The ballet master and the composer indicate with great care the diverse movements of the dance and the pantomime. The rehearsals last sometimes two or three hours, which does not keep the artist or the figurant from taking a dance lesson, or sometimes even from remaining on one's feet for the length of an entire performance.[28]

This description brings to life the choreographer, surrounded by the chaotic preoccupations of dancers waiting to be embroiled in the action. While some dancers read, others ate, and others playfully parodied those who were dancing, the choreographer demonstrated phrases of movements to the accompaniment of the music. Dancers, responding with movements determined by the vocabulary and style established in their training, might contribute many of the specific phrases of movement or at least suggest movement that the choreographer would then alter or shape in some way. Where the musical score would provide the choreographers with clear indications of durations for movement phrases, for interactions between characters, and for entire scenes, the scenario, through its examination of the characters and their motives, would guide the choice of vocabulary and style.

Just as the pas de deux took on a new appearance as a result of the dimorphic vocabularies for male and female dancers, so the large group massings and trajectories developed new visual momentum. Bodies wove more intricately around one another,

75. A pas de quatre from *Les Bayadères* (1821).

76. Filippo Taglioni, Mlle. Pierson, and M. Stiasny in the *Ballet die Weintese*.

using changes of level to create dynamic massings. (See figs. 75, 76, and 77.) Choreographers increasingly worked the diagonals of the stage, posing and moving dancers along them. Unlike the rectilinear paths that eighteenth-century dancers followed, across the stage and from back to front, these diagonals contained the energy suspensefully upstage and then ushered it forward propulsively as dancers moved toward the downstage opposite corner. Soloists or groups moving along these paths pressed forward with an urgency that the eighteenth-century right-angled orientations, for all their exuberance, had not achieved. Similarly, the large circular paths, instead of designating the regulated embroidery of bodies along its edges, became a swirling mass, its speed or sometimes

77. Mlle. Pierson, John Taglioni, Marie Taglioni, and Herr Stullmüller as Amazons and Greek swordsmen in the *Ballet Scherdt und Lanze*.

ragged edges reflecting the maelstrom-like force of its energy. As much as they solicited and responded to dancers' suggestions for specific phrases, choreographers necessarily entered each rehearsal with prepared strategies for moving large groupings of dancers across and around the stage in these basic patterns.

Throughout the rehearsal process the choreographer divided attention between the nuances of dramatic scenes enacted by principal dancers and the logistics of large ensemble dances, between the high-strung temperaments of soloists and the rebellious absences and inertia of the corps, and between the sections of danced acting and those of virtuoso dancing. The integration of dramatic scenes with virtuoso pas, even under the guidance of the scenarist's plan for the ballet, remained elusive, in part because of the practice of allowing principal dancers to insert their own solos and duets designed to showcase their most brilliant accomplishments, and also because of the tumultuous

78. The leap from the opening scene of Jean Coralli's *La Péri* (1843).

response of the audience to spectacular moments in the production. Elssler's *La Cachucha,* for example, fit unusually well into the Spanish setting of *Le Diable Boiteux* as a private performance by renowned Opéra dancer Florinda. As the only moment in the story when Florinda performed, viewers could easily rationalize any discrepancies between Elssler's style and that of Jean Coralli, the ballet's principal choreographer. And the occasion of a performance excused the exceptional dancing Elssler presented. Still, the solo evoked such enthusiastic response that she was required to repeat it, thereby breaking the continuity of the action. Similarly, Carlotta Grisi's sensational fall as the peri into the arms of Lucien Petipa in the ballet *La Péri* (1843) provoked such audience expectation that if the couple did not perform it perfectly, they were required to repeat it until the audience was satisfied.[29] (See fig. 78.)

If these spectacularly arresting moments pulled the audience away from the narrative, the scene design helped to reimmerse them in the action. Set designers like Daguerre and Ciceri relied on technical advances in lighting intensity and carefully arranged translucent fabrics to create a world onstage that drew viewers into it.[30] In sharp contrast with eighteenth- and early-nineteenth-century sets that most often presented broad, open, symmetrical, public spaces spilling action out toward the audience, these sets created a sense of interiority. Instead of uniformly embossed columns lining the stage, their landscapes often placed some prominent architectural or natural feature downstage—an outcropping of rock, a bridge or landing—that viewers looked past or through in order to arrive at the interior of the stage space. (See fig. 79.) Vegetation was likewise arranged so as to define a volume or series of receding volumes within the confines of the stage.

Drawn into such spaces viewers became engulfed by a mysterious melancholy as low levels of light caused the enigmatic appearances and disappearances of glimmering

79. Pierre-Luc-Charles Ciceri's sketch for the scene design for Filippo Taglioni's *La Fille du Danube* (1836).

maidens. "The Ballet of the Nuns," a cloistered, midnight ritual that summoned nuns from their graves in act 3 of the opera *Robert le Diable,* marked the inauguration of this new kind of choreographic collaboration with lighting and scene design. (See fig. 80.) As one of the first acts of his directorship at the Opéra, Louis Véron made the decision to expand the section in order to develop fully a mood of somber foreboding as the nuns rose from the dead, arched and lunged and glided through the space to create a menacing swirl of light and motion. In subsequent ballets containing supernatural beings, the lighting against the dancers' layered skirts as they floated through the profuse forest vegetation achieved a shimmering, translucent effect. Elaborate machinery allowed dancers to fly, literally, from one side of the stage to the other. The choreography could build on the optical indefiniteness afforded by the technology so as to keep viewers engrossed in deciphering shadow, image, and motion. This prolonged meditation on illusoriness itself performed to the haunting strains of the music drew viewers into an alterity that enhanced enormously what plot and character could provide.

80. The Ballet of the Nuns from *Robert le Diable* (1831).

These scenic designs along with the new variable lighting throughout the theatre emphasized the degree to which audience and performers now assumed separate functions. The theatre remained an ideal place for audience members to see and be seen, but their performance of socializing became restricted to before and after the presentation. During the ballet viewers felt less a part of the spectacle and more a voyeuristic presence that looked in upon it. Nor did they see on stage any movement that they could connect with their own. Dancers manifested feminine and masculine attributes embraced in daily life, but the highly trained bodies and even the choreographic arrangement of those bodies had come to be governed by aesthetic regulations unrelated to quotidian protocol.

Dance, now the perfect emblem of muteness, no longer struggled to reconcile image and word, to embody both poetry and painting in motion. A ballet, no longer called an action ballet, specified that genre of spectacle that presented feelings inexpressible through words. It "told" a story, but that story had become a pretext for the display of a lightness, fragility, sensuousness, and evanescence that surpassed, as it resided outside of, all verbal description. In the segregation and inequivalence of writing and dancing, movement lost some of its power to provide critical or satiric commentary. The territory of the nonverbal, inhabited by sylphs and gypsies and also by pierrots, seemed to satisfy, instead, a need to signal inexpressibility. Pierrot, the immensely popular clown figure who performed, costumed in white silk, a long-suffering everyman,[31] was never capable of specifying the injustices wrought upon him or the hopes that motivated his pitiful schemes. Where eighteenth-century Harlequin had satirized speech in his gesticulated circumventions of it, Pierrot occupied a fragile and pathetic space outside the domain of words. Pierrot invited endless commiseration, just as the sylph, his counterpart across town, provoked countless fantasies.[32] Viewers, attaching themselves to her, left language behind in order to enter a sensual cynosure, thereby reactivating the initial decision they had made in choosing to attend a performance of that consummately nonverbal art, the ballet. Dancing, either through critique or example, no longer manifested an imminent possibility for perfection. The ballet thus suggested itself as a magnificent escape, one that evoked an ideal yet ephemeral world that needn't be taken too seriously.[33]

Dancing the object of desire

By the 1840s the popularity and prevalence of the female dancer and the resonances between key values in dancing—lightness, evanescence, decorousness—and those central to female identity had created of ballet a feminine art. Ballet's exquisite femininity staged gendered roles ascribed to men and women as unique in keeping with the consolidation of masculine and feminine domains accomplished throughout French society in the early decades of the nineteenth century. Yet the alignment of masculine with public and feminine with private spaces framed ballet as one of the few and certainly the most remarkable display of women and of feminine values that occurred in public. And the masculine public space that constituted ballet's surround began to inflect with new identities these performances, the gender roles they represented, and the viewing public who witnessed them.

Critic Jules Janin intimated some of the new gendered implications for male and female dancers in this hyperbolic description of ballet:

> The *grand danseur* appears to us so sad and so heavy! He is so unhappy and so self-satisfied! He responds to nothing, he represents nothing, he is nothing. Speak to us of a pretty dancing girl who displays the grace of her features and the elegance of her figure, who reveals so fleetingly all the treasures of her beauty. Thank God, I understand that perfectly, I know what this lovely creature wishes us, and I would willingly follow her wherever she wishes in the sweet land of love. But a man, a frightful man, as ugly as you and I, a wretched fellow who leaps about without knowing why, a creature specially made to carry a musket and a sword and to wear a uniform. That this fellow should dance as a woman does—impossible! That this bewhiskered individual who is a pillar of the community, an elector, a municipal councillor, a man whose business it is to make and above all unmake laws, should come before us in a tunic of sky-blue satin, his head covered with a hat with a waving plume amorously caressing his cheek, a frightful *danseuse* of the male sex, come to pirouette in the best place while the pretty girls stand respectfully at a distance—this was surely impossible and intolerable, and we have done well to remove such great artists from our pleasures. Today, thanks to this revolution which we have effected, woman is the queen of ballet. She breathes and dances there at her ease. She is no longer forced to cut off half her silk petticoat to dress her partner with it. Today the dancing man is no longer tolerated except as a useful accessory. He is the shading of the picture, the green box trees surrounding the garden flowers, the necessary foil.[34]

Janin's caustic diatribe summarizes concisely the expectations concerning gender that circulated widely in society and then locates dance and dancers within the system of gendered values. As he saw it, the female dancer affirmed and even enhanced the assumptions concerning feminine docility and attractiveness, but at the same time, she announced a kind of sexual availability. This "lovely creature" enticed the viewer who "willingly followed her into the land of love." In contrast, the male dancer, now embarrassingly effeminate, contravened the requirements made on him to legislate, uphold, and defend social order. His sensuality, his dedication to physical rather than mental labor, the decorous, diversionary context for his actions—all inappropriate to his social stature and calling—could no longer be tolerated. He posed a threat both to masculine identity and to heterosexual normalcy that could only be mollified by reducing his participation in the ballet to that of an animate prop.

Although Janin exaggerated the general response to male performers, his observations did accurately reflect the divisions of labor that governed male and female participation within the profession. Male choreographers and administrators continued to direct the development of the art, and male critics evaluated its success. A small number of male dancers came up through the ranks to star as partners of the celebrated ballerinas, but their roles either as masters of pantomimic gesture or as virtuoso dancers had been leached of any serious or persuasive meaning.[35] The female characters consistently magnetized the viewer's attention and claimed the bulk of space in the critics' appraisals.

The ballet's choreography framed and developed the ballerina's performance as the central focus, but it also figured her as the gratifying object of the viewer's desiring gaze. Her costume, vocabulary of skills, and her centrality within the story invested her with a charisma that no other characters shared. Male dancers and even female corps de ballet deferred to her, their gazes and postures functioning like directionals that guided the viewer's attention toward her. Her disappearance into the corps de ballet during scenes of group dancing only fueled the need, reinforced by the male dancer's search for her, to see her once again. She flirted with him and with the audience. She danced for those onstage and with those seated out front.

In figuring the ballerina as the central and most desired subject and her partner as a prosthetic extension of the viewer's gaze, the production engendered the presumed viewer as masculine and oriented "his" desire as heterosexual. Eighteenth-century ballets had endowed both male and female performers with sexual charisma and even intimated the possibility of homosexual attachments.[36] Female viewers swooned over male dancers in the same way that male viewers adored female dancers. Consonant with the more fluid mores prescribing sexual behavior up through the end of the century, viewers might also find themselves gratified by the possibility of same-sex attractions.[37] Nothing in the choreography deterred the viewer from channeling desire toward dancers of either sex or from purposefully recasting male/female relations as same sex partnerships. By the 1840s, however, the kinds of strictures that defined each gender's behavior both on- and offstage constrained severely the directions in which desire might travel. Both male and female viewers witnessed a performance intended to appeal to the masculine desire for the female body.

One complication to this basic structuring of the viewer's identity existed through the figure of the female dancer *en travesti*, a practice increasing in popularity since the beginning of the century.[38] Neither an ephemeral sylph nor a seductive exotic, this largish woman played male corps de ballet roles and sometimes took the part of the male principal dancer in ballets with comic plots. (See fig. 81.) Where the tragedy continued to require the seriousness that a man's performance would lend to the production, the comedies utilized the travesty dancer as partner to the ballerina, a hero who gestured adoringly toward his love and also showed remarkable competence at the battery of male steps. Tantalizingly exposed, a female body clad in men's breeches, but displaying a confident mastery of her part, the travesty dancer resolved the threat of the effeminate male onstage. In enacting his unmanly activities, she substituted for the anxiety he provoked a faithful and charming replication of his duties.

81. Costume for a page from act 1 of Filippo Taglioni's *La Fille du Danube* (1836).

The female travesty performer, prevalent in all boulevard entertainments, achieved high visibility at the Opéra through the phenomenal success of Thérèse Elssler's partnering of her sister Fanny. Thérèse choreographed specialty duets and at least one entire ballet, *La Volière* (1838). She then performed as her sister's escort, a young and daring hero, tall, well-built, and ever solicitous of the heroine's needs. Reviews complemented Thérèse on her skillful partnering and her graceful ability to display her sister's talents. They praised her shapely legs and, equally, her choreography, which contributed new complexities of interlocking shapes to the partnering vocabulary as well as deftly drawing the viewer's attention to Fanny's exceptional skills. According to reviewers, Thérèse's presence, perfectly acceptable, even desirable because the two bodies worked so well together, signaled no intimation of homoerotic possibility, no sense of illicit, much less scandalous behavior. Nor did the reviews register a sense of relief at the handy substitution of a manly woman for an effeminate man. Instead, they situated the Elsslers' duets within the tradition of such performances so that the correct execution of the role mattered and the gendered deviance it implied did not.

Still, the female travesty dancer's unique position, in no way comparable to male travesty performances in the acrobatic roles of witch or hag, must have complicated the viewer's response. In one way, she increased the availability of the ballerina because she stood as a mere woman in between the masculinized viewer and the object of desire. In another, she further excited the masculinized viewer by signaling the eroticism of a female couple. In still another, she provided a safe, tacit attachment for men or women inclined toward homoerotic fantasy. Thus she loomed in and out of focus: a coquettishly aggressive woman asserting a male identity, a plausible attachment for both heterosexual and homosexual desire, but also a talented dancer competent at the codes of male dancing, and a charming cipher for the labor entailed in displaying the ballerina.[39] Just as the ballet vacillated between pathos and tours de force, the travesty dancer pulled viewers into the mystery of her "becoming a man" and then pushed them back away at every moment where the divergence between character and sexual identity became apparent. She thereby enhanced viewers' ability to indulge in the seductive perversion of bending the narrative. They could move in and out of it, flirting with nihilistic abandon at the contradictions embodied before them. Located at the very heart of the ballet, as partner within the pas de deux, she fueled the ballerina's charisma and also trivialized the possible impact of ballet as an art form.

The ballerina, her travesty partner, and the female corps de ballet all derived a certain notoriety from their highly visible location as women in public who put their bodies on display. This violation of gendered roles and spaces positioned them as one of the several varieties of *femmes publiques*, signaling in some degree their sexual availability. As public women they participated in and were subject to the economies that regulated all public expressions of sexuality, tacit and explicit forms of advertisement, and all controls governing availability and procurement.[40] This status for female dancers was graphically documented in writings about dance, especially at the Opéra, and also in the changed institutional identity of the Opéra itself. Ballet thrived or declined as one of the products the Opéra put on sale, and the female dancer, both product and purveyor of the performance as product, likewise endured the economic vicissitudes that a capitalist market produces.

In the 1830s and '40s two related kinds of literature about dance that reported these changes began to enjoy unprecedented popularity and to circulate in far greater quantity than ever before.[41] One kind of publication profiled operations behind the scenes at the Opéra and the other summarized gossip, usually in the guise of short biographical entries, about well-known performers. These pamphlets and books exuded an aura of mystery and intrigue. Full of innuendoes that seemed to refer to scandalous amorous liaisons, they blurred professional persona and personal life as defined by affairs of the heart. Always promiscuous, life in the theatre now appeared more bohemian than ever, debauched but also joyous, impoverished but free, poignant and risqué. (See fig. 82.)

These publications, often titled anatomies or physiologies of the Opéra,[42] detailed in sentimental terms the various constituencies who appeared daily at the side door of the Opéra house to contribute their talents and labor to the productions of ballet: costume and scene designers and their staff; machinists and their crew; composers, conductors, and musicians; writers hoping for the opportunity to present their scenario to a member of the administration; the approximately forty machine operators, twenty lamplighters, fifteen messenger boys, six firemen, and twelve dressers required for a given performance; the leader of the claque,[43] there to receive instructions as to when and how loudly his paid group of audience members should applaud; critics from the newspapers who were also paid by Opéra administrators and dancers to mention favorably their latest efforts; the Opéra doctor there to treat an injury or to deliver his report on the claim to illness or injury made by a given dancer; female dancers usually accompanied by their mothers or other female relatives and by hopeful suitors; a smaller number of male dancers; and most notorious of all, the *petits rats*, prepubescent girls, always hungry and poor, who studied dance and aspired to a career on the stage.

82. Backstage at the Opéra.

These young girls figured prominently in accounts of the Opéra as a symbol of the hardships entailed by the life of a dancer and also the dedication it required. With their bony knees, their enormous dark eyes, the crust of bread in their pocket, these children exceeded all criteria for poignancy. They walked several miles to their early morning dance class with little to eat or to wear. They hovered in the wings eagerly soaking in all the action that took place both on- and offstage during rehearsals and performances. They assimilated the performance styles of the great ballerinas and their infinitely nuanced styles of coquetry as well. Some eventually qualified for positions as *figurantes,* the lowest rank within the corps de ballet. Like the gypsies or sylphides they so admired, the petits rats combined adventurous assertiveness with fragile innocence. Their half-clothed bodies and long, tangled hair gestured tantalizingly toward the women they would become, yet also like the sylph they remained for the moment sexually unavailable.

Once a member of the Opéra staff, young dancers still faced a serious problem of financial support. Opéra salaries could not begin to pay for food and lodging, much less dance classes and costume accessories.[44] Consequently, most found it necessary to enter into negotiations with a wealthy businessman or aging aristocrat with whom they contracted to exchange sexual favors for monetary security. Usually arranged by a mother, aunt, or older sister, these affairs procured for the young dancer an apartment, a substantial monthly allowance, and sometimes the political influence to advance rapidly through the ranks. They assured the bourgeois businessman or the aristocrat a reputation for wealth and potency. This arrangement between dancer and protector, as he was called, could last a few months or several years. Both the specifics of the each contract and the system itself garnered considerable attention in the gossip literature on performers' lives.

Throughout the eighteenth century female performers had always used their independent status to engage in liaisons at will, but financial security had not determined their sexual availability. Salaries at the Opéra had covered basic needs, and the hierarchies of genre and seniority ensured advancement and an adequate pension after fifteen years of service. Dancers used liaisons to enhance their wealth and power, not to prevent destitution.[45] Their actions took place in a context where extramarital relationships were normative and public. By the 1830s, however, the growth of the middle class with its emphasis on the nuclear family privatized extramarital affairs and gave both dancers and their liaisons a desperate aura.[46]

The financial plight of dancers worsened with the 1831 leasing of the Opéra, to Louis Véron as an independent business capable of fully funding its own productions. Taking into account the large governmental subvention Véron negotiated as part of the contract, he nonetheless made the Opéra into a successful income-generating institution in the four years of his directorship, and the changes he initiated, consonant with the conversion to a capitalist economics that overtook the country during these years, endured for decades. Writing about his artistic successes of the 1830s, Véron offered this concise summary of ballet's aesthetic role:

> I acquired, however, the conviction that ballets representing a dramatic action cannot be counted on for a grand success. . . . Dramas and tableaux of social mores are not part of the domain of choreography; the public demands above all else in the ballet varied and gripping music, new and curious costumes, great variety, contrasting decors, surprises, visible changes, a simple plot, easy to understand, but where the dance is the natural development of the situations. It is also necessary to add the seductions of a beautiful and young artist, who dances better and differently from those who preceded her. When one does not speak either to the spirit or the heart, it is necessary to speak to the senses and especially to the eyes.[47]

Véron rejected as unmarketable any attempts to present social customs or complex messages through dance. Rather than "speak to the soul" he hoped to fill the eyes and the senses. As a good entrepreneur, Véron understood that his ability to "sell" the ballet depended upon a smooth integration of the ballet's component parts using a simple plot that could transcend the tension between storytelling and dancing. Even more important the ballets required a lavish attention to production values—newness, functionality, and tastefulness of costumes and decor, suitability of the music, and the beautiful appearance and skills of the dancers, especially the women.

In order to accomplish this, Véron had the entire Opéra house refurbished and installed Locatelli astro lamps that permitted a greater range of light levels. He also added to the glamour of the Opéra by arranging entertainment and unusual set designs for the weekly public balls held there.[48] (See fig. 83.) He cultivated new talent by establishing a school for young children, and used his medical expertise to influence the selection of those students whose "health, temperament, bodily proportions, and flexibility of limbs promised the most success at dancing."[49] Véron also took a strong hand in the selection and realization of ballet scenarios.[50] And he negotiated individually contracts for all members of the corps de ballet and eliminated pensions altogether, while at the same time creating a star system for the leading ballerinas.[51]

Véron's administrative actions caused the complete collapse of the genre system, already weakened by the emphasis on generic virtuoso competence. He actively recruited foreign principal dancers, thereby subverting the Opéra's system of fixed salaries

83. Staircase at the Opéra during a masked ball at Carnival time.

for each rank. Although dancers from other countries had often appeared for limited periods at the Opéra, Véron consistently favored the exotic imports over dancers who had come up through the ranks of the Opéra, and he paid them stunning fees. Local dancers, who had once been compared only with earlier stages in their own development or with their repertoire of characters, now competed with fresh talent from abroad.[52]

If this practice contributed to low morale among mid-ranking dancers, it also diminished the audience's ability to evaluate their dancing. With new ballerinas arriving regularly, the criteria for evaluation shifted to the fresh physique, the latest tours de force, the immediately apparent elements of the dancer's style. No sooner had audiences become accustomed to Taglioni's incomparable fluidity, for example, than Elssler was contracted to arrive in Paris. Véron, a masterful publicist, orchestrated a rivalry between the two dancers that embroiled critics, poets, illustrators, portraitists, and designers of women's fashion in a delirium of enthusiasms that compared the two dancers by focusing on the relative merits of body parts, skills en pointe, and a narrow range of character traits. When attendance declined slightly Véron would announce falsely that a given production was in its final week of performances.[53] In order to keep attention focused on the dancers, he conferred nightly with Auguste, leader of the claque, over new orchestrations for the timing and fervor of applause.[54]

Véron also increased support for the Opéra by opening the Foyer de la Danse as a meeting place for dancers and their admirers. Here, in front of an elite group of bankers, businessmen, aristocrats, and critics, dancers warmed up and rehearsed their parts one last time before going on stage. By subscribing to a season ticket, these men enjoyed the exclusive privilege of the ballerinas' intimate company before, during, and after the performance. An enchanted land of enticingly dressed sylphs, peasant maids, and svelte nobles, the Foyer de la Danse structured the patrons' escapist reveries around the objectified physique and coquetry of the dancers. For them the Foyer de la Danse offered one of the few civilized forums for appreciation and flirtation. For the dancers it also created a marketplace for the display of wares they hoped to exchange for financial security.

The nightly pre-performance preparations proceeded as if choreographed for the stage. First figurantes, then *coryphées,* then the mid-level dancers, and finally the stars entered the room and embarked on their routine as male admirers seated throughout the space looked on:

> The dancers lift one after the other each leg until they are able to place the foot horizontally on the wooden barre and to leave it to stretch for a while; then they abandon this position, and, grasping the barre with one hand, they practice their *battements* and *jetés-battus.* After these preliminary exercises, they water the floor with a charming little watering can; then, posing in front of the mirror which is full-length, they attempt numerous *pirouettes, entrechats,* and rehearse more or less seriously before appearing onstage the steps they will dance. [55]

This well-established sequence, by keeping dancers occupied with but not invested in their roles, provided an excellent vehicle for the coquettish exchange of comments and glances and the objective appraisal of a dancer's compatibility. The mother, "an accessory as necessary as the watering can," mediated the interactions.[56] The surrounding mirrors, still a novelty especially in this quantity, multiplied the voyeuristic, self-admiring, and envious gazes collected in the room.[57]

Observing these displays of feminine form and often participating in the flirtatious banter, the critics could not help but be influenced by the aestheticization of sexual desire. They were influenced by the sexual climate of the Foyer de la Danse, but as professional journalists they also necessarily responded to performers as clients. Since the establishment of the newspaper industry at the beginning of the century, it had been common practice for theatre managers and star performers to hire favorable exposure. Shopkeepers paid the newspapers to praise the quality of their merchandise, and similarly, principal dancers paid for laudatory commentary. The critics' function thus combined aesthetic evaluation and the reportage of erotic intrigue with advertisement. Their reviews reflected the same fascination with dancers' erotic power evident in the biographies and incidental literature on the Opéra. Plot summaries dominated the writing with their length and prominent location as they had throughout the eighteenth century. But in their appraisal of the performers, critics adopted a tone both familiar and calculating, one that specified as much about the physical attributes of the dancers as their dancing and acting prowess.[58]

With the demise of the genre system, each dancer could, through her physique and accomplishments, establish her own style. Yet overall standards, especially regarding physical attributes, endured. One dancer was simply too skinny; another's shoulders too rounded; another's legs a treasure but her bosom unremarkable. At the same time that critics encouraged viewers to savor a dancer's elegant bodily proportions and attributes, they demonstrated how to decode the dancer's physique for evidence of her character. For them she could only be successful if she had the right demeanor for the part. Gautier, for example, offered this comparison of Elssler, Lucile Grahn, and a new American dancer, Augusta Maywood, on the occasion of her debut:

> Mlle. Augusta Maywood has a quite clear-cut type of talent. It is not the melancholy grace, dreamy abandon, and carefree lightness of Mlle. Grahn, in whose eyes are reflected Norway's cold and clear blue sky, and who suggests a valkyrie dancing over the snow; still less the inimitable perfection, glittering poise, bearing of a classic Diana, and sculptural purity associated with Mlle. Fanny Elssler; there is something abrupt, unexpected, fantastic about Mlle. Maywood which sets her quite apart. . . . She is of medium height, well formed, and very young . . . with black eyes and small features with an alert and untamed expression which gambles strongly on being beautiful; add to this sinews of steel, the knee-joints of a jaguar, and an agility almost equal to that of a clown. . . . she might be compared to an India rubber ball bouncing on a racket; she had a great deal of elevation and spring: her small deer-like legs can bound as far as those of Mlle. Taglioni.[59]

For Gautier, the actual proportions of the limbs and color of the eyes or hair signaled a character type. The ballet's story, rather than offering a dancer the opportunity to "become the character," served as a pretext for putting into action her telling physiognomy.

Although summarized comprehensively in the reviews, the ballet stories seemed to merit little critical attention. Eighteenth-century critics had examined in detail the integrity of characters' motivations and the effectiveness of the sequence of scenes in order to rate the empathic connection of performer to character and character to audience. Now critics evidenced the same distance from characters and their situations that they maintained from the female body. It was only when they perceived the fortuitous conjunction of a well-proportioned physique, a pretty countenance, expertise at mime and dancing, and a plausible story exquisitely produced that they felt transported by the performance. The plight of characters mattered far less than the dancer's waist or her smile.

Gautier, although more obsessed with the physical detail than most,[60] reflected the typical gaze directed toward female dancers in his anatomical rapture over Fanny Elssler's body:

> Mlle. Fanny Elssler is tall, supple, and well formed; she has delicate wrists and slim ankles; her legs, elegant and well-turned, recall the slender but muscular legs of Diana, the virgin huntress; the knee-caps are well-defined, stand out in relief, and make the whole knee beyond reproach; her legs differ considerably from the usual dancers' legs, whose bodies seem to have run into their stockings and settled there; they are not the calves of a parish beadle or of a jack of clubs, which arouse the enthusiasm of the old *roués* in the stalls and make them continuously polish the lenses of their Opéra-glasses, but two beautiful legs like those of an antique statue, worthy of being cast and studied with care.
>
> We shall be pardoned, we hope, for having discoursed at such length on legs, but we are speaking of a dancer.
>
> Another praiseworthy feature is that Mlle. Elssler has rounded and well-shaped arms, which do not reveal the bone of the elbow, and have nothing of the angular shape of the arms of her companions, whose awful thinness makes them resemble

lobster-claws dabbed with wet-white. Her bosom is full, a rarity among dancers, where the twin hills and mountains of snow so praised by students and minor poets appear totally unknown. Neither can one see moving on her back those two bony triangles which resemble the roots of a torn-off wing.

As to the shape of her head, we must admit that it does not seem to us to be as graceful as it is said to be. Mlle. Elssler is endowed with superb hair which falls on each side of her temples, lustrous and glossy as the two wings of a bird; the dark shade of her hair clashes in too southern a manner with her typically German features; it is not the right hair for such a head and body. This peculiarity is disturbing and upsets the harmony of the whole; her eyes, very black, the pupils of which are like two little stars of jet set in a crystal sky, are inconsistent with the nose, which, like the forehead, is quite German."[61]

By breaking down the body into specific parts, Gautier and other critics claimed a strange intimacy with the dancers but also an objective distance. They knew every curve of each dancer's flesh, but they also compared, curve for curve, all dancers' attributes.

The analytic procedures at the Opéra that constructed a physiology of performance production applied to the principal dancer's body in the extreme. Subject to such analysis, she no longer exemplified a physiological type such as the petit rat, who contributed her unique talents to the overall functioning of the Opéra organization. Instead, the parceling of her body into its various delicious and less adequate parts obscured the dancer's personhood both on- and offstage and opened up the dancer's body to the viewer's consuming gaze. The body's parts, salaciously separated from the whole, became subject to symbolic purchase. Moving through the dance, knees, shoulders, neck, or ankles suggested themselves as available for a price. By equating to the abstract category of capital, the dancer's various physical attributes assimilated to the category of commodity, advertising more ostensibly than most their erotic allure. Their every movement repeated the cycle of erotic attraction of goods on the market: the enticement to purchase and the failure of the possession once acquired to sate desire. They did, after all, vanish, transporting themselves to the next move just as the viewer's eyes attempted to grasp them.

An entrepreneur like Louis Véron apprehended the erotic space that the ballet could occupy and worked hard to construct an economic and physical surround that could support it. In his *Mémoires* he never mentioned the opening of the Foyer de la Danse as one of his achievements, but he did take great pride in the fact that during his years as director no dancer incurred an injury as the result of faulty machinery. The ropes, pulleys, trapdoors, flies, and freestanding scenery that composed the mechanical infrastructure of the theatre presented serious hazards to both dancers and crew who traversed the backstage areas under dimly lit conditions. Scenery easily collapsed and ropes hauling dancers through the air eventually frayed. Véron, like the good businessman he was, inspected all the ropes every night in order to ensure the peak condition of all his merchandise.

The dissolving object of the gaze

The early-nineteenth-century consolidation of masculine public and feminine private spaces feminized all the arts. Construed as less serious or consequential than the domains of government and business, the arts then reproduced among themselves the same gendered and functionalist hierarchies, based on the valuing of abstract and concrete, logical and emotional, textual and visual, through which their relegation to the feminine had been accomplished. Sentiment-filled and evanescent, the dance's display of bodily movement earned it a position as the most feminine art of them all. Yet the fact that it was produced within the public realm and not within the domestic sphere forced a version of the feminine defined by masculine values and expectations.

Untainted by, because incapable of expressing, issues with social or moral relevance, the ballet entertained and diverted its audience, and at its best enchanted them with its ephemeral beauty. An eclectic group of spectators—business men and their wives, artists, shopgirls, students, aging aristocrats—looked past the seamy backstage life with its poverty, frivolous expenditures, and mothers serving as pimps in order to adore the ballerina or become lost in the landscape. The spectacle they encountered presumed a homogeneous vectoring of desire on their part. The female dancer, even as she celebrated the feminine attributes of grace and lightness, also functioned as the object of a masculine desire. Ballets, in all their exquisite invention and wondrous fragility, also stuffed the stage with scantily clad women for a masculine gaze to admire.

At the same time that audience members exercised a masculine and heterosexual role in viewing the ballet, they also identified as consumers. The arts, including dance, no longer set standards of aesthetic excellence through which the state partially defined itself; rather, they offered an array of aesthetic experiences for spectators to select. Viewers at the ballet elected to purchase what it offered. The production team at an institution like the Opéra, which included administrators, artists, artisans, and even the claque, manufactured an event that critics evaluated for viewers' consumption. If the ballet was successful, the critic might comment, verifying the objecthood of the female dancer: "Nothing was lacking—not invention, poetry, music, the arrangement of new dances, the number of beautiful women dancers, harmony, liveliness, grace, energy, Adèle Dumilâtre, and especially Carlotta Grisi."[62] The prime ingredients for success—inventiveness, grace, and beautiful women dancers—could all be catalogued with no regard to the choreographer's labor or the ballerina's personhood.

The capitalist marketing of dancers and ballet worked alongside the dimorphism of gender roles to further commodify the female dancing body. The female body's parts, increasingly separated from the dancing person, presented themselves as objects of a fetishistic reverie. Several years in advance of the opening of the first Parisian department stores, ballet functioned to invest the dancer's body with the viewer's desire and to dramatize the spending of that desire in the form of the transience of dancing itself. This cycle of acquisitiveness and dissipation occurring at the site of the dancer's body robbed it of any status or intrinsic worth. Instead, the dancing body filled the momentary need for erotic reverie before resuming more serious social obligations.[63]

Nothing very risqué took place in such moments of erotic investment. The ballerina and even the female travesty dancer both facilitated conservative prescriptions for social and gendered behavior. The ballerina in all her incarnations preserved and enhanced male sexual potency as she danced out the desirability of heterosexual coupling. When partnering her, the male dancer directed the viewer's gaze toward her but nonetheless remained in control of this spectacularly charismatic object. In comic plots the ballerina's vivacity heightened the control of the man who would be her mate and confirmed male hegemony as she passed in exchange between father and husband. When the travesty dancer played a principal role, this female hero evinced no threat of uncontrollable sexual appetite or uncontainable passion, and she charmingly burlesqued the ballerina's intimidating sexual potency, thereby provoking only perverse delight rather than the apprehension of a monstrous feminine otherness. In tragic plots where the leading couple failed to unite, the impediment could be traced to the impossibility of achieving union across class or blood lines. This tacit affirmation of the boundaries of race and class exerted a quiet control over the inebriating sensuality of the ballet's visual and corporeal splendor.

Could female dancers implement any tactics of resistance to the scopophilic packaging of their life and art? Certainly the travesty dancer offered no affront to the certitude of gendered social roles or to the market that purveyed them. Unlike the boulevard theatres, circuses, and hippodromes that continued to introduce outrageous contestations of normative values and behavior, the ballet upheld the strict codes that authorized its theatricality. In its unique role as the supreme orchestration of muteness, ballet had no access to the blending of discourses on which the boulevard theatres based their satire. It steadfastly displayed the authenticity of gesture and the perpetual vanishing of charm. Any liberatory impulses the ballet might offer thus marked their own futility by dissolving even as they drew dancer or viewer toward them.

Interlude

Making Merry / Gazing On

While the premiers danseurs and danseuses exhibit their talents, the corps de ballet looks on appreciatively. Each privileged display of dancing by a soloist, couple, or small group is framed by an affable group of supporters. Clumped in intimate groupings around the periphery of the stage, these onlookers create the illusion of a festive gathering. They bow and nod to one another, stand or sit alongside one another, and sometimes even wander the half-circle along which they are decorously strewn in imitation of participants at some party or celebration. They meet and greet, lift their glasses in a toast, hide coyly behind their fans, or whisper discreetly, mostly between dances. During the sequences of spectacular virtuosity, they remain almost frozen, attending only to the dancing. They encourage the audience to do likewise. Their bodies collect the gazes of spectators and redirect them toward the tours de force. At the same time, they serve as movable scenery, an animated backdrop to the principal action, full of variety, asymmetry, and contrast. Most important, however, these pedestrian bodies exemplify the raw corporeal matter out of which the virtuosity on display has been wrought.

Within the centerstage world of the premiers danseurs and danseuses there exist varieties and degrees of perfection. These dancers compete playfully amongst themselves, their danced exchanges not unlike a salon's lively repartee. Their dialogue builds to the inevitable and quintessential bon mot—the solos or pas de deux of hero and heroine. These two garner the most demanding vocabulary and demonstrate the most refined execution. Their performance climaxes the narrative of accomplishment laid out in the successive solo and group displays. The corps de ballet, enthusiastic amateurs, reiterate and reinforce the narrative of virtuosity. They constitute the "before" and the soloists exhibit the "after." With their laudatory gazes, they justify the entire process through which some bodies have acquired more skill and nobility than others. Their deferential demeanor combines with the bolstering and focusing effect of their disposition in space to validate the hierarchy on display.

La Sylphide (1832)[1]

With *La Sylphide* choreographer Filippo Taglioni found the perfect vehicle for displaying the unprecedented dancing style and prowess of his daughter Marie. But he also realized one of the most powerful scenarios, written by the renowned tenor Adolphe Nourrit, ever conceived for the ballet stage. Acknowledged as registering an epistemic shift in the fundamental conventions on which ballet productions were based, *La Sylphide* catapulted theatrical dance into a romantic modality. As Gautier observed:

> After *La Sylphide, Les Filets de Vulcain* and *Flore et Zéphire* were no longer possible; the Opéra was given over to gnomes, undines, salamanders, elves, nixes, wilis, peris—to all that strange and mysterious folk who lend themselves so marvellously to the fantasies of the *maître de ballet*. The twelve palaces in marble and gold of the Olympians were relegated to the dust of the store-rooms, and the scene painters received orders only for romantic forests, valleys illumined by the pretty German moonlight reminiscent of Heinrich Heine's charming ballads.[2]

Although following in arrears of literary romanticism, the new productions with their waters and forests and the creatures that inhabited them revitalized the oppositions between reality and aspiration and between transitory earthly pursuits and immortal, abstract ideals, making the dual life of humankind more palpable than ever.

La Sylphide opens on James asleep in his chair as the sylphide kneels at his feet, ethereal yet adorable, her hair ringed with flowers, tiny wings protruding from her back. She rises and dances around him, and as if she were a dream, he follows her motions in his sleep. Her kiss awakens him and he pursues her around the room, but she takes flight up the chimney; he is left wondering whether her presence was real or imagined. James's companion, Gurn, has seen nothing, but soon fixes all his attention on his love, Effie, who enters with James's mother. James and Effie are to be married on this day and kneel for the mother's blessing. James remains distracted, even when Effie's girlfriends arrive with gifts and she dances for and with them. Suddenly the old hag and soothsayer, Madge, materializes at the fireplace, and at the girls' request she reads Effie's palm. Yes, she will be happy in marriage, but no, James does not love her. Gurn, however, thrusting his palm in front of the hag, does. James rages at the old sorceress and she departs. The others exit, disturbed by the incident, and James becomes reimmersed in his fantasies. The sylphide appears at the window and then floats into the room. As they dance together she conveys her love and need for him. Hearing guests approaching, he hides her under his scarf on the chair and when accosted by Gurn, lifts it to find her gone. Yet as villagers begin a lengthy celebration, she returns, flitting in and out of the action, often pursued by James. At the crucial moment where the couple's rings are to be exchanged, the sylphide deftly snatches James's ring and rushes out the window, James in hot pursuit. The wedding company, abandoned, gather around Effie to ease her despair.

Act 2 opens on a forest in dense fog. Madge and then her companions dance menacingly around a cauldron, eventually pulling out of it a long, shimmering scarf. As the mist clears and with it the witches, James enters, still pursuing the sylphide. Suddenly she is beside him, and just as suddenly many more sylphides appear in the trees above and on the ground, surrounding him. The sylphide's elusiveness is now compounded by the presence of so many similar beings. She vanishes into the group, and James searches for her in vain. Then he comes across Madge, who, at his request for help in securing the sylphide's companionship, proffers the scarf. Once entwined around the sylphide's wings, Madge explains, she will fly no more. In a final pas de deux, the sylphide chases after the scarf, thinking it an enticing present from her sweetheart. Finding his opportunity, James wraps it around her, and her wings flutter to the floor. But their loss also entails her death. She sinks slowly into his arms as her supernatural sisters gather mournfully around. They bear her body heavenward. James remains utterly desolate and prostrate on the ground as Gurn's and Effie's wedding party passes by in the distance.

The deep appeal of this scenario resided in the powerfully contrasting categories—castle and forest, evil witch and innocent bride, supernatural others and real villagers—that shaped striking spectacle and diverse dancing. The witches' dance at the beginning of act 2 vivified the extreme difference between the castle's culture and a mysterious and unruly nature. Their pulsing circle propelled bodies in a grotesque contortion of classical values—hunched torsos, ponderous but menacing leaps, fingers in spidery disarray. Following on the well-ordered and buoyant festivities of villagers in act 1, who expressed their gaiety in symmetrical sequences of jumps, beats, and gallops, all with a Scottish flair, the witches summoned up a dark and tragic netherworld. The ragged edges of their sleeves and capes slicing through the fog presented the antithesis of the neat plaid kilts and skirts and the simple rounded arms of the villagers. The castle's gothic features likewise opposed the profusion of trees and bushes in which the sylphides made their home. Their costume and movement vocabulary, one that included flying, transported viewers to a land unlike anything they had ever seen.

The vaporous muslin skirts, the darting sissonnes and effortless runs, the floating arms, all gave the sylphides their ethereal look. Elaborate machinery aided in their exploration of aeriality, suggesting the possibility of lightness and flight to an unprecedented degree. At the end of her opening solo as the sylphide, Taglioni rushed into the fireplace and reached out of sight for a bar that pulled her up through the chimney, her pointed feet disappearing as the last trace of a single gesture that converted horizontal into vertical motion. Stepping from the window onto a table just inside, she maintained a coy pose as a section of that table lowered her smoothly to ground level. These arresting moments, enhanced by Taglioni's own skill at producing lightness in the extended limb or the balance en pointe, rendered all the more credible the daring flights across the entire stage span by members of the corps de ballet in act 2. While others of their kind perched high in the trees that framed the forest glade, sylphides in arabesque with arms unfolding to the front would glide from one side of the stage to the other, creating the sense that their community inhabited comfortably both ground and air. Other dancers, fastened to pushcarts wheeled upstage of the bushes at the back of the glade, floated in and out of sight. Many of these contrivances had been used in earlier ballets; for example, Charles Didelot's *Flore et Zéphire* had electrified audiences with the nymphs' flight. But never had these effects integrated so fluidly with character and movement to create a world, thoroughly convincing but radically different from contemporary or historical settings.

Played out across these oppositional categories of virtuous and wicked, real and supernatural, and intensified by their extreme distinctiveness, the differing attachments among the four principal characters moved the plot forward with a new dynamism. The triangular attachment of two female characters for the same man, itself an innovative configuration for ballet scenarios, created new drama and fresh choreographic possibilities. Filippo Taglioni mined these with special effectiveness in a pas de trois in act 1, where both sylphide and bride-to-be competed for James's attention. The sylphide insinuated herself into the couple's classic shapes, causing James to abandon Effie in order to partner her. When, in her proprietary impetuousness, Effie reappropriated her partner's support, the sylphide soon found a way to lure James back into dancing with her. Because the sylphide was only visible to James, the perpetually evolving, complex shapes created by the three dancers could be read by viewers as two dances occurring at the same time: one a duet between Effie and her preoccupied and irresponsible fiancé, and the other a trio where the cause of his distraction coalesced as the sylphide.

The nuances inherent in such a triangle, more concentrated in the pas de trois, proliferated over the course of the first act and were augmented by the inverse rivalry between Gurn and James over Effie. Alternately despairing and insistent, Gurn applied pressure on both Effie and James to change their feelings. He repeatedly reminded Effie of his affections, giving her a beautiful feather, asking the witch to read his palm, and trying to dance with and for her. Having witnessed James dancing with the sylphide, or at least the act of James hiding something under the tartan, Gurn demanded an investigation. The fact that it proved nothing only intensified James's quandary. Gurn's vigilance in combination with the competing attentions of sylphide, fiancée, and village expectations forced an escalation in James's ambivalence. His confusion did not even resolve itself when the sylphide peremptorily seized the ring from his hand and fled. The quickness of her action and his response could be attributed either to his decision to follow her or to his need to retrieve the ring.

The sylphide, especially as realized by Marie Taglioni, presented one of the most complex and intriguing characters yet to appear on the ballet stage. Shy, retiring, desperate for James's attention and love, she was also capriciously aggressive. Flitting with demure chasteness away from him, resting chin on hand in a pose that signified fragility and meekness, she nonetheless repeatedly returned, interrupting the social status quo with increasingly urgent demonstrations of her love. These conflicting sets of character traits helped to support her identity, made clear in James's pantomimed confusion as to the nature of her being, as both a female character and an abstract version of love. From her opening solo as James followed her in his sleep to the moment of her death, the sylphide functioned both as creature and as concept. She stood for another kind of woman, another kind of love, and for love in its abstract perfection. James longed for her just as he longed to experience an ideal love.

The fact that viewers could interpret the dancing on all these levels—just as they could see two dances within the pas de trois, or the sylphide chasing after a shawl that was a charming present and the instrument of her death—gave *La Sylphide* a depth that few earlier ballets had attained. At many moments the performance even became a metaphor for the workings of desire itself. The sylphide, oscillating between realizable female romantic partner and unrealizable dream of perfect love, remained always in motion. Even more confounding, she repeatedly vanished only to reappear, more desirable than ever. Containing or immobilizing this desired object stilled its magnetic attraction. The sylphide's inevitable death verified this principal law of desire.

The tragic ending to *La Sylphide,* as striking an innovation as the aerial world of the sylphides, reverberated with the deadly accuracy of this choreographic analysis of desire.

James, ambitious in his contract with the witch yet naively unaware of desire's destiny, was nonetheless responsible for the sylphide's death. His pathetic and forsaken body lay in the foreground while in the background social reality marched gaily forward, torches raised to stave off nature's gloom. Above him hovered the constellation of sylphides, their own most ambitious member prone and lifeless in their midst. Like James she had adventured into a world outside her own and suffered the consequences. Or was she nothing more than his own self-validating dream of desire, as fantastical as the twelve dancing girls floating decorously in midair?

Up through the 1820s the equation of dancing with lightness and happiness had necessitated a comic plot. Now the possibility that dancing could metaphorize transitivity and loss pivoted theatrical dance conventions toward new plots and new characters. These new formulae for danced action positioned man as dreamer, caught between social banality and a utopistic dream world. They positioned woman as the attractive force that divided man between these two worlds. The male character, sensitive but also indecisive, indulged in the inner conflict produced by these two competing lives. The female character, with little social identity of her own, kept desire in circulation by serving alternately as the object of its attachment and the corporeal trace of its path.

Maybe Yes; Maybe No

"I will try to see what you are holding, letting curiosity overtake me, or I will affect disinterest because I should not care." "I will let you come nearer because I like you, or I will recoil knowing it is improper to be near you." "I will consider your request because I am kind, or I will shy away because you frighten me." "I will allow you to kiss my hand, feeling things I have never felt before, or I will withdraw it because you have gone too far." "I will stay near you because it makes me so happy, or I will run away because this should not go on." "I will dance with you because I love you, or I will stop dancing because I should not reveal my love."

The female character dances out these thoughts while the male character engages in courtly pursuit of her heart and her body. He displays ingenuity in devising activities or projects that intrigue her—he initiates games, picks flowers, offers her presents, ribbons, or bouquets. He responds with admirable alacrity to each of her forms of refusal—blocking her exits, circling around her, entreating her on bended knee. Above all he shows an eloquent use of the rhetoric that will persuade her his love is deep and pure. He must master this rhetoric because he cannot dance with her—that is, make love with her—until he has assured her that his love for her is eternal.

But how can he prove his devotion to her? Sometimes she, in the form of the invigilant dancer, sees him alone, longing for her, caressing a flower she has given him, tracing her initials on the tree. More often, he must signal his feelings with a certain form of docility: he must show himself overriding his burning desire for her by not coming too close too often, by appearing distraught and supplicatory, by acting overjoyed when she acknowledges in some small way his devotion. In this way he shows her power over him and his fidelity to her.

He restrains himself in accordance with her wishes and thereby appears courageous and sensitive. She restrains herself in conformance with the rules of both social propriety and desire itself and thereby appears confused. The social code prohibits her from all intercourse with a potential lover. She should act as an obedient and responsible daughter unless she can find essential, true love. The man must be tested to determine whether he is this true love. The code of desire prohibits her from acting overeager. She must frequently feign indifference to keep his desire active. Each time she remembers the social code, she is seized with guilt. Each time she remembers the code of desire, she connives. Her two forms of refusal appear slightly different from each other. When guilty, she moves with quick, impelled directness. When conniving, her body divides; she looks longingly toward him while withdrawing, or she leaves an arm behind to be grasped as she turns to leave.

In the end, of course, she capitulates. After many minutes of dithering—pulled in one direction, tugged in another—her determination dissolves under his sustained pressure.

La Volière, ou les Oiseaux de Boccace (1838)

TOP: 84. Costume design for Gunima in Thérèse Elssler's *La Volière* (1838).

MIDDLE: 85. Fanny Elssler as Zoe in *La Volière,* from an American performance in 1840. Courtesy of the Victoria and Albert Museum.

BOTTOM: 86. Costume design for Domingo in *La Volière.*

The one-act ballet *La Volière* was created for and premiered at the 1838 benefit concert for the Elssler sisters. Thérèse Elssler had constructed innumerable pas de deux and solos for herself and her sister since their debut in Paris, but this was her first ballet. The commission to choreograph an entire ballet, however, may not have been such an honor, since it was awarded because of the incidental occasion of a benefit concert. The right to hold a benefit concert was accorded to principal dancers as part of their contracts with the Opéra. From these long evenings composed of many small selections from operas and ballets, stars received a portion of ticket revenues and additional gifts that permitted them to lead a more comfortable life. *La Volière*, although the centerpiece of the Elsslers' benefit, did not succeed, and it was eliminated from the repertoire after only four performances.

Set on a colonial estate in San Domingo, *La Volière* introduces Thereza (played by Thérèse), who has been seduced and abandoned by Don Alonzo; her black servant Gunima (see fig. 84), who was also deserted by her husband; and Thereza's younger sister Zoe (played by Fanny), who as a consequence of the older women's experiences with romance, has never laid eyes on a man. (See fig. 85.) Thereza attempts to interest Zoe in dancing, but she remains listless and apathetic. A dialogue between Thereza and Gunima over the nefarious ways of men produces love letters written by Don Alonzo. As Thereza reviews them regretfully, a knock at the door announces the arrival of Ferdinand, accompanied by Domingo, Gunima's former husband. (See fig. 86.) The men have been separated from the hunt and ask for refreshments; Thereza refuses. After they leave, Thereza succeeds in giving Zoe her dancing lesson, and the two sisters enjoy a lively and affectionate duet. Ferdinand, who has glimpsed Zoe during his brief stay in the house, now climbs high in the tree outside the garden wall in order to see more. Zoe, entering the garden, spies him. She asks Gunima, who is serving tea, to identify this strange creature, and Gunima informs her that Ferdinand is an exotic bird. Gunima ushers Zoe back inside, but Ferdinand audaciously angles a fishing rod to retrieve keys left behind on the table and enters through the garden gate. Zoe sneaks up from behind and captures him in a large bird cage. She leaves and Domingo enters, much amused by his master's plight. When Domingo finally opens the cage, Ferdinand pushes him inside. Now Don Alonzo arrives, angry at the shenanigans, but Ferdinand persuades him to hide in the bushes as Zoe returns to find her exotic white bird changed into a black one. She runs in fright to find her friends as Ferdinand releases Domingo from the cage. When all the girls and Thereza return, they are perplexed to find the cage empty, but Don Alonzo, seeing Thereza from afar, is seized with remorse.

As the others exit, Zoe remains intent on recapturing her prize. Ferdinand compliantly emerges from the bushes. She tracks him and throws a silk rope around his neck. He begs her to release him, promising to obey all her commands. She moves, he follows; she calls, he comes. Delighted with her pet, she feeds and strokes him. Then conceiving of further training, she teaches him the gallantries of walking, bowing, and finally dancing. Their joyful duet ends in an impetuous embrace that troubles Zoe with the new feelings of love it produces. Again Gunima arrives and ushers Zoe inside, but she soon returns, this time to find Ferdinand surrounded by her friends, with whom he dances one after another. This scene provokes the new sensation of jealousy in Zoe. After the girls depart, Ferdinand settles down for a nap in the garden. Zoe, driven by revenge, approaches sword in hand to stab the creature who has caused her such pain, but finds that she cannot. Thereza arrives and questions her sister, and Zoe mimes the alternations of joy and dismay that her creature has inspired. Thereza then spots the contrite Don Alonzo, and the girlfriends rush in with a captured Domingo. The stage erupts with scenes of forgiveness, reconciliation, and exuberance. The curtain closes on festive dancing in celebration of the three joyful couples.

Contrived to suit the talents of the Elssler sisters, *La Volière* switched genders for the principal characters in its adaptation of a tale from Boccaccio about the innocent young man who knows nothing of the opposite sex. Regardless of which gender occupied which role, the tale crystallized the tension between the two sexes in its fantastical making over of the one by the other. In Elssler's production the story allegorized the feminine fantasy of teaching men courtship. But it also summoned up the darker desire for vengeance against male domination. The man—caged, roped, and instructed—endured a thinly veiled hostility. Even his complicity may not have mitigated entirely the tacit humiliation intrinsic to his role.

The perception of this denigration of the male character may have fueled critics' negative reviews of the ballet. In his review Janin flatly asserted that the role of the bird belonged more appropriately to a woman.[1] Only Gautier, intent on his support of the Elsslers, offered this perverse evaluation of the production:

> We will not offer the slightest literary criticism of the framework of this ballet, which is the product of the intelligent legs of Mlle. Thérèse Elssler. It is quite an adequate excuse for amusing and varied dances. We shall begin, therefore, by praising Mlle. Thérèse Elssler for the taste she showed in not giving the male performers anything to dance in her choreography. Indeed, there is nothing more disagreeable than a man showing his red neck, great muscular arms, parish beadle legs, and the whole of his heavy frame shuddering with leaps and pirouettes. We were spared that tedium at the performance of *La Volière*. The pas that Mlle. Thérèse Elssler and her sister performed is charmingly designed. There is one moment in particular, when the two sisters run forward from the back of the stage holding hands and shooting out their legs in unison. It is as if one were the shadow of the other, or there were only one dancer, advancing alongside a mirror that reflects her every movement. There could be no more delightful or harmonious sight than this dance, which was performed with great speed and precision.[2]

Simultaneously derogatory and laudatory, Gautier assumed, as usual, that ballet provided only an occasion for amusing dancing. His attempts to praise the production relied on a series of derisive observations: that Elssler's legs and not she herself showed intelligence; that ballets should never aspire to more than entertainment; and that the great advantage of this ballet, apart from the sisters' dancing, was the absence of men dancing. If the viewer concurred with these assumptions, then the ballet would satisfy, especially because of the doubling of pleasure the mirror-opposite sisters provided. Certainly no denigration of the male dancer was evident, since men's effortful execution of steps, their heavy frames shuddering as they leapt, produced such a repugnant effect.

For viewers less feverish in their allegiances than Gautier, the charm of the ballet's characterizations lay in Ferdinand's ironic self-mastery over his masquerade, which also rectified his vulnerable position. As in Sallé's *Pygmalion*, the vehicle for the developing romance between hero and heroine was the dancing lesson. In each ballet, although for different reasons, the students clearly knew more than they initially let on. How otherwise could they ever master so complicated a vocabulary in such a short time? In *La Volière* Ferdinand, thoroughly civilized already, recuperated his control over the romance by demonstrating his ability to appear untutored. In the quick deftness of his responses, coupled undoubtedly with sidelong knowing glances to the audience, he signaled both his own amusement at his tutelage and the naiveté of the tutor.

In his flirtations with the other girls and his carefree nap, Ferdinand resumed the stereotypic masculine identity referenced throughout the production. Despite all civilizing efforts, as both Thereza and Gunima could attest, men seemed destined to fickle flirtations. Ferdinand's behavior rationalized Zoe's original treatment of him and inspired an even more dramatic scheme for revenge. Yet much to her surprise, Zoe found herself unable to execute her own plan. In this moment of discovery Ferdinand became the static vehicle that enabled Zoe's character to develop. She experienced the contradictory emotions of love and hate, empathy and jealousy, while he slept.

Typically, the female character served as the object whose stasis illumined the male hero's depth of character and his self-knowledge. In ballets where the heroine did exhibit an analogous depth of character, her development occurred in response to a situation, not an individual. Furthermore, it took the form of madness, a hyper-awareness of injustice, from which no useful self-knowledge could be retrieved. In its use of Ferdinand to enable Zoe's full emotional maturation, *La Volière* not only presented an unusually rich female interiority, but also violated normative gendered patterns for the production of self-identity. It is possible that this subtle yet profound violation unnerved its male viewers sufficiently to determine its failure as a ballet.

If *La Volière* contested gender expectations, it did not offer any new configuration of race relations. As in earlier ballets, the inferior status of the dark-skinned servants was demonstrated in the crudeness of their interaction with each other. Where Don Alonzo showed remorse and Thereza agonized over her love letters, the black couple simply reunited. Although it was impossible to imagine as mimed communication, viewers were also informed via the program notes that Domingo had, prior to the action on stage, bartered his wife for a keg of rum. This barbarous yet comic allegation deepened the colonizing ideological intent of the San Domingan setting even as it could be dismissed as preposterous hilarity. The comic identity of the black couple thus helped to reinforce the ballet's clearest message: that men will be men and women will forgive them, in all places and regardless of race or class.

Dark Spaces

In a forest glade, by the mouth of a cave, at the very jaws of hell—these are the settings for aberrant dancing. In these dark, enclosed environs furies wield their vipers, witches concoct their brews, the deranged dwell in agonized introspection, ghostly apparitions flicker in and out of visibility. Such settings always contrast effectively with the open, airy, rectilinear forms of the city and the generous rolling curves of village or country estate. They surround a gloomy center with serpentine, entangled, obscure paths of light and vegetation, offering no tangible certitude, providing no exit. The dancing that occurs in these spaces—angular, contorted, grotesque, or eerie—likewise bears no resemblance to the easeful, buoyant interactions of public space. Here, the values of the sociable body are mutilated, stretched in some direction so as to warp the scale of qualities that measures propriety and even virtuosity.

What is the purpose of these spaces? Like their oppositional counterpart, the heavens, they secure the possibility for drama in affairs on earth. Yet where the heavens operate as pristine alternative to earthly life, dark places symbolize the source of drama. Those who have lost their reason find themselves in the forest glade, delirious, struggling against and within the fullest volume of their interiority to find an identity. The forest closes in like a second skin, symbolizing the exterior of the character's body so that his/her whole repertoire of movement comes to represent the internal turmoil. The listless gesture, the frenetic turn, the head twisted back—these actions embody the wellspring of the conflict occurring within the soul. Alternatively, those who wander into the dark clearing may fall prey to the quixotic, appetitive energy that these spaces generate. Quickened with desire, they suddenly witness the beings that inhabit these spaces. Are they real? Are they a dreamlike projection? As if in response to the character's interrogations, they dart menacingly near, then out of reach, summoning up the very problems that the story must solve.

This is not a revelation. Nor is the fact that most creatures dancing and living in these spaces are feminine and from an obscure racial origin. (The dark makes it easy to transpose racial attributes onto gendered ones and vice versa.) Circe, brooding in front of her cave, plots to entrap Télémaque. The Furies, enlivened by Don Juan's arrival in hell, dance toward him enticingly, only to thrust a viper at him when he tries to partner them. Madge the witch manufactures a scarf that will capture the sylphide but also cause her death. The evils these women are capable of, all in order to affect the viewers' commiseration with a masculine predicament and to perpetuate the progress of a masculine good. What would the story do without them?

Dark spaces and the creatures that inhabit them press in on the narrative, suffocating the story with their unspeakable powers. At the very moment of strangulation, however, the narrative always springs free. Triumphant, it turns its full weight against the dark and vanquishes its inhabitants, not forever, but at least until dusk, until it needs to prove itself once again. Is there another way for narrative to flex its muscles? Perhaps, but this duel with and in the dark is so handy. So much scenery in the storeroom could simply be repainted and used for the next show. The lights know their perfect setting, the music its ominous strains. Ah, here they come again.

Giselle, ou les Wilis (1841)

Giselle,[1] the most highly acclaimed and popular ballet of the mid nineteenth century,[2] achieved a remarkable synthesis of the styles and vocabularies of dancing. In act 1 it presented a girl who loved to dance and who involved everyone around her in dancing, and in act 2 it transformed her into a supernatural being whose modus operandi was dancing. The range of dramatic and choreographic styles suggested by this character afforded Carlotta Grisi, who originally danced the part of Giselle, an opportunity to blend the approaches of Taglioni and Elssler. The production likewise involved several very talented and powerful artists in a complex collaboration: Théophile Gautier conceived of the ballet's theme and Jules Vernoy de Saint-Georges, a professional scenarist for the vaudeville, structured the scenes; Adolphe Adam provided an innovative musical score that used rhythmic patterns to imitate dialogue and specific combinations of instruments to identify certain characters, and also developed the use of reiterated key motifs later in the piece; Paul Lormier worked out the costumes; Pierre L. C. Ciceri constructed sets in consultation with the machinist who worked out the aerial choreography; and finally, Jules Perrot choreographed the solos and pas de deux while Jean Coralli crafted the large group dances.

Such a large-scale collaboration could easily have run amok and required the strongest of themes to galvanize a cohesive product. Gautier, always probing ballet's strengths and limitations, found in Heinrich Heine's recounting of a Slavic legend of female spirits called "wilis" the perfectly captivating premise around which the entire production revolved:

> These are affianced young women who die on the eve of the wedding; these poor creatures cannot rest tranquilly in their tombs. In their extinguished hearts, in their dead feet, remains the love of dancing that they could not satisfy during their lives, and at midnight they rise, assemble into groups on the highway, and woe to the young man who encounters them: he must dance with them until he falls dead.[3]

The legend assumes that a young woman, presumably a virgin, whose sexual desire has been stimulated during courtship, has, on the eve of her wedding, attained the zenith of unclaimed, unchanneled sexual energy. Legally, she is in transition between her father's and husband's jurisdictions. Her love of dancing both reinforces and contributes to her desire by cultivating her preference for play over work and body over mind. Interrupted at death, this desire, now unattached and unfulfilled, does not dissipate. Instead, it motivates these women to return from the grave and dance throughout the night. Any man foolish enough to pass by their nightly home must die seemingly in retribution for their sexual frustration: "They laugh with a joy so perfidious, they call you with so much seductiveness, their attitude contains such sweet promises, that these dead Bacchantes are irresistible."[4] Innocent in life, they have become in death insatiable and full of duplicity. But this is part of their attraction: the blatant sexual appetite apparent beneath their winsome, youthful appearance requires no promise of love, no commitment beyond a dance or two. As in *La Sylphide, Ondine, La Fille du Danube* and other ballets, the existence of the wild and haunting supernatural figure created a powerful format for spectacle in the contrasts between culture and nature, earthly and aerial. *Giselle* added

87. Act 1 of Jean Coralli and Jules Perrot's *Giselle* (1841).

to this the characterological development of girl into wili, and also the menacing temperament of the wilis against which Giselle would struggle.

The act 1 curtain opens on a rural, agrarian village scene sometime between the sixteenth and eighteenth centuries, somewhere (according to publicity for the ballet) in central Germany. (See fig. 87.) Two cottages, one with a thatched roof and the other larger and more solid, open their doors onto a common area. Two statuesque trees mingle their branches above the cottages, framing the common area and also distant fields, above which a castle perches high on a hill. Giselle, who lives in the house on the left, is enamored of Loys, recently settled in the cottage on the right. Giselle is in turn loved by Hilarion, who indicates all this in his opening pantomime. His brooding, ponderous gestures intimate failure in matters of the heart. Jealous and suspicious, he hides in order to spy on events as the door of Loys' cottage opens. Loys, clad in peasant garb, is detained by Wilfrid, a companion in noble dress who nonetheless defers to Loys in his posture and comportment. But with a curt, authoritative wave of the hand, Loys dismisses him and runs to Giselle's door. She skips jauntily out, and they begin to dance out her momentary fears and demure shyness, his calm and solicitous reassurances, and the joyful celebration of their mutual affection. She seizes a flower and plucks the petals to determine Loys' love, and when the results are unfavorable runs from him in dismay. Loys picks a second flower, which returns a favorable prediction, and the two happily reconcile. Hilarion, whose jealousy can no longer be contained, bursts onto the scene to accuse the two lovers of excessive intimacy. Giselle merely laughs while Loys rushes angrily toward him. A group of young women harvesters then enter in search of Giselle, and rather than accompany them to work, Giselle begins a waltz which they cannot resist. She leads one line and Loys another in a lively series of circles, braids, and serpentines. Their raucous gamboling rouses Berthe, Giselle's mother, who marches out of the house with angry reproaches. The other girls listen in genuine fear as Berthe, hunched in concentration, her arms deftly carving the space, depicts the fate of all those who loved to dance too much. Giselle alone remains impervious to her mother's warning. Laughing as she did at Hilarion, she reaffirms her love for Loys and for dance as he departs for the harvest and she, pulled along by her mother, enters the house. Hilarion, now alone, seizes the opportunity to enter Loys' cottage in the hopes of discovering some evidence that would compromise his rival.

A hunting party arrives in the village—the Prince and his daughter Bathilde accompanied by the ladies and gentlemen of the court and the falconers. Their grand procession fills the stage with rich velours and glittering jewels. The Prince requests refreshments from Berthe, and Giselle converses with Bathilde as she serves her. Bathilde takes such pleasure in Giselle's dancing that she gives her a necklace, which Giselle proudly displays to her mother. Then the Prince and Bathilde retire to the house to rest, advising the hunting party to continue without them. The stage has just emptied when Hilarion appears at the door of Loys' cottage, jubilantly waving the sword and cape he has found within. They identify Loys as Albert, the Duke of Silesia. Hiding them in the bushes, Hilarion exits to await the proper moment for revenge. First Loys-Albert and then the rest of the villagers return from the completed harvest. The adults bear huge baskets of grapes and a palanquin supporting a young child dressed as Bacchus. Children with garlands of flowers and even a horse drawing a large barrel for the grapes circle the stage in anticipation of the harvest festival. Giselle runs to embrace her lover, and they begin a celebratory dance joined by the other villagers, during which Giselle is crowned queen of the harvest. At the height of the festivities Hilarion enters, triumphantly waving Albert's sword and cape. Giselle along with the villagers respond to this revelation with doubt and confusion. Loys-Albert lashes out at Hilarion, yet the Prince coming out of Giselle's house and the other courtiers arriving from the hunt pay homage to Albert, an act which confirms for Giselle his noble origins. She runs from him in horror toward her mother's house only to confront Bathilde in the doorway, suddenly realizing that they are both affianced to the same man.

Under the strain of these revelations Giselle loses her reason and begins a dance that interweaves her memories of the past and her love of dancing and of Loys with the horror and grief caused by his deception. Each image—counting the flower petals, leaping in a circle—disintegrates during its execution, mutilated by the convulsive surge and sudden depletion of Giselle's energy. At one point she seizes Albert's sword in an attempt to kill herself and is saved by the quick response of her mother. Giselle's delicate health, however, cannot sustain the shock of learning Albert's true identity, and she finally collapses, dead, in her mother's arms. Albert, who has looked on in horror, runs to Giselle and kisses her passionately in an attempt to bring her back to life. Realizing his ineffectiveness he seizes his own sword in attempted suicide. The Prince stops him and pulls him away. Bathilde kneels in tears at Giselle's feet. Villagers and courtiers assembled around her body look on in dismay as the curtain closes.

The scenery for act 2 could hardly achieve a stronger opposition with that of the first act. (See fig. 88.) It sets the action at night in a forest clearing adjacent to a lake. A chaotic profusion of vegetation surrounds the stage, at times so abstractly suggested as to become a swirling play of light and shadow. The only straight lines appearing in this gnarled and foreboding landscape are those of a cross with the name Giselle written on it. A few gamekeepers arrive looking for a place to camp, but Hilarion admonishes them to move on as the clock strikes midnight and a mysterious music is heard. A parting in the rushes

88. Act 2 *Giselle.*

reveals Myrtha, queen of the wilis. Lightly, restlessly, she transits the stage, a luminous nocturnal figure, touching each plant with her wand and causing her female companions to appear. Two among them, Moyna from the Orient and Zulme from India, perform exotic solos that blend movements from their native traditions with the ethereal vocabulary of the wilis. The others then join in, darting throughout the forest until Myrtha calls them to assemble in order to summon the new initiate. A shrouded Giselle slowly ascends from her grave and comes before Myrtha. A touch of her wand causes the shroud to vanish and wings to appear. Giselle, becoming more animated, begins to dance with the same enthusiasm and dedication as before but now with an added lightness. A noise in the distance disperses the wilis. Several young village men arrive in the clearing on their way home from a neighboring village festival. Slowly, seductively, the wilis surround them and entice them to dance. One old peasant in the group recognizes their danger and rallies the men to depart. They escape, pursued by the spirits, who are furious at having lost their captives.

Albert enters, stricken with grief, carrying an armful of flowers and followed by his page, Wilfrid. Crying as he kneels at the grave, Albert perceives Giselle floating above him. As if in a dream, he reaches toward her and she vanishes, reappearing on the other side of the clearing. Repeatedly and with great tenderness Giselle approaches him, but just as he moves to embrace her she slips past him. Suddenly, Hilarion runs in pursued by wilis. He rushes toward one exit but finds his way barred; he quickly changes direction but to no avail. The wilis circle him until Myrtha with a touch of her wand causes him to dance. Albert now witnesses Hilarion's death by dancing as he is forced by Myrtha's magic power to partner one spirit after another. Exhausted, Hilarion rushes down the diagonal line formed by his partners toward Myrtha and pleads with her to spare his life, but she and the others offer only a relentless and ruthless charm. They whirl him toward the lake and his death. Joyful at his demise, the wilis commence a macabre bacchanal led by Myrtha.

In the course of this dance, Albert is discovered. Myrtha raises the sceptre that will enchant Albert with the same fatal desire to dance, when Giselle runs in to stay her hand. Giselle quickly guides Albert to the marble cross on her grave. Here he remains protected from their influence as the wilis swirl around him. Myrtha, whose wand has no effect near the cross, now devises a more insidious strategy for capturing Albert. She commands Giselle to dance in front of him. Giselle unwillingly obeys, and in her seductive role as wili quickly causes Albert to leave the cross, happy to join Giselle in a final pas de deux. Their rapid, vertiginous duet eventually begins to drain Albert's resources. He stumbles, falters, and then resumes the dance inspired by Giselle's grace. Seeing him finally exhausted, Giselle runs to him in tears, but Myrtha commands her to continue the dance. At length, completely exhausted, Albert lies dying when the first light of dawn appears and the wilis' power begins to diminish. They fade slowly back into the forest. No longer in danger, Albert clings to Giselle as she moves inexorably toward her grave. Happy in the knowledge that she has saved him, Giselle implores Albert to release her. Wilfrid runs in followed by Bathilde, and Giselle indicates to Albert that his future lies with them. As she disappears forever, Albert plucks flowers from her grave, kissing them, pressing them to his heart, and then falls back into the arms of his companions, holding Bathilde's hand.

Giselle not only worked to great advantage the structural oppositions between nature and culture and human and supernatural, but also made excellent use of distinctions between pagan and Christian, youth and age, and peasant and aristocrat. The uniqueness of the two acts, one set in the sunny space of clearly cultivated pathways and the other in a morass of foreboding shapes that required supernatural navigational skills, worked to deepen the dramatic tension. The impetuousness of youth threatened to overturn the aged wisdom of the peasant community as exemplified by Berthe and the older peasant, who knew the wilis' ways. The pagan impulses of Giselle with her flower and her dancing in act 1 and the wilis in act 2 seemed on the verge of triumphing over a religion that barely held them in check. Both peasants and aristocrats suffered the same fate in the wilis' supernatural world, but once the night had passed, they returned to a class-differentiated society in which costume and comportment added to the diverse spectacle onstage.

Class differences provided a clear rationale for distinctive group massings in act 1. During the peasant celebrations each performer assumed a unique stance and interacted sporadically with neighbors while watching the central action. Small intrigues and flirtations occurred at the periphery of the group, creating a lively hubbub. In contrast, the nobility, laden with their rich attire, made a strong, dynamic impression with the entrance of their hunting procession through the ornate costumes and sudden numbers of people and horses onstage. Where the peasants moved into the air with abandon and gusto, directing their weight with strength and vitality in simple skips, gallops, or more complicated patterns of beats and higher leaps, the nobility moved with alacrity forward and back or swayed from side to side, never leaving the ground. Their dignified configurations appeared uniform and remote in comparison with the casual and resilient elasticity of the peasants. The contrast between older and more youthful characters of both classes added to this variety.

To move from the variegated textures of comportment presented in act 1 to the mellifluous melancholy of act 2 pulled viewers into an even more profoundly contrasting, yet still credible, spectacle. And act 2 developed its own impressive range of contrasting vocabularies and styles through the characters of the wilis, the peasants, and Hilarion and

Albert. When the wilis danced with Hilarion, they swirled around him exerting a sustained forward momentum that knocked him off balance first in one direction and then another, his staggering lurches isolated against their constant gliding, pressing motion. The wilis' circular paths, although reminiscent of the patterns established in the harvest dances, appeared far more uniform and vaporous. Their billowing white skirts ornamented by the graceful shapes of their bare arms elaborated a filmy aerial tracery which likewise highlighted Albert's progressive fatigue. These differing styles condensed in Giselle's own body as she struggled to keep Albert alive even while dancing him to death. Her performance oscillated between a Christian altruistic love and a pagan sensuous desire.

This dramatic struggle, the last in a series of choreographic syntheses between pantomime and the classical repertoire of steps, underscored further the effectiveness of her character. Because she loved to dance so much, she could glissade "he loves me" in one direction, and glissade "he loves me not" in the other. She could grand jeté in response to Bathilde's questions and infect the village girls with pas de basques when they came to take her to the fields. Her enthusiasm interjected a rationale different from the usual reliance on celebrations for dancing into both dialogues and large group actions. This same passion for dancing enabled a choreographic depth and coherence seldom achieved through variations and reiterations on earlier dance material. Her mad scene, for example, interpolated variations in dynamics of previously performed phrases into the progressive dissolution of her being. Then in her act 2 pas de deux with Albert, she performed some of the same phrases, but this time the buoyant energy that had played across her body transformed into an even more delicate and attenuated style of execution. The duple meter, in contrast to the lyrical waltz in their first adagio, created a more stately, sober, nostalgic context for the expression of their commitment to each other.

Giselle, not the typical robust and bawdy peasant character but an innocent and refined beauty, responded with confusion and then hurt and humiliation to Loys' true identity. Had Loys been the object of Giselle's desire, she would undoubtedly have been enraged by this revelation, her pride and her heart shattered, her world jeopardized but not decimated. Loys, however, was not the man she loved so much as her partner in love. Because Giselle developed no sense of herself as other than one member of a pas de deux, she fell into a delirious, tormented review of her past. Her body, racked by the indulgence in and withdrawal from its accustomed dancing, eventually collapsed. But in death Giselle's love evolved into a selfless, protective concern for Albert. As a wili she experienced a distinct gap between self and other that deepened as she was forced to dance seductively before Albert. The erotic power of their last pas de deux derived from the conflict within Giselle herself. Her ability to sustain this conflict eventually saved Albert's life. Yet she guided him even further. In a final loving gesture she implored him to release her and reconcile with Bathilde.

Albert's obsessive passion for Giselle motivated all his actions. Her death rendered him suicidal and impotent—having failed in his attempt to kiss her back to life, he tried to take his own. Unlike Giselle, whose love matured, Albert's love only increased in intensity. He arrived at her grave distraught and disordered, dressed as a nobleman but unable to resume his aristocratic life. He looked on in a voyeuristic trance at Hilarion's demise, making no attempt to save either himself or his rival. Whatever prompted Albert to masquerade as a peasant had occurred before the action of the ballet. This enigmatic decision on his part enriched his passive, single-minded behavior throughout the ballet:

his suicidal impulses could result from remorse or from a manic desire to join her in death. His reclining position at the end suggested reverie—it could all have been a dream—as well as exhaustion.

Both Albert and Hilarion loved Giselle, and both sought to attain her love selfishly. Both Hilarion (through his brutish jealousy) and Albert (through his naive arrogance) caused Giselle's death. Each trespassed, Albert by assuming a peasant's guise and Hilarion by entering Albert's cabin, in order to gain knowledge or experience outside his own realm. Each at a different moment occupied a privileged place outside the main action of the ballet where he could see without being seen. Hilarion watched Giselle dance with Albert in act 1; and in an ironic reversal, one that conformed to the classic workings of revenge, Albert witnessed Hilarion danced to death by the wilis in act 2. Exiting from his hidden location in act 1, Hilarion blunderingly attempted to win Giselle's affections, or more precisely to discourage her from giving them to another; this was the first of three poorly calculated but nonetheless concrete actions taken by Hilarion to attain the object of his desire. By comparison, Albert remained transfixed, frozen in horror at every moment that demanded action from him. He consistently submitted to the events taking place before his eyes. In act 1 Giselle similarly yielded to the events that revealed Albert's identity. With no trace of anger, no thoughts of revenge, she responded simply by disintegrating. In act 2, however, Giselle seized control of events by leading Albert to the cross and resisting, however feebly, Myrtha's commands. Albert, however, remained caught throughout act 2 in a love that left him powerless. His initial social transgression opened up to him two worlds, that of the peasant village and that of the fantastical forest, within which he had no control. In the first an innocent and sincere affection destroyed itself before him. In the second a wanton and ruinous attraction devoured any who crossed its path. Albert's sensitive spirit, his excess of feeling in the face of each of these feminine types, stilled his body.

Giselle and Myrtha, the public facets of the feminine, found their counterparts in Christian Bathilde and all-providing Berthe, representatives of the private sphere of feminine life. Bathilde, a generous and humane aristocrat, genuinely moved by Giselle's death, accepted Albert without retribution in the end. Berthe, stable, wise, and cautious, stood as the very emblem of hospitality. In comparison with the principal male characters, whose motivations remained ambiguous and subject to a considerable range of interpretation, the female characters manifested simple and clearly defined types. They represented a full spectrum of dramatic action that defined feminine participation in narrative: piety, nurturance, madness, and seduction.[5]

The seduction performed by Myrtha and her wilis acquired increasingly horrific dimensions over the course of the ballet. Initially, this international community of female spirits manifested the most ethereal grace, the most delicate and dignified organization. But as Myrtha icily rejected both Hilarion's and Giselle's pleas for mercy, and the wilis rushed to execute her commands, their charisma took on an evil cast. Finally, in the most perverse and insidious of gestures, she commanded Giselle to seduce Albert while she and the other wilis looked on. This complex staging of desire, reminiscent of the contractual negotiations for dancers undertaken by their mothers in the greenroom,[6] recast Giselle as masochistic love object. Forced to submit to Myrtha's dominating will, Giselle was commanded not to be still, but to dance. Yet her very nature impelled her into dancing. Thus while Myrtha and Albert watched and directed viewers' attention toward her, Giselle struggled to redefine the dancing that no longer meant what it had.

The wilis assembled into a single compelling image several lineaments of a masculine desire. They combined innocence with an overt interest in sex to produce an alluring fantastical creature. Their ephemeral presence also implied an absence of social or even monetary obligations. Available—unlike proper young ladies or even prostitutes, who each required some form of contractual negotiation—they flexed their voracious sexual appetites. Raising fears of physical and sexual adequacy, they exhausted the men they danced with, but at the same time they satisfied both a masochistic impulse toward sexual depletion and a bravado impulse to flirt with sexual challenge and even death.

If the wilis both delighted and threatened male sexual desire, they worked a similar charm on female desire. Their destiny as wilis, with its cycle of seduction and destruction, reminded all young women of the perils of excessive desire, yet their open and aggressive display of sexual interest and their joyful vengeance provided a thrilling embodiment of violated social codes, just as the fact that they lived communally, apart from any male influence and ruled by a female leader, offered a scandalous but intriguing alternative social organization. As symbols of a mysterious, terrifying female power, they permitted, from both masculine and feminine perspectives, an indulgent repetition in the syntax of desire. Like the sylphides, they floated, unattainable and insatiable, in the space between desire and its object.

All four principal characters—Albert in his ideal search, Giselle in her playful innocence, Hilarion in his jealous blundering, and Myrtha in her rapacious vengeance—operated as sexually charged, desiring subjects. Their movements tracked those they desired across the stage space just as the aristocrats sought after their prey in act 1 and the wilis after theirs in act 2. Albert had embarked on his hunt, naively, recklessly hoping to escape the binding network of obligations within his own class in order to find a more pure and unconstrained reciprocity. Giselle responded by undergoing a transformation of her desire from a self absorbed in love to a self that could give lovingly. The image of the hunt played against Giselle's character development toward altruism and across all other structural oppositions of the ballet. Gamekeeper Hilarion, commissioned both to regulate nature and to protect the rights of the aristocracy, immediately detected Albert's violation, yet his selfish attachment to Giselle destabilized his own regulatory abilities. Or perhaps a class-based resentment toward the privileges of the rich motivated his response, a brutish gesture that only fueled the disruptions to class and culture that Albert's initial transgression had set in motion.

Hilarion's ambiguous motivations—signaled in part by his failure ever to grieve at Giselle's grave—pointed toward two genuses of power vividly staged through the ballet's combined movement vocabularies. The one, a hierarchical structuring of society that passed authority hereditarily from one generation to the next, signaled its existence through the clearly delineated codes of behavior and comportment displayed by Duke, Prince, page, gamekeeper, and peasant. The other, transitory and unpredictable, yet capable of obliterating all class-based hierarchies, found embodiment in the shifting movements of the wilis. Succinctly symbolized in the props of sword and wand, these two formations of power were placed on a collision course by Albert's initial violation of class boundaries. Where his sword and cape passed to him as the enduring material metonym for his noble entitlement, Myrtha's wand of rosemary, picked fresh each evening, provided a directional device for channeling an otherworldly power, one that leveled all social distinctions. The organic alterity of the dark forest's creatures rose up at a flick of that wand to challenge the very foundations of civilized society. Only the generous acts of two women, Giselle and Bathilde, worked to appease or abate the forces whose final confrontation would result in utter disaster. Unlike *La Sylphide,* where the hero's restless desire caused his complete downfall, Albert recuperated both social and personal entitlements. At the end of the ballet and at Giselle's behest, he sank back into Bathilde's arms, sadder and wiser but no less rich or loved. His encounter with the most formidable Other the ballet would ever construct, like Giselle's process of self-discovery, was made possible by the multiple meanings that dancing could support.

Premised on the equation of dancing and sexual desire, *Giselle* nonetheless elaborated for dance an impressive array of choreographic incarnations: dancing staged itself as innocent flirtation, as buoyant celebration, and as a demented unraveling of self; dancing also represented the consummation of a mature love, the path traced by desire itself, and the movement of the soul toward the ideal. This range of significance gave dancing a passionate intensity and poetic power that extended far beyond the reflexive appeal of a ballet like *La Dansomanie* where dance both stood for and commented upon the exotic and the virtuoso, but it never articulated the character's inner journey towards dissolution or transcendence. *Giselle*'s credible integration of so many dancings into a scenario of mythic proportions produced a work that subsequent ballets might copy but never surpass.

Still, *Giselle* proffered a conservative message, especially when compared with a ballet like *La Sylphide.* Ballet's first major supernatural heroine, the sylphide, had enacted a maverick sexual desire, so unruly and unpredictable that it could bring down the nobleman who pursued it. The wilis, in contrast, remained contained within their nocturnal forest world, and this containment, more than Giselle's courage, permitted the eventual restoration of a patriarchal and striated social organization. Thus the feminine, rather than perform incomprehensibly as the sylphide had, accomplished instead all the labor necessary to the development and completion of the narrative. As demonic sexuality, the feminine hosted characters' explorations of the antisocial forces of desire. As nurturant, altruistic support, the feminine guided the male soul on its journey to self-discovery. Like the many meanings that dancing conveyed, the feminine functioned in several distinct capacities to give the narrative sustenance. Yet where the resonances among dancings imbued dance with new representational depth, the confining operations of the feminine only reaffirmed the severe limitations to female participation in the public, social, and political spheres. It also underscored the availability of the feminine for use as an Other on which dominant patriarchal structurings of power could continue to thrive.

CONCLUSION
Ballet's Bodies and the Body of Narrative

With *Giselle* the action ballet realized a highly effective synthesis of pantomimic and classical vocabularies. Each of its characters exhibited strong, clear motivations, and the scenic changes from village to forest, along with the kinds of spectacle that each scene presented (festive peasant dances, an aristocratic hunting procession, a young girl's suicide, wilis' revels) offered the perfect blend of poignancy and excitement. Even the scenario, an original story (although it built upon dozens of similar scenarios played out on boulevard stages), translated easily to the stage, leaving no disconcerting discrepancies between print and action. The tragic plight of the heroine reverberated with layers of love stretching from the mundane pagan ritual of consulting a flower to the sublime Christian sacrifice of self for another. In short, *Giselle* manifested a kind of greatness, the danced equivalent of the classical myths, that mid-eighteenth-century pioneers in the genre would have been gratified to see.

Giselle would have impressed them with its brilliant integration of virtuosity, drama, and spectacle, and it would have confirmed the validity of their impulse to divorce dance from opera and constitute ballet as an autonomous art form. But the aesthetic climate in which *Giselle* occurred would equally have provoked their dismay. Why had the male dancer become an object of such disgust and the female dancer a variety of public woman? Why and how had dance acquired its reputation as highly sexualized yet frivolous diversion? Did choreographers and viewers no longer believe in gesture's capacity to convey the deepest movements of the soul? Why was the contribution of dance to a performative sociality, to the creation of decorous social intercourse, no longer evident?

Had the incorporation of narrative itself wrought these changes on dance? Partially, yes. Certainly, the mandate to tell a story *using* bodily movement alone forced a divide between the ambitious yet playful probing of physicality evident in the repertoire of danced steps and the empathic sensibility evoked by the vocabulary of dramatic gestures. As these two domains within dancing moved farther apart, each was reduced in the breadth and depth of its possible significance. The virtuoso, depleted of the aplomb and deftness through which it had connected to social protocols and all dexterous human activities, could only impress through higher, faster, or longer versions of otherwise meaningless steps. The pantomimic, standing predictably for mute moments of coquetry or angst, revitalized itself only through the delectable execution by the newest or comeliest dancer. Together, they showed a body that the dancer deployed merely to act the part or to display its tricks. Any sense of physicality as a discourse, and of dance as an endeavor that investigated and then celebrated that physicality, had vanished.

Certain ballets, most notably *La Sylphide* or *Giselle*, or *Coppelia* (1887) or *Swan Lake* (1877), pitched their plots so as to reabsorb into a single theatrical presence the disparate domains of virtuosity and drama. *Coppelia* resuscitated the Pygmalion premise and *Swan Lake* reinvented the supernatural creature in a habitat that provided breathtaking spectacle. Yet these plot types, quickly exhausted, could not provide a steady source of images and actions. Numerous derivative storylines left all the more evident the mechanical sterility and merchandised sexuality of the dancer. The archetypal dramas capable of substituting for a depleted physicality could only revitalize the tradition once in a generation at most.

But it was not only the expulsion of meaning-filled physicality from the dancing body as it mastered storytelling that determined ballet's sorry stature. The action ballet might have incarnated a different theatrical presence had it not developed in tandem with the enormous social and political changes that transpired during the same period. In politics, the absolutist regime that had scripted carefully each body's performance transformed into a nation-state whose effective governance demanded that each citizen hold his or her own body in place. In society, the marked presence and participation by both men and women in the public sphere gave way to a gendering of public space as masculine and private space as feminine. In the economy, capitalist enterprise slowly gained momentum and with it, new approaches to the presentation and marketing of goods and even the value of money. In science, the increasing scrutiny of the body produced an objectified physicality. The body's participation in passionate expression became known down to the tiniest muscle, just as the body's structural foundation for a unique and functionalist differentiation of gender was discovered in bone-deep and other physiological distinctions between men and women.

The action ballet registered and participated in all these changes. The pervasive, metadisciplinary status of dance, its interstitial relations to health, comportment, appearance, and sociability evaporated under the double gazes of scientific inquiry and professional standardization. The body acquired thing-ness, and dancing specialized in the most intricate maneuvering of this newly objectified body. The physicality that had played across stage, ballroom, and street compartmentalized into endeavors that had little relevance one for another. Sports no longer related to social dance, which no longer shared values with theatrical dance, which no longer contributed to good health or proper appearance and comportment. What all these newly discrete physical endeavors shared was the individuated subject who signaled its self-propelling, self-motivated status by directing the body in each of these activities. Such a subject met the disciplinary requirements of the new nation-state that relied on individuated bodies to evaluate their own behavior.

In the action ballet, subjects proved their individuality through dramatic soliloquies where they prevaricated or remonstrated with themselves, through the causal logic of exchanges they held with other bodies, and through their display of virtuoso skills. Both drama and dancing presumed an interiorized subjectivity that directed the body in expressive or virtuoso acts. The dancers who performed these acts increasingly demonstrated their individual control over the body with a daily regimen of exercises that constructed a geometrized volume over which each dancer presided. First they paced the body through a standardized set of exercises, and then they danced. In dancing their performances divided along the lines that marked gendered difference. No longer dancing side by side, male and female characters displayed different sets of skills and unique kinds of roles. Female dancers, delicate, ethereal, and vulnerable, required support from their male partners. They never refused their partners' declarations of love, as Diana's nymphs had, but instead invited attachment with their seductive bravado or their pitiable plights, or their mute and languorous lightness.

These changes to the dancing body stimulated new routings of desire for the viewing public who attended and supported the ballet. Desire, rather than play across a physicality that both rebuffed and incited it, drew the viewer into the character's internalized subjectivity. Viewers learned in the first decades of action ballet production to delight in the arousal to passion exemplified in the amorous exchanges between hero and heroine. But as dancing feminized and female dancing bodies punctuated a masculine public space, desire focused fetishistically on specific women's capacities and attributes. Their bodies' parts, seemingly available, even purchasable, charged with the wantings of so many eyes, congealed momentarily as the object of desire and then vanished. The suffusion of eros through body, character, and spectacle that the first action ballets had offered came to be replaced by cycles of enticement and disappearance whose specific focus was female anatomy. In purchasing the pleasure of the spectacle, viewers replicated the act of consumption, its eagerness to possess and the subsequent evacuation of the desired object's attraction, that they witnessed onstage.

Desire not only shifted locations and trajectories over the course of the action ballet's development, but it embroiled newly gendered viewing identities in the acts of empathy and evaluation. Just as the action ballet came to elaborate distinct vocabularies and character types that signaled unique roles for male and female dancers, so the performance stipulated sexual and gender identities for those who viewed it. The male heterosexual gaze dominated, and female viewers were asked to channel through that gaze in order to gain access to the dancing's significance. Same-sex attractions were accommodated only through complex and oblique codings that required viewers seeking same-sex love interest to unravel the narrative almost completely with their aggressive counter-readings.

Opera-ballets of the early eighteenth century had not legislated these kinds of pathways for desire. Male and female dancers carried equal valence and invited more openly the attachments of both heterosexual and homosexual viewers. Diana's nymphs, for example, independent and content with their own company, preserved a whimsical distance from the fauns' love even as they capitulated to it. The fauns similarly suggested both an attachment to their own masculine ways and to the pursuit of their female counterparts. With the inauguration of the action ballet, male and female leads continued to manifest an equal charisma, although the opportunities for same-sex attraction diminished because the story depended upon the propulsion that male-female union provided. Only with the rigid alignment in the early nineteenth century of the masculine with public, discursive, and legislative functions and of the feminine with private, bodily, and decorative pursuits did the ballets choreograph such a singular pathway for desire to travel.

The first pioneers who had argued for the development of the story ballet had alleged that it would elaborate upon a universal language of gesture. All men (and women) and animals, they presumed, would sign and decipher its messages. Such a universal language, even as it was designed to subvert the hierarchical privileges of lineage, nonetheless masked critical differences in gender, race, and class that the subsequent evolution of the action ballet inevitably revealed. Although its bourgeois characters seemingly appealed to a wider audience than the opera-ballet, the action ballet soon distributed specific functions across character types in ways that contradicted any presumption of universality. Female characters, for example, "spoke" the language of love. They functioned to arouse and propel the narrative forward, whereas their stoic male counterparts restored events to the status quo. Orientalist characters "spoke" in exotic foreign tongues that stimulated the senses and pleasurably disoriented the viewer before they became absorbed into or excluded from European normalcy. Peasants "spoke" an earthy yet vital language that entertained the more refined aristocracy even as it remained respectfully subservient to it.

Ballets depended upon these differentiated "languages" to provide both the obstacles and the mechanisms for overcoming those obstacles that would enable the story to get told. But ballets themselves had lost their capacity to "speak." Where the first action ballets had claimed a transparent relation between theatrical action and printed program, with the choreographer's authorship of both works as proof of their exchangeability, the nineteenth-century ballets increasingly lost their discursive status. Shunted into the diminished realm of the bodily and the nonconsequential domain of the feminine and dismissed as evanescent and amorphous, lacking even the capacity to be notated, ballet arrived in the land of love. Here it had much to say, all of it frivolous, lighthearted, and utterly transient. Where it achieved something more profound, as in Giselle's sublime gestures of self-dissolution and self-sacrifice, the effect endured only briefly and always outside a realm where it could wield influence or even be described.

This is not to say that the ballet had no formal attributes. Within the sequestered, because nonsubstantial, space of the dance studio, practitioners of the art of ballet continued to test the generativity of its regulatory and principled foundations. They found that the possible combinations and sequences of positions and steps were far from exhausted, and that the larger, higher, and faster specifications for combinations left them challenged but undaunted. The hierarchical organization of steps based on their complexity and the orderly connections that all steps maintained with basic bodily positions continued to endow ballet with a clear rationale for bodily cultivation. The logic of this organization informed both the pedagogical approach within the dance class and the general aesthetic criteria used to evaluate correct execution. The dance class proceeded from simpler to more complex combinations of steps, always monitoring students to ensure that steps were performed properly and also that the correct guidelines for transiting from one step to the next were implemented.

But it was not simply the lucid organization of the ballet vocabulary that dancers and dance teachers found compelling. It was also the application of that vocabulary to a brand new conception of body, a body that had the capacity to embed within its musculoskeletal structure a geometry of forms. Dancers had begun construction on this body when they first engaged in lengthy preparatory exercises, prior to and separate from dancing, that developed the strength, flexibility, and internally fortified erectness necessary for the body to dance. This kind of training regimen, although initially cognizant of individual proclivities, came eventually to privilege a single ideal body that its exercises would effectively and efficiently produce. As in the capitalist manufacturing and marketing practices that developed alongside this training regimen, no possibility for distinct types or styles of dancing, such as those elaborated by the genre system, existed. Bodies looked different from one another, not because their individual predispositions had been analyzed and cultivated, but because the uniform training exposed each body's innate capacities and deficiencies. The genre system had provided an overarching organization for individual difference, one that embraced distinct sets of natural talents and specified a process of acculturation for them. The new star system, in contrast, capitalized on the opposition between natural endowments and cultural training. Whatever survived the training process as the dancers' nonconforming attributes became the marks of their distinctive and marketable character.

The new training regimen contoured the exterior surfaces of the body, and it also established, for the first time, an interior on whose proper alignment and functioning the appearance of the body depended. It was this new interior, composed of the bones and muscle groups associated with each region of the body, that hosted the set of abstract lines that verified ballet's formal existence. With the dissolution of a physicalized sociability, a gesture such as the brush of the foot no longer resonated with the significance of a regulatory system for general comportment. But if that brush of the foot could also signal the movement of the leg's line from one angle to another, then ballet would achieve a new aesthetic rationale and grounding for its own enterprise. The arduous task of inculcating this geometry within the body absorbed dancers' energies and attention as never before.

The eighteenth-century dancing body had embedded itself spatially within horizontal and vertical grids and temporally within the meter and phrasing of the music. All bodies inhabited these spatial and temporal markers and moved individually and communally through them. The body's trajectories through space as well as the gestures of each body part referenced, through the traces that they made, a geometry of up and down, back and front, and sideways. The timing of its movements likewise established a dialogue with the rhythmic structures articulated in the music. This exterior spatial and temporal grid provided physicality with an orientation. It served as the ultimate ordering principle against which all bodies' movements registered a difference. Not only was bodily motion measured against these markers, but the relationality of bodies, one to another, could be tracked because of them.

Nineteenth-century pedagogical practice removed the spatial geometry of the stage to the body's interiority. There it erected not a grid, but a central core line with appendages. This schemata of head, torso, arms, and legs underlay the graceful shapes and metered movements that each body performed, changing its geometric configuration with every motion the body made. Bodies exhibited their geometry through the straight or curved shapes they articulated and also through a quality of presentation in which the line seemed almost to attract the musculature toward it as a way of signaling its embodiment.

The body's job—to manifest the line's presence—altered radically the appearance and functioning of the ballet vocabulary. Many of the steps, although called by the same name, looked nothing like their eighteenth-century ancestors. The principles that governed their sequencing likewise changed. Choreography directed the geometric ensemble as much as the actual shape of the body into pleasing configurations. Independent, self-propelling bodily geometries were asked to create unisons or variations with one another. Dialogue with the music no longer figured as a major choreographic goal. Instead, the music served to discipline and measure the geometry, just as the narrative manipulated it to serve dramatic purposes. Thus, the body moved responsively to meet the demands of music and story, its geometrized interior lending depth and structure to its efforts.

The internal bodily geometry secured for ballet the same kind of Pythagorean potential—an eternal, formal, rational, and abstract essence—that the invention of harmony had given to music. It gave dancing a masculine substantiality and erectness that offset, ever so slightly, its absolute femininity. The geometric schemata dwelt behind the sensuous, frivolous, and evanescent qualities of the ballet like a ghostly rational presence. Its presence infused ballet with a charisma that continued to attract and charm viewers in spite of the worn-out stories, recycled costumes, or even the absence of new and inviting female flesh.

By grounding the ephemerality of danced spectacle in a formal and rational design, the internal bodily schemata preserved for ballet a foothold within the arts. It nonetheless eradicated almost entirely the possibility for a physicalized semiosis. By the mid nineteenth century, the body not only told a story, but it also denoted a mathematics. Placed in the position of conveying these ideas, both dramatic and geometric, the body largely did what it was told. It did not initiate or carry on a discourse, and ballet did not cultivate its impulses. Sporadic rambunctious initiatives on the body's part such as those manifest in the can-can or the tango could only be interpreted as licentious and lacking in all aesthetic value.

The instantiation of an internal bodily geometry profoundly affected the encoding of sexuality and the routing of desire. In the early eighteenth-century hierarchy of venues, sexuality was given far freer reign in the parodic fair theatres than in the king's patented houses, yet currents of bodily sensuality and sexuality ran through all genres of spectacle. The fair theatres graphically explored references to sexual desire and behavior, but the opera-ballets in their abstruse and ponderous way likewise acknowledged the body's sexual presence. Once the ballerina had become a variety of public woman, however, the ballet had to cloak her sexuality. Instead of the high art form that refined sexuality, ballet became the genre of dance that repressed it. The ballet staged a body that was both disciplined and frivolously decorous whose carnal and inchoate desires lurked underneath.

Thus the divide within ballet productions between the discursive dramatic actions and the figural danced steps spawned another: the body as disciplined, obedient, and aesthetic, and the body as unruly, lascivious, and entertaining. And each of these divides was buttressed by the conception of the dancing body as geometry. By the mid nineteenth century bodily playfulness and initiative were construed not only as sexual but also as nonaesthetic. The eighteenth-century genre system had cultivated different physiques and the hierarchy of venues had addressed different aesthetic registers, all with the effect of enhancing both the sexual presence and articulability of the dancing body. The nineteenth-century star system, in contrast, thrived on a single culturally produced ideal physique and its natural variants. The body that danced within that system maintained the illusion of pristine, disciplined form, even as sexual desire circulated clandestinely all around it.

Attempts to suture these divides, all too predictable and limited in their success, could not prevent a serious decline in the tradition over the latter half of the nineteenth century. The vacuousness of virtuosity and the insubstantiality of ballet even as diversion left little room for it to move amidst the many popular provisions for entertainment available to the Parisian public. Although an independent and autonomous art, ballet's strength no longer resided in the promise to deliver a unique aesthetic experience, the perfect synthesis of painting and poetry. Instead, it coasted along on the institutionalized production of highly trained bodies, still needed to flesh out the operas and to represent through ballet a feminine presence in the range of theatrical spectacles.

Ever capable of reflecting critically on its aesthetic situation, the tradition produced its own eloquent summary of this dilemma as part of the revitalization to ballet accomplished by the Ballets Russes in the forms of Michel Fokine's 1911 adaptation of the Pygmalion story, *Petrouchka*. Opening on the hubbub of a mid-nineteenth-century Russian fair, *Petrouchka* introduces an ancient wizardlike puppeteer whose mysterious allure charms the populace into attending his small theatre. The curtains are drawn back to reveal three puppets: the exotic, brutish Moor; the mechanical, virtuoso Columbine; and the contorted, sincere Petrouchka. In this brief display Petrouchka's love for Columbine enrages the Moor, and the puppets burst the boundaries of the theatre only to be restrained by the discontented puppeteer. Petrouchka, now banished to his private cell, acts out the mournful tale of his unrequited love and his frustrated incarceration at the hands of the puppeteer. Then, in his own cell the Moor, in the midst of absurd devotion to a coconut, is visited by Columbine, who kicks and pirouettes around him in an effort to attract his attention. Having finally succeeded by sitting on his lap, she is annoyed to see Petrouchka enter. His further entreaties toward her enrage the Moor, and their frantic chase spills out into the street, where, much to the crowd's dismay, the Moor kills Petrouchka. The wizard, exhausted and irritated, shoves his way through the concerned onlookers to demonstrate that Petrouchka is only a puppet, a bag of straw he yanks from the ground with a speed that verifies its nonhuman weight. Dragging the puppet back to his theatre, he closes for the night. But as he begins to exit the stage he suddenly sees the apparition of Petrouchka gesturing menacingly from the rooftop above the theatre. Overwhelmed with fear, he runs out as Petrouchka persists in a melancholy yet taunting laugh.

Instead of Pygmalion's statue, the realization of the sculptor's every artistic ideal, Fokine's puppeteer had created three puppets whose actions made him his living. He did not love or worship them or find in them an exalted representation of human achievement. Neither art nor life held that promise of perfectability. Instead, he put the puppets through their paces. The three miniature figures, unlike Galathea, who magically awakened into a human life, wavered ambiguously between the mechanical and the human, sometimes manifesting needs and desires but then resuming their identities as bags of straw. No exterior divine force brought them to life. Only their maker, a crafty sorcerer with plausible connections to mysterious forces, or else their own overwhelming need to act, brought about the transition into the human. Neither noble nor good, and alienated from their own means of production, they performed their small dramas, whose impact only resonated in the hollow laugh of a ghostly afterlife.

As in *La Fille de Marbre* the simple narrative drive toward love accomplished narrative closure. Petrouchka's desire for Columbine led to his demise. Yet unlike St. Léon's scenario, *Petrouchka* offered a powerful and moving political critique. In *La Fille de Marbre,* the heroine fell in love with a young prince who subsequently led a successful rebellion against his oppressors. Yet the story of his liberation packed no political punch. The circumstances of the young prince, never exposed in the ballet, only provided an excuse for further spectacle. In Fokine's ballet, however, Petrouchka's miserable and dejected motions beneath the portrait of the puppeteer on the wall could be read on two levels simultaneously. The poor puppet aspired to love Columbine, but also to be free. By using the figure of the puppet, a pitiful doll operated on by external forces, Fokine vividly evoked the oppressive conditions of the peasantry in czarist Russia. By situating the story within the small puppet theater, he reinforced the poignancy of the peasants' plight. The puppets/peasants danced out their lives on a stage not of their own making.

Petrouchka, the most palpable counterpart to Galathea because of his nearly human hopes and his brave initiatives, communicated his innermost feelings to the audience from the sequestered confines of his cell, and he attempted to move out and beyond the puppeteer's stage, attracting the crowd's interest and sympathy. Unlike Sallé's *Pygmalion,* which elaborated on the felicitous interchange between artmaker and work of art, Petrouchka engaged in hostile and unresolved dialogue with his maker. Obviously at a disadvantage in the power relation, established by the kick from the puppeteer that relegated him to the cell and the yank that pulled his body up from the street, Petrouchka persevered in his desire for equal status. Even after death, his final menacing laugh threatened the puppeteer with the possibility of retaliatory gestures, causing him to flee the stage in fright.

But as engineer of the spectacle, the puppeteer was running away from something more than the ghost of a rebellious creation or even the Russian populace. He ran from an aesthetic rupture in the making, one that Petrouchka's introverted and pathos-filled body symbolized with extraordinary precision. Where Sallé had brought her uncorseted and unwigged Galathea to life in order to emblazon a choreographic future on the stage, Fokine cannily used his three puppets to sum up his own period's choreographic predicament. The Moor referenced ballet's use of exotic and lavish trappings from otherworldly places to activate desire. A stupid, blundering brute, impressive only for the exotic way he brandished his scimitar and capable only of worshiping a coconut, the Moor's character measured the shallow and sluggish contribution of exoticized spectacle to current choreographic needs. Columbine, like a wind-up doll, impressed herself as much as others with her astonishing but utterly mechanical prowess at the ballet vocabulary. Her mindless performance signaled the diminished resources, the sterility, of the classic repertoire of steps. Neither character expressed feelings or desire credibly, nor did they invite the viewer's attachment to them.

Only Petrouchka, pathetic and lacking all erectness, evinced a genuine emotional life. Yet the vocabulary used to express that life was nowhere aligned with ballet tradition, but rather negated ballet's aesthetic ideals at every turn. Internally rotated at hip and shoulder joints, hunched, crooked, and deflated, he performed without a Pythagorean core. Even more problematic, the absence of a geometrized interior was what enabled him to achieve his expressivity. The welling up of movement from within his concave torso, the struggling, stretching erectness he occasionally achieved, gave his motions authentic pathos. But the expanding and contracting torques that conveyed his feelings could never map onto the lines and shapes that ballet had developed.

The irreconcilability of geometry and expressivity demonstrated in Petrouchka's performance gave his character its magnificent ambiguousness, half-human and half-puppet, bound by love and servitude. It also referenced the impending confrontation between ballet and the new expressivist agendas proposed by the early modern choreographers. Fokine, captivated by the dancing of Isadora Duncan only a few years earlier, configured within Petrouchka's character a modernist approach to dramatic representation.[1] Unlike the exotic Moor and the virtuoso Columbine, who performed predictably for their choreographer, Petrouchka burst through the representational boundaries set by his maker. In keeping with the experimental tradition he symbolized, Petrouchka behaved uncontrollably and with open antagonism toward the ballet tradition.

At the turn of the century, Duncan, alongside several other women artists, most notably Loïe Fuller, Maud Allen, and Ruth St. Denis, introduced radical new movement vocabularies and methods of composition that established the grounds on which a new synthesis of the discursive and the figural might occur. Pioneering in one of the few vocations that would tolerate female leadership, they constructed of the stage a space where the self might unfold rather than a place where the self was depicted. Their performances, partaking of neither the virtuoso nor the pantomimic, bridged the divide that had hobbled ballet for decades. Unabashedly hostile to the geometrized ballet body, to its pedagogical practices, and its unseemly reputation, they argued for an alignment of all of dance practice with the natural. "Culture" had produced ballet's deformed bodies and insipid scenarios. "Nature," if liberated within the body, could manifest itself in new organic pathways for movement that would tune body, soul, and world once again.

Earthbound, preoccupied with flow from core to peripheral body and back, rather than with shape of core and appendages in space, these women occupied the stage as soloists. They choreographed and performed their own dances and thereby reactivated a choreographic connection between scenario and composition. Their unpartnered performances, the product of no other choreographic vision than their own, detonated the ballet stage and its sexual politics. Yes, they were gazed upon, but they did not die at the end of their dances. Instead, arms plunging upwards and legs shooting down into the ground, they stood proudly, sensual and articulate in the same moment. Moving with uninhibited voluptuousness, dressed in practically nothing, their nobility did not permit viewers to exercise the standard fetishizing gaze. Their charisma thus resulted not only from the refreshing aesthetics they proposed, but also from their ability to capitalize on and, at the same time, disrupt the sexual economy of viewing to which their audiences were accustomed.

Vaslav Nijinsky, who played the part of Petrouchka and whose subsequent choreography expanded upon the introverted and contorted vocabulary he performed as puppet, stood as brother to this sororal initiative, similarly disrupting and reenergizing the viewers' gaze. Deviant yet magnificent, always cast in the role of the exotic, Nijinsky specialized in a serpentine, even contorted bodily shaping combined with the highest leaps ever made. It was he who had internalized the feminine ability to feel and to be guided by one's feelings, he who died or vanished at the end of Fokine's ballets. Lacking the modern dancers' earnestness, reluctant to confront the viewer directly, he vanished into thin air, much like the nineteenth-century ballerina. His manly leaps, his sinewy yet sensuous flesh encouraged attachments from multiple sexual orientations. Clearly identified as homosexual in an age that had recently recognized homosexuality as a category, he eroticized the male dancer for the first time in over a century. Whereas the female travesty dancer of the nineteenth century masqueraded as a man who everyone knew was a woman, Nijinsky performed as a heterosexual hero who everyone knew to be the liaison of Serge Diaghelev. Along with his untamable modernism, Nijinsky's swerving sexuality haunted the stage at the end of *Petrouchka* like a queer male "wili."

Petrouchka's puppeteer, anticipating the dancer's rebellion against the choreographer and the modernists' revolt against ballet—but also the immunity of the Pythagorean body to new modes of expressivity and the open closet of homosexuality on the twentieth-century stage—could only respond by throwing up his arms and running away. As a sorcerer with prescient abilities, he may also have been responding to the future of expressivity forecast by the ballet: *Petrouchka* portended a division of labor between ballet and modern dance in which ballet no longer provoked empathic connections to its danced characters so much as to the superbly moving beauty of its form. Modern dance, by contrast, explored the authenticity of human feeling whether embodied in identifiable characters or in movement qualities. Yet each tradition remained haunted by the divide between the figural and discursive that the storying of dancing bodies had choreographed.

In its effort to account for that divide, this history has focused on the choreographic initiative that narrativized theatrical dancing, and it has made of that initiative a story. In so doing, this history has staged its own theoretical "origin" and its own narrative trajectory for the development of the action ballet. Where the eighteenth-century choreographers who aspired to found a genre located an origin for the action ballet in ancient Greek and Roman performances, this history identifies as its "origin" not a specific historical occasion of dancing but a choreography of choreographies, a theorization of theories of embodiment. Like Sallé's *Pygmalion*, this history aspires to reflect on the actions that produced its subject matter. According to eighteenth-century notions of ancient dance, Greek and Roman performances faithfully translated language into gesture. This history's conception of dance similarly manifests linguistic attributes and capabilities, yet it also acknowledges that dance could never copy precisely the written or the spoken, any more than it could be rendered fully in verbal form. The decision to imbue dancing with the linguistic and discursive power it maintains throughout this text is designed to place dance on equal footing with the words that describe it, so that dance can manifest an integrity actively resistant to the reductive power of descriptive language. Ballet's "fall" out of language and its enslavement to narrative, the story this history tells, thereby come into view as a series of cultural operations on and through dance rather than an ontological property of dance.

The trajectory of this history's story, the momentum and weight of its own narrative, push toward the tragic. It records with regret the loss of physicality as discourse, the loss of respect for both male and female dancers, and the loss of status for dance. Yet the early eighteenth century offered no utopian space where all bodies spoke freely and eloquently. Its massive hierarchies of status and protocols for behavior legislated every pathway, every gesture that a body could make. In its attentiveness to the body's movement, the eighteenth-century state accorded the body a rhetorical power that diminished when the nineteenth-century body was removed from social concern to individual property and disciplined as subservient object through the practices of dance, physical education, fashion, and etiquette. Yet the privilege to exercise that rhetorical power, accorded only to a very few, went hand in hand with the presumption that neither individual nor social identity existed outside of the monarchic organization of power. Thus, unlike the eighteenth-century historians who contoured the development of dance after the ancient performances as a sharp decline and slow rise toward perfection, this history traces the supplanting of certain aesthetic forms of subjugation and celebration by others.

In their descriptions of ballet's development, eighteenth-century historians did not attempt to analyze the relation of dance to its cultural surround more than to equate barbarous dances with barbarous peoples or to presume the sophistication of the court in cultivating danced spectacle. Their taxonomic ordering of sacred, ritualized, social, and theatrical forms sufficed to connect a dance to its social context. In spite of its emphasis on ballet's developing autonomy, this history has conceptualized dance *as* a cultural practice and not as a formal endeavor that must be situated *within* culture. Neither the passive reflection nor the active initiator of cultural values, the action ballet participated as one of the ensemble of practices that danced out the social and political choreography of its time. At times performing a prescient solo, at other times lagging behind as part of the corps de ballet, it always danced on the stage of culture and *in relation* with the ensemble. Like Sallé's Galathea, the action ballet took on a life of its own, but one that could never exist apart from the choreographic dialogue through which it discovered itself.

Sallé's ballet barely told a story. The dialogue between sculptor and artwork kept either character from coalescing into a personage that could exercise influence or control over the other, nor did their exchange produce an obvious climax. This history similarly refrains from identifying a single causal explanation for the events it describes, or a golden age for ballet. It does not, for example, account for the surge of interest in virtuoso dancing that accompanied the rise of the action ballet or for the almost seamless continuity of ballet's development throughout the turbulent decade of the 1790s. And if it identifies in ballets like *La Sylphide* or *Giselle* a powerful realization of an aesthetic agenda, it does not follow them with a celebratory conclusion. Instead, it has focused on the body, bridge among the various practices that go into one moment's cultural choreography, as a way of rendering more apparent the location and trajectory of ballet in relation to other practices on the cultural stage. In this focus it shares with the eighteenth-century opera-ballets an awareness of the spatialized network, shot through with the coercive momentum of power itself, within which bodies move in order to negotiate their mutual identities.

Although an instantiation of that power, Sallé's *Pygmalion* opened a space where sculptor and artwork could playfully resist as well as reflect upon their own destinies.

Their bodies, never free from nor totally determined by the poetics of power, found ways to initiate changes in the staging of culture. Tinged with the tragic weight that their dancing bodies acquired as they reincarnated in Milon's, Saint-Léon's and even Fokine's ballets, this history holds out hope for the kind of choreographic agency that Sallé performed. She, along with Petrouchka and Columbine, might yet arrive in the dance studio where the ballerina, after staring long and hard at her seesaw, has just made her first moves.

APPENDIX

The *Collection des chorégraphies et musiques de divers ballets et exercices* includes exercises for dance classes from 1833, 1834, 1835, and 1836. The following is the complete list for 1833 in order and labeled as they appear in the manuscript according to the air which accompanied them. This transcription retains original spelling and punctuation.

Air No. 7
Jeté devant, restez *à la 2de* demie h. rapprochez sur le coup de pied, sans plier, et faites un grand rond de jambe, lentement, baissez le pied derrière contre le mollet et développez *à la 2de* h. de la h. pliez dans cette position. C. P.

Autre air No. 50
Pliez *à la 5eme* bien bas relevez en mettant le pied de devant sur la cheville, développez *à la 2de* h. de la h. baissez ensuite à la demie h. faites 4 petits ronds de jambe sur la pointe et très vifs terminés *à la 2de* h. de la h. rebaissez à la demie h. et répétez ces ronds de jambe finis à la h. de la h. Ensuite portez, lentement, la jambe derrière en attitude posez derrière pour recommencer du C. P.

Autre même air
Coupé dessous 2 petits ronds de jambe sans sauter 3 emboités derrière entrechat à 4. pliez sur le pied de devant pour le C. P. ou fait le contraire en avant.

Air No. 22
Assemblé devant sissonne, de la même *à la 2de* 2 petits ronds de jambe sautés jeté devant. C. P. faites le contraire en arrière.

Autre même air
Assemblé derrière sissonne du pied de devant *à la 2de* deux ronds de jambe sautés tems levé en soutenant la jambe tendu. C. P. On fait le contraire.

Autre même air
Tems de cuisses devant sissonne *à la 2de* du pied de derrière 2 petits ronds de jambe en dedans sautés et tems levé. C. P. tout à la bien ballonné de même en arrière ou fait le contraire.

Autre air No. 8
Pas de bourré battu en avant assemblé soutenu fini plié, pirouette en dedans (en vous relevant), de la jambe de derrière en attitude et développez *à la 2de* h. de la h. tems de pirouette 2 tours *à la 2de* et un grand développé en tournant fini *à la 2de* posez derrière. C. P.

Autre air No. 28
Entrechat *à 5* pris sur 2 pieds, assemblez derrière entrechat *à 6* et entrechat *à 4*. C. P.

Autre même air
Assemblez devant du pied de devant, jeté *à la 4eme ouverte*, bien enlevé en attitude les bras opposés, pendant que vous êtes en l'air brisé en place sur l'autre fini en attitude et coupez dessous. C. P.

Autre air No. 26
Entrechat à 3 pris sur les deux pieds terminé sur le gauche qui se trouvait devant et le droit bien enlevé *à la 2de* posez vivement derrière *à la 5eme* et entrechat à 4. quatre fois du même coté, la dernière fois changement de jambe, au lieu d'un entrechat à 4. C. P.

Autre air No. 4
Coupé en arrière rapprochez le pied sur la cheville, les bras ronds et bas; développez en avant *à la 4eme* h. de la h. en même tems les bras, portez la jambe *à la 2de* et *à la 4eme* derrière en attitude, posez en suite le pied derrière *à la 4eme* pliez et relevez (en faisant un tour en dehors en attitude) sur la jambe de devant et retournez-la en dehors en la tendant *à la 2de* h. de la h. baissez derrière pour le C. P.

Autre air No. 54
Jeté 4 petits battemens, assemblez devant sissonne rebondie, *idem.* derrière. C. P. Ensuite: même. On fait le contraire en montant.— On répette cet exercise en Rond de jambe.

Autre même air
Jeté devant et dégageant la jambe *à la 2de* restez ferme; 2 petits ronde de jambe sautés et beaucoup de petits battemens finis *à la 3eme* C. P. plusieurs fois de même.

Air No. 6
Pliez bien bas *à la 5eme* relevez sur la pointe et le pied de devant sur la cheville, développez en avant *à la 4eme* h. de la h. les bras opposés, un ballonné dans cette position, et portez la jambe bien tendue *à la 2de* pour faire un grand developpé en dehors en tournant un tour terminé la jambe en avant *à la 4eme* les bras opposés, faite de même (sans ballonné) un grand développé en tournant 2 tours finis en avant, passez ensuite, (en pliant la jambe) de devant derrière, un tour en dehors et levez les bras au demi tour en les opposant, retournez les mains en dessous sans changer d'attitude, pliez et relevez sur la pointe. Posez derrière. C. P.

Autre air No. 2 (bis)
Attitude en tournant sur la pointe un tour en dedans et un peu en montant, développez en avant, toujours sur la pointe, plusieurs fois de même. De chaque Pied. Ensuite en descendant jeté sur la pointe un tour en dedans *à la 2de* h. de la h. et un grand développé en tournant en dehors, fini *à la 2de* C. P. de celui qui est en l'air.

Exercise sur les airs No. 6 ou 11 (bis)
Tems de pirouette relevez, en faisant, un petit foité, en tournant en dehors développez à la h. de la h. et foité en dedans en tournant du même coté développez de même *à la 2de* tems de pirouette de la même 2 tours en dehors *à la 2de* arrêttée ferme. Posez derrière. C. P.

Autre air No. 6
Attitude jêté en tournant en descendant, préparez le bras de la jambe qui fait le jeté en avant; le corps bien placé et les bras *idem* en attitude en fillant sur la pointe et bien arrêtée, envoyez le bras par dessus pour le C. P. et arrondissez-le pour l'élant du jeté attitude. &. On les fait en montant et après le jeté attitude on baisse les bras en tournant et on les relève au dernier demi tour. Baissez-les pour le C. P.

Autre air Variation du No. 43
Jeté en avant entrechat *à la* 5eme dessous et sisonne devant sur le coup de pied de celui derrière C. P. On fait le contraire en arrière.

Autre No. 54
Pas de bourrée dessous bien serrés et 2 imboités en arrière. C. P. plusieurs fois de même. On fait le contraire en avant.

Autre même air
Jeté 2 petits battemens finis *à la* 2de et la pointe par terre; 2 emboités en avant bien vifs *idem.* du C. P. plusieurs fois en avant et de même en arrière.

Autre No. 43
Le corps posé sur le pied de devant et l'autre derrière sur la pointe *à la* 4eme appuièz sur celui de derrière pour faire: Un brisé (en montant) en arrière avec la jambe de devant, sissonne *à la* 2de du p. de devant 2 ronds de jambes sautés coupé dessous et un grand jeté en avant *à la* 4eme. Posez le pied derrière pour le C. P.

Autre air No. 43
Assemblé devant entrechat à 6 échappé *à la* 2de pirouette, en vous relevant, à petits battemens. C. P. plusieurs fois de suite. On fait le même pas en changeant les petits battemens En Ronds de jambe.

Exer. sur No. 11
Relèvez *à la* 2de petit foité en face, développez *à la* 2de baissez lentement la jambe à la demi h. beaucoup de petits battemens et relevez en attitude posez derrière pour le C. P.

Autre sur l'air No. 34
Entrechat à 5 pris sur 2 pieds, assemblé derrière et entrechat à 6 C. P.

Autre air No. 46
Brisé dessus de coté fini sur un pied, *idem* dessous, 6 fois de même; Ensuite: coupé dessous, petit foité en retournant le corps du coté opposé pour le C. P.

2me manière même Air
Brisez de Même dessus et dessous trois fois et foité derrière en retournant le corps de même pour le C. P.

Autre air No. 7
Jeté devant terminé *à la* 2de levez à la h. de la h. rond de jambe de pied ferme en dehors, possez la même en attitude tournez lentement un tour en dedans en levant les bras bien arrondis baissez-les pour le C. P. On fait le contraire. Jeté *à la* 2de derrière du pied de devant levez à la h. de la h. grand rond de jambe en dedans, de pied ferme, développez en avant les bras opposés (tout cela cambré et bien marqué) tournez lentement un tour en dedans en passant la jambe de devant derrière en attitude et levant les bras biens ronds au dessus de la tête baissez-les C. P.

Autre air No. 51
Préparation du pied et du bras en devant, une pirouette jetée en avant en attitude développez immédiatement, *à la* 2de Un ou 2 tour, en dedans, pas de bourée, vivement, dessus et dessous en tournant, un tour en dehors *à la* 2de. demi h. [illegible] de pirouette *à la* 2de et 2 tours en dehor à petits battemens, coupé dessous pour 6 C. P.

Autre No. 51
Coupé en arrière en passant la jambe de devant derrière en attitude, tournez lentement un tour en dedans en développant la jambe *à la 2ᵈᵉ*. enface, foité, en tournant en dedans, un tour vivement et développez *à la 2ᵈᵉ* restez ferme. C. P.

Autre No. 51
Posez attitude tournez un tour en dehors développez *à la 2ᵈᵉ* foitez derrière, jeté pirouette renversée à tirre-bouchon, développée *à la 2ᵈᵉ* Coupez dessous.

Exercise No. 51
Port de bras un tour en dedans *à la 2ᵈᵉ* un rond de jambe en dedans (vivement) et pirouette en dedans à plusieurs tours sur le coup de pied. passez ensuite le pied de devant arrière, port de bras. C. P.

Autre Ex. Par V. air No. 51
Tems de pirouette relevez en faisant 3 tours *à la 2ᵈᵉ* h. de la h. *idem* tems de pirouette 3 tours sur le coup de pied développés *à la 2ᵈᵉ* et tems de pirouette trois tours en attitude. posez derrière C. P.

Autre par le même
Pirouette *à la 2ᵈᵉ* rond de jambe enface (vivement) posez derrière *à la 4ᵉᵐᵉ* relevez en faisant (vivement) un tour en dehors avec un rond de jambe p. der. C. P.

Autre par le même
Pirouette en dedans en attitude et developpée *à la 2ᵈᵉ* pirouette de la même *à la 2ᵈᵉ idem* pirouette en attitude developpée en avant pour le C. P.

Autre du même No. 51
Grand balloté (lentement) dessus et dessous levez la jambe bien haut en avant, et pliez-là passer derrière en arabesque, et tournez un tour en dedans, (lent) posez derrière pour le C. P.

Autre Alb. air No. 54
Brisé en montant, pris du pied de derrière fini devant sur les deux; sissonne derrière de celui de derrière. C. P. plusieurs fois. Ensuite: on en fait 2 avec une sissonne et 4 sans sissonne. On fait le contraire en descendant.

Exer. de C air No. 2 (bis)
Développez en avant passez *à la 2ᵈᵉ* posé derrière *à la 4ᵉᵐᵉ* port de bras 2 tours en dedans *à la 2ᵈᵉ* h. de la h. foité en dedans, devant et derrière développez *à la 2ᵈᵉ* pirouette, de la même, en attitude à 2 tours terminée en Arabesque. posez derrière pour le C. P.

Exercise du même air No. 51
Pirouette *à la 2ᵈᵉ* h. de la h. changée en attitude arretée, assemblé soutenu derrière en tournant un tour en dehors sur les 2 pointes et passant le pied de devant derrière sur les orteils, posez les talons, pliez pirouette, en vous relevant, en dehors à 2 tours sur le coup de pied developpez *à la 2ᵈᵉ* et placez la jambe en atttitude posez derrière pour le C. P.

Autre du même No. 46
Foité en sautant devant et derrière, demi h. glissade derrière, le tout sans changer d'épaulement brisé derrière du pied de devant, bien enlevé en changeant d'épaulement. C. P.

Autre même air No. 46
Tems de pirouette relevez en faisant: 2 ronds de jambes de pied ferme, et un en dedans fini en attitude. C. P.

The *Collection des chorégraphies et musiques de divers ballets et exercices* also includes description of the steps for several short dances of which the pas des deux from *La Vestale* (1807), *Les Pages de Duc de Vendôme* (1820), and Albert's debut in Munich (1835) offer the most complete instructions for both male and female dancers. The manuscript indicates that the pas de deux from *La Vestale* was choreographed by Pierre Gardel; the choreographer of the other two dances is not specified.

Pas de deux de *La Vestale* par M. Gardel

Andante

L'homme à le pied gauche devant la dame. L'homme commence—par echo. Les bras bas et arondis, porte le pied de devant derrière en y appuyant le corps tenus pour la préparation aux double bras, reportez le corps sur la jambe de devant, coupez dessous développez la jambe movant *à la 4eme* portez-la *à la 2de* et tournez le corps à gauche en attitude la jambe de derrière tendre le bras par dessous. Restez dans cette attitude le tems que la D . . . répette le pas. Ensuite posez la jambe derrière, très lentement, port de bras 2 tours en dedans *à la 2de* coupez dessous développez en avant, posez attitude, devant la Dame. (perdez un tems) Coupez dessous du pied droit foité derrière coupez *à la 2de*. Sept ronds de jambe en dedans finis en attitude, restez ferme pendant que la D . . . répette l'Écho. Coupez dessous jetez derrière sur le coup de pied, coupez *à la 2de*. Sept ronds de jambe en dedans-restez ferme (la Dame répette). Développez (lentement) essavant à la demi [illegible] un tour en dehors *à la 2de* sans plier, 2 petits ronds terminés *à la 2de* sur la pointe (le bras de la jambe haut le corps un peu tourné à droite) Coupez dessous sans changer d'épaulement un emboité en changeant d'épaulement pas marché en avant tems de cuisse devant battement tendu derrière en vous levant sur la pointe revenez *à la 4eme* pliée avec préparation de bras pour tourner un quart de tour à droite en rapprochant le pied droit sur la gauche ou jeter coupez (du même) à droite, pirouette à 2 tours en dedans (vite) à tirré-bouchon, sur le coup de pied terminée en développant *à la 2de* hauteur de la h. coupez dessous assemblez derrière *à la 4eme* avec préparation de bras le corps un peu tourné à gauche, un tour en dehors en vous relevant battement derrière et devant liez la préparation pour une pirouette en dedans à 2 tours à la seconde coupez dessous développez la jambe en avant (lentement) en forçant le talon en dehors, et le genoux bien tourné. posez attitude devant la D . . . Les bras haut (opposés) du côté à l'attitude.

(Pendant que la D . . . répette le pas le C. remonte)

Le pied Gauche devant *à la 4eme* posez le corps dessus (comme préparation) brisé derrière sur un pied. Entrechat à 5 sur 2 pieds sissonne devant sur le coup de pied de la jambe de derrière, jetez *à la 2de* en passant la jambe devant et un grand jeté (bien enlevé) en avant *à la 4eme* une fois de chaque jambe trois fois de même. Ensuite assemblez derrière 2 grand ronds de jambe en dehors de celle de devant pas de basque à droite, les bras opposés et la tête à la Danseuse (la D répette le pas) Ensuite: pas tombé derrière pas marché *à la 2de* coupé croisé relevez en attitude en faisant un tour en dehors. restez ferme. La D . . . *idem.* Ensuite: pas de bourrée dessous et dessus en face, glissez immédiatement, le pied de devant *à la 4eme* rapprochez l'autre derrière en y portant le corps dessus développez l'autre lentement *à la 2de* tems de pirouette trois tours *à la 2de* et une quatrième en développant en dehors fini en avant posez attitude pas de bourée dessous et dessus en face en glissant le pied *à la 4eme* devant, pliez pour faire (en vous relevant) un tour en dehors en attitude retournez en dehors la même *à la 2de* le bras droit haut et arrondi, posez le pied *à la 4eme* ouverte. pliez immédiatement, pour faire un tour en vous relevant en tire bouchon, et developé *à la 2de* h.

de la h. pas tombé derrière pas marcher en avant tems de cuisse devant. La D . . . fait le même l'enchainment. :$: [Da capo sign notated with no further instructions.]

Allegro

Le pied gauche devant. Levez sur les pointes entrechat à 6 pas marché en arrière brisé derrière du pied de devant, levez sur les pointes. 2 grand ronds de jambes en l'air foité jeté en attitude tems de cuisses en avant. (La D . . . *idem*) Ensuite: Le pied droit jeté derrière 5 petits battemens de l'autre en commençant devant, sans s'arrêter brisez derrière de la même 3 fois de même. Ensuite: jeté dessous foité derrière jeté attitude et passez vivement la jambe devant en y portant le corps dessus. La D . . . *idem.* Le Pied Droit. Pirouette jetée en dedans *à la 2de* pas de bourrée dessus et dessous 2 tours en dehors *à la 2de* et 3 tours en attitude finie par un pas de bourrée dessous et dessus. La D . . . *idem.* (observez de bien vous cambrer au dernier demi tour en faisant le pas de bourrée dessous et dessus)

Le pied Droit devant. brisé derrière du pied de derrière en montant *idem* du contre pied, changement de jambes soubre saut échapé *à la 2de* pirouette en dehors sur le coup de pied et pas de basque. La D . . . *idem.* Le Droit devant. Appuiez le corps sur celui de derrière brisé derrière de celui de devant assemblez devant entrechat à sept jeté dessous. 2 fois de même. Ensuite: jeté en avant entrechat à 5 changement de pied (bien serré) jeté en avant pour le C. Pied coupé dessous pirouette *à la 2de* h. de la h. à deux tours et un grand rond de jambe à chaque tour, bien vifs et arretée en attitude. Le Ballet danse. L'homme commence le pied Droit devant. Developpez *à la 2de* assemblez devant 2 grand ronds de jambe en dedans du pied de derrière La D . . . *idem.* (pendant ce peu de tems) le Cavalier développe la jambe *à la 2de* fait un tour renversé en dedans pas tombé derrière pas marché en avant *à la 4eme* (les bras opposés) coupé dessous foité pirouette, renversée pas tombé derrière et portez le corps sur la jambe de devant rapprochez l'autre derrière, reportez celle de devant derrière, port de bras 2 tours en dedans sur le coup de pied finis en pas de basque (la D. et le Cav. ensembles) pas marcher en arriere brisé derrière du pied de devant, jeté attitude la jambe tendue et sur la pointe le bras gauche opposé, pas de bourrée dessous et dessus fini en attitude devant la D . . . 2 fois de même. Ensuite en montant; pas de bourée dessous et dessus en tournant finis en attitude et tournant un tour et demi et en achevant les 2 tours, faites (vivement) pas de bourrée dessous et dessus (2 fois de même) Jeté dessus et dessous 5 brisés en arrière assemblez derrière du pied gauche 2 grand ronds de jambe en dedans du même, tems levé *à la 1ere* trois petits jetés tendus en avant assemblez devant du pied droit, *idem* 2 ronds de jambe en dedans de celle de derrière tems levé *à la 1ere* trois petits jetés tendus en avant et jeté attitude sur le pied droit, coupé dessous foité en face et attitude toujours ensembles. Coupé foité pirouette renversé pas tombé derrière pas marcher tems de cuisses en avant, coupé dessous pirouette *à la 2de* et sur le coup de pied finie par un pas de basque, portez la jambe de devant derrière port de bras 2 tours en dedans sur le coup de pied finie (également) par un petit pas de basques, coupé dessous du pied droit ballonné du gauche sur le coup de pied posez attitude, plusieurs fois en sortant *adlibitum.* Fin.

Pas de Deux des *Pages du Duc de Vendôme* (1820)

Andante moderato

La dame commence. L'homme entre du coté droit du public par des pas de bourrée volés terminés dessous et dessus le Pied gauche devant. Trois petits battemens *le 1ere* derrière, devant et derrière en finissant sur le pied de derrière l'autre sur le coup de pied (le corps retourné à gauche) développez en avant *à la 4eme* h. de la h. les bras opposés, passez la jambe de devant derrière par un développé en dedans fini en attitude, tems de cuisses, sans sauter fini sur la jambe de devant; 2 petits battemens derrière et devant sur le coup de pied, développez immédiatement la même en avant *à la* 4eme avec opposition de bras, et passez de même la jambe derrière en attitude, tems de cuisses sans sauter fini sur la jambe Droit *à la* 4eme. battemens derrière devant et lâchez le pied à *la* 4eme *idem.* du Contre pied 3 fois de même, coupé *à la* 2de du pied gauche, coupé croisé du droit portez y le corps dessus et un tour en dehors: en faisant en même tems un grand développé fini à *la* 2de portez la même (bien en dehors) en avant *à la* 4eme et pliez-là pour la passer derrière en attitude tourné devant la Dx. les bras opposés.

La Dx commence de la jambe droite. Ensuite le Cav. de la gauche fait: Pirouette *à la* 2de et un grand développé en dehors et en tournant fini *à la* 2de posé derrière. Entrechat à 6 coupé à droite plusieurs petits battemens finis pliés devant, coupé à gauche rapprochez sur le coup de pied développez en avant *à la* 4eme h. de la h. un ballonné en place grand dévelopé en tournant en dehors terminée en avant, grand ballotté tems levé passez la jambe jeté dessus coupé dessous (en montant) brisé derrière du pied de devant jeté attitude pirouette renversée à 2 tours posez derrière pas marcher en avant rapprochez l'autre derrière, pour prendre une pirouette *à la* 2de changée en attitude et terminée par un pas de bourée dessous et dessus.

La Dx commence une mesure. Le Cavalier répette c'est à dire: Se léve sur les pointes plié grand rond de jambe en l'air en dehors. Maintenant Ensembles jusqu'a la fin de *l'andante*. Développez la jambe qui est en attitude pirouette à tirre bouchon à un tour développée *à la* 2de pas tombé derrière pas marcher en avant 3 fois de même et tems de cuisses en avant. Levez-vous sur la pointe gauche portez le pied de derrière *à la* 4eme pliez relevez en faisant, du pied de devant, petits battemens devant et derrière et assemblez devant de la même. Levez de même sur le pied de devant dégagez celui de derrière *à la* 4eme pliée, relevez sur le pied de derrière en faisant un tour en dehors, en même tems battemens derrière et devant (bien moëlleux) dévellopez ensuite *à la* 2de un grand rond de jambe de pied ferme et la Flêche pas tombé derrière pas marcher en avant tems de cuisses: Ensuite sur le point d'orgue portez la jambe de devant derrière port de bras pirouette en dedans à *la* 2de h. de la h. développé en attitude en pliant la jambe pour la passer derrière et arretée devant la Dx. Le Cavalier prend la Dx par la main et montent ensembles le théâtre et l'invite à danser l'allegro.

Allegretto

La Dx commence. Le Cavalier fait ensuite du pied Droit devant. Un développé à la seconde assemblé devant grand rond de jambe en dedans (bien enlevé) du pied de derrière, jeté attitude, passez la jambe du pied de derrière, jeté attitude, passez la jambe de derrière devant, en faisant un tems levé et formant un demi cercle en passant *à la* 2de et *à la* 4eme entrechat à 5. dessus et coupez dessous. assemblez devant, rond de jambe en dedans, pour répéter la phrase 2 fois. Ensuite: un petit battement sur le coup de pied fini plié, et relevez la même en attitude derrière sur la pointe, beaucoup épaulé et cambré, très gracieusement, coupez dessous pour faire de même du C. P. coupé dessous foité pirouette renversée (à tire bouchon) pas tombé derrière pas marcher et tems de cuisses. La Dame danse. Ensuite le Cavalier fait: du Pied Droit devant Tems de coup de pied restez un tems sur les pointes posez les talons entrechat à 6 bien enlevé, idem tems de coup de pied brisé derrière du pied de derrière fini sur les deux, levez sur les pointes 2 grands ronds de jambe en l'air en dehors, posez devant et glissez, immédiatement, le pied en avant *à la* 4eme rapprochez l'autre derrière pirouette *à la* 2de en attitude et développez en avant en l'air, posez en avant tems levé passez la jambe jeté dessus brisé derrière sur un pied. (2 fois de même) Ensuite: jeté à gauche en rapprochant le p. droit sur le coup de pied, glissade derrière à droite et jeté derrière, jeté (encore) à gauche sur le coup de pied glissade à droite derrière, portez le pied de devant, derrière pour une préparation d'une pirouette en dedans sur le coup de pied finie par un pas de basques. (La Dx danse) Ensuite le Cav. le pied Droit dev. en l'air sur le *1er* tems Jeté dessus glissade derrière en tournant (à gauche) jeté dessus pas tombé derrière lâchez le pied en avant *à la* 4eme plié, tems de cuisses coupez dessous (3 fois le même pas) la 3eme fois le tems de cuisses fini en l'air, jeté dessus.

:𝄋: [Note in margin: ici commence le changement transporté à la Coda de suite] 2 entrechats à 5 en l'air sur le pied de devant coupé dessous Brisé brisé dessous à droite du pied de devant, jeté derrière *à la 4*eme sur le coup de pied, jeté en avant *à la 4*eme (la jambe de derrière préparée pour) brisé dessus et brisé dessous coupé dessous pour recommencer l'enchainement du triangle.

(Entrechat à 5 dessus et sur un pied, glissez derrière à gauche (presqu'en place) jeté derrière sur le coup de pied) trois fois le même enchainement pris de 5eme. la 3eme fois l'entrechat à 5 fini sur 2 pieds. Grande pirouette *à la 2*de sur le coup de pied terminée en pas de basques. La Dame danse et fini par une pirouette sur les 4 premiers accords. Le Cavalier prend ensuite du pied gauche sur les 4 derniers accords. Pirouette *à la 2*de grand rond de jambe vivement en tournant, changée sur le coup de pied et terminée par un pas de basques (dans le vide de l'air). [Note in margin: allez à la Coda]

Ensuite on recule un peu ou se prend (tout deux) la main gauche, et la Dx appuie la droite sur l'épaule du Cav. tous deux ont le pied gauche en avant *à la 4*eme sur la pointe appuiez dessus pour faire:

Jeté sur la jambe de derrière en passant l'autre derrière en attitude, tems de cuisses en avant fini en l'air 3 petits jetés tendus en avant et jeté dessus, un peu épaulé à gauche, on se quitte les mains, jeté *à la 2*de à gauche un peu en montant, portez la jambe droite par dessus l'autre tournez un tour sur les 2 pointes, pliez immédiatement, sur le pied de devant et levez l'autre derrière contre la cheville, jeté en place passez l'autre en attitude pour recommencer l'enchainement.

La seconde fois après avoir tourner sur les deux pointes on appuiera le corps, en pliant, sur le pied de derrière et on levera l'autre devant sur la cheville; assembleé devant entrechat à 5 sur un pied (on sissonne derrière) jeté attitude en passant du même tems la jambe de derrière devant (vivement) assemblé devant entrechat à 5 pour recommencer l'enchainement 3 fois, la dernière fois après l'entrechat à 5 (on fera simplement) jeté attitude pas tombé derrière pas marcher en avant tems de cuisses. coupé dessous pirouette *à la 2*de changée sur le coup de pied et terminée en pas de basques, tournée devant la Dame. On lui prend les mains on la fait tourner à gauche en l'enveloppant avec son bras droit on se place en attitude derrière la Dame on sort ensembles.

Coda

La Dame commence à danser les 8 premieres mesures de la (Coda) en descendant le théâtre en faisant a peu près le même pas que le Cav. Ensuite le Cav. descend diagonalement le théâtre en faisant du pied Droite devant = Pas marcher en avant du Pied droit jetez et attitude en tournant (bien en levée) pas de bourrée dessous et dessus, pas tombé derrière tachez le pied de devant *à la 2*eme sissonne en avant jeté tendu fini plié et assemblez soutenu avec opposition de bras, baissez la jambe en dehors, en appuyant le corps sur le pied de derrière pour recommencer le pas du même pied 4 fois de même. Ensuite en remontant Pas de bourrée dessous et dessus (en tournant à droit) coupez dessous assemblez derrière *à la 4*eme coupez encore du pied de derrière pour recommencer le même pas de bourée en tournant coupez dessous et jetez dessus du P. gauche au lieu d'assembler derrière, Tems de cuisse du Droit, jetez du même en avant (bien enlevé) en passant et développant en même tems la jambe de derrière devant, jetez dessus; 3 ou 4 fois de même en descendant en tenant la D. de la même droite la faisant tourner au tour de Soi (Elle fait des petits contre tems en avant et jetés tendus jusqu'au milieu du théâtre) Le Cav. l'invite à danser. Ensuite le Cav. du P. gauche devant. Brisé attitude sur place tems levé en passant la jambe devant 3 jetés tendus en avant Jetez dessus jetez *à la 2*de passez la jambe croisée par dessus l'autre tournez un tour sur les 2 pointes, brisez encore sur place fini en attitude tems levé en passant la jambe en avant, 7 jetés tendus en avant en passant devant la D. et formant un grand demi cercle, pour venir se placer à sa droite et lui prendre la main droite avec votre droite, le bras gauche arrondi derrière la D. et le P. droit devant; dans cette position vous faites en descendant: Tems de cuisses (du pied de derrière) jetez tendu du même tems, jetez dessus (pour le 2eme) et brisez en place en passant (vivement) le pied de derrière devant (3eme P.) 4 fois le même pas. Ensuite, en remontant, pas de bourrée dessous et dessus, en tournant un tour et assemblez derrière 2 fois de même, grande pirouette *à la 2de* et sur le coup de pied terminée en pas de basque. On prend la D. par la main et on fait un attitude pour sortir ensembles.

Pas de deux dansé par Arthur pour son second début à Munich le 12 août 1835

La Dame commence et danse 32 m. jusqu'au 𝄐.

Le Cav. entre du même coté, c'est-à-dire, de la coulisse à droite du public - Brisé à trois pas terminé en attitude à l'arabesque du coté de la D. posez le pied devant pour refaire le pas deux fois, la seconde fois coupez dessou, au lieu de poser devant, jetez dessus jetez *à la 4eme* ouverte derrière et un tour de pirouette renversée, posez derrière pour recommencer le tout du même coté. Ensuite, brisez derrière du pied de derrière en montant, *idem* du C. P. tems de coup de pied deux grands ronds de jambes en l'air assemblé derrière. C. P. pour toute la phrase, la D. fait un tour de pirouette en dedans (finie au public) le Cav. répète du C. pied la pirouette en dedans, et immédiatement après deux tours en tire bouchon, ensemble avec la D. et un troisième tour en continuant la pirouette finie en attitude. (On va se placer au grouppe) [Diagram indicating pose:]

Allegretto

La D. commence: le Cav. sur le pied gauche devant, assemblé devant du pied de devant, grand rond de jambe, en l'air, en dedans fini un peu plié, développez en avant *à la 4eme* en retendant le genou et l'épaulement devant la D. posez devant (pour faire en tournant) glissade derrière, jeté bien enlevé coupez dessous retenez l'épaulement pour répeter. L'assemblé devant du pied G. grands ronds de jambe en dedans développez la jambe en avant *à la 4eme* sans changer d'épaulement, portez la jambe *à la 2de* tems de piroutte 3 tours sur le coup de pied pas de basque, bien ferme la. D. danse.

Le Cav. du P. gauche, assemblez devant entrechat à 4. fini plié et relevez (vivement) la jambe de devant entrechat *à la 2de* h. de la h. restez un tems ferme; tems de pirouette de la même 2 tours *à la 2de* finis lentement, à l'arabesque tourné devant la D. La Dame dance. Ensuite le Cav. le P. droit devant, Entrechat à 3, posez le pied derrière et à 4 en allant à droite 4 fois de même, la dernière fois on fait un changement de jambes au lien d'un entrechat à 4 pour prendre le C. P. et faire le même pas 2 fois seulement pour revenir à gauche et une pirouette à 4 tours sur le coup de pied prise du G (la D. dance). Le Cav. monte le théâtre pendant ce tems. Ensuite il descend, diagonalement en faisant: Un pas marcher du pied G. brisé à 3 pas à droite revenez sur la gauche en filant un tour de pirouette renversée, finie au public, posez derrière, pas marcher devant pour répeter le pas 3 fois desuite, la dernière fois jetez devant, au lieu du pas marcher, trois brisés en arrière assemblez devant pirouette de la jambe G. 2 tours à la seconde et 4 tours en attitude terminés par un pas de bourrée dessous et dessus. (La D. *idem*) Le Cav. tourne au tour de la D. en faisant: assemblé devant du P. gauche tournant 1/4 de tour sissonne en attitude pas de bourée dessous et dessus, fini croisé un peu plié, relevez-vous en développant la jambe de derrière devant par un rond de jambe, et en achevant le tour, assemblez devant pour répeter le pas trois fois pour tourner au tour de la D. pirouette sur le coup de pied bien arretée, et restez en place (la D. tourne au tour du Cav.)

Le Cav. du P. gauche devant. 2 entrechats à 4 petits ronds de jambe sautés, pas de bourée dessous et dessus, 2 fois de même; glissade derrière ronds de jambe sautés jetez dessus lâchez le pied derrière *à la 4eme* pliée, relevez en développant devant posez devant pour le C. P. Ensuite pas tombé derrière pas marchez en avant tems de cuisses en l'air jetez devant posez le pied derrière *à la 5ᵉᵐᵉ* Entrechat a 5 tems levé petit battement sur le coup de pied, brizez dessous de la même, fini sur un pied, assemblez derrière pour le C. P. 3 fois le même enchainement, jetez derrière la dernière fois *à la 4ᵉᵐᵉ*, ouverte du pied de derrière, croisez l'autre en même tems devant, assemblez derrière en tournant; grand changement de jambes fini plié relevez (vivement) la jambe de devant *à la 2ᵈᵉ* h. de la h. posez devant, 4 élévations et grande pirouette *à la 2ᵈᵉ* et sur le coup de pied terminée en pas de basque. La D. danse. Le Cav. le pied droit devant, Brisez dessous fini en l'air, 2 jetés tendus devant glissade derrière en tournant 1/4 de tour levez la jambe de devant *à la 4ᵉᵐᵉ* h. de la h. passez-là derrière en attitude en tournant le corps d'1/4 de tour et le bras opposé, pas tombé derrière lâchez le pied en avant plié, sissone devant du pied de derrière 3 jetez tendus en avant et jetez dessus, pas de bourrée dessus et dessous jetez attitude à la Dame. glissade derrière en tournant à gauche, foitez derrière pas de bourée (encore) dessus et dessous jetez attitude à la D. glissade derrière en tournant assemblez derrière; face au public, pirouette *à la 2ᵈᵉ* et sur le coup de pied, attitude à l'arabesque à la D. on sort ensemble.

Pas de la Dame du pas de deux précédent

Brisé à 3 pas attitude à droite en descendant le théâtre diagonalement, posez et recommencez le brisé de la jambe de derrière comme ci dessus, la 2ᵈᵉ fois coupez dessous jetez dessus, jetez *à la 2ᵈᵉ* en montant, coupez croisé tournez un tour à gauche, sur les pointes (Dacapo du tout) Ensuite: 2 petits ronds de jambe sur la pointe assemblez soutenu posez derrière. *idem* du C. P. pirouette à petits battemens finie devant *à la 5ᵉᵐᵉ* changez de pied sans quitter la terre; on recommence la phrase des ronds de jambe. Ensuite: relevez derrière en attitude développez en avant grand rond de jambe en tournant fini par un pas de bourrée dessous et dessus, battement devant et derrière; développez du pied de derrière en avant h. de la h. ballonné grand rond de jambe en tournant assemblé, soutenu devant sur les pointes; posez les talons. 4 petits ronds de jambe sur la pointe finis *à la 2ᵈᵉ* deux fois de même. Ensuite, 2 petits ronds de jambe sautés 3 fois de même, jetez derrière fini *à la 2ᵈᵉ* deux petits battements sur le coup de pied terminés *à la 2ᵈᵉ* deux fois de même, et 5 emboites en allant de coté, sur les orteils, pirouette à la seconde terminée du coté la coulisse pour voir le Cav. Il entre. Ensuite, la D. port de bras un tour renversé en dedans (en tire bouchon) le Cav. *idem* la D. deux tours, ensembles et un troisième en continuant la pirouette, changée en attitude à l'arabesque, Grouppe. La D. le P. gauche devant: glissade devant à droite petit battement devant du pied de derrière jeté derrière sur le coup de pied fini plié, developpez *à la 2ᵈᵉ* (moeleusement) coupez dessous 2 petits ronds de jambe sur la pointe 3 emboités entrechat à 4. glissade à 3 pas à gauche revenez en faisant sissonne derrière 2 brises dernière coupé dessous assemblé devant entrechat à 4. Le C. danse.

2. Le P. D. devant. Assemblez (du pied D.) devant fini plié-relevez (vivement) le pied de devant *à la 2ᵈᵉ* tenus de pirouette de la même 2 tours *à 2ᵈᵉ* terminés lentement à l'arabesque devant le Cavalier. (le C. répête)

3. Ensuite du P. G. D. Entrechat à 5 derrière (ou sissonne) 1 petit battement en faisant un tems levé sans changer d'épaulement, brisé dessous bien enlevé en changeant l'épaulement assemblé derrière. C. P. Ensuite entrechat à 5 (encore) derrière coupez derrière *à la 4ᵉᵐᵉ* ouverte sur la pointe posez (vivement) devant pliez pour recommencer l'entrechat à 5 et le coupé sur la pointe 2 fois en montant, coupez dessous pirouette sur le coup de pied finie, les bras sur le coté.

4. Le P. D. devant: Pas tombé derrière pas de basques en avant *idem* du C. P. coupé dessous 2 petits battements (sautés) derrière et devant *idem.* du C. P. coupé dessous glissade derrière pas de Basques en avant *idem.* du C. P. coupé dessous 2 petits battements (sauter) derrière et devant *idem* du C. P. coupé dessous jeté derrière assembleé derrière. *le C danse.*

5. du P. D. une pirouette à 2 tour *à la 2ᵈᵉ* et 4 tours en attitude terminée par un pas de bourrée dessous et dessus.

6. Le P. D. devant pas marcher un peu croisé du P. D. en avant glissade devant croisée finie pliez,

relevez sur le pied de devant en filant un tour en dehors en mettant le pied gauche devant sur la cheville, jeté sur le pied du devant (sans dégager) et jeté attitude pour répéter le même pas; la seconde fois après le jeté et attitude; glissade devant à gauche jeté devant glissade à droite coupé dessous assemblé devant et royale.

7eme et dernier. La Dame se trouve du coté opposé le P. gauche dev. 3 entrechats à 4 changement de jambes *idem* du C. P. Glissade derrière à gauche ronds de jambe sautés jeté devant glissade derrière a droite ronds de jambe sautés jeter dessus assemblé devant entrechat à 4 brisé—à 3 pas de coté à droite ramenez le pied derrière jeté dessus assemblé devant; *idem.* du C. P. ensuite–7 emboités sur les orteils, en avant, près du pied de derrière (finis dans l'épaulement contraire) Un pas de bourrée dessous pris du pied de derrière sans changer d'épaulement, 3 pas de bourrée et un grand tems-levé en haut d'épaulement, ensuite 2 pas de bourrée dessous glissade derrière à gauche assemblé derrière, *idem* du C. P. sissonne derrière du P. de derrière, coupé dessous assemblé devant changement de jambes, sissonne derrière coupé dessous assemblé devant changement de jambes coupé en avant coupé dessous pirouette *à la 2de* et sur le coup de pied finie dernière; traversez avec le Cav. en faisant: (ensembles) brisé dessus fini en l'air 2 jetés tendus devant glissade derrière en tournant un quart de tour levez la jambe de devant *à la 4eme* h. de la h. portez-la derrière en attitude du tournant le corps d'1/4 de tour. Le bras opposé, pas tombé derrière lâchez le pied de devant à la 4eme pliée, sissonne devant du pied de derrière 4 jetés tendus en avant pas de bourrée dessus et dessous jeté attitude au Cav. glissade derrière en tournant à droite foité derrière *idem* pas de bourrée dessus et dessous jeté attitude au Cav. glissade derrière en tournant assemblé derrière (face au public) Grande pirouette *à la 2de* et sur le coup de pied: donnez la main au Cav. et sortez ensembles.

NOTES

PREFACE

1. Giselle, along with a large majority of the female heroines of the romantic era, engaged in dancing as both an innocent pleasure and a sensual seduction, as I will argue in chapter 5. I refer the reader also to Théophile Gautier's definition of the wili as a young girl "who loved to dance too much."

2. Throughout this text I will use "narrative" in the highly restricted sense of a story that tells of the causally related, emotionally motivated actions among characters shaped into a beginning, a middle, and an end. This definition of narrative shares with Hayden White's analysis of history (as distinct from chronicle or annals) a sense of narrative's moralizing effects. See his essay "The Value of Narrativity in the Representation of Reality." It also draws on studies of the novel, its origins and development, as analyzed by Ian Watt in *The Rise of the Novel* and Michael McKeon in *The Origins of the English Novel, 1600–1740*.

3. I am deeply indebted to several superb reconstructionists of eighteenth- and nineteenth-century dance, whose work I have been privileged to view: Elizabeth Aldrich, Regina Beck-Fris, Ivo Cramer, Francine Lancelot, Sandra Noll Hammond, Wendy Hilton, Linda Tomko, Catherine Turocy, and Shirley Wynne. Their theorizations of historical dancing bodies have profoundly influenced the analysis presented here.

4. Recent dance histories that do engage the interconnectedness of dance with the body politic include Sally Banes's *Greenwich Village: 1963*, Mark Franko's *Dance as Text*, Lynn Garafola's *Diaghilev's Ballets Russes*, Susan Manning's *Ecstasy and the Demon*, Cynthia Novack's *Sharing the Dance*, and Marta Savigliano's *Tango and the Political Economy of Passion*.

5. For a fuller account of the motivations for and consequences of conceptualizing written and danced discourses as equivalent, see my essay "Choreographing History."

6. In *Reading Dancing* I argue that Cunningham's choreography from the 1950s and 1960s breaks from modernist approaches to dance-making by incorporating all human movement as dance movement, by de-centralizing bodily phrasing and stage space, and by pursuing a choreographic trajectory independent from music, costumes, or scenic design. Cunningham's insistence on the value of dance as the organization of physical events helped to expose as roles the gendered vocabularies and styles assigned to male and female dancers. It also provided a rigorously non-narrativized dance practice, one that serves as the point of reference for this study's deconstruction of narrative and its impact. As amusing evidence of my claim for Cunningham's disinterest in narrative, I refer the reader to his work entitled *Story* (1976), a dance that implemented improvisational structures performed by entirely autonomous and unrelated characters, and lacking a beginning, middle, or end. Despite its antinarrative stance, *Story* is able to allude to and summon up various states of feeling and kinds of interactions among danced characters.

7. Recent dance criticism has frequently presumed a distinction between abstract movements that demonstrate grace, virtuosity, or form, and representational movements that connote feelings or dramatic actions. This study attempts to historicize the distinction between the "abstract" and the "representational" and to study the influence of this opposition on choreographic practice. In order to excavate assumptions leading to this distinction, I have moved both halves of the opposition into the realm of representation. As in *Reading Dancing*, where all four choreographic modes are construed as varieties of representation or as tropological operations, here the "abstract" steps and the "representa-

tional" gestures, the virtuoso tours de force and the dramatic attitudes, the classical vocabulary and the pantomimic actions operate as representational strategies. I take this analytic move to be one of the great strengths of Norman Bryson's study of eighteenth-century painting. For his treatment of the difference between the figural and the discursive, which has much in common with the approach taken here, see *Word and Image*, pp. 1–28.

INTRODUCTION

1. M***. *Mercure de France,* April 1734, pp. 770–772. For more information on Sallé, see her biography, *Une Danseuse de l'Opéra sous Louis XV: Mlle. Sallé (1707–1756),* by Émile Dacier.

2. One such production took place at the Comédie Italienne in Paris two months later. Renée Viollier's book *Mouret, Le Musicien des Graces, 1682–1738* (on the composer Mouret) provides a detailed account of the Paris performance, whose scenario by Panard and l'Affichart was danced by Mlle. Roland and Sr. Riccoboni to music by Mouret, who, according to Viollier, may also have composed the music for Sallé's *Pygmalion* (p. 145).

3. In his writings on ballets from the 1750s and '60s, Ange Goudar commented that a ballet should never last more than twenty-five minutes because dancers would tire and the energy would die (*Observations sur les trois derniers ballets pantomimes qui ont paru aux Italiens & aux François: sçavoir, Télémaque, Le sultan généreux, La mort d'Orphée*, 1759, p. 44).

4. Theatres in London and in many Italian cities would have been the most likely sites for such an experiment because there pantomime had for many years played a more prominent role in many kinds of productions. For an indication of pantomime's success in England, see Richard Ralph's biography of the early-eighteenth-century choreographer John Weaver, *The Life and Works of John Weaver,* who used pantomime frequently in his ballets. Pantomime was also highly developed in Italy. For some sense of its prominence there, see Marion Hannah Winter's *The Pre-Romantic Ballet.*

5. The trajectory of ballet's development as I will present it follows the contours of three large arguments that focus on the enormous political changes that occur in eighteenth- and early-nineteenth-century France: first, the epistemic shift in political power as elaborated by Michel Foucault in *Discipline and Punish*, *The Order of Things*, and *The Birth of the Clinic,* in which the locus of power moves from an absolutist regime that organizes monarch, aristocracy, and populace to the bureaucratic state whose governmental initiatives supervise the individual's control over his or her own body; second, the changing conception of public and private space as identified principally by Jurgen Habermas in *The Structural Transformation of the Public Sphere: An Inquiry into a Category of Bourgeois Society,* tying the rise of capitalism and the bourgeoisie to the re-formation of state power; and third, the redefinition of masculine and feminine genders as observed by, among others, Joan Scott in *Gender and the Politics of History,* which demonstrates the centrality of gender constructs to the formation of the body politic. Much in these arguments was popularized by Richard Sennet in *The Fall of Public Man.* I give Sennet credit for his willingness to engage with theatrical practices, fashion, and comportment as part of his argument.

6. L. J. Milon, *Pygmalion, ballet-pantomime, en deux actes*. Paris: L'Imprimerie à Prix-Fixe, An VII.

7. The reviewer in the *Courrier des Spectacles* found it one of the most interesting spectacles ever produced. In separate reviews on the fifth, eighth, and ninth of Fructidor, he praises Vestris, who danced the role of Pygmalion, and the choreographic manipulation of groups and tableaux. In evaluating the first act, he writes:

> Le gout triomphe complettement, l'essai devient un coup de maître et l'action de ce premier acte paroîtra toujours étonnante. Toutes idées anacréontiques parfaitement liées, tous tableaux d'une fraîcheur incomparable, cette allégorique des Amours de caractère opposé, ce combat que le Dieu de l'Inconstance livre au coeur de l'amante de Pygmalion, l'empire consolateur que l'Amour constant, rival du Dieu volage, prend sur l'esprit de l'amant trahi, au point de lui offrir les arts pour dédommagement d'une illusion malheureuse, enfin, cette foule de détails qui, nécessaires aux principaux incidens, reposent néanmoins de l'attention que ces derniers commandent; tout flatte, soutient, augmente à chaque instant l'intérêt; tout rit à la pensée qui,

satisfaite et préparée, passe avec une disposition plus favorable au sujet purement mythologique dont se compose le second acte.

B***, *Courrier des Spectacles,* An VIII de la République, 9 Fructidor, no. 1271, p. 2.

8. Jean-Jacques Rousseau, *Oeuvres Complètes,* Vol. II. Paris: Bibliotèque de la Pléiade, 1961, pp. 1926–1940.

9. This interpretation of the fate of Galathea is inspired by and supports Teresa de Lauretis's claim in *Alice Doesn't* concerning the sadistic nature of narrative and its uses of the female character. See also Catherine Clément's impassioned traverse of similar territory with regard to grand opera in *Opera, or the Undoing of Women.*

10. Two crucial works that focus specifically on body, subjectivity, and the state during the eighteenth century are Norbert Elias's *The Civilizing Process: The History of Manners* and Dorinda Outram's *The Body and the French Revolution.*

11. Arthur Saint-Léon, *La Fille de Marbre, ballet-pantomime en deux actes et trois tableaux*. Paris: Michel Levy Frères, 1847.

12. See Charles Maurice's review "La Fille de Marbre," in *Coureur des Spectacles,* October 21, 1847, pp. 1–2.

13. My analysis here draws upon the work of economist Jean-Joseph Goux, whose attempts to bring together psychoanalytic and Marxist perspectives on cultural exchange have provided me with insight into how the dancing body might function at a level of abstraction analogous to that of money. See *Symbolic Economies: After Marx and Freud.*

14. This analysis alludes to Eve Sedgwick's proposal in *Between Men* that nineteenth-century narratives most often revolved around the homoerotic desire felt by two male protagonists camouflaged as the devoted attachment that each expressed for the same female character.

15. Francis Sparshott, in his book *Off the Ground,* describes in compelling and comprehensive terms the treatment of dance in relation to the other arts by nineteenth-century aestheticians. Sparshott argues that the failure of nineteenth-century philosophy to acknowledge dance as an art form comparable to music, painting, and poetry resulted from the inability of ballet to manifest a unique mode of communication. Because of the irreconcilability of virtuoso and mimetic trends, ballet evidenced no substantive medium through which to convey an argument.

16. Artur Michel traces her influences through Hilverding, who saw her in Paris in 1735, and through her partner Lany, who produced a version of her *Pygmalion* in Berlin in 1745 which Noverre saw ("The *Ballet d'Action* before Noverre," p. 65). Deryck Lynham presumes an association between Noverre and Sallé during the early 1740s though their alliances with the director of the Opéra Comique, Jean Monnet. See Lynham, *The Chevalier Noverre,* pp. 13–15.

17. Noverre's *Lettres sur la Danse et les Ballets* was published in 1760 and expanded and revised as *Lettres sur les arts imitateurs en général, et sur la danse en particulier,* published in 1807. Cyril W. Beaumont's translation of the 1760 edition is a fine one, widely accessible, and I have used it throughout this text. For closer study of Noverre's text, I recommend the 1952 edition by Lieutier, which documents the differences between 1760 and 1807 editions.

1. ORIGINARY GESTURES

1. "Un geste n'est beau que quand il a peint la douleur, la tendresse, la fierté, l'âme en un mot." Batteux, *Les Beaux Arts réduits à un même principe,* p. 346.

2. See, for example, Burette, "Premier Memoire pour servir a l'histoire de la danse des anciens," in *Histoire de l'Académie Royale des inscriptions et belles lettres, avec les mémoires de littérature tirés des registres de cette Académie,* pp. 100–116; Du Bos, *Réflexions critiques sur la poésie et sur la peinture,* 1719, pp. 188–199; *Recherches historiques et critiques sur quelques anciens spectacles, et particulièrement sur les mimes et sur les pantomimes, avec des notes,* pp. 3–127; Cahusac, *La Danse ancienne et moderne ou traité historique de la danse,* vol. 2, pp. 2–32; Algarotti, *Essai sur l'Opéra* (1757), pp. 64–66; Gallini, *A Treatise on the Art of Dancing,* 1762, p. 235; Laus de Boissy, *Lettre Critique sur notre Danse Théâtrale, adressée à l'Auteur du 'Spectateur français' par un homme de mauvaise humeur,* pp. 9–13; Maximilien

Gardel, *L'Avènement de Titus à l'Empire, ballet héroïque*, pp. 8–12; and the *Encyclopédie* entries for "Ballet," "Danse Théâtrale," "Geste," and "Pantomime." Even a critic for the *Mercure de France* comments on the multitude of texts associating ancient practices with the new pantomimic dance: "The genre of heroic pantomime is little known here. It merits encouragement, given the resources it will contribute to the variety of spectacles. It is, besides, the only true theatrical dance. Others have remarked on it before us; and to support this idea one can find powerful authorities among the ancient authors and in several of the modern authors who have written about spectacle." ["Le genre de la Pantomime Héroïque est peu ou mal connu ici. Il méritoit d'être encouragé, attendu les ressources qu'il forniroit pour la variété des spectacles. C'est d'ailleurs, peut-être, la véritable et la seule danse théâtrale. D'autres l'ont remarqué avant nous; et pour soutenir ce sentiment on trouveroit de puissantes autorités dans tous les Auteurs anciens, et dans plusieurs des modernes qui ont écrit sur les spectacles."] November, 1765, p. 213.

3. Michel makes the point that aestheticians throughout the eighteenth century justified their arguments for improvements in dance through an appeal to the dances of ancient Greece and Rome in "The *Ballet d'Action* before Noverre," p. 52.

4. The implications of the prominence of the painting metaphor for all the arts and music in particular is the subject of Rex, "À Propos of the Figure of Music in the Frontispiece of the *Encyclopédie*: Theories of Musical Imitation in d'Alembert, Rousseau and Diderot."

5. "Mais il y a ici une chose à remarquer: c'est que de même que les Arts doivent choisir les desseins de la Nature & les perfectionner, ils doivent choisir aussi & perfectionner les expressions qu'ils empruntent de la Nature. Ils ne doivent point employer toutes sortes de couleurs, ni toutes sortes de sons: il faut en faire un juste choix & un mélange exquis: il faut les allier, les proportionner, les nuancer, les mettre en harmonie. Les couleurs & les sons ont entr'eux des sympathies & des répugnances. La Nature a droit de les unir selon ses volontés, mais l'Art doit le faire selon les règles." Batteux, *Les Beaux-Arts réduits à un même principe*, pp. 60–61.

6. The most vigorous arguments are made by Algarotti in his *Essai sur l'Opéra*; by Angiolini in his preface to *Dissertation sur les Ballets Pantomimes des Anciens, Pour Servir de Programme de "Semiramis"*; by Cahusac in his article on "Danse" for the *Encyclopédie* and also in his *La Danse ancienne et moderne*; and by Diderot in his *Entretiens sur "Le Fils Naturel,"* which is discussed in greater length later in this chapter.

7. Cahusac, in his article on "danse" in the *Encyclopédie* and in his *La danse ancienne et moderne*, quoted below, orchestrates a similar beginning. Charles Pauli, in his *Elémens de la Danse*, stages the new origin for dance in these terms: "Un accès de joie qui prend sur son âme, s'empare de tout son corps, le fait tressailler, le pousse à des bonds, à des sauts qui, quoique sans art et sans préceptes ressemblent assez bien à la danse," pp. 33–34; also, Jean-Jacques Rousseau, in a description strikingly similar to Pauli's and Cahusac's, proposes that the first gestures, if not dancing, resulted from primitive man's response to the soul's feelings (*The First and Second Discourses*, pp. 154–55).

8. Condillac establishes the contours for this dramatic scene representing the first human cries and gestures in his discussion of the origins of language. See his *Essai sur l'origine des connaissances humaines, Oeuvres philosophiques*, I, p. 61. For an overview of Enlightenment philosophers' interest in gesture, see Josephs' *Diderot's Dialogue of Language and Gesture: "Le Neveu de Rameau,"* pp. 2–28.

9. I expand on the epistemological differences between this new origin for dance and the origins for dance established in an earlier dance history by Jean Claude Menestrier in my essay "Textual Evidances."

10. "L'Homme a eu des sensations au premier moment qu'il a respiré, et les sons de la voix, le jeu des traits du visage, les mouvemens du corps ont été seuls les expressions de ce qu'il a senti.

Il y a naturellement dans la voix des sons de plaisir et de douleur, de colère et de tendresse, d'affliction et de joie. Il y a de même dans les mouvemens du visage et du corps, des gestes de tous ces caractères; les uns ont été les sources primitives du Chant, et les autres de la Danse.

C'est-là ce langage universel entendu par toutes les Nations et par les animaux même; parce qu'il est antérieur à toutes les conventions, et naturel à tous les êtres qui respirent sur la terre.

Ces sons inarticulés qui étoient une espèce de chant; et (si on peut s'exprimer ainsi) la Musique naturelle, en se développant peu à peu, peignirent d'une manière non équivoque, quoique grossière, toutes les différentes situations de l'âme, et ils furent précédés et suivis à l'extérieur de gestes relatifs à toutes ces diverses situations.

Le corps fut paisible ou s'agita, les yeux s'enflammèrent ou s'éteignirent; le visage se colora ou palit;

les bras s'ouvrivrent ou se fermèrent, s'élevèrent vers le ciel ou retombèrent vers la terre; les pieds formèrent des pas lents ou rapides; tout le corps enfin répondit par des positions, des attitudes, des sauts, des ébranlemens aux sons dont l'ame peignoit ses mouvemens. Ainsi le Chant, qui est l'expression primitive du sentiment, en a fait développer une seconde qui étoit dans l'homme, et c'est cette expression qu'on a nommée la Danse." Cahusac, *La danse ancienne et moderne,* Vol. 1, pp. 13–15.

11. Claims for the universality of the language of movement are made not only by Cahusac but also by Batteux, *Les Beaux-Arts réduits à un même principe*, pp. 337–38, and by Noverre. His description of painting and dancing is characteristic of aesthetic thought of the period: "Painting and dancing have this advantage over the other arts, that they are of every country, of all nations; that their language is universally understood, and that they achieve the same impression everywhere." Noverre, *Letters on Dancing and Ballets*, p. 28.

12. See Le Brun, *Méthode pour apprendre à dessiner les passions*.

13. Pauli commences his lengthy categorization of dance with the distinction between the original or natural dance of primitive human beings and the artificial dance developed by civilized humans: "Artificial dance at its foundation is only the disciplining of the movements and gestures of the first motions that humankind made naturally and without reflection." ["La danse artificielle ne fait dans le fond que discipliner les mouvemens & les gestes brutes tels que l'homme les fait naturellement & sans réflexion."] And he praised the artificial dance as "a science that shows humanity how to regulate the movements of the body; to make gestures with freedom, steps with firmness and lightness; and all with measure and cadence. . . ." [". . . une science qui montre à l'homme à régler les mouvemens de son corps; à faire des gestes avec liberté, les pas avec fermeté et légèreté; et le tout mésuré et cadencé. . . ."] *Elémens de la Danse*, p. 37.

14. "On apprend ainsi à danser, quoiqu'on ait en soi tous les pas dont se forme la Danse, comme on apprend à chanter, quoiqu'on ait dans la voix tous les sons dont se forme le chant." Cahusac, *La danse ancienne et moderne*, Vol. 1, pp. 17–18.

15. "Les ballets, dont il me reste à vous parler, sont la partie la plus brillante de cet Opéra. . . . Dans chaque acte l'action est ordinairement coupée au moment le plus intéressant par une fête qu'on donne aux acteurs assis, et que le parterre voit debout. Il arrive de là que les personnages de la pièce sont absolument oubliés, ou bien que les spectateurs regardent les acteurs qui regardent autre chose. La manière d'amener ces fêtes est simple : si le prince est joyeux, on prend part à sa joie, et l'on danse; s'il est triste, on veut l'égayer, et l'on danse. J'ignore si c'est la mode à la cour de donner le bal aux rois quand ils sont de mauvaise humeur; ce que je sais par rapport à ceux-ci, c'est qu'on ne peut trop admirer leur constance stoïque à voir des gavottes ou écouter des chansons, tandis qu'on décide quelquefois derrière le théâtre de leur couronne ou de leur sort. Mais il y a bien d'autres sujets de danse : les plus grave actions de la vie se font en dansant. Les prêtes dansent, les soldats dansent, les dieux dansent, les diables dansent; on danse jusque dans les enterrements, et tout danse à propos de tout.

La danse est donc le quatrième des beaux-arts employés dans la constitution de la scène lyrique; mais les trois autres concourent à l'imitation; et celui'là, qu'imite-t-il? Rien." Rousseau, *Julie; ou La Nouvelle Héloïse: Lettres de deux amants habitants d'une petite ville au pied des Alpes.* Second Partie, Lettre XXIII, pp. 265–66.

16. See also the more sympathetic analysis of the problems offered by an opera lover who located the lack of narrative coherence in "the ancient habit of repeating in the dance that which the preceeding scene had depicted, and during this time it is necessary for the god and the goddess, the shepherd and the shepherdess to wait more than a quarter of an hour for their turn to sing, propped up on a bench where they make conversation to entertain themselves, which does not help the theatrical illusion but rather destroys it, since the hero or the shepherd abandon all the dignity or naivety that a moment before had been their charm." [" . . . l'ancienne habitude de répéter par la Danse, ce que la Scène précédente a représenté, & il faut pendant tout ce tems que le Dieu & la Déesse, le Héros & l'Héroïne, le Berger & la Bergère attendent plus d'un quart d'heure leur tour pour chanter, assis sur une banquette, appuyés aux loges, où ils font la conversation pour se dessenuyer, ce qui ne prête point à l'illusion théâtral, la détruit au contraire, puisque le Héros ou le Berger quitte alors en face de tout le public cette dignité, ou cette naïveté qu'un moment auparavant l'avoir séduit."] *Examens des causes destructives du Théâtre de l'Opéra, et des moyens qu'on pourroit employer pour le retablir; ouvrage spéculatif, par un Amateur de l'Harmonie*, p. 19.

17. Diderot, *Entretiens sur "Le Fils Naturel,"* in Green, ed., *Diderot's Writings on the Theatre*, pp. 97–98.

18. "La Danse ne fut donc dans les premiers tems qu'une expression naïve de la joie & de la reconnaissance. Des yeux plus pénétrans, un génie plus étendu, l'amour du plaisir, tout fit découvrir les effets plus frappans dont elle était susceptible. Bientôt l'arrivée du Boeuf apis fournit d'autres sujets plus élévés; on célébra la naissance d'Osiris, ses exploits, ses amours & son couronnement." Maximilien Gardel, *L'Avènement de Titus à l'Empire, ballet allégorique*, pp. 12–13.

19. The failure of dance to enliven its audience is even evident in Toussaint de Rénard de Saint-Mard's comments on the Opéra from 1741. He writes that dances have "une certaine uniformité qui me lasse & qui m'ennuye: Nos Dances sont presque toutes dessinées les unes comme les autres. Nul varieté, mal esprit," p. 93. Although he complains that dancers currently look like machines, he does not advocate that dancers learn pantomime, for that would taint their nobility. He also complains about recent duets that substitute the libertine for the voluptuous, the indecent for the graceful. Recent ballets he admires include *L'Europe galante*, *Les Eléments*, and *Les Fêtes Vénitiennes*. Rénard de Saint-Mard, *Réflexions sur l'Opéra*, p. 93.

20. "Tout d'un coup j'entends le parterre qui claque des mains à l'apparition d'un grand et beau danseur masqué avec une perruque noire à longues boucles qui descendaient jusqu'à la moitié de sa taille, et vêtu d'une robe ouverte par devant qui lui allait jusqu'aux talons. . . . Je vois cette belle figure qui s'avance à pas cadencés, et qui parvenue au bord de l'orchestre élève lentement ses bras arrondis, les meut avec grâce, les étend entièrement, puis les resserre, remue ses pieds, fait des petits pas, des battements à mijambe, une pirouette ensuite, et disparaît après entrant à reculons dans la coulisse. Tout ce pas de Duprés n'a duré que trente secondes. Le claquement du parterre et des loges était général; je demande à Patu ce que cet applaudissement signifiait, et il me répond sérieusement qu'on applaudissait aux grâces de Duprés, et à la divine harmonie de ses mouvements. Il avait, me dit-il soixante ans et il était le même qu'il était quarante ans auparavant.

— Quoi? Il n'a jamais dansé autrement?

— Il ne peut pas avoir dansé mieux; car ce développement que tu as vu est parfait. Y a-t-il quelque chose audessus du parfait?" Casanova, *Histoire de ma vie*, vol. 3, pp. 140–41.

21. In the analysis that follows, I have purposefully chosen Dupré to illustrate early-eighteenth-century dance aesthetics in order to underscore the masculine presence in dance and the high status accorded to both male and female dancers of that period. In *Sexual Suspects* Straub argues that English actors and possibly dancers had acquired an effeminate character early in the century. I find no evidence of this in France, where male dancers and actors and the professions of dance and theatre remained resolutely masculinized until the end of the century.

22. ". . . l'Art de la Danse ait toujours été reconnu l'un des plus honnêtes & plus nécessaires à former le corps, & lui donner les premières & plus naturelles dispositions à toutes sortes d'Exercices, & entr'autres à ceux des armes, & par conséquent l'un des plus avantageux & plus utiles à notre Noblesse, & autres qui ont l'honneur de Nous approcher, non-seulement en tems de Guerre dans nos Armées, mais même en tems de Paix dans le divertissement de nos Ballets. . . ." *Lettres patentes du roi pour l'établissement de l'Académie Royale de Danse en la ville de Paris*, reprinted in *Danseurs et Ballet de l'Opéra de Paris depuis 1671*, p. 27.

23. *Statuts de l'Académie Royale de Danse, annexés aux lettres patentes pour l'établissement de ladite Académie*, Mars 1661; reprinted in *Danseurs et Ballet de l'Opéra de Paris depuis 1671*, p. 28.

24. For summaries of the literature on comportment and comprehensive bibliographies, see Wildeblood and Brinson, *The Polite World*, and Aresty, *The Best Behavior*.

25. Bryson offers a particularly vivid account of the intensive drills in etiquette to which all except Louis himself were subjected, in *Word and Image: French Painting of the Ancien Regime*, pp. 42–55.

26. Hogarth, *Analysis of Beauty*, p. 147.

27. One of the most comprehensive descriptions of the *menuet* is provided by Chavanne, *Principes du menuet et des révérences, nécessaires à la jeunesse de savoir, pour se présenter dans le grand monde*, pp. 31–49.

28. Wynne translates the impervious, unflappable, and accomodating stance of the eighteenth-century courtier as "cool" in her article "Complaisance, An Eighteenth-Century Cool."

29. I am indebted to John Jordan for this overview of notational principles.

30. Rameau, *The Dancing Master*, p. 2.

31. "La France la [la Danse] reconnoit depuis long-tems pour le commencement nécessaire de tous les beaux Exercices; c'est elle qui corrige les défauts naturels du corps, & qui en change les mauvaises

habitudes; répandent tant d'agrément dans toutes ses actions; c'est elle qui enseigne à ceux qui la cultivent, l'art d'entrer agréablement dans les Compagnies, & d'y gagner cette premiere & prompte approbation qui fait quelque fois leur fortune, & toujours leur joye avec celle des Spectateurs; c'est elle qui leur apprend à se démêler avec bienséance, & sans désordre, des lieux les plus embarrassez; c'est elle qui leur facilite l'Exercice de monter à cheval, & celui de faire des armes; c'est elle qui les rend plus propres à servir leur Prince dans les batailles, & à lui plaire dans les divertissements." *Discours académique pour prouver que la Danse, dans sa plus noble partie n'a pas besoin des instruments de Musique, et qu'elle est en tout absolument indépendante du violon*, reprinted in *Danseurs et Ballet de l'Opéra de Paris*, p. 34.

32. "Pour être pleinement convaincu de la nécessité de l'exercice en général . . . il ne faut qu'envisager avec attention la structure du corps humains. C'est un assemblage merveilleux de tuyaux de différents diamêtres entrelacez & repliez sur eux-mêmes en milles manières, au travers desquels différents liquides doivent rouler sans cesse pour leur donner divers ébranlements, que ces liquides en reçoivent à leur tour. Or il est certain que l'exercice met en mouvement tous les muscles du corps, & donne des secousses réitérées à toutes les autres parties tant intérieures qu'extérieures. Par-là, les fibres acquirent une flexibilité, qui en facilite les vibrations; & le sang subtilisé & comme broyé par la fréquente percussion de ces mêmes fibres, parcourt avec plus de vitesse les routes embarrassées d'une circulation, qui doit le porter jusques dans les derniers replis de ce labyrinthe de vaisseaux. Il résulte de tout cela plusieurs avantages, qui contribuent à maintenir la machine dans le meilleur état où elle puisse être . . ." Burette, "Premier Mémoire pour servir à l'histoire de la danse des anciens," in *Histoire de l'Académie Royale des inscriptions et belles lettres, avec les mémoires de littérature tirés des registres de cette Académie*, p. 97.

33. "Mais ce qui distingue la Danse, & la met fort au dessus des autres exercices, c'est que sans sortir du naturel, & sans s'abandonner à cette véhémence d'action, qui caracterise la plus part des espèces de Gymnastiques; elle sait distribuer une agitation médiocre à toutes les parties du corps, qu'elle remue en cadence & avec mesure; en sorte qu'il n'y a pas un muscle qui n'agisse, & qui n'entre pour sa part dans le jeu nécessaire à former les figures, les gestes, et les attitudes du Danseur." Burette, "Premier Mémoire pour servir à l'histoire de la danse des anciens," in *Histoire de l'Académie Royale des inscriptions et belles lettres, avec les mémoires de littérature tirés des registres de cette Académie*, p. 99.

34. Hilton demonstrates the substantial overlap in her analysis of early eighteenth-century social and theatrical forms in *Dance of Court and Theatre: The French Noble Style, 1690–1725*: "Dance in the serious or noble style had two aspects for the French courtiers. They performed social dances in the ballroom, where it was usual for only one couple to dance at a time, and theatrical dances in court entertainments. In the latter the content of the dances approximated those composed for the ballroom, but the costumes were elaborate and symbolic of the dancers' roles" (p. 3). She also observes that "the audience, most of whom danced themselves, would have been kinesthetically aware of the difficulties they were watching and able to appreciate apparent ease in a performer" (p. 37).

35. This point is made effectively in the film collaboration by Shirley Wynne and Allegra Fuller Snyder entitled *Baroque Dance, 1675–1725*.

36. The choreography performed by the masked dancer may have functioned analogously to the melancholy and ambiguous characters depicted by Watteau in his paintings. In *Word and Image* Norman Bryson argues that Watteau's emphasis on the eyes of his characters lend a passionate quality to the face, whereas the body is always depicted in a more stately and formal posture. The simultaneous conflicting messages allow the viewer to engage in endless reverie about the character. The masked dancer achieved the same results by presenting just the inverse of Watteau's characters—a passionately expressive body and a motionless face. See pp. 58–88.

37. I am grateful to Linda Tomko, whose historical and analytical understanding of the sarabande informed this section of the essay.

38. This description of a sarabande performance appears in Father François Pomey's *Le Dictionaire Royal Augmenté* (Lyons, 1671), p. 22 (copy now in Bibliothèque municipale Rodez). Translation into English by Patricia M. Ranum. The passage is quoted in full in Little and Jenne's *Dance and the Music of J. S. Bach*, pp. 93–94.

39. Many viewers, of course, despaired the increasing obsolescence of Dupré's style, as in the review from the *Mercure de France* in 1762 that observed, sadly, that Mlle. Camille, one of the last representatives of Dupré's style, was retiring. May 1762, p. 181.

40. For a description of the full terrain implied by the term, see the entry on "Sensibilité" in the *Encyclopédie.* For an analysis of the parallel development in fiction of Diderot's concept of sensibility, see Brissenden, *Virtue in Distress: Studies in the Novel of Sentiment from Richardson to Sade.* For a historical overview of sensibility as it operated in literature and drama, see Vincent-Buffault's *The History of Tears.*

41. For a comprehensive listing of the key elements that Diderot hoped to change, see Green's introduction to his edition, *Diderot's Writings on the Theatre,* pp. 8–9.

42. Diderot especially disdains the sudden interventions by gods or natural forces, known as "coups de théâtres," that radically altered or suddenly resolved the dramatic plot. See his *Entretien sur "Le Fils Naturel"* in Green, p. 29.

43. In several of his descriptions of the new drama, Diderot presents an evocative blend of dialogue, pantomime, and still life. See *Entretiens sur "Le Fils Naturel"* in Green, p. 53, and *De La Poésie Dramatique,* also in Green, p. 193.

44. Josephs argues that it was precisely these qualities about gesture that attracted Diderot. See *Diderot's Dialogue of Language and Gesture: "Le Neveu de Rameau,"* pp. 50–58.

45. Le Brun, *A Method to Learn to Design the Passions,* pp. 13–14.

46. For an excellent summary of this theory of the passions, see Roach, *The Player's Passion,* pp. 93–115.

47. Diderot, "Lettre sur les sourds et muets," p. 359.

48. For an excellent summary of the bodily conventions used in acting throughout Europe in the early eighteenth century, see Golding, *Classicistic Acting: Two Centuries of a Performance Tradition at the Amsterdam Schouwburg,* pp. 72–138.

49. For a summary of Garrick's visits to Paris and his continuing and close friendships with Diderot, Mme. Riccoboni, Monnet, and Noverre, see Hedgcock, *A Cosmopolitan Actor, David Garrick and His French Friends.*

50. For a full description of Garrick's approach to acting, see Woods, *Garrick Claims the Stage: Acting as Social Emblem in Eighteenth-Century England,* pp. 41–46. On Garrick's use of a mechanical wig for his performance of Hamlet, see Roach, *The Player's Passion,* pp. 58–59.

51. See Woods, *Garrick Claims the Stage,* p. 81.

52. In *Farce and Fantasy: Popular Entertainment in Eighteenth-Century Paris,* Isherwood describes the fair theatres performances in great detail and sets them in the context of other types of entertainment available to citizens of Paris during the period. See pp. 20–54.

53. Anon., *Lettre de Madame *** à une de ses amies sur les spectacles, et principalement sur l'Opéra Comique,* p. 9.

54. Michel emphasizes the influence that the English mime tradition had on the French fair theatres by citing the number of English mimes who were imported to perform in Paris, especially between the years 1720 and 1729. "The *Ballet d'Action* before Noverre," p. 55. The Italian as well as English influence on the development of pantomime must not be underestimated. The profusion of pantomimic techniques may have resulted from the amount of travel back and forth between England, France, and Italy undertaken by all the players.

55. Michel, "The *Ballet d'Action* before Noverre," p. 67.

56. For a detailed discussion of these subversive conventions, see Crow, *Painters and Public Life in Eighteenth-Century Paris,* pp. 49–67, and Goodden, *Actio and Persuasion,* pp. 94–111.

57. The scenario indicates that the first performance took place at the Comédie Italienne on September 26, 1743.

58. Folly's final speech in the production gives a good indication of the satire and of dance's relationship to other arts of self-presentation:

> I intend to lead you
> If Folly is your prop,
> You can be sure to be pleased today.
> I have already retained in advance
> In order to show you the beautiful dance,
> A pantomime ultra-montain.
> In order to teach you the important art,
> Of frittering with ease,

At your morning toilette
Must come a dandyish abbot.
An Italian musician
With an amphibious voice,
Is going to show you with success,
How to sing in French;
But when one wants to be accomplished
One must have a beautiful soul;
So finally, in order to build morals,
I have hired an Actress from the choirs.
Through my care you will carry
Into the world where you will shine,
Your talents will create a frenzy,
And everyone will adore your charms
there.
Of all my favorites you will please
You will flutter,
You will sing,
You will dance.
Always, finally, you will imitate,
you will babble,
You will talk slang,
You will trifle.
Graces, come and guide the steps,
Upon them you will form yourself;
At every place you present yourself
And everyone will adore your charms
there.

[Je prétens te conduire,
Si la Folie est ton appui,
Sois sûr de plaire aujourd'hui.
J'ai déjà retenu d'avance
Pour te montrer la belle danse,
Un Pantomime ultra-montain.
Pour t'enseigner l'art d'importance,
De minauder avec aisance,
A ta toilette le matin,
Doit venir un Abbé poupin.
Un Musicien d'Italie,
Avec une voix amphibie,
Va te montrer avec succès
Comme on doit chanter en François;
Mais quand on veut être accomplie,
Il faut avoir l'âme embellie;
Afin de te former les moeurs,
J'ai pris une Actrice des choeurs.
Par mes soins tu l'emporteras
Dans le monde tu brilleras,
Tes talents feront du fracas,
Et l'on fera de tous tes appas
las.
A tous mes Favoris tu plairas
Tu voltigeras,
Tu chanteras,

Tu danseras.
Toujours enfin, tu imiteras,
Tu babilleras;
Jargoneras,
Persifleras.
Graces, venez guider ses pas,
Sur elles tu te formeras;
En tout point tu l'emporteras
Et l'on fera de tous tes appas
las.]

(*Brioche; ou l'Origine des Marionettes, Parodie de Pigmalion,* pp 18–19.) The graces then enter and execute the ballet Pantomime of the puppet's education.

59. One of Isherwood's main theses is that popular entertainment in Paris consistently appealed to and was viewed by all classes of people, and that at such entertainment the rich and poor brushed shoulders constantly. See *Farce and Fantasy*, p. 37.

60. "Un jeune Mousquetaire un genou en terre déclamoit tragicomiquement aux pieds d'une assez jolie Actrice, & lui baisoit une main qu'on lui abandonnoit sans façon; une autre Actrice combattoit foiblement avec un fade Conseiller, qui vouloit absolument lui remettre sa jarretière, qu'elle avoit détachée pour lui faire admirer la beauté de l'ouvrage; une troisième badinoit avec un Petit-maître impudent, qui lui passoit la main sur la gorge." Anon., *Lettre de Madame *** à une de ses amies sur les spectacles, et principalement sur l'Opéra Comique*, pp. 9–10.

61. ". . . que je changeai vingt fois de visage, mon embarras leur fournit quantité de mauvaises plaisanteries, qu'ils débitèrent assez haut pour être entendue." Anon., *Lettre de Madame ****, p. 11.

62. ". . . fit des mines, prit du tabac, parla bas à une espèce de Suivante qu'elle avoit avec elle, tira d'un sac brodé une navette d'or qu'elle fit briller aux yeux des Spectateurs, la remit dans son sac après avoir fait un noeud; & pour se délasser de la fatigue que lui avoit causé ce pénible exercice, & montrer un portrait enrichi de diamans qu'elle portoit en forme de bracelet, elle appuya sa tête sur son coude, & essaya assez long-tems une attitude intéressante. Malheureusement pour elle, les Acteurs parurent, & lui enlevèrent la plus grande partie des Spectateurs." Anon., *Lettre de Madame ****, pp. 15–16.

63. See Aubry and Dacièr, *"Les Caractères de la Danse." Histoire d'un Divertissement pendant la première moitié du XVIIIe siècle*, p. 17.

64. Many eighteenth-century authors identify Sallé's work as the direct source and inspiration for the reforms in dance advocated by mid-eighteenth-century choreographers. Algarotti, for example, cites her ballets *Pygmalion* and *Les Ballets de la Rose* as the ones choreographers should emulate in his *Essai sur l'Opéra*, p. 66. Compan describes her as the innovator of the genre of ballet d'action in his *Dictionnaire de danse*, p. 4. Rénard de Saint-Mard also speaks highly of her *L'Europe galante* in his *Réflexions sur l'Opéra*, p. 93. Twentieth-century scholars who have argued persuasively for her central influence on the establishment of narrative dance include Brinson in *Background to European Ballet*, pp. 164–66, as well as Michel.

65. Even Sallé's ballets were not the first to utilize pantomime to depict a classical theme. One of the earliest experiments cited by choreographers and scholars occurred in 1715 at the summer home of the Duchesse du Maine. Sallé's mentor, Françoise Prévost, and Jean Balon, both principal dancers at the Opéra, recreated the last scene from the fourth act of Corneille's *Les Horaces*, unmasked and without resort to any verbal explication. The fourth act begins when Camille's brother returns from war having slain her lover, and continues with an exceptional range of highly emotional moments. The audience, entirely familiar with the plot, would have had no difficulty following the action. One difference between this early experiment with danced narrative and Sallé's is the degree of closeness to the text that the dancing achieved. Prévost's and Ballon's version of *Les Horaces* seems to have followed the play faithfully, almost line by line, whereas Sallé functioned as both dramaturg and choreographer, creating a danced scenario version of Pygmalion.

An additional and crucial influence on experimentation with gestured narrative came from productions by Jean-Nicolas Servandoni. A stage designer, Servandoni conceived and produced several spectacles that conveyed a story through simple gesture, lighting, and scenic changes. See his scenarios and also Goodden, *Actio and Persuasion*, pp. 96–97.

66. In 1725 John Rich, director of Lincoln's Inn Fields Theatre and a close associate of Garrick, engaged Sallé to appear along with several other French dancers trained at the fair theatres in "dramatic entertainments of dancing." Rich, influenced by the wordless pantomimes of choreographer and scholar John Weaver, had produced his own plagiarized versions of Weaver's ballets, to which he added harlequinade scenes, some speech, and song. Where Weaver's visionary yet austere works had failed to garner substantial acclaim, Rich's blended divertisements proved very successful. If Garrick did not see Sallé's performances in London or similar experiments integrating pantomime into ballet, he certainly witnessed Rich's productions and other more popular displays presented in the street theatres that capitalized on the vivid and telling gesture. His performances onstage and in the salons of Paris resonated with these populist strategies developed in alternative theatre. For a comprehensive study of Weaver's work as a choreographer, Dancing Master, and dance scholar, see Ralph, *The Life and Works of John Weaver*.

67. DeHesse seems to have been a very ambitious choreographer and created work in several different genres. In his 1754 review of the arts in Paris, *Les Cinq Années Littéraires*, Clément cites one critic who commented on DeHesse's work as follows: "There is something amazing in the prolificacy of this DeHesse. No year goes by in which he does not produce twelve to fifteen ballets, either for the court or for the capital. All are delightful and spirited, with intriguing plots that are easily comprehensible and sharply defined. And almost all are totally different each from the other." Quoted in Michel, "Two Great XVIII Century Ballet Masters: Jean-Baptiste DeHesse and Franz Hilverding; *La Guinguette* and *Le Turc généreux* seen by G. de St. Aubin and Canaletto," p. 277.

68. For descriptions of these ballets, see Lynham, *The Chevalier Noverre*, pp. 21–24.

69. One exception to this general stance can be found in the work of Abbé du Bos, who writes: "It seems to me nevertheless that viewers who are pleased to see the Italian Comedy, and principally the actors who play the old Octave, the old Scaramouche, and their friends Harlequin and Trivelin, are persuaded that one can very well execute many scenes without speech. But one can specify certain facts that prove even better than reasoning that such an execution is possible. Troops of mimes from England and even some actors who have performed in Paris at the Opéra Comique have produced mute scenes that everyone has seen. Even though Roger never opens his mouth, we comprehend fully what he wants to say. What apprenticeship has Roger had in comparison with the ancient mimes? Roger only knows that he never had a Pylade or a Bathylle." ["Il me semble néanmoins que les personnes qui se plaisent à voir la Comédie Italienne, et principalement celles qui ont vu jouer le vieil Octave, le vieil Scaramouche, et leurs camarades Arlequin et Trivelin, sont persuadées que l'on peut bien exécuter plusieurs scènes sans parler. Mais nous pouvons alléguer des faits qui prouveront mieux que des raisonnemens, que cette exécution est possible. Il s'est formé en Angleterre des troupes de Pantomimes, et même quelques-uns de ces Comédiens ont joué à Paris sur le théâtre de l'Opéra Comique, des scènes muettes que tout le monde entendoit. Quoique Roger n'ouvrit point la bouche, on comprenoit sans peine tout ce qu'il vouloit dire. Quel apprentissage Roger avoit-il fait en comparaison de celui que faisoient les Pantomimes des Anciens? Roger sçavoit-il seulement qu'il y eût jamais eu un Pylade et un Bathylle."] *Réflexions critiques*, pp. 311–312. Laus de Boissy also mentions productions at the Théâtre Ambigu Comique as having a resemblance to ancient pantomime. See *Lettre critique sur notre Danse Théâtrale addressée à l'Auteur du Spectateur français, par un homme de mauvaise humeur*, p. 14.

70. Published scenarios for the new genre used a variety of subheadings to signal the approach they were undertaking. These include: Spectacle orné de machines, animé d'acteurs pantomimes & accompagnés d'une Musique; Ballet sérieux, héroï-pantomime; Tragédie-Lyrique; Ballet-allégorique; drame lyrique; tragédie-pantomime, ballet anacréontique; ballet héroï-pantomime; and ballet tragique. These terms seem to indicate specific types within the larger category that I am calling the action ballet.

Télémaque dans l'isle de Calipso

1. Pauli called him "the most famous dancer and composer of our century" (*Elémens de la Danse*, p. 49). Pitrot evidently provoked strong reactions, both positive and negative. One anonymous letter addressed to him but published to take issue with his abilities, claimed that *Télémaque* was not only a disaster but that it ruined the Comédie Italienne. It also alleged that Pitrot lied repeatedly about his age

by having given the same age for the past four-and-a-half years. *Lettre d'un des petits oracles de M. Campion au Grand Pitrot,* p. 15.

2. The *Mercure de France* reviewed Pitrot's *Ulysse dans l'île de Circé* in glowing terms: "the magnificence of this ballet, the beauty of its scenes, the grace and variety of the designs, the ensemble evident in the execution, all answered to the celebrity that M. Pitrot has acquired in all the countries of Europe where they admire his talents." ["la magnificence de ce Ballet, la beauté des situations, les grâces & les variétés du dessein, l'ensemble de l'éxécution, tout a répondu à la célébrité que M. Pitrot s'est acquise dans tous les Pays de l'Europe où il a fait admirer ses talens."] The reviewer continued by expressing satisfaction that Pitrot had come back to Paris, where he had left a void when he departed. Pitrot's wife also received considerable praise. November 1764, p. 192.

Grimm, although satisfied with the production, took issue with Pitrot's own performance as Ulysse: "He is a bad Ballet Master, this M. Pitrot; as a dancer his torso is nice enough, but his huge legs with much force, peculiar steadiness, lack of grace, no softness or resiliency, that are abrupt and hard: he will never arrive at the perfection of Vestris. Upon reflection, I think that there is no dancer in Europe who performs a pirouette as vigorously as he." ["C'est un mauvais maître des ballets que M. Pitrot; comme danseur, il a le buste assez bien; mais la jambe grosse, beaucoup de force, des à plombs singuliers, point de grâce, rien de doux ni de mœlleux dans ses mouvemens, qui sont brusques et durs: il n'arrivera jamais à la perfection de Vestris. En revanche, je crois qu'il n'y a point de danseur en Europe qui fasse une pirouette aussi vigoureusement que lui."] *Correspondance littéraire,* vol. 4, November 1764, p. 263.

Grimm's review of Pitrot's *Pouvoir des Dames,* however, excoriated choreographer and theater: "It was a masterpiece of stupidity. It was besides of such excessive length that the spectators, overwhelmed with boredom and fearing to fall asleep during the comedy, began to groan loudly, especially toward the end, when Pitrot advanced toward the front of the stage in order to perform a pirouette which itself must have lasted half an hour." ["C'était un chef-d'œuvre de bêtise. Il était d'ailleurs d'une longueur si excessive, que le parterre, assommé d'ennui et craignant de coucher à la comédie, se mit à pousser de profonds gémissemens, surtout lorsque vers la fin, Pitrot s'avança sur le bord du théâtre pour faire une pirouette qui dura elle seule une demi-heure."] *Correspondance littéraire,* vol. 5, December 1765, p. 113.

3. The review of *Télémaque* in *Mercure de France* claimed that Pitrot had difficulty in translating the poem by Fénelon into dance: "but there are scenes which were not possible to express: the one, for example, where Calipso wants to know from Télémaque whether Mentor is not a god. It is the same with Mentor's lessons whose infinite details are announced in the program. But the most inevitable disadvantage was the character of Mentor, who it was ridiculous to have dance and whose cold and silent action was out of place in the middle of the ballet." ["mais il y a des Scènes qu'il n'étoit pas possible d'exprimer: telle est par exemple celle ou Calipso veut sçavoir de Télémaque si Mentor n'est pas une Divinité. Il en est de même des leçons de Mentor, d'une infinité de détails annoncés dans le Programme. Mais l'inconvénient le plus inévitable étoit le personnage de Mentor, qu'il eût été ridicule de faire danser, & dont l'action froide & muette est déplacée au milieu d'un Ballet."] April 1759, pp. 201–202.

Goudar found innumerable problems with the production. He accused Pitrot of being one of those choreographers who sacrificed dramatic integrity for virtuoso display. He also complained that the spectator had constantly to refer to the program in order to comprehend the action and that individual characters were given too little variation in their steps to signify their changing feelings. His hilariously damning critique, one of the most detailed descriptions of any ballet of the period, mercilessly satirized Pitrot's production, as in this brief excerpt:

> I carefully examined all the pantomimed pictures, and I cannot find a single one that characterized in this moment Eucharis's situation: the only thing that corresponds exactly to the poem is that the nymph, following her agitation, falls on the grass where she gives herself over to rest. Télémaque comes in dancing to find her, and he falls to her feet after a *demi-cabriole;* he moves from one place to another making several declarations of love in dance and promises her while *cabrioling* his eternal fidelity.
>
> Mentor catches them in the act, Eucharis retires for fear of him seeing her passion. Here the moral becomes the farce: Mentor-Pantomime reprimands Télémaque-Buffoon.
>
> ["J'ai examiné avec attention toutes ces peintures pantomimes, & je n'en ai pas trouvé une seule qui caractérisat dans ce moment la situation d'Eucharis: tout ce qu'il y a d'exact avec le

Poëme, c'est qui la Nymphe, après son agitation, se laisse tomber sur le gazon ou elle se livre au repos. Télémaque l'y vient trouver en dansant, il tombe à ses pieds à la suite d'une demi-cabriole; il se fait de part & d'autres dans cet endroit plusieurs déclarations d'amour par des danses, & on se promet en cabriolant une fidélité éternelle.

Mentor les prend sur le fait, Eucharis se retire, de crainte de laisser voir sa passion. Ici la Morale entre dans la farce: Mentor Pantomime fait une réprimande à Télémaque Baladin."]

Observations sur les trois derniers ballets pantomimes qui ont paru aux Italiens & aux François: Sçavoir, Télémaque, le sultan généreux, La mort d'Orphée, pp. 16–17.

4. "Qu'entend-je, s'écrie-t-il? Quoi Mentor m'abandonneroit, c'est fait de moi. O! Eucharis, si Mentor me quitte je n'ai plus que vous. Que dis-tu, Télémaque, cruel Ingrat, reprend Calipso? Je jure par le Stix, que tu sortiras de mon Isle; & toi Amour, tyran des coeurs, fuis de ma presence." Pitrot, *Télémaque dans l'isle de Calipso*, p. 13.

5. ". . . l'inquiétude, la crainte, l'espérance, la joie sont autant de différentes mouvements qu'elle ressent & qui l'agite à tel point, qu'elle se laisse tomber sur un lit de gazon pour prendre du repos." Pitrot, *Télémaque dans l'isle de Calipso*, p. 10.

6. ". . . avec frayeur, la joie succede bientôt à sa crainte: ces deux tendres Amants expriment leur amour par des Danses caraterisées." Pitrot, *Télémaque dans l'isle de Calipso*, p. 10.

Arlequin Soldat Magicien, ou le Canonier, Pantomime

1. For background on early eighteenth-century developments of Arlequin and other Comedia characters see Griffiths, "Sunset: From *Commedia Dell'Arte* to *Comédie Italienne*."

2. Charles Favart and his wife pioneered in the genre of musical comedy, ushering in many new initiatives in theatrical production, ranging from costuming to the integration of spoken and sung dialogue with pantomimed action. See his autobiography, *Mémoires et Correspondences Littéraires, dramatiques et anecdotiques*.

3. Bakhtin's notion of the carnavalesque body is applicable here. See *Rabelais and His World*, pp. 196 277.

4. For a good overview and analysis of the significance of this nineteenth-century mime tradition, see Storey, *Pierrots on the Stage of Desire*.

2. STAGING THE CANVAS AND THE MACHINE

1. Noverre, *Letters on Dancing and Ballets*, p. 33.

2. Even Rousseau grudgingly admitted to the popularity of the ballets. And a host of other critics, tourists, and interested viewers concurred. See, for example, Anon., *Etat actuel de la musique du roi et des trois spectacles de Paris*, p. ii; Anon., *Examen des causes destructives du Théâtre de l'Opéra, et des moyens qu'on pourroit employer pour le rétablir; ouvrage spéculatif, par un Amateur de l'Harmonie*, p. 17; DeChernier, *Observations sur le théâtre*, pp. 84–85; and Maillet-Duclairon, *Essai sur la Connoissance des Théâtres François*, p. 29. At the Opéra, where the popularity of the ballets threatened all other contributions to the productions, one reviewer summed up the ballets' impact in this way: "Dancing, for once, didn't singlehandedly secure the success of the opera, but it contributed a great deal." ["La danse, pour cette fois, n'a pas fait seule le succès de l'opéra—mais elle y a beaucoup contribué."] *Mercure de France*, April 1769, p. 145.

3. For a good overview of the development of these theatres, see Root-Bernstein, *Boulevard Theatre and Revolution in Eighteenth-Century Paris*, pp. 1–136.

4. For a general account of activities at private theatres, see Jullien's *L'Opéra Secret au XVIIIe Siècle*, and for a fascinating analysis of early eighteenth-century private performances and their relationship to public life, see Crow, *Painters and Public Life in Eigtheenth-Century Paris*, pp. 51–65.

5. The danced entre-actes at the Comédie Française were exceedingly popular. DeHesse also choreographed there, and the cleverness and success of his productions undoubtedly contributed to

fears that dance was fast becoming the principal attraction at the Comédie. One anonymous letter published in 1753 pleads with the administration at the Comédie Française not to move forward with the proposed ban on ballets there. See *Très-humbles et Très-respectueuses Remonstrances de MM les Comédiens Français Au Roi Pour obtenir de Sa Majesté la suppression d'un Arrêt du Conseil qui leur deffend les Ballets sous peine de 1000 liv. d'amende, etc.*, p. 10. Another testimony to the popularity of dance is given by Grimm in his description of ballets at the Comédie Française: "Their plays are followed by ballets and pantomimes that represent more or less the subject, executed by Italian dancers Cosimo, Maranies, and Mlle. Bagiani who show expression and surprising force in their thighs, but who do not approach the grace, precision and justice of our dancers, especially our Lany. It is because of the popularity of these ballets that the spectators suffer through the master-pieces." ["Ces pièces sont . . . terminées par des ballets et par des pantomimes à peu près conformes au sujet, et exécutés par Cosimo, Maranies, et Mlle. Bagiani, danseurs Italiens, qui ont de l'expression et une force surprenante dans les jarrets, mais qui n'approchent pas des grâces, de la précision et de la justesse de nos danseurs, et surtout de nos Lany. C'est en faveur de ces ballets que le public semble souffrir encore qu'on lui représente les chefs-d'œuvre."] Grimm, *Correspondance Littéraire*, July 1753, vol. 1, pp. 35–36.

6. Pitrot's ballets produced at the Comédie Italienne are one such example.

7. Noverre, *Letters on Dancing and Ballets*, p. 16.

8. As in earlier periods, a significant percentage of the Opéra's productions were revivals of earlier works.

9. Surviving records of the correspondence among various administrators at the Opéra reflect the complicated influences governing the production of work there. Decisions to produce new work as well as revive existing repertory were made on the basis of artistic opinions of best works mixed with practicalities of performers' schedules and contracts, the wishes of the queen, the cost of any given production, spectators' opinions, and productions at boulevard theatres. See, for example, the duties of administrators as documented in correspondence entered into the *Journal de l'Académie Royale de Musique*, April–June 1782.

10. Pay sheets for Opéra employees indicate that musicians in the orchestra were better paid and also outnumbered members of the corps de ballet. See *Sommaire Générale 1785–88* and *1788–90*.

11. As late as 1782 director of the Opéra Papillon de la Ferté cautions that the popularity of the action ballet will enhance the popularity of the dance and hence undermine the traditional relationships between music and dance, and the intended purpose of the Opéra itself. See *Journal de l'Academié Royale de Musique*, April 13–June 15, 1782, p. 38.

12. Noverre wrote extraordinarily eloquent scenarios for these ballets, which he compiled in eleven volumes dedicated to the Duke of Wurtemberg and published in 1766. See *Théorie et pratique de la danse simple et composée; de l'Art des Ballets; de la Musique; du Costume & des Décorations.*

13. These included *Balet [sic] intitulé le Combat de l'Amour et de la Raison* (1763), *Le Retour D'Apollon au Parnasse, Ballet allégorique pour la fête de sa majesté Catherine II* (1763), and *Le Départ D'Enée ou Didon Abandonnée, ballet tragique pantomime* (1766).

14. For a comprehensive overview of the architecture and mechanics of the eighteenth-century stage, see Baur-Heinhold, *Baroque Theatre,* and Gruber, *Les Grandes Fêtes et leurs Décors à l'Époque de Louis XVI.*

15. Penzel's *Theatre Lighting Before Electricity* gives a good account of eighteenth-century lighting conditions on stage and in the auditorium.

16. Gallini provides drawings of floor patterns for some of these configurations in *A Treatise on the Art of Dancing,* p. 164.

17. Most dancing manuals from the period begin with an identical enumeration of the basic positions and steps. See, for example, Magny, *Principes de chorégraphie, suivi d'un traité de la cadence, qui apprendra les tems & les valeurs de chaque pas de danse, détaillés par caractères, figures, & signes démonstratifs*, p. 1; Malpied, *Traité sur l'art de la danse*, p. 9–10; Chavanne, *Principes de Menuet*, pp. 12–15; Magri, *Theoretical and Practical Treatise on Dancing*, pp. 63–147; Guillemin, *Chorégraphie*, pp. 7–8; Clément, *Principes de Corégraphie [sic]*, pp. 4–5; and the *Encyclopédie* entry on "Chorégraphie."

18. I am indebted to Linda Tomko for this insight into the relationship between dance and music. Personal communication.

19. In his Preface to the ballet *Sémiramis,* Angiolini provides a detailed analysis of four genres: "grotesque, comic, demi-caractère, et haute," paying particular attention to the grotesque. That genre, he argues, is well suited for the representation of countryfolk, herdsmen, and those from Germany, Turkey, Spain, and England. Dancers expert in this genre, equivalent to the Pierrot, Polichinelle, and Scaramouche

characters in theatre, undertake "leaps and jumps, out of meter, and perilous leaps" ["sauts et bonds, hors de cadence, et sauts périlleux"]. Their performances are intended to produce "astonishment blended with fear, in seeing their likeness exposed to death at each instant" ["étonnement mêlé de crainte, en voyant leurs semblables exposés à se tuer à chaque instant"]. The comic genre, not as forceful as the grotesque, is suitable for amorous intrigues or national dances. Its characters include shepherds, gardeners, villagers, and workers. Always lively and fast, performers in this genre ask viewers to "admire the joining of force with precision and lightness, and also to enjoy how they artistically contrive the wry faces and contracted gestures that are indespensable to their effort" ["admirer la force jointe à la précision et la légèreté, et même faire rire quelquefois en tournant artistement en grimaces les gestes de contraction qui leur sont indispensables pour leur effort"]. The *demi-caractère* characters include those of pastoral, anacreontic, or Roman ballets. They are notable for the larger vocabulary of arm movements they perform and for their "justness, lightness, equilibrium, alacrity and softness, and gracefulness" ["justesse, lérèreté, l'équilibre, le moeleux, les grâces"]. The *haute* genre, exemplifed by Dupré and Vestris and revolutionized by Noverre, "makes the spectators shiver inwardly with the language of horror, pity, and terror inside ourselves, and bestirs us to pale with sighing, to tremble, and to shed tears" ["fasse sentir aux Spectateurs ces frémissements intérieurs, qui sont le langage avec lequel l'horreur, la pitié, la terreur parlent au-dedans de nous, et nous secouent au point de pâlir, de soupirer, de tressaillir, et de verser des larmes"], pp. C–5 through D–1. In his effort to pay Noverre a compliment and to rationalize the action ballet, Angiolini misrepresents to a certain extent the noble genre. What does ring true about his description is the genre's ability to evoke passions associated with the tragic. See also Noverre's description of the genres in *Letters on Dancing and Ballets*, pp. 88–90.

20. "M. Vestris, malgré le service de la Cour, a dansé dans la passacaille du quatrième acte avec l'applaudissement ou plutôt l'admiration des connoisseurs, qui sentent tout le prix et toute la difficulté d'un genre de danse, simple en apparence, mais qui réunit toutes les perfections de ce talent." *Mercure de France*, October 1765, p. 204.

21. Guimard, who went on to be one of the great dancers of the century, excelling in both the action ballet and the opera-ballet, apparently suffered a fall and danced for several weeks with her arm held in a scarf. See the *Mercure de France* reviews of her performances for February 1766, p. 161, and March 1766, p. 170. Guimard was one of the Opéra's most notorious and influential dancers. She had a flamboyant affair with the painter Fragonard, who decorated some of her lavish house and private theatre. She also went on to marry the boulevard writer Jean-Étienne Despréaux. For a good summary of her life, see Goncourt, *La Guimard*.

22. Accounts of dancers' private lives read like scripts for dramatic action. The lawyer for Mlle. Louise Regis, wife of Dancing Master Antoine Pitrot, described his treatment of her in these vivid terms: "It was July 29, 1765, that a cruel scene reduced her to this extreme. Her throat grabbed violently by Mr. Pitrot, lifted up into the air by her hair, thrown on the floor, *while in a state of being pregnant*, hit several times causing multiple contusions, and all this verified by a public officer, she was in danger of losing her life, if her neighbors, arriving at the sound of her cries, had not procured her liberty so that she might flee to her mother's house." ["Ce fut le 29 Juin 1765 qu'une scène cruelle la réduisit à cette extrèmité. Prise violement à la gorge par le sieur Pitrot, soulevée en l'air par les cheveux, jetée sur le plancher, *quoique dans un état de grossesse*, frappée de plusieurs coups qui lui firent plusieurs contusions très-graves, & constatées par l'Officier public, elle étoit en danger de perdre la vie, si les voisins, accourus à ses cris, ne lui eussent procuré la liberté de s'enfuir dans la maison maternelle"] Barentin, *Mémoire pour demoiselle Louise Regis*, p. 8.

He also provides this background information on Pitrot's first wife: "She saw him abandon himself with fury to the vices to which he was enslaved, gambling and debauchery. Then she found it necessary to sell part of her household furniture, in order to pay off his gambling debts, and after that to free him from the entanglements wrought by the disorderliness of his conduct. But what grieved the supplicant most, was to find herself the victim of an illness that she cannot even name without shame, and that was the product of Pitrot's dissolute and improper behavior. He was not content merely to render her a victim of his debauchery; he forced her to become a witness, to see it with her own eyes and to support it in her own house." ["Elle l'a vu . . . s'abandonner à la fureur des vices dont il étoit esclave, pour le jeu & la débauche. Tantôt elle s'est vu exposée à vendre partie de son mobilier, pour acquitter les dettes qu'il contractoit au jeu, tantôt pour lui rendre la liberté, dont il se privoit par la nature de ses engagemens & part les desordres de sa conduite. Mais ce qui afflige la Suppliante davantage, ça été de se sentir frappée d'une maladie dont elle ne peut sans honte nommer, & qui étoit le fruit de l'excès de dérèglement & de l'inconduite dudit Pitrot. Il ne s'est pas contenté de la rendre victime de ses débauches; il l'a forcée d'en être témoin, & de soutenir, sous ses yeux, dans sa maison."] Barentin, *Mémoire pour demoiselle Louis Regis*, p. 6.

23. Arguing on behalf of his client, who is suing a female dancer at the Opéra for not paying for renovations he made to her house, one lawyer describes the dancers' status in these terms: "The performers at the Académie Royale de Musique are a privileged type, almost indescribable. Ineffective, yet unfortunately regarded as necessary, less empowered than protected, the political government and not the law tolerates them. Isolated in the middle of civil society, they rule in a sphere that is separate from all others. Nature and familial and marital rights can exert no power over them. They are not allied with their parents or a husband: they depend only on themselves. Their associations formed more out of interest or fantasy than inspired by taste or by a sincere attachment of feelings, never last long." ["Les Actrices de l'Académie Royale de Musique sont des espèces d'être privilégiées & presque indéfinissables. Inutiles, & malheureusement regardées comme nécessaires, moins autorisées que protégées, le Gouvernement politique, & non la législation, les tolère. Isolées au milieu de la Société civile, elles règnent dans une sphère qui est séparée de toute autre. La nature, la puissance paternelle & maritale ont comme perdu leurs droits sur elles. Elles n'appartiennent ni à Parens, ni à Epoux: elles ne dependent en quelque sorte que d'elles-mêmes. Leurs engagemens plutôt formés par l'intérêt ou la fantasie, que par le goût & que par un rapport légitime de sentimens, ne sont jamais de longue durée. "] Carsillier, M. and Guiet, *Mémoire pour le Sieur Blanchard, Architecte, Juré-Expert*, p. 6.

The dossier continues by comparing the dancer's stage and daily lives this way: "She takes arbitrarily in civil society as many roles as each time in the theatre she changes her habits and her characters. Having forgotten her family or her husband, she goes by only a fantasy name, and for each civil action that effects her, will she have difficulties? Any man whom she might employ for projects or goods, would he be in a position to interogate her or to inform himself as to whether she is married or not?" ["Elle prend arbitrairement vis-à-vis de la Société civile, autant de formes, qu'elle change quelque fois sur le Théâtre, d'habits & de roles différents. Si oubliant sa Famille ou son Mari, elle ne porte qu'un nom de fantasie, à chaque acte de la vie civile qu'on passera avec elle, lui faudra-t-il faire des difficultés? Tout homme qu'elle voudra employer pour les choses d'usage ou de consommation, sera-t-il dans le cas de l'interroger ou de s'informer si elle est mariée ou non?"] M. Carsillier and M. Guiet, *Mémoire pour le Sieur Blanchard*, p. 7.

24. Several anonymous pamphlets, lascivious in tone, offer feigned objections to the amorous adventures of the female Opéra dancers. See *Le Code Lyrique, ou Règlement pour l'Opéra de Paris*, and *Constitution du Patriarche de l'Opéra*, in which the author observes, "The girls at the Opera have sorted out among themselves the government: one has the Ministry of War, another that of Finance, another that of Religious affairs, and that one there the mangagement of Foreign Affairs." ["Les filles d'Opéra ont partagé entr'elles le Gouvernement: l'une a le département de la Guerre, l'autre celui des Finances, celle-ci les affaires de Religion, & celle-là le maniement des affaires étrangères."] P. 17. See also Capon, *Les Vestris, le 'diou' de la danse et sa famille,* for an account of the amourous adventures of the Vestris family; and Capon and Yve-Plessis, *Fille d'Opéra, vendeuse d'amour, Histoire de Mlle. Deschamps (1730–1764)*, and Houssaye, *Men and Women of the Eighteenth Century*.

25. Laus de Boissy claims that Dauberval made all the ladies "susceptible to love," and tells the story of one count who took his mistress to see Dauberval at the ballet and was very successful afterwards. *Lettre critique sur notre Danse Théâtrale, adressée à l'Auteur du 'Spectateur français, par un homme de mauvaise humeur*, p. 12.

26. According to Isherwood, "Towards the middle of the century, entertainments usually of the bawdiest kind, were hired by the rich for presentation in their private theaters. In these private theaters the mistresses of aristocracy, primarily dancers, singers, and actresses mixed company with ladies of high birth," p. 37. He concurs with Capon and Yve-Plessis, who argued that the ladies "found it deliciously evil to play the role of slut and actress. They did not have to bear the stigma of sexual freedom under the guise of being patrons of the arts," quoted in Isherwood, p. 37.

27. *Mercure de France*, July 1762, p. 116.

28. ". . . il en resultera que ce qu'on apelle *Pas* dans notre talent, tient lieu des mots pour notre langage; que lesurs combinaisons forment des phrases plus ou moins bien tournées; que tout cela méthodiquement ordonné, ce fera avoir ecrit correctement; mais que l'exécution de ces parties, quelque

parfaite qu'elle puisse être, ne sera autre chose, par comparaison, que lire regulièrement, avec les inflexions convenables, & très-bien prononcer: il n'y aura en tout ceci rien qui provienne du genie, rien qui puisse lui être relatif. Pour me servir de l'hyperbolique expression des Applaudisseurs, les Danseurs ou les Danseuses dont les pas *ecrivent* les nottes, ont sans doute, à un très-grand degré, le merite de bien articuler. Mais qu'articulent-ils? Voilà de quoi il s'agit, pour savoir s'il y a non seulement du genie, mais même simplement de l'esprit dans leur Danse. On doit plaire aux yeux, sans contredit, lorsque l'on danse; c'est la première condition: mais comme la Danse doit, par un autre langage auxiliaire, prêter un coloris, une nouvelle *intelligibilité* à celui de la Musique, il faut donc nécessairement que la Danse parle à l'esprit, qu'elle excite ou rappelle des idées, & que dans les occasions, elle détermine l'âme aux mouvemens que le Poëte & le Musicien auront voulu lui faire prendre." *Mercure de France*, July 1762, pp. 119–20.

29. "On remarque particulièrement dans le Couplet du *Crescendo* une manière de pas précipités et enchainées par lesquels ce jeune Danseur écrit exactement aux yeux les notes de ce Couplet. Il joint à cette fidelle et vive expression dans tout le morceau, une légéreté facile et un à-plomb surprenant, avec une force qui laisseroit croire, à la fin de cette Entrée, une des plus fortes et des plus longues qu'on ait encore vu danser au Théâtre." *Mercure de France*, January 1763, vol. 1, p. 162.

30. Ballets performed at the Opéra were regularly reviewed in the *Mercure de France* and also in small published pamphlets, usually written in the form of a letter, that described a given performance. Many of these pamphlets seem to have been available for purchase in the lobbies of the theatre and elsewhere.

31.The son of the famous Dancing Master Marcel, in defending his father's profession from the perceived attack offered by Jean-Jacques Rousseau in his *Emile*, argues that Dancing Masters, by imparting graceful, clear actions and firm steps, contribute to "la perfection de l'espèce." *Lettre à M. J.-J. Rousseau, C. de Genève*, p. 9.

32. This enthusiasm is evidenced, in part, in the large number of dance manuals published during this period that consist largely of notated scores for dances. See, for example, Guillemin, *Chorégraphie, ou l'art de décrire la danse*; La Cuisse, *Suite du Répertoire des Bals*, Magny, *Principes de chorégraphie*; and Malpied, *Traité sur l'art de la danse*.

33. Pauli's *Elémens de la Danse*, for example, divides dance into "danse simple" for exercise, self-improvement, and good conduct; "la danse de bal" to be used in solemneties and ceremonies; "la contre-danse" designed for permissible pleasures; and "haute danse" utilized in theatrical representations, p. 5. And Giovanni-Andrea Gallini succinctly summarizes the advantages of dancing this way: "In the view of a genteel exercise, it strengthens the body; in the view of a liberal accomplishment, it visibly diffuses a graceful ability through it; in the view of a private or public entertainment, it is not only a general instinct of nature, expressing health and joy by nothing so strongly as by dancing; but is susceptible with all of the most elegant collateral embellishments of taste, from poetry, music, painting, and machinery." *A Treatise on the Art of Dancing*, pp. xii–xiii.

34. Chavanne, *Principes de Menuet*, pp. 16–25.

35. It could easily be argued that the term "machine" in eighteenth-century French had such widespread and general acceptance as a colloquial expression for the body that its use by Dancing Masters is insignificant. Still, in the context of other references to the body such as springs and as levers, and the frequent scientific experiments on the body, its use seems to indicate that the concept played a formative role as a central and generative metaphor.

36. Noverre, *Letters on Dancing and Ballets*, p. 218.

37. Gallini, *A Treatise on the Art of Dancing*, p. 235.

38. Much of the argument I am making here supports, and is framed to complement, the analysis undertaken by Roach in *The Player's Passion* on the interactions between science, rhetoric, and acting theory in the seventeenth and eighteenth centuries. Roach argues persuasively for the centrality of the machine metaphor in acting theory during the early and middle eighteenth century. See pp. 58–92. I am also indebted to Roach for the interpretation of the Pygmalion figure, which was as popular in eighteenth-century drama as it was in dance.

39. See Roach, *The Player's Passion*, pp. 62–66.

40. "Je voudrais qu'un maître expliquat à son écolier la cause de tout, qu'il lui fit sentir que ce qu'on lui demande est naturel, conforme à la raison et qu'une attitude ou un mouvement désagréable ne l'est pas. Par exemple, en marchant, le centre de pesanteur du corps est alternatif sur les pieds: cela est

conforme aux lois mécaniques, cela est naturel; si la tête et les épaules tombent en avant, si les hanches restent plus en arrière que les jambes ce sont des mouvements non naturels." C. F. O. de Brucourt commenting on the appropriate method of teaching postural alignment in his 1747 volume *Essai sur l'éducation de la noblesse.* Quoted in Georges Vigarello, "Posture, Espace et Pedagogie," p. 46.

41. "Si l'on vouloit faire attention à la manière dont un homme est construit, on verroit qu'il n'est jamais plus aisément composé, & plus sûrement bien dessiné, que dans le tems ou posant également sur ses deux pieds, peu distans l'un de l'autre, il laisse tomber ses bras & ses mains ou leur propre poids les porte naturellement; c'est ce qu'on appelle, en terme de danse, être à la seconde position, les mains sur les poches. C'est la situation la plus naturelle & la plus simple; cependant on a toujours une peine infinie à y bien poser quelqu'un qui apprend à danser. Il semble que la nature s'oppose perpétuellement à elle-même." Riccoboni, *L'Art du Théâtre, à Madame ****, p. 10.

42. Gallini, *A Treatise on the Art of Dancing,* p. 137.

43. Harking back to seventeenth-century Dancing Master Ferdinand de Lause, Nivelon writes, "The Head, being the principal Part of the human Figure, must be first considered, because it entirely governs all the Rest . . . a Person whose Head is rightly placed, is capable of Standing, Walking, Dancing, or performing any genteel Exercise in a graceful, easy and becoming Manner," *The Rudiments of Genteel Behavior,* pp. 1–2.

44. Noverre writes, "The sole of the foot is the true base which supports the whole body. A sculptor would run the risk of destroying his work if he supported it on a round and moving body. The fall of his statue would be inevitable, for it would infallibly snap and break. For the same reason the dancer must make use of all the toes of his feet as so many branches of which the spreading out on the ground will increase the size of his base, consolidate and maintain his body in a fit and proper equilibrium." *Letters on Dancing and Ballets,* p. 121.

45. "Il vous auroit dit que pour faire un pas assuré, il faut fléchir le jarret de la jambe dont on veut partir; lever le pied de cette même jambe à un pouce de terre; le porter en avant en étendant le jarret, de façon que la jambe, bien tendue, se trouve sur la même direction que la hanche. Ensuite il vous auroit fait poser le pied totalement à terre en avançant le corps sur la jambe dont vous êtes parti, & il vous auroit dit 'Monsieur, voilà un pas de fait.'" Marcel, *Lettre à M. J.-J. Rousseau,* p. 7.

46. Guillemin, *Chorégraphie,* p. 35.

47. See Wildeblood and Brinson's extensive list of procedures for bowing in *The Polite World,* pp. 267–72.

48. A critic writing on the performance of Mlle. Heinel, one of the foremost dancers of the period, comments that nothing could improve her dancing unless she were to "incline a little less her head to the back so that her neck would not appear as shortened nor her head fitted too low between the shoulders. It is with confidence that we risk this observation." [". . . penche un peu moins la tête en arrière, ce qui fait quelque fois paroître le cou trop raccourci & la tête emmanchée trop bas dans les épaules. C'est avec confiance que nous osons risquer cette observation."] *Mercure de France,* June 1769, p. 175.

49. Noverre, *Letters on Dancing and Ballets,* p. 125.

50. Gallini argues similarly for the many improvements in one's sociability to be derived from dancing: "But besides the effect of the moment in pleasing the spectators; the being well versed in this dance especially contributes greatly to form the gait, and address, as well as the manner in which we should present ourselves. It has a sensible influence in the polishing and fashioning the air and deportment in all occasions of appearance in life. It helps to wear off anything of slowishness in the carriage of the person, and breathes itself into otherwise the most indifferent actions, in a genteel and agreeable manner of performing them." Gallini, *A Treatise on the Art of Dancing,* p. 172.

51. Gallini, *A Treatise on the Art of Dancing,* p. 121

52. Gallini, *A Treatise on the Art of Dancing,* p. 154.

53. Guillaume, *Almanach dansant ou positions et attitudes de l'allemande avec un discours préliminaire sur l'origine et l'utilité de la danse dédié au beau sexe par Guillaume, maître de danse pour l'année 1770,* p. 10.

54. Reviews often evaluated performers in terms of their success at exemplifying a given genre or the primary attributes of that genre, as in this commentary: "The happy blend of different genres, noble, galant, gay, and mimetic, excites curiosity and contentment. M. Gardel appeared to advantage in a *chaconne* in the second act, where he develops all the force, sureness, and nobility of his dance. Mlle.

Heinel is always admirable in the fierce and majestic genre that she executes with such superiority. It is also necessary to place in the first rank Mlle. Guimard for the gracious and voluptuous genre; Mlle. Allard for the strong and pantomimic dance and her student Mlle. Peslin; M. Dauberval surprises and charms the viewer each time with the boldness and picturesque art of his steps." ["L'heureux mélange des différens genres de danse noble, galante, gaie et pantomime, exécutés par les plus grands talens, excite la curiosité et la contente. M. Gardel paroît avec avantage dans la chaconne du second acte, où il développe toute la force, la sûreté et la noblesse de sa danse. Mlle. Heinel est toujours admirable dans le genre de danse fière et majestueuse qu'elle exécute avec tant de supériorité. Il faut placer aussi au premier rang Mlle. Guimard, pour le genre gracieux et voluptueux; Mlle. Allard pour la danse forte et pantomime, et Mlle. Peslin, son émule; M. Dauberval étonne et charme en même tems le spectateur par la hardiesse et l'art pittoresque de ses pas."] *Mercure de France,* October 1772, vol. 1, p. 152.

55. Noverre, *Letters on Dancing and Ballets,* p. 33.

56. Even Papillon de la Ferté plagiarized Noverre in his summary of the necessary attributes of a successful and talented choreographer. See *Manuscript sur la composition des ballets et le role du maître de ballet,* pp. 1–4.

57. Throughout this text I am using "choreography" in its twentieth-century meaning to refer to the art of making dances. Eighteenth-century definitions of the term emphasized the transcription of the dance into notated form, rather than the actual invention and sequencing of movements.

58. Noverre, *Letters on Dancing and Ballets,* pp. 68–69.

59. In an undated letter (possibly from the end of the eighteenth century or as late as the 1820s) to the Opéra administration asking for his pension, Pierre Gardel summarized the Ballet Master's duties by comparing the job to orchestra or choir conductor. Although he argued that the Ballet Master took a far more active role in the creation of dances than conductors who merely oversaw the execution of the composer's work, the list of responsibilities belies the subsidiary part played by the choreographer within the Opéra organization: "Conductors only execute what the composers have created; but the Ballet Master composes the solos, pas de deux, trios, quartets, and the corps, the fights, the processions, the drama, the ceremonies, etc. . . . Once a work is established by the Masters of the Choir or the Orchestra they can rest easy; but the Ballet Master is almost always forced to compose for the alternate cast choreography completely different from that for the principal artists. The Master is also obliged to be at the theatre every morning and evening to fix up last minute changes." ["Ces derniers font exécuter ce qui les (compositeurs) ont composé; mais le Chef de la Dance compose les pas seule, les pas de deux, de trois, de quatre, les corps de Ballet, les combats, les marches, les actions, les cérémonies, etc . . . Lorsqu'un ouvrage est établie les Chefs du Chant et de l'Orchestre se reposent; mais celui de la Danse est presque toujours forcé de composer pour les Doubles tout différemment qu'il a composé pour les premiers artistes. Il est obligé aussi d'être tous les matins et tous les soirs au Théâtre afin de parer aux fréquents événements."] Pierre Gabriel Gardel, "Dossier artiste," p. 2.

60. Grimm carefully explains the choreographic imperative to exaggerate the observable world in order to create a viable representation of it this way: "All passion has without doubt its signs, the gestures that are appropriate to it; it is for pantomime to discern them and to use them; but you must believe that pantomime would have very little effect in the theatre it if did not depict them with more force and energy than that found generally in nature." ["Toute passion a sans doute des signes, des gestes qui lui sont propres; c'est au pantomime à les discerner et à les saisir; mais croyez qu'il ferait peu d'effet au théâtre s'il ne les rendait pas avec plus de force et d'énergie qu'on n'en trouve communément dans la nature."] P. 86–87, January 1776, vol. 1, pp. 85–87.

61. Noverre, *Letters on Dancing and Ballets,* pp. 32–33.

62. Noverre, *Letters on Dancing and Ballets,* pp. 35–36.

63. Noverre, *Letters on Dancing and Ballets,* p. 33.

64. Noverre, *Letters on Dancing and Ballets,* p. 35.

65. Noverre, *Letters on Dancing and Ballets,* pp. 71–72.

66. Noverre, *Letters on Dancing and Ballets,* pp. 188–96.

67. Noverre, *Letters on Dancing and Ballets,* p. 16 and p. 53.

68. The potential conflict between dancers' traditional training and the new action ballet's demands was highlighted by Laus de Boissy, who specifically noted Vestris's inability to act. Claiming that Vestris has never really danced, because dance should be an imitation and he has always been himself, Laus de Boissy continues: "This man might well change his headpiece, his costume, and his mask, but it is always

he that one sees in the character that he wants to represent." ["Cet homme a beau changer de casque, d'habit & de masque, c'est toujours lui qu'on voit dans le personnage qu'il veut représenter."] *Lettre Critique sur notre Danse Théâtrale,* p.8.

69. Noverre, *Letters on Dancing and Ballets,* p. 156.

70. Michel summarizes the new expertise required of both choreographers and dancers in this description of DeHesse's career: "Witnesses, in surprising agreement, attest that DeHesse trained the young dancers to combine with their movements an expressive power 'by means of which they touched on the art of the actor.' Moreover, it was a remarkable phenomenon to witness in his ballets that the second and third dancers, and even the corps de ballet, were brought to the point where they were able to contribute their share to this art of natural and vivid expression. Thus he developed a style of stage dancing that the critics lauded as 'pittoresque.' They meant, by this, that each of DeHesse's ballets had its individual 'picturesque' character, that is, a specific character of movement which was shared by all the dancers on the stage, so that their movements seemed to be part of a unified, balanced, living painting with finely graduated tones." "Two Great XVIII Century Ballet Masters: Jean-Baptiste DeHesse and Franz Hilverding; *La Guinguette* and *Le Turc généreux* seen by G. de St. Aubin and Canaletto," p. 274.

71. Noverre, *Letters on Dancing and Ballets,* p. 91.

72. Noverre, *Letters on Dancing and Ballets,* p. 29.

73. Noverre, *Letters on Dancing and Ballets,* p. 114.

74. Noverre, *Letters on Dancing and Ballets,* p. 121.

75. Noverre, *Letters on Dancing and Ballets,* p. 127.

76. Noverre, *Letters on Dancing and Ballets,* pp. 100–108.

77. Noverre, *Letters on Dancing and Ballets,* p. 107.

78. Noverre, *Letters on Dancing and Ballets,* p. 100.

Jason et Médée

1. This, according to Deryck Lynham, *Le Chevalier Noverre,* pp. 60–61.

2. See Grimm's comment, quoted in full below.

3. "Il a, dit-on, été vu dans les Cours étrangères, mais bien postèrieurement à l'idée qu'avoit eu le charmant Auteur de *Daphnis et Cloé, d'Eglé,* et de *Silvie,* de l'annexer à cet Ouvrage et l'introduire sur la scène, puisqu'en 1755 la musique était faite et en 1763 l'Opéra fut donné à Choisi devant leur Majestés, avec le même Ballet, dont Vestris a très-bien saisi l'historique et l'esprit en le remettant au théâtre." *Mercure de France,* January, vol. 1, 1771, pp. 187–88.

4. See Capon's biography of the Vestris family, *Les Vestris, le 'diou' de la danse et sa famille, 1730–1808,* for a summary of his life accomplishments.

5. For example, his *Don Juan.*

6. Lynham describes the effect of one production on the audience in these terms: "During one of them, *Les Danaïdes,* it has been said the scene in which *Death, Parcae* and a number of spectres appeared, was so terrifying that a number of the audience, seized with a sudden terror, hastily left the theatre." *The Chevalier Noverre,* p. 63.

7. "L'inconstance de Jason qui abandonne Médée pour épouser Creuse, ses nouvelles amours, le dépit de Médée, les efforts qu'elle fait pour réveiller le tendresse de son époux infidèle, en lui présentant ses enfans; les fureurs de cette femme jalouse, ses enchantemens, les fêtes du mariage de Creuse, la réconciliation insidieuse que Médée paroit faire avec sa rivale, les présens empoissonnés qu'elle lui donne; les tourmens & la mort de Creuse; le désespoir de Jason, les furies qui l'agitent, la rage insultante de Médée enlevée dans un char trainé par des dragons; le meurtre de ses enfans qu'elle poignarde à la vue de leur père; une pluie de feu & l'embrasement du Palais; toute cette action & ce spectacle produisent le plus grand effet." *Mercure de France,* January, vol. 1, 1771, p. 188.

8. "Les principaux personnages, savoir Jason (Vestris), Médée (Allard), Creuze (Guimard), sont chacun dans leur caractère, d'une expression qui étonne. La Jalousie, La Vengence, et le Désespoir, les trois Divinités infernales forment une scène dont le tableau est du grand effet." *Mercure de France,* January, vol. 1, 1771, pp. 187–88.

9. The score by Rodolphe is filled with markings indicating pauses in the musical score that accompanied tableaux. See Rodolphe, J., *Médée et Jason,* 1776.

10. "Le ballet que Noverre a donné à Vienne était imité par Vestris qui a dansé à Vienne dans ce ballet de Noverre. Il fallait en conserver au moins la musique qu'on dit superbe; mais M. de la Borde a mieux aimé y substituer la sienne sans génie et sans goût. Vestris n'a pas observé une autre chose aussi essentielle que la musique: c'est que dans les ballets de Noverre la danse et la marche cadencée sont très-distinctes; on ne danse que dans les grands mouvemens de passion, dans les momens décisifs; dans les scènes on marche en mésure à la vérité, mais sans danser. Le passage de la marche mésurée à la danse et de la danse à la marche mésurée, est aussi nécessaire dans ce spectacle, que dans celui de l'Opéra le passage du récitatif à l'air et de l'air au récitatif; mais danser pour danser ne peut avoir lieu que lorsque la pièce en danse est finie. . . . Son imitateur Vestris, n'ayant pas pris garde à ces élémens n'a paru avoir fait un ballet sans aucun effet. Malgré cela, la nouveauté du spectacle l'a fait réussir et a attiré beaucoup de monde à l'Opéra. Les uns ont dit que c'était bien, les autres que les contorsions de Vestris-Jason étaient ridicules et celles de Médée-Allard effroyables. Creuse-Guimard, après avoir été empoisonnée dans ce ballet par sa rivale, a dansé dans le troisième acte comme simple bergère, en robe si élégante que nos dames ont quitté le domino du carnaval pour danser en robes à la Guimard. Ce n'est pourtant autre chose qu'une robe retroussée avec élégance sur un jupon d'une autre couleur. La première invention en est due aux actrices de la Comédie Italienne qui ont jouées les rôles de l'Opéra Comique avec ces habits; une demoiselle Guimard, ou son décorateur, n'a fait qu'y ajouter beaucoup de pompons, d'agrémens et de guirlandes." Grimm, *Correspondance Littéraire,* January 1771, vol. 1, pp. 401–402.

Apelles et Campaspe

1. According to Papillon de la Ferté, "M. Gardel appeared very disatisfied that Noverre would stay on until the month of July, and he sent Dauberval to speak to me about it, but I reminded Dauberval that he owes his talent to Noverre; and what is more, he cannot ignore the fact that Noverre had the honor to teach the Queen to dance, and that he has enjoyed their protection and would not want them deceived by having them think he had stayed at the Opéra when in reality he had taken his leave three months earlier." ["Le S. Gardel paroît très mécontent que le S. Noverre reste encore jusqu'au mois de juillet, il en a envoyé le S. Dauberval pour m'en parler, mais j'ai cru devoir lui rappeller que lui Dauberval doit son talent à Noverre; qui est plus il ne peut ignorer que Noverre, ayant eû l'honneur de montrer à la Reine à danser, qu'il a été honoré de la protection de Ses Majestés et que même il n'en veut point abuser, pour rester à l'Opéra ayant pris réellement son parti de quitter dans trois mois."] *Journal de l'Académie Royale de Musique,* April 21, p. 48.

2. According to Grimm, Mlle. Guimard asked for a new dress for her appearance in a production of *Castor et Pollux,* but "the economical director having refused her, she cut the old dress into a million pieces and sent him the sorry scraps. De Vîsmes was obliged to have another made for her, and only after many entreaties was he able to persuade her to resume her role." ["L'économie du directeur ayant osé la refuser, elle découpa l'ancien en mille pieces et lui en renvoya les tristes lambeaux. Le sieur de Vîsmes fut obligé d'en faire faire un autre, et ce n'est qu'après beaucoup de prières qu'il put l'engager à reprendre son rôle."] *Correspondance Littéraire,* March 1779, vol. 4, pp. 366–67.

3. Those advocating the changes in the Opéra were impressed with Noverre's production, as exemplified in this anonymous reviewer's comments: "Noverre's ballets are hardly composed of these monotonous designs, these eternal pinwheels, these balances, these astonishing steps, so difficult, but which say nothing to the appearance or the spirit of the viewer; his are made of magnificent tableaux, ingenious groupings, striking attitudes that give way rapidly one to the next; and they make regular actions that, for the sensitive, can often compete with the masterpieces of French drama." ["Les Ballets de M. Noverre ne sont point uniquement composés de ces dessins monotones, de ces tournoiemens éternels, de ces balancemens, de ces pas si étonnans, si difficiles; mais qui ne disent rien au coeur ni à l'esprit du spectateur: ce sont des tableaux magnifiques, des groupes ingénieux, des attitudes piquantes qui se succèdent rapidement les uns aux autres; et font des actions régulières qui, pour le pathétique, peuvent souvent entrer en concurrance avec les chef-d'œuvres du Théâtre Français."]

He continues: ". . . a pantomime ballet that was received with much applause; it is in the gracious genre. . . . the diverse attitudes that Apelles asks Campaspe to take in order to represent her on the canvas make so many tableaux whose concepts would do honor to our best painters; so many scenes that imply a most rich and most poetic imagination. . . . The music, also by Rodolphe, created the greatest effect; one could search in vain for an expression more truthful, noble, or varied than that of the celebrated Vestris, more fiercely imposing and majestic than that of Mlle. Heinel, and with more graces, seductive and voluptuous, than those of Mlle. Guimard." [". . . en Ballet pantomime, qui a été accueilli avec beaucoup d'applaudissements; il est dans le genre gracieux. . . . les diverses attitudes qu' Apelles fait prendre à Campaspe, afin de les retrouver sur la toile, forment autant de tableaux, dont les idées feroient honneur à nos meilleurs Peintres; autant de scènes, qui supposent l'imagination la plus riche & la plus poétique. . . . La musique aussi est de M. Rodolphe, produiroit le plus grand effet; on cherchoit peut être en vain une expression plus vraie, plus noble, plus variée que celle du célèbre Vestris, une fierté plus imposante & plus majestueuse que celle de Mlle. Heinel, & des grâces plus voluptuesses & plus séduisantes que celles de Mlle. Guimard."] *L'Esprit des Journaux,* November 1776, pp. 276–78.

4. "Cependant si l'on veut trouver quelque chose à désirer dans cette magnifique composition; c'est que le Peintre pantomime ait refermé un double sujet dans le même cadre; c'est que le couronnement de Roxane fasse une seconde action qui, noble & imposante, contraste peut-être trop avec celle, pleine de grâces, des amours d'Apelles & de Campaspe; c'est qu'il ait fait en même temps un tableau digne de l'Albane, du Corrège, avec un tableau de Raphael ou de Michel-Ange. Osons même demander à ce grand Maître, si'il étoit à propos qu'Alexandre, Ephistion & Roxanne figurassent dans la danse, s'il ne suffisoit pas qu'ils parussent comme des personnages dramatiques pleins de passions & intéressés à l'action, mais qui y fussest distingués par leur rang & par leur contenance. Il est certain que l'on voit avec peine Alexandre, Ephestion, & Roxanne danser chacun leur entrée, & figurer avec Apelles, Campaspe, les Elèves d'Apelles & les Guerriers. Au reste nous ne pouvons pas assez marquer notre admiration pour ce genre de danse, qui s'approche de la bonne poétique & des règles de la peinture." *Mercure de France,* October 1776, p. 169.

5. A staunch supporter of Noverre, Grimm took Gardel to task for ignoring his duties as an actor playing the role of Alexandre in order to display his virtuoso talents: "Heinel produces a pantomime of anxiety and jealousy that infuses variety into the subject and gives the scene warmth and life. Apelles restrains Roxanne's concern, reassures Campaspe, and conceals her in order to avoid a confrontation. Since this Apelles does not cease being M. Gardel for one moment, that is to say, one of the premier dancers in all Europe but one of the coldest actors who ever appeared in any theatre, this situation, although admitting of interest, made only the slightest impression." [". . . elle [Heinel] produit une pantomime d'inquiètude et de jalousie, qui, jette de la variété dans le sujet, et donne à la scène de chaleur et de vie. Alexandre modère l'importement de Roxanne; rassure Campaspe, et dissimule pour éviter un éclat. Comme cet Alexandre ne cesse pas un moment d'être le sieur Gardel, c'est-à-dire un des premiers danseurs de l'Europe, mais un des plus froides acteurs qui ait jamais paru sur aucun Théâtre, cette situation, quoique très susceptible d'intérêt, ne fait que peu de sensation."] Grimm goes on to comment that Alexander is shown dancing in act 2 because "Alexandre Gardel would rather renounce his world empire than his *entrechats.*" ["Alexandre Gardel aimerait mieux renoncer à l'empire du monde qu'à ses entrechats."] *Correspondance Littéraire,* October 1776, vol. 3, pp. 276–78.

6. In his evaluation of *Apelles et Campaspe,* Grimm asserts that the decorations and costuming were not realistic and in very poor taste and that the administration should have allotted more funds for sets. *Correspondance littéraire,* October 1776, vol. 3, p. 274.

7. A typical example was Noverre's *Les Caprices de Galathea,* whose review provides insights into the general kind of action that these short pieces contained: "The caprices of a young shepherdess who sometimes invites and sometimes refuses a shepherd, who receives with ecstasy the present of a bird which she disdains the next instant; who refuses and rejects with disgust a bouquet that her lover has just offered; who picks it up and possesses it with pleasure once the young shepherd, reduced to despair, has left in order to hide his suffering; all this would not seem at first to lend itself to the making of an interesting pantomime; nevertheless one finds interest and agreeableness in the ballet we have described. The scenes where the inconsequential shepherdess abandons herself to all her fantasies are interrupted with episodic scenes that offer the most striking contrast. The manner in which Galathea is crowned, for that matter, the lightness of her character, is extremely ingenious . . . . the figures in dance that make a suite of action have the double advantage of being striking and new." ["Les caprices d'une jeune Bergère qui tantôt attire, & tantôt repousse son Berger; qui reçoit avec transport le present d'un oiseau qu'elle dédaigne à l'instant même; qui refuse & rejette avec mépris le bouquet que son amant

vient de lui offir; qui le ramasse & s'empare avec plaisir, quand le jeune Berger, reduit au désespoir, est sorti pour cacher sa douleur; tout cela ne paroît pas d'abord devoir former une Pantomime bien intéressante; cependant on trouve de l'intérêt & de l'agrément dans le Ballet dont nous rendons compte. Les Scènes où l'inconséquente Bergère se livre tour-à-tour à tous ses caprices, sont coupées par des Scènes épisodiques qui offrent le contraste le plus piquant. La manière dont Galathée est couronnée, pour ainsi-dire, la légèreté de son caractère, est extrêmement ingènieuse. . . . les figures des danses qui font une suite de l'action, ont le double avantage d'être piquantes & neuves."] *Mercure de France,* July 1, 1780, pp. 37–38.

8. Another review of *Apelles et Campaspe* exemplifies the guarded praise Noverre consistently received, taking issue with Noverre's realization of the plot: "No matter how great a painter Apelles was, he could never have passed for a god. It is therefore ridiculous to disguise his students as Amours, Zephirs, Graces, etc." ["Tout grand Peintre que fût Apelles, jamais il ne passa pour demi Dieu. Il est donc ridicule de déguiser ses Elèves en *Amours,* en *Zéphirs,* en *Grâces,* &c."] And in the scene where Alexandre decides to have Apelles paint Campaspe's portrait, "one was surprised to see dance for such a long time the Prince, who probably had not had much time to learn dancing; and given that in his station as Prince would have known dancing since birth, would hardly have come to the painter's studio to practice." ["on a été surpris d'y voir si bien & si longtems danser un Prince, qui probablement n'avoit pas beaucoup de tems pour apprendre la danse; & quantd [sic], en sa qualité de Prince, il auroit su danser en naissant, il se serait bien gardé de venir l'exercer dans l'atelier de son Peintre."] The reviewer then claims that the second act is devoid of all interest because all the intrigue of the piece terminates in the first. The reviewer suggests that "Noverre could have remedied this inconvenience by reserving for the second act the pardon that [Alexandre] accords to Apelles and Campaspe at the end of the fifth scene, and this is how I imagine the catastrophe could have been brought about in the second act so as to hold in suspense the minds of the spectators and to leave them something to desire." ["M. Noverre auroît pu remédier à cet inconvénient, en réservant pour le second Acte le pardon qu'il accorde à Apelles & Campaspe à la fin de la Ve. Scene; & voici comment j'imagine que cette catastrophe auroît put être amener au second Acte, afin de tenir en suspens l'esprit des Spectateurs & de leur laisser quelque chose à désirer."] *Journal des Théâtres; ou le Nouveau Spectateur.* Numero XIII, October 1, 1776. pp. 292–94.

3. NARRATING PASSION AND PROWESS

1. "Les premiers hommes, fortement émus par les objets environnants, exprimèrent leurs sensations par des métaphors, par des articulations vives et accentuées, par des gestes énergiques. La Poésie, la Musique, la Danse, naquirent avec la langue primitive, ou plutôt elles en faisoient l'essence." L'Aulnaye, *De la saltation théâtrale,* p. iv.

2. Reforms in costuming undertaken by Mme. Favart at the Opéra Comique and later by actors Lekain and Clairon at the Comédie Française dressed characters of a given social class, age, and profession in versions of clothing very much like those worn by real people of those backgrounds. Opéra costumes, however, continued through the 1770s to signal differences only through tiny alterations in the ornamentation of standardly cut garments.

3. The ballet *Palmire et Zélénor,* produced in November 1765, included a three-act "Pantomime Héroique" at the end that featured a number of pantomimed tableaux. See *Mercure de France,* November 1765, pp. 212–14. The opera *Thésée* also included a long concluding celebration in which pantomime played a significant role: "a ballet of a new theatrical genre, and more natural than the others. A tumultuous multitude, where the youths, the old people, and the children of both sexes mixed together in their songs and dances, representing far more accurately the effervescence of the crowd than in the solos, duets and particular airs that one customarily uses in between the other divertissements. . . . The natural gaity, supported by the antique instruments on which the dancers play, summoned the attention and pleasure of the spectators throughout the duration of the ballet. In all imitation, the truth has laws superior to the rules, especially when one knows how to present it. That is what M. Lani has done in the composition of his ballet.

In the middle of these popular dances, they bring in Thésée, seated on a bundle of pikes, shields and other arms. He is surrounded by a number of sodiers not in formation around which the people continue to rejoice until the moment the troops ordered by the hero organize to go defend their posts. There prevails so much variety, so much movement, and a kind of novelty for the theatre in all this scene that the eyes never rest for an instant. . . .

Effects even more forceful and of a completely different genre strike the viewers' eyes and seize their souls in the third act. The desert. . . . It is here that Medea invokes the infernal beings. One sees the earth rise up and open as they form into a group to make their passage. This means, never before seen at the theatre, adds to the illusion and prepares for the horror of the spectacle that follows. The infernal beings exit with some effort from the bosom of the earth in picturesque and characteristic attitudes. Medea liberates them from their chains. They express very strongly in their steps and clear manner the cruel pleasure of souls tormented by crimes and remorse. . . . The flaming torches, with which they arm themselves, augment the terror. In waving the torches, the flames increase prodigiously, so that they seem to envelope those who carry them in torrents of fire, ready to consume the interested victim of their fury. This effect, so enormous in appearance, is that of a powder contained within capsules inside the torches; this powder is subtly inflammable, so that it produces no smoke, no odor, and does not risk burning even lightly during its lively explosion; the discovery of this effect is the result of M. Laval's ardent zeal."

[". . . un ballet d'un genre nouveau au théâtre, & plus naturel que les autres. Une multitude tumultueuse, où les jeunes, les vieillards & les enfans des deux sexes, mêlent ensemble leurs chants & leurs danses, représente bien mieux la vérité d'une effervescence populaire, que les pas seuls, les pas de deux, & les airs particuliers dont on a coutume de couper les autres divertissements. . . . La gaieté naturelle, soutenue par le son des instrumens antiques, sur lesquels frappent les danseurs, entretient l'attention & le plaisir du spectateur pendant toute la durée de ce ballet. Dans toute imitation, le vrai a des droits superieurs aux règles, surtout quand on sçait le bien présenter. C'est ce qu'a fait M. Lani dans la composition de son ballet.

Au milieu de ces danses populaires on aporte Thésée assis sur un faisceau de piques, de boucliers et d'autres armes. Il est environné d'un nombre de soldats sans ordre, à travers lesquel le peuple continue ses réjoissances, jusqu'au moment où, par l'ordre du héros, les troupes de soldats se reforment pour aller en bon ordres aux postes qu'il faut défendre. Il règne tant de variété, tant de mouvement, & une sorte de nouveauté pour le théâtre, dans tout ce tableau, qu'il semble ne rester qu'un instant sous les yeux. . . .

Des touches bien plus fortes, & d'un tout autre genre, frappent les yeux & saisissent l'âme du spectateur au troisième acte. Le désert. . . . C'est la que Médée évoque les êtres infernaux. On voit la terre se soulever, s'entrouvrir, en se pelotonnant, pour leur faire passage. Ce moyen, qui n'avoit pas encore été pratiqué au théâtre, ajoute à l'illusion & prépare à l'horreur du spectacle qu'on attend. Les êtres infernaux sortent avec quelqu'effort du sein de la terre, dans des attitudes pittoresques & bien caractérisées. Médée les délivre de leurs chaines. Ils expriment très fortement par leurs pas & d'une manière assez claire ce plaisir cruel des âmes tourmentées de crimes & de remords. . . . Les flambeaux, dont s'arment les habitans des enfers, en augmentent la terreur. En agitant ces flambeaux, la flamme s'en accroit si prodigieusement, qu'elle semble tantot envelopper dans des torrens de feu ceux qui s'en servent, & tantot prête à consumer l'interessante victime de leur furie. Cet effet, si prodigieux en apparence, est celui d'un poudre contenue dans les capsules des flambeaux; cette poudre est si subtilement inflammable, qu'elle ne produit nulle fumée, nulle odeur, & n'est d'aucun risque pour brûler, même légèrement, dans sa plus vive explosion; la découverte de ce moyen est dû aux soins & au zèle ardent de M. de Laval." *Mercure de France,* January 1766, pp. 201–204.

4. Dauberval seems to have taken the initiative on several occasions to introduce aspects of dramatic action, thereby accustoming viewers slowly to the new look of the action ballet. As early as 1766 he appeared "in a solo notable for its strange character, shown with an attack and a lightness almost inconceivable. Not only does he please, he awakes and sustains within the spectator a pleasure through the spiritual play that he puts into the dance, animating it throughout the rest of the divertissement in which he seems never to cease taking part. The merit in this genre is that of the actor who plays the nonspeaking scene." [". . . dans un pas fort singulier et d'un caractère qui paroît tout-à-fait étranger, fait briller une adresse et une légèreté inconcevables. Non-seulement il plaît, il éveille et soutient le plaisir du spectateur par le jeu spirituel qu'il met dans sa danse, mais il anime encore, il égaye tout le reste du divertissement auquel il semble ne cesser de prendre part. C'est le mérite, en ce genre, de l'acteur qui joue la scène muette."] *Mercure de France,* July 1766, p. 200.

His duets with Allard within larger opera-ballet productions also helped to introduce the new genre, as indicated in this review: "These two dancers have introduced to the theatre the dramatic dance. They are actors; they act, they express through their steps and through their gestures the different feelings of the soul; they speak to the eyes, they have a veritable eloquence of the body, that makes so great an impression on our senses and our hearts! This art studied, practiced, and applied, gives us the pantomimed spectacles that enchanted the ancient Romans. It is a genre of which Dauberval and Allard are the founders and the most excellent examples." ["Ces deux danseurs ont introduit sur le théâtre la danse dramatique. Ils sont acteurs, ils jouent, ils expriment par leur pas et par leur gestes les différentes affections de l'âme; ils parlent aux yeux, ils ont cette véritable éloquence du corps, qui fait tant d'impression sur nos sens et sur notre coeur! Cet art étudié, exercé, pratiqué, nous donneroit les spectacles pantomimes dont les Romains étoient enchantés. C'est un genre dont le sieur d'Auberval et la Dlle. Allard auront été les fondateurs et les plus excellens modèles."] October 1768, p. 150.

5. The chapter heading appeared in the November issue, vol. 1, from 1777.

6. A drawing of *Les Adieux* (1784) presented at the Théâtre Ambigu-Comique shows a tableau-vivant in which all bodies, organically spaced, register different emotions.

7. Isherwood offers the following playbill for one of Nicolet's performances as an indication of the typical bill of fare at one of the boulevard theaters: "La Troupe des Grands Danseurs de Roi will present today, Thursday 1 September 1785 the fourth performance of Roi Lu, parody of Roi Lear, tragi-comedy. *[Les] sauteurs* will do the leaps of the carp, the eel, the bear, and the lion; performing *Deux Figaro,* Sieur Ribie will play the role of the father and Sieur Mayeur that of the son: for the third time *[Con]tentement passe richesses,* proverb; Sieur Fonpré will play the role of Sans-Quartier; *l'Heureux désespoir, la Taverne enchantée, Un voleur qui vole l'autre,* pantomime *divertissement.* Between acts the balance of the ladder, the little allemande, the Basque, and so on will be given. [One] will begin with *Arlequin Soldat Deseurteur,* pantomime with machines in three acts without interval," p. 170. See also Rahill's *The World of Melodrama* for a concise summary of changes in the boulevard theatre offerings in the late eighteenth century, pp. 18–38.

8. For his 1778 production *Momie, opéra burlesque, parodie d'Iphigénie, opéra, en trois actes, en prose et en vaudevilles,* Despréaux listed among others the following character types: Danseur Chinois (played by Dauberval), Danseuse Chinoise (played by Heinel), Pirouetteurs (Vestris and Fabre), Sauteurs (Marcadet, Abraham, Ledoux), Gladiateurs and Cuisineurs, and Péruviennes (played by Gardel and Dauberval *en travesti*). The performance took place before the court at Choisy as one of several productions by boulevard authors whose popularity had piqued the King's interest. Many of the productions summoned to court used the performers from the boulevard, but this one embroiled dancers from the Opéra whose scandalous behavior in their various roles, including travesty, would have added to the hilarity. The title of Despréaux's treatment of Jason and Médée, produced the same year as Noverre's version, also gives a sense of strategies of satire: *Medea and Jason, terrifying ballet, ornamented with dance, suspicion, blackness, pleasure, stupidity, horror, treasonous gaiety, joking, poison, assassination, and fireworks.* [*Médée et Jason, ballet terrible, orné de danse, soupçon, noirceur, plaisir, bêtise, horreur, gaité trahison, plaisanterie, poison, assassinat, & feu d'artifice*.]

9. The scenario for *L'Elève de la Nature, Comédie en un acte, mêlée de musique,* presented at Nicolet's Théâtre des Grands-Danseurs de Roi, included specific instructions for the actor playing the student as follows: "It is necessary that the actor who takes this role pay attention not to play the savage with stiffness or with the manners of a civilized man; one must put in it the greatest naturalness and in each situation that one finds oneself, demonstrate great *astonishment, sweetness,* and *sensibility.*" ["Il faut que l'Acteur qui se chargera de ce rôle, ait l'attention de ne pas le jouer avec la roideur d'un Sauvage, ni avec les manières d'un homme policé; il doit y mettre le plus grand naturel, et dans chaque situation où il se trouve, il témoigne beaucoup d'*étonnement,* de *douceur,* et de *sensibilité.*"] P. 8.

10. The preface to the libretto for *Fameux Siège* describes how pantomime and music worked together: We warn the reader that the informative couplets that can be found in the program do not merit public attention; they were only imagined and sketched out in an instant, in order to animate and set the silent performance of each actor, who could say to him- or herself words analogous to the situation and measured more or less according to the character that must be followed and fulfilled so as to achieve more expression in the performance and in all that is not dialogue or recitation. But the spectators seemed curious to know about the discourse that each actor was to express, however neglected it might be, and we thought we could not do better than to satisfy them at once." ["On prévient le lecteur que les couplets informés qu'il trovera dans ce Programe ne méritoient pas de devenir publics; ils n'ont été imaginés & tracés qu'en un moment, que pour animer & fixer le jeu muet que chaque Acteur, qui pouvant dire en lui-même des paroles analogues à la situation, & mesurées tant bien que mal sur les avis qu'il doit

suivre & remplir, doit en avoir plus d'expression dans son jeu, & tout ce qui n'est ni dialogue ou récit. Mais le Public a paru curieux de savoir les discours que chaque Acteur veut exprimer, quelque négligés qu'ils puissent être, & l'on a cru ne pouvoir pas mieux faire que de le satisfaire sur le champ."] *Programe du "Fameux Siège, Pantomime,"* p. 1.

11. For a good summary of the history of tightrope walking acts at Nicolet's theatre from 1760–1787, see Manne and Ménétrier, *Galerie Historique des Comédiens de la Troupe de Nicolet,* pp. 15–30.

12. Isherwood accords this function to the private theatre entertainments in *Farce and Fantasy,* p. 37. For an overview of their functioning, see Capon and Yve-Plessis, *Les Théâtres Clandestins au XVIIIe siècle.*

13. The *Mercure de France* reviewer applauds *Le Ballet des Suivans de la Jalousie* because "It is of a new genre of composition. Rapid movements, crossing without confusion, and irregular figures produce an ingenius image of what one wants to represent." ["Il est d'un genre nouveau de composition. Les mouvemens rapides, croisés sans confusion, et les figures irrégulières y produisent ingénieusement l'image de ce qu'on veut représenter."] January 1763, vol 2, p. 143. See also the review of Laval's choreography for *Thésée,* quoted above.

14. ". . . rompu l'ordre symétrique des figures, usité dans toutes les entrées ordinaires. Les personnages sont distribués par groupes inégaux de nombre, qui varient & se reforment sans cesse, comme par le seul hasard. C'est une multiplicité infinie de ballets différens, qui produisent un ensemble toujours pittoresque, toujours vrai, & formé en apparence par des positions fortuites, qui ne peuvent être cependant que le résultat d'une combinaison profonde de l'art & de l'ordre cachés avec un génie & une adresse qu'on ne peut trop applaudir. Les Danseurs, de tailles graduées pour la perspective, & placés au fond du théâtre, y soutenoient un mouvement, qui ne laissoit de vuide dans aucune partie du ballet, & qui concouroit à l'illusion, sans distraire des objets dominans du spectacle." The review continues by commending Dauberval for his performance as one of the athletes in competition in the second act, and by complementing Allard who, despite her graceful figure, becomes a perfectly terrifying fury in the third act. The reviewer characterizes the overall effect of the ballet in these terms: "A rapid movement, a perpetual variety, a kind of bizarreness and caricature carried out with justness that gives all the scenes their subject and clear character and a force and uniqueness appropriate to the occasion.

It is with joy and eagerness that we offer our praise and that we exhort all lovers of the theatre to applaud the talents and efforts of the composer of the ballets that work to paint, that seek to make the dance speak, thereby contributing to the general good of the opera and stepping outside the monotonous habits of the art to approach the grand rules of drama."

["Un mouvement rapide, une variété perpétuelle, une sorte de bisarrerie & de caricature placée avec justesse, donnent à toutes les scènes de son sujet, le véritable caractère, la force & la singularité de spectacle qui conviennent en cette occasion.

C'est avec joie, c'est avec empressement, que nous comblons d'éloges, & que nous exhortons tous les amateurs de théâtre à applaudir aux talens & aux efforts d'un Compositeur de ballets qui s'attache à peindre, qui cherche à faire parler la danse, à la faire contribuer au but général de l'opéra, & qui s'écarte des habitudes monotones de son art, pour se rapprocher des grandes règles de l'art dramatique."] *Mercure de France,* April 1765, pp. 180–82.

15. Noverre claimed that this was one of his important innovations in early ballets choreographed at the Opéra Comique. See *Letters on Dancing and Ballets,* p. 46. See also the *Mercure de France* review of *Castor and Pollux* by Laval, quoted above.

16. Although the issue was debated, most choreographers agreed that the new ballet could not sustain the visual variety and contrast necessary for its appeal if it could not present diverse locations and multiple events. Almost always, the successful realization of all these factors required choreographers to abandon the classic unities of time and place that governed drama, and it was generally agreed that they could do so. All scenic changes were nonetheless required to converge toward a single end. Angiolini, for example, argued that in order to enrich the spectacle and not hamper the development, the ballet must be excused from obeying the unity of place, and he concluded that the twenty-four-hour time limit typically used to limit the amount of time the drama was supposed to represent was inappropriate for dance because what it took actors three hours to say could be danced in five minutes. *Dissertation sur les Ballets Pantomimes des Anciens, Pour Servir de Programme de 'Semiramis',* pp. 8–19. On the need for the ballet to operate under a single theme, see Noverre, *Letters on Dancing and Ballets,* p. 53.

17. Ange Goudar's delightful and detailed review of Pitrot's *Télémaque* takes up each of these issues

in turn. *Mercure de France* criticism of Noverre's *Jason et Médée* also raised these issues: "The ceremony of Jason's crowning gives a grand feeling that forms an admirable opposition with the horror that inspires Medea's revenge. This composition that demonstrates an artist truly a master of his art is nonetheless not without reproach. One observed that the figures executed by the dancers in the first act, formed around several stakes that supported trophies placed throughout the space, did not produce any illusion; and that the first two scenes in the second act, that is, where Creon reflects on the necessity to abdicate his throne, and the following, where he confides in his daughter Creuse his plan to make her marry Jason, are not intelligible except to those who keep their eyes on the ballet program." ["La cérémonie du couronnement de Jason porte un grand caractère, elle forme une opposition admirable avec l'horreur qu'inspire la vengeance de Médée. Cette composition, qui annonce un Artiste vraiment maître de son Art, a pourtant essuyé quelques reproches. On a observé que la course figurée du premier Acte, exécutée par deux Danseurs, formant des pas autour de quelques piquets chargés de trophées, & placés d'espace, ne pouvoit produire aucune illusion; que les deux premières Scènes du second Acte, c'est-à-dire, celle où Créon réfléchit seul sur la nécessité d'abdiquer sa couronne; & la Suivante, où il confie à Creuse sa fille, le dessein qu'il a de lui faire épouser Jason, ne sont intelligibles que pour ceux qui ont sous leurs yeux le programme du Ballet."] February 12, 1780, pp. 89–90.

18. Rarely were Opéra dancers criticized in print for their performances. The following acerbic review makes one of the few derogatory remarks ever published: "We viewed two of the pas des deux executed in the most pleasing manner by M. Vestris and Mlle. Théodore. Truly these duets must be fatiguing because at the production on Sunday the ninth, the two dancers hardly danced them, they barely sketched them, which is undoubtedly more convenient for the dancers, but much less agreeable for the spectators." ["On y a vu deux pas de deux exécutés de la manière la plus satisfaisante par M. Vestris et Mlle. Théodore. Vraisemblablement ces deux pas sont fatiguans, car à la représentation du Dimanche 9, les deux Sujets que nous venons de citer, ne les ont point dansés, ils n'ont fait qu'en indiquer le dessin; ce qui sans doute est beaucoup plus commode pour les Exécutans, mais beaucoup moins agréable pour le Public."] *Mercure de France*, July 15, 1780, p. 138.

19. The *Mercure de France* observes that the debut of Mlle. Compain give great hopes for the genre of Mlle. Allard; January 1772, p. 154. Mlle. Théodore makes her debut in the genre of Mlle. Lany; January vol. 2, 1778, p. 165. And M. Hus debuts in the genre of M. Dauberval; May 15, 1779, pp. 179–80.

20. For example, Guimard, normally known for her grace and lightness, was praised in *Ninette à la Cour* for the stupidity and clumsiness she showed in portraying the peasant Ninette; *Mercure de France*, September 5, 1778, pp. 66–67. When Mlle. Saulnier made her debut in 1784, the reviewer, sensing the subtle erosion in the persuasive power of the three genres, characterized her performance in these terms: "Nature has given her all that is needed for the noble dance, a precious genre that it is important to maintain in this theatre, and that requires all at the same time an elegant and lifted figure, force and lightness, correctness and ease at the steps and a perfect accord throughout all the movements: this union, as rare as it is difficult, can only be acquired through self-willed and patient work, but without it one remains mediocre in the only genre of dance where one is not permitted to be so." ["La Nature lui a donnée tout ce qui est nécessaire pour la Danse noble, genre précieux qu'il importe de maintenir sur ce Théâtre, & qui demande tout-à la-fois une taille élégante & élevée, la force & la légèreté, la correction & la facilité dans les pas, & l'accord le plus parfait dans tous les mouvements: cette réunion aussi rare que difficile, ne peut s'acquérir que par un travail opiniâtre & patient, mais sans elle on reste médiocre dans le seul genre de Danse où il ne soit pas permis d l'être."] *Mercure de France*, October 2, 1784, pp. 40–41.

21. Dancers exercized their considerable clout by bringing formal complaints against various administrators, as in the 1779 hearing of grievances against De Vîsmes by "Le Gros, Geslin, Vestris, Gardel, d'Auberval, Noverre, Acteurs et Danseurs; Levacœur, Duplain, Beaumesmil, Durancy, Guimard, Heinel, Allard, Peslin, Actrices & Danseuses." See *Instruction du Procès, Entre les premiers Sujets de l'Académie Royale de Musique & de Danse. Et le Sr. de Vismes, Entrepreneur, jadis public, aujourd'hui clandestin, & Directeur de ce Spectacle.*

These complaints resulted in a restructuring of the administration, in which the Director no longer functioned as "the soul of the machine" [l'âme de la machine] but instead deliberated as part of a committee of six persons on all productions. The Director's voice counted for two. Each member of the committee was responsible for a different aspect of the production: Legros oversaw lighting; Durand worked as machine inspector; Vestris surveyed the proper functioning of technicians during the spectacle; Gardel reported on scenery and props; Dauberval was in charge of costumes; and Noverre advised on the viability of reviving productions and on issues of redundancy from one production to the next. *Mercure de France,* June 10, 1780, pp. 76–77.

22. New regulations issued in 1776, added to the *Réglement concernant l'Opéra* that had originally been drafted in 1713, reflect a concern for the growing disobedience of artists. See Des Essarts, *Le trois théâtres de Paris, ou abrégé historique de l'établissement de la Comédie Françoise, de la Comédie Italienne & de l'Opéra,* for a complete list of all regulations.

In his prison diary, the Intendant Papillon de la Ferté reflects back on his career as "contrôleur de l'argenterie menus-plaisirs et affaires de la chambre du roi" from 1756–1780. He notes numerous examples of dancers indulging in outrageous behavior, secure in the knowledge of their immense popularity. He recalls that for one performance at Fontainebleau, "Vestris made much noise wanting to be lodged and conveyed in a manner more distinguished than his colleagues. I was obliged to be somewhat rigorous with him because he is always the leader of the pack." ["Le sieur Vestris a fait beaucoup de bruit, voulant être logé et voituré d'une manière plus distinguée que ses camarades. J'ai été obligé de sévir un peu contre lui, car il est toujours le chef de la meute."] He also recounts a Mlle. Hus, who was completely drunk by the time she arrived at Fontainebleau for a performance and required a great deal of coffee. See Boysse, *Journal de Papillon de la Ferté,* pp. 30–31.

23. Mlle. Théodore, for example, excelled in the roles of the romantic heroine, yet offstage she proved to be a hardheaded business woman who was dedicated to a moral life in the theatre. At a young age she wrote to Rousseau to ask his advice about entering the theatre. She also took the initiative to organize a benefit concert for Moslem Indians being held captive on a boat in the Bordeaux harbor. Swift, *A Loftier Flight,* p. 26. For details of her life, see DuBois, *Une page de la vie d'une danseuse française au XVIIIe siècle (Mlle. Théodore).*

24. Surviving administration records from the Opéra indicate that each rank of dancer was assigned a specific salary, with female dancers in each rank receiving the same or slightly less than their male counterparts. See, for example, the list of salaries and pensions paid for 1785–86 in the *Académie royale de musique. Sommaire général, 1785–88.*

25. The construction of new routings for desire in the action ballet characters parallels the domestication of sexuality outlined by Nancy Armstrong in her book *Desire and Domestic Fiction.* Armstrong argues that bourgeois characters in the novels of this time perform the fiction of the social contract. Furthermore, the union of male and female characters manifests the underlying narrative paradigm on which novels of the period are based.

26. "La danse a acquis de nos jours une perfection qui la fait dominer dans nos opéras. . . . quoiqu'elle ne soit par la constitution des poëmes qu'un accessoire de l'action. Mais lorsqu'elle en fera partie, et qu'elle prendra un rôle, c'est alors que plus essentielle, et même nécessaire, elle fera sentir d'avantage combien, secondée par une musique éloquente et pittoresque, elle a de ressources pour exprimer toutes les passions et tous les sentimens. Elle pourroit même devenir le premier des arts; car il est d'expérience que la vue est de tous les sens celui qui frappe l'âme avec le plus de rapidité et d'énergie." *Mercure de France,* July 1773, vol. 1, pp. 162–63.

27. One reviewer, disgruntled at the visibility the action ballet had achieved for dance, remarked with satisfaction that dance in the spectacles offered this past year had now "returned to its rightful place, that of an agreeable accessory." ["rentrée dans la place qui convenoit, celle d'agrément accessoire."] *Mercure de France,* April 14, 1787, p. 77.

28. Le Brun, *A Method to Learn to Design the Passions,* pp. 6–7.

29. For background on Le Brun's role and status in the art world, see Bryson, *Word and Image,* pp. 30–95; on his importance to eighteenth-century debates over the correct representation of the passions, see Crow, *Painters and Public Life in Eighteenth-Century Paris,* p. 42; and for an overview of his significance for the acting community, see McKenzie, "The Countenance You Show Me: Reading the Passions in the Eighteenth Century," pp. 762–66 and Roach, *The Player's Passion,* pp. 66–73.

30. Playwright and aesthetician Johan Jakob Engel was inspired by Otto Lessing's philosophical works and also his theatrical presentations. Engel's two-volume work on theatrical gesture presented the most exhaustive consideration of gesture—its origins, types, capacity to signify worldly events—of any eighteenth-century text.

31. According to Engel, "If gestures are the exterior and visible signs of our body, through which one learns of the interior modifications of our souls, then it follows that one can consider them from a double

point of view: first, as changes visible in and of themselves; and second, as the means that indicate the interior operations of the soul." ["Si les gestes sont des signes extérieurs et visibles de notre corps, par lesquels on connoît les modifications intérieures de notre âme, il s'ensuit qu'on peut les considérer sous un double point de vue: d'abord, comme des changemens visibles par eux-mêmes; en second lieu, comme des moyens qui indiquent les opérations intérieurs de l'âme."] *Idées sur le Geste et l'action théâtrale*, vol. 1, pp. 62–63.

32. Engel, *Idées sur le Geste et l'action théâtrale*, vol. 1, p. 5.

33. ". . . les mines et les mouvemens décèlent ensemble l'inquiétude, et le combat intérieur de l'âme avec le sentiment douloureux du mal. L'homme qui souffre n'est plus, comme le mélancolique, foible et abattu; il est oppressé, il éprouve des angoisses; les angles des sourcils s'élèvent vers le milieu du front ridé, et vont, pour ainsi dire, au-devant du cerveau troublé et agité par une forte tension; tous les muscles du visage sont tendus et en mouvement; l'oeil est rempli de feu, mais ce feu est vague et vacillant; la poitrine s'élève rapidement et avec violence; la marche est pressée et pesante, tout le corps s'allonge, s'étend et se contourne, comme s'il avoit un assaut général à soutenir; la tête, jetée en arrrière, se tourne de côté en s'élevant avec une violente contraction; (mouvement facile, par conséquent assez ordinaire, . . . comme à la pitié et à la plainte ironique) tous les muscles des bras et des pieds se roidissent; les mains fermées, qui se tiennent avec force, se quittent, et souvent elles se retournent en se détachant du devant du corps, où elles pendent vers la terre avec les doigts fortement entrelacés. Lorsqu'enfin les pleurs inondent le visage, ce ne sont pas les larmes pleines, gonflées et isolées qui s'échappent des yeux de l'homme qui n'a pu assouvir sa colère; ce ne sont pas non plus les larmes douces et taciturnes du mélancolique qui coulent d'elles-mêmes des vaisseaux pleins et relâchés; c'est un torrent, qu'une commotion visible de la machine entière et des secousses convulsives de tous les muscles du visage expriment avec force des glandes lacrymales."] Engel, *Idées sur le geste et l'action théâtrale*, vol. 1, pp. 255–56.

34. Roach notes the shift in metaphors and its influence on acting theory in *The Player's Passion.*

35. Engel, *Idées sur le geste et l'action théâtrale*, vol. 1, p. 40.

36. Magli identifies this distinction as crucial to eighteenth-century acting theory in her article "The System of the Passions in Eighteenth Century Dramatic Mime," p. 34.

37. Engel, *Idées sur le geste et l'action théâtrale*, vol. 1, pp. 40–46.

38. The two approaches, outlined below, along with a number of sophisticated compromise positions, captivated actors and aestheticians throughout the century. Many of the positions are eloquently summarized in Roach, *The Player's Passion*, pp. 93–115.

39. These terms are taken from an anonymous text, *L'Art du Comédien*, written in 1782, pp. 17–19.

40. Samuel Foote, for example, evaluated David Garrick's performance on the match of his physique to that of the character this way: "As G's Person is so insignificant and trifling, Q's is too cumbersome and unweildy [sic]; as the first is deficient in Characters that require Consequence and Dignity, so is the last in those that demand Ease. . . ." *A Treatise on the Passions, so far as they regard the Stage*, p. 24.

41. "Le Danseur ne rend compte aux Spectateurs que des mouvemens de son corps. L'Acteur doit faire tomber toute leur attention sur les affections de son âme. Celui qui danse doit toujours se montrer dans une attitude à peindre, & toutes les positions de cette espèce sont recherchées. Celui qui joue ne doit employer les positions brillantes que rarement & lorsqu'il s'y voit forcé. Pour l'ordinaire il doit se présenter simplement. Voilà pourquoi je dis qu'il ne faut point étudier ses gestes devant un miroir. Un homme qui se regarde dans une glace, s'habitue à trop compasser & trop ralentir ses mouvemens, ce qui lui ôte la liberté; à demeurer trop long-tems dans les attitudes qui flattent le plus ses yeux, à y revenir plus souvent qu'à celles qui lui paroissent moins frappantes, & par-là il devient maniéré. Le Danseur, au-contraire, ne peut jamais choisir un meilleur maître que le miroir, parce que toutes les choses qui jouent, deviennent des perfections lorsqu'elles se trouvent dans celui qui danse." Riccoboni, *Lettre de Mr. Riccoboni, Fils, à Monsieur ***, au sujet de l'Art du Théâtre*, in *L'Art du Théâtre*, pp. 7–8.

42. Noverre, *Letters on Dancing and Ballets*, p. 100.

43. Noverre described the dancer's responsibilities in these terms: "Dancers, like players, should devote themselves to depict and feel, they have the same object to attain. If they cannot be really moved by the part they have to fill, they cannot present the character with any degree of truth, and they cannot hope to succeed and please; they must likewise captivate the public by the force of the illusion and make it experience all the emotions by which they are swayed. That realism, that enthusiasm which distinguishes the great actor and which is the life-blood of the fine arts is, if I may so express myself, like

an electric spark. It is a fire which spreads rapidly, and in a moment captivates the imagination of the spectator, stirring his soul and rendering his heart susceptible to every emotion. . . . Does the spectator put himself in the actor's place, if the latter do not take that of the hero he portrays? Can he hope to move and cause tears to flow, if he do not shed them himself? Will his condition arouse sympathy if he do not make it affecting and be not himself greatly moved by it?" *Letters on Dancing and Ballets*, pp. 107–108.

44. See Noverre, *Letters on Dancing and Ballets*, pp. 111–27, and Gallini, *A Treatise on the Art of Dancing*, pp. 160–61.

45. Noverre, *Letters on Dancing and Ballets*, p. 114.

46. See Noverre, *Letters on Dancing and Ballets*, pp. 110–11, and Magri, *Theoretical and Practical Treatise on Dancing*, pp. 176–78.

47. Gallini, *A Treatise on the Art of Dancing*, p. 159.

48. Magri, *Theoretical and Practical Treatise on Dancing*, p. 176.

49. Noverre, *Letters on Dancing and Ballets*, pp. 119–20.

50. For an overview and critical analysis of these changing conceptions of posture and postural pedagogy, see Vigarello, *Le corps redressé*.

51. Magri, *Theoretical and Practical Treatise on Dancing*, pp. 175–76.

52. Papillon de la Ferté writes with enthusiasm about the establishment of the school which will "assure service to the court, the Queen's amusements, and that will satisfy at the same time the Parisian public." ["assurera le service de la Cour, les amusemens de la Reine, et qui satisfera en même temps le public de Paris."] *Académie royale de musique, Lettres et règlements*, pp. 49–50.

The school was deemed an immediate success. It provided a reliable source of dancers for the corps de ballet. See the *Mercure de France* report of December 1, 1781, pp. 36–37. Its value is reiterated in a summary of its activities in 1784 where the reviewer concludes that its only failings are that students cannot live there; that the curriculum is not coordinated among disciplines; and that the students never get the opportunity to perform an entire opera (*Mercure de France*, September 23, pp. 175–81). Another dance enthusiast also remarked on the school's effectiveness in this description: "one encounters often in the grand foyer of the dance and even in the theatre, a crowd of dancers among which one can discern the top talents. Everyone exercises as they see fit, and they share among themselves their discoveries concerning their art." ["on rencontre souvent, au grand foyer de la danse et même au théâtre, une foule de danseurs et de danseuses, parmi lesquels on distingue les premiers talens. Tous s'exercent à l'envi et se communiquent mutuellement les découvertes qu'ils font dans leur art."] Anon., *Réflexions, sur les causes de la dégradation du Chant, à l'Opéra, comparée avec les succès brillans de la danse, au même théâtre. Par un observateur, ami des deux arts*, p. 4.

53. In the review of *Electre*, the *Mercure de France* lists the latest accomplishments of dancers as follows: "There has arisen in recent times among our dancers a rivalry for force and lightness, the abuse of which seems contrary to good taste and the ultimate goal of the dance. These turning entrechats, these double and triple pirouettes in the air or on the tip of the toe, cannot help but please when they are well placed; but if one repeats them endlessly, if one produces them everywhere, whether in the heroic dance or that of the herdsmen, if one only performs them with an effort that is incompatible with the beautiful development of the body and the accord of all its parts, with the correctness even of the steps; these tours de force that impress the crowd, must shock those with taste. In producing them thus, one confounds all the genres, one is fatigued by their monotony, one loses the sentiment of grace that all their effort makes disappear and that nothing can replace without loss." ["Il s'est élevé depuis quelques temps parmi les Danseurs une émulation de force & de légèreté, dont l'abus semble contraire au bon gout & au véritable but de la Danse. Ces entrechats tournans, ces doubles & triples pirouettes en l'air ou sur la pointe du pied, ne peuvent manquer de plaire quand ils seront placés; mais si on les répète sans cesse, si on les prodigue par-tout, depuis la Danse Héroïque jusqu'à celle des Pâtres, si on ne les exécute qu'au moyen d'efforts incompatibles avec les beaux développemens du corps & avec l'accord de toutes ses parties, avec la correction même des pas; ces tours de force, qui ébluissent la multitude, doivent choquer les gens de goût. En les prodiguant ainsi, on confond tous les genres, on fatigue par la monotonie, on perd le sentiment de la grâce, que tout air d'effort fait disparoître & que rien ne remplace qu'avec perte."] August 31, 1782, pp. 227–28.

54. ". . . il en resultera que ce qu'on appelle *Pas* dans notre talent, tient lieu des mots pour notre langage; que leurs combinaisons forment des phrases plus ou moins bien tournées; que tout cela méthodiquement ordonné, ce fera voir écrit correctement; mais que l'éxécution de ces parties, quelque

parfaite qu'elle puisse être, ne sera autre chose, par comparaison, que lire régulièrement, avec les inflexions convenables, & très-bien prononcer: il n'y aura en tout ceci rien qui provienne du génie, rien qui puisse lui être relatif. Pour me servir de l'hyperbolique expression des Applaudisseurs, les Danseurs ou les Danseuses dont les pas *écrivent* les notes, ont sans doute, à un très-grand degré, le mérite de bien articuler. Mais qu'articulent-ils? Voilà de quoi il s'agit, pour savoir s'il y a non seulement du génie, mais même simplement de l'esprit dans leur Danse. On doit plaire aux yeux, sans contredit, lorsque l'on danse; c'est la première condition: mais comme la Danse doit, par un autre langage auxiliaire, prêter un coloris, une nouvelle *intelligibilité* à celui de la Musique, il faut donc nécessairement que la Danse parle à l'esprit, qu'elle excite ou rappelle des idées, & que dans les occasions, elle détermine l'âme aux mouvemens que le Poëte & le Musicien auront voulu lui faire prendre."] *Mercure de France*, July 1762, pp. 119–20.

55. "Nous trouverons, pour les Danseurs, suivans de la Haine, plusieurs actions à faire sous les yeux d'Armide présente, telle que de déchirer avec fureur entr'eux un bandeau, de reverser un carquois, de s'en distribuer les flêches, & de les briser en diverse manières: l'éxécution du flambeau de l'Amour, pourroit produire seul un Ballet figuré en mille manières différentes; le jeu de ce flambeau avec ceux des Furies, après l'avoir présenté à Armide; tout enfin produiroit la plus féconde matière d'un Poëme entier en danse." *Mercure de France*, August 1772, pp. 178–79.

56. Noverre, *Letters on Dancing and Ballets*, p. 19.

57. "Il faut que le Lecteur, pour bien juger cet essai, se fasse une juste idée des tableaux, des grouppes, des attitudes, & de l'action que doit produir chaque situation. Ces tableaux, ces grouppes, ces attitudes, sont au Maître de Ballet, ce que le style & la versification sont au Poëte, l'on conviendra que quand le fond de l'ouvrage est fait, il ne faut pour l'exécution, que du feu, du goût, la connaissance de sont art, celle de l'effet théâtral & du caractère de ses personnages." Maximilien Gardel, *L'Avènement de Titus à l'Empire, ballet héroïque*, p. 8.

58. This relationship between dancing and scenario became one of the central points of contention in a famous exchange of letters among Gasparo Angiolini, the reknowned choreographer of action ballets in Vienna, Noverre, and their advocates. Their published letters developed the correspondences between danced steps and vocabulary, their sequencing and verbal syntax. Noverre agreed with Angiolini, who wrote that "in the pantomime dance, it is necessary first to learn the steps or the alphabet of our language; this apprenticeship is already long and difficult. In addition, it is necessary to acquire grace, nobility, elegance of attitude, which is a study of design. Finally, one must acquire expression, or the art of speaking in dance." ["Dans la Danse Pantomime il faut d'abord apprendre les pas ou l'Alphabet de notre langage; cet apprentissage est déjà long & pénible. Il faut encore se donner la grâce, la noblesse, l'élégance des attitudes, cela vaut bien une étude du dessein. Enfin, il faut acquérir l'expression, ou l'art de parler en dansant."] *Dissertation sur les Ballets Pantomimes des Anciens, Pour Servir de Programme de "Semiramis,"* p. 19. They also debated the applicability of Aristotelian unities, agreeing that unity of action was essential. But the focus of their concern and disagreement centered on the relationship between program and danced action. Angiolini preferred to provide background information on characters, whereas Noverre advised choreographers to write out the action of each scene as preparation for the rehearsal in which it would be choreographed as a direct translation of story into movement and as a draft of the printed program. Angiolini's followers accused Noverre of choosing stories far too complex to be enacted in ballets. The abstract dialogue and subtle motivations portrayed in Noverre's program notes, they argued, could not possibly be danced. See *Lettre d'un des petits oracles de Monsieur Angiolini au Grande Noverre*, p. 16.

59. The debate over the function of the ballet program was further complicated by the fact that choreographic changes might continue to occur even after the scenario went to press. Beffroy de Reigny, *Les Ailes de l'Amour*, p. 71.

60. *Lettre de Monsieur le Baron****, p. 12.

61. "Il seroit donc fort ridicule, selon moi, de voir Terpsichore exprimer sa douleur, en dansant & en pirouettant tristement autour d'un tombeau." *Lettre de Monsieur le Baron ****, p. 8.

62. Engel's text includes frequent references to gesture's capacity as a language. For example, "Metaphors are expressed" by the body (vol. 1, p. 50), muscles "speak" with "eloquence" (vol. 1, p. 53).

63. "Je pourrois accumuler à l'infini les exemples des gestes figurés. Voulez-vous une métonymie qui emploie l'effet pour la cause? Le laquais, en parlant de la récompense desagréable avec laquelle son maître pourroit payer ses fredaines, se frotte avec le dessus de la main le dos, comme s'il sentoit déjà la

douleur des coups de baton. En demandez-vous une autre, qui, au lieu de la chose, indique un rapport extérieur? Pour désigner le vrai Dieu, ou les dieux du paganisme, le langage du geste se sert de leur prétendue demeure dans le ciel. De la même manière, les mains élevées, les yeux dirigés vers le ciel, appellent les dieux à témoin de l'innocence, implorent leur secours, & sollicitent leur vengeance. Ou aimez-vous mieux une synecdoque? On désigne une seule personne présente pour indiquer toute sa famille; on montre un seul ennemi qu'on voit losqu'on veut parler de toute l'armée ennemie. Ou bien voulez-vous une ironie? La jeune beauté qui refuse la main de l'amant qu'elle méprise, lui fait une révérence profonde, mais ironique. Le nombre des allusions n'est pas moins grand dans le langage des gestes. L'action de laver les mains constate l'innocence; deux doigts plantés devant le front indiquent l'infidélité de la femme; en soufflant légèrement par-dessus la main ouverte, on désigne l'idée de rien." Engel, *Idées sur le geste et l'action théâtrale*, vol. 1, pp. 78–79.

64. Engel, *Idées sur le geste et l'action théâtrale*, vol. 2, p. 50.

65. Engel, *Idées sur le geste et l'action théâtrale*, vol. 2, p. 48.

66. Engel, *Idées sur le geste et l'action théâtrale*, vol. 2, pp. 49–60.

67. Engel, *Idées sur le geste et l'action théâtrale*, Préface du Traducteur, pp. 22–29.

68. Engel, *Idées sur le geste et l'action théâtrale*, vol. 2, pp. 33–34.

69. Engel, *Idées sur le geste et l'action théâtrale*, vol. 2, p. 41.

70. Engel, *Idées sur le geste et l'action théâtrale*, vol. 2, p. 290.

71. Even the reviewer for the *Mercure de France* admitted the need to use a well-known plot in his review of Maximilien Gardel's *La Chercheuse Esprit*: "M. Gardel has retained as much as possible the airs from the Opéra Comique; he has given his pantomime a development, figures, character and expression the most appropriate for speaking to the eyes, and for replacing speech with dance. It would be useless to give an analysis of the ballet, since it differs only slightly from the action and the organization of scenes at the Opéra Comique, so well known to those who love spectacle.

It is a great advantage for the pantomime to represent only subjects already well known to the spectators, and to let them have the pleasure of interpreting the airs, the gestures, and the dances. We would add that the pantomime dancer must always regulate gestures and steps with the music, and that if one abandons it sometimes for a free and nonmeasured locomotion; one betrays the art, it becomes a comedy pantomime; the play, disfigured by negligence, no longer has the same interest or agreeableness. This is a fault that we reveal here because we have noticed it in several pantomime ballets where the mixture of free pantomime with measured pantomime creates an overly long production and a disparate sensibility."

["M. Gardel a conservé, autant qu'il a été possible, les airs de l'Opéra Comique; il a donné à sa pantomime les développemens, les figures, le caractère & l'expression les plus convenables pour parler aux yeux, & remplacer la parole par la danse. Il seroit inutile de donner ici l'analyse de ce Ballet, qui diffère très-peu, pour l'action & pour la coupe des scènes, de l'Opéra-Comique, si connu de tous ceux qui aiment le Spectacle.

C'est un très-grand avantage pour la Pantomime de ne représenter que des sujets déjà bien sus des Spectateurs, & de leur laisser le plaisir de faire eux-mêmes l'interprétation des airs, des gestes & des danses. Ajoutons que le danseur pantomime doit toujours régler ses gestes & ses pas sur la musique, & s'il abandonne quelquefois à une marche libre & non mesurée; il trahi alors son art, il devient un Pantomime de Comedie; son jeu, défiguré par cette négligence, n'a plus le même intérêtt ni le même agrément. C'est un défaut que nous relevons ici, parceque nous l'avons remarqué dans plusieurs Ballets Pantomimes, où ce mélange de Pantomime libre avec la Pantomime mesurée, faisoit longueur, & un disparate sensible."] April 1778, pp. 165–66.

Some critics apparently felt that the need to use a well-known plot proved the ballet's derivative nature: ". . . an incontestable truth: it is that dance never could be, nor is, nor will ever be anything more than an accessory in whatever piece it is introduced; and that even the action ballet is in essence only an accessory, that it cannot by itself produce a sustained interest without the aid of a plot, based on a well-known subject with situations whose details are equally well known or easy to comprehend; because articulating nothing, unable to announce anything, the ballet is obliged in making itself understood to have recourse to the more expressive sounds however inarticulate of the music." [". . . une vérité incontestable: c'est que la Danse n'a pu être, n'est, et ne sera jamais qu'un accessoire dans telle espèce de pièce qu'on l'introduise; que dans le Action ballet même elle n'est essentiellement qu'accessoire, qu'elle ne peut par elle-même y produire un intérêt soutenu qu'à l'aide d'un plan, d'un fond de sujet connu, et de situations de détail également connues, ou faciles à connoître; car n'articulant rien, ne pouvant rien annoncer, elle est obligée pour se faire comprendre d'avoir recours aux sons plus expressifs quoiqu'inarticulés de la Musique."] Anon., "Lettre de l'Amateur du Vaudeville, sur la prochaine dissolution de ce Spectacle," *Le Censeur Dramatique*, vol. 4, no. 29, p. 66.

The practice of borrowing plots from other kinds of productions was so deliberate and frequent that it caused the Comédie Italienne to seek and obtain an injunction against the Académie Royale de la Musique to the effect that the Opéra was no longer able to borrow either subjects or music for its action ballets. *Mercure de France*, March 3, 1787, p. 40.

72. *Le Déserteur* was adapted scene by scene from Sedaine's highly popular *opéra comique* of the same name. Grimm thought that the faithfulness of the adaptation created many awkward moments although the overall structure seemed effective. See *Correspondance littéraire*, March 1788, vol. 4, p. 495.

73. "En générale, cette Pantomime est très-interessante, et a beaucoup réussi. Quoiqu'elle ne soit autre chose que la Pièce si connue, suivie d'un bout à l'autre, elle semble produire plus d'effet que la Pièce même; soit parce que les événemens plus rapprochés donnent à l'air une secousse plus vive; soit parce que la Pantomime, obligée, à défaut de paroles, d'exagérer l'expression, a des moyens plus pouissans de nous électrifier, que le simple discours." *Mercure de France*, January 26, 1788, p. 177.

74. The reviewer of Gardel's *Télémaque dans l'isle de Calipso* observed that even though it was an action ballet, the author had introduced more dancing than is typical in those sorts of works. *Mercure de France*, March 2, 1790, p. 94.

75. A review of Noverre's book in the *Mercure de France* encourages all dance students to renounce "cabrioles" in favor of noble Pantomime. May 17, 1883, p. 136.

76. One critic expressed the dilemma after viewing Gardel's *Télémaque* in these simple terms: "We submit also to the author a reflection that is dictated by our love of the art. Télémaque, the Nymphs, and Amour do not walk, they dance: which must be in effect the mode of action in the pantomime ballet. Gestures and cadenced steps form a kind of language of the country, like song for the opera and verse for tragedy. Why, then, do Mentor and Calypso only walk? Is it to preserve their nobility and dignity? They should have been given a noble and serious dance; but once again, the dance is in a ballet whose essential language is received and hypothetical." ["Nous soumettrons aussi à l'Auteur du Ballet une réflexion qui ne nous est dictée que par l'amour de l'art. Télémaque, les Nymphes, l'Amour ne marchent point, ils dansent: tel doit être en effet le mode d'action dans le Ballet-Pantomime. Les gestes & les pas cadencés y forment en quelque sorte le langage du pays, comme le chant dans l'Opéra, comme les vers dans la Tragedie. Pourquoi donc Mentor & Calypso ne font-ils que marcher? Est-ce pour conserver plus de noblesse & de dignité? Il fallait leur donner une danse noble & grave; mais encore une fois, la danse est dans un Ballet de l'essence même du langage reçu & hypothétique."] *Mercure de France*, October 1, 1791, p. 40.

77. "On peut observer d'aprés une telle composition, que la danse pantomime est l'art qui s'approche le plus de la peinture. Elles parlent l'une & l'autre aux yeux, & elles forment pareillement des tableaux où les passions & les sentimens des personnages sont rendus par le secours des gestes, des attitudes, des positions & des groupes. La peinture fixe ses compositions. La danse pantomime varie les siennes. La peinture ne peut saisir qu'un moment intéressant d'une composition simple; la danse pantomime doit au contraire chercher une action susceptible d'une suite de tableaux. La première emploie le coloris, les ombres & les clairs pour donner du relief & de la vie à ses figures; la seconde emprunte l'art de la musique pour donner l'intelligence de ses dessins. C'est tous ces rapports principaux qu'il faut juger du mérite de la danse pantomime, & c'est en rapprochant le plus qu'il est possible la danse de la peinture, que M. Noverre est parvenu à un art nouveau, ou, du moins, à rappeler la danse pantomime des Anciens, ou à perfectionner les ébauches imparfaites que l'on avoit esquissées grossièrement. Demandons, d'après les principes de la danse, qui doit toujours peindre & faire partie d'une action ou d'une composition raisonnée, ce que signifient ces solo, ces duo, ces pas compliqués, dans lesquels un ou plusieurs Danseurs viennent développer, avec grâce, si l'on veut, leurs jambes & leurs bras, battre des entre-chats, aller successivement de gauche à droite, s'élancer en avant & en arrière, tourbillonner sur eux-mêmes, & faire des évolutions comme des gens dans le délire. On sent que tous ces divers mouvemens sont de bonnes études pour les appliquer dans l'occasion; mais lorsqu'ils ne sont point placés dans une action principale, ils ne peignent rien. Que diroit-on d'un Peintre qui voudroit composer un tableau avec des essais qu'on appelle des *Académies*? Chaque figure séparement pourroit être coloriée merveilleusement, &

dessinnée avec beaucoup de précision & d'élégance; mais l'ensemble de ces figures ne seroit-il pas ridicule & insoutenable?" *Mercure de France,* October 1776, pp. 169–71.

78. "J'en ai vu aussi, de ce genre, de très-beaux à la Cour de Mannheim; mais ces ballets ont tout un autre système que ceux de l'opéra français. On y marche bien plus qu'on ne danse. On y voit bien moins de pas et de danses symétriques que de gestes et de groupes; on n'y connaît point ces deux files de danseurs et de danseuses rangées de chaque côté du théâtre. Cet arrangement de bal ne peut tout au plus avoir lieu qu'après le dénoûement, lorsqu'il n'est plus question que de terminer la pièce par un divertissement général." Grimm, *Correspondance littéraire,* November 1765, vol. 5, pp. 50–51.

Mirza

1. For the Versailles production, see *Mirza, ballet en action* (Paris: Ballard, 1779) and for the Opéra production, see *Mirza* (Paris: Chez les Marchands de Pièces de Théâtre, 1779). The ongoing debate over the role of program notes surfaced this way in one reviewer's comments: "the program which one absolutely must read in order to inform oneself of the subject and learn the details, is sold at Delormel . . . and in the Opéra house. Price 12 francs." ["le Programme qu'il faut absolument lire pour se mettre au fait du sujet & pour en saisir les détails, se vend chez Delormel . . . & dans la Salle de l'Opéra. Prix. 12*f*."] *Affiches, Annonces, et Avis Divers,* no. 48, December 1, 1779, p. 192.

2. In *The Surprising Effects of Sympathy,* Marshall argues that the momentary helplessness of the female character creates the condition that inspires an onrush of empathic attachment to her from the male character. Marshall demonstrates the use of this structuring of desire in eighteenth-century French literature, but it applies equally well to the action ballet.

3. "Cette pantomime a eu le plus grand succès; on peut assurer qu'elle en est digne. On a dit avec raison que l'intrigue étoit peu de chose; peut-être auroit-on du ajouter qu'une intrigue trop compliquée ne sauroit convenir à un ballet; qu'une action simple, facile à développer par la succession des scènes, où le secours de la gesticulation n'est employé que pour peindre des choses & non pas des mots, doit seule être admise dans des Ouvrages de cette espèce: peut-être devoit-on ajouter encore que l'Auteur a eu l'art d'employer très-habilement les contrastes, de présenter des tableaux d'un genre opposé, sans blesser les convenances & sans sortir du sujet. On rit au premier acte, au second on est vivement ému; au troisième, on est partagé tour à tour entre l'admiration & la joie: il nous semble qu'on ne peut exiger rien de plus d'un Compositeur. Il y auroit sans doute quelques nuances à désirer encore, quelques retranchemens à faire; car, où la perfection se trouve-t-elle? Le choix des airs qui sont mis en action, est fait avec beaucoup d'esprit & de discernement; on ne peut pas en dire autant du choix des airs de danse." *Mercure de France,* November 27, 1779, p. 181.

4. Grimm was less impressed with Gardel's craft: "There is nevertheless in the composition of this ballet very little invention, very little spirit or interest, but the execution was very well done. Mlle. Guimard, costumed as a Creole, has all the graces of a sixteen-year-old. The combat between Vestris and Nivelon creates an extraordinary illusion, and the huge noise in the third act is well suited to seduce the ears of those accustomed to the charm of the French Opéra." ["Il n'y a néanmoins dans la composition de ce ballet, ni beaucoup d'invention, ni beaucoup d'esprit, ni beaucoup d'intérêt, mais l'exécution en a été très-soignée. Mlle. Guimard, habillée en créole, a toutes les grâces de seize ans. Le combat de Vestris et de Nivelon fait une illusion extraordinaire, et le grand bruit du troisième acte est bien fait pour séduire des oreilles accoutumées au charme de l'Opéra Français."] *Correspondance littéraire,* February 1781, vol. 5, p. 57.

5. The *Mercure de France* review of Gluck's *Iphigénie en Tauride* with ballets by Noverre reveals the simultaneous demands placed on the foreign or "savage" population both to augment the sense of terror and suspense and to enliven the action: "The first act, albeit of great simplicity, is worthy of this celebrated choreographer; it paints with truth and force the cruel joy of a savage people who triumphantly lead these two victims, and who rejoice in anticipation of seeing their blood run. It is very well executed by all the dancers, and especially by Gardel and Dauberval who render marvelously, by steps and simple movements, but energetic and well characterized, the dance of the two savage chiefs." ["Le premier, quoique d'une grande simplicité, est digne de ce célèbre Compositeur; il peint avec vérité & avec force la joie cruelle d'un peuple sauvage, qui amène en triomphe ces deux victimes, & se réjouit d'avance de voir bientôt couler leur sang. Il est très-bien exécuté par tous les Danseurs, & principalement

par MM. Gardel & Dauberval, qui rendent à merveille, par des pas & des mouvements simples, mais energiques & bien caractérisés, la danse de deux Chefs de Sauvages."] June 15, 1779, p. 170.

6. "un prétendu Ballet-pantomime, dans lequel on déjeune au premier Acte; ou, au second, l'on tue des Sauvages à coups de fusil, spectacle digne des Cannibales; dont le troisième Acte représente quelques Soldats manoeuvrant sur une place d'armes, les apprêts d'un supplice, & les angoisses d'une femme implorant la grâce de son mari prêt à périr sur un bûcher; dont le quatrième Acte enfin, par un miracle d'autant plus frappant qu'il n'est opéré par aucune puissance apparente, fait voir des sourds qui entendent & des muets qui chantent. . . ."] *Mercure de France,* March 3, 1782, p. 30.

7. "Pantomime a fait pencher vers sa chute le Théâtre de Rome, elle doit nécessairement entrainer celle du nôtre; qu'à l'Opéra elle ne peut exister sans la Danse; qu'elle ne doit être qu'un accessoire." *Mercure de France,* March 3, 1782, p. 32.

Le Premier Navigateur, ou le Pouvoir de l'Amour

1. See the *Mercure de France* review from February 12, 1780, pp. 89–90.

2. The success of *Le Premier Navigateur* seems to have depended upon the perfect combination of simple plot, spectacle, and brilliant dancing, as this review summarizes: "the success of this work has perfectly responded to the choice of subject, which, without being complicated, lends itself in a singular manner to the richness of the decorations, the grand movements so necessary in the genre of pantomime, and the variety of situations. M. Gardel knew how to employ in a very ingenious manner the different airs that aid in the expression that situations require. . . . one has known for a long time the finesse of Mlle. Guimard's performance; but M. Vestris shows, in the terrible movement where his mistress is separated from him by the sea, an intelligence and sensibility rarely united to the degree of perfection of his talent for dance, of which he gives the most surprising proofs in this same ballet. Mlle. Masson renders to great advantage the role of Sémire; the vision of the boat and of the island where Mélide is confined during Daphne's sleep evoked the greatest applause." ["le succès de cet ouvrage a parfaitement répondu au choix du sujet, qui sans être compliqué, prête singulièrement à la richesse des décorations, aux grands mouvemens si nécessaires dans le genre de la pantomime, & à la variété des situations. M. Gardel a su y employer d'une manière très ingénieuse différens airs qui aident à l'expression qu'exigent les situations. . . . on connoît depuis long-tems la finesse du jeu de Mlle. Guimard; mais M. Vestris montre, dans le mouvement terrible où sa maîtresse est séparé de lui par la mer, une intelligence & une sensibilité qui se trouvent rarement unies au degré de perfection de son talent pour la danse, dont il donne les preuves les plus surprenantes dans ce même ballet. Mlle. Masson rend avec beaucoup d'avantage le rôle de Sémire; l'apparition de la barque & de l'îsle où Mélide est confinée pendant le sommeil de Daphnis, a excité les plus grands applaudissemens."] P. 326–27. *L'Esprit des Journaux,* October, 1785, pp. 324–27.

Grimm agreed with reservations: "one would have experienced more involvement and more fright in seeing this lover embark in a fragile and primitive skiff than in the pretty gondola that Gardel seemed obliged to substitute. As for the rest, the plan of this ballet is well conceived, the action is easy to grasp, of a graduated interest, and after some long periods, rather engaging. The airs, taken from our best *opéra comiques,* are a fortuitous choice and very appropriate to characterize the expression so often vague and too insignificant of the gesture and the pantomime." ["on eût éprouvré plus d'intérêt et plus d'effroi en voyant cet amant s'embarquer dans une nacelle infirme et sauvage, que dans la jolie gondole que le sieur Gardel a vu devoir substituer. Au reste, le plan de ce ballet est bien conçu, l'action en est facile à saisir, d'un intérêt gradué, et, à quelques longueurs près, assez attachant. Les airs, tirés de nos meilleurs opéras comiques, sont d'un choix heureux, et très-propre à caractériser l'expression souvent trop vague et trop insignifiante du geste et de la pantomime."] *Correspondance littéraire,* September 1785, vol. 3, pp. 317–18.

3. "On désireroit que son génie, excité seulement par le songe, lui inspirat à son réveil l'idée d'abattre un arbre creusé, en se faisant aider s'il le faut par ses amis, d'en former un frêle canot dans lequel on ne pourroit le voir entrer sans frémir. Alors, dit-on, les alarmes qu'il inspire seroient justifiées; peuvent-elles exister avec une protection si visible de la part des Dieux?" *Mercure de France,* August 13, 1785, p. 87.

4. ". . . celui du songe, où l'agitation de son âme, très différente de celle qu'il éprouvoit éveillé, laisse distinguer l'égarement du sommeil; & celui où dans son délire il repousse Sémire avec fureur, & tombe au même instant à ses genoux pour lui demander pardon de sa dureté. Ces endroits nous semblent

préférables à l'expression même du désepoir; non que M. Vestris ne l'ait très bien rendue, mais nous croyons que les passions violentes n'exigent, pour être bien exprimées, que de l'énergie, de la sensibilité naturelle & que ces qualités sont moins rares que la finesse & la profondeur de conception." *Mercure de France*, August 13, 1785, pp. 87–88.

5. "Depuis quelques années on représente, & le Public voit avec plaisir la représentation des Ballets-Pantomimes. Ces Ballets sont des Ouvrages à part qui demandent de grands soins, de grandes dépenses, des études multipliées, & qui ne peuvent être exécutés que par les premiers Sujets de la Danse . . . Mais ce genre convient-il à l'Opéra, & ne peut-il pas, au contraire, lui devenir très-nuisible?" *Mercure de France*, April 22, 1786, p. 200.

6. "La Danse n'est qu'un accessoire du Théâtre de Polymnie, un accessoire très-utile & très-indispensable . . . mais nous n'en regardons pas moins comme une innovation dangereuse pour ce spectacle, le parti reçu depuis quelque temps d'en faire un genre à part, parce qu'il est à craindre que tôt ou tard il ne cherche à prendre le pas sur celui dont il ne doit considéré que comme membre. Au surplus, comme il est certain qu'il y a plus de mérite peut-être à plier avec art ses idées à celles des autres, à se subordonner en quelque manière pour faire briller les richesses de son génie, qu'à créer au hasard dans des sujets donnés, ou imaginés plus pour l'effet que pour la raison." *Mercure de France*, April 22, 1786, p. 200.

7. *Mercure de France*, April 22, 1786, p. 215.

Escape into the Heavens

1. If all goes well, the characters glide along magically. Occasionally, however, the machinery fails, and what had been a majestic moment disintegrates into chaos, as in this description of a benefit performance for Pierre Gardel: "In sum, the ballet *Psyché* is far from amusing. A single incident provoked hilarity among the spectators; at the moment where Jupiter, accompanied by Venus, Amour, and Psyche, wants to climb onto a large cloud daubed with yellow and white, which, according to its old and solemn usage served as the mount for gods at the Opéra, the aforementioned cloud showed itself to be stubborn, the orchestra recommenced its reprise, but the machine remained motionless. Finally the poor immortals, completely out of character, were obliged to walk across stage and exit into the wings, much to the amusement of the public, which accorded them a resounding acclamation." ["En résumé, le ballet de *Psyché* est loin d'être amusant. Un seul incident a excité l'hilarité du public; au moment ou Jupiter, accompagné de Vénus, de l'Amour et de Psyché, veut monter sur un grand nuage barbouillé de jaune et de blanc, qui, suivant l'usage antique et solennel, sert de monture aux divinités de l'Opéra, ledit nuage s'est montré rétif, l'orchestre avait beau recommencer sa reprise, la machine restait immobile. Enfin les pauvres immortels, tout décontenancés, ont été obligés de prendre la traverse pour regagner la coulisse, au grand divertissement du public qui les saluait de ses bruyantes acclamations."] Anon., *Le Figaro*, February 25, 1829, p. 2.

Hercule et Omphale,Pantomime en 1 Acte

1. This is my interpretation of the handwritten draft of the scenario that survives in the Collection Rondel at the Bibliothèque de l'Arsenal. It shows the ending scratched out and written over in the same handwriting as that of the censor de Cromer, who gave permission for the production and for the printing of the scenario on the same day, January 5, 1787.

4. GOVERNING THE BODY

1. Kleist, "On the Marionette Theatre," p. 1212.

2. Dancing manuals throughout the eighteenth century had made the argument for dance's applicability to general social skills in public. As late as 1797, Dancing Master J. J. Martinet offers this class-based

protocol for public greetings: "When a young lady encounters someone in the street whom she would like to greet, if it is a person who is in no way different, whether by age or rank, and who she does not want to stop, once close to the person she wishes to greet, she will place her right leg in second position, and bringing the left leg soon after into first position, she will make a bow." ["Lorsqu'une demoiselle rencontrera dans la rue quel-qu'un qu'elle voudra saluer, si c'est une personne dont on ne diffère aucunement, soit par l'âge soit par la condition, et que l'on ne veuille pas s'arrêter, étant près de la personne qu'elle veut saluer, elle portera le pied droit à la deuxième position, et raprochant de suite le pied gauche à la première position, elle fera sa révérance."] *Essai ou principes élémentaires de l'art de la danse,* pp. 34–35.

3. Vivid documentation of the blending of public life and performance comes from a comentator named Le Brun, whose astute observations convey the theatricality of public space: "All Paris is under the sway of the empire of fashion; patriotism and reason are not exempt; one saw it these last days at the champ de Mars, Sunday the fourth of this month, some citizens of both sexes, at the moment of the workers' retirement, amused themselves by carrying wheelbarrows full of earth. They were not long alone; a crowd gathered and suddenly five or six thousand persons digging or dragging carts with much gaiety created a charming spectacle. This scene continued until ten o'clock at night.

The next day one could see the good effects of the nightly labor. For several days one had felt that the rotation and transport of earth could not be accomplished by July 14 by the only workers that were employed; still the idea had not occurred to anyone to work at it; but the example of the first impulse once given, the concurrence was prodigious. Delicate women, in linen dresses and hats, took charge of the carts; others rolled the wheelbarrows, or attached themselves to wagons that they pulled with a courage beyond all expression. The wheelbarrows empty, the men made the women climb in, and they carried them triumphantly to their different lodgings. The following days the eagerness was universal; all the workers, all the corporations of Paris, colleges, etc. as well as the inhabitants of the surrounding countryside, came to contribute to the erection of the patriotic altar." ["Tout à Paris est soumis à l'empire de la mode; le patriotism et la raison n'en sont pas exempts; on l'a vu, ces jours derniers, au champ de Mars. Dimanche quatre de ce mois, quelques citoyens des deux sexes, au moment de la retraite des ouvriers, se sont amusés à transporter des brouettes de terre. Ils n'ont pas été long-temps seuls; la foule s'est accrue, et tout de suite cinq à six mille personnes piochant ou trainant des tombereaux avec beaucoup de gaieté, ont formé le plus charmant spectacle. Cette scène a duré jusqu'à dix heures du soir.

Le lendemain on s'est apperçu des bons effets du travail de la veille. Depuis quelques jours on sentoit bien que le dessolement et le transport des terres ne pourroient pas être operés au 14 Juillet par les seuls ouvriers qu'on y employoit; il ne venoit cependant à l'idée de personne de mettre la main à l'oevre; mais l'exemple et la première impulsion une fois donnés, le concours a été prodigieux. Des femmes delicates, en robe de linon et en chapeau, chargeoit des tombereaux; d'autres rouloient la brouette, ou s'atachoient à des camions qu'elles tiroient avec un courage au-dessus de toute expression. Les tombereaux vides, les hommes y faisoient monter les femmes, et les ramenoient comme en triomphe aux différens atteliers. Les jours suivans l'empressement a été universel; tous les ouvriers, toutes les corporations de Paris, colleges, etc. ainsi que les habitans des campagnes qui l'entournent, sont venus contribuer à l'érection de l'Autel de la patrie." *Journal de la Mode et du Goût, ou Amusemens du Salon et de la Toilette,* no. 14, 15 July 1790, pp. 3–5.

4. For overviews of public space and public activities during the French Revolution, see Ozouf, *Festivals and the French Revolution,* and Huet, *Rehearsing the Revolution.*

5. For a detailed analysis of many of the codes and conventions that governed the new public theatricality, see Hunt, *Politics, Culture, and Class in the French Revolution.*

6. According to Goodden, "The meetings of the national assembly after the events of 1789 enjoyed great favour among the populace as a form of entertainment, as well as being relished by serious political observers and cultivated amateurs of debate; and a part of this favour seems to have derived from the 'actorly' comportment of députés." *Actio and Persuasion,* p. 19.

7. Goodden, *Actio and Persuasion,* 19–20.

8. According to the *Mercure de France* review, when the royal family visited the Opéra for a presentation of *Castor and Pollux,* audience members cheered them constantly. In the fourth act during the lighting of the Devils' torches, the young prince seemed especially excited, and everyone applauded his enthusiasm. Then when the Demons started to chant "Break all our chains," ["Brisons tous nos fers"]

the crowd chanted along with the singers for a long time, and then cheered the king. October 1, 1771, pp. 36–39.

9. The sense of group participation in performance is emphasized in Poyet's *Idées Générales Présentées par le Sieur Poyet*: "In a celebration of this genre, the most important point is to reunite the spectators as much as possible, because in that way, all spectators will become actors in the most august scene." ["Dans une fête de ce genre, le point le plus important est de réunir le plus de spectateurs possible, parce que là, tout spectateurs deviendra acteurs dans la scène la plus auguste."], p. 7.

Revellière-Lépeaux offers substantial advice to those who would attempt to orchestrate a patriotic fête. He admonishes them to be orderly and not dirty and chaotic and to inspire enthusiasm. In order to have full effect, all participants should be involved in seeing, saying, singing, and doing everything. Instead of standing up all day as they did at the Champs de Mars, they should build wooden seats, and also provide opportunities for participants to move around. The circle in the center, like an altar for patriotic activities, should be draped in colors visible from far away, as should all actors within the circle. Each section of seats should have its own orchestra and orators. Different participants should take turns going to the altar to pronounce part of the ceremony. Movements made on the altar should be visible, and details should be explicitly narrated at the same moment they are executed. The beginning and ending should be kept the same so everyone learns it, and at the end "when the cortege leaves the area, citizens should return to their homes and entertain themselves with dancing and games." ["le cortège sort du cirque, et les citoyens regagnent leurs foyers ou se livrent à la danse et aux jeux particuliers."] He further advises that the ceremony may last all day but that there must be breaks. "In this way two or three thousand spectators will be able to take part in the same feelings and share the same joy, all becoming actors themselves." ["Par un tel concours de moyens, deux ou trois cent mille spectateurs éprouvent à la fois les mêmes impressions et partagent les mêmes jouissances, tous ensemble ils soient acteurs eux-mêmes."] Revellière-Lépeaux, *Essai sur les Moyens de Faire Participer l'Universalité des Spectateurs à tout ce qui se practique dans les Fêtes Nationales*, pp. 7–20.

10. This description synthesizes accounts of various fêtes such as *Programme de la Fête de la Souveraineté du Peuple, qui doit se célébrer le 30 ventôse, an 7 de la République, dans l'enceinte du palais du Conseil des Anciens; Détails des Cérémonies, Jeux, Courses de Bateaux, Joutes, Spectacles, Concerts, Illuminations et Danses . . .* (whose very title gives a sense of the melange of activities); David's *Rapport et Décret sur la fête de la Réunion républicaine du 10 Août*; *Détail de la Véritable Marche des Cérémonies et de l'Ordre à Observer dans La Fête à L'Être Suprême*; *La Confédération Nationale. Détail exact de cette fête, et de tout ce qui s'est passé dans la journée mémorable du 14 Juillet 1790*; *Grand Détail. De l'Ordre et la Marche, avec toutes les Cérémonies qui doivent être observées demain dans la Ville de Paris . . .* ; and *Détail Des Cérémonies faites à l'Ouverture des Etats-Généraux.*

11. Boissy d'Anglas's *Essai sur les Fêtes Nationales suivi de quelques idées sur les arts* makes a comprehensive argument for the improvements to morality, imagination, and social memory that the fêtes contribute; pp. 14–18. And Marcoz, in the preface to his *Objet et ordre des Fêtes Décadaires de la République Française,* explains that "The natural objects, political, moral, and intellectual that are the most important for human society, must become the subjects of the ten-day celebrations. In that way, the celebrations will be adopted unconsciously by all nations and all sects without a spirit of national jealousy or dissident religous opinions creating insurmountable obstacles. In this way the French people will propagate, as much through their celebrations as their laws, their political influence and their commerce, a new order of things that must render to humanity a dignity and happiness for all humankind." ["Les objets naturels, politiques, moraux et intellectuels, les plus importans pour l'homme en société, doivent devenir ceux des fêtes décadaires. Par là, ces fêtes seront adoptées insensiblement par toutes les nations et par toutes les sectes, sans que l'esprit de jalousie nationale ou de dissidence d'opinions religieuses puisse y apporter des obstacles insurmontables. Ainsi le peuple français propagera, autant par ses fêtes que par ses lois, son influence politique et son commerce, le nouvel ordre des choses qui doit rendre sa dignité à l'homme et le bonheur au genre humain."] Pp. 1–2.

12. Reveillière-Lepeaux, *Réflexions sur le Culte*, p. 34.

13. Boissy D'Anglas, *Essai sur les Fêtes Nationales suivi de quelques idées sur les arts*, p. 71.

14. Boissy d'Anglas also suggests that agricultural labor should be celebrated with dances. *Essai sur les Fêtes Nationales,* pp. 54–55.

15. "A l'Être-Suprême
A la Nature et a l'Univers
Au Genie-Humain

A l'Amour conjugal
A l'Amour des Parens et des Enfans
A l'Amour de la Patrie

A l'Amitié
A la Bienveillance entre tous les hommes
Aux Bienfaiteurs de l'Humanité

Au Soutien du Foible et de l'Opprimé
Au Soulagement de l'Indigence
A la Consolation des Affligés et des Malheureux

A la Liberté
A l'Egalité
Aux Martyrs des Droits de l'Homme

A la Souveraineté et a l'Independance des Peuples
A l'Union entre les Nations libres
A la Paix parmi les Hommes

Aux Lois
A la Justice
A l'Ordre publique

A l'Education
Aux Moeurs
A la Vertu

A la Verité
A la Raison
Au Genie

A l'Instruction
Aux Sciences
Aux Découvertes utiles

Au Travail
A l'Industrie
Aux Arts et Metiers

A l'Antiquité
A la Posterité
A l'Immortalité"

Marcoz, *Objet et Ordre des Fêtes Décadaires de la République Française*, pp. 3–5.

16. In his *Réflexions sur la Festomanie,* Didier B*** objects to the popularity of the festivals, claiming that they are on their way to becoming a "culte religieuse," p. 1.

17. The decree, however, encouraged a new kind of awareness of the relations between choreographer and dancers by introducing a distinction between the score of the dance and its interpretation by a given performer.

18. For a good overview of the impact of the revolution on theatrical productions, see Carlson, *Theatre of the French Revolution.*

19. "Plan de régénération du spectacle de l'Opéra National présenté au Comité du Salut Public," reprinted in *Danseurs et Ballet de l'Opéra de Paris,* p. 97.

20. The *Mercure de France* reviewer of *Psyché* makes a startling statement about his own inability to describe the production. This speechless response breaks with the tradition of criticism that willingly and easily transcribed action into words, and it intimates the new decorous space that dancing would come to occupy in order to avoid scrutiny from the state: "It is necessary to see a Pantomime in order to judge it well: all analysis destroys its effect. We content ourselves with saying that this one reunites all that can charm the eyes and interest the soul; that the disposition of the subject, the charming tableaux that the Ballet Master introduced there, that the ingenious ideas of the machinist, the aptitude of the scenarist, the prodigious talent of the performers, all conspired to make the most beautiful spectacle in the world." ["Il faut voir une Pantomime pour la bien juger: toute analyse en détruit l'effet. Nous nous contenterons de dire que celle-ci réunit tout ce qui peut charmer les yeux et intéresser l'âme; que la disposition du sujet, les tableaux charmans que le Maître de Ballet y introduit, que les idées ingénieuses du Machiniste, l'habilité du Décorateur, le talent prodigieux des Exécutans, tout concourt à en faire le plus beau Spectacle du Monde."] December 25, 1790, pp. 159–60.

21. For a good overview of choreographers' contributions to festivals and to other patriotic programming, see Chazin-Bennahum, *Dance in the Shadow of the Guillotine.* The *Détails des Cérémonies, Jeux, Courses de Bateaux, Joutes, Spectacles, Concerts, Illuminations et Danses* mentions that "allegorical dances by the Artistes du Théâtre des Arts" occurred during the evening, followed by a presentation of *Fêtes des Vendanges,* a ballet-pantomime at the Théâtre du Carré Marigny; p. 2.

22. See, for example, *La Fête de l'Égalité, mélodrame pantomi-lyrique, en un acte et en vers,* presented at the Théâtre de la Cité on November 14, 1793.

23. The Opéra was threatened as an institution associated with the monarchy, and also because of the grand scale of its productions. The following diatribe against funding for the Opéra indicates the political message it sent to "le peuple" in the mid 1790s: "During the reign of the tyrants, the fanaticism and enslavement of peoples, the government needed a spectacle absolutely under its orders, so as to praise willingly a victory obtained at the price of the people's blood, the birth of a tyranny. It was necessary therefore to create a spectacle imposing enough to shock the people and numb them to the expenditures made by the state, it was necessary to persuade them still that humans destined for the honor of representing gods, emperors, kings, even ministers and satraps, could never be ordinary men, it was necessary to distinguish by the pompous declamations of academic actors, pensioners of the king, and the titles sometimes accorded to merit, but most often to intrigue, were the base of this kind of supremacy that one seeks to perpetuate inappropriately in the reign of liberty." ["Lors du règne des tyrans, du fanatisme et de l'esclavage des peuples, il fallait au gouvernement un spectacle absolument sous ses ordres, afin de le louanger à volonté pour une victoire remportée à prix de sang du peuple, la naissance d'un tyranneau, etc . . . Il fallut alors rendre ce spectacle assez imposant pour étonner le peuple et l'étourdir sur les dépenses qu'il coûtait à l'état, il fallut lui persuader encore que les hommes destinés à l'honneur de représenter des dieux, des empereurs, des rois, enfin des ministres et des satrapes, ne pouvoient être des hommes ordinaires, il fallut les distinguer par les fastueuses déclamations d'académiciens-comédiens ordinaires et pensionaires du roi, et ces titres accordés quelquefois au mérite, mais bien plus souvent à l'intrigue, furent la base de cette espèce de suprématie que l'on cherche à perpetuer mal-à-propos dans le règne de la liberté."] *Encore 7 millions pour le grand opéra? Ça ne prendra pas: Rendez la salle à Montansier,* pp. 7–8.

24. For example, the liberal impulse that had instigated theatrical reform in order to "elevate" the taste and sensibilities of the common people by providing access to great texts came to be perceived instead to have resulted in an "erosion of values." The Hébériste government responded by reinstating censorship and mandating patriotic content. As Robespierre's government assumed power, it revised the literalist standards for theatrical presentations while still asserting control over quality of the production.

Certain classics, banned under Hébériste law because they did not depict the immediate political situation, were reintroduced if they demonstrated high moral standards.

25. De Gouges wrote several plays as well as political tracts. For a sense of the larger political and literary context in which she worked, see Kadish and Massardier-Kenney, eds., *Translating Slavery.*

26. By the end of the 1790s, the boulevard theatres were again producing highly satiric commentary on government, as the plot from *Kiki* suggests: On an imaginary island, a benign but naive emperor entertains shipwrecked guests. Informed by a scoundrel that on this island masters and servants must reverse roles, a servant couple is treated by the emperor as aristocracy. Their dialogue parodies the flamboyant phrasing of the emperor and a whole set of aristocratic presumptions. See Bernard-Valville and Hus, *Kiki, ou l'Ile Imaginaire, Comédie-Folie en trois actes, en prose, Mêlée de chant, danse, pantomime, cérémonies burlesques, etc.*

27. This is a reference to Outram's analysis of the emergence of the model of *homo clausus* in the late eighteenth century. Building on Norbert Elias's work, she discusses the relationship of stoic behavior such as that assumed by those on their way to the guillotine to generalized public behavior during this critical period of change in conceptions of body and society. See *The Body and the French Revolution,* pp. 68–123.

28. Lavater's *Essai sur la physiognomie destiné à faire connaître l'homme et à le faire aimer* was republished numerous times in France between 1781 and 1803. For an overview of his work and especially its impact on the representation of Parisian life in literature such as that undertaken by Balzac, see Wechsler's A Human *Comedy.* On the role of anatomists, including the German anatomist Felix Camper, in establishing research strategies that would identify unique differences between men and women and also members of distinct races, see Sheibinger's *Nature's Body,* pp. 113–83.

29. Scheibinger summarizes this research in her article "Skeletons in the Closet" and expands the argument in her book *The Mind Has No Sex?* Scheibinger's argument is discussed in more detail below.

30. Austin's *Chironomia, or A Treatise on Rhetorical Delivery,* for example, contains extremely precise observations concerning the varieties and effects of oratorical gestures, of which this description of the hand in its most "natural" position is exemplary: "The hand, when unconstrained in its natural and relaxed state, either hanging down at rest or raised moderately up, has all the fingers a little bended inwards towards the palm; the middle and third finger resting partly on the nail of the third. The fore finger is separated from the middle finger and less bended, and the little finger separated from the third, and more bended," p. 336. See also Jelgerhuis, an actor and acting teacher from Amsterdam, whose *Theoretische Lessen over de Gesticulatie en Mimik* contains an extraordinary number of drawings of facial expressions, postures, and gestures designed to guide the actor. The great actor Talma, in his quest for precise renditions of human feelings, even prescribed a kind of self-interrogation and observation while in the midst of the passion: "In the expression of the passions there are many shades which cannot be devined and which the actor cannot paint until he has felt them himself. The observations which he has made on his own nature serve at once for his study and example; he interrogates himself on the impressions his soul has felt, on the expression they imprinted upon his features, on the accents of his voice in the various states of feeling. He meditates on these, and clothes the fictitious passions with these real forms. I scarcely know how to confess that, in my own person, in any circumstance of my life in which I experienced deep sorrow, the passion of the theater was so strong in me that, although oppressed with real sorrow, and disregarding the tears I shed, I made, in spite of myself, a rapid and fugitive observation on the alteration of my voice, and on a certain spasmodic vibration which it contracted as I wept; and, I say it, not without some shame, I even thought of making use of this on the stage, and, indeed, this experiment on myself has often been of service to me." *Reflections on the Actor's Art,* p. 39.

31. Bell, *Essays on the Anatomy of Expression in Painting,* pp. 97–98.

32. Bell, *Essays on the Anatomy of Expression in Painting,* p. 2.

33. See Scheibinger, *The Mind Has No Sex?* pp. 160–244.

34. Bell, *Essays on the Anatomy of Expression in Painting,* p. 167.

35. Bell, *Essays on the Anatomy of Expression in Painting,* p. 172.

36. For additional sources and observations on ballet vocabulary in the early nineteenth century, see Hammond, "Clues to Ballet's Technical History from the Early Nineteenth Century Ballet Lesson."

37. "Celui qui est jarreté doit s'appliquer continuellement à éloigner les parties trop resserrées; le premier moyen pour y réussir, est de tourner les cuisses en dehors, et de les mouvoir, dans ce sens, en profitant de la liberté du mouvement de rotation du fémur dans la cavité cotyloide des os des hanches.

Aidé par cet exercice, les genoux suivront la même direction, et rentreront, pour ainsi dire, dans leur place. La rotule qui semble destinée à limiter le rejet du genou trop en arrière de l'articulation, tombera perpendiculairement sur la pointe du pied; et la cuisse et la jambe ne sortant plus de la ligne, en décriront alors une droite qui assurera la fermeté et la stabilité du tronc." Blasis, *Traité Elémentaire, Théorique et Pratique de l'Art de la Danse,* p. 48.

38. Théleur's *Letters on Dancing reducing This Elegant and Healthful Exercise to Easy Scientific Principles* evidences an impressive mastery of anatomical terms. See especially pp. 54–55 and p. 85.

39. "La plante du pied est la vraie base sur laquelle porte tout le poids du corps; mais c'est la ceinture qui renferme réellement l'à-plomb et facilite l'exécution de la danse. On ne peut être bon danseur sans être ferme sur les reins: si on les abandonne, il est impossible de se soutenir dans une ligne droite; on risque à chaque instant de perdre le centre de gravité . . . Le danseur bien assis sur les hanches, doit montrer sa poitrine à découvert par l'effacement des épaules, et la position de la tête légèrement en arrière: le menton doit être un peu rentré en dessous de la machoire." Gourdoux, *Principes et notions élémentaires sur l'art de la danse pour la ville, suivi des manières de civilité qui sont des attributions de cet art,* p. 12.

40. "Les effets de cet art sur le physique de certains individus sont infiniment intéressans; qu'on se peigne une jeune personne d'un tempérament faible, dont l'éducation aura été négligée; elle aura naturellement la tête en avant, enfoncée dans les épaules, la poitrine retirée, les genoux crochus et butans, les pieds en dedans, l'habitude du corps chancelante, conservant à peine le centre de gravité; voyez la sortir après six mois de leçons, d'entre les mains d'un bon maître, les pieds en dehors, le jarrêt tendu, la hanche bien placée, la poitrine en avant, l'air de tête fier et gracieux, les membres déliés en avant et les mouvemens aisés." Martinet, *Essai ou principes élémentaires de l'art de la danse,* pp. 22–23.

41. The growing conception of the body as consisting of a central core and secondary cores for limbs is also evident in Austin's analysis of rhetorical arm gestures: "The arm, the hand, and the fingers united in one flexible line of several joints, which combine together their mutual action, form the grand instrument of gesture, or as Cicero calls it, 'the weapon of the orator.' The centre of motion of this compound line, is the shoulder, which does not move all together in the manner of an inflexible line; but each separate joint becomes often a new centre of motion for the portion between it and the extremity." *Chironomia,* p. 375.

42. Although many instructors continued to invoke the terms "arqué" and "jarreté" to refer to knock-kneed and bowlegged conditions, Blasis, building upon Noverre's initial insights, replaced these descriptive terms with the distinction between the hip's tendency to rotate outward or inward. This propensity of the hip was seen by Blasis to cause the shape of the leg. Blasis's analysis provides further evidence of the new volumetric integrity of the leg with its linear interior. See Noverre, *Letters on Dancing and Ballets,* pp. 111–12, and Blasis, *Traité Elémentaire,* pp. 40–41.

43. As demonstration of this set of linear guidelines, Blasis recounts a conversation with Gardel, who proposed that the instructor stop the dancer at any point in the execution of an exercise in order to examine the lines of the body. *Traité Elémentaire,* p. 24.

44. Blasis, *Traité Elémentaire,* pp. 15–16.

45. Blasis expressed his discontent with the disappearance of the noble genre in *Traité Elémentaire,* pp. 89–91. Pierre Gardel, Milon, and Aumer asserted the importance of the genres in their "Observations de MM, les Maîtres de Ballets," reprinted in *Danseurs et Ballets de L'Opéra de Paris,* p. 67.

46. In his *Idées Générales sur l'Academie Royale de Musique,* Deshayes asserts that because all students study the same regimen they develop only mediocre skills; p. 40. He also condemns the system for only developing stars instead of a well-trained corps de ballet; p. 14.

47. Deshayes claims that he and others sent petitions to the Opéra in 1819 asking for funds to reinstitute the genre system. *Idées Générales sur l'Academie Royale de Musique,* p. 42.

48. ". . . de placer ses élèves, de les tourner, de faire une attention particulière à leurs pointes; de faire ployer en dehors, et surtout de faire tendre extrêmement les genoux; de veiller scrupuleusement à ce que les mouvements de la tête, ceux des bras et du corps soient en parfaite harmonie avec les pas que forment les jambes tels difficiles qu'ils soient." Coulon, "Rapport sur l'enseignement donné par M. Coulon," reprinted in *Danseurs et Ballets de L'Opéra de Paris,* p. 82.

49. The number of male and female corps remained approximately equal in the early decades of the nineteenth century, and salaries were determined by rank, as indicated in these rosters from 1811:

Gardel	maître de ballet	5210
Despreaux	maître de danse	2600
Vestris	1st danseur	2600
Beaulieu	2nd danseur	2082
Beaupré	3rd danseur	1736
Bromiliu	3rd danseur	1736
Albert	3rd danseur	1736
Mme. Gardel	1st danseuse	2600
Clotilde	1st danseuse	2600
Bigottini	2nd danseuse	2082
Chevigny	2nd danseuse	2082
Reiune	3rd danseuse	1736
rehearsal master		600
Lanner		600

Pierre Gardel, "Court Ballet under Napoleon Bonaparte" n. p.

50. See "Règlement de l'Ecole de Danse," reprinted in *Danseurs et Ballets de L'Opéra de Paris,* p. 80.

51. See "Pétition des élèves du Conservatoire royal de Danse au Ministre de l'intérieur," reprinted in *Danseurs et Ballets de L'Opéra de Paris,* p. 84.

52. *Journal de l'Empire,* March 10, 1808, p. 1.

53. "On a défini la danse une suite de pas dirigés par la musique, et accompagnés de divers mouvemens de corps. La danse, naturelle à l'homme, exista dans tous les tems et dans tous les lieux. Dans son principe, elle était, comme le geste, la manifestation des sentimens intérieurs; muet langage, qui, par des attitudes, des bonds, des ébranlemens, exprimait le plaisir ou la douleur, la colère ou la tendresse, l'affliction ou la joie. Peu à peu, ces mouvemens simples et désordonnés devinrent plus réglés et plus sages; l'imitation, ce principe des arts, s'en empara, les combina, les transporta sur le théâtre; et les ébauches, d'abord rudes et grossières, mais, avec le tems, épurées, agrandies, perfectionnées, présentèrent enfin le dessin le plus correct, les couleurs les plus brillantes." Baron, *Lettres et Entretiens sur la Danse,* pp. 9–10.

54. The heterodox varieties of spectacle even included ballets on the tightrope. See, for example, *Introduction à la Danse sur la Corde au Sérail, ou Le Dey D'Alger.* The history of the Fioroso family also documents the popularity of tightrope acts and the intermingling of genres within their performances. Their tightrope act at the Théâtre Louvois in 1801 used a cord inclined to the middle of the parterre and then doubled back toward the third loges forming a V out over the heads of the main floor. Pierre Forioso and his sister danced "l'allemande sur deux cordes paralèles" while playing the violin, and Mustapha danced with fireworks that went off while he performed. Alternatively, Pierre and his sister, costumed in military outfits, would do drill exercises. Pierre was compared to Vestris and was said to have more grace on the wire than Vestris on a solid floor. In 1808 the family again appeared alternating wire acts with "petits intermèdes muets." The Fioroso family found a rival in the person of Ravel, with whom they had a contest in 1807 that Vestris and Paul Duport judged. Ravel was hired twice by Montansier, in 1807 and 1808, after she had received permission to produce theatre. He performed "danses de corde and exercizes de voltige, des scènes pantomimes & des arlequinades." Manne and Ménétrier, *Galerie Historique des Comédiens de la Troupe de Nicolet,* pp. 200–203.

55. In *Précis Historique sur les Fêtes, les Spectacles, et les Réjouissances Publiques,* Ruggieri gives a wonderfully succinct account of the different royal fêtes and public entertainments of late-eighteenth- and early-nineteenth-century Paris.

56. The most detailed and comprehensive analysis of masked balls and public dances is provided by Cordova in "Poetics of Dance: Narrative Designs from Staël to Maupassant."

57. Mayer provides vivid descriptions of the English pantomime productions during this period in his *Harlequin in His Element: The English Pantomime, 1806–1836.* Many of the values—the fast scenic changes, the acrobatic display, the hyperbolic passions- apply equally to the French stage.

58. Guilcher makes this observation as part of his explanation concerning the importance and popularity of social dance in postrevolutionary France. See *La contredanse et les renouvellements de la danse française,* p. 151.

59. For good overviews of social dance conventions throughout this period, see Aldrich, *From the Ballroom to Hell;* Cordova, "Poetics of Dance"; and Guilcher, *La contredanse et les renouvellements de la danse française.*

60. ". . . cette légèreté dans les mouvemens, ces manières civiles, aimables et gracieuses, ces grâces séduisantes qui, après avoir été portées dans les beaux jours de la France à un haut degré de perfection, furent, dans les temps désastreux, contraintes chez les uns, méconnues chez les autres, et remplacées chez plusieurs par un ton déformé et grossier, bien éloigné de la galanterie et de l'urbanité française. . . ."] Gourdoux, *Principes et notions élémentaires,* p. 6.

61. ". . . on ne vit plus que cette partie matérielle qui défiguroit un art plein de graces et de charmes: on se tourna alors vers la danse de théâtre, et on s'en occupa entièrement comme d'un seul moyen suffisant pour briller en société, et la méthode des anciens maîtres fut tournée en ridicule." Gourdoux, *Principes et notions élémentaires,* p. 7.

62. Gourdoux points out that in pursuing theatrical training, the social dance enthusiasts deceive themselves because "the manner in which the style of steps is executed" [la manière dont ils exécutent la qualité de leur pas] is so different." *Principes et notions élémentaires,* p. 11.

63. See Guilcher, *La contredanse et les renouvellements de la danse française,* pp. 122–26.

64. Guilcher makes a compelling argument for this shift by comparing diagrams for floor patterns and lists of steps in both eighteenth- and nineteenth-century dance manuals. See *La contredanse et les renouvellements de la danse française,* pp. 87–186.

65. Faget argues that "dance is one of the motives that has most served the coming together of the two sexes and the consequent conduct of men—to soften the rudeness of their manners. Dance has created politesse, urbanity, a good tone, elegant manners, and introduced into society this reciprocal exchange of elegant manners that had established so highly throughout Europe the gallant reputation of the French nation." ["La danse est une des causes qui ont le plu servi à rapprocher les deux sexes, et à conduire par consequent les hommes—à adoucir la rudesse de leurs manières. La danse a créé la politesse, l'urbanité, le bon ton, l'élégance des manières, et introduit dans la societé cet échange réciproque d'élégantes manières qui avaient établi si haut en Europe la réputation galante de la nation française."] *De la Danse,* p. 12.

66. Walker, *Exercises for ladies,* p. 132.

67. Voarino, *A Treatise on Calisthenic Exercises,* p. 65.

68. Albert's essay on social dance emphasizes its benefits to posture and good health. See *L'Art de Danser à la Ville et à la Cour, ou Nouvelle Méthode des vrais principes de la Danse Française et Etrangère. . .*

69. My analysis of the role of gesture in melodrama is indebted to two important works on the topic, Brooks, *The Melodramatic Imagination: Balzac, Henry James, and the Mode of Excess,* and Pryzbos, *L'Entreprise Mélodramatique.* Both argue that gesture in melodrama took on the special function of communicating the ineffable and inexpressible. Brooks even extends his analysis to Romantic drama in general, arguing that "emblematic, then, of the Romantic dramatic enterprise are those plays constructed precisely around a central dumbness, an unspeakable darkness, which is not so much the void of meaning as the over-fullness of awful meaning, the fully sublime," p. 107. For a general overview of productions and themes, see also Rahill, *The World of Melodrama.*

70. A succinct definition of melodrama and its obvious relevance to ballet is offered by Charlemagne in this poem:

> It is a saturnale where the obscure citizen,
> Is, for thirty cents, equal to the patrician.
> Hortense is ecstatic at the word "humanity,"
> And swoons at those with "sensibility,"
> But what are these words? Tableaux mean more.
> The object of melodrama is to speak to the eyes.
> Of what is offered, Madame is satisfied:
> It is an illusion, one can add no more to,
> A real panorama, in which the moving subjects

Seem by turns agitated, agitating,
Moved, impassioned, persecutors, victims,
Models of virtue, monstrous convents of crime.
It gives you all the colors.
You will have noblemen, princes, thiefs,
Soldiers, ninnies, clod hoppers, pirates,
Handsome shepherds carressing their shepherdesses.
The breathless actor, pressed to have his turn
One crushes, poisons, kills, makes love,
One conspires, fights, exiles a head,
One erects a scaffold and one gives a party.

[C'est une saturnale, où l'obscur citoyen,
Est, pour ses trente sols, l'égal d'un patricien.
Hortense s'extasie au mot *humanité,*
Et se pâme à celui de *sensibilité,*
Mais que sont les mots? Des tableaux valent mieux.
L'objet du mélodrame est de parler aux yeux.
De ce qu'on offre aux siens, Madame est satisfaite:
C'est une illusion, on ne peut plus compléte,
Un vrai panorama, dont les sujets mouvans
Paraissent tour-à-tour agités, agissans,
Émus, passionnés, persécuteurs, victimes,
Modèles de vertus, monstres couvents de crimes.
On vous en donnera de toutes couleurs.
Vous aurez des menins, des princes, des voleurs,
Des soldats, des niais, des manants, des corsaires,
Et de jolis bergers caressant leurs bergères.
L'acteur est haletant, pressé d'avoir son tour
On pille, on empoisonne, on tue, on fait l'amour;
On conspire, on se bat, on proscrit une tête,
On dresse un échaffaud et l'on donne une fête.]

Le Mélodrame aux Boulevards Facétie Littéraire, Historique et Dramatique, pp. 6–8.

71. Blasis registered the difference in this way: "By gesture we present to the eyes all that we cannot express through the ears; it is a universal interpreter that follows us to the very extremities of the globe, and makes us intelligible to the most uncivilized hordes. It is understood even by animals. Speech is the language of reason: it convinces our minds; tones and gestures form a sentimental discourse that moves the heart. Speech can only give utterance to our passions, by means of reflections through their relative ideas. Voice and gesture convey them to those we address, in an immediate and direct manner. In short, speech, or rather the words which compose it, is an artifical institution, formed and agreed upon between men, for a more distinct reciprocal communication of their ideas; whilst gestures and the tone of voice are, I may say, innate in us, and serve to exhibit all that concerns our wants and the preservation of our existence, for which reason they are rapid, expressive, and energetic." *The Code of Terpsichore,* pp. 113–14.

72. In her analysis of melodrama, Pryzbos proposes a function for this immensely popular form deriving from Girardian notions of sacrifice. Melodrama, symbolizing the Revolution itself, offered a victim, symbolizing the guillotined, a villain, standing for Robespierre and other members of the Terrorist government, and a deceived populace. The happy resolution of events in the melodrama allowed viewers to affirm their innocence, and also to see in contemporary society a final and just end to the conflict of the 1790s.

73. Faget, *De la Danse, et particulièrement de la danse de société,* pp. 22–23.

74. The Porte Saint-Martin production *Les artistes, ballet-pantomime en deux actes* likewise acknowledged the new role for the choreographer by casting him alongside painter and musician as one of the three principal characters.

75. This observation by Genlis gives some indication of the vocabulary that dancers and audience loved, but that connoisseurs rejected: "Theatrical dance has been spoiled for several years because it

distances itself from nature. It is without doubt very difficult to do ronds de jambes that begin at the thigh, and to lift the leg to the height of the shoulder without bending the knee, but this manner of cutting short the joint is a very disagreeable tour de force to see because it denaturalizes the human figure; one would have better left it to the tightrope dancers, who do it all the time, and one would do well to return it to them." ["La danse théâtrale se gâte depuis plusieurs années, parce qu'elle s'éloigne de la nature. Il est sans doute très-difficile de faire des ronds de jambes qui partent des hanches, et d'élever sa jambe à la hauteur de son épaule sans ployer le genou, mais cette manière de se retrancher une articulation est un tour de force fort désagréable à l'œil, parce qu'il dénature la figure humaine; on auroit du le laisser aux danseuses de corde, qui l'ont fait de tout temps, et l'on feroit bien de le leur restituer."] *Dictionnaire critique et raisonné des étiquettes de la cour*, p. 117.

76. "Elle rappelle des aventures si touchantes, elle offre des tableaux si frappans et si variés, que quand même on supprimeroit les trois ou quatre pas qui s'y trouvent, elle n'en réussiroit pas moins, tant chaque situation est adroitement amenée, tant les scènes sont pleines d'effet, et la catastrophe habilement ménagée. . . . Enfin cette pantomime est exécutée avec tout l'ensemble désirable. On y danse peu, car tout est en action depuis le premier acte jusqu'au dernier; cependant on a beaucoup applaudi, au premier acte, le pas nègre, dont l'exécution est parfaite. M. Sevin, qui conduit cette troupe de Noirs, s'y fait remarquer par sa force et son adresse à manier le bamboo. C'est un des meilleurs combattans du Boulevard." *Courrier des Spectacles*, June 30, 1806, p. 2.

77. "L'effet que produit à la lecture ou à la scène, le charme d'une pièce aisée et harmonieuse, d'un style naturel, délicat et gracieux, de ces pensées ingénieuses, exprimées avec énergie et châleur, cet effet, dis-je, est souvent incertain, quand on veut porter à l'âme, par les yeux seulement, les impressions qu'elle est habituée de recevoir d'une oreille attentive. Cependant le sujet des amours d'Héro et Léandre offre une situation si touchante, qu'il m'a paru susceptible d'inspirer un intérêt réel, en le mettant en action, sans emprunter les secours d'une plume exercée, et les talens du déclamateur.

En le présentant dans sa simplicité historique, j'avois à craindre qu'il n'offrit trop de monotonie. J'ai cru lui donner un caractère plus aimable, et une marche dramatique, en y ajoutant des épisodes allégoriques, qui forment une liaison de scènes variées, sans altérer la vérité du fait.

L'Amour que j'ai introduit, et qui joue un role principal, m'étoit nécessaire pour activer l'ardeur qu'il fait naître dans Héro; pour amener l'incident où il rappelle, par une danse allégorique, le plus beau triomphe de Vénus, celui où sa beauté seule lui fit adjuger par Paris le prix qu'envioient Junon et Palla, pour donner plus de vraisemblance aux moyens mythologiques qui, au dénouement, rappellent les deux amans à la vie et au bonheur." Milon, *Héro et Léandre, ballet-pantomime, en un acte*, pp. 3–5.

78. "Chaque instant lui parait être le dernier de sa vie. Que va-t-il devenir? seul dans un désert, sans secours, repoussé de la nature entière; errant sans but, sans espérance, trahi par ses amis, ingrat, parjuré, couvert d'opprobre; toutes ses idées l'accablent à la fois!" Gardel, *L'Enfant Prodigue*, p. 46.

79. Another vivid example of the scenario's representation of interior thoughts comes from Gardel's *Vertumne et Pomone* (1810): "Vertumne paled at the severity of his destiny, he wants to distance himself from a place that seems made for happy lovers. Pomone's severity causes him to despair and fleeing seems to him the surest means to remove himself from her scorn. But why flee? Doesn't the power of Vertumne surpass that of Pomone?" ["Vertumne se palint de la rigueur de son sort, il veut s'éloigner d'un lieu qui pourtant semble fait pour des amans heureux. La rigueur de Pomone le désespère, et fuir lui paraît le moyen le plus sûr de se soustraire à ses mépris. Mais pourquoi fuir? Le pouvoir de Vertumne ne surpasse-t-il pas celui de Pomone?"] P. 9.

80. Continued tension between acting and dancing in the ballets was reflected in comments like these: "Let us add that the action ballet at the grand Opéra theatre will only attain perfection when the actors who are called upon to perform forget that they are before all else *dancers*: it is necessary that they become immersed in the representation of the actions ballets, that they are actors, and that they entirely undo the stiff manners of these academic poses and of convention that leads the spectator to believe that they are about to perform an *entrechat* at the moment, often the most emotional, of the action." ["Ajoutons que le ballet d'action, sur le théatre du grand Opéra, n'atteindra à la perfection que quand les acteurs qui sont appelés à la représenter oublieront qu'ils sont avant tout des *danseurs*: il faut qu'ils se pénètrent, dans la représentation des ballets d'action, qu'ils sont seulement acteurs, et qu'ils se défassent entièrement de ces manières guindées, de ces poses académiques et de convention qui prêtent à croire au spectateur qu'ils vont passer un entre-chat au moment souvent le plus pathétique de l'action."] Viollet-Leduc, *Précis de Dramatique ou de l'Art de Composer et Exécuter les Pièces de Théâtre*, p. 177.

81. For a good overview of early-nineteenth-century administrative regulations affecting costume and scenery production of the Opéra, see Wild, *Décors et Costumes du XIXe Siècle à L'Opéra de Paris*, in *Opéra de Paris*, vol.1.

82. "Virginie, à l'Opéra, est décente, modeste, quoique vive et spirituelle; à la Porte Saint-Martin, cette Virginie, sous le nom de Zoé, est froide et niaise, mais beaucoup moins scrupuleuse sur la bienséance; elle reçoit même assez facilement les caresses d'un colon inconnu qu'elle rencontre par hasard: il est vrai qu'on peut dire que son intention est bonne, et qu'elle se sacrifie à l'humanité; c'est pour délivre une malheureuse négresse que Zoé s'apprivoise avec le maître.

Quant à Paul, si simple, si ingénu, si bien élevé par M. Bernadin de Saint-Pierre, c'est, dans *Les Deux Créoles*, un petit libertin, entreprenant et déterminé, qui se fait appeler Théodore. . . .

A l'Opéra, c'est un nègre qui s'est enfui avec ses deux enfans, pour se dérober à la cruauté de son maître; à la Porte St. Martin, c'est une négresse avec un seul enfan. On a négligé, à l'Opéra la circonstance du portrait de Paul, que Virgine porte sur son coeur; à la Porte Saint-Martin, on a mis quelqu'importance à cette bagatelle sentimentale; mais une grande différence entre Paul et son représentant Théodore, c'est que Paul est un homme, et Théodore une femme. Quoique cette femme soit madame Quériau, elle n'en fait pas plus d'illusion; et cette passion de deux femmes l'un pour l'autre est fort peu touchante. . . .

On a remarqué, il est vrai, dans le ballet de la Porte Saint Martin plus de noir, et du plus beau noir; plus de dévotions, de priéres et de génuflexions; plus de caresses et d'attouchements; plus d'agitations, de mouvemens et de courses désordonnées; le tableau des jeunes Amours est beacoup plus chargé; l'orage fait un plus grand tintamarre; Zoé reste plus long temps évanouié au sortir de la mer; elle a plus de peine à reprendre ces esprits: voilà les seuls avantages que je réconnoisse dans la composition d'Aumer. Mais le ballet de l'Opéra me paroit avoir une immense superiorité du côté du goût, de la précision, de la justesse, et d'élégance dans le dessin comme dans l'exécution . . . Le ballet d'Aumer est à celui de Gardel, comme le théâtre de la Porte Saint Martin est au théâtre de l'Opéra." *Journal de l'Empire*, July 4, 1806, pp. 1–2.

83. "Il est peu de pièces qui soient jouées avec autant d'ensemble, et il n'en est qu'une, celle de *Jenny*, où Mad. Quériau déploi autant de talent. Dans *Les Deux Créoles*, elle joue le rôle de Théodore, et y met toute la chaleur, tout l'abandon, tout le pathétique dont elle peut résister à tant de secousses. À mesure qu'on approche du dénouement, à l'instant même où elle paroit épuisée, elle semble acquérir de nouvelles forces." *Courrier des Spectacles*, June 30, 1806, p. 2.

84. The degeneration of the action ballet into a decorative art is evident, as early as 1798, in these remarks by Pierre Gardel: "I have always remarked that in the action ballets the effects of the decorations, the varied and agreeable divertissements, were what attracted the crowd of spectators and their quick applause; after this remark, I looked for a subject that could be bent to validate the grand talents of the Opéra that Paris alone possesses in dance. . . ." ["J'ai toujours remarqué dans les Ballets d'action que les effets de décorations, et les divertissemens variés et agréables, étoient ce qui attiroit le plus la foule des spectateurs, et les vifs applaudissemens; d'après cette remarque, j'ai cherché un sujet qui pût se plier à faire valoir les grands talens que l'Opéra, de Paris seul, possède en danse. . . ."] Avant-Propos for *Le Jugement de Paris, ballet-pantomime en trois actes*.

It is equally evident in comments from the Avant-Propos of Dauberval's *Le Page Inconstant, ou Honi soit qui mal y pense, ballet heroï-comique, Tiré du Mariage de Figaro, en trois actes*: "If the art of pantomime produced vivid sensations among the Greeks and Romans, we can only attribute it to the address of their mimes, and to their choice of striking subjects that would be of interest for the Republic and known by all people. Convinced of this truth, I chose a subject less serious, which, by its gaiety, would conform better to my nation." [Si l'art de la pantomime produisit de vives sensations chez les Grecs et les Romains, ne l'attribuons qu'à l'adresse qu'avaient leurs mimes, de ne choisir que des situations frappantes, bien intéressantes pour la République et que tout le peuple savait. Pénétrée de cette vérité, j'ai choisi un sujet moins grave, qui, par sa gaîté, convient mieux à ma nation."] Pp. 1–2. On the ballet as a form of diversion, see also A!A!A!, *Traité du Mélodrame*.

85. Blasis, *The Code of Terpsichore*, p. 7. Blasis goes on to present an elaborate analysis of dancing as "pleasurable, voluptuous, and delightful," that aligns dance with Southern temperaments and with the feminine. See pp. 7–11.

86. Baron, *Lettres et entretiens sur la danse*, p. 13.

87. Théleur, *Letters on Dancing reducing This Elegant and Healthful Exercise to Easy Scientific Principles*, p. 1.

88. Théleur, *Letters on Dancing reducing This Elegant and Healthful Exercise to Easy Scientific Principles*, p. 1.

89. Because of its length and substantial detail, Baron's historical documentation of dance would seem to be the exception, yet his account of dance's past differs in two important ways from eighteenth-century texts. Populated with scenes of naked or sparsely clad women dancing their excessive feelings, Baron's text treats history as a pretext for the seduction of the reader, Sophie, to whom the work is addressed. Second, Baron inverts the eighteenth-century strategy of justifying contemporary practices through evidence of similar ancient practices. Instead of bolstering the present with the past, he enlivens the past by showing its similarities to the present. See, for example, his discussion of Emilie Bigottini, whose work exemplifies in spirit if not in form the ancient Roman mime performances. *Lettres et entretiens sur la danse*, pp. 125–28.

Les Royalistes de la Vendée, ou les Époux Républicains, Pantomime en Trois Actes

1. The Collection Rondel of the Bibliotèque de l'Arsenal lists ninety-four entries of different productions he directed through 1824. The following titles are indicative of the kind of spectacle he typically created: *Martial et Angélique, ou le Témoin irrécusable, scènes pantomimes, équestres et anecdotiques, en 3 parties* (1810); *L'Enfant d'Hercule, ou les Deux temples, tableaux mythologiques et allégoriques, à grand spectacle, en 2 actions* (1811); *L'Asile du silence, ou Gloire et sagesse, mimologue et tableau allégorique en 1 acte et à grand spectacle* (1811); *L'Entrée des chevaliers français dans Sévica, prologue mélodramatique en 1 acte et à grand spectacle* (1811); *Le Sac et la corde, ou la Funambulomanie, divertissement pantomime grotesque en 2 parties* (1812); *La Pucelle d'Orléans, pantomime historique et chevaleresque, en 3 actes, à grand spectacle* (1813).

2. "J'ai vu et m'écris . . . puissent les tableaux affreux que ma foible main a essayé de tracer, redoubler dans tous les coeurs, la haine de la tyrannie et du fanatisme! puissent les nuages de sang qui s'agglomèrent encore sur nos têtes, se dissiper bientôt aux rayons bienfaisans du soleil de la Liberté!" Cuvelier de Trie, *Les Royalistes de la Vendée*, p. 4.

La Dansomanie

1. I am fortunate to be able to include as part of the documentation on which this analysis of *La Dansomanie* is based a superb reconstruction of the ballet by Swedish choreographer Ivo Cramer, as performed by the Paris Opera Ballet in 1988.

2. The ballet's success was proved, in part, by the fact that it remained in the repertoire of the Opera until 1826.

3. As inspiration for the character of M. Duléger, Gardel may have retained an image from his older brother's production of *Mirza,* in which Dauberval played the part of an older officer attempting to dance: "Nothing is more gay, more real, and more agreeable than M. Dauberval in the *forlane* he dances in the first act: he perfectly seized the costume, the tone, the manners of an old officer who seeks to reestablish the suppleness, ease, habits or his first youth." ["Rien de plus gai, de plus vrai, de plus agréable que M. Dauberval dans la forlane à qu'il danse au premier acte: il a parfaitement saisi le costume, le ton, les manières d'un vieil Officier qui cherche à remettre en oeuvre la souplesse, l'aisance, les habitudes de sa première jeunesse."] *Mercure de France,* November 27, 1779, p. 182.

4. Auguste Vestris, like his father, was notoriously self-aggrandizing about his own expertise at dancing. He unreliably appeared for performances and dramatized his artistic temperment at social gatherings as well as in the theatre. For a summary of the Vestris family's many accomplishments, see Gaston Capon's *Les Vestris, le 'diou' de la danse et sa famille.*

5. ". . . on supplie M. Duléger, qui voit à ses genoux jusqu'à son fils, à peine âgé de cinq ans. Tout ce qui, dans ce groupe, frappe l'attention de M. Dulèger, c'est que l'enfant, dans cette attitude, n'a pas le pied assez en-dehors, et il court corriger cette faute." B***, "Review of *La Dansomanie* by Pierre Gardel," *Courrier des Spectacles,* An VIII, 26 Prairal, No 1198, p. 2.

Nina, ou La Folle par Amour

1. This is Beaumont's translation as published in his *Complete Book of Ballets*, p. 7.

Les Pages du Duc de Vendôme

1. Aumer claims in his preface to the program that he is presenting this ballet "to yield to the desire evinced by the adminstration to see produced a ballet 'in harmony with the actual theatre space.' " ["pour céder au désir que lui a témoigné l'administration de voir monter un ballet *en harmonie avec la salle actuelle*."] *Les Pages du Duc de Vendôme*, p. 2.

2. According to Guest, *Les Pages* was repeated 126 times, a number exceeded only by Aumer's *Astolphe et Joconde* (1827), and by *La Sylphide* (1832) and *Giselle* (1841). See Guest's very helpful appendix enumerating ballets produced at the Opéra between 1820 and 1847 in *The Romantic Ballet in Paris*, pp. 268–69.

3. One reviewer, following on Aumer's claim that he was presenting a ballet appropriate to the theatre, wrote: "It would be injust to say that the actual theatre space being shabby, tedious, and unpleasant, the ballet is perfectly in harmony with it; but the indulgence with which the spectators received this bagatelle is one more motive for advising M. Aumer to deserve it, by deleting from his ballet several useless details. He will feel then the necessity of abridging some long pas, and deleting others that produce little effect because they are poorly framed. In short, in rendering the beginning more rapid, the middle less long and the ending more lively, one can hope that the public will not see other than with pleasure a ballet where one dances. . . ." ["Il seroit injuste de dire que la salle actuelle étant mesquine, maussade, et déplaisante, le ballet est parfaitement en harmonie avec la salle; mais l'indulgence avec laquelle le public a reçu cette bagatelle, est un motif de plus pour conseiller à M. Aumer de la mériter, en faisant disparaître de son ballet plusieurs détails oiseux. Il sentira encore la nécessité d'abréger quelques pas longs, et d'en supprimer d'autres qui produisent peu d'effet, parce qu'ils sont mal encadrés. Enfin, en rendant le commencement plus rapide, le milieu moins long et le dénoûement plus vif, on peut espérer que le public ne verra pas sans quelque plaisir un ballet où on dansent. . . ."] *Le Drapeau Blanc*, 20 October 1820, No. 294, p. 2. Another found fault with the weak and superficial subject: "This new choreographer should make a point of forgetting the vaudeville from the Rue de Chartres. The action is entirely based on the known work. Before it begins, interminable divertissements, while executed with rare perfection, retard the ballet too long. The ballet obtained little success, and what is more, the grand Opéra possesses a silly little trifle." ["Ce nouveau chorégraphe ne fera point oublier le vaudeville de la rue de Chartres. L'action est entièrement calquée sur l'ouvrage connu. Avant qu'elle commence, des divertissemens interminables, quoiqu'exécutés avec une rare perfection, la retardent trop long-tems. Le ballet a obtenu peu de succès, et le Grand-Opéra possède une petite niaiserie de plus."] *Journal des Théâtres, de la Littérature et des Arts*, No. 183, 19 October 1820, p. 2.

4. "[M]ais, comme cela doit toujours arriver au dénouement d'une comédie, d'un opéra, d'un vaudeville, voire même d'un ballet, le héros, après avoir fait de la colère avec des entrechats, se calme, pardonne, et le page insolent et la fille séduite ne trouvent d'autre opposition de leur conduite, que les baisers de leur papa et de leur maman.

Une aussi faible composition, si peu digne d'un grand théâtre, ne pouvait se distinguer que par le mérite de la danse, que par des tableaux différents et variés; rien de tout cela ne se trouve dans le nouveau ballet; à peine seroit-il digne du théâtre de la Porte Saint-Matin. Les pages dansent souvent comme des sabotiers, ou du moins ils cherchent à produire des effets en frappant du pied et en faisant raisonner le plancher du théâtre." *Journal des Théâtres, de la Littérature et des Arts*, No. 183, 19 October 1820, p. 2.

5. Virginie Dézajet (1797–1875) initiated a range of travesty roles at the Théâtre des Varietés. For thirty years she played roles as "street urchin, dandy, stevedore, duke, marquis, actor, young timid man, drummer, and even an artillery officer." ["gamin de Paris, coquette, débardeur, duc, marquis, acteur, jeune homme timide, tambour et meme officier d'artillerie."] She even played Napoléon with a huge army. From Grand-Carteret, J., *XIXê Siècle: Classes, Mœurs, Usages, Costumes, Inventions*, p. 177.

5. FUGITIVE DESIRES

1. "Art charmant! art enchanteur! que te manque-t-il pour égaler les autres arts qui empruntent souvent ton secours? le pouvoir, comme eux, de fixer et de perpéuer tes séductions. Mais, hélas! aussi fugitif que la pensée, tu n'existes qu'un moment, et un souvenir que le tems efface chaque jour, est la seule trace que tu laisses après toi." Faget, *De la Danse, et particulièrement de la danse de société*, p. 17.

2. Gautier, *La Presse*, September 11, 1837. Trans. Ivor Guest, *Gautier on Dance*, p. 16.

3. "Il arrive donc que l'homme imprudent qui s'égare à l'heure de ce bal funèbre, à l'instant où la wili est lachée, voit venir à lui une petite main qui l'invite à la danse. . . . prenez garde. Fermez les yeux! Non seulement la main est brûlante, et le sourire brûlant comme la main, mais encore le regard est mouillé et plein de feu, la taille est élancée et svelte, et l'épaule . . . rendue plus blanche et plus éclatante dans le pâle manteau de la lune—frêle dentelle découpée à toutes les feuilles de l'arbre, à tous les profils de la fleur—le moyen de résister à la wili ainsi faite, quand elle vous dit: "Veux-tu?" c'en est fait, il faut entrer dans la danse. Vous savez l'air et le refrain de cette ronde de nos beaux jours:—*Entrez dans la danse*, et le reste? O les wilis de dix-sept ans, où sont-elles! O les blanches filles de nos rondes poétiques, quand elles chantaient en dansant: -*entrez dans la danse!* et puis, misérable que je suis, je ne sais plus le reste des vers, mais cela voulait dire: *Embrassez qui vous aimerez!*" Janin, *Journal des Débats*, p. 2.

4. The work of choreographer Charles Didelot undoubtedly had a profound influence on the Romantic ballet's cultivation of flying techniques. His famous *Flore et Zéphyr* enjoyed immense popularity in Paris in the early 1800s. For a carefully researched account of his life, see Swift, *A Loftier Flight: The Life and Accomplishments of Charles-Louis Didelot, Balletmaster*.

5. For his review of *La Tarentule*, Gautier comments that what he liked about costumes was the legs visible beneath the layers of gauze, "outlined clearly and lightly like the pistils of a red flower." ["se dessiner nettes et légères comme les pistils d'une fleur rouge."] Gautier, *L'Art Dramatique*, p. 284.

6. Here I am paralleling the research conducted by Laqueur on the transition from a one-sex/two-gender model of sexual difference to a two-sex/two-gender model. Summarizing a wealth of anatomical and medical research, Laqueur argues that this fundamental change in the conception of gender occurred across the eighteenth century. See *Making Sex*, pp. 149–243.

7. See, for example, Bruyères, *La Phrenologie, le geste, et la physionomie*.

8. "Les prédispositions particulières de l'homme et de la femme sont telles, que le premier, ayant la force en partage, semble né pour commander et être obéi. Par là il doit être sujet à des passions plus violentes que la femme, qui, faible douce et soumise, ne semble créée que pour aimer et consoler, obéir et plaire. Par conséquent l'attitude de l'homme doit être noble, fière et impérieuse; sa pose pleine de fermeté, la rectitude du tronc invariable, et la position de la tête fixe; tandis que la position de la femme doit être timide, remplie de mollesse et d'agrément: tout chez elle est souplesse et ondulations gracieuses; sa tête, mollement penchée, a toute la candeur de la pose enfantine.

Dans les fonctions ordinaires de la vie, l'homme est plus froid; il est d'une sensibilité plus profonde que la femme au milieu des grandes influences; s'il emploie le geste, c'est toujours avec une supériorité d'expression et d'entraînement, surtout pour les manifestations des sentiments énérgiques. La femme, dont les idées sont plus nombreuses et plus nuancées, les mouvements plus souples et plus faibles, emploie des gestes variés et sans energie.

Dans la démarche et l'expression, l'homme, dont la taille est moins balancée et l'attitude plus ferme, se meut avec plus de force et d'aplomb que la femme; sa démarche prend un caractère de virilité et de résolution; son regard est ferme et méditatif; sa diction, énérgique, positive et régulière; sa voix, sonore, impérieuse et sans éclat. Chez la femme la démarche est légère et élégante; son regard plein de douceur, de sensualité et de finesse. Douée d'une sensibilité dont les modifications sont infinies, elle parle souvent avec excès, presque toujours d'une manière agréable; son élocution est gracieuse et brillante; sa voix, douce, flutée et claire; sa respiration, active et variée, prend un caractère particulier en conséquence des déplacements qu'elle fait éprouver aux seins."

B*** and Bell, *Histoire pittoresque des passions chez l'homme et chez la femme, et particulièrement de l'amour*, pp. 41–42.

9. "Lorsque l'on tient la tête haute, et que l'on efface les épaules, de manière que la poitrine soit toujours ouverte, on respire avec une grande facilité; les canaux n'étant obstrués par aucune courbe, et le buste étant continuellement bien tenue, les poumons se remplissent d'air aisément, et font leurs

fonctions sans obstacles." Alerme, *De la danse considérée sous le rapport de l'éducation physique*, p. 86.

10. Vigarello makes this point in *Le corps redressé*, pp. 81–154.

11. Guest describes at length the intensity of Taglioni's training regimen, which included two hours of slowly developed poses with extended balances, two hours of stretches, and two hours of work on jumping. See *The Romantic Ballet in Paris*, pp. 74–75. See also Levinson's *Marie Taglioni*. Levinson notes that her father, Filippo Taglioni, fashioned grueling regimes of daily exercises to improve her dancing in general and her pointe work in particular (p. 136). Véron compared Filippo Taglioni's approach as a teacher to that of Vestris in these terms: "Vestris taught grace, seduction; he was a sensualist. Taglioni required a gracious facility with movements, a lightness, certainly an elevation, buoyancy; but he did not permit his daughter a gesture, an attitude lacking in decency and modesty." ["Vestris enseignait la grâce, la séduction; c'était un sensualiste . . . Taglioni exigeait une gracieuse facilité de mouvements, de la légèreté, de l'élévation surtout, du ballon; mais il ne permettait pas à sa fille un geste, une attitude qui manquât de décence et de pudeur."] *Mémoires* vol. 3, p. 135.

12. The remarkable fluidity of her style and its various aspects are the subject of this review: "her talent differs from that which is dedicated to our stage, in that it offers an *impossible* assemblage of graces customary at the theater and of those that are required in the world. Her dance is all together that of the Opéra and of the ballroom. By this fusion conducted with as much art as nature, the telegraphic lines, the geometric figures disappear; no more of these laboriously voluptuous poses, no more so-called lascivious scenes, that play with a smile and the eyes; no more pointed ankles, broken wrists, detached little fingers; in a word nothing that feels like the profession's work, the job's artifices, or the school's characters. All her proportions are full of harmony; she designs, in her totality, the deliciously rounded contours or lines of admirable purity. There is in all her person a remarkable softness, in all her movements a lightness that distances her from the earth; if one could express it thus, she dances everywhere as if each of her parts was carried by wings." [". . . son talent diffère de celui qui est mécaniquement consacré sur notre scène, en ce qu'il offre l'assemblage *impossible* des grâces d'habitude au théâtre, et de celles qui sont obligées dans le monde. Sa danse est toute ensemble celle de l'Opéra et la danse des salons. Par cette fusion opérée avec autant d'art que de naturel, les lignes télégraphiques, les figures géométriques disparaissent; plus de ces poses laborieusement voluptueuses, plus de ces scènes soi-disant lascives, qui jouent avec le sourire et les yeux; plus de coudes pointus, de poignets cassés, de petits doigts détachés; en un mot, rien qui sente le travail d'une profession, les artifices d'un métier, ou les caractères d'une école. Toutes ses proportions sont pleines d'harmonie; elle dessine, dans son ensemble, des contours délicieusement arrondis ou des lignes d'une pureté admirable. Il y a dans toute sa personne une souplesse remarquable, dans tous ses mouvemens une légèreté qui l'éloigne de la terre; si l'on peut s'exprimer ainsi, elle danse de partout, comme si chacun de ses membres était porté par des ailes."] Anon., *Les Adieux à Mlle. Taglioni, suivis d'une notice biographique sur cette célèbre danseuse.*

13. Elssler developed roles as the Spanish dancer Florinda in *Le Diable boiteux* (1836), as the Chinese princess in *La Chatte métamorphosée en femme* (1837), as the Italian peasant Lauretta in *La Tarentule* (1839), and proved a great success as the dumb girl Funella in the opera *La Muette de Portici*. For details of her life, see Guest, *Fanny Elssler*.

14. An anonymous, handwritten record of exercises used in ballet classes, some with musical notation referencing the air that accompanied them, survives in the *Bibliothèque de l'Opéra* Reserve collection. The document records exercises for 1833, 1834, and 1835. The exercise routines are remarkable for the difficulty and complexity of the sequences involving substantial balances en relevé, numerous dévelopés and ronds des jambes, and large numbers of repetitions of each exercise. See a sampling of these exercises in the Appendix.

15. This discussion applies equally to the grand jeté and the sissone.

16. A close analysis of Saint-Léon's notation for the pas de deux from *Giselle* indicates to what extent the uniqueness of male and female roles had consolidated by this time. The opening consists largely of unison dancing by the male and female dancers performed on the same or on opposite sides. In the adagio the female dancer performs more dancing and is consistently in front and on pointe. For the last eleven measures, the couple performs in unison. For the coda the female dancer dances alone, and then the male dancer joins her. They perform fast circling sequences around each other alongside one another on opposite sides until the last section, which combines unison with partnered shapes. See Saint-Léon, *Pas de deux de "Giselle Sténochorégraphié.*

The *Collection des chorégraphies et musiques de divers ballets et exercises* records pas des deux from ballets, including one choreographed by Pierre Gardel for *La Vestale* (1807), one danced by Julie Aumer and Albert in *Les Pages de Duc de Vendôme* (1820), and one danced by Arthur at his debut in Munich in 1835. These three pas des deux show a steady evolution in the form toward the uniqueness of male and female roles evident in Saint-Léon's Giselle. For example, Gardel's duet consists of seven sections, each of which is performed first by the male dancer and then repeated in its entirety by the female dancer. *Les Pages* contains long sections of unison or repetition for male and female dancers but also short sections of distinctive vocabularies where the dancers perform for one another. The coda includes several sequences where either the female dancer is directed and presented by the male dancer or the partnering positions place the female dancer slightly in front of the male dancer as they perform in unison. The duet for the debut of Arthur shows a substantial divergence in vocabularies for male and female dancers. Although there is little partnering in the record for this duet, the female dancer performs smaller and more complicated footwork where the male dancer executes larger and grander steps and entrechats with multiple beats and pirouettes with three and four turns. See Appendix.

Even accounting for the discrepancies in the amount and detail of the notation, these duets demonstrate a marked increase in the amount of pointe work, in the partnering techniques, and in the discreteness of male and female vocabularies of movement.

17. Gautier wrote: ". . . and here, as on many other occasions, tribute must be paid to Petipa. How devoted he is to his dancer! How he looks after her! How he supports her! He never endeavours to attract attention to himself, he dances solely for his partner." Quoted in Guest, *The Romantic Ballet in Paris*, p. 67.

18. *La Presse*, September 11, 1837. Trans. Ivor Guest, *Gautier on Dance*, pp. 15–16.

19. "Mais ce qui rend Taglioni inimitable, c'est cette légèreté aérienne, ce fluide indéfinissable qui n'appartiennent qu'à elle; elle vous berce de poésie; c'est une ombre ossianique, une fleur balancée par le zéphyr, une idéalité, un rêve, mais un rêve réel. . . . En deux mots: les unes semblent des anges déchus, tandis que l'autre [Taglioni] est l'ange dans toute sa pureté primitive." "Mademoiselle Taglioni" in *L'Annuaire Historique et Biographique*, 1844, p. 7.

20. "Un tact délicat, une grace infinie distinguent Mlle. Noblet; sa danse est légère et correcte; sa pantomime savante et vive. Nul effort, nulle fatigue ne trahit le travail; tout au contraire cache l'art aux yeux les plus clairvoyants." "Louise Noblet—Extraits des presse, 1823–24," Folio, Collection Rondel, 11792.

21. "De tous les êtres qui ont vie sur la terre il n'y a que nous qui subissons une semblable oppression; nous ne recevons le jour que pour entrer dans une espèce de prison; mais que dis-je une prison! il n'en existe pas, je pense, qui ne laisse au malheureux qu'on y renferme la faculté de mouvoir librement." Alerme, *De la danse considérée sous le rapport de l'éducation physique*, p. 97.

22. *Cahier des charges de la Direction de l'Opéra en régie intéressée*. February 28, 1831. Reprinted in *Danseurs et Ballet de l'Opéra de Paris*, p. 42.

23. Gautier, *L'Art Dramatique*, p. 328.

24. Spanish theatre was put in crisis by the struggle for leadership that ensued after the death of King Ferdinand VII in 1833. Véron took this opportunity to import Spanish dancers, rarely ever seen abroad, to perform at the *bal masqués* held regularly at the Opéra. These dancers—Francisco Font, Mariano Camprubi, Manuela Dubinon, and Dolores Serral—also performed in *La Muette de Portici* in 1834, galvanizing a vogue for Spanish dancing that endured for several years. Dolores Serral and Manuela Dubinon were invited back two years later and again created a rage of interest. Guest, *The Romantic Ballet in Paris*, pp. 132–33 and 149. Gautier, enormously taken with the Spanish dancers, reviews them several times. He also discusses at length other types of dancers and physical acts occurring at the circuses and other minor theatres. See *L'Art Dramatique*.

25. Boigne, *Petits Mémoires de l'Opéra*, p. 132. Translated and quoted in Guest, *The Romantic Ballet in Paris*, p. 152.

26. The success of collaborations between writer Eugene Scribe and choreographer Jean Aumer, beginning with *La Somnambule* in 1827, had helped to institutionalize this new form of collaboration. Scribe introduced a new style of writing in the scenarios, more colloquial and conversational in tone when reporting individual characters' thoughts and feelings, as in this description from *La Belle au Bois Dormant, pantomime-féerie en trois actes*: "It is true that if he does not enter into the chateau, another will also marry her; and she is so pretty! Come on, take courage. . . . Why can't I be like everyone else?

He becomes excited, animated. . . . Come along, let's go . . . no, it's too powerful for me, my knees are giving way, I tremble in all my limbs. It's finished, I could never. Oh, my good angel! he cried, throwing himself to his knee, give me the courage that I lack." ["Il est vrai que s'il ne pénètre pas dans le château, un autre l'épousera aussi; et elle est si jolie! Allons, du courage. . . . Pourquoi n'en aurai-je pas comme tout le monde? Il s'excite, il s'anime. . . . Allons, partons . . . non, c'est plus fort que moi, mes genoux fléchissent, je tremble de tous mes membres. C'est fini, je ne pourrai jamais. O mon bon ange! s'écrie-t-il en se jetant à genoux, donne moi le courage qui me manque."] P. 144.

27. Véron was certainly the most effective as this type of strong-handed producer. Subsequent directors, less willing or able to exert such clear aesthetic guidance, nonetheless oversaw the collaborative process among choreographer, scene designer, composer, and costumer.

28. "C'est dans le foyer de la danse qu'ont lieu les études de pantomime pur les premiers sujets; mais les répétitions du corps de ballet, hommes et femmes, ne peuvent se fair sur le théâtre. Ces études et ces répétitions des ballets ne ressemblent guère aux répétitions du foyer du chant; ce n'est que bruit, babil, tapage, éclats de rire; aussi le maître qui commande à tout ce personnel tient-il constamment à la main un énorm bâton, dont les coups redoublés sur le plancher parviennent avec peine à rétablir le silence. . . . C'est un tableau des plus comiques et digne du pinceau d'un peintre habile et spirituel. Luxe et misère! . . . Les unes sont venues en voiture, les autres en socques; mais un esprit de fraternité règne dans ce petit monde: celle qui n'a pas le sou ne se montre pas humble, celle que le luxe environne n'est point insolente. . . .

Dans tous les coins, on grignote, on mange des bonbons et des gâteaux; quelques-unes lisent un roman de Paul de Kock ou d'Eugène Sue; de jeunes enfants parodient entre eux la scène de pantomime qui vient d'être répétée. . . .

Les premiers répétitions de ballet ne se font qu'avec un bien triste orchestre: un premier et un second violon; le soir ou dans le jour, à la lueur de deux ou trois quinquets pour éclairer tout le théâtre et la salle. Le maître de ballet et le compositeur de la musique indiquent avec grand soin les divers mouvements pour la danse et pour la pantomime. Les répétitions durent quelquefois deux ou trois heures, ce qui n'empêche ni artiste, ni figurante de prendre exactement sa leçon de danse, et souvent même de se tenir le soir sur les jambes pendant toute une représentation." Véron, *Mémoires d'un Bourgeois de Paris,* vol. 3, pp. 218–20.

29. Guest, *The Romantic Ballet in Paris,* pp. 223–24.

30. Daguerre had used the newly installed gas lighting system for the first time at the Opéra in the production of *Aladin* (1822), which enjoyed an enormous success. In April of 1827, a special committee at the Opéra formed to update practices for scenery design and construction. The committee's most influential member, Henri Duponchel, later to become director of the Opéra from 1835 to 1840 and from 1847 to 1849, initiated reforms that included bringing the front curtain down in between each act so that scenery could be more substantial and therefore more realistic. He also gave Ciceri full license to compose sets for *Robert le Diable* and *La Sylphide,* among others. For a good overview of these changes, see Guest, *The Romantic Ballet in Paris,* pp.13–15. For a more detailed discussion of the use of translucent fabrics and various other lighting and scenic effects, see Allevy, *La Mise en Scène en France dans la première moitié du dix-neuvième siècle* and Join-Diéterle, *Les Décors de Scène de l'Opéra de Paris à l'Époque Romantique.*

31. Jean Deburau, the most famous Pierrot figure of the 1820s and '30s, was taken up by the young Romantic movement and especially by critic Jules Janin as a symbol of the people. See Storey, *Pierrots on the Stage of Desire*, pp. 4–5. It is possible to see Deburau and Taglioni as embodiments in separate genres of many similar values.

32. In *L'Art Dramatique* Gautier remarks on the similarities between Elssler's performance in *La Muette de Portici* and Deburau's productions. See p. 45.

33. My analysis here draws upon and is consonant with Erik Aschengren's monograph, *The Beautiful Danger,* in which he identifies the Romantic ballet as a divertissement, but one with complex appeal. For writers and intelligentsia who never wrote about but frequently attended the ballet, it offered the most primitive expression of Romantic issues—the drama of a young man who seeks in vain for an ideal love. For the growing middle- and upper-middle-class population, Véron's emphasis on female flesh and opulent decor created a titillating spectacle. For a small number of disenfranchised artists, the ballet afforded a true escape, a haven of beauty in an otherwise alienating world.

34. Guest, *The Romantic Ballet in Paris,* p. 21.

35. In *The Romantic Ballet in Paris* Guest claims that hostility toward the male dancer ran so high that *Alfred le Grand,* a five-act heroic ballet choreographed by Aumer in 1822, was the last ballet for more than a hundred years to feature as the principal character a male hero played by a male dancer, p. 45.

36. For example, Maximilien Gardel's 1787 production, *Le Coq d'Or,* contained a scene where two men dressed as women came to blows over a young man. The *Mercure de France* critic was thoroughly entertained although admitted that the action for this scene was too exaggerated given that the two female characters commenced a fistfight which ended in their rolling in each others arms on the floor. April 14, 1787, p. 39.

37. Cross-dressed characters enhanced the opportunities for same-sex attractions. In the fêtes for Marie Antoinette's marriage, for example, women played the male roles of both Amour and Hymen. See Fromageot, "L'Opéra à Versailles en 1770 pour les fêtes du mariage de Marie Antoinette," in *Versailles Illustré,* p. 24.

38. Lynn Garafola first brought the travesty dancer to attention in her article "The Travesty Dancer in Nineteenth Century Ballet."

39. The critics seem to have been very matter-of-fact about Thérèse Elssler's performances. Janin described her as "a tall and beautiful creature with an admirably shaped leg, who will become the best male dancer at the Opéra, not excepting Perrot, over whom Thérèse has the advantage of a very delicate figure and lovely features. As a *danseuse* Mlle. Thérèse is a little tall, particularly when compared to her sister who is so tiny. . . . Without thought for herself, Thérèse has generously given Fanny the most beautiful poses and the liveliest pieces of music, she shows off her sister as much as she can, and dances herself only to give her time to recover her breath. . . . The pit . . . rapturously applauded them both, particularly at the conclusion of the pas, when the two of them link arms back to back, a very novel and lively effect." *Fanny Elssler,* pp. 67–68. Guest also quotes a review by Charles Maurice: "Mlle. Thérèse Elssler makes a fine looking Styrian man, but if the eyes are persuaded that she is a man, the heart does not want to believe it." *Fanny Elssler,* p. 68.

40. For a concise analysis of governmental and other strictures regarding the regulation of prostitution, see Corbin, "Commercial Sexuality in Nineteenth-Century France."

41. Publications that disseminated gossip about primarily female artists include the following: Second's famous *Les Petits Mystères;* Touchard-LaFosse, *Chroniques Secrètes et Galantes de l'Opéra, 1665–1845; Le foyer de l'Opéra; Le Monde d'Amour; Les Filles d'Opéra et les Vertus de Table d'Hote;* and Flaneur, *Petite Biographie Dramatique.* Remarkably, Flaneur lists names and addresses of all "nymphes de l'Académie Royale aux appointemans de 500 francs," pp.181–82. For no other group of actors or performers is this information provided. Publications intimating that the opera served as a site fostering sexual liaisons between female performers and male patrons endure from the eighteenth century as well. See chapter 2, note 24. Yet the proliferation of these texts in the 1820s, '30s, and '40s is remarkable as is their blatant expression of lascivious interest.

42. For example, *Physiologie de l'Opéra, Du carnaval, du Cancan et de la Cachucha, par un Vilain Masqué.* See also Véron's reference to the Opéra as a body for which he will provide an anatomy of its three parts, the stage, the house, and the administration. *Mémoires,* vol. 3, p. 211. Véron's commodification of the female dancer was also informed by his training in anatomy. Véron established a school for young children and attended the exams held every few months: "Nevertheless my medical studies allowed me to distinguish, more surely perhaps than other judges, those whose health, termperament, bodily proportions, fineness of attachments for the hands and feet, made them the most eligible to study the art of dance." ["Cependant mes études médicales me faisaient distinguer, plus sûrement peut-être que les autres juges, celles que leur santé, leur tempérament, les proportions de leur corps, la finesse des attaches des pieds et des mains, rendaient les plus propres à étudier l'art de la danse."] *Mémoires,* vol. 3, p. 300.

43. One of the best summaries of the claque's function comes from its leader Auguste's memoirs. See Castel, *Mémoires d'un Claqueur.* A vivid description of the claque is offered by a devotee of Taglioni: "In this room, more or less full of people, there to find a release from their labor, a recreation for the spirit, a spectacle for the eyes, emotions for the soul: there are scattered here and there; without order among the good public: beings whose job it is to chide brutally our sensations, our sentiments: through a violent call for applause. . . . They attack at the raising of the curtain, at the *entrée* of a scene." ["Dans cette salle, plus ou moins pleine du monde . . . là venu pour y trouver un délassement à des travaux, une récréation de l'esprit, un spectacle pour les yeux, des émotions pour l'âme: il y a semé ça et là; par ordre, pêle-mêle

avec ce bon public: des êtres dont l'office est de brutalement gourmander nos sensations, nos sentimens; par un appel violent à des applaudissemens. . . . Ils attaquent à un lever de rideau, à une entrée en scène."] Anon., *A mes demoiselles Taglioni et Noblet, Excuse pour une prétendue offense, ou plûtot, à cause d'un moment de déplaisir à elles involontairement causé Homage,* pp. 10–11.

44. A letter dated February 18, 1841, from students of the Royal Conservatory of Dance, claims that students would receive entirely insufficient training were they only to enroll in the three free weekly classes offered in the school curriculum. In order to study effectively, they had to pay for several additional lessons per week. See *Pétition des élèves du Conservatoire royal de Danse au Ministre de l'Intérieur,* reprinted in *Danseurs et Ballet de l'Opéra de Paris,* pp. 84–86. According to Guest, dancers were even expected to pay critics and the claque. See *Fanny Elssler,* pp. 64 and 104.

45. One anonymous samaritan writing in 1842 observes that the young women who enter the Opéra are almost always without fortune. Because they cannot possibly support themselves on the theatre salaries, they succumb to a perpetual dissipation. Only by consenting to sell themselves do they find the means to exist and to escape misery. They are usually very proud and when they reach the age of thirty have lost their beauty and enter a very sordid life. The author proposes the establishment of a foundation that would include a bank, a collective lending program, and an emergency fund for these women and their children. This institution would be funded by the state and by collections from the women themselves. *Des Femmes Élégantes, et attachées aux théâtres et d'une association mutuelle ayant pour but d'assurer leur présent et de garantir leur avenir,* pp. 10–19.

46. For crucial new insights into their daily living conditions, see Robin-Challan, "Danse et Danseuses l'envers du decor, 1830–1850."

47. "J'acquis toutefois la certitude que les ballets représentant une action dramatique ne peuvent compter sur un grand succès. . . . Les drames, les tableaux de moeurs ne sont pas du domaine de la chorégraphie; le public exige avant tout dans un ballet une musique variée et saisissante, des costumes nouveaux et curieux, une grande variété, des contrastes de décorations, des surprises, des changements à vue, une action simple, facile à comprendre, mais où la danse soit le développement naturel des situations. Il faut encore ajouter à tout cela les séductions d'une artiste jeune et belle, qui danse mieux et autrement que celles qui l'ont précédée. Quand on ne parle ni a l'esprit ni au coeur, il faut parler aux sens et surtout aux yeux." Véron, *Mémoires,* vol. 3, pp. 224–25.

48. Véron hired the highly popular orchestra conductor Musard to take charge of the public balls held at the Opéra. See Bouteron, *Danse et Musique Romantiques,* p. 65. Boigne claims that Véron was also a genius at publicity, repeatedly announcing that a production was close to its final performance. See *Petits Mémoires de l'Opéra,* p. 8.

49. Louis Véron, *Mémoires,* vol. 3, p. 300.

50. See, for example, Véron's description of final cuts and changes he made to *Robert le Diable* in his *Mémoires,* vol. 3, p. 231.

51. Guest observes that the dancers received no pension in *The Romantic Ballet in Paris,* p. 25.

52. Boigne comments on the inadequacies of Véron's system by observing that "At the Opéra advancement is not given to the most senior, but to the chosen. One does not win each rank one by one; in a single bound one seizes it, one raises the sceptre. One arrives from London, Naples, or Vienna with a name already made, sometimes with a talent too made." ["A l'Opéra l'avancement ne se donne pas à l'ancienneté, mais au choix. On ne gagne pas ses grades un à un; d'un bond on saisit, on enlève le sceptre. On arrive de Londres, de Naples ou de Vienne avec un nom tout fait, quelquefois avec un talent trop fait."] See *Petits Mémoires de l'Opéra,* p. 20.

53. Boigne, *Petits Mémoires de l'Opéra,* p. 8.

54. Véron, *Mémoires,* vol. 3, p. 232 and pp. 313–22.

55. "Les danseuses élèvent l'une après l'autre chaque jambe jusqu'à pouvoir poser le pied horizontalement sur ces rouleaux de bois et l'y laisser étendu un certain temps; puis elles quittent cette position et, saisissant d'une main un de ces rouleaux, elles s'appliquent à des battements et à des jetés-battus. Après ces exercices préliminaires, elles arrosent le parquet avec un petit arrosoir coquet; puis, se posant devant les glaces qui sont de plain-pied, elles essaient de nombreuses pirouettes, des entrechats, et répètent plus ou moins sérieusement avant de paraître en scène le pas qu'elles vont danser." This is Véron's own description of Foyer de la Danse activities from his *Mémoires,* pp. 295–96.

56. Boigne writes: The mother or sister is an essential piece of the ballerina's equipment, "a required piece of furniture like the watering can." ["un meuble de rigueur comme l'arrosoir."] *Petits Mémoires de*

l'Opéra, p. 19. The watering can was used to wet the floor so as to achieve the necessary degree of friction.

57. An in-depth study of the mirror would undoubtedly yield very interesting results. A biography of Mme. Vestris indicates that her refurbishing of Covent Garden in 1839 included a greenroom with "a full length movable swing-glass so that on entering from his dressing room an actor could see himself from head to foot at one view, and get back, front, and side views by reflection all around." Appleton, *Madame Vestris and the London Stage*, p. 124.

58. Discussions by male admirers of the ballerinas include an astonishing number of references to them as horses. Boigne's comments are representative. Horses, he claims, look good after battle but the dancer after her performance is "exhausted, breathless, almost dead, she barely holds herself up; she wheezes like a vapor machine; her face, glued on, has slackened and resembles a rainbow; her corsage is wet, soiled with sweat; her mouth grimaces, her eyes look haggard; what a spectacle!" ["Epuisée, haletante, presque morte, elle se soutient à peine; elle souffle comme une machine à vapeur; son visage, peint à la colle, a déteint et ressemble à un arc-en-ciel; son corsage est mouillé, souillé par la sueur; sa bouche grimace, ses yeux sont hagards; quel spectacle!"] P. 33.

Dancers, he continues, unlike horses, never get a vacation: "Eight days of rest condemns them to a month of forced entrechats. The dance class has replaced the inquisition, with the difference that for the class, the patients pay fifty francs a month each. The dancing master has no pity for his victims: he drives them, torments them, harasses them, scolds them. Never a moment of rest! Never an encouraging word: He commands and they obey.

"Turn out!" he shouts; and they all continue, as well as they can, shoulder to shoulder; their knees stretched and their feet on the same line.

"Split yourselves!" he adds; and you see all the feet and all the hands execute the maneuver with a perfect ensemble. It is a question, all the while holding the barre with the right hand, of placing the left foot on the same barre, and of changing, at the command, the leg and the hand; and in the middle of these tortures, one must smile." ["Huit jours de repos les condamnent à un mois d'entrechats forcés. La classe de danse a remplacé l'inquisition, avec cette différence qu'à la classe, pour se faire administrer la question, les patientes payent cinquante francs par mois et par tête. Le maître de danse est sans pitié pour ses victimes: il les presse, les tourmente, les harcèle, les gronde. Jamais un moment de repos! Jamais un mot d'encouragement: Il commande et elles obéissent.

Tournons-nous! s'écrie-t-il; et toutes de rester, tant qu'elles peuvent, talon contre talon; les genoux tendus et les pieds sur la même ligne.

Cassons-nous! ajoute-t-il; et vous voyez tous ces pieds et toutes ces mains exécuter la manœuvre avec un ensemble parfait. Il s'agit, tout en tenant la barre de la main droite, de poser le pied gauche sur la même barre, et de changer, au commandement, de pied et de main; et au milieu de ces tortures, il faut sourire."] *Petits Mémoires de l'Opéra*, p. 35.

59. Gautier, *L'Art Dramatique*, p. 330.

60. Gautier was particularly fond of breaking down the female body into parts and connecting the anatomized body to other stylistic attributes, as in this description of the Noblet sisters: "Imagine the haunches wiggling, the backs arching, the arms thrown in the air, movements the most provocatively voluptuous, a mad ardor, a diabolical warmth, a dance to wake the dead." ["Figurez-vous des frétillements de hanches, des cambrures de reins, des bras et des jambes jetés en l'air, des mouvements de la plus provoquante volupté, une ardeur enragée, un entrain diabolique, une danse à réveiller les morts."] *L'Art Dramatique*, pp. 41–42. But other critics also singled out body parts as a way of patronizing the dancer with their praise: "It is not then Mlle. Carlotta Grisi who takes something from someone, it is her ravishing legs that reclaim, wherever they find it, the good that one might have tried to take from them in making part of her fortune." ["Ce n'est donc pas Mlle. Carlotta Grisi qui prend quelque chose à quelqu'un, ce sont ses jambes ravissantes qui ressaisissent, par tout où elles le trouvent, le bien qu'on avait essayé de leur dérober en faisant partie de sa fortune."] Drouaire, "Nouvelles de Paris," *Courrier des Théâtres,* February 18, 1841, p. 2.

61. Guest, *The Romantic Ballet in Paris*, p. 21.

62. Janin, *Journal des Débats,* June 30, 1841, p. 4.

63. Brooks makes this point in analyzing Zola's characterization of women in his novel *Nana*. He writes: "Zola perceives that the logic of his various projects of seeing and knowing the woman's body requires that this body should eventually become a cult object, like any truly sacred object unknowable

but worshipped through its icons. He perceives also that in modern capitalist economies, these icons belong to the marketplace: they require expenditure. Commodities are invested with passion, and passion spends itself in purchasing commodities, acquired not from need or for their intrinsic worth or even for their social status function—as in Balzac's world—but to fill the void of erotic revery." *Body Work*, p. 154. I am arguing that the ballet vivified a similar commodification of the dancer's body as early as the 1830s.

La Sylphide

1. My analysis of *La Sylphide* has benefited enormously from the production, based on the original, staged by Pierre Lacotte that first premiered at the Paris Opéra in 1976 and was filmed for video distribution by KULTUR films international in 1982. Lacotte studied carefully all extant documents concerning the costumes, machinery, scenery, and choreography for the ballet and achieved, in my opionion, a remarkably sensitive reconstruction.

2. Beaumont, *Complete Book of Ballets*, p. 82.

La Volière, ou les Oiseaux de Boccace

1. *Journal des Débats*, May 7, 1838.

2. *Gautier on Dance*, trans. Ivor Guest, pp. 35–36.

Giselle, ou les Wilis

1. Two books about *Giselle*, historical studies occasioned by centenary performances, provide a wealth of information about this immensely popular ballet. In *Giselle: Apothéose du Ballet Romantique*, Lifar, dancer and choreographer, undertakes a detailed compositional analysis. He focuses on the resonances between movement vocabulary and character, innovations in the use of the corps de ballet and of pantomime, and the nature of the collaboration among scenarists, choreographers, and composer. In *The Ballet Called Giselle*, Beaumont, critic and aesthetician, approaches *Giselle* as an aesthetic object requiring explication and evaluation. He presents biographies of all the artists involved and a viewer's guide to the action. In addition to these texts, there is an abundance of video documentations of contemporary versions of the ballet. Among these, the production by Alicia Alonzo for the National Ballet of Cuba distinguishes itself as one of the most moving.

2. According to Guest, *Giselle* was performed 381 times between its premiere and the end of 1865. See *The Romantic Ballet in Paris*, p. 269. Critics raved about the production, noting especially Grisi's bravura performance. Writing for the *Moniteur des Theatres*, Chaudes-Aigues commented on the frequent applause that caused interruptions in the action (July 3, 1841, p. 1). Both Maurice in the *Courrier des Théâtres* (June 30, 1841) and Janin writing for the *Journal des Débats* (June 30, 1841) gave it the highest praise. One added perspective on the production comes from Maurice's review of July 1, in which the critic describes his annoyance at the machinist: "One should have thought to urge the machinist, when he is managing the contrivances, to not speak so loudly during the performance when he communicates his orders to his workers. In the land of the wilis, one probably doesn't hear words so discouraging to their illusion: 'Go! Go ahead! Softly! Leave! Again! Enough! . . .' This monologue is not part of M. de St.-Georges' program, and it goes so far as to dishonor the Opéra where formerly the machinist gave his orders by signs, handkerchief in his hand and with every precaution necessary never to make the public aware of the strings." ["On ne saurait trop engager le machiniste de l'Opéra à ménager ses *moyens*, à ne pas donner autant de voix, quand il communique, pendant les représentations, ses ordres aux subalternes. Chez les Wilis, on n'entendait probablement pas ces mots décourageans pour l'illusion: 'Allez! allez donc! doucement! partez! encore! assez! . . .' Ce monologue ne fait pas partie du

programme de M. de St.-Georges, et il va jusqu'à déshonorer l'Opéra où, jadis, le machiniste commandait par signes, le mouchoir à la main et avec toutes les précautions nécessaires pour ne jamais mettre le public dans la confidence des ficelles."] *Courrier des Théâtres,* p. 3.

3. "Ce sont des fiancées mortes avant le jour des noces; ces pauvres créatures ne peuvent demeurer tranquilles sous leur tombeau. Dans leurs coeurs éteints, dans leurs pieds morts, est resté cet amour de la danse qu'elles n'on pu satisfaire pendant leur vie, et à minuit elles se lèvent, se rassemblent en troupes sur la grande route, et malheur au jeune homme qui les rencontre: il faut qu'il danse avec elles jusqu'à ce qu'il tombe mort." Saint-Georges, Gautier, and Coralli, *Giselle, ou les Wilis,* p. 8.

4. "Elles rient avec une joie si perfide, elles vous appellent avec tant de séduction, leur air a de si douce promesses, que ces Bacchantes mortes sont irrésistibles." Saint-Georges, Gautier, and Coralli, *Giselle, ou les Wilis,* p. 8.

5. In this assertion I am following de Lauretis, who observes that the personalities and social roles allowed women in most Western cultures are as follows: "service functions within male structures, adherence to the feminine mystique of charity, sacrifice, and self-denial, and madness." *Technologies of Gender,* p. 89.

6. I am indebted to Susan Manning for this interpretation of Myrtha's role in *Giselle.* Personal communication.

CONCLUSION

1. Fokine's manifesto on the future of ballet is translated and reproduced in Cohen's *Dance as a Theatrical Art,* pp. 102–108.

BIBLIOGRAPHY

SOURCES—GENERAL

***, Marquis de. *Lettre Critique de M. le Marquis de *** A M. de Servandoni, Chevalier de l'Ordre du Christ, Peintre & Architecte du Roi & de son Académie Royale. Au sujet du Spectacle qu'il donne au Palais des Tuileries.* 1754.

A! A! A!, MM. *Traité du Mélodrame.* Paris: Delaunay, 1817.

"A Son Excellence le Ministre, Secrétaire d'Etat au département de l'Intérieur," from "Les Elèves du Conservatoire Royal de Danse." February 18, 1841. Bibliothèque de l'Opéra, Archives 19, no. 282.

A Une des Rivales de Terpsichore. London: Chez Emslay, Paris: Chez Esprit, 1775.

Abbate, Carolyn. "Opéra; or, the Envoicing of Women." In *Musicology and Difference: Gender and Sexuality in Music Scholarship,* edited by Ruth A. Solie, 225–258. Berkeley and Los Angeles: University of California Press, 1993.

Abelove, Henry. "Some Speculations on the History of Sexual Intercourse during the Long Eighteenth Century in England." *Genders* 6 (November 1989): 125–130.

"Académie Royale de Musique." Extrait de presse. June 6, 1834. Bibliothèque de l'Arsenal, Collection Rondel, 11696.

Académie Royale de Musique. Lettres et Règlements. 1781. Bibliothèque de l'Opéra, Res. 1027 (1–2).

"Académie Royale de Musique. Représentation au bénéfice de M. Gardel." *Le Figaro,* Feb. 25, 1829, p. 2.

Académie royale de musique. Sommaire général, 1785–88. Bibliothèque de l'Opéra, Res. 1025 (1).

Académie royale de musique. Sommaire général, 1788–90. Bibliothèque de l'Opéra, Res. 1025 (2).

Adice, G. Léopold. *Théorie de la gymnastique de la danse théâtrale.* Paris, Napoleon Chaix, 1859.

Les Adieux à Mlle. Taglioni, suivis d'une notice biographique sur cette célèbre danseuse. Paris: l'Imprimerie de J.-A. Boudon, 1837.

Affiches, Annonces, et Avis-Divers, no. 48, Dec. 1, 1779, p. 192.

Albert (Ferdinand Albert Decombe). *L'Art de Danser à la Ville et à la Cour, ou Nouvelle Méthode des vrais principes de la Danse Française et Etrangère; Manuel à l'usage des Maîtres à danser, des Mères de familles et Maîtresses de pension.* Paris: La Harpe, 1834.

Albert, Maurice. *Les Théâtres des Boulevards (1789–1848).* Paris: Société Françoise d'Imprimerie et de Libraire, 1902.

Albert, Victor. *Aquarelles de Victor Albert (1831–35).* Bibliothèque de l'Opéra, Res. 978.

Alderson, Evan. "Ballet as Ideology: *Giselle,* Act II." *Dance Chronicle* 10:3 (1987): 290–304.

Aldrich, Elizabeth. *From the Ballroom to Hell: Grace and Folly in Nineteenth-Century Dance.* Evanston, IL: Northwestern University Press, 1991.

Alerme, P.-E. *De la danse considérée sous le rapport de l'éducation physique.* Paris: Imprimerie de Goetschy, 1830.

Algarotti, Francesco. *Essai sur l'Opéra.* Translated from Italian into French by M.*** [F. J. de Chastellux]. Paris: Chez Rualt, 1773. Originally published as *Saggio sopra l'Opéra in musica,* 1755.

Allen, James Smith. *Popular French Romanticism: Authors, Readers, and Books in the 19th Century.* Syracuse: Syracuse University Press, 1981.

Allevy, Marie-Antoinette. *La mise en scène en France dans la première moitié du dix-neuvième siècle.* Paris: E. Droz, 1938.

Almanach du Théâtre du Palais-Royal. Paris: de l'Imprimerie de Cussac, 1791.

Almanach Forain, ou les différens Spectacles des Boulevards et des Foires de Paris. Paris: Chez Valleyre, 1773–75.

Amanton, C. N. *Notice sur Mme. Gardel.* Paris: Imprimerie de Frantin, 1835.

Amelot. *Mémoire pour servir à l'histoire de l'Académie Royale de Musique vulgairement l'Opéra depuis son établissement jusqu'en l'année 1758.* 1781.

Angiolini, Gaspare. *Dissertation sur les Ballets Pantomimes des Anciens, Pour Servir de Programme de "Semiramis."* Vienna, 1765.

Angiolini, Gasparo. *Lettere di Gasparo Angiolini a Monsieur Noverre sopra i Balli Pantomimi.* Milan, 1773.

Annuaire Dramatique [ou Étrennes Théâtrales]. Paris: Delaunay, 1805–1822.

Apelles et Campaspe—review in *L'Esprit des Journaux.* November 1776, pp. 276–78.

Apelles et Campaspe—review in *Journal des Théâtres; ou le Nouveau Spectateur.* No. XIII. October 1, 1776, pp. 292–94.

Appleton, William W. *Madame Vestris and the London Stage.* New York: Columbia University Press, 1974.

Archer, William. *Masks or Faces?* London, 1788.

Aresty, Esther B. *The Best Behavior: The Course of Good Manners—From Antiquity to the Present—As Seen through Courtesy and Etiquette Books.* New York: Simon and Schuster, 1970.

Armstrong, Nancy. *Desire and Domestic Fiction: A Political History of the Novel.* New York: Oxford University Press, 1987.

———, and Leonard Tennehouse. *The Ideology of Conduct: Essays on Literature and the History of Sexuality.* New York: Methuen, 1987.

L'Art du Comédien, vu dans ses principes. Amsterdam and Paris: Chez Caillean and La Veuve Duchesnes, 1782.

Aschengreen, Erik. "The Beautiful Danger: Facets of the Romantic Ballet." *Dance Perspectives* 58 (Summer 1974): 1–52.

Au, Susan. "The Shadow of Herself: Some Sources of Jules Perrot's *Ondine.*" *Dance Chronicle* 2, no. 3 (1978): 159–171.

Aubry, Pierre, and Émile Dacier. *"Les Caractères de la Danse," Histoire d'un Divertissement pendant la première moitié du XVIIIe siècle.* Paris: Honoré Champion, 1905.

Auerbach, Nina. *Woman and the Demon: The Life of a Victorian Myth.* Cambridge and London: Harvard University Press, 1982.

Austin, Gilbert. *Chironomia, or A Treatise on Rhetorical Delivery.* 1806. Reprint. Edited by Mary Margaret Robb and Lester Thonssen. Carbondale and Edwardsville: Southern Illinois University Press, 1966.

Ayrenhoff, Cornelius. *About the Theatrical Dances and the Ballet Masters Noverre, Muzzarelli, and Vigano.* Vienna, 1792.

B***, A., and J. Boll. *Histoire pittoresque des passions chez l'homme et chez la femme, et particulièrement de l'amour.* Paris: Imprimerie d'Alexandre Bailly, 1846.

B***. "Review of *La Dansomanie* by Pierre Gardel." *Courrier des Spectacles.* An VIII, 26 Prairal, no. 1198, p. 2.

B***. "Review of *Pygmalion* by Louis Milon." *Courrier des Spectacles* An VIII de la République, 5 Fructidor, no. 1265, p. 2; 8 Fructidor, no. 1270, p. 2; 9 Fructidor, no. 1271, pp. 2–3.

B., C.-J. *Précis historique et analytique des arts du dessin, avec sept planches; suivi d'un précis de la danse ancienne et moderne.* Paris: Chez Audot, Cherbuliez, et Olivier, 1836.

B., J. D. *Essai sur l'état actuel des Théâtres de Paris.* Paris: Chez S.-C. L'Huillier, n.d.

Babbitt, Irving. *Rousseau and Romanticism.* Boston and New York: Houghton Mifflin, 1930.

Bacon, Albert. *A Manuel of Gesture.* Chicago: S. C. Griggs and Company, 1875.

Bakhtin, Mikhail. *Rabelais and His World.* Translated by Helene Iswolsky. Bloomington: Indiana University Press, 1984.

Bal, Mieke. *Murder and Difference: Gender, Genre, and Scholarship on Sisera's Death.* Translated by Matthew Gumpert. Bloomington: Indiana University Press, 1987.

———. *Narratology: Introduction to the Theory of Narrative.* Translated by Christine van Bohecmen. Toronto: University of Toronto Press, 1985.

Ballets, Opéra, et autres ouvrages lyriques, par ordre chronologique depuis leur origine; avec une table alphabétique des ourvrages et des auteurs. Paris, 1760. Reprint. London: H. Baron, 1967.

Bals de l'opéra: costumes du quadrille historique. Paris: Rittner et Goupil, 1834.

Banes, Sally. *Greenwich Village 1963: Avant-Garde Performance and the Effervescent Body.* Durham and London: Duke University Press, 1993.

Bann, Stephen. *The Clothing of Clio*. Cambridge: Cambridge University Press, 1984.
Barbier, Patrick. *La vie quotidienne à l'Opéra au temps de Rossini et de Balzac, Paris/1800–1850*. Paris: Hachette, 1987.
Barentin, M., Avocat Général, M. Marguet, Avocat, M. de Recicourt, Procureur. *Mémoire pour Antoine-Bonnaventure Pitrot. . . .* Paris: l'Imprimerie de Ch. Et. Chenault, 1766.
———, Avocat-Général, M. Ellie de Beaumont, Avocat, M. Babaud, Procureur. *Mémoire pour demoiselle Louis Regis. . . .* Paris: l'Imprimerie de Louis Cellot, 1776.
Barish, Jonas. *The Anti-Theatrical Prejudice*. Berkeley and Los Angeles: University of California Press, 1981.
Barker, Francis. *The Tremulous Private Body: Essays on Subjection*. London: Methuen, 1984.
Baron, Auguste Alexis Floreal. *Lettres et entretiens sur la danse, ancienne, moderne, religieuse, civile, et théâtrale, accompagnés d'une lithographie chorégraphique*. Paris: Dondey-Dupré Pere et Fils, 1824.
Barrows, Susanna. *Distorting Mirrors: Visions of the Crowd in Late Nineteenth-Century France*. New Haven, CT: Yale University Press, 1981.
Barthes, Roland. *On Racine*. Translated by Richard Howard. New York: Performing Arts Journal Publications, 1983.
———. "Introduction to the Structural Analysis of Narratives." In *Image, Music, Text*. Translated by Stephen Heath. New York: Hill and Wang, 1977, 79–124.
Baschet, Roger. *Mademoiselle Dervieux, fille d'Opéra*. Paris, Flammarion, 1943.
Batteux, Charles. *Les beaux-arts réduits à un même principe*. Paris, 1746.
Baur-Heinhold, Margarete. *Baroque Theatre*. Translated by Mary Whittal. London: Thames & Hudson, 1967.
Beaumont, Cyril W. *Ballet Design Past and Present*. London: The Studio, 1946.
———. *Complete Book of Ballets: A Guide to the Principal Ballets of the Nineteenth and Twentieth Centuries*. New York: Grosset and Dunlap, 1938.
———. *The Ballet Called Giselle*. 1945. Reprint. Brooklyn: Dance Horizons, 1969.
———. *Three French Dancers of the XVIIIth Century: Camargo, Sallé, Guimard*. London: C. W. Beaumont, 1934.
Beffroy de Reigny, Louis-Abel. *Les Ailes de l'Amour*. 1786. Bibliothèque de l'Arsenal, Collection Rondel, 10180.
Bell, Charles. *Essays on the Anatomy of Expression in Painting*. London: Longman, Hurst, Rees, and Orme, 1806.
Berchoux, Joseph de. *La danse ou La Guerre des Dieux de l'Opéra*. Paris: L.-G. Michaud, 1829.
Bergman, Gösta M. "La Grande Mode des pantomimes à Paris vers 1740 et les spectacles d'optique de Servandoni." *Recherches théâtrales* 2 (1960): 71–81.
Bernardin, Napoléon-Maurice. *La Comédie Italienne en France et les théâtres de la foire et du boulevard, 1570–1791*. Paris: Éditions de la Revue Bleue, 1902.
Bernier, A. *Théorie de l'art du comédien ou manuel théâtral*. Paris, 1826.
Bertelsen, Lance. "David Garrick and English Painting." In *Eighteenth Century Studies* 11 (Spring 1978): 308–324.
Bichat, Xavier. *Physiological Researches on Life and Death*. Translated by F. Gold. Boston: Richardson and Lord, 1827. Reprinted in *Significant Contributions to the History of Psychology, 1750–1920*, edited by Daniel N. Robinson. Washington, DC: University Publications of America, 1978.
Binney, Edwin. *Glories of the Romantic Ballet*. London: Dance Books, 1985.
———. *Royal Festivals and Romantic Ballerinas, 1600–1850*. Washington, DC: Smithsonian Institution, 1971–1973.
Blair, Hugh. *Lectures on Rhetoric and Belles Lettres*. London, 1783.
Blasis, Carlo. *The Code of Terpsichore: A Practical and Historical Treatise, on the Ballet, Dancing, and Pantomime; with a Complete Theory of the Art of Dancing: Intended as Well for the Instruction of Amateurs as the Use of Professional Persons*. Translated by R. Barton, 1828. Reprint. New York: Dance Horizons, 1976.
———. *Traité Elémentaire, Théorique et Pratique de l'Art de la Danse*. Milan, 1820. Reprint. Bologna: Forni, 1969.
Blaze, François Henri Joseph (Castil-Blaze). *La danse et les ballets depuis Baccus jusqu'à Mademoiselle Taglioni*. Paris: Paulin, 1832.

Blessington, Lady Marguerite. *The Idler in Italy*. London, 1839.
Bloch, Maurice, and Jean H. Bloch. "Women and the dialectics of nature in eighteenth-century French thought." In *Nature, Culture, and Gender*, edited by Carol P. MacCormack and Marilyn Strathern. Cambridge: Cambridge University Press, 1980.
Boigne, Charles de. *Petits Mémoires de l'Opéra*. Paris, 1857.
Boisquet, François B. *Essai sur l'art du comédien chanteur . . .* Paris, 1812.
Boissy D'Anglas. *Essai sur les Fêtes Nationales suivi de quelques idées sur les arts; et sur la nécessité de les encourager, adressé à la Convention Nationale*. Paris: De l'Imprimerie Polyglotte, 1794.
Bonnet, Jacques. *Histoire Générale de la Danse*. Paris: Chez d'Houry, fils, 1724.
Bonquiot, Marc-François. *Opinion sur l'organisation des Fêtes comiques*. Paris: De l'Imprimerie Nationale, 1795.
Bouce, Paul-Gabriel, ed. *Sexuality in Eighteenth-Century Britain*. Totowa, NJ: Manchester University Press, 1982.
Boulenger de Rivery, Claude Françoise Félix. *Recherches historiques et critiques sur quelques anciens spectacles*. Paris, 1751.
Bournonville, August. *My Theatre Life*. [1848] Translated by Patricia N. McAndrew. Middletown, CT: Wesleyan University Press, 1979.
Bouteron, Marcel. *Danse et Musique Romantiques*. Paris: Le Goupy, 1927.
Boysse, Ernst. *Journal de Papillon de la Ferté, intendant et contrôleur de l'argenterie menus-plaisirs, et affaires de la chambre du roi, 1756–1780*. Paris: Paul Ollendorf, 1887.
Brazier, Nicholas. *Chroniques des Petits Théâtres de Paris, (1783–1838)*. Paris: Rouvegre et G. Blond, 1883.
Brenner, Clarence D. *The Théâtre Italien: Its Repertory, 1716–1793*. Berkeley and Los Angeles: University of California Press, 1961.
Brinson, Peter. *Background to European Ballet*. 1966. Reprint. New York: Arno Press, 1980.
Brissendon, R. F. *Virtue in Distress: Studies in the Novel of Sentiment from Richardson to Sade*. New York: Barnes and Noble, 1974.
Broadbent, R. J. *A History of Pantomime*. 1901. Reprint. New York: B. Blom, 1964.
Brockett, Oscar G. *History of the Theatre*. Boston: Allyn and Baron, 1968.
Brookner, Anita. *Jacques-Louis David*. New York: Harper and Row, 1980.
Brooks, Lynn Matluck. "Court, Church, and Province: Dancing in the Netherlands, Seventeenth and Eighteenth Centuries." *Dance Research Journal* 20, no. 1 (Summer 1988): 19–27.
Brooks, Peter. *Body Work: Objects of Desire in Modern Narrative*. Cambridge: Harvard University Press, 1993.
———. *The Melodramatic Imagination: Balzac, Henry James, Melodrama, and the Mode of Excess*. New Haven: Yale University Press, 1976.
Brown, Marilyn R. *Gypsies and Other Bohemians: The Myth of the Artist in Nineteenth-Century France*. Ann Arbor: University of Michigan Press, 1985.
Bruyères, Hippolyte. *La Phrénologie, le geste, et la physionomie*. Paris: Aubert et Cie, 1847.
Bryson, Norman. *Word and Image: French Painting of the Ancien Régime*. Cambridge: Cambridge University Press, 1981.
Bucci, Moreno. *Drawings for the Stage; Italian Set Designs from 1790 to 1860*. New York: Wheelock Whitney, 1984.
Buckle, Richard. "Monsters at Midnight." Parts 1–3. *Dance and Dancers*. 17 (April, May, June 1966): 36–38, 22–27, 22–27, respectively.
Buffon, George-Louis Leclear. *Histoire Naturelle*. 44 vols. 1749. Translated by William Smallie. London, 1785.
Bunn, Alfred. *The Stage*. London: Bentley, 1840.
Burette, Pierre Jean. *Treize mémoires sur la gymnastique des anciens: premier mémoire pour servir à l'histoire de la danse des anciens; second mémoire pour servir à l'histoire de la danse des anciens; mémoire pour servir à l'histoire de la sphéristique ou de la paume des anciens*. [s. l.] 1710. Reprinted in *Histoire de l'Académie Royale des inscriptions et belles lettres, depuis son établissement jusqu'à présent, avec les mémoires de littérature tirés des registres de cette Académie, depuis son renouvellement jusqu'en M. DCCX*. Paris: Imprimerie royale, 1761, pp. 93–116, 117–135, 153–177.
Burnim, Kalman A. *David Garrick, Director*. Pittsburgh: University of Pittsburgh Press, 1961.

Bushaway, Bob. *By Rite: Custom, Ceremony and Community in England, 1700–1880*. London: Junction Books, 1982.
Buteux, Charles-Joseph. *Précis historique et analytique des arts du dessin, avec sept planches; suivi d'un précis de la danse ancienne et moderne*. Paris: Chez Audot; Cherbuliez; or Ollivier, 1836.
Cabinet des Modes. 4 vols. Paris: Chez Buisson, 1785–1789.
La Cacophonie, ou projets relatifs au lustre de l'Opéra. 1767. Bibliothèque de l'Opéra.
Cahusac, Louis de. *La danse ancienne et moderne ou traité historique de la danse*. 3 vols. The Hague, 1754.
Camper, Petrus. *The Works of the late Professor Camper, on the Connexion between the Science of Anatomy and the Arts of Drawing, Painting, Statuary . . .* Translated by Dr. T. Cogan. London: C. Dilly, 1794.
Capon, G., and R. Yve-Plessis. *Fille d'Opéra, vendeuse d'amour. Histoire de Mlle. Deschamps (1730–1764)*. Paris: Plessis, 1906.
Capon, Gaston, and R. Yve-Plessis. *Paris galant au dix-huitième siècle: les théâtres clandestins au XVIII siècle*. Paris: Plessis, 1905.
Capon, Gaston. *Les Vestris, le 'diou' de la danse et sa famille, 1730–1808, d'après des rapports de police et des documents inédits*. Paris: Société de Mercure de France, 1908.
Carlson, Marvin. *The French Stage in the Nineteenth Century*. Metuchen, NJ: Scarecrow Press, 1972.
———. *The Theatre of the French Revolution*. Ithaca: Cornell University Press, 1966.
Carsillier, M., and M. Guiet. *Mémoire pour le Sieur Blanchard, Architecte, Juré-Expert*. Paris: l'Imprimerie L. Cellot, 1760.
———. *Mémoire pour le Sieur Blanchard Architecte, Juré-Expert*. Paris: l'Imprimerie L. Cellot, 1760.
Casanova de Seingalt, Jacques. *Histoire de ma vie*. 12 vols. in 6 port. Wiesbaden: F. A. Brockhaus, 1960.
Castel, Louis (Robert). *Mémoires d'un Claqueur, Contenant la théorie et la pratique de l'art des succès; des jugements sur la talent de plusieurs auteurs, acteurs, actrices, danseurs, danseuses, et un très-grand nombre d'anecdotes historiques toutes inédites*. Paris: Constant-Chantpie, 1829.
Castle, Terry. *Masquerade and Civilization: The Carnivalesque in Eighteenth-Century English Culture and Fiction*. Stanford: Stanford University Press, 1986.
Challamel, Augustin. *Album de l'Opéra*. Paris: Ducessois, 1845.
Chapman, John. "An Unromantic View of Nineteenth Century Romanticism." *York Dance Review* 7 (Spring 1978): 28–40.
Chapman, John V. "Auguste Vestris and the Expansion of Technique." *Dance Research Journal* 19, no. 1 (Summer 1987): 11–17.
Charlemagne, Armand. *Le Mélodrame aux Boulevards: Facétie Littéraire, Historique et Dramatique*. Paris: l'Imprimerie de la rue Beaurepaire, 1809.
Chaudes-Aigues, J. "Review of *Giselle*." *Moniteur des Théâtres*, July 3, 1841, p. 1.
Chavanne, J. M. de. *Principes du menuet et des révérences, nécessaires à la jeunesse de savoir, pour se présenter dans le grand monde*. Luxembourg: les Héritiers d'André Chevalier, 1767.
Chazin-Bennahum, Judith. *Dance in the Shadow of the Guillotine*. Carbondale and Edwardsville: Southern Illinois University Press, 1988.
———. "*Livrets* of Ballets and Pantomimes during the French Revolution (1787–1801)." Ph.D. diss., University of New Mexico, 1981.
Chenier, M. J. *Essai sur les Principes des Arts*. 1818.
Chesterfield, Philip Dormer Stanhope. *Lord Chesterfield's Advice to his Son*. London, 1774.
Chevrier, M. de (François Antoine de). *Observations sur le théâtre dans lesquelles on examine avec impartialité l'état actuel des Spectacles de Paris*. Paris: De Bure le Jeune, 1755.
Chorégraphie de divers ballets. N.p., n.d. Bibliothèque de l'Opéra, C515.
Christout, Marie Françoise. *Le merveilleux et le "théâtre du silence."* Paris: Editions Mouton, 1965.
Chroniques de l'Académie Royale de Musique, 1836–1838. 3 vols. Bibliothèque de l'Opéra, Res. 658.
Ciceri, Pierre-Luc-Charles. *Album des Dessins*. Bibliothèque de l'Opéra, Res. 1018.
Clairon, Hyppolite. *Mémoires d'Hyppolite Clairon et réflexions sur l'art dramatique*. Paris, 1799.
Clark, Timothy J. *The Absolute Bourgeois: Artists and Politics in France, 1848–51*. London: Thames and Hudson, 1973.
———. *Image of the People: Gustave Courbet and the 1848 Revolution*. Princeton: Princeton University Press, 1982.

Clément, Catherine. *Opera, or the Undoing of Women*. Translated by Betsy Wing. Minneapolis: University of Minnesota Press, 1988.

Clément, Charles François. *Principes de Corégraphie [sic], ou l'Art d'Écrire et de Lire la Danse par Caractères Demonstratifs*, Paris: Chez Denis, 1771.

Clement, Nemours Honoré. *Romanticism in France*. New York: The Modern Language Association of America, 1939.

Cobban, Alfred. *A History of Modern France: Volume Two: From the First Empire to the Second Empire, 1799–1871*. 2nd ed. London: Penguin, 1965.

Le Code Lyrique, ou Règlement pour l'Opéra de Paris. Utopie: Chez Thomas Morus, 1743.

Collection de Costumes. réunissant la Ressemblance and la Physionomie Théâtrale des Acteurs du spectacle de la rue Feydeau. Paris: Chez Huet. Bibliothèque de l'Opéra, Res. 967.

Collection des chorégraphies et musiques de divers ballets et exercises. N.p., n.d. Bibliothèque de l'Opéra, Res. 1140.

Compan, Charles. *Dictionnaire de danse*. Paris: Chez Cailleau, 1787.

Compardon, Émile. *L'Académie royale de musique au XVIIIe siècle*. 2 vols. Reprint. New York: DaCapo Press, 1971.

———. *Les spectacles de la foire*. Paris: Berger-Levrault et Cie, 1877.

Condillac, Etienne Bonnot de. *Oeuvres philosophiques*. Paris: Presses universitaires de France, 1947–52.

———. *Traité de Sensations*. 2 vols. London and Paris, 1754.

Condorcet, Jean-Antoine-Nicolas de Caritat, marquis de. *Condorcet: Selected Writings*. Edited by Keith Michael Baker. Indianapolis: Bobbs-Merrill, 1976.

La Confédération Nationale. Détail exact de cette fête, et de tout ce qui s'est passé dans la journée mémorable du 14 Juillet 1790. Paris: De l'Imprimerie de Caillot et Courgier, 1790.

Constitution du Patriarche de l'Opéra. Cytheropolis, 1754.

Cooter, Roger. "The Power of the Body: The Early Nineteenth Century." In *Natural Order: Historical Studies of Scientific Culture*, edited by Barry Barnes and Steven Shapin, 73–92. Beverly Hills, CA: Sage Publications, 1979.

Cope, Jackson I. *Dramaturgy of the Demonic: Studies in Antigeneric Theater from Ruzante to Grimaldi*. Baltimore: Johns Hopkins University Press, 1984.

Corbin, Alain. "Commercial Sexuality in Nineteenth-Century France: A System of Images and Regulations." In *The Making of the Modern Body: Sexuality and Society in the Nineteenth Century*, edited by Catherine Gallagher and Thomas Laqueur, 209–219. Berkeley and Los Angeles: University of California Press, 1987.

———. *The Foul and the Fragrant: Odor and the French Social Imagination*. Cambridge: Harvard University Press, 1986.

———. *Women for Hire: Prostitution and Sexuality in France after 1850*. Cambridge: Harvard University Press, 1990.

Cordova, Sarah Penelope Davies. "Poetics of Dance: Narrative Designs from Staël to Maupassant." Ph.D. diss., University of California, Los Angeles, 1993.

Cornu, Paul. *Gallerie des Modes et Costumes Français dessinés d'après nature, 1778–1787*. 3 vols. Paris: Libraire Centrale des Beaux-Arts, n.d.

Costumes et Annales des Grands Théâtres de Paris, accompagnés de notices intéressantes et curieuses. Paris: Couturier, 1786.

Cournand, Gilberte. *Beauté de la Danse*. Paris: Gautier-Languereau, 1977.

Courtois, Clément. *L'Opinion du Parterre ou Censure des Acteurs, auteurs et spectateurs du Théâtre Français*. Paris: Chez Martinet, 1840.

Creech, James. *Diderot, Thresholds of Représentation*. Columbus: Ohio State University, 1986.

Crompton, Louis. *Byron and Greek Love: Homophobia in 19th Century England*. Berkeley and Los Angeles: University of California Press, 1985.

Crow, Thomas E. *Painters and Public Life in Eighteenth-Century Paris*. New Haven: Yale University Press, 1985.

Dacier, Émile. *Les Dernières années d'une Danseuse du XVIIIe Siècle*. Paris: Société de l'Histoire de Paris, 1907.

———. *Une Danseuse de l'Opéra sous Louis XV: Mlle. Sallé (1707–1756)*. Paris: Plon-Nourrit et Cie, 1909.

Daniels, Barry, W. *Revolution in the Theatre: French Romantic Theories of Drama*. Westport, CT: Greenwood Press, 1983.

"La Danse à l'Opéra, comment on devient danseuse." N.d. Bibliothèque de l'Arsenal, Collection Rondel 9975.

Danseurs et Ballet de l'Opéra de Paris: depuis 1671. Paris: Archives Nationales et Bibliothèque Nationale, 1988.

Darnton, Robert. *Mesmerism and the End of the Enlightenment in France*. Cambridge: Harvard University Press, 1968.

———. *The Great Cat Massacre and Other Episodes in French Cultural History*. New York: Basic Books, 1984.

Darwin, Charles. *Expression of the Emotions in Man and Animals*. Chicago: University of Chicago Press, 1965.

David, Jacques Louis. *Rapport et Décret sur la Fête de la Réunion républicaine du 10 Août*. Paris: De l'Imprimerie Nationale, 1793.

Davies, Thomas. *Memoirs of the life of David Garrick, esq., interspersed with characters and anecdotes of his theatrical contemporaries*. Boston: Wells and Lilly, 1818.

Davis, Natalie Zemon. *Society and Culture in Early Modern France*. Stanford: Stanford University Press, 1975.

Davis, Tracy C. "The Spectacle of Absent Costume: Nudity on the Victorian Stage." *New Theatre Quarterly* 20 (November 1989): 321–333.

Dawson, Robert L. "The *Mélange de poésies diverses* (1781) and the Diffusion of Manuscript Pornography in Eighteenth-Century France." In *'Tis Nature's Fault: Unauthorized Sexuality during the Enlightenment*, edited by Robert Parks Maccubbin, 229–39. Cambridge: Cambridge University Press, 1987.

De la Boullaye, Ferdinand. "Notice Biographique. Mme Carlotta Grisi (Perrot)." *L'Independant*, July 7, 1841, p. 1.

de Lauretis, Teresa. *Alice Doesn't: Feminism, Semiotics, Cinema*. Bloomington: Indiana University Press, 1984.

———. *Technologies of Gender: Essays on Theory, Film, and Fiction*. Bloomington: Indiana University Press, 1987.

Deburau, Jean Gaspard. *Pantomimes de Gaspard et Ch. Deburau*. Paris: E. Dentu, 1889.

Delaforest, M. A. *Théâtre moderne*. Paris, 1836.

Delon, Michel. *The Priest, The Philosopher, and Homosexuality in Enlightenment France*. Translated by Nelly Stéphane. In *'Tis Nature's Fault: Unauthorized Sexuality during the Enlightenment*, edited by Robert Parks Maccubbin, 122–131. Cambridge: Cambridge University Press, 1987.

Demuth, Norman. *French Opéra: Its Development to the Revolution*. Sussex, UK: Artemis Press, 1963.

Des Essarts, Nicolas Toussaint Lemoine. *Les trois théâtres de Paris ou abrégé historique de l'établissement de la Comédie Françoise, de la Comédie Italienne & de l'Opéra* . . . Paris: Lacombe, 1777.

Deshayes, André. *Idées Générales sur l'Académie Royale de Musique, et plus spécialement sur la Danse*. Paris: Chez Mongie, 1822.

Despréaux, Jean-Étienne. *Mes Passe-Temps: Chansons suivis de l'Art de la Danse, Poëme en Quatre Chants, Calqué sur l'Art poétique de Boileau Despréau*. Vol. 2. Paris: Imprimerie Crapelet, 1806.

Desprèz de Boissy, Charles. *Lettres de M. Desp. de B*, Avocat au Parlement, sur les Spectacles; avec une histoire des ouvrages pour & contre les théâtres*. 4th ed. Paris, 1771.

Desrat, G. *Traité de la danse contenant la théorie des danses françaises & étrangères, anciennes et modernes, le cotillon & des figures*. Paris: Delaru, 1865.

Dessins de décorations de Théâtre. Bibliothèque de l'Opéra, Res. 517.

Dessins du décor du théâtre. Bibliothèque de l'Opéra, Res. 914.

Détail de la Véritable Marche des Cérémonies et de l'Ordre A Observer dans la Fête à l'Être Suprême. Paris: Imprimé par Ordre de la Convention Nationale, 1794.

Détails des Cérémonies faites à l'Ouverture des Etats-Généraux. N.p., n.d.

Détails des Cérémonies, Jeux, Courses de Bateaux, Joutes, Spectacles, Concerts, Illuminations et Danses. Paris: de l'Imprimerie du Dépôt, 1801.

Les Deux Créoles—review in *Courrier des Spectacles, Journal des Théâtres et de Littérature. June 30, 1806, p. 2.*

Devéria, Achille. *Costumes historiques de ville ou de théâtre et travestissemens*. Paris: l'Imprimerie Lith. de Cattier, n.d.

Diderot, Denis. *Diderot's Writings on the Theatre*. Edited by F. C. Green. Cambridge: Cambridge University Press, 1936.

———. *Discours de la Poésie dramatique*. Paris: Larousse, 1970.
———. "Lettre sur les sourds et muets." [1751]. In *Oeuvres Complètes de Diderot,* edited by J. Assézat. Paris: Garnier Frères, 1875.
———. *Lettres à Sophie Volland.* Edited by A. Babelon. Paris: Gallimard, 1938.
———. *Paradoxe sur le comédien* (c. 1780). Paris: Garnier-Flammarion, 1958.
Didier B***. *Réflexions sur la Festomanie, qui nous a été laissée en partant, par Robespierre, Chaumette, Pache, Payan, Saint-Just, Hebert, et autres philosophes de la même volée.* Paris: l'Imprimerie de Boulard, n.d.
Dollet, Lacauchie, and Lassalle. *Galerie Dramatique; Costumes des Théâtres de Paris.* 10 vols. Paris: Maison Martinet, 1844–1853.
Dorat, Claude Joseph. *L'art de la déclamation théâtrale, précédé d'un discours et de notions historiques sur la danse.* Paris: Imprimerie de S. Jorry, 1766.
"Les Drames dansants." In *Le Radoteur.* Vol. 2: 3–19. Paris: Chez J.-Fr. Bastien, 1776.
Le Drapeau Blanc. 20 October, 1820. No. 294, p. 2.
Drouaire. "Nouvelles de Paris." *Courrier des Théâtres,* Feb. 18, 1841.
Du Bos, Jean Baptiste. *Réflexions critiques sur la poésie et sur la peinture.* 2 vols. Paris: Jean Mariette, 1719.
Du Faget. *Costumes pour l'Opéra, Gaité, Théâtre Français, St. Martin, 1823–1838.* 2 vols. N.p., n.d. Bibliothèque de l'Opéra, Res. 216.
DuBois, Albert. *Une Page de la vie d'une danseuse française au XVIIIe siècle. (Mlle. Théodore*). Bruxelles: P. Weissenbruch, 1896.
Duden, Barbara. *The Woman Beneath the Skin: A Doctor's Patients in Eighteenth-Century Germany.* Translated by Thomas Dunlap. Cambridge: Harvard University Press, 1991.
DuFresnel. *Essai sur la perfection du jeu théâtral contenant les principes nécessaires à la bonne représentation théâtrale.* Liege, 1782.
Dumesnil, Marie-Françoise. *Mémoires de Marie-Françoise Dumesnil, en réponse aux mémoires d'Hyppolite Clairon.* Paris: Chez Dentu, 1796.
Dumont, Gabriel Pierre Martin. *Parallèle de Plans des plus Belles Salles de Spectacles D'Italie et de France, avec des Détails des Machines Théâtrales.* Paris, 1774. Reprint. New York: Benjamin Blom, 1968.
Duplain. *Guimard, ou l'Art de la Danse-Pantomime, Poème.* Paris: Chez Merigot, 1783.
Duthé, Rosalie. *Souvenirs de Mlle. Duthé de l'Opéra.* Paris: Louis-Michard, n.d.
Elias, Norbert. *The Civilizing Process: The History of Manners.* Translated by Edmund Jephcott. New York: Urizen Books, 1978.
Elshtain, Jean. *Public Man, Private Woman: Women in Social and Political Thought.* Princeton, NJ: Princeton University Press, 1981.
Encore 7 millions pour le grand opéra? Ça ne prendra pas: Rendez la salle à Montansier. Paris: l'Imprimerie de la Vérité, 1794.
Encyclopédie; ou Dictionnaire raisonné des sciences, des arts et des métiers, par une société de gens de lettres. Edited by Denis Diderot. 17 vols. Paris, 1751–65.
Engel, Johann-Jakob. *Idées sur le geste et l'action théâtrale.* French translation by H. Jensen. 2 vols. Paris: Barrois l'âiné, 1788–89.
Entretiens sur l'État Actuel de l'Opéra de Paris. Amsterdam and Paris: Chez Esprit, 1779.
L'Esprit des Journaux. November 1776, pp. 276–278.
L'Esprit des Journaux. August 1779, pp. 292–294.
Essai sur l'état actuel des Théâtres de Paris . . . Par J. D. B. Paris: Chez S.- C. L'Huillier, 1813.
Etat actuel de la musique du roi et des trois spectacles de Paris. Paris: Chez Vente, Libraire, 1771.
Etiennez, Hippolyte. "Histoire de la danse." *Musée des Familles,* vol. 13. Part I—November 1845, pp. 41–48; Part II—February 1846, pp. 136–142; Part III—June 1846, pp. 280–287; Part IV—August 1846, pp. 315–319.
Examen des causes destructives du Théâtre de l'Opéra, et des moyens qu'on pourroit employer pour le rétablir; ouvrage spéculatif, par un Amateur de l'Harmonie. London and Paris: La Veuve Duchesne, 1776.
Faget, Jean. *De la Danse, et particulièrement de la danse de société.* Paris: l'Imprimerie de Pillet, 1825.
Falvey, John. "Women and Sexuality in the Thought of La Mettrie." In *Woman and Society in Eighteenth-Century France,* edited by Eva Jacobs and others, 55–68. London: Athlone Press, 1979.

Favart, Charles S. *Mémoires et Correspondences Littéraires, dramatiques et anecdotiques*. 3 vols. Paris: Chez Léopold Collin, 1808.

Fayolle, M. *Sur les Drames Lyriques, et leur exécution*. Paris: De l'Imprimerie de J. B. Sajon, 1813.

Des Femmes Élégantes; et attachées aux théâtres et d'une association mutuelle ayant pour but d'assurer leur présent et de garantir leur avenir. Paris: Chez l'Éditeur, Quai des Augustins, 49, 1842.

Fénelon, François de Salignac de la Mothe. *Dialogues sur l'Eloquence*. Paris, 1718.

Ferrêre, Auguste Frederic Joseph. *Partition et Chorégraphie*. Valencienne, 1782.

Les Filles d'Opéra et les Virtuoses de Table d'Hote. Paris: J. Labitte, 1846.

Fletcher, Angus. *Allegory: Theory of a Symbolic Mode*. Ithaca, NY: Cornell University Press, 1964.

Flourens, Pierre. *Phrenology Examined*. Translated by Charles de Lucena Meigs. Philadelphia: Hogan & Thompson, 1846. Reprinted in *Significant Contributions to the History of Psychology, 1750–1920*, edited by Daniel N. Robinson. Washington, DC: University Publications of America, 1978.

Foote, Samuel. *A Treatise on the Passions, so far as they regard the Stage*. London: C. Corbett, 1747.

Foster, Susan Leigh. *Reading Dancing: Bodies and Subjects in Contemporary American Dance*. Berkeley: University of California Press, 1986.

———. "Choreographing History." In *Choreographing History*, edited by Susan Leigh Foster, 3–21. Bloomington: Indiana University Press, 1995.

———. "Textual Evidances." In *Bodies of the Text*, edited by Ellen Goellner and Jacqueline Shea Murphy, 231–246. New Brunswick: Rutgers University Press, 1995.

Foucault, Michel. *Discipline and Punish*. Translated by Alan Sheridan. New York: Vintage Books, 1979.

———. *The Birth of the Clinic: An Archaeology of Medical Perception*. Translated by A. M. Sheridan Smith. New York: Pantheon, 1973.

———. "Of Other Spaces." *Diacritics* (Spring 1986): 22–27.

———. *The History of Sexuality: Volume 1: An Introduction*. Translated by Robert Hurley. New York: Vintage, 1980.

———. *The Order of Things: An Archaeology of the Human Sciences*. New York: Vintage, 1970.

———. *The Use of Pleasure: Volume 2 of The History of Sexuality*. Translated by Robert Hurley. New York: Vintage, 1985.

Le Foyer de l'Opéra. Paris: Hippolyte Sourverain, 1842.

France, Peter, and Margaret McGowen. "Auteur du *Traité du récitatif* de Grimarest." *XVIIe Siècle* 132 (1981): 303–317.

Franko, Mark. *Dance as Text: Ideologies of the Baroque Body*. Cambridge: Cambridge University Press, 1993.

Fried, Michael. *Absorption and Theatricality: Painting and Beholder in the Age of Diderot*. Berkeley and Los Angeles: University of California Press, 1980.

Fromageot, Paul. "L'Opéra à Versailles en 1770 pour les fêtes du marriage de Marie Antoinette." In *Versailles Illustré*, 1–33. Versailles: Imprimerie Aubort, 1902.

Fulcher, Jane F. *The Nation's Image: French Grand Opéra as Politics and Politicized Art*. Cambridge: Cambridge University Press, 1987.

Furst, Lilian R. *Romanticism in Perspective: A Comparative Study of Aspects of the Romantic Movements in England, France, and Germany*. New York: St. Martin's Press, 1969.

Galerie Théâtrale. Collection de 144 Portraits en Pied des Principaux acteurs et actrices. 2 vols. Paris: Chez Barraud, 1872.

Gallagher, Catherine. "The Body Versus the Social Body in the Works of Thomas Malthus and Henry Mayhew." In *The Making of the Modern Body: Sexuality and Society in the Nineteenth Century*, edited by Catherine Gallagher and Thomas Laqueur, 83–106. Berkeley and Los Angeles: University of California Press, 1987.

———, and Thomas Laqueur, eds. *The Making of the Modern Body: Sexuality and Society in the Nineteenth Century*. Berkeley and Los Angeles: University of California Press, 1987.

Gallini, Giovanni-Andrea Battista. *A Treatise on the Art of Dancing*. London: Printed for the Author and sold by R. and J. Dodsley, T. Becket, and W. Nicholl, 1762.

———. *Critical Observations on the Art of Dancing*. London: R. Dodsley, 1770.

Galuppi, Giovanni. *Alla celebratissima danzatrice Fanny Cerito*. Rome, 1843.

Garafola, Lynn. *Diaghilev's Ballets Russes*. New York: Oxford University Press, 1989.

———. "The Travesty Dancer in Nineteenth Century Ballet." *Dance Research Journal* 17, no. 2; and 18, no. 1 (Fall–Spring 1985–86): 35–40.

Gardel, Pierre Gabriel. *Court ballet under Napoleon Bonaparte, (1806–1811).* New York Public Library of the Performing Arts at Lincoln Center. Dance Collection.

———. "Dossier artiste." Bibliothèque de l'Opéra.

Garrick, David. *An Essay on Acting.* London, 1744.

———. *The Journal of David Garrick, describing his visit to France and Italy in 1763 . . .* New York: Modern Language Association, 1939.

Gauthier, François Louis. *Traité contre les danses et les mauvaises chansons; dans lequel le danger & le mal qui y sont renfermés sont démontrés par les Témoignages multipliés des saintes Ecritures, des SS. PP. des Conciles, de plusieurs Evêques du siècle passé & du nôtre, d'un nombre de Théologiens moraux & de Casuistes, de Juris consultés, de plusieurs Ministres Protestans, & enfin des Païens même.* Paris: Chez Antoine Bondet, 1769.

Gautier, Théophile. *Les Beautés de l'Opéra.* Paris: Soulié, 1845.

———. *Gautier on Dance.* Edited and translated by Ivor Guest. London: Dance Books, 1986.

———. *Mademoiselle de Maupin.* Translated by Joanna Richardson. New York: Boni and Liveright, [1918].

———. *The Romantic Ballet as Seen by Théophile Gautier.* Translated by Cyril W. Beaumont. London: C. W. Beaumont, 1932.

———. *Théâtre: mystère, comédies et ballets.* Paris, 1872.

———. *Histoire de l'art dramatique en France depuis vingt-cinq ans.* Leipzig: 1858–59.

Gelfand, Toby. *Professionalizing Modern Medicine: Paris Surgeons and Medical Science and Institutions in the Eighteenth Century.* Westport, CT: Greenwood Press, 1980.

Genest, Émile. *l'Opéra Connu et Inconnu.* Paris: E. de Boccard, 1920.

Genlis, Stéphanie Félicité Ducrest de Saint Aubin, comtesse de. *Dictionnaire critique et raisonné des etiquettes de la cour.* 2 vols. Paris: P. Mongie, 1818.

Geoffroy. *Journal de l'Empire.* July 4, 1806, pp. 1–2.

George, David J., and Christopher J. Gossip. *Studies in the Commedia Dell'Arte.* Cardiff: University of Wales Press, 1993.

Gerard, Kent, and Gert Hekma, eds. *The Pursuit of Sodomy: Male Homosexuality in Renaissance and Enlightenment Europe.* New York: Harrington Park Press, 1989.

Gilbert. *Histoire du théâtre de l'Académie de Musique en France, depuis son établissement jusqu'à présent.* 2nd ed. 2 vols. Paris: Chez Duchesnes, 1757.

Gillot, Claude. *Nouveaux desseins d'habillements à l'usage des Balets, Opéras, et Comédies.* Paris: Duchange, n.d.

Ginisty, Paul. *Le Théâtre des Rois.* Paris: Société des Éditions Louis-Michaud, n.d.

———. *Le Théâtre romantique,* Paris: Morance, 1922.

Giraudet, A. *Mimique, Physionomie, et Gestes; méthode pratique d'apres le système de F. Del Sarte pour servir à l'expression des sentiments.* Paris: Ancienne Maison Quantin Librairies-Imprimeries Réunis, 1895.

Goldberg, Rita. *Sex and Enlightenment: Women in Richardson and Diderot.* Cambridge: Cambridge University Press, 1984.

Golding, Alfred Siemon. *Classicistic Acting: Two Centuries of a Performance Tradition at the Amsterdam Schouwburg to Which Is Appended an Annotated Translation of the "Lesson on the Principles of Gesticulation and Mimic Expression of Johannes Jelgerhuis, Rz.* Lanham, MD: University Press of America, 1984.

Goncourt, Edmond de. *Histoire de Marie-Antoinette.* New ed. Paris: Charpentier, 1879.

———. *La Guimard, d'après les registres des menus-plaisirs de la Bibliothèque de l'Opéra. . . .* Paris: Charpentier & Fasquelle, 1893.

———. *L'Amour au dix-huitième siècle.* Paris, 1875.

———. *La Femme au dix-huitième siècle.* Paris: E. Flammarion, 1923.

Gonzague, Pierre Gothard. *Information à mon Chef, ou éclaircissement convenable du décorateur-théâtral.* St. Petersburg: L'Imprimerie d'Alex Pluchart, 1807.

Good, Kathleen F. "Truth and Signification in Marivaux's 'Monde Vrai.'" *Eighteenth-Century Studies* 19, no. 3 (Spring 1986): 355–372.

Goodden, Angelica. *Actio and Persuasion: Dramatic Performance in Eighteenth-Century France.* Oxford: Clarendon Press, 1986.

———. "The Dramatising of Politics: Theatricality and the Revolutionary Assemblies." *FMLS* 20 (1984): 193–212.
Goudar, Ange. *De Venise—Remarques sur la Musique et la Danse*. Venise: Chez Charles Palese, 1773.
———. *Lettres sur l'état présent de nos spectacles, avec des vues nouvelles sur chacun d'eux; particulièrement sur la Comédie Françoise & l'Opéra*. Amsterdam, 1765. Paris: Chez Duchesne, 1765.
———. *Observations sur les trois derniers ballets pantomime qui ont paru aux Italiens & aux François: sçavoir, Télémaque, Le sultan généreux, la mort d'Orphée*. 1759.
———. *Suplément aux Remarques sur la musique, et la danse ou lettres de M. G*** à Milord Pembroke*. Venise: Chez Charles Palese, 1773.
Goudar, Sara. *Remarques sur les anecdotes de Madame la Comtesse DuBarri*. London, 1777.
———. *Oeuvres Mélées de Madame Sara Goudar, Angloise, Divisées en deux tomes. Tome premier: lettres sur les divertissements du Carnaval de Naples et de Florence. Tome second: Remarques sur la Musique Italienne et sur la Danse à Monsieur Pembroke*. Amsterdam, 1777.
Gouges, Olympe de. "Declaration of the Rights of Woman and Citizen in 1791." In *Women, the Family and Freedom: The Debate in Documents, Vol. 1, 1750–1880*, edited by Susan Bell and Karen Offen. Stanford: Stanford University Press, 1983, pp. 104–111.
Gourdoux, J. H. *Principes et notions élémentaires sur l'art de la danse pour la ville, suivi des manières de civilité qui sont les attributions de cet art*. Paris: Dondey-Dupré, 1811.
Gourdoux-Daux, J. H. *De l'Art de la danse considéré dans ses vrais rapports avec l'éducation de la jeunesse*. Paris: Dondey-Dupré, 1823.
Goux, Jean Joseph. *Symbolic Economies: After Marx and Freud*. Trans. Jennifer Curtis Gage. Ithaca: Cornell University Press, 1989.
Grand Détail. De l'Ordre & la Marche, avec toutes les Cérémonies qui doivent être observées demain dans la Ville de Paris, pour la Proclamation de l'Acte Constitutionnel, & la Fête publique décrétée par l'Assemblée Nationale, ainsi que le "Te Deum" qui sera chanté en l'Eglise de Notre-Dame, où Le Roi, la Reine & la Famille Royalle assisteront. Paris: Limodin, 1790.
Grand-Carteret, J. *XIXe Siècle: Classes, Moeurs, Usage, Costumes, Inventions*. Paris: Librarie de Firmin-Didot et Cie, 1893.
Grasset de Saint-Sauveur, J. *Costumes des représentations du peuple*. Paris: Chez Deroy, 1795.
Griffiths, Bruce. "Sunset: From *commedia dell'arte* to *comédia italienne*." In *Studies in the Commedia Dell'Arte*, edited by David J. George and Christopher J. Gossip, 91–105. Cardiff: University of Wales Press, 1993.
Grimarest, Jean Léonor le Gallois de. *La vie de M. de Molière*. Geneva: Slatkine Reprints, 1973.
Grimm, Fréderic Melchior. *Correspondance littéraire, philosphique et critique addresée à un souverain d'Allemagne*. 16 vols. Paris: Garnier frères, 1877–1882.
Gros de Besplas, Joseph-Marie. *Essai sur l'Eloquence de la Chaire*. Paris: Vallet la Chappelle, 1767.
Gruber, Alain-Charles. *Les Grandes Fêtes et leurs Décors à l'Époque de Louis XVI*. Paris: Librairie Droz, 1972.
Guérard, Eugène. *Les annales de l'Opéra ou Recueil des premières danseuses*. Paris: Delarue, 1844.
La Guerre de l'Opéra. Lettre écrite à une dame en province, par quelqu'un qui n'est ni de l'un, ni de l'autre. 1755. Bibliothèque de l'Arsenal, Collection Rondel 656.
Guest, Ivor, ed. *La Fille Mal Gardée*. London: The Dancing Times Limited, 1960.
———. *A Gallery of Romantic Ballet, A Catalogue of the Collection of Dance Prints at the Mercury Theatre*. London: New Mercury, 1965.
———. *Fanny Elssler*. Middletown, CT: Wesleyan University Press, 1970.
———. *The Ballet of the Second Empire*. Middletown, CT: Wesleyan University Press, 1974.
———. *The Romantic Ballet in Paris*. Middletown, CT: Wesleyan University Press, 1966.
———. *Victorian Ballet Girl*. London: Adam and Charles Black, 1957.
Guicciardi, Jean-Pierre. "Between the Licit and the Illicit: The Sexuality of the King." Translated by Michael Murray. *Eighteenth-Century Life* 9, no. 3 (May 1985): 88–97.
Guilcher, Jean-Michel. *La contredanse et les renouvellements de la danse française*. Paris: Mouton, 1969.
Guillamot, Auguste Étienne. *Costumes de l'Opéra des XVIIe–XVIIIe Siècles*. Paris, 1883.
Guillaume, M. *Note remise à Monsieur le Ministre Secrétaire d'Etat de l'Intérieur, dans le but d'obtenir l'organisation d'un Conservatoire de Danse*. 1842.

Guillaume, Simon. *Almanach dansant ou positions et attitudes de l'allemande avec un discours préliminaire sur l'origine et l'utilité de la danse dédié au beau sexe par Guillaume maître de danse pour l'année 1770*. Paris: Chez l'Auteur, 1770.

Guillaumot, A. *Costumes des Ballets du Roy*. Paris: Ed. Monnier and Cie, 1885.

Guillemin. *Chorégraphie, ou l'art de décrire la danse*. Paris: Chez Petit; l'Imprimerie Ve Herrisant, 1784.

Guimard, Marie-Madeleine. *Dossier artiste*. Bibliothèque de l'Opéra.

Habermas, Jurgen. *The Structural Transformation of the Public Sphere: An Inquiry into a Category of Bourgeois Society*. Translated by Thomas Burger with the assistance of Frederick Lawrence. Cambridge, MA.: MIT Press, 1989.

Hagstrum, Jean H. *Sex and Sensibility: Ideal and Erotic Love from Milton to Mozart*. Chicago: University of Chicago Press, 1980.

Hammond, Sandra Noll. "Clues to Ballet's Technical History from the Early Nineteenth Century Ballet Lesson." *Dance Research* 3, no. 1 (Autumn 1984): 53–66.

Hannetaire, Jean-Nicholas Servandoni de. *Observations sur l'art du comédien*. 1774. Paris: Ribon, Duchesne, and Costard, 1786.

Harari, Josué. *Scenarios of the Imaginary*. Ithaca, NY: Cornell University Press, 1987.

Harris, Jennifer. "The Red Cap of Liberty: A Study of Dress Worn by French Revolutionary Partisans, 1789–94." *Eighteenth-Century Studies* 14, no. 3 (Spring 1981): 283–312.

Heartz, Daniel. "*Les Lumières*: Voltaire and Metastasio; Goldoni, Favart and Diderot." In *International Musicological Society; Report of the Twelfth Congress: Berkeley 1977*, edited by Daniel Heartz and Bonnie Wade, 233–238. Bärenreiter Kassel: American Musicological Society, 1981.

———. "The Beginnings of the Operatic Romance: Rosseau, Sedaine, and Monsigney." *Eighteenth Century Studies* 15, no. 2 (Winter 1981–82): 149–178.

Hedberg, Gregory, and Marion Hirschler. "The Jerome Hill Bequest: Corot's *Silenus* and Delacroix's *Fanatics of Tangiers*." *Minneapolis Institute, Arts Bulletin* 61 (1974): 93–103.

Hedgcock, Frank Arthur. *A cosmopolitan actor, David Garrick and his French friends*. London: S. Paul & Co., 1912.

Hemmings, F. W. J. *Theatre and State in France, 1760–1905*. Cambridge: Cambridge University Press, 1994.

Hill, John. *The Actor*. London: R. Griffiths, 1755.

Hillairet, Jacques, and Auguste André Coussillau. *Gibets, Piloris, et Cachots de Vieux Paris*. Paris: Les Éditions de Minuit, 1956.

Hilton, Wendy. *Dance of Court and Theatre: The French Noble Style, 1690–1725*. Princeton: Princeton Book Publishers, 1981.

Hobsbawm, Eric J. *The Age of Revolution: Europe 1789–1848*. London: Wiedenfeld and Nicolson, 1962.

Hobson, Marian. Review of *The Archeology of the Frivolous: Reading Condillac*, by Jacques Derrida. Translated by John P. Leavey, Jr. *French Studies* 43, no. 3 (July 1989): 329–331.

———. *The Object of Art: The Theory of Illusion in 18th-Century France*. Cambridge: Cambridge University Press, 1982.

Hogarth, William. *The Analysis of Beauty*. 1753. Reprint. Edited by Joseph Burke. Oxford: Oxford University Press, 1955.

Holland, Vyvyan Beresford. *Hand Coloured Fashion Plates, 1770–1899*. London: Batsford, 1955.

Holmström, Kirsten Gram. *Monodramas, Attitudes, Tableaux Vivants: Studies on Some Trends of Theatrical Fashion, 1770–1815*. Stockholm: Almqvist & Wiksell, 1967.

Home, Henry (Lord Kames). *Elements of Criticism*. 2 vols. Edinburgh: A. Kincaid, 1762.

Hopkins, Albert, A. *Magic: Stage Illusions and Scientific Diversions, Including Trick Photography*. New York: Munn, 1901.

Houssaye, Arsene. *Men and Women of the Eighteenth Century*. 2 vols. New York: Redfield, 1857.

Howarth, William Driver. *Sublime and Grotesque: A Study of French Romantic Drama*. London: Harrap, 1975.

Huckenpahler, Victoria. "Confessions of an Opéra Director: Chapters from the *Mémoires* of Dr. Louis Véron." Parts 1–3. *Dance Chronicle* 7, nos. 1–3 (1984): 50–106, 198–228, 345–370.

Huet, Marie-Helène. *Rehearsing the Revolution: The Staging of Marat's Death*. Translated by Robert Hurley. Berkeley and Los Angeles: University of California Press, 1982.

Hugo, Victor. *Preface to "Cromwell"*. 1827. In *Revolution in the Theatre: French Romantic Theories of Drama*, edited by Barry Daniels. Westport, CT: Greenwood, 1983, pp.152–190.

Hunt, Lynn. *Politics, Culture, and Class in the French Revolution*. Berkeley and Los Angeles: University of California Press, 1984.

Hutchinson, Francis. *An Essay on the Nature and Conduct of the Passions and Affections with Illustrations on the Moral Sense*. 1742.

Hytier, Adrienne D. "The Decline of Military Values: The Theme of the Deserter in Eighteenth-Century French Literature." In *Studies in Eighteenth-Century Culture*, vol. 2, edited by Harry C. Payne, 147–162. Madison: University of Wisconsin Press, 1982.

Indicateur Dramatique, ou Almanach des Théâtres de Paris. Paris: chez le Fort, an VII.

Instruction du Procès, Entre les premiers Sujets de l'Académie Royale de Musique & de Danse. Et le Sr. de Vismes, Entrepreneur, jadis public, aujourd'hui clandestin, & Directeur de ce Spectacle. 1779. Bibliothèque de l'Opéra, C 6688.

Instruction sur la Danse, Extraite des Stes. Ecritures, des Sts. Pères, des Sts. Conciles, et des Théologiens les plus recommandables par leur piété et leur science; Par un Prêtre du Diocèse de Metz. Charlesville: De l'Imprimerie de Rancourt, 1821.

Introduction à la Danse sur la Corde au Sérail, ou le Rey D'Alger. 1812. Bibliotèque de l'Arsenal, Collection Rondel, 10130.

Isherwood, Robert M. *Farce and Fantasy: Popular Entertainment in Eighteenth-Century Paris*. New York: Oxford University Press, 1986.

Janin, Jules Gabriel. *Deburau, histoire du théâtre à quatre sous; pour faire suite à l'histoire du théâtre-français*. 3d ed. Paris, 1833.

———. "Review of *Giselle*," *Journal des Debats*. June 30, 1841, p. 1.

Jelgerhuis, Johannes. *Theoretische lessen over de gesticulatie en mimick*. Amsterdam: P. M. Warnars, 1827–29.

Jimack, P. D. "The Paradox of Sophie and Julie: Contemporary Response to Rousseau's Ideal Wife and Ideal Mother." In *Woman and Society in Eighteenth-Century France*, edited by Eva Jacobs and others, 152–165. London: Athlone Press, 1979.

Join-Diéterle, Catherine. *Les Décors de Scène de l'Opéra de Paris à l'Époque Romantique*. Paris: Picard Editeur, 1988.

Jordanova, Ludmilla. *Sexual Visions: Images of Gender In Science and Medicine Between the Eighteenth and Twentieth Centuries*. New York: Harvester Wheatsheaf, 1989.

Josephs, Herbert. *Diderot's Dialogue of Language and Gesture: "Le Neveu de Rameau."* Ohio State University Press, 1969.

Journal de l' Académie Royale de Musique. April 13–June 15, 1782. Bibliothèque de l'Opéra, Res. 657.

Journal des Débats, 1838–1841.

Journal des Spectacles, représentés devant leur majestés, sur les Théâtres de Versailles & de Fontainebleau, pendant l'année 1765. Paris: Ballard, 1766.

Jowitt, Deborah. *Time and the Dancing Image*. New York: William Morrow and Co., 1988.

Juillet. *De la danse. Considérations sur les causes de sa défaveur actuelle et moyens de la mettre en rapport avec le gout du siècle*. Paris: Chez l'auteur, 1825.

Julien, Jean-Auguste (Desboulmiers). *Histoire du théâtre de l'opéra-comique*. 2 vols. Paris: Lacombe, 1769.

Jullien, Adolphe. *Histoire du Costume au Théâtre*. Paris: G. Charpentier, 1880.

———. *Histoire du théâtre de Madame de Pompadour dit théâtre des petits cabinets*. Paris, 1874.

———. *L'Opéra Secret au XVIIIe Siècle*. Paris: Edouard Rouveyre, 1880.

———. *La comédie à la cour. Les Théâtres de société royale pendant le siècle dernier*. 1885. Reprint. Geneva: Slatkine Reprints, 1971.

———. *La Cour et l'Opéra sous Louis XIV*. Paris: Didier et Cie, 1878.

Kadish, Doris Y., and Françoise Massardier Kenney, eds. *Translating Slavery: Gender and Race in French Women's Writing, 1783–1823*. Kent, OH: Kent State University Press, 1994.

Kelly, George Armstrong. "Conceptual Sources of the Terror." *Eighteenth-Century Studies* 14, no. 1 (Fall 1980): 18–36.

Kirstein, Lincoln. *Dance: A Short History of Classic Theatrical Dancing*. 1935. Reprint. Westport, CT: Greenwood Press, 1970.

———. *Movement and Metaphor: Four Centuries of Ballet*. New York: Praeger, 1970.

Kivy, Peter. *Sound and Semblance*. Princeton: Princeton University Press, 1984.

Kleist, Heinrich von. "On the Marionette Theatre." Translated by Idris Parry. *TLS*, October 20, 1978. p. 1212.

Kusch, Manfred. "The River and the Garden: Basic Spatial Models in *Candide* and *La Nouvelle Héloïse*." *Eighteenth-Century Studies* 12, no. 1 (Fall 1978): 1–15.

L'Aulnaye, Françoise Henri Stanislas de. *De la saltation théâtrale, ou recherches sur l'Origine, les Progrès & les Effets de la Pantomine chez les Anciens*. Paris: Chez Barrois, 1790.

L'Epée, Charles Michel de. *Institutions des sourds et muets, par la voie des signes méthodiques*. Paris: Chez Nyon, 1776.

La Cépède, M. le Comte de (Bernard Germain Étienne de la Ville sur Illon). *La poétique de la musique*. Paris, 1785.

La Cuisse, S. de. *Le Répertoire des bals, ou théorie-practique des contre danses, décrites d'une manière aisée avec des Figures démonstratives pour les pouvoir danser facilement, auxquelles on a ajouté le Airs notés*. Paris: Chez Cailleau, 1762.

———. *Suite du Répertoire des Bals ou Recueil de Contredanses*. Paris: Chez Mlle. Castagnery, 1762.

La Mettrie, Julien Offray de. *La Mettrie's L'Homme Machine*. Edited by Aram Vartamian. Princeton: Princeton University Press, 1960.

Lacey, Alexander. *Pixerécourt and the French Romantic Drama*. Toronto: University of Toronto Press, 1928.

Lacotte, Pierre. "Looking for *La Sylphide*." *Dance and Dancers* (October 1982): 14–16.

Lacroix, Paul. *The Eighteenth Century*. New York: Scribner, Werford and Armstrong, 1876.

Laforêt, Claude. *La vie musicale au temps romantique: salons, théâtres et concerts*. 1929. Reprint. New York: Da Capo Press, 1977.

Lairesse, Gérard. *Groot Schilderboek*. Amsterdam: H. Desbordes, 1712.

Lambranzi, Gregorio. *New and Curious School of Theatrical Dancing*. 1716. Reprint. New York: Dance Horizons, 1966.

Landes, Joan B. *Women and the Public Sphere in the Age of the French Revolution*. Ithaca, NY: Cornell University Press, 1988.

Lang, Franciscus. *Dissertatio de Actione Scenica, cum Figuris eandem explicantibus, et Observationibus quibusdam de Arte Comica*. The Hague, 1727.

Lang, Paul Henry. "French Opera and the Spirit of the Revolution." In *Studies in Eighteenth-Century Culture; Volume 2: Irrationalism in the Eighteenth-Century*, edited by Harold E. Pagliaro, 321–342. Madison: University of Wisconsin Press, 1982.

Langlade, Émile. *Rose Bertin, the creator of fashion at the court of Marie Antoinette*. London: J. Long, 1913.

Laqueur, Thomas. "Orgasm, Generation, and the Politics of Reproductive Biology." In *The Making of the Modern Body: Sexuality and Society in the Nineteenth Century*, edited by Catherine Gallagher and Thomas Laqueur, 1–41. Berkeley and Los Angeles: University of California Press, 1987.

———. *Making Sex: Body and Gender from the Greeks to Freud*. Cambridge: Harvard University Press, 1990.

Larbouillat, Léger. *Receuil de Décorations Théâtrales et autres objets d'ornement*. Paris: Imprimerie de J. Tastu, 1830.

Laus de Boissy, Louis de. *Lettre Critique sur notre Danse Théâtrale, addressée à l'Auteur du Spectateur français, par un homme de mauvaise humeur*. Paris: Chez Louis Jorry fils, Lesclapart, 1771.

Lavater, Johann Caspar. *Essai sur la Physiognomonie, Destiné a faire Connoître l'Homme & à le faire Aimer*. The Hague: Chez Jaques van Karnebeek, n.d.

Laver, James. *The Age of Illusion: Manners and Morals, 1750–1848*. New York: David McKay Company, Inc., 1972.

Le Brun. *Journal de la Mode et du Gout, ou Amusemens du Salon et de la Toilette*. 3 vols. 1790–93. Bibliothèque de l'Opéra, Res. 714.

Le Brun, Charles. *A Method to Learn to Design the Passions*. 1734. Translated by John Williams. Reprint. Los Angeles: William Andrews Clark Memorial Library, University of California, Los Angeles, 1980.

———. *Méthode pour apprendre à dessiner les passions*. 1702. Reprint. Hildesheim, Germany: Georg Olms Verlag, 1982.

Le Faucheur, Michel. *Traité de l'action de l'orateur*. Paris, 1657.

Le Flaneur, Guillaume. *Petite Biographie Dramatique, silhouettes des acteurs, actrices . . . des théâtre. . . .* Paris: Chez Paul Domère, 1821.

Le Vacher de Charnois, Jean Charles. *Costumes et annales des grands théâtres de Paris*. Paris, 1786–89.

le Huray, Peter, and James Day, eds. *Music and Aesthetics in the Eighteenth and Nineteenth Centuries*. Cambridge: Cambridge University Press, 1981.

Lecomte, Henry. *Histoire des Théâtres de Paris: Le Théâtre de la Cité, 1792–1807*. Paris: Daragon, 1910.

Lecomte, Nathalie. "L'exotisme dans le ballet: les chinoiseries au XVIII siècle." *La Recherche en Danse* no. 3 (June 1984): 29–41.

Lee, Vera. *The Reign of Women in Eighteenth-Century France*. Cambridge, MA: Schenkman, 1975.

LeGates, Marlene. "The Cult of Womanhood in Eighteenth-Century Thought." *Eighteenth-Century Studies* 10, no. 1 (Fall 1976): 21–39.

Legendre, Pierre. *La Passion d'Être un Autre: Étude pour la Danse*. Paris: Éditions de Seuil, 1978.

Leroux, J. J. *Rapport sur l'Opéra, présenté au Corps Municipal le 17 Août 1791*. Paris: l'Imprimerie de La Becq, 1791.

Lessing, Gotthold Ephraim. *Laocoon: An Essay on the Limits of Painting and Poetry*. Translated by Edward Allen McCormick. Baltimore: Johns Hopkins University Press, 1984.

Lesure, François. *L'Opéra Classique Français*. Geneva: Éditions Minkoff, 1972.

*Lettre de Madame *** à une de ses amies sur les spectacles, et principalement sur l'Opéra Comique*. N.p., 1745. Bibliothèque de l'Opéra.

*Lettre de Monsieur le Baron ***. Ancien Capitaine de Cavalerie. Chevalier de l'Ordre Royal & Militaire de Saint Louis, Pensionaire du Roi. A une des rivales de Terpsichore*. London: Chez Emslay; Paris: Chez Espril, 1775.

*Lettre d'un Amateur de l'Opéra, à M. ***, Sur quelques objets relatifs à ces Spectacles*. 1789. Bibliothèque de l'Arsenal, Collection Rondel 943.

Lettre d'un des petits oracles de Monsieur Angiolini au Grand Noverre. Milan: Chez Jean Baptiste Bianchis, 1774.

Lettre d'un Parisien, à son ami, en province, sur le nouveau Spectacle des Élèves de l'Opéra, ouvert de 7 janvier. Paris: Chez les Marchands de Nouveautés & audit Spectacle, 1779.

Lettre d'une comédienne, à une danseuse de l'Opéra. and Réponse d'une danseuse de l'Opéra à une comédienne. N.p., n.d. Bibliothèque de l'Opéra, C5931 (7).

Lettres et règlements sur l'Académie Royale de Musique, 9 avril 1781–26 jan. 1782, vols. 1–2. Bibliothèque de l'Opéra, Res. 1027.

Levi, Anthony. *French Moralists: The Theory of the Passions, 1585–1649*. Oxford: Clarendon Press, 1964.

Levinson, André. *Marie Taglioni*. Paris: Librarie Félix Alcan, 1929.

Levy, Darline Gay, Harriet Branson Applewhite, and Mary Durham Johnson, eds. *Women in Revolutionary Paris, 1789–1795*. Urbana, IL: University of Illinois Press, 1979.

Lifar, Serge. *Giselle: Apothéose du Ballet Romantique*. Paris: Éditions Albin Michel, 1942.

Locke, Arthur Ware. *Music and the Romantic Movement in France*. London: Kegan Paul, Trench, Trubner and Co., 1920.

Locke, Ralph, P. *Music, Musicians and the Saint-Simonians*. Chicago: University of Chicago Press, 1986.

Longing for the Ideal: Images of Marie Taglioni in the Romantic Ballet. Cambridge: Harvard Theatre Collection, 1984.

Longyear, Rey Morgan. *Nineteenth-Century Romanticism in Music*. Englewood Cliffs, NJ: Prentice-Hall, 1969.

Lormier, Paul. "Dossier artiste." Bibliothèque de l'Opéra.

Lough, John. *Paris Theater Audiences in the 17th and 18th Centuries*. London: Oxford University Press, 1957.

Louise Noblet. Extraits des presse, 1823–1824. Bibliothèque de l'Arsenal, Collection Rondel 11792.

Louisy, Paul. *Le Théâtre—Mystères, Tragédie, Comédie, et la Musique—Instrumens, Ballet, Opéra Jusqu'à 1789*. Paris: Librairie de Firmin-Didot et Cie, 1887.

Lowinsky, Edward E. "Taste, Style, and Ideology in Eighteenth-Century Music." In *Aspects of the Eighteenth Century*, edited by Earl R. Wasserman, 163–205. Baltimore: Johns Hopkins Press, 1965.

Lukács, Georg. *Essays on Realism*. Edited by Rodney Livingstone. Translated by David Fernbach. London: Lawrence and Wishart, 1980.

———. *The Theory of the Novel*. Translated by Anna Bostock. Cambridge: MIT Press, 1971.

Lynham, Deryck. *Ballet Then and Now: A History of the Ballet in Europe*. London, Sylvan Press, 1947.

———. *The Chevalier Noverre*. 1950. Reprint. London: Dance Books, 1972.

Mably, Gabriel Bonnot de. *Lettres à Madame la Marquise de P . . . sur l'Opéra*. Paris, 1741. Reprint. New York, AMS Press, 1978.
MacCormack, Carol P., and Marilyn Strathern, eds. *Nature, Culture, and Gender*. Cambridge: Cambridge University Press, 1980.
"Mademoiselle Taglioni," in *L'Annuaire Historique et Biographique*. 1844. Pp. 1–7.
Magli, Patrizia. "The system of the passions in eighteenth century dramatic mime." *Versus: Quaderni di studi semiotici* 22 (January-April 1979): 32–47.
Magny, Claude Marc. *Principes de chorégraphie, suivi d'un traité de la cadence, qui apprendra les tems & les valeurs de chaque pas de la danse, détaillés par caractères, figures, & signes démonstratifs*. Paris: Chez Duchesne, 1765.
Magri, Gennaro. *Theoretical and Practical Treatise on Dancing*. Naples, 1779. Translated by Mary Skeaping, Anna Ivanova, and Irmgard E. Betty. London: Dance Books, 1988.
Maillet-Duclairon, A. *Essai sur la Connoissance des Théâtres François*. Paris: Chez Prrult père, 1751.
Maligny, Aristippe Bernier de. *Théorie de l'art du comédien: ou, manuel théâtral*. Paris, 1826.
Malpied, N. *Traité sur l'art de la danse*. Paris: Chez M. Boüin, [ca. 1785].
Manne, Edmond de and Charles Ménétrier. *Galerie Historique des Comédiens de la Troupe de Nicolet*. Lyon: N. Scheuring, 1869.
Manning, Susan. *Ecstasy and the Demon: Feminism and Nationalism in the Dances of Mary Wigman*. Berkeley: University of California Press, 1993.
Manuel, Frank E. "From Equality to Organicism." *Journal of the History of Ideas* 17, no. 1 (January 1956): 54–69.
Marcel, M. *Lettre à M. J.-J. Rousseau, C. de Genève*. N.p. 1763.
Marcoz. *Objet et Ordre des Fêtes Décadaires de la République Française*. Paris: De l'Imprimerie Nationale, 1794.
Marmontel, Jean François. *Les Eléments de la Littérature*. 19 vols. Paris: Verdière, 1818–20.
Marquet. *Mémoire pour Antoine-Bonnaventure Pitrot, maître des ballets, & premier danseur de la Comédie Italienne*. Paris: Ch. Est. Chenault, 1765.
Mars, Francis O. "Ange Goudar, Cet Inconnu (1708–1791) — Essai bio-bibliographique sur un aventurier polygraphe du XVIIIeme Siècle." *Casanova Gleanings* 9 (1966).
Marshall, David. *The Surprising Effects of Sympathy*. Chicago: University of Chicago Press, 1988.
Martin, Jean-Baptiste. *Collection de figures théâtrales*. Paris, n.d. Bibliothèque de l'Opéra, Res. 2262.
Martin, Wallace. *Recent Theories of Narrative*. Ithaca: Cornell University Press, 1986.
Martinet, J. J. *Essai ou principes élémentaires de l'art de la danse, Utiles aux personnes destinées à l'éducation de la jeunesse*. Lausanne: Chez Monnier et Jacquerod, 1797.
Mason, H. T. "Women in Marivaux: Journalist to Dramatist." In *Woman and Society in Eighteenth-Century France*, edited by Eva Jacobs and others, 42–54. London: Athlone Press, 1979.
Maudit-Larive, Jean de. *Réflexions sur l'art théâtrale*. Paris, 1801.
Maurice, Charles. "La Fille de Marbre." In *Le Coureur des Spectacles*. October 21, 1847, pp. 1–2.
———. "Mademoiselle Legallois, premier sujet, et le journaliste mauvais . . ." *Courrier des Théâtres*, January 7, 1825, p. 1.
———. "Review of *Giselle*," *Courrier des Théâtres*. June 30, 1841, p. 1.
———. "Review of *Giselle*," *Courrier des Théâtres*. July, 1841, p. 3.
Maury, Jean S. *Principes d'Eloquence pour la Chaire et le Barreau*. Paris: T. Warée, 1804.
Mayer, David. *Harlequin in His Element: The English Pantomime, 1806–1836*. Cambridge: Harvard University Press, 1969.
Maza, Sarah C. *Servants and Masters in Eighteenth-Century France: The Uses of Loyalty*. Princeton: Princeton University Press, 1983.
La Mazourka, Album à la Mode dessins composés et executés par Guérard, chorégraphie de M. Laborde, fils. Paris: Chez Albert et Cie, n.d.
Mazzinghi. *The Favorite Opéra Dances for the Year 1788 also 1789–90 performed at the Kings Theater Hay Market*. London: Longman & Broderip.
McClary, Susan. *Feminine Endings: Music, Gender, and Sexuality*. Minneapolis: University of Minnesota Press, 1991.
McKenzie, Alan T. "The Countenance You Show Me: Reading the Passions in the Eighteenth Century." *The Georgia Review* 32 (Winter 1978): 758–773.

McKeon, Michael. *The Origins of the English Novel, 1600–1740*. Baltimore: Johns Hopkins University Press, 1987.

Meisel, Martin. *Realizations: Narrative, Pictorial and Theatrical Arts in Nineteenth-Century England*. Princeton: Princeton University Press, 1983.

Mémoires Secrèts de Bachaumont. Paris, 1859.

Mémorial Dramatique, ou Almanach Théâtral. Paris: Barba, 1807–1819.

Ménestrier, Claude-François. *Des ballets anciens et modernes selon les règles du théâtre*. Paris: Chez René Guignard, 1682.

Le Mercure de France. Paris, 1760–1820.

A mesdemoiselles Taglioni et Noblet, Excuse pour une prétendue offense, ou plutôt, à cause d'un moment de déplaisir à elles involuntairement causé Hommage. Paris: Éverat, 1833–34.

Michel, Artur. "The *Ballet d'Action* before Noverre." *Dance Index* 6, no. 3 (March 1947): 52–72.

———. "Two Great XVIII Century Ballet Masters: Jean-Baptiste DeHesse and Franz Hilverding; *La Guinguette* and *Le Turc genereux* seen by G. de St. Aubin and Canaletto." *Gazette des Beaux-Arts* (May 1945): 270–286.

Michelet, Jules. *History of the French Revolution*. Translated by Keith Botsford. Wynnewood, PA: Livingston Pub. Co., 1972.

———. *Women of the French Revolution*. Philadelphia: Henry Carey Baird, 1855.

Migel, Parmenia. *Great Ballet Prints of the Romantic Era*. New York: Dover, 1981.

———. *The Ballerinas from the Court of Louis XV to Pavlova*. New York: Macmillan, 1972.

Milhouse, Judith. "Dancers' Contracts at the Pantheon Opera House, 1790–1792." *Dance Research* 9, no. 2 (Autumn 1991): 51–75.

Miller, D. A. "*Cage aux folles*: Sensation and Gender in Wilkie Collin's *The Woman in White*." In *The Making of the Modern Body: Sexuality and Society in the Nineteenth Century*, edited by Catherine Gallagher and Thomas Laqueur, 107–136. Berkeley and Los Angeles: University of California Press, 1987.

Miller, J. Hillis. *Versions of Pygmalion*. Cambridge: Harvard University Press, 1990.

Miller, Nancy K. "Changing the Subject: Authorship, Writing, and the Reader." In *Feminist Studies/Critical Studies*, edited by Teresa de Lauretis, 102–120. Bloomington: Indiana University Press, 1986.

———. "Female Sexuality and Narrative Structure in *La Nouvelle Héloïse* and *Les Liaisons dangereuses*." *Signs* 1, no. 3, part 1 (Spring 1976): 609–638.

Milon. "Dossier artiste." Bibliothèque de l'Opéra.

Mittman, Barbara G. *Spectators on the Paris Stage in the Seventeenth and Eighteenth Centuries*. Ann Arbor, MI: UMI Research Press, 1984.

Le Monde d'Amour. Geneva: Lepondril, 1842.

Monnet, Jean. *Mémoires*. Reprint. Paris: Louis-Michaud, 1908.

Montaiglon, M. de, avocat. *Quelques Réflexiones pour MM. Ciceri et Lébé-Gigun, Peintres Décorateurs; contre M. Véron, Directeur du grand Opéra de Paris*. Paris: Imprimerie Porthmann, 1833.

Montmorency, Duc, de. *Lettres sur l'Opéra (1840–1842)*. Paris, 1921.

Moore, Lillian. "The Duport Mystery." *Dance Perspectives* 7 (1960).

Moreau de la Sarthe, Jacques Louis. *Histoire naturelle de la femme . . .* Paris, 1803.

Moreau de Saint-Méry, Médéric Louis. *De la danse*. À Parme: Bodoni, 1801.

Morporgo, J. E., ed. *The Autobiography of Leigh Hunt*. London: The Cresset Press, 1949.

Moses, Clair Goldberg. *French Feminism in the 19th Century*. Albany: State University of New York Press, 1984.

Mullan, John. "Hypochrondria and Hysteria: Sensibility and the Physicians." *The Eighteenth Century: Theory and Interpretation* 25, no. 2 (Spring 1984): 141–174.

Le Musée Philipon. Paris, Chez Auber, Place de la Bourse, 1841–1842.

Nares, Robert. *Remarks on the nature of pantomime, or imitative dance, ancient and modern*. London: John Stockdale, 1789.

"Nécrologie sur Marie-Jeanne Saulnier (1783–1825)." *Pandore*, July 23, 1825, p. 2.

Nettl, Paul. *The Dance in Classical Music*. London: Peter Owen, 1963.

Nicolet, Jean Baptiste. *La littérature renversée ou l'art de faire des pièces de théâtre sans paroles; Ouvrage utile aux poètes dramatiques de nos jours*. Berne and Paris: Chez les Débitans de Brochures nouvelles, 1775.

Nicoll, Allardyce. *The Garrick Stage: Theatres and Audiences in the Eighteenth Century*. Manchester: University of Manchester Press, 1980.

Nivelon, F. *The Rudiments of Genteel Behavior*. N.p. 1737.

Nougaret, Pierre Jean Baptiste. *De l'art du théâtre en général*. Paris: Cailleau, 1769.

Le Nouveau Spectateur, ou examens des nouvelles pièces de théâtre servant de repertoire universel des spectacles. Paris: Chez Esprit, 1776.

Novack, Cynthia. *Sharing the Dance: Contact Improvisation and American Culture*. Madison: University of Wisconsin Press, 1990.

Noverre, Charles Edwin. *The Life and Works of the Chevalier Noverre. . . .* London: Jarrold and Sons, 1882.

Noverre, Jean Georges. *Letters on Dancing and Ballets*. 1803. Translated by Cyril W. Beaumont, 1930. Reprint. New York: Dance Horizons, 1966.

———. *Lettres sur la Danse et les Arts Imitateurs*. Paris: Éditions Lieutier, 1952.

———. *Lettres sur les arts imitateurs en général, et sur la danse en particulier*. 2 vols. Paris: Léopold Collin, 1807.

———. *Recueil des programmes de ballet*. Vienna, 1776.

———. *Théorie et pratique de la danse simple et composée; de l'Art des Ballets; de la Musique; du Costume & des Décorations*. 11 vols. Louisbourg, 1766.

O'Connell, Michael, and John Powell. "Music and Sense in Handel's Setting of Milton's *L'Allegro* and *Il Penseroso*." *Eighteenth-Century Studies* 12, no. 1 (Fall 1978): 16–46.

Olivier, Jean Jacques, and Willy Norbert. *Une étoile de la danse au XVIIIe siècle, Barbarina Campanini (1721–1799)*. Paris: Société français d'imprimerie et de librarie, 1910.

Ong, Walter J. *Ramus, Method and the Decay of Dialogue: From the Art of Discourse to the Art of Reason*. Cambridge: Harvard University Press, 1958.

L'Opinion du Parterre, ou Revue de tous les théâtres de Paris. Paris: Chez Martinet, 1811.

Outram, Dorinda. *The Body and the French Revolution: Sex, Class and Political Culture*. New Haven: Yale University Press, 1989.

Ozouf, Mona. *Festivals and the French Revolution*. Translated by Alan Sheridan. Cambridge: Harvard University Press, 1988.

Les Pages du Duc de Vendôme—review in *Journal des Théâtres, de la Litterature et des Arts*. No. 183. October 19, 1820, p. 2.

Palache, John Garker. *Gautier and the Romantics*. London: Jonathan Cape, 1979.

Pantomime dramatique, ou Essai sur un nouveau genre de spectacle. Florence and Paris: Chez Jombert, 1779.

Papillon de la Ferté. *Détail des fêtes et spectacles donnés à Versailles à l'occasion du Mariage de Monseigneur le Dauphin le 16 Mai 1770*. Bibliothèque de l'Opéra, Res. 574.

———. *Manuscript sur la composition des ballets et le role du maître de ballet*. N.d. Bibliothèque de l'Opéra, Res. 60.

Pateman, Carole. *The Sexual Contract*. Stanford: Stanford University Press, 1988.

Pauli, Charles. *Elémens de la Danse*. Leipsic: d'Ulr. Chret. Saalbach, 1756.

Paulson, Ronald. *Emblem and Expression*. Cambridge: Harvard University Press, 1975.

———. *Representation of Revolution, 1789–1820*. New Haven, CT: Yale University Press, 1983.

Peaden, Catherine Hobbs. "Condillac and the History of Rhetoric." *Rhetorica* 11, no. 2 (Spring 1993): 135–156.

Pélisse, Paul. *Histoire administrative de l'Académie Nationale de Musique et de Danse*. Paris: Imprimerie Bonvatot-Jouve, 1906.

Penzel, Frederick. *Theatre Lighting Before Electricity*. Middletown: Wesleyan University Press, 1978.

Peroux, Joseph Nicolaus. *Pantomimische Stellingen von Henriette Hendel*. Frankfurt, 1810.

Perrot, Phillippe. *Le Travail des Apparences: ou Les Transformations du Corps Féminin, XVIIIe–XIXe Siècle*. Paris: Éditions du Seuil, 1984.

Peters, Dolores. "The Pregnant Pamela: Characterization and Popular Medical Attitudes in the Eighteenth Century." *Eighteenth Century Studies* 14, no. 4 (Summer 1981): 432–451.

Petit Courrier des Dames: Journal des Modes. Paris. January 1839–August 1841.

Petites observations sur deux grands Théâtres, dont la réunion doit coûter dix millions au Gouvernement. Par un sans-culotte de Perpignan, qui ne veut pas payer sa part des violins de l'Opéra, sans danser. Paris: l'Imprimerie des Enfans-Aveugles, n.d.

Les Petits Spectacles de Paris. Paris: Chez Guillot, 1786–87.
Physiologie de l'Opéra, du Carnaval, du Cancan et de la Cachucha, par un Vilain Masqué. Paris: Raymond-Bocquet, 1842.
Pitou, Spire. *The Paris Opéra: An Encyclopedia of Opéras, Ballets, Composers, and Performers. Rococco and Romantic, 1715–1815*. Westport, CT: Greenwood Press, 1985.
Le Porte-Feuille de Madame Gourdan. Paris, 1783.
Pougin, Arthur. *L'Opéra-Comique: Pendant la Révolution, de 1788 à 1801, D'Après des Documents inédits, et les sources les plus authentiques*. Paris: Nouvelle Librairie Parisienne, 1891.
Poyet. *Idées Générales presentées par le Sieur Poyet, Architecte du Roi et de la Ville, sur le Projet de la Fête du 14 Juillet, à l'occasion du Pacte-Fédératif, entre les Gardes Nationales et les Troupes de Ligne de la France; pour célébrer l'époque de la Révolution*. Paris: l'Imprimerie de la Ve Delaquette, 1790.
Przybos, Julia. *L'Entreprise Mélodramatique*. Paris: Librarie José Corti, 1987.
Pujoulx, J.B. *Paris à la fin du XVIIIe siècle*. Paris: Librairie Economique, 1801.
Querelle de Saint-Roch et de Saint-Thomas sur l'ouverture du Manoir céleste à Mademoiselle Chameroy. Paris: Pierre, 1802.
Rabinbach, Anson. *The Human Motor: Energy, Fatigue, and the Origins of Modernity*. New York: Basic Books, 1990.
Racinet, Albert Charles Auguste. *Le costume historique*. Paris, 1888.
Rahill, Frank. *The World of Melodrama*. University Park: Pennsylvania State University Press, 1967.
Ralph, Richard. *The Life and Works of John Weaver*. New York: Dance Horizons, 1985.
Rameau, Pierre. *The Dancing Master*. [1725] Translated by Cyril W. Beaumont. New York: Dance Horizons, 1970.
Rawson, Claude. *Henry Fielding and the Augustan Ideal under Stress: "Nature's Dance of Death" and other Studies*. London: Routledge and Kegan Paul, 1972.
Recherches historiques et critiques sur quelques anciens spectacles, et particulièrement sur les mimes et sur les pantomimes, avec des notes. Paris: Chez Jacques Merigot, 1751.
Recueil complet de tout ce qui s'est passé à la Fête de l'Unité et l'Indivisibilité de la République Française. Bibliothèque Nationale, 8° Z Le Senne 9. 438.
Recueil d'Opéra. Lyon: l'Imprimerie d'Aimé Delaroche, 1743.
Recueil de Croquis de Décorations Italiennes. N.p., n.d. Bibliothèque de l'Opéra, Res. 945.
Recueil des costumes. Bibliothèque de l'Opéra, D 270.
Recueil des Costumes de tous les Ouvrages Dramatiques représentés avec succès sur les Grands Théâtres de Paris. Paris: Chez Vizentini Editeur, 1820–1824.
Réflexions d'un Peintre sur l'Opéra. The Hague: Chez Pierre Gosse, 1743.
Réflexions, sur les causes de la dégradation du Chant, à l'Opéra, comparée avec les succès brillans de la danse, au même théâtre. Par un observateur, ami des deux arts. Paris: De l'Imprimerie du Courrier des Spectacles, Ventose An VI.
Règles pour faire des Balets. Bibliothèque de l'Opéra, C4844.
Rémond de Sainte-Albine, Pierre. *Le Comédien*. Paris: Chez Vincent, Fils, 1749.
Rénard de Saint-Mard, Toussaint de. *Réflexions sur l'Opéra*. A la Haye: Chez Jean Neaulme, 1741.
Réponse d'un Artiste à un homme de lettres, qui lui écrit sur les Waux-halls. Amsterdam and Paris: Chez Defour, 1769.
Réponse de Saint-Roch et de Saint-Thomas à Saint-Andrew. Paris: J. F. Girard, 1802.
Reveillère-Lépeaux, Louis-Marie. *Réflexions sur le Culte, sur les cérémonies civiles et sur les fêtes nationales*. Paris: Chez H. J. Jansen, 1797.
———. *Essai sur les Moyens de Faire Participer l'Universalité des Spectateurs à tout ce qui se pratique dans les Fêtes Nationales*. Paris: H. J. Jansen, 1797.
Rex, Walter E. "A Propos of the Figure of Music in the Frontispiece of the *Encyclopédie*: Theories of Musical Imitation in d'Alembert, Rousseau and Diderot." In *International Musicological Society; Report of the Twelfth Congress: Berkeley 1977*, edited by Daniel Heartz and Bonnie Wade, 214–225. Bärenreiter Kassel: American Musicological Society, 1981.
Rey, Michael. "Parisian Homosexuals Create a Lifestyle, 1700–1750: The Police Archives." Translated by Robert A. Day and Robert Welch. In *'Tis Nature's Fault: Unauthorized Sexuality during the Enlightenment*, edited by Robert Purks Maccubbin, 179–191. Cambridge: Cambridge University Press, 1987.

Reynaud, Charles. *Musée Rétrospectif de la Classe 18; Théâtre.* Saint-Cloud: Imprimerie Belin Frères, 1900.
Ribeiro, Aileen. *Dress in Eighteenth-Century Europe, 1715–1789.* New York: Holmes and Meier Publishers, 1985.
Riccoboni, François. *L'Art du Théâtre, à Madame ****. Paris: Chez C. F. Simon, Fils, 1750.
Richards, Kenneth, and Laura Richards. *The Commedia dell'Arte: A Documentary History.* Oxford: Basil Blackwell, 1990.
Roach, Joseph R. *The Player's Passion: Studies in the Science of Acting.* Newark: University of Delaware Press, 1985.
Robida, Albert. *"Yester-year": Ten Centuries of Toilette.* New York: C. Scribner's Sons, 1891.
Robin-Challan, Louise. "Danse et Danseuses: l'envers du décor (1830–1850)." Thèse de doctorat (sociologie), Université de Paris 7eme,1983.
Robinson, Paul. *Opera and Ideas.* New York: Harper and Row, 1985.
Roche, Daniel. *The People of Paris: An Essay in Popular Culture in the 18th Century.* Translated by Marie Evans and Gwynne Lewis. Leamington Spa, UK: Berg, 1987.
Rodolphe, J. *Médée et Jason.* Partition pour l'orchestre. Choreography by Noverre. 1780. Bibliothèque de l'Opéra.
———. *Médée et Jason.* Partition pour l'orchestre. Choreography by Vestris. 1776. Bibliothèque de l'Opéra.
Rollin, Charles. *Methods of Teaching and Studying the Belles Lettres or an Introduction to Language, Poetry, Rhetoric, History, Moral Philosophy, Physics, etc.* London: Bettesworth and Hitch, 1742.
Root-Bernstein, Michèle. *Boulevard Theatre and Revolution in Eighteenth-Century Paris.* Ann Arbor, MI: UMI Research Press, 1984.
Rosenfeld, Sophie. "The Language of Primitive Dance: Towards a Semiotic Anthropology in late-18th-century France." Unpublished manuscript, n.d.
Rougemont, Martine de. *La vie théâtrale en France au XVIIIe siècle.* Paris: Librairie Honoré Champion, 1988.
Roullet. *Notice historique des évènements qui se sont passés dans l'administration de l'Opéra, la nuit du 13 Février 1820.* Paris: l'Imprimerie de P. Diderot, l'ainé, 1820.
Rousseau, Jean-Jacques. *Emile; or, On Education.* Translated by Allan Bloom. New York, 1979.
———. *Julie; ou La Nouvelle Héloïse: Lettres de deux amants habitants d'une petite ville au pied des Alpes.* Paris: Éditions Garnier Frères, 1960.
———. *Le Devin du Village, intermède.* Paris: Chez la V. Delormel & Fils, 1753.
———. "Pygmalion, Scène Lyrique." In *Collection Complète des Oeuvres de J.-J. Rousseau.* Vol. 15: 289–300. Edited by P. A. du Peyrou. Geneva, 1782–1789.
———. *The First and Second Discourses: Together with the Replies to Critics, and Essay on the Origin of Languages.* Edited and translated by Victor Gourevitch. New York: Harper and Row, 1986.
Ruggieri, Claude. *Précis Historique sur les Fêtes, les Spectacles, et les Réjouissances Publiques.* Paris: Chez Barba, 1830.
Russett, Cynthia Eagle. *Sexual Science: The Victorian Construction of Womanhood.* Cambridge: Harvard University Press, 1989.
Saint-Hilaire, Amable Vilain de. *Petite biographie dramatique.* Paris: Chez Lemonnier, 1821.
Saint-Léon, Arthur Michel. *Exercices de 1829, 2me Cahier des Exercices de 1830, Cahier des Exercises pour LL. AA. Royales les Princesses de Wurtemburg, 1830.* Bibliothèque de l'Opéra.
———. *Pas de deux de "Giselle" Sténochorégraphié.* Bibliothèque de l'Opéra, Res. 234.
———. *La Sténochorégraphie.* Paris, 1852.
Saisselin, Rémy. *The Role of Reason and the Ruses of the Heart.* Cleveland, OH: The Press of Case Western Reserve University, 1970.
Saunier, P. M. *Tableau Historique des Cérémonies du Sacre et du Couronnement de S. M. Napoléon 1er Empereur des Français.* Paris: Chez Rochette, 1805.
Savigliano, Marta. *Tango and the Political Economy of Passion.* Boulder: Westview Press, 1994.
Schiebinger, Londa. "Skeletons in the Closet." In *The Making of the Modern Body: Sexuality and Society in the Nineteenth Century*, edited by Catherine Gallagher and Thomas Laqueur, 42–82. Berkeley and Los Angeles: University of California Press, 1987.
———. *The Mind Has No Sex?: Women in the Origins of Modern Science.* Cambridge: Harvard University Press, 1989.

———. *Nature's Body: Gender in the Making of Modern Science*. Boston: Beacon, 1993.

Schimmelpennick, Mary Anne. *Theory on the Classification of Beauty and Deformity, and their Correspondance with Physiognomic Expression*. London: John and Arthur Arch, 1815.

Schneider, Louis. "L'accident d'une Danseuse à l'Opéra en 1807." Bibliothèque de l'Arsenal, Collection Rondel 11673.

———. "Le squelette de l'Opéra." 1841. Bibliothèque de l'Arsenal, Collection Rondel 11771.

Schor, Naomi. *Breaking the Chain: Women, Theory, and French Realist Fiction*. New York: Columbia University Press, 1985.

Schwartz, Judith L., and Christena L. Schlundt. *French Court Dance and Dance Music: A Guide to Primary Source Writings, 1643–1789*. Stuyvesant, NY: Pendragon Press, 1987.

Scott, Joan Wallach. *Gender and the Politics of History*. New York: Columbia University Press, 1988.

Sedgwick, Eve. *Between Men: English Literature and Male Homosocial Desire*. New York: Columbia University Press, 1985.

Seigel, Jerrold E. *Bohemian Paris: Culture, Politics and the Boundaries of Bourgeois Life, 1830–1930*. New York: Viking, 1986.

Sennett, Richard. *The Fall of Public Man*. New York: Vintage Books, 1978.

Sévigné, Madame de. *Lettres*. Paris: Gallimard, 1953.

Sheriff, Mary D. "For Love or Money? Rethinking Fragonard." *Eighteenth-Century Studies* 19, no. 3 (Spring 1986): 333–353.

Siddons, Henry. *Practical illustrations of rhetorical gesture and action; adapted to the English drama: from a work on the subject by M. Engel*. London, 1822.

Skeaping, Mary. "Giselle—Discovery and Tradition." *Dance and Dancers* 22, no. 5 (May 1971): 20–22.

Smith, Horatio. *Festivals, games, and amusements, ancient and modern*. London, 1831.

Souveraineté des Peuples dans leurs fêtes publiques, prouvé par l'histoire ancienne et moderne. Paris, 1797.

Sparshott, Francis. *Off the Ground*. Princeton: Princeton University Press, 1988.

Les spectacles de Paris, ou calendrier historique & chronologique des théâtres. Paris: Chez la Veuve Duchesne, 1789.

Spurzheim, Johann Gaspar. *Outlines of Phrenology*. Boston: Marsh, Capen and Lyon, 1832. Reprinted in *Significant Contributions to the History of Psychology, 1750–1920*, edited by Daniel N. Robinson. Washington, DC: University Publications of America, 1978.

Staël, Madame de (Anne-Louise-Germaine). *Considerations on the Principal Events of the French Revolution*. 2 vols. New York: James Eastburn and Co., 1818.

———. *Oeuvres complètes*. Paris: Didot, 1871.

Stafford, Barbara Maria. *Body Criticism: Imaging the Unseen in Enlightenment Art and Medicine*. Cambridge, MA: MIT Press, 1991.

Stambolian, George, and Elaine Marks, eds. *Homosexualities and French Literature: Cultural Contexts/Critical Texts*. Ithaca: Cornell University Press, 1979.

Starobinski, Jean. *Portrait de l'artiste en saltimbanque*. Geneva: Editions d'Art Albert Skira, 1970.

———. *The Invention of Liberty, 1700–1789*. Translated by Bernard C. Swift. Geneva: Editions d'Art Albert Skira, 1964.

———, and others. *Revolution in Fashion: European Clothing, 1715–1815*. New York: Abbeville Press, 1989.

Stebbins, Genevieve. *Delsarte System of Expression*. 1902. Reprint. New York: Dance Horizons, 1977.

Storey, Robert F. *Pierrots on the Stage of Desire: Nineteenth-Century French Literary Artists and the Comic Pantomime*. Princeton: Princeton University Press, 1985.

Straub, Kristina. *Sexual Suspects: Eighteenth-Century Players and Sexual Ideology*. Princeton, NJ: Princeton University Press, 1992.

Swift, Mary Grace. *A Loftier Flight: The Life and Accomplishments of Charles-Louis Didelot, Balletmaster*. Middletown, CT: Wesleyan University Press, 1974.

Taglioni, Filippo. *Note des représentations faites depuis mon départ de l'Italie pour la Suede le 1er Décembre 1817*. Bibliothèque de l'Opéra, Fonds Taglioni R 85.

Talma. *Papers on Acting IV: Réflexions on the Actor's Art*. New York: Dramatic Museum of Columbia University, 1940.

Taplin, Diana Theodores. "On critics and criticism of dance." 7th Dance in Canada Conference, Waterloo, Ont., 1979. *New Directions in Dance*, pp. 77–93. Toronto, 1979.

Taylor, George. "The Just Delineation of the Passions: Theories of Acting in the Age of Garrick." In *Essays on the Eighteenth-Century English Stage*, edited by Kenneth Richards and Peter Thomson, 51–72. London: Metheun, 1972.
Tessier, André. "Louis Bouquet, dessinateur et inspecteur général des menus-plaisir." *La Revue de l'Art* (n.d.): 15–26, 89–100, 173–184.
Théleur, E. A. *Letters on Dancing reducing This Elegant and Healthful Exercise to Easy Scientific Principles*. London: Sherwood & Co., 1831.
Tilly, Charles. *An Urban World*. Boston: Little, Brown and Co., 1974.
———. *The Contentious French*. Cambridge, MA: Belknap Press, 1986.
Tissot, Amédée de. *L'Albionade, ou Mademoiselle Noblet à Londres, poëme, en un chant*. Paris: Chez Delaunay, Barba, Dentu, 1822.
Tocqueville, Alexis de. *The Old Régime and the French Revolution*. 1856. Translated by Stuart Gilbert. New York: Anchor Books, 1955.
Tomlinson, Kellom. *The Art of Dancing Explained by Reading and Figures*. London. 1735.
Touchard-LaFosse, G. *Chroniques secrètes et galantes de l'opéra, 1665–1845*. Paris: Gabriel Roux et Cassanet, 1846.
Très-humbles & Très-respectueuses Remonstrances de MM les Comédiens Français Au Roi Pour obtenir de Sa Majesté la suppression d'un Arrêt du Conseil qui leur deffend les Ballets sous peine de 1000 liv. d'amande, etc. Paris, 1753.
Tudor, J. M. "Goethe's Conception of Music as Mediator and 'Element.'" In *Studies in Eighteenth-Century Culture, Vol. 2*, edited by Harry C. Payne, 321–342. Madison: University of Wisconsin Press, 1982.
Undank, Jack. *Diderot: Inside, Outside, and In-Between*. Madison, WI: Coda Press, 1979.
Vaillat, Léandre. *La Taglioni, ou la vie d'une danseuse*. Paris: Éditions Albin Michel, 1942.
Vaïsse, Léon. *De la Pantomime, comme Langage Naturel et moyen d'instruction du sourd-muet*. Paris: L. Hachette et Cie, 1854.
Vallière, Louis-César, Duc de la. *Ballets, opéra et autres ouvrages lyriques*. Paris: C. J. B. Bouche, 1760.
Verlet, Paul. "Décors et Costumes de l'Opéra de Versailles pours les Spectacles de 1770." *Les Monuments Historiques de la France*, no. 1 (January-March 1957): 28–34.
Véron, Louis, *Mémoires d'un bourgeois de Paris, par le docteur L. Véron, comprenant: la fin de l'empire, la restauration, la monarchie de juillet, et la république jusqu'au rétablissement de l'empire*. Paris: Gabriel de Gonet, [1853–] 1855.
Vestris, Désiré. *Les Danses d'Autrefois; de la Pavane à la Gavotte*. Paris: C. Marpon et E. Flammarion, n.d.
Vigarello, Georges. "Posture, Espace et Pédagogie." *Dix-Huitième Siècle* 9 (1977): 39–48.
———. *Le corps redressé*. Paris: J. P. Delarge, 1978.
Vincent-Buffault, Anne. *The History of Tears: Sensibility and Sentimentality in France*. Translated by Teresa Bridgeman. New York: St. Martin's Press, 1991.
Viollet-Leduc. *Précis de Dramatique ou de l'Art de Composer et Exécuter les Pièces de Théâtre*. Paris: Au Bureau de l'Encyclopédie Portatif, 1830.
Viollier, Renée. *Mouret, Le Musicien des Graces, 1682–1738*. Reprint: Geneva: Minkoff, 1976.
Voarino, G. P. *A treatise on calisthenic exercises*. London: N. Hailes, 1827.
Voiart, Elise, *Essai sur la danse antique et moderne*. Paris: Audot, 1823.
Le Vol Plus haut, ou l'Espion des Principaux Théâtres de la Capitale; Contenant une Histoire abrégée des Acteurs et Actrices de ces mêmes théâtres, enrichie d'Observations Philosophiques & d'Anecdotes récreatives. Memphis: Chez Sincère, 1784.
Vuillier, Gaston. *A History of Dancing*. 1898. Reprint. Boston: Millford House, 1972.
Walker, Donald. *Exercises for ladies; calculated to preserve and improve beauty, and to prevent and correct personal defects, inseparable from constrained or careless habits: founded on Physiological Principles*. London: Thos. Hurst, 1836.
Walker, John. *Elements of Elocution . . . A Complete System of the Passions*. London, 1781.
Watelet, Claude Henri. *L'Art de peindre: poëme: avec des réflections sur les différentes parties de la peinture*. Paris: H. L. Guerin & L. F. Delatour, 1760.
Watt, Ian. *The Rise of the Novel: Studies in Defoe, Richardson, and Fielding*. Berkeley and Los Angeles: University of California Press, 1957.
Weaver, John. *An essay towards an history of dancing: in which the whole art and its various excellencies are in some measure explain'd: containing the several sorts of dancing, antique and modern, serious,*

scenical, grotesque. . . . London: J. Tonson, 1712.
———. *The Fable of Orpheus and Eurydice, with a dramatick entertainment in dancing thereupon; attempted in imitation of the ancient Greeks and Romans. As perform'd at the Theatre Royal in Drury-Lane. Written, collected . . .* London: Mears, 1718.
———. *The history of the mimes and pantomimes, with an historical account of several performers in dancing, living in the time of the Roman Emperors. To which will be added, A list of the modern entertainments that have. . . .* London: Printed for J. Roberts (etc.), 1728.
———. *The Loves of Mars and Venus: a dramatic entertainment of dancing, attempted in imitation of the pantomimes of the ancient Greeks and Romans. As perform'd at the theatre in Drury-Lane.* London: Mears, 1724.
Wechsler, Judith. *A Human Comedy: Physiognomy and Caricature in 19th Century Paris.* London: Thames and Hudson, 1982.
White, Hayden. *Metahistory: The Historical Imagination in Nineteenth-Century Europe*. Baltimore and London: Johns Hopkins University Press, 1973.
———. *The Content of the Form: Narrative, Discourse, and Historical Representation*. Baltimore and London: Johns Hopkins University Press, 1987.
———. "The Value of Narrativity in the Représentation of Reality." *Critical Inquiry,* Autumn 1980, pp. 5–27.
Wild, Nicole. *Décors et Costumes du XIXe Siècle, Vol. 1: Opéra de Paris.* Paris: Bibliothèque Nationale, 1987.
———. "La Recherche de la précision historique chez les décorateurs de l'Opéra de Paris au XIXeme siècle." *International Musicological Society: Report of the Twelfth Congress: Berkeley 1977*. 453–463. Bärenreiter Kassel: American Musicological Society, 1977.
Wildeblood, Joan, and Peter Brinson. *The Polite World: A Guide to Manners and Deportment from the Thirteenth to the Nineteenth Century*. London: Oxford University Press, 1965.
Williams, David. "The Fate of French Feminism." *Eighteenth-Century Studies* 14, no. 1 (Fall 1980): 37–55.
Williams, Raymond. *Culture and Society, 1780–1950*. London: Chatto and Windus, 1958.
———. *The Sociology of Culture*. New York: Schocken Books, 1982.
Winter, Marian Hannah. *The Pre-Romantic Ballet*. London: Pitman, 1974.
———. *The Theatre of Marvels*, New York: Benjamin Blom, Inc., 1964.
Witherell, Anne, L. *Louis Pécour's 1700 "Recueil de danses."* Ann Arbor: UMI Research Press, 1983.
Woods, Leigh. *Garrick Claims the Stage: Acting as Social Emblem in Eighteenth-Century England*. Westport, CT: Greenwood Press, 1984.
Wynne, Shirley. "Background research in dance, music and costume. Support materials for use by teachers" students viewing Baroque Dance 1675–1725. Made under the sponsorship of Department of Dance, UCLA, funded by NEH. EH–25011–76–859–@ UCLA 1977.
———. "Complaisance, An Eighteenth-Century Cool." *Dance Scope* 5, no. 1 (Fall 1970): 22–35.
———. "From Ballet to Ballroom Dance in the Revolutionary Era." *Dance Scope* 10, no. 1 (1975): 65–73.
Zorn, Friedrich, Albert. *Grammar of the Art of Dancing*. Brooklyn, NY: Dance Horizons, 1976.
Zorn, John W., ed. *The Essential Delsarte*. Metuchen, NJ: Scarecrow Press, 1968.

SOURCES—SCENARIOS

Aeglé, ballet-héroïque en un acte. Paris: Ballard, 1770.
Albert [Ferdinand Albert Decombe]. *Le Séducteur au Village, ou Claire et Mectal, ballet-pantomime en deux actes*. Paris: Chez Roullet, 1818

Alexandre aux Indes, opéra en trois actes. Paris: P. de Lormel, 1783.
Andromache, tragédie-lyrique en trois actes. Paris: Lormel, 1780.
Angiolini, Gasparo. *Le Départ D'Enée ou Didon Abandonnée, ballet tragique pantomime*. St. Petersbourg: De l'Imprimerie de l'Academie Impériale des Sciences, 1766.
———. *Les Nouveaux Argonautes, ballet pantomime-allégorique*. St. Petersbourg: de l'Imprimerie du Noble Corps des Cadets de la Marine, 1770.
Aniel, Pierre-Jean. *Fleurette ou les Premières Amours de Henri, ballet pantomime historique en deux actes*. Lyons: Chambet Fils Ainé, 1830.
———. *Les Marchandes de Modes ou Une Soirée de Carnaval, pantomime-folie en deux actes, mêlée de danse*. Paris: Chez Bezou, 1825.
Aniel, Pierre-Jean, and Jean Coralli. *La Fiancée de Sarnen, ou Retour au Chalet, ballet-pantomime en trois tableaux*. Lyon: Chambet, 1830.
Arnould, Jean-François Mussot. *Arlequin Soldat Magicien, ou Le Canonier, Pantomime*. Paris: Chez Claude Harissant, 1764.
———. *Les Quatre fils Aymons, pantomime en trois actes*. Paris: l'Imprimerie de P. de Lormel, 1779.
———. *Les Deux Amis, ou l'Héroïsme de l'Amitié, pantomime en trois actes*. Paris: Chez Brunet, 1781.
———. *Pierre de Provence et la Belle Maquelonne, pantomime en quatre actes*. Paris: l'Imprimerie de P. de Lormel, 1781.
Audinot, Nicole-Medard. *Hercule et Omphale, Pantomime en 1 Acte*. Théâtre de l'Ambigu Comique, 1787. Collection Rondel, Bibliothèque de l'Arsenal.
Aumer, Jean Pierre. *Aline, Reine de Golconde, ballet-pantomime en trois actes*. Paris: Chez Roullet, 1823.
———. *Astolphe et Joconde, ou Les Coureurs d'Aventures, ballet-pantomime en deux actes*. Paris: Chez Barba, 1827.
———. *La Belle au Bois Dormant, ballet-pantomime-féerie en trois actes*. In Eugène Scribe, *Oeuvres Complètes*. Paris: E. Dentu, 1874–75, ser. 3, v. 1, pp. 131–158.
———. *Jenny ou Le Mariage Secret, ballet-pantomime en trois actes*. Paris: Hocquet, 1823.
———. *Les Amours d'Antoine et de Cléopatre, ballet historique en trois actes*. Paris: Hocquet et Comp., 1808.
———. *Les Pages du Duc de Vendôme, ballet en un acte*. Paris: Chez J. N. Barba, 1820.
———. *Partie de ballet pour "Les Bayadères, Opéra en Trois Actes."* 1810.
Belfort, Mme. *L'Artemise Française, ou les heureux effets de la Paix, comédie en un acte, en prose, avec un divertissement*. N.p., n.d.
Bignon, D. *Marie Millet, ou l'Héroïne Villageoise, pantomime*. Paris: Chez Valleyre l'aîné, 1780.
Billioni. *Les Quatre Parties du Jour, ballet pantomime, de Meuniers Provençaux*. Paris: l'Imprimerie de Ballard, 1759.
Blache, Frédéric-Auguste. *Cocambo, ou l'Ambassade à Smyrne, divertissement-pantomime en deux actes*. Paris: Théâtre de l'Ambigu-Comique, 1829.
———. *Polinchinel Vampire, ballet-pantomime et Divertissemens burlesques en un Acte et à Spectacle*. Paris: Pollet, 1823.
Blache, Jean-Baptiste. *Scylla et Glaucus, grand ballet d'action, en trois actes*. Lyon: Pelzin et Devron, an XII.
Céphale et Proscris, ou L'Amour Conjugal, Tragédie-Lyrique en Trois Actes. Paris: Ballard, 1773.
Chimène, ou Le Cid, Tragédie en trois actes. Paris: P. de Lormel, 1784.
Cogniard, Hypolite et Théodore. *Les Farfadets, ballet pantomime en trois actes*. Paris: Marchant, 1841.
Coralli, Jean. *Les Artistes, ballet-pantomime en deux actes*. Paris: Chez Bezou, 1829.
———. *Lisbèll, ou la Nouvelle Claudine, pantomime en trois actes, mêlée de danse*. Paris: Chez Bezou, 1825.
———. *Le Mariage de Raison, ballet-pantomime en trois tableaux*. Paris: Chez Bezou, 1827.
———. *La Neige, ballet-pantomime en trois actes*. Paris: Chez Bezou, 1827.
———. *M. de Pourceaugnac, ballet-pantomime-comique en deux actes*. Paris: Chez J.-N. Barba, 1826.
———. *La Visite à Bedlam, ballet-pantomime en deux tableaux*. Paris: Chez Bezou, 1826.
Curmer. *La Laitière Polonaise, ou le coupable par Amour. pantomime en trois actes*. Paris: Chez Barba, 1798.
Cuvelier de Trie, Jean Guillaume-A. *Le Damoisel et La Bergarette, ou La Femme Vindicative. Historiette du XVI Siècle, Divisée en trois Chapitres*. Paris: Cailleau, 1795.

———. *Les Royalistes de la Vendée, ou les Epoux Républicains, pantomime en Trois Actes.* Paris: Limondin, 1794.

Dauberval, Jean. *Le Déserteur, ballet d'action, en trois actes.* Paris: Chez Barba, 1804.

———, Remis par Jean Aumer. *Les Jeux D'Églé, ballet anacréontique.* Paris: Chez Barba, 1802.

———. *Le Page Inconstant, ou Honi soit qui mal y pense, ballet héroï-comique, Tiré du Mariage de Figaro, en trois actes.* Paris: Chez Barba, 1805.

Dauvergne, Antoine. *La tour enchantée, ballet figuré, mêlé de chant et de danse; representée à Versailles, devant sa Majesté.* Paris: Pierre-Robert-Christophe Ballard, 1770.

de Blamont, Colin. *Les Caractères de l'Amour, ballet héroïque.* Paris: Ballard, 1738.

Deshayes, A. J. J. *Zémire et Azor, ballet féerie en trois actes.* Paris: Chez Roulet, 1824.

Despréaux, Jean Étienne. *Médée et Jason, ballet terrible, orné de danse, soupçon, noirceur, plaisir, bêtise, horreur, gaieté, trahison, plaisanterie, poison, assassinat & feu d'artifice.* Paris, 1780.

———. *Momie, opéra burlesque, parodie d'Iphigénie, opéra, en trois actes, en prose et en vaudevilles.* Paris: P. P. C. Ballard, 1778.

Desriaux. *La Toison D'Or, Tragédie en Trois Actes.* Paris: P. de Lormel, 1786.

Didelot, Charles. *Sapho & Phaon: Grand Ballet Erotique, en quatre actes.* London: Baylis, 1797.

Dubut, Laurent. *Le Bienfait Recompensé, pantomime espagnole.* Paris: Chez Claude Herissant, 1764.

———. *Pierrot, Roi de Cocagne, pantomime.* Paris: Chez Claude Herissant, 1764.

Duhamel l'aînée, Mlle. *L'Agnès: divertissement Mêlé de chants & de Danses, en un Acte.* Paris: Chez Claude Herissant, 1763.

Duport, Louis. *Figaro, ou la Précaution Inutile, ballet-pantomime en trois actes.* Paris: Bertin et Lautour, 1806.

L'Élève de la Nature, Comédie en un acte, mêlée de musique. Paris: Desanges, 1781.

Elssler, Thérèse. *La Volière ou les Oiseaux de Boccace, ballet-pantomine en un acte.* Paris: Imprimerie d'Adolphe Éverat, 1838.

Les Festes de l'Himen et de l'Amour ; ou Les Dieux D'Egypte, ballet héroïque. Paris: L'Academie Royale de Musique, 1748.

Fiochi. *Sophocle, Opéra en Trois Actes.* Paris: Roullet, 1811.

Franconi, Jeune. *Robert le-Diable ou Le Criminel Repentant, pantomime en trois actes et à grand spectacle.* Paris: Hocquet, 1818.

———. *La Dame du Lac, ou l'Inconnu, pantomime en trois actes, à grand spectacle.* Paris: Barba, 1813.

———, et Mme. Bellemont. *Arsène ou le Génie Maure, pantomime en trois actes, à grand spectacle et à machines.* Paris: Chez Barba, 1813.

Gallet. *Bacchus et Ariane, ballet héroïque.* Paris: De l'Imprimerie Civique, 1791.

Gardel, Maximilian. *L'Avènement de Titus à l'Empire, ballet héroïque.* Paris: Chez Musier, 1775.

———. *Mirza, ballet en action.* Paris: Ballard, 1779.

———. *Mirza.* Paris: Chez les Marchands de Pieces de Théâtre, 1779.

———. *Phaon, drame lyrique, en deux actes.* Paris: Ballard, 1778.

Gardel, Pierre. *Achille à Scyros, ballet-pantomime en trois actes.* Paris: Chez Ballard, 1804.

———. *La Contre-Révolution, ballet national, en trois actes.* Vienna: De l'Imprimerie des Fugitifs, n.d.

———. *La Dansomanie, Folie-Pantomime, en deux actes; Du Citoyen Gardel, membre de la société philotechnique.* Paris: Ballard, 1800.

———. *Daphnis et Pandrose, ou la vengeance de l'amour, ballet-pantomime en deux actes.* Paris: Ballard, 1803.

———. *Diane et Endymion.* 1810. Dance Collection, New York Public Library at Lincoln Center, *MGZM - Res. Gar P.

———. *Le Déserteur, ballet-pantomime en cinq actes.* Paris: Ballard, 1788.

———. *L'Enfant Prodigue, ballet-pantomime, en trois actes.* Paris: l'Imprimerie D'Adrien Égron, 1812.

———. *Le Jugement de Paris, ballet-pantomime en trois actes.* Paris: De Lormel, 1793.

———. *La Morte de Cléopatre.* 1809. Dance Collection, New York Public Library at Lincoln Center, *MGZM - Res. Gar P.

———. *Le Premier Navigateur, ou le Pouvoir de l'Amour, ballet d'action, en trois actes.* Paris: De Lormel, 1785.

———. *Proserpine, ballet pantomime en trois actes.* Paris: Chez Roullet, 1818.

———. *Psyché, ballet pantomime en trois actes.* Paris: l'Imprimerie Civique, 1795.

———. *Télémaque dans l'îsle de Calipso, ballet héroïque, en trois actes*. Paris: Salle de l'Opéra, 1790.
———. *Vertumne et Pomone, ballet-pantomime en un acte*. Paris: Fain, 1810.
Gaubier. *Brioché; ou l'Origine des Marionettes, Parodie de Pigmalion*. Paris: Chez Duchesne, 1753.
Gautier, Théophile. *La Péri, ballet fantastique en deux actes*. Paris: Mme. de Jonas, n.d.
———. *Paquerette, ballet-pantomime en 3 actes et 5 tableaux*. Paris: Mme. de Jonas, n.d.
La Gitana, A Grand Ballet in Two Acts. London: H. N. M. Millar, 1839.
Gougybus. *Mioco et Filoli, ou le Triomphe de l'Humanité, pantomime en deux actes*. Paris: Chez Barba, an V.
Grandi, Thomas and Antoinette Grandi. *Pigmalion: de Monsieur Jean-Jacques Rousseau*. Milan: Chez Jean Baptiste Branchi, 1775.
Grétry, André Ernest Modeste. *La Double Epreuve, ou Colinette à la Cour, Comédie-Lyrique en Trois Actes*. Paris: P. de Lormel, 1782.
———. *L'Embarras des Richesses, Comédie-Lyrique en trois actes*. Paris: P. de Lormel, 1782.
Hapdé, Jean-Baptiste. *Le Troubadour, ou l'Enfant de l'Amour, Pantomime en trois actes, à grand spectacle, marches, combats, évolutions militaires; musique nouvelle du C. Guebar; décors du C. Moenk; costumes du tems, incendré, explosions, démolitions, etc*. Paris: Chez Lacouriere, 1800.
Hilverding, Franz Anton Christoph. *Ballet intitulé le Combat de l'Amour et de la Raison*. 1763.
———. *Le Retour D'Apollon au Parnasse, ballet allégorique pour la fête*. St. Pétersbourg: De l'Imprimerie de l'Acadmie Impériale, 1763.
Hus le jeune, Citoyen. *Tout Cède à l'Amour, ballet Pantomime-Anacréontique en trois actes*. Théâtre de Bordeaux, Fructidor l'An VI.
Le Boeuf, Jean-Joseph. *Jérusalem délivrée, ou Renaud et Armide, tragédie-pantomime en quatre actes*. Paris: de l'Imprimerie de P. de Lormal, 1779.
Leuven, Adolphe de (1800–1884). *Le diable à quatre, ballet pantomime en deux actes*. Paris: Mme. de Jonas, 1845.
Lockroy, Joseph-Philippe and Léon Appiani. *Les Amours de Faublas, Ballet-Pantomime en Trois Actes et Quatre Tableaux*. Paris: Marchant, 1835.
Mazzinghi. *The Favorite Opera Dances for the Year 1789 Performed at the King's Theatre Hay Market*. London: Longman & Broderip, n.d.
Milon, Louis Jacques Jessé. *Clari, ou la Promesse de Mariage, ballet-pantomime en trois actes*. Paris: Dondey-Dupré, 1827.
———. *Héro et Léandre, ballet-pantomime, en un acte*. Paris: Prix-Fixe, 1799.
———. *Le Carnaval de Venise, ou la Constance à l'Épreuve, ballet-pantomime en deux actes*. Paris: L'Imprimerie de Dondey-Dupré, 1816.
———. *Les Noces de Gamache, ballet-pantomime-folie en deux actes*. Paris: Chez D.-Dupré, 1801.
———. *Nina, ou la Folle par Amour*. Paris: Chez Dondey-Dupré, 1813.
———. *Ulysse, ballet-héroïque, en trois actes*. Paris: Chez Dondey-Dupré, 1807.
———. *L'Enlèvement des Sabines, ballet-pantomime-historique en trois actes*. Paris: Chez Dondey-Dupré, 1811.
———. *Pygmalion, ballet-pantomime, en deux actes*. Paris: L'Imprimerie à Prix-Fixe, An VII.
Noverre, Jean Georges. *Apelles et Campaspe*, in Noverre, *Lettres sur les Arts Imitateurs*, vol. II, pp. 503–514.
Parisau, Pierre-Germain. *Sophie de Brabant, pantomime en trois actes*. Paris: Chez Thomas Brunet, 1781.
Perrot, Jules. *L'Illusion d'un Peintre: ballet-pantomime en deux tableaux*. Havre: Imprimerie de H. Brindeau, 1846.
Pitrot, Antoine Buonaventure. *Ulysse dans l'île de Circée, ballet sérieux, héroi-pantomime*. Paris: Ballard, 1764.
———. *Télémaque dans l'îsle de Calipso, ballet sérieux, héroï pantomime; De l'invention & composition du Sr. Pitrot (maître de ballet pour sa majesté le roi de Pologne)*. Paris: Ballard, 1759.
Planterre. *La Fête de l'Égalité, mélodrame pantomime-lyrique, en un acte et en vers*. Paris: à la Salle de Spectacle du Théâtre de la Cité, 1793.
Pleinchesne, R.-T. Regnard de. *Programme des Aventures de Don Quichotte, pantomime en trois actes, précédée d'un prologue, pantomime; le tout sur des airs connus*. Paris: Se Trouve Au Spectacle des Grands Danseurs du Roi, & à toutes les Adresses ordinaires, 1778.
Programme du "Chat-Botté, Pantomime." Paris: Théâtre de l'Ambigu-Comique, 1772.

Programme du "Fameux Siège, Pantomime." Paris: P. R. C. Ballard, 1778.
Saint-Georges, Vernoy de, Théophile Gautier, and Jean Coralli. *Giselle ou les Wilis, Ballet fantastique en 2 Actes*. Paris: Mme. Ve Jonas, Libraire de l'Opéra, 1841.
Saint-Léon, Arthur. *La Fille de Marbre: Ballet-pantomime en deux actes et trois tableaux*. Paris: Michel Lévy Frères, 1847.
Scribe, Eugene, and Jean Aumer. *Manon Lescaut, ballet-pantomime en trois actes*. Paris: Bezou, 1830.
———, and Jean Aumer. *La Somnambule, ou l'Arrivée d'un Nouveau Seigneur, ballet-pantomime en trois actes*. Paris: Chez Barba, 1827.
———, and Jean Coralli. *L'Orgie, ballet en trois actes*. Paris: Bezou, 1831.
Servandoni, Jean-Nicolas. *La Forêt Enchantée, Représentation tirée du Poème Italien de la Jerusalem délivrée. Spectacle orné de machines, animé d'acteurs pantomimes & accompagnés d'une Musique (de la composition de M. Geminiani) qui en exprime les différentes actions*. Paris: Ballard, 1754.
———. *La Descente D'Énée aux Enfers, représentation*. Paris: Chez la veuve Pissot, 1740.
———. *Le Triomphe de l'Amour Conjugal. Spectacle orné de Machines, animés d'Acteurs Pantomines & accompagnés d'une Musique qui en exprime les differentes actions.* Paris: Ballard, 1755.
Spectacles représentés devant leurs Majestés à Versailles, 1786. Paris: Ballard, 1786.
Taconnet, Toussaint-Gaspard. *La Mariée de la Courtille, ou Arlequin Ramponeau, ballet pantomime, orné de Chants et de Danses*. Paris: Ballard, 1760.
Taglioni, Filippo. *La Sylphide: ballet en deux actes*. Paris: J.-N. Barba, 1836.
———. *La Fille du Danube, ballet-pantomime en deux actes et en quatre tableaux*. Paris: D. Jonas, 1836.
Tibule, ou les Saturnales. Paris: Lormel, 1777.
Titus, Antoine. *La Laitière Suisse, ballet-pantomime en deux actes*. Paris: Chez Bezou, 1823.
Vestris, Auguste. *The Sorceress & the Knight, a grand magic ballet in three acts*. London: 1833.

INDEX

SUSAN LEIGH FOSTER,

choreographer, dancer, and writer, is Professor in the Department of Dance at the University of California, Riverside. She is the author of *Reading Dancing: Bodies and Subjects in Contemporary American Dance*; editor of *Choreographing History* and *Corporealities*; and a coeditor of *Cruising the Performative: Interventions into the Representation of Ethnicity, Nationality, and Sexuality.*

DATE DUE			
DEC 12 1998			
AUG 8 2005			